# Wild, High
# and Tight

BOOKS BY PETER GOLENBOCK

*Dynasty: The New York Yankees 1949–1964*
*The Bronx Zoo* (with Sparky Lyle)
*Number 1* (with Billy Martin)
*Guidry* (with Ron Guidry)
*Balls* (with Graig Nettles)
*Bums: An Oral History of the Brooklyn Dodgers*
*Bats* (with Davey Johnson)
*Pete Rose on Hitting* (with Pete Rose)
*Personal Fouls*
*How to Win at Rotisserie Baseball*
*Teammates* (illustrated by Paul Bacon)
*The Forever Boys*
*Fenway: An Unexpurgated History of the Boston Red Sox*
*American Zoom*

# WILD, HIGH

AND

# TIGHT

## The
## Life and Death
## of Billy Martin

PETER GOLENBOCK

St. Martin's Press / New York

WILD, HIGH AND TIGHT: THE LIFE AND DEATH OF BILLY MARTIN.
Copyright © 1994 by Peter Golenbock. All rights reserved. Printed
in the United States of America. No part of this book may be used
or reproduced in any manner whatsoever without written permission
except in the case of brief quotations embodied in critical articles
or reviews. For information, address St. Martin's Press, 175 Fifth
Avenue, New York, N.Y. 10010.

Design by Richard Oriolo

Library of Congress Cataloging-in-Publication Data

Golenbock, Peter.
    Wild, high and tight: the life and death of Billy Martin /
  c Peter Golenbock.
      p.   cm.
    ISBN 0-312-10575-4
    1. Martin, Billy, 1928–   . 2. Baseball managers—United
  States—Biography.   I. Title.
GV865.M353G65   1994
796.357'092—dc20
[B]                                                    93-44904
                                                          CIP

First Edition: June 1994

10  9  8  7  6  5  4  3  2  1

Books are available in quantity for promotional or premium use.
Write to Director of Special Sales, St. Martin's Press, 175 Fifth
Avenue, New York, N.Y. 10010, for information on discounts and
terms, or call toll-free (800) 221-7945. In New York, call (212)
674-5151 (ext. 645).

This book is dedicated to my parents,
Jerome and Annette Golenbock,
in celebration of their fiftieth wedding anniversary;
and to Neil Reshen,
who is my Eddie Sapir and Bill Reedy
all rolled into one.

# CONTENTS

# INTRODUCTION

The issue of control is central to most lives. People need to feel in control. No one likes to helplessly sit by and be buffeted by events. It is far more comforting to call the shots, even if what you're deciding on isn't very significant.

The more decisions a person makes during the course of the day, the more he *feels* in control.

To have a working relationship, you have to give up some of your decision-making power. In order to relate to another person, you have to *trust* that other person. You have to let that other person make some of the decisions, big and small, *for you*. To do that, you have to be secure in the love of the other person for you and trust the decision will also be good for you.

For a business relationship to work—whether you work above, under, or with someone else—you often have to put away your own personal desires and do what is best for the group. To get along, you have to take advice, listen to others, and make the others feel that you at least have an interest in what they are saying.

People with healthy egos interact in just such a way.

Emotional harm results when the decision maker believes, for whatever reasons, that he is the *only* one capable of making decisions, that no one else counts, and that he is right even when he is wrong and that others are wrong even when they are right.

In world history, these men are known as tyrants. In America, the corporate world supplies our dictators.

As a leader, the CEO has two choices. He can run the company either as a democracy or as a dictatorship. It is up to him whether his underlings will be consulted when it comes time to make decisions. He decides whether responsibility will be delegated. He sets the policy of the entire company.

If that CEO is self-assured and values the input of the people below him, he will empower his underlings, give them responsibility, and make them feel both wanted and needed.

If that man is weak and unsure of himself (often characteristic of sons of company founders—in this case, George Steinbrenner), he will see those below him as threats to his position. The more capable the person below him, the more of a threat he becomes until the threat becomes overwhelming and he talks himself into "having" to fire him.

This was the type of man for whom Billy Martin went to work as manager of the New York Yankees.

In the corporate world there are brilliant men unfit to be Organization Men. For them, having to work within such an organization becomes frustrating and difficult. These men may know their field as well or better than their superiors do, but they are constitutionally unfit to work with other people, hard as they try, unless they are allowed to make all the decisions. Their skills help them become noticed until their unwillingness to work as a team member provokes them to either leave the company or be beaten down and ultimately discarded by the company.

Billy Martin was just such an employee.

Billy and George. It was the Clash of the Warped Titans, the unstoppable driving force meeting the immovable vindictive object, as one talented man bent on controlling the lives of others was hired to work for a more powerful man intent on taming him, controlling him, and owning his soul.

This is a book about an intimidating, brilliant maverick, insistent on doing things his way, who joins a company to work for a powerful but weak, self-centered tyrant who not only is unable to delegate responsibility but who resents the success of his employees and who punishes them emotionally as if they were the enemy.

It is also a book about what happens to men who are incapable of sharing love and whose emotional barrenness ruins their lives and destroys those of everyone around them.

This book is also about the choices these men make, how the Sirens of sex, fame, and fortune draw one of them, a seemingly strong man, into a whirlpool he cannot control, spinning him toward an untimely death.

Finally, this is a story about manipulation. Billy Martin was one of the two or three most intimidating managers in the history of the game of baseball. Only John McGraw and maybe Leo Durocher were more intimidating. Billy was a master at manipulating players and umpires, even opposing managers, but in handling the rest of his life, in his desire to attract beautiful women and powerful men to his side, Billy made terrible, self-destructive choices.

During the last ten years of Billy's life, the two people with whom he was most closely entwined were George Steinbrenner and Jill Martin, his fourth and last wife. As tough a guy as Billy seemed to be, in the hands of these two master mind-benders, one his boss, the other his wife, Billy Martin was putty, mush, as they contributed to the unhappiness which plagued him during the final years of his life.

In my search to discover what motivated the three principal players, Billy, George, and Jill, finding the real Billy was a lot easier than learning about the other two, because Billy, unlike George and Jill, had no interest in covering his tracks and rewriting history. Billy had no interest in image. Billy had no interest in piling up meaningless awards.

Billy was Billy.

Deep down, Billy Martin was not a deceitful, vindictive person, unless he felt cornered, which happened periodically throughout his life. Some team owners and general managers will disagree, and there are sportswriters who put up with his enmity and sarcasm too long to believe *anything* good about Billy. Billy handled sportswriters abominably because he was afraid of them, fearful of their power over him. But the sportswriters, though influential, were a small group. The majority of the people Billy interacted with over the years, his many players and his cadre of loyal friends, spoke as one when they said that they loved Billy because he was a brilliant manager and a straight shooter.

As for the people who know George Steinbrenner and Jill Martin, from them I received only dire warnings, repeated over and over: Beware of their distortions, the PR gloss, and watch out when you don't buy into their version of events. With George, moreover, I was warned to be prepared for possible retaliation, including threats of lawsuits, character assassination, and other harassment.

The most difficult task in writing history is trying to determine what really happened when two people give different versions of events.

The easiest method is to merely give both sides. But if one of the tellers is lying, does giving both sides give a distorted version of what happened? Indeed it does.

If you as a journalist determine that X is believable and Y is not, do you have the right to disbelieve Y? It's a question debated in journalism schools everywhere.

In *Wild, High and Tight* I have been faced with a similar scenario. George Steinbrenner and Jill Martin have their versions of their relationships with Billy Martin, and everyone else has a different version. *Wild, High and Tight* is what really happened to Billy.

In a sense, I began writing this book in 1979, when I began working with Billy on his autobiography, *Number 1*. In six months together Billy and I developed a solid respect for each other, based on our love of the game of baseball and a shared interest in the life of one Alfred Manuel Martin.

Baseball was all he cared about (except for sex with young, well-built girls). Every once in a while he would talk about his interest in the Civil War, but I never saw any books on the subject in his home, and he never mentioned any general except Douglas MacArthur, whom he adored because General "I Shall Return" MacArthur stood up to that pansy Harry Truman (who, of course, fired him).

Billy allowed me a look at his private life, dragging me to some of his bar haunts, where we drank Perrier during his year on the wagon, and he provided me with thrills and chills. I can remember when he was driving down the interstate highway around Minneapolis before a ball game. His young girlfriend, Heather, was sitting in the passenger seat. I was in the back.

Heather, who came from the South Bronx, said to him, "You know, Billy, I've never driven a car before."

"Shove over," said Billy, and before my heart was able to skip a beat, Heather slid behind the wheel, and Billy sat as her passenger.

"Hold her steady," Billy said. It was his one piece of driving advice.

We rode about five miles as Heather resolutely motored down Interstate 35, the six-lane superhighway, not moving from her lane, not swerving from the cars coming at us from the off-ramps. I imagined the headlines: BILLY MARTIN, BLONDE BOMBSHELL, WRITER DEAD IN CRASH.

Billy praised her driving skill, and just before the turn-off for the ballpark, they switched back. We made it in one piece.

To give this young girl her first taste of the open road, Billy had chivalrously risked our lives. His charm was that after the danger had passed, you forgot about his recklessness and remembered the fun. They called him Billy the Kid, and that's what he was, a little kid.

Ten years later he was dead, the victim of a car accident. Remembering Minneapolis, I wasn't surprised. Inexplicably I felt sad for him. Billy Martin had a kid's charm that deeply affected those few people he allowed to get close to him.

Through the years I kept up with Billy mostly through Billy's lawyer, Judge Eddie Sapir, who has become a close friend. A half-dozen times I dropped by to see Billy at Yankee Stadium, and he always had a warm smile. For years we mulled over a sequel. I told him to wait until after he retired. So long as he was still a Yankee working for George, I knew his tongue was tied.

I guess, in some way, this is our sequel. Knowing Billy, I suspect there are a couple of anecdotes he would have asked me to take out, but that's all, just a couple. Billy was funny. When I was researching *Number 1,* there were incidents about his life I learned from interviewing others. A few were not flattering. Billy never sought to protect his image and deny them. He'd say, "That's the way it was, pard." And he'd shrug.

*Wild, High and Tight* is Billy's life as it was. It's about his brilliance as a manager and the control he had over his environment in the dugout and about his total lack of control away from it. It's about the people who drove him crazy and reduced him to a hopeless alcoholic and about the loyal friends who felt powerless to save him.

If Billy had had any PR skills, he would have become a martyr. His place in the Hall of Fame would be assured.

He was as great a manager as they come, but because Billy was an alcoholic who drank and fought publicly, and because the man for whom he worked destroyed his reputation through his constant public denigrations and multiple firings, he may never join the hallowed hall where he should rightfully be placed next to his mentor, Casey Stengel.

My one wish is that though *Wild, High and Tight* recounts Billy's off-the-field adventures, it will above all rekindle the memory of the baseball genius that was the hallmark of Alfred Manuel Martin.

\* \* \*

There are so many wonderful people to whom I wish to express my deepest gratitude for their time and cooperation.

I wish to thank the late Jenny Downey, Ken and Pat Irvine, Joan Holland, Ruben DeAlba, Trivio Torrez, Sam and Lois Curtain, Kelly Martin, Billy Joe Martin, Sam Pedone, Bruno Andrino, George Metkovich, Phil Rizzuto, Whitey Ford, the late Eddie Lopat, Jerry Coleman, Bob Turley, Ralph Terry, Ryne Duren, Lewis Figone, Vicki Figone, Bill and Carol Reedy, Greer Johnson, Jim Burris, Graig Nettles, Sparky Lyle, Dock Ellis, Lenny Randle, Roy Howell, Toby Harrah, Bill Denehy, Dr. Irving Kolin, Bernardo Leonard, Ron Pruitt, Barry Halper, Rick Cerrone, Eddie and Peggy Sapir, Bill Kane, Matty Keough, Pearl Davis, Shane Rawley, Katheryn Marrero, Marty Blackman, the late Cedric Tallis, Heather Coyles, Ed Linn, Tex Gernand, Mike and Katie Klepfer, David Falkner, Bill Fischer, and Dave Ballard.

Thanks also to George and Jenny Sehringer, Joe Bennett, Frank Treadway, Bill Gabriel, Bob and Patsy Stecher, Paul Hensil, Ketmann Barber, George Steiner, Jim Beardsley, Lee Robinson, Bill Callaghan, A. Coke Smith, Don Martin, Tony Butterfield, Dr. Jack Brody, Steve Blasky, Fred Goldstein, Dick Kraft, Bill Mason, Charlie Glass, Peter Callahan, Bruce Breckinridge, Edward W. Jones, Colonel Marion Mixson, Jerry Adams, Lou Lyle, Sam Romano, Colonel Hal Connors, Jeanette Montgomery, Lou Berliner, Tom Keyes, Tony DeSabito, John LeCorte, Ben Froelich, Len Dawson, Robert Sauvey, William Crippen, Dr. James Hull, Bob August, Paul Hornung, Otto Graham, John McClendon, John Nagy, Jack Adams, Mike Cleary, Dick Brott, Bill Sharman, Mary Stouffer, Bob Sudyk, Ben Flieger, Robert Ferry, Louis Mitchell, Jerry Lucas, Dan Swartz, Rob Franklin, Maury Allen, Fred Bachman, Howard Berk, the late Mike Burke, Gabe Paul, David Halberstam, the late Joe Flaherty, Larry Wahl, Marty and Pat Appel, the late Neale Roach, Tom McBride, Tom Evans, Jack Melcher, Herb Kalmbach, Rodney Dammeyer, Judge Leroy Contie, David Dorsen, Jim Polk, and Roy Meyers.

Jill Martin declined to be interviewed, either in writing or in person.

Thanks to Bill Deane and Matt Reese at the Baseball Hall of Fame, and to Bill Adler, whose idea it was to do this book, and to my editor, George Witte, who had the confidence in me to buy it even though another Billy book loomed on the horizon. Also to Mark Rifkin, a fine copy editor, and to Paul Sleven, thanks for your care and legal expertise.

Thanks finally to Rhonda, the love of my life, to Charles, my tee-ball star, and to our beloved Sparky and Mickey, both of whom we miss very much.

# THE DEATH OF
# BILLY MARTIN

**B**illy Martin *was* driving, despite everything written to the contrary. It was Christmas Day 1989, and as he sat behind the wheel of his Ford F250 four-wheel-drive ¾-ton pickup truck, he was heading back to his farm just outside Binghamton, New York, to celebrate a holiday he hated with a wife he despised, except when they were in bed together.

Christmas ordinarily was a sad time for Billy, who habitually shunned celebrating holidays. Only two weeks earlier, his mother, Jenny Downey, had died, and he had sunk into a deep depression. Billy had loved and hated his mother—it was the way he felt about women in general, but Billy had known that life for him would be hard once his mother passed away. He would tell friends, "When my mother dies, I will either get drunk for a month, or I will die."

On this Christmas Day he would do both. It was around five in the afternoon. He had four hours of booze poured down him, but if his driving was impaired, it was impossible for his passenger to detect. Darkness had fallen, the roads were icy, and Billy was driving cautiously.

Billy was talking animatedly to his closest friend, Bill Reedy, who was visiting him and his wife Jill for the Christmas holidays, and as a result he missed the highway exit he usually took to go home, so he had to take a longer, more circuitous route. He didn't mind. He and Bill Reedy were talking, and another five minutes wouldn't make any difference. Billy had taken the back way before, on days when he was trying to avoid the local cops who habitually were on the lookout for the always-sloshed Billy Martin.

He was seconds from his driveway off Potters Field Road when he began driving down a steep decline that ended only yards from the large metal gates with the impressive golden B.M. initials proclaiming the entrance to the Martin farm.

Billy never made it home. His truck slid into a ditch and crashed head-on into a concrete culvert. The impact caused his neck to snap, and on Christmas Day in the year 1989, Billy Martin, one of the great managers and one of the most controversial figures in the history of the game of baseball, died.

During a managerial career that lasted sixteen years, Billy won five divisional titles. He led four teams, the Minnesota Twins, the Detroit Tigers, the Oakland A's, and the New York Yankees, to victory.

Every stop along the way, Billy would teach a new crop of players how to play the game the way it should be played. He won 1,253 games during his career, with a .553 winning percentage, a remarkable figure considering that with each new job, Billy started with bad or inexperienced teams.

Billy's major problem in baseball was that he never could forge a strong enough alliance with a general manager to allow him to stay in one place very long. The reason, his bosses said, was that *he* always wanted to be the general manager. Billy, they said, never had enough no matter what he had, and this especially included sex, of which he never seemed to get enough. The flaunting of his sex life made them very, very nervous.

And yet, even though he was fired often, his influence over a generation of managers today is not disputed. Billyball, as the press called it, has spawned a significant group of men—including Buck Showalter, Jim Essian, Tony La Russa, Toby Harrah, Lou Piniella, Mike Hargrove, and Jim Fregosi—who emerged as managers after learning the game from Billy Martin.

Only a few managers have left their imprints on the game. Three of the most influential, John McGraw, Casey Stengel, and Billy Martin, came to us one from the other.

John McGraw, considered by many the greatest manager in the history of the game, had a similar personality to Billy's. The Great McGraw was a son of a bitch to play for, a perfectionist who whipped his players and made them be perfect. Many of them hated him as a person, but they loved what he could do for their careers. But John McGraw, a devoted family man, had the complete devotion of Giants owner John T. Brush, and he stayed as Giants manager from 1902 until 1932, when he retired.

McGraw's protégé, Charles Dillon "Casey" Stengel, managed the New York Yankees from 1949 until 1960. During that twelve-year period he won ten pennants and seven world championships. He was able to do it because general manager George Weiss allowed him to manage his way without criticism or interference.

Billy Martin, who was taught by Stengel, never had that luxury. Baseball is a team sport, on the field and in the front office. Billy could play and manage the game on the field, but he was a failure in the way he dealt with the front office. He made enemies, and those men, always more powerful than he, caused him to be a managerial nomad.

Billy got fired for two reasons. First he believed that as long as he did his job and won, nothing else mattered. He was wrong about that. Billy's private life was personally offensive to his bosses, and some of them fired him because of that, even though he won.

The other reason he got fired was that Billy always thought that he was the master of all men and all situations. No matter what bind he was in, he felt, "I can handle it."

He believed himself to be a master of mind games. In the end, he was convinced, if you went up against him, he would win, and you would lose.

It turned out there were others who played the game of life his way but did it even better. During the last ten years of his life, Billy Martin took on two very powerful entities, one a rich, jealous, egocentric man who paid his salary and reduced his public image to that of a lackey, the other a beautiful, avaricious woman who separated him from most of his friends and loved ones and killed his spirit. Together they reduced Billy Martin to a shell of what he once had been. Together they took one of the great managers in the game and ruined his life.

Billy died for a number of reasons, all of which had exacerbated his alcoholism. Billy died because at the time of the crash his blood-alcohol level was .18, high enough to blitz the average American tippler, and the alcohol had affected his judgment. He died because he had been fired as manager by the Yankees once too often, and his unhappiness made him drink. He died because he was stuck living in a small town away from his New York City world, and his loneliness made him drink. He died because his wife and he didn't get along, and their fighting made him drink. He died because he was an alcoholic, and no one understood that well enough to save him from himself.

Near the end, Billy Martin's life had become an ordeal. After he was fired for a fifth time by George Steinbrenner and the New York Yankees in July 1988, Billy found himself isolated and imprisoned on his estate. When he stayed home, Castle Martin was a constant irritant to him, a reminder that his wife Jill was spending every dime of his money improving the place, trying to make it a showplace for her and her stable of horses.

Billy Martin's public reputation was that of a roughneck and a tough guy, but the truth was that he was a wimp when it came to his demanding wife. Whatever she wanted, she got, and Billy was powerless against her. Martin would tell all his friends over and over how much he longed to be back in New York, or to be back in Northern California with his childhood friends and family, but he had become a prisoner of his fame and his wife's pleasures.

Life's important decisions were no longer his to make. The few visitors to their Binghamton farm could glimpse the famed ex-manager sitting morosely in the distance by his pond with a fishing pole waiting for a smallmouth bass to swim by, a tall glass filled with straight V.O. by his side.

When he wasn't fishing, he was fighting with his wife. His friends, who never could figure out why he married her in the first place, shook their heads when they considered the toll this union had taken on him. Years ago George Steinbrenner had turned him into a pathetic drunk. Those friends were saddened that the constant fighting with Jill Martin at home had ensured that he continue that way.

In the months after Billy was fired for the last time, it had become his habit to spend the entire day at one of the local Binghamton bars, Morey's or the Bull and Bear, where he would drink Stolichnaya with his bar friends until nightfall. His constant state of inebriation was such that his prodigious intake of Stoli barely fazed him when he got behind the wheel.

"Look out." Or maybe it was "Watch out." Those were Billy's last words. They weren't said with any urgency. The truck was sliding into a ditch on the right, but it wasn't going very fast. There was nothing life-threatening about what was happening.

But Billy was in a ditch, and he had to make a split-second decision. Other men might have hit the brakes. Had he braked, the truck would have halted in the ditch, atilt but intact.

Billy died because he drove the way he lived, with his foot on the accelerator, on the edge of being out of control. All he needed this night was a little moderation, and he would have been fine. Unfortunately, Billy was too high-strung, too combative, too impulsive—and too sauced—to have considered a safer alternative. To Billy, sliding into that ditch was a personal affront. How dare that ditch put him in such a position! Billy Martin doesn't get stuck in any goddamn ditch.

Martin, who felt himself the master of every situation, especially when stoked with a day's supply of liquid refreshment, attacked the ditch. He rammed his foot on the accelerator, turned the steering wheel hard left, and willed the truck out of the ditch.

Dusk had set in. Snowflakes were falling on already-packed snow. Visibility was poor.

The truck's back tires spun quickly. The left-side tires raised up as the truck sped forward, but because of the slickness and the downward pitch of the culvert, the truck could not escape the ditch and the large sluice pipe at the end of it.

Martin saw the pipe too late. The forward motion of the truck was halted like it had been punched in the nose by a powerful unseen force.

Though the side window of the truck had warned its occupants to "buckle up," neither rider ever did. Real men don't buckle their seat belts.

When the truck hit the pipe, Bill Reedy, who was sitting in the middle of the long bench seat, struck his head first on the rearview mirror, shearing it off, and then on the windshield, leaving a spiderweb of broken glass. He lacerated his left hand on the gearshift that protruded from the floor in an attempt to grab anything that would hold him upright.

Failing that, Reedy was slammed back against the seat and was immediately thrown forward and downward, his large body compressing in great pain under the passenger-side dashboard.

While Reedy was experiencing the crushing of his hip, beside him Billy Martin had grabbed the steering wheel tightly, hoping it would stop his forward motion. Martin pitched forward, hitting the steering wheel with his head and snapping the wheel off in his hands. He then struck the windshield, forming a round web on the glass where he hit.

Because the truck was canted at a steep angle, virtually lying on its right side, he rebounded backward and was propelled down toward the passenger side of the truck cab, behind Reedy's wedged body. When the paramedics arrived at the scene, Martin was found by the passenger door of the truck.

After the crash, the truck lay angled on its right side. Reedy saw that Billy wasn't moving. He talked to him, but when Billy didn't respond, he decided to get help. Reedy, a powerful man, tried to open his door, but the right side of the cab lay against the ground. The door would not open.

Ignoring the searing pain in his hip, Reedy reached up and grabbed the steering wheel in an attempt to pull himself to the driver's window and out of the mangled truck. The uphill effort made his progress slow.

Reedy was still struggling to extricate himself when a passerby stopped and summoned paramedics from the local fire department.

When the first wave of help arrived, one of the paramedics asked Bill Reedy, "Who was driving?"

For fifteen years Bill Reedy had acted the bodyguard and protector for Billy Martin. Bill Reedy didn't hesitate.

"I was," he said.

When Reedy discovered in the hospital that Billy had died, there was no longer a need to cover for him. He told investigators the truth—that Billy was driving. That should have been the end of it. There was an accident. Billy was dead. Turn the page.

It wasn't to be. In the end, just as Billy Martin paid the price for putting a high premium on fortune and fame, so Bill Reedy was to pay the price for his friendship. That seemed to be the way it was with those who loved Billy Martin. It was fun while it lasted, but in the end, what remained were tears and sadness.

# THE ZENITH

From the cover of *Time* magazine, dark, piercing, intelligent eyes stare at you. The crow's-feet around the eyes and the leathery face and neck reflect high anxiety and hard living. In profile the subject has a mustache and is wearing the green and gold colors of the Oakland A's. There is no joy or anger in his face. Rather, he is watching, waiting. If you play for him, it's a face that tells you that you better not screw up. If you're playing against him, it warns that you better be on your toes.

In 1979, the year before this man came on board as manager, the A's won 54 games, lost 108, and drew only 306,000 fans. The team owner, Charlie Finley, was desperate to find a way to sell his lackluster team, and so he hired as manager Billy Martin, who had won or dramatically improved teams and then been fired at Minnesota, Detroit, Texas, and twice with the New York Yankees under the frenetic ownership of George Steinbrenner. Martin had a reputation for succeeding and then trying to build his power base, attempting to make decisions about the farm system and the choice of players, undermining the general managers and farm directors—actions that inevitably got him fired. Charlie Finley didn't care about any of this. Finley, who fired managers as often as Steinbrenner did, didn't need Martin for the long run. A quick fix was all he needed to unload his team. Martin was given a two-year contract. For $125,000 a year, Charlie Finley was getting the biggest drawing card in the game. Martin was Finley's eleventh manager since he moved the team from Kansas City in 1968.

During the 1980 season Billy Martin cemented his reputation for his ability to teach players how to win. When he arrived in spring training, he discovered that Finley was running such a lean operation that the office didn't even have a Xerox machine or a blackboard or a piece of chalk. The A's were so pathetic that Rickey Henderson, a young player with outstanding potential, said he preferred to play at Tacoma in the minor leagues.

No one in the A's organization could spend a penny without Finley's express okay. Billy called his lawyer, Eddie Sapir, and asked Sapir to call American League president Lee MacPhail to tell him of the situation. MacPhail asked Sapir to make sure Finley was supplying the bats and balls mandated by the league. MacPhail promised Sapir he would make sure the A's were adequately equipped for spring training.

By the start of May, Billy Martin's Oakland A's were doing things on the field they hadn't done in a long time, playing tight defense, stealing bases, executing the hit-and-run, hustling. May was but a week old, and A's runners had stolen home three times, a Billy Martin trademark.

Attendance rose dramatically. Martin, who came from nearby West Berkeley, once again became a local hero. Oakland Mayor Lionel Wilson directed his comments to Billy during a banquet honoring the A's when he said, "You've really excited our community. I can't think of anyone who can excite our community like you have."

He added, "You are a hustling club. You can't play for Billy Martin unless you are a fighter."

Martin had the talent-thin A's in first place by midsummer.

On August 14, 1980, Charles Finley, who before Billy arrived hadn't been able to find a buyer at $7 million, sold his team to Levi Strauss blue-jeans mogul Walter Haas and his son-in-law Roy Eisenhardt for $12.7 million.

At one of their first meetings Martin told Eisenhardt, "Roy, I'm going to tell you this is a wicked game. One day you will reach up to scratch your ear, and your head might be gone. Roy, I'll always watch it for you. I'll never let that happen. We'll get every edge we can get."

Roy Eisenhardt told the public, "We are depending on Billy Martin's knowledge of baseball."

On Billy Martin Appreciation Day that summer Charlie Finley sent him a card—no money, no boat, no nothing, just a card, thanking Billy for making him the extra five and a half million.

By year's end Martin's A's could not overcome the powerful Kansas City Royals, but they finished second, a remarkable feat. Billy Martin was named Manager of the Year by both the Associated Press and United Press International. At season's end the A's rewarded Martin by giving him use of an expensive home in exclusive Danville, California, for ten years and extending his contract. Billy had wanted a ten-year deal, but the final draft provided for only five. In front of Wally Haas and Roy Eisenhardt, a naive Billy said, "We don't have to put those last five in writing. Their word is their bond. We'll do it for five, know it's for ten, and when we get to year six, we can deal with real figures."

His lawyer, Ed Sapir, was against doing it that way, but he couldn't go against Billy's wishes in front of Haas and Eisenhardt. What was he going to say, "My guy trusts you, but I don't"?

Sapir remembered, "So we did it Billy's way, and Billy might have cost himself $2 million with that statement."

Either way, Billy was happy with his new deal, and when Billy came to spring training camp in 1981, his players learned quickly that Martin's desire for winning was intense.

The A's opened their exhibition schedule in Scottsdale, Arizona, against a Japanese professional team. Before the ball game started, Martin gathered his players together in the clubhouse and said, "I just want everyone to remember one thing about today's ball game: Pearl Harbor."

The young guys looked at one another, wondering what Pearl Harbor had to do with winning an exhibition game in 1981.

Rickey Henderson, his left fielder, with little experience but huge potential, opened the first inning for the A's by getting on base. Martin had him steal second, then third, and he sent him home on a short fly ball to right field to score a run. It was a pattern of aggressive baseball Martin instilled into the entire team.

When his A's opened the season with eleven straight wins, Billy was rewarded with the *Time* magazine cover and the headline IT'S INCREDIBLE. His picture on the May 11, 1981, issue of *Time* was proof of Martin's managerial genius and an affirmation that Billy Martin was the number-one figure in America's Pastime, a more renowned figure than any player or owner.

Martin fashioned his team around the strong arms of his five young starting pitchers—Mike Norris, Rick Langford, Matt Keough, Steve McCatty, and Brian Kingman—and his strong young outfield of Rickey Henderson, Dwayne Murphy, and Tony Armas.

There was a long strike in the middle of 1981, and the A's were in front when the picket lines went up. After the season resumed and ended, it was decreed that the winners of the first half would play the winners of the second half for the division title. Martin's A's defeated second-half winner Kansas City and then played for the pennant but lost three straight to his old team, the New York Yankees.

For the second year in a row Martin was named Manager of the Year, tying a record set by his mentor, Casey Stengel.

As the manager of Oakland, Billy Martin had everything he could have wanted. When the new A's management took over, they gave him carte blanche to make *all* the decisions, setting up the organization so that Billy could pick the minor league personnel and show them how to teach Billyball throughout the organization.

Living in Oakland, Billy was surrounded by people who loved him—his mom, his brothers and sisters, and his old friends. He and his young wife Heather lived for free in a beautiful home in the exclusive Blackhawk community in Danville. He was as far away as he could be from the pressures of the New York press and nemesis George Steinbrenner, who twice had hired him and twice publicly ridiculed and humiliated him before firing him. Martin, in fact, got a good chuckle when it was reported during the 1981 World Series that Steinbrenner had gotten into a fracas with two young men.

Martin sent him a telegram: "Just heard the bad news. You're fired."

At Oakland, Martin had peace and tranquillity. Had he desired, he could have finished out his career surrounded by friends and family in the luxury and comfort of Northern California. For once, Billy Martin seemed to have it all.

# JENNY

In 1879, Nicholas Salvini traveled by boat from La Brusse, Italy, and landed in San Francisco, where his brother lived. As was typical for Italian society of the times, Salvini, a fisherman, was matched with a woman thirty-five years younger. This woman, Raphaella, married him because she had no choice.

When Raphaella first saw this older man, she demurred.

"I am not going to marry him," she said. But in her Italian society, women were subservient, and custom prevailed over individual will.

Her family told her, "You came from Italy, and that's who you're going to marry." The match was made.

The Salvinis lived in San Francisco on the corner of Mason and Chestnut streets. Three months before the great earthquake of 1906, they moved to one of the less affluent Bay Area suburbs, West Berkeley, California, joining a society of immigrants who had escaped poverty in Italy.

After the earthquake, which leveled their former home, many of their less fortunate San Francisco relatives moved in with them, filling the small two-story house to the extent that some cousins had to sleep under tables until they could find housing.

The Salvinis re-created their life in Italy. They grew vegetables and fruit on the arable land. On his small plot Nicholas grew grapes. In the back of the house he built a large tank for making wine, and at the dinner table Nicholas always had a gallon jug sitting next to him on the floor.

There were ten Salvini children, including Juvan, who was born in 1901.

The Salvinis raised their children in a strict household. Nicholas was a commercial fisherman who for months at a time traveled to Anchorage, Alaska, but when he was in port, he ruled absolutely. To disobey was to risk physical punishment.

Raphaella ruled when Nicholas was away fishing. She ordered. The children listened. If a child disobeyed, she also would become physical. She would fly into a rage, grab the miscreant by the hair, and bite that child's arm until it bled.

Because of the nature of Nicholas's work, the family lived frugally. When Nicholas was away for several months, times would get very tough. Raphaella kept everyone eating by working for the rich up on the hill as a maid and cook. She also took in a boarder or two.

When the fleet finally came home, Nicholas might have two hundred dollars in his pocket, and money worries would temporarily disappear. Then it would be time for him to leave, and as the months passed, money would again become tight. It was a cycle that would repeat itself until his death in 1918.

Raphaella, who was called Nonna, lived thirty more years. Nonna was deeply religious. She had an altar in her bedroom with a statue of Christ on the cross nailed to the wall, and every night she would say her prayers in Italian and light votive candles that burned all night.

During the remainder of her life she experienced real tragedy. Her most successful daughter, Theresa, ran a three-girl whorehouse and a bootlegging joint in neighboring Emeryville. She made a substantial income during the Depression, as much as a thousand dollars a week, but she died prematurely when she was murdered by a jealous boyfriend who could not accept that she was going with another man.

Another sister, Antoinette, died when she was twenty-five. Her husband was killed on the ship *State of California* when it sank. Antoinette was distraught. She would say to her younger sister, Juvan, who cared for her daily for more than a year, "When you come home from school, I'm going to be dead."

"Netta, you are not going to die."

But one day when Juvan returned home, Antoinette was dead. After lingering for a year after her husband's death, she died of what doctors said was a broken heart.

From her childhood, Juvan, a tiny woman not even five feet tall, was independent and headstrong. When she was old enough, she decided she wanted a more American name.

She asked her mother, "Why do you call me 'Juvan'? What is it in American?"

"I don't know," said Nonna.

Juvan said, "Okay, call me Jenny Catherine."

She was Jenny for the rest of her life.

In 1917, when Jenny was sixteen, she came home from school one afternoon and noticed that her mother was sewing, making sheets.

"Gee, Mom, that's nice. Who are you sewing them for?"

"You," she said.

"Me? Why?"

"You're going to get married."

At the time Jenny had been courting a fellow in San Francisco named Vittorio.

"I'm going to marry Vittorio?" she asked.

"No," said her mother, "you're marrying Donato."

Donato was one of her mother's boarders. They were married for three years and had one son, Frank, who his whole life was known as Tudo (pronounced TOO-doo).

Jenny has given two versions of what happened to her first marriage to Donato Pisani.

The first: "He was a bum who ran around with women. One day he told me he was leaving. He took off. We got a divorce."

The second: "I told my mother, 'I don't like him, but I'll marry him because you want me to, but if I find another guy, I'm going to leave him.' And sure as hell, I found another guy, and I left him."

Shortly after Donato and Jenny split, Donato Pisani died a violent death.

According to Jenny, "Tudo stayed with me, and Donato went back to Italy, where he got married. Then he came back to America and moved to Little Rock, Arkansas, where he was murdered. He had a bad habit of shaking his pockets with money, and I guess he was shaking it too much. They found him in the snow a year later."

The man who cost Donato Pisani the affection of Jenny was a smoothy named Alfred Manuel Martin. Jenny met him through a friend of hers named May, a Hawaiian woman who was giving her hula lessons. Al Martin was a tall man with a pencil mustache, a Hawaiian of Portuguese descent. He played guitar and sang in neighborhood clubs. According to Jenny, he had a way with words that would find their way to a woman's heart.

Jenny didn't go with Alfred Martin long before she married him. She fell for his charm, hard, loved him as she had never loved a man before. But Al Martin enjoyed the conquest of a woman better than the rest of the relationship, and soon after they were married, there were cracks in their relationship when he began staying out drinking in the local bars until two or three in the morning.

Jenny, in part because he stayed out late, had suspicions that Al Martin wasn't faithful. One day she noticed he no longer was wearing the wristwatch she had given him as a present.

"Where's your wristwatch?"

"I don't know."

When she was three months pregnant, one of her network of gossipy friends visited her at home to inform her that Al had given the wristwatch to a fifteen-year-old girl who was going to Burbank High School.

Jenny Salvini Pisani Martin was not the type of woman to turn the other cheek. Her expressed motto throughout life was "Don't Take Shit from No-body," and true to her colors, she took the trolley to Burbank High School, located the girl, pulled the watch off her wrist, and pummeled her with her fists. As she would describe later, "I beat the holy hell out of her."

Jenny returned home, took all her husband's clothes, stomped all over them, dumped them in a suitcase, and tossed them onto the lawn.

When he came home from work, he asked her, "What's the matter?"

"You're not chipping on me," she said. "Out you go, and you stay out."

Al Martin's car sat at the curb. Jenny took a hand mirror, and like an out-of-control tornado she relentlessly smashed every window on that car. Then she screamed, "Get out, and don't ever come back again!"

Martin, who was a lover, not a fighter, didn't argue. He got in his open-air car and drove off.

Jenny, who loved him dearly, was devastated. Even after Alfred moved out, she continued to monitor his whereabouts. During their separation, another of her spies came to tell her that Al had a girl in his room.

Jenny described what happened next: "I shouldn't have done this, but I put my coat on and went up there. And I'm telling you, I beat the hell out of him. Beat her, too. I beat both of them, and before you knew it, there were all these cops downstairs.

"This policeman said to me, 'Let her go.' Al didn't say a word. I said to him, 'I'm still married to you, you son of a bitch. We're not divorced yet.'

"I guess that's the way I was, and I couldn't help it. I felt better after I beat him up. I punched him. He was a tall sucker. But I got up there to punch him."

When Jenny went to a lawyer and received a court order for Alfred Martin to pay her sixty-five dollars a month child support for her child-to-be, Al Martin disappeared. He had fled to Hawaii, abandoning Jenny and the baby. He never sent his family a penny. For fifteen years he was gone. He wouldn't know his wife had given birth to a son until long after the son hated him for abandoning them.

The baby conceived by Alfred and Jenny Martin didn't want to come out. "I never thought I'd have him," Jenny said. She was a month overdue when she was hanging clothes, the line broke, and she fell backward into the coal bin.

The next day, cut and bruised, she felt the pains and gave birth.

Despite Jenny's degradation and Al's abandonment, the name she gave on the birth certificate read Alfred Manuel Martin, Jr. Once the boy was old enough to understand, Jenny would tell the boy that his father had been nothing but a bum. "The Jackass" was how she referred to him.

Obsessed by what he had done to her, she recited a litany whenever she talked about him. She would tell the boy, "When he dies, I am going to piss on his grave. I know he's going to die before me, and when he does, I'm going to go right there before all his family and friends and pee right on him."

When the boy grew old enough, he would bloody the face of anyone who made the mistake of calling him Alfred.

The Martin boy was born on May 16, 1928. When he was eight months old, Jenny met another man, a kindly, quiet Irishman by the name of Jack Downey.

He was a cook on the ferryboat going from San Francisco to Sausalito. All during the boat trip he flirted with her. She would smile back.

After the boat docked, she met her girlfriend, Peggy, who was fixing her up on a blind date. As they waited, she could see the cook coming toward the car.

"That's the guy who was flirting with me," Jenny said.

"Well, that's the guy you're going out with," Peggy said.

As they rode in the car Downey, who had sung professionally in Chicago, began crooning the song "True Blue."

"I fell in love right there and then," Jenny said.

They were married on November 5, 1929, seven days after the stock market crashed. In the next few years Jenny would give birth to three more children, Joanie, Pat, and Jackie.

If Jenny had one regret it was that she didn't have Jack Downey adopt Alfred, whom everyone called Billy. Grandma Nonna one day picked up the boy from his crib, and she began talking about how beautiful he was.

"Bellissimo" or "Bellino" she called him, and after a while the family started calling him Billy. Jenny was glad no one called him Alfred, a name she came to detest even though it was the name she had bestowed upon him, and she was always sorry that fame didn't come to Billy Downey rather than to Billy Martin.

From the time Billy was a year old Jack Downey raised him like he was his own son. Jack Downey was the only father Billy ever knew. But Jenny Martin for the rest of her life would talk about Alfred Manuel Martin, the Jackass, and she would tell their boy what he had done. When asked about his father, Billy Martin did not talk about Jack Downey. Rather, he talked about the Jackass, the father who had left him.

Times were hard in West Berkeley once the country became gripped by the Depression, but except for one month, Jack Downey's bills got paid, and there was always plenty of food.

Jack Downey was employed at a series of jobs, working for the McCormer ciderworks, then shoveling prunes, then lumping, which involves throwing three-hundred-pound sacks. He graduated to driving a truck, making nine dollars a day.

When Billy was about eight, Jack Downey began to suffer a recurrence of asthma, which had halted his singing career. It became so bad he had trouble breathing, and he had to stop working. The family needed to go on welfare for three weeks.

After those three weeks Jenny stopped reporting to the welfare office. The week before, the welfare worker had told her that she wasn't supposed to spend any welfare money on cigarettes. The worker was holding a cigarette when she told her.

"Who the hell are you to tell me not to smoke?" Jenny told her. "Go to hell. I'll starve to death first."

So she didn't go back. While Jack Downey continued his recuperation the family was helped out with groceries by Mary Figone, a family friend, and Father Moore of the St. Ambrose Church.

Father Moore knew the Martins because Billy went to the church. Jenny had gone as a youngster but refused to go as an adult. Jenny's vocabulary had always been liberally sprinkled with colorful four-letter words, and she didn't feel it right that someone who swore as much as she did should be hypocritical and go to church.

When Father Moore came to visit her, Jenny told him this. Father Moore asked her, "Do you have God in your heart?"

"Yes."

"That's good enough for me."

Father Moore donated food to the Downeys, and in return Jack Downey worked in the church, sweeping floors and cleaning. He was never paid for his work. Jenny would not allow Father Moore to pay him. She felt that Father Moore had been more than generous.

For the rest of his life Billy would tell the story of how he had swept the church floor for Father Moore in exchange for bags of groceries. He made it sound like during his entire childhood his family was just scraping along, one step from the poorhouse.

In fact, although the Downeys certainly were not well off, they were no different from most of the families in the lower-class stratum of their society. They certainly had not been as poor as Billy led others to believe.

Said his sister Pat, "Billy dreamed up certain events, including his poverty-stricken youth. He had a romantic streak when it came to telling the story of his life. He was always trying to make himself seem poorer than he was, to make his rise to the top seem even more impressive. And pretty soon, after telling this story of how he grew up in a slum often enough, he began to believe his own story.

"My dad worked for the church. Billy and I went with him, and we thought it was wonderful to go into church and pull up the kneelers and then be able to walk on the side of the altar. But as far as *his* going there and working? It never happened.

"When his books started coming out, about how he had worked for Father Moore, I questioned him on it. I said, 'You didn't go to the church and work with Dad cleaning up. You *never* did that.' And he said, 'I never said I did.'

"I said, 'How did the writer find this out?'

"He said, 'I'm telling you. I never said it.' And the next book would come out, and it would say the same thing. We finally got wise to it. We began to understand that that was the story Billy wanted everyone to believe."

The monthlong crisis ended when Jack's health improved enough for him to get a job working for the Works Progress Administration, President Franklin Roosevelt's program to put the country back to work.

Jack Downey worked as a handyman and carpenter making eighty-five dollars a month. Money was tight toward the end of each month, so to supplement his income, Jack attached a gas-powered saw to the back of his Model T Ford, collected branches from the California shore, and cut them into firewood, which he sold.

Billy's stepfather was a hard worker his whole life. His family didn't often have a lot of money to spend on entertainment, but there was always food on the table, and Jenny bought Billy new jeans and corduroys, not clothing that was secondhand. He may have grown up without many material possessions, but as a young boy he wasn't fazed by what he lacked. In West Berkeley during the 1930s he had exactly what all the rest of his friends had—the clothes on his back. It wasn't until he went to junior high school and met the children of Berkeley's upper-class society that he discovered what he had been missing.

When he was a preteen, Billy's greatest influence was his half brother, Frank, who was called Tudo. Tudo was born ten years before Billy, and from the time Billy was about six years old, the two found a common bond in the game of baseball. Sister Pat remembers that when Billy was a youngster, the two boys talked baseball constantly.

Tudo had grown up with Augie Galan, a talented athlete who became an outfielder for the Chicago Cubs from 1934 to 1941. Galan played with four other teams until he retired in 1949. Tudo, a pitcher, and Augie had been best of friends in high school, and their friendship has continued to this day. When Billy was growing up, Tudo and Galan talked baseball, discussing the fine points of the game, which Galan learned from his experience with the Cubs. Tudo passed down this information to his younger brother.

In the 1930s, an era before the invention of television and the proliferation of the automobile, children went outside the home for their entertainment. The meeting place was often the local park. In West Berkeley the playground, a long block down and a short block over from the Downey home, was known as James Kenney Park.

Kenney Park was the place to go for those athletically inclined, who wanted to play baseball, football, basketball, kickball, dodgeball, or Ping-Pong. Kids played sports for hours for the sheer pleasure of playing the games. There were no adults coaching them, telling them what they were doing wrong, ruining their fun. In those days sports meant fun, and if you were a talented player, you had plenty of opportunity to improve your game through competition.

From the time he could remember, Billy's home away from home was Kenney Park. On weekends, and especially summer vacations, Billy and his closest childhood friends, Howard Noble, Ruben DeAlba, and Babe Firman, would meet there in the morning and stay until nightfall.

"I'd say, 'Billy, get home in time to eat,' " said Jenny. " 'Oh, Ma, I don't care if it gets cold.' Then he'd get in about seven o'clock, he'd eat, and it'd be time to go to bed."

Because of his brother Tudo and Augie Galan, Billy decided as early as the age of six that he was going to be a baseball player when he grew up. At James Kenney Park a young Billy was able to watch Tudo and Augie and their friends play on the A field against teams from other towns. Before long he was playing and starring against kids his own age.

"He was crazy about baseball from a kid," said his mother. "To tell the truth, I didn't pay no attention to baseball until Billy got into it, and then I started liking it. There was nobody in his family that ever thought about baseball except Tudo."

What Billy learned from Tudo and Augie Galan was aggressiveness. Tudo, a pitcher, wasn't afraid to pitch inside and wasn't afraid of contact on the bases if contact was called for. Ken Irvine, who grew up with Billy and later married his sister Pat, remembers Tudo running from the pitcher's mound, covering first on a play, and shouldering the runner in order to make the out.

"A lot of pitchers avoid contact," said Irvine. "Tudo didn't worry about contact. If he had to make it, he made it."

Tudo was good enough to play major league baseball, but he was a shy, introverted man who couldn't leave home.

"Tudo was a minor league player for the Giants in 1940 and 1941," said sister Pat. "They wanted him to go back East to play baseball. He wasn't used to being away from home, and he went for a couple months and got homesick. Maybe if he had been with Augie, he would have made it."

Augie Galan, because he was a major leaguer, may well have had the strongest influence on Billy's early baseball education. Galan was such an aggressive player that one time he ran into the center-field wall in Chicago's Wrigley Field and broke both his knees. Galan's reputation was that of a player who went all out regardless of consequence, and it was just such aggressiveness that Billy exhibited from the time he began playing the game.

"I met Billy in the third grade," said Ken Irvine, "and when I moved into the neighborhood, his habits were already there. From a young age Billy knew the things you had to know to play good baseball. He was one of those little boys who picked up on baseball at a very early age.

"He knew you didn't let anyone intimidate you. From the time Billy learned to pull up his pants, he knew this stuff. Augie, more than anyone else, had the strongest influence on Billy. Billy played the way Augie Galan played ball.

"From the time we were in grammar school, there was marble season, tops season, in addition to basketball and football, but regardless of the season, Billy had a mitt and a ball with him. When he was eight years old if we didn't have a pickup game, he'd be looking for someone to throw him grounders, and this could be in the dead of winter. He never wanted anyone to hit him fly balls. He wanted grounders, because he wanted to be an infielder."

Billy had a strong throwing arm, but he didn't have the patience to play the outfield. He didn't want to be involved in three plays in a game, even if they were important plays. He wanted to be where the action was, and to Billy that was the infield.

By the age of thirteen, Billy was playing in the A games in Kenney Park, competing against men in their twenties and thirties, including Tudo, Augie

Galan, and other major leaguers including Les Scarsella, Bill Rigney, and Ernie Lombardi.

Billy was gaunt and looked ungainly, but he displayed unusual talent and a desperate passion for the game, and he was accepted into the men's world as a ballplayer.

"Billy did not have the classic movements of a ballplayer," said childhood friend Ruben DeAlba, "but he'd go after any ball hit to him, and he had a great arm. He looked so awkward, but he got the job done. In the field he would stop line drives the average player wouldn't even attempt to go after, and at the plate he was aggressive, would stand in there, and when he hit the ball, he had exceptional power."

One of Billy's early ball-playing friends was Bruno Andrino. Bruno and Billy played together on the same YMCA basketball team.

Remembered Bruno, "Billy showed his temper, but it was a winning temper. He wanted to win, wanted to beat you. He didn't care whether you were big or little, he wanted to beat you, and he did. He was a winner. Didn't matter what sport. If you wanted to go bowling, he'd beat you in bowling. Ping-Pong, same.

"On the basketball court, you had better not miss a shot, especially a layup. He'd say, 'What's the matter, you big dummy? Christ, we laid it up for you.'

"No matter how the play was, he would overshadow you. It was just that he played so hard."

Sam Curtain met Billy when they were about thirteen. Sam played basketball for the San Pablo park teams, and Billy played for James Kenney Park. They also opposed each other when Sam played for St. Joseph's in Berkeley and Billy played for St. Ambrose in the church league.

Said Sam about Billy, "Billy was more dedicated to sports than anything else, other than screwing around."

Since he was a student in elementary school, Billy had chafed at criticism or any attempt to discipline him. Like his mother, Billy had no respect for authority, and hardly a day went by when Billy wasn't either arguing with or being lectured or punished by a teacher. And when he'd get in trouble in school and he'd get his knuckles rapped with a ruler as punishment, his mother would complain to the principal that her son was being picked on.

Said Jenny, "I didn't fool around with none of them teachers, none of them. I'd go in there and let them have it."

His behavior never changed, even in high school. Ruben DeAlba remembered, "In high school never a day went by that he wasn't into something, whether in the classroom or during lunch hour."

What Billy loved most was Sturm und Drang. When things got too quiet, Billy became restless and antsy. He was a youngster who could barely sit still. Always he had to be *doing* something, and what he enjoyed most were activities involving physical competition with a definite outcome.

He loved team sports, but what he enjoyed most as a young boy was fist-fighting. It was a skill he learned from his mother, with whom he would argue fiercely, four-letter words careening around the house with a verbal violence that only two people as alike and devoted to each other as Jenny and Billy could summon. It was Jenny who taught him that life was a struggle and that to earn the respect you deserved you had to use your fists. It was from her that he learned that a strong right hand was the most satisfying way to solve disputes.

Said Jenny, "I'll tell you, when I would hear anyone say anything about me, I wouldn't ask twice. I'd start swinging. I beat up three or four ladies. Why? Because as soon as they said something about me I didn't like, I'd hit them.

"One time we had a neighbor who was picking on Tudo, because Tudo hit his kid, or so he said. The guy grabbed Tudo. I ran out and shoved the guy. I told him, 'I'm his father. I'm his mother. Now you're going to have to fight me.'

"There were men fixing the sewers at the time, and I said, 'Nobody move. I don't want anybody to help me.' And he and I went at it. When he picked up some dirt and threw it in my face, that made me madder. And I really beat the hell out of him. He didn't give me a scratch, nothing.

"He went home, and the next day I found out the guy had been in the war, and they were poor, so I sent food over there.

"Later the guy said, 'I was in the war, and I never had anyone beat me like you did.' That's the God's honest truth."

There were other lessons Billy learned from his mother. He learned from her that the police were an enemy, not a friend. She taught him too that people were out to get you, and you'd better be on guard.

As a boy he understood that no matter what he did, his mom would defend him and even make excuses for him. She was judge and jury, and she would respond with fury at the lawmen whenever Billy would get into mischief. Billy answered to only one higher authority: his mother.

Jack Downey had little influence over Billy, even though he had raised him from the time he was eight months old. Part of it was that like most hardworking blue-collar fathers, Downey was working twelve to fourteen hours a day, and when he came home at night, he was too tired to provide much parental guidance. And, in the 1940s, parenting was less hands-on than it is today.

Said Ruben DeAlba, "You didn't get the encouragement in those days. Not that our parents didn't love us, but it was a different lifestyle: The kids were on their own. Home was just a base. We spent most of our childhood growing up in the streets and the playground."

When Billy was around fifteen, an event occurred that changed his relationship with his stepfather. Alfred Martin showed up one day in front of Billy's home and announced himself to Billy.

Tudo, who was twenty-five at the time, told him, "Don't you come around here. Stay away from this house."

Billy kept his real father at arm's length out of deference to his mother, whose hatred for him continued to burn, but one by-product of the meeting was that Billy's affection for his stepfather cooled noticeably from that time, and Jack's influence on the boy became nonexistent.

As a boy Billy didn't get in *serious* trouble. Few kids did back then, when crime wasn't nearly as violent as it is today. Kids stole from the apple cart or the grocer, and when they fought they used their fists rather than guns and knives. Gangs protected their turf but usually didn't seek trouble. Police were not under the constant threat of death the way they are today, and they responded to provocation with patience rather than force. Billy would get in trouble with the police, but there were few consequences. Mom defended him from all outside attempts to discipline him.

One time Billy was visiting his closest friend, Howard Noble, during school hours, when the truant officer showed up at the Nobles' house. When the truant officer accused Billy of skipping school, Billy punched him. The officer drove Billy back to his house to discuss what happened with his mother. His mother told the truant officer, "Don't you ever put a hand on my son."

Another time a neighborhood boy stole money and blamed it on Billy. The police took Billy to a detention center for a day.

When the police came to the Downey house, Jenny angrily told them, "You look in every goddamn room, look everywhere, cause you won't find a goddamn thing, because if he'da stole it, I'da beat the hell out of him."

Said Jenny, "Billy knew the other kid had done it, but he wasn't going to squeal on him, but finally, he told me."

On a third occasion Jenny got a call from the police in nearby Albany, California. They had Billy at the station. Jenny wanted to know why.

According to Jenny, the only reason he was there was because he was from West Berkeley, and West Berkeley boys had a bad reputation.

Said Jenny, "One of the cops was fresh, and he took Billy and knocked him into the wall, and Billy hit him back. See, Billy didn't like it. Billy wasn't going to take that shit from no cop.

"They called me and said, 'We have your kid. Come and get him.'

"I said, 'You took him, you bring him back the same way.' They left him off a block away. They wouldn't come to the house, because I would have knocked the shit out of them myself. Ha!

"I wouldn't take nothing from nobody. Billy took after me, to tell you the truth. I was a son of a gun. I'd tell him, 'Nobody is better than you.'

"And that's how I raised Billy. Time and time again, I told him, 'Never take shit from nobody.' "

Billy took his mother's lessons to heart. By the time he was fifteen years old, Billy Martin had earned a reputation for picking fights and finishing them with one punch. All his life Billy would talk about the fights he got into as a youngster. He told me, "From the time I was twelve until I was maybe fifteen, I awoke every morning knowing that there was a good chance I was going to have to get into a fight with somebody."

But according to his friends, few blows were ever exchanged in Billy's fights. Usually they were one-punch KOs, with Billy doling out the punishment. If you looked at him funny or he didn't like your body language, or if he decided there was something about you he didn't appreciate, he would say something provocative, and if you took the bait, he would attack you and hurt you, connecting with a Sunday punch before you knew what hit you.

To say Billy was a fighter as a boy doesn't do him justice. His reputation was more that of a vicious thug, a person to be avoided if he wasn't your friend.

"You always had to be a little leery of what he was going to do," said Sam Curtain. "Nobody ever knew what the hell was going through Billy's mind."

Said Ruben DeAlba, "The demons—he had them. Billy could be so nice, like an angel, so pleasant and congenial, and then minutes later he'd be a raving maniac, ready to do battle."

One of his early tutors was a professional boxer by the name of Dick Foster. Foster had been an up-and-coming professional fighter when he was a student at Berkeley High. Because he was brought along too fast, he took too many beatings and never became the champion he should have been. But before his managers destroyed him, he had a reputation for being able to hit and take a hit.

Foster, like Augie Galan, was a close friend of Tudo's, and on the playground of Kenney Park, Foster would teach Billy how to fight.

Ken Irvine remembers Billy's workouts. "A professional fighter wasn't any better on the speed bag than Billy," says Irvine.

One lesson Billy took to heart was Foster's admonition, "Make the first punch count." To this advice Billy added his own interpretation. To Billy, who had no respect for authority or rules, every fight was war. Winning the fight was all-important. Billy's motto became "Don't Let the Other Guy See the First Punch Coming."

University Avenue begins by the San Francisco Bay and the Berkeley marina, and it heads due east intersecting the streets of West Berkeley in the flats and then climbing steeply for several miles. It passes Shattuck and Telegraph streets near Berkeley High School until it reaches the sprawling, beautiful campus of the University of California, Berkeley.

Before junior high school, Billy's world was limited to the flatland of West Berkeley. His friends were Italian and also Mexican, after a flood of Mexican immigrants came into the area in the 1940s. Some of Billy's closest friends were Mexican, including Ruben DeAlba and Jesse Garcia.

Few if any of Billy's friends even considered climbing the hill to go to college because tuition was beyond their means and also because of racism and classism, with the high school advisers tending to steer the poorer Italian, Mexican, and the sprinkling of black kids away from college prep classes and into courses such as shop, car repair, and physical education.

The children who lived up on the hill grew up in expensive houses, drove fancy cars, had more money and education, and dressed better.

To the upper-class kids, the children from the bottom of the hill were ruffians to be avoided or ignored, as though they were invisible. The upper-class kids did not allow the Italian and Mexican kids to join their social clubs. Snubbed, the kids from West Berkeley snidely referred to the wealthy kids from up on the Hill as "the Goats."

Billy hadn't been aware of these class differences until he went to Burbank Junior High School. There he was thrown in with sons and daughters of professionals and UCal-Berkeley professors. Billy and many of the poorer West Berkeley kids were awed by what these kids had, and they reacted to them by withdrawing from them, sticking with each other. And when they withdrew, these richer kids didn't bother to reach out to the West Berkeley kids, in effect snubbing them, so that the school was segregated into two groups.

"They just wouldn't have anything to do with us," said Ruben DeAlba. "To the Goats, we were garbage."

Race was never an issue when Billy Martin was growing up. No one blinked that the Downey family was close with several Mexican families. Rather, what affected Billy deeply when he went to junior high school was class. The distinction stayed with him the rest of his life. The Goats had money, and he didn't. They had education and opportunities that he didn't. He felt an ambivalence toward these monied WASPs that would never leave him. He admired them, wanted to be like them, and wanted to have what they had, but even more deeply he hated them for making him feel inferior.

Puberty coincided with his arrival into junior high school. Adding to his resentment of the Goats was his discovery that the boys with the money and the snappier clothing were more apt to attract the prettiest girls. Suddenly what had seemed good enough no longer was. Fifteen is a tough enough age for most adolescents, but when Billy began comparing his clothes and his material belongings with those of the richer kids on the hill, for the first time in his life he felt shabby.

"My clothes was one of the reasons I didn't date much," Billy told me. He stared at the floor, humiliation on his face. Not measuring up was his greatest fear, and in junior high school and later in high school there was a whole unapproachable society out there rejecting and excluding him and his friends. In defiance of the Goats, who sported crew cuts and wore cotton button-down shirts and saddle shoes, Billy and his friends affected DA haircuts, long-haired and greasy, and they went to school wearing clothes that foreshadowed *The Blackboard Jungle*.

The coming of pubescence also awoke strong feelings of self-pity that came as a result of his large Roman nose. Other kids called him names like Pinocchio, Big Nose, and the one the sportswriters printed every day in the papers after he became a professional player, Billy the Horn. His acute sensitivity led him to react violently to what he perceived to be the barest slight.

Said his sister Pat, "Billy was always on his guard to see whether you were going to insult him. One time I wrote him a letter that ended, 'See you soon, Goon.' Billy took it seriously. I had to explain that I was only joking. He took everything very seriously and to heart."

His nose was a daily reminder that he felt ugly.

A close family friend, Lewis Figone, remembers that comments about his nose usually led to fisticuffs.

"I didn't think his nose was that bad," said Figone, "but a lot of guys used to tease him about it, and he got in a lot of fights about it."

His friend Sam Curtain remembers that as Billy's reputation as a fighter grew, fewer and fewer were willing to taunt him.

"He did have an exceptionally large nose," said Curtain, "but no one who knew him would take a chance in joking about it. Billy probably weighed 135, but nobody who knew Billy would take a chance of saying something like that because he was so goofy. He'd punch you right off the bat without even thinking about it. He would wait for a guy to say something, and a lot of guys would get punched for not even meaning what they said.

"Billy picked most of the fights. They really weren't fights. He'd just punch somebody—to hurt him, not just to punch him. Billy didn't want anybody getting up. He wanted to make sure the fight was over."

Ruben DeAlba remembered, "In high school I saw Billy take after guys and pummel them, beat them till they fell in a heap, and if you didn't pull him off, he'd keep swinging."

Said his sister Pat, "Picking fights was in Billy's blood. There was no need for what Billy and his friends did. They had a wild streak. For them, fighting was the thing to do."

In high school Billy was part of a gang called the West Berkeley Boys.

"We gained quite a reputation as being really bad boys, mean boys," said Ruben DeAlba. "You didn't fool with the guys from West Berkeley."

The West Berkeley Boys liked to snatch beanies off the heads of the UCal freshmen, and for fun the group enjoyed isolating sailors visiting town and beating them up.

"I remember one time I was at the Paramount Theater," said Sam Curtain. "This was during the war. I was a junior, and Billy was a sophomore, and he was running with a bunch of kids from Kenney Park. We came out of the theater, and Billy came running up. He said, 'Sam, we just beat the shit out of some sailors down there.' They'd go out and get some poor goddamn sailor and beat the shit out of him, and they thought that was fun. Well, that wasn't fun as far as I was concerned. That wasn't my game, but Billy would enjoy that. He had a tendency to be violent, but he picked his spots."

One of their favorite targets was the rich kids from Berkeley and neighboring towns.

Said Ruben DeAlba, "For entertainment, we liked to crash parties in other towns—Albany, Oakland, Richmond. Most of us walked or went by bus. The cops in the other towns didn't like us. They hassled us because they knew we were up there looking for mischief, trouble, whatever.

"Usually we'd go to a party to instigate a brawl. We were looking for a fight. There'd be fisticuffs and bloody noses. If the cops came, we fled on foot.

"See, we had no identity. But soon, everyone knew who we were, that we could take care of ourselves and that nobody better mess with us. In fact, nobody did."

"I remember it was graduation day. Billy and I both graduated. We walked down, got our diplomas, and right after the ceremony a bunch of us headed off to crash a Goats party.

"We walked in, raided the icebox, just took over, and no one said a word. And when we got our fill of this hell-raising, we went up to the Berkeley Hills to Lake Anzo, where the Goats hung out to swim. We were drinking beer, and we passed out.

"We woke up the next day and went home. That's how we spent our graduation."

When Billy first began showing an interest in girls in junior high, he found he was very vulnerable to rejection by the girl Goats, and it scarred him.

"I remember one school dance we had in the junior high school gymnasium," Billy told me. "All the girls stood on one side of the gym, and all the boys on the other. It had been quite a while before I got up the courage to ask this one girl, who I had been eyeing for a long time, to dance. I walked up to her, asked her for a dance, and she said no. Then a little later another guy went over and asked her, and she said yes to him. I said to myself, 'That's the last time I'll ever ask a girl to dance.' I'll never forget because it made such a great impression on me. It was such a blow to my ego, and it was embarrassing because when I came back the guys hoorahed me. I said to myself, 'That's it,' and so I went through high school and didn't date one girl from there."

Billy discovered that with the girls from his own social class there was something about his personality that made him attractive and popular despite his lack of wealth and his floppy ears and big nose.

"Billy was an ugly duckling," said Ruben DeAlba, "but women liked him. Billy would go after the good-looking girls, and somehow he got a date with them. I always wondered, How in the hell is he doing it? Billy was an extrovert. He had a line.

"Most boys wonder, Does she like me? but they never find out because they don't make a move. Billy was making the moves. And he was scoring.

"And when he had his eye on a particular girl, he was always very persistent. Very persistent. He wouldn't take no for an answer. He'd wear 'em down to the point where they would finally go out with him."

Getting a girl to go out with him became the object. The chase became everything. Getting a woman to say yes became a lifelong obsession.

"Most of anything else," said DeAlba, "Billy loved a challenge. Quoting Clint Eastwood, that's what made his day. And you know what, as soon as he had a woman in the palm of his hand, he'd get rid of her. She would become boring to him."

"In one of the books Billy wrote," said his sister Pat, "he said that in his first love affair, he didn't know where to put his you-know-what and almost put it in her belly button. Maybe that was when he was three. But in high school, the girls were always after him. He didn't have to chase them. They went after him. The phone used to ring all the time. He was just a young kid. The girls would say to Joannie and me, 'Please fix us up with your brother.'

"He had this need to conquer. I had girlfriends I wouldn't fix him up with, because he'd love you, and then he'd be gone. A couple of them wouldn't believe me. I would tell them, 'If you go out with him, don't come and cry to me.'

"And after they went out with him, they'd say, 'I should have listened to you.'

"I'd say, 'I don't want to hear it.' "

In school, say his friends, Billy was a desultory student who took mostly shop and phys-ed courses. Billy had a good mind, but to him and most of the kids from the flats, schooling was a waste of time in that all the adults they knew held blue-collar jobs that didn't require any more than a high school diploma. What was the point of going to college, they figured, if they were going to be a postman, fireman, or truck driver? Or in Billy's case, a professional baseball player.

Billy did just well enough academically to stay in school and graduate. One reason he didn't drop out was so he could play on the Berkeley High basketball and baseball teams.

He was a good enough basketball player to make the high school junior varsity team as a junior and the varsity as a senior, but it was in baseball that he excelled. Though he didn't play much, he made the varsity as a freshman, which was and is very unusual, and he started and starred for three years on the Berkeley High School varsity baseball team.

Berkeley High had an enrollment of about 1,100 students. At the time it was one of the finest high schools in the state of California, rated among the top ten academically. It had a very good baseball team. Outfielder Babe Van Huitt signed with the Cincinnati Reds when he graduated, and Billy, Ruben DeAlba, and Babe Firman all signed with the Oakland Oaks of the Pacific Coast League.

When Billy played, Berkeley High never won a county title as it should have because Billy and his teammates Ruben DeAlba and Babe Van Huitt were hot-headed and often out of control.

The coach of the Berkeley High team was Elgin Erickson, an old-timer whom his players remember best for scratching his balls while he coached on third base during the ball games. Erickson was soft-spoken. He didn't teach fundamentals but enjoyed watching the kids play the game. Also, he was a sportsman, a coach who believed that how you played the game was more important than whether you won or lost.

But according to Ruben DeAlba, winning baseball games and becoming famous in school circles was what Billy and the West Berkeley boys needed to overcome their intense feelings of rejection and lack of self-worth.

"We always loved to see our names in print," said DeAlba. "We loved that. Billy had his scrapbook, and I had mine."

Added DeAlba, "Because of his nose, his ears, his bad teeth, he was abused and ridiculed all his young life, and he was very, very self-conscious about that. What made Billy was the abuse he took. From this abuse came the desire to prove himself and make something of himself. To compensate for that, he drove to prove himself in sports. Every loss in high school was just like a personal affront to him. He just hated to lose."

Coach Erickson and Billy didn't get along because there was nothing gentlemanly about the way Billy played the game. Billy, who played shortstop and third base for Berkeley High, *never* wanted to lose. The WIN column was the way Billy was able to find his own self-worth. Winning acted on him like a drug. If he won, he could bury for a short time his feelings of self-loathing while he basked in the satisfaction of victory. If he lost, those negative feelings would surface, and his frustration and anger would simmer.

In high school Billy competed at a frenzied emotional level from start to finish, and if his team got behind, he would become sullen and nasty and often would do something antagonistic, ignoring sportsmanship and civility, those qualities that sports are supposed to teach high school players.

"He always did the one little thing extra that he shouldn't have done, like tagging a guy in the face," said Sam Curtain. "There was something about him. He had that little shit-disturbing quality where he *had* to do those things that infuriated people all the time. It was his nature."

In one game against Haywood High School, Billy was playing shortstop, and the star Haywood player, whose name was George Legorio, came into second base as Billy was covering on the double play. Billy thought Legorio had come in with his spikes a little too high.

The next time Legorio came into second, Billy was waiting. He took the ball but made no attempt to make the out. He smashed the ball into Legorio's teeth. Legorio slid under the tag and was safe, but Billy had made his point and gained an edge.

Said Ken Irvine, who followed the team closely, "George Legorio never tried to go into Billy with his spikes high again. And because George was their big star player, that impressed the rest of the players on the Haywood team. They didn't do it either."

Elgin Erickson had a team of talented players, but he could not handle Billy and his friends. The rivalry with the Goats within the team was a continual problem. The Goats tolerated the West Berkeley players on the field but shunned them off the diamond. The West Berkeley players felt that Erickson sometimes played Goats who weren't as talented as the West Berkeley players.

One time the center fielder, Babe Van Huitt, was angry because Erickson played a Goat at first base instead of one of the West Berkeley kids. A fly ball was hit to center, and Babe just looked at the ball and watched it drop in front of him. He stood there as the ball rolled past him, and then he went and chased it down. Erickson never said a word.

DeAlba's senior year Erickson had to kick him off the team after he shoved an umpire. DeAlba hit what he thought was a home run, and the umpire called it foul. DeAlba, who had a temper, instinctively ran up and shoved the umpire.

Billy made the all-star Alameda County Athletic League team as a junior in 1945, playing in the all-star game. In 1946 he again was named an all-star, but he was barred from playing in the prestigious game his senior year because of an incident in a game against Richmond High about two weeks before the end of the season.

One of Richmond's rooters along the third-base stands had been heckling him, continually calling him Pinocchio, making fun of his nose. Billy took the abuse late into the game, when he no longer could stand it. He dropped his glove by the third-base bag, ran up to the heckler, and began slugging him. When the umpire went to break up the fight, Billy struck him, too. Erickson, appalled, kicked him off the team.

And when he got in trouble, Billy would tell his mother about his fights. Always the other person started it, and always Billy would finish it. And always his mother understood and approved because after all, he was only doing what Jenny Downey had always told him: "Billy, don't *ever* take no shit from nobody."

# HENRY

Around the same time Billy Martin's grandfather was traveling steerage in the hull of a steamship from Italy to the United States, the great-grandfather of George Steinbrenner III, a man by the name of Philip Minch, ran his own steamship company on the Great Lakes. Minch himself had been an immigrant, having sailed from Blankenheim, Germany, in 1840 and landed in Vermilion, Ohio. In 1842, Minch, a carpenter by trade, built his first ship and, after building up a fleet of ships, in 1875 moved his operation to Cleveland, the Lakes' busiest port, where the steel and petroleum industries had been booming since iron ore was discovered in the Masabe region of northern Michigan.

When Minch died in 1887, he left a large fleet. His daughter, Sophia, and her husband, Henry Steinbrenner, took over control. Henry, who had emigrated from Stuttgart, Germany, had a background in law and real estate, and in 1905 he reorganized the company, calling it the Kinsman Transit Company.

Henry died in 1929, just before the stock market crash, and Sophia died four years later. With the Crash, the demand for steel declined, and the need for the huge fleets disappeared, bankrupting many of the fleet owners.

Kinsman, however, did not go under, and it survived because of the penny-pinching, the organizational ability, and the sheer will of one man: Henry Steinbrenner, the grandson of Sophia and Henry and father of George III.

Henry as a boy had gone to Culver Military Academy and then on to the Massachusetts Institute of Technology, where he starred at track. His times in the high hurdles were good enough for him to make the 1928 Olympic track team, but his girlfriend, Rita, insisted Henry choose between marrying her and training for the Olympics, and Henry chose her. After they married, on July 4, 1930, their first child, George, was born.

At six foot three, with white hair, Henry had a regal bearing. He was known as a man who kept his word. If he said a boat would be at a certain place at a certain time to pick up your grain, you could count on it being there, even if he could have made more advantageous use of the boats in a subsequent deal. Henry was not a liar, nor was he a double-crosser. His word was his bond.

Around the Great Lakes he was famous for his eccentricities. He was the sort of man about whom the people in the business whispered stories. Because he was powerful and rich, they feared him too much to tell the stories out loud. The one attribute talked about most prevalently was his penury. It was said that Henry once found a three-cent stamp on the floor of the office and began screaming at the secretaries over the need not to be wasteful. Another story seems straight out of Charles Dickens's *A Christmas Carol*. It occurred one Christmastime, when one of the secretaries in the office asked Henry if she could leave early so she could sing Christmas carols.

"Sing a carol right now," the Scrooge-like Henry Steinbrenner ordered. She did so, and he had her sit back down in her chair and keep working.

The other attributes possessed by Henry Steinbrenner that the old salts liked to gossip about were his temper and his penchant for firing people. He ran his boat company like a South American dictatorship. You did things his way—or else.

One of his rules was that a boat could not travel faster than ten miles an hour, in order to cut down on fuel costs.

"Henry fired quite a few guys for not doing that," said Robert Sauvey, a first mate who had worked for Kinsman. "Also for mouthing back to him. He was a bitchy old bastard," he added.

What Sauvey remembered best about Henry was that there actually were two Henrys, the one who was tyrannical during times of crisis and stress, and the other one who was gentlemanly and even gentle if everything was going smoothly.

"I was doing winter work in Cleveland," said Sauvey. "We were unloading the *James E. Ferris* at Montana Mills, and it was the first time in twenty-five years that the Cleveland River had frozen over. We had five inches of ice, and there was no way we could move the boat close enough to the elevator to unload the grain.

"All the longshoremen had turned out, standing around because they couldn't do their work, and it was costing Mr. Steinbrenner money.

"I called the tugs, but they wanted two weeks' pay to break the ice. I couldn't use the fire tugs because of a city ordinance. Henry was feuding with G&W Welding, so we couldn't use their icebreaker.

"I finally went to the Coast Guard. They had to fit out a boat in Detroit and send it to us.

"I was talking to Henry on the phone. He said, 'What the hell is going on down there?'

"I said, 'We can't move the boat. We can't break the ice.'

"He said, 'Goddamn it, Sauvey, you have to do something about it.'

"And just then, I saw the icebreaker coming down. I said, 'Mr. Steinbrenner, here comes the icebreaker now.'

"And it was like a switch had been pulled. His voice became calm, and he said, 'Robert, that just goes to show you. The pollution program is working.' In other words, because of the pollution program, the lake was clean enough to freeze over. When he saw the job was going to get done, that's how quickly his mood shifted. Remember the old piston-ring commercials: 'So tough but yet so gentle'? That's the way Henry Steinbrenner was.''

Henry and Rita Steinbrenner lived on a twenty-acre farm across the road from the shores of Lake Erie in the town of Bay Village, Ohio, about a half an hour west of downtown Cleveland. The farmhouse, built in 1874 and remodeled by Henry before he moved into it in 1939, was simple and tasteful. In front of the house on the broad green lawn stood a gazebo covering a water well. In front of the well rested a large boat anchor. Henry called his home Kinsman Anchorage.

A caretaker lived in the back, and Henry and he would dig in and work on the gardens of flowers and vegetables, which Rita canned. There was a stand by the road for selling the produce. The farm had ponies, lambs, guinea pigs, and chickens. It was a fun place for the neighborhood children to play.

Despite his considerable wealth, Henry was as fiscally conservative at home as he was with his business. He drove around in an old Ford, the equivalent of a Pinto at the time. One time a tree branch or something else heavy fell on the car's roof and put a dent in it, and it was a long time before Henry fixed the dent, because the car ran fine and he didn't feel it was necessary.

Henry, the product of Culver Military Academy, ran his fleet with precision and ran his family the same way. Henry had rules that had to be followed.

"His father was very Prussian, and he would fix the rules, and you better do it his way," said Patsy Stecher, a close friend of the Steinbrenners'. "Henry could be a tyrant."

Henry dictated when the radio could be listened to. He outlined the various chores for the children.

Frank Treadway, a Bay Village neighbor who grew up with George, remembered Henry Steinbrenner as "a tough old German." Treadway remembers his own mother once telling him a story told to her by Rita about how shortly after their honeymoon, Rita had made Henry a casserole made of leftovers, and he had thrown it at her. Apparently she thought a casserole was a legitimate form of food, and he didn't.

One story George himself told Treadway concerned Henry's edict that there be no running water in the Steinbrenner home after eight P.M.

"One night George came home from a date and started to go downstairs," said Treadway. "He heard a splashing of water in the basement. George said, 'Mother, is that you?'

"Poor Rita was giving herself a sponge bath in the laundry tub because it was eight-thirty and Henry didn't want to hear the water running."

Treadway remembers that Henry didn't want to have anything to do with George's young friends. "My father was the same way," said Treadway. "He was polite to my friends, but he didn't care to have much to do with them."

And yet, says Treadway, he can remember after not seeing Henry for a period of time, Henry would put his arm around him and glad-hand him "as though you had just gotten back from the Ethiopian war."

"As tough as Henry was," said Treadway, "he could charm the pants off a virgin."

Joe Bennett, another close childhood friend of George's, also saw Henry's dual nature.

"Henry was an autocrat, a tough son of a bitch," said Bennett. "From a child's perspective he was overbearing. It was his way or no way. I would say Henry ruled the roost with an iron hand. Rita was a very timid person. She had to go along with it. My impression was that she could be scared of him, and so could George.

"We all feared him. I was scared to death of him. He was just a tough guy, tougher than most fathers. I was petrified of the guy."

According to Bennett, Henry Steinbrenner didn't ask George to do anything. He told him, "Do it," and George jumped. In fact, Bennett was so scared of Henry that when he came into the house, Bennett often ran out.

"He was difficult to all the people who knew George," said Bennett.

In the same breath Bennett will say that Henry Steinbrenner on the inside was sentimental and gentle, the same description as that given by Kinsman First Mate Robert Sauvey. "Inside he was pretty much of a pussycat," said Bennett.

There were times when George experienced both the sympathetic and the difficult characteristics of his father. George went to junior high school in Bay Village, and he was the only boy in the eighth grade who wore a jacket and tie to school. As part of his education Henry made him go into the egg business. George would collect the fresh eggs from the chicken coop, and he would sell the eggs to neighbors, and he would also take the eggs to school and sell them to his teachers. With the money from the eggs, George earned his allowance.

One afternoon George brought his report card home after school, and in one course George got a lower grade than he thought he deserved. "The teacher doesn't like me," George told his father. The next morning Henry drove to the school to talk to the principal about George's unfair grade.

According to the story told by George to many of his friends, that morning George carried the eggs to school, and before he could unload them he was called into the principal's office to testify about the grade. His father and the principal started arguing, and during the discussion, as George's story went, his father, enraged at the way his son was being treated, began shaking him, because, apparently, he couldn't shake the principal. All the eggs in his pockets broke, according to George's story.

Like Billy, who as an adult made his childhood seem poorer than it was, George liked to tell stories to show how tough this rich kid, who went to summer camp and private school, had it as a child.

As Frank Treadway remembered, "If you are rich when you grow up and are still rich when you're fifty, it's no big deal, so what George did was make out that he had a few mountains when he was a kid and make the stories sound all that much better."

The egg story is one of the stories George likes best, to show how tough his father had been on him.

But as his father's actions would indicate over and over in the years ahead, the egg story illustrated something else: that Henry never trusted George enough to let him fend for himself and get out of his own scrapes. The father's subliminal message to George was: You're not capable. You can't handle this.

During his adolescence, whenever young George got into any sort of trouble and couldn't get out of it by himself, old man Henry would always come to his rescue. In much the same way that Billy Martin's mother excused whatever he did, George Steinbrenner's father, using his power, influence, and money, was able to "fix it" anytime young George got into a bind. Self-reliance was not the answer, George learned; using one's connections and influence was.

Beginning in the ninth grade, George attended Culver Military Academy, located on beautiful Lake Maxinkuckee in Culver, Indiana, about forty-five minutes south of South Bend and about three hours from George's Bay Village home.

Once George entered Culver Military Academy, Henry Steinbrenner's specter hovered over the entire school. Yes, his father would yell at him to do better, but for George his father became his avenging guardian angel. With his father only a phone call away, he didn't have to do better to do better. He only had to call.

Culver was a male-only private school with an excellent academic reputation when George entered as a freshman in the fall of 1944. Not all the students came from wealthy families, but tuition was steep, and so a lot of the kids came from money. Among the kids who went to school with George were Pitt Oakes from Bimini in the Bahamas, who at the time, as one classmate put it, "owned all the sugar in sight," and Peter Plant, who was movie actress Barbara Stanwyck's son. Money and status abounded at Culver.

The school was divided into units. Most of the students were members of the infantry. A select few rode horses as members of the cavalry. The school had stables for the horses and an indoor polo ring.

George, who loved music and theater, was a drummer in the band unit. The band held little status on campus. On Sunday mornings when the entire school went into parade formation, eight hundred students put on a show of military smartness. The infantry marched past the reviewing stand, raised sabers, saluted, presented arms, turned eyes right, and the Black Horse troop cavalry would ride past, the riders looking sharp atop their mounts. Providing the music was the sixty-member band unit, playing John Philip Sousa marches and some compositions penned by Culver's band director. At Culver the band unit was considered in the same way band members are at most high schools. As young boys are wont to do, they see music and arts as being less than macho, and they react accordingly.

The school was a paragon of discipline. The students were awakened at 6:25 in the morning, and everyone had three minutes to get his feet onto the floor. After breakfast there was a white-glove inspection, then there were classes, and then sports in the afternoon, and after dinner there was a mandatory study period during which the students had to be silent and do their homework.

Like at West Point, the system was designed to terrify the freshmen into obedience. Under the strict plebe–old man network, you could be subjected to harassment and intense intimidation. You had to be tough to survive that first year emotionally.

George was not tough. He admitted years later, "There was more than one night when I would go to bed more than misty-eyed. Because it was tough; really tough."

Lee Robinson, George's freshman-year roommate, remembered that George very much resented the authority of the upperclassmen.

"At the dining table he would often do things out of line," said Robinson. "You're supposed to sit on the edge of your chair, and he would not do that. They'd yell at him. There wasn't much he could say. He'd end up doing it."

In later years, when he became the inspector, there were times when he would bend down to check a plebe's shoes to see how well they were shined, only to take the laces and tie them together. At the first command the unknowing plebe would fall over and get a demerit.

One of his classmates remembers a young George enjoying the practice of taking a pat of butter, putting it on the end of his knife, and flicking the knife in such a way that the butter would be launched skyward until it hit the high ceiling, where it would stick, and then melt, dripping onto whatever or whomever was below. On this day George had managed to launch three butter patties when his counselor came over to question him about it.

George looked the counselor in the eye and denied having done it. He looked at the other students and said, cool as a cucumber, "Now you guys gotta quit flicking the butter patties on the ceiling."

The counselor suspected that George was lying, but he couldn't prove it. He told him if he did it again and was caught, he would be in deep trouble.

George, an average student, was argumentative in class. He had great difficulty dealing with the autocratic military system.

George got demerits, as many of the youngsters did that first year, but George received more than his share, enough that on a couple of occasions he had to walk to the square with a rifle on his shoulder as punishment.

But by his junior year his classmates saw George had devised, by accident or design, a system that got him all he wanted out of Culver without having to do the work. It was a system that earned George dislike from some and loathing from others. But getting his way was what mattered to George. How the others felt about him never seemed to mean very much to him.

His classmates began to notice that George's father, Henry, was showing up on campus a great deal, and his appearance often coincided with a problem that George had created for himself, whether it was a poor grade or a potential punishment for his undisciplined behavior.

And what they saw was that after his father's visit, George's problem often would evaporate.

"If his father felt the faculty was treating George unfairly," said Ket "Pete" Barber, George's senior-year roommate, "he'd come over and address his complaints to the faculty and embarrass George somewhat. He would chew George out good and proper. Of course, the other students never saw the chewing out."

What they saw were the results.

"George used his father and his father's influence any chance he could to further his career at Culver," Lee Robinson said. "At least that's how the students looked at it. There was a group of us, maybe fifteen including George, who went through the four years of Culver together, and most of that group felt that way.

"He'd get in trouble. For instance, he wouldn't have his shoes shined, and he'd get demerits, and the kids would joke with him and say, 'George, you don't have to worry about that. Pop will get those wiped off for you.'

"It didn't upset George. He'd say about demerits, 'I don't have to worry about those things.'

"He would sass the teachers. It was only after his father developed a close relationship with the band director, Colonel Payson, and some of the other teachers, that his grades improved his last year.

"Even back then at Culver, when he had a goal to reach, he didn't hesitate to use his or anyone else's money or power to achieve that goal."

Robinson was so convinced of George's effectiveness in using Henry's money and influence to corrupt the system that he felt there were times when George's father got specific tormentors of George's in trouble.

"A lot of us suspected that," Robinson said.

"It's understandable the others would think that," said Pete Barber, "because they knew George's dad was there and stuck up for George's rights and got aggressive about it. Henry was a rather large man with a stentorian voice, and he wasn't the kind of guy who would speak in whispers. He'd go to the superintendent's office or the counselor's office, and people knew he was there, and even the faculty members would sometimes talk about it."

The most egregious example of George's getting something he didn't deserve occurred in the spring of his senior year when he was promoted to lieutenant. He was named aide to the commandant.

Some of his classmates raised their eyebrows. He had been an average student, didn't seem to work hard, showed little leadership, and here he was, being awarded the rank of lieutenant, a promotion many felt he didn't deserve.

Said one band-member classmate, who like some of George's former acquaintances preferred anonymity, "It was obvious that Pop had a heavy hand
in whatever George did, and that brought some reactions from faculty members
to try not to accept that kind of interference. I know it was resisted for quite a
while. But I always thought George got his lieutenancy through Dad's influence."

Said Robinson, "It was almost a special rank created for him just to give
him a position of authority. The other kids couldn't understand that. And it
came after a visit by his father, December of 1947. Some of the kids were
unhappy."

At the end of his senior year George was awarded the Callahan Award, chosen
by the band director, Colonel Payson, as the most dedicated member of the
band.

Again his classmates were amused and not at all surprised that he won the
award because of the special connection between Payson and George's father,
who visited Payson often when he arrived on campus.

Said Lee Robinson, "The Callahan Award was a very minor sort of award.
That's why I don't think anyone got overly upset at George winning it. There
were obviously better musicians in the band than George. George really wasn't
that good a musician. I can swear to that. I played the drums myself."

But what was important to George, even at that young age, was the award.
Trophies were what counted, not how he ended up getting them. How the others
felt about him getting them was also not important.

Henry Steinbrenner, using his power and influence to buy George the grades
and honors no one else felt he deserved, taught George Steinbrenner his most
important lesson in life: Winning is everything. George learned that if you have
money and power, you can play by your own rules. And finally, George learned,
if you have money and power and play by your own rules, there is absolutely
nothing the poor suckers can do about it.

# BILLY STENGEL

hen Billy Martin graduated from high school, his goal was to play for the best. He was different from the majority of the California players who aspired to play in the Pacific Coast League, which fielded teams throughout the West Coast from San Diego to Vancouver. Though it was considered by Easterners to be only minor league at the Triple A level, for Californians it was their major league, because the majors were half a country away. The closest major league baseball teams at the time were the St. Louis Cardinals and Browns, and for those California kids, cities like New York, Boston, and Philadelphia seemed as far away and exotic as London, Paris, and Rome.

To the boys of the Oakland Bay area, the Oakland Oaks *were* the major leagues. If you could play for the Oaks, you could make just as much money as the major leaguers, and you could play at home.

For Billy Martin, however, making the PCL wasn't shooting high enough. Most kids wanted to stay at home. Billy didn't care if he did or not. Ever since he had been a little boy old enough to think about his future, his goal had been to play at the top. He would tell anyone who cared to listen that when he grew up he was going to be a baseball player, an infielder, and play for the New York Yankees.

"From the third grade, he wanted to go to the Yankees," said childhood friend Ken Irvine. "He knew about Babe Ruth and Lou Gehrig. He was born with a baseball in his hand. From the time he learned to read, he read baseball. He knew all about the players, and the biggest stars were Yankees.

"Augie Galan and Billy used to talk about it, but Billy had no desire to go to the Cubs. He wanted to be a Yankee.

"I can remember one time at Kenney Park the ball took a bad hop and hit him right between the eyes. He had a huge lump. It was a wonder he could still see. But he wouldn't come out of the ball game because he wanted them to hit him another ground ball. That's what got Billy to where he went."

Said his friend Ruben DeAlba, "All through high school, he was telling me he was going to be a Yankee."

The Yankees were baseball's dominant team, and winning was everything to Billy. Beginning when he was eight years old, around the time kids pay attention to these things, the Yankees won pennants in 1936, 1937, 1938, 1939, 1941, 1942, and 1943. Who was Billy Martin going to root for if not the Yankees?

He also liked the Yankees because of their Italian tradition. The Yankees featured two of the greatest players of the day, Joe DiMaggio and Phil Rizzuto, and boasted Tony Lazzeri and Frank Crosetti. If you were a great Italian player, who had the greatest Italian players? DiMaggio and Crosetti, moreover, came from the San Francisco Bay Area.

Few, however, thought Billy had the talent or the temperament to make the Pacific Coast League, never mind the Olympian New York Yankees. But Billy, despite his societal insecurities, had no self-doubts about his abilities as a ballplayer. Billy *knew* he would be a big-leaguer. Somehow, through the strength of his will, Billy Martin intended to battle all the way to the big leagues.

The route was a circuitous one. In May 1946, during his senior year at Berkeley High, Billy and teammates Ruben DeAlba and Babe Firman traveled to San Mateo for a tryout with the Brooklyn Dodgers. Branch Rickey was running the Dodgers at the time, and his policy was to look first at the character of a player before signing him. Had Rickey gone to the trouble, he would have discovered their reputations as fighters and troublemakers. The Dodgers said they would contact him if they were interested. They never called. It was around this time that Rickey was signing another controversial shortstop, Jackie Robinson, who came from the Southern California town of Pasadena.

Senior year customarily is the time for the major league scouts to come around to express interest in prospects. Billy received no inquiries. His getting kicked off the Berkeley High team hurt him not only because it cost him two weeks of the season and kept him from playing in the prestigious all-star game but also because it left a lasting impression on the scouts—the boy, undisciplined and unmanageable, appeared to be a hoodlum.

Fortunately for Billy, a savvy baseball man by the name of Red Adams had watched Billy play for Berkeley High and had managed him on a team called the Junior Oaks, a team designed to nurture local talent. Adams, the trainer of the Oakland Oaks, was able to look beyond labels or youthful behavior and concentrate on the talent underneath.

Adams had seen the positive attributes Billy brought to the Junior Oaks: his love of the game, his will to win, his killer instinct, and his solid batting and fielding skills.

Red Adams pushed hard for the Oaks to sign Billy. Red would invite Billy to come down to Oaks Field at the corner of San Pedro and Park streets in Emeryville, buy him a hamburger, give him a locker, and make sure Billy had transportation to and from home.

The man that Adams wanted Billy to impress was the Oaks manager, an old-timer by the name of Charles Dillon "Casey" Stengel, who in 1946 was beginning the first of three seasons with the Oaks.

It was during an afternoon when Billy had come down to Oaks Field at Adams's invitation that Martin, the eighteen-year-old kid who loved to field ground balls, fell in love with Stengel, the fifty-six-year-old man who loved to hit them.

Billy had spent much of his childhood begging his friends to hit him grounders. Some kids practice the piano or ballet or tennis or study geology or political science. Billy Martin took his Ph.D. in fielding ground balls. It was his passion. He loved the rhythm of the exercise, getting into position, reacting to the ball, making the catch, and throwing it back to the batter. For lovers of the game, playing pepper can be a religious experience.

As a kid Billy had eschewed the games of one o'cat or hit-the-bat because those games featured catching fly balls. Fly balls were for outfielders. He envisioned himself an infielder, so when he practiced, he demanded ground balls.

The manager, Casey Stengel, had been a major leaguer as far back as 1912, when he was a rookie with the Brooklyn Dodgers. He played for Pittsburgh, Philadelphia, the New York Giants and the Boston Braves until his retirement in 1925.

As a Dodger, Stengel injured his arm in spring training in 1914 and, while incapacitated, agreed to coach baseball at the University of Mississippi for a few weeks when his old high school coach, who had become the UMiss athletic director, asked him to help out. Stengel was appointed a full professor for his short stay.

Casey returned to his Dodger team just as spring training ended, but his nickname, the Professor, remained with him the rest of his career. In later years he became known as the Old Professor, or Perfessor.

Stengel, however, did not have the demeanor of a professor. He was a hard-nosed brawler who could drink anyone else under the table. After one late-night bar brawl engaged in by Stengel and a half-dozen other Dodger players, Brooklyn owner Charles Ebbets wanted to know, "What kind of hoodlums do we have on this club?"

Ebbets overlooked Stengel's bar fights because the Dodger outfielder was talented, always hustled, and showed great desire on the field, developing an excellent reputation as an entertaining player. Back then bar fights did not become headlines. Newspaper writers covered the games, nothing else.

Some of Stengel's comical performances are legendary. After he was traded from Brooklyn to Pittsburgh in 1917, he returned to Ebbets Field with the Pirates to play the Dodgers. Just before his first at bat, as the formerly Brooklyn faithful booed him as vociferously as they had once cheered him, Casey bowed low to the crowd and removed his cap, where underneath, perched on Stengel's head, was a sparrow, which flew away. Stengel had found the small bird dazed in the outfield during batting practice. He knew the Brooklyn fans were going to boo him, so he figured that if they were going to give him the bird, he would give them one in return.

Stengel had played on the National League champion Brooklyn Dodgers under manager Wilbert Robinson, but it wasn't until he played for John J. McGraw in 1922 and 1923 that he got his real baseball education.

McGraw taught Stengel the importance of learning the fundamentals, of throwing to the right base, of hitting behind the runner, of not making mental mistakes. If a player did something stupid, McGraw would stand in front of the player before his teammates and give him a humiliating tongue-lashing. Many of McGraw's players hated him for it, but the Giants under McGraw managed ten pennant-winning teams in one twenty-one-season stretch, including the ones Stengel played on in 1922 and 1923.

It was from John McGraw that Casey Stengel learned the art of platooning, batting a right-hander against a left-handed pitcher and vice versa. McGraw had platooned him and outfielder Bill Cunningham, and Stengel, who preferred to play every day and resented McGraw's platooning, nevertheless realized that his career-high .368 and .339 averages were because of McGraw's strategy.

Something else he learned from McGraw: that each player had to be handled differently. Stengel saw that no one got the most out of each of his players like McGraw did. Among the little things McGraw did was hand out cash bonuses after the game to players who did something special, like getting hit by a pitch in a crucial situation or laying down a squeeze bunt.

John McGraw was Casey Stengel's hero. There was no one Stengel admired and praised like McGraw. "I learned more from McGraw than anybody," he would say. During Stengel's two years on the Giants, McGraw had become equally fond of him, and the manager would invite Casey to his home in Pelham, New York, and they would sit for hours talking baseball.

From 1934 to 1943, Stengel used all of McGraw's strategies during his major league managing career with the Brooklyn Dodgers and Boston Braves, but he never had very good talent, and all his teams finished in the second division, usually in seventh place.

As a manager he never stopped clowning, hoping the fans would concentrate on his antics and ignore the lack of talent of his players.

While managing the Dodgers, Stengel made himself visible on the third-base coaching lines, delivering impromptu orations, conversing with the opposition, performing an occasional soft-shoe, and badgering the umpires, thus providing more entertainment than his players did.

Stengel drove his players hard and tried to instruct them, but most of them had neither the talent nor the intellect to take advantage of his guidance.

It is said that Stengel invented a pickoff play that he taught his team, a play to be used in a situation when there was a runner on third and a right-handed batter up. Stengel instructed the pitcher to throw over the head of the batter and then yell, "Look out," as he released the pitch. Stengel figured that the runner on third would take his lead and then be so concerned about the welfare of his fallen teammate that he would freeze, allowing the catcher to pick him off third. Stengel finally had to discard the play, however, because his third baseman froze along with the base runner, and the left fielder always ended up chasing the throw, which sailed by third base into the left-field bullpen!

"Managing the team back then," Stengel would say years afterward, "was a tough business. Whenever I decided to release a guy, I always had his room searched first for a gun. You couldn't take any chances with some of them birds."

Casey was fired by Brooklyn after the 1936 season, and because he had a two-year contract, he sat out the 1937 season while getting paid by the Dodgers.

In 1938 Stengel signed a contract to manage the Boston Braves, another collection of ragtags and has-beens. Again he became the center of attraction in order to divert the minds of the fans from the poor quality of the baseball being played. One dreary, rainy afternoon Stengel appeared on the field to exchange the lineup cards with the umpires, wearing a raincoat and holding an umbrella in one hand and a lantern in the other. It was classic Stengel, and most of the writers loved him for his antics, his colorful stories, and his congeniality. Once Stengel was relating to a group of writers an incident concerning a catcher who had once played against him back in the twenties. The catcher's nickname was Horseface.

"When Casey showed how the catcher used to look," said a writer who was there, "he not only looked more like a horse than a catcher, he looked more like a horse than Whirlaway."

"For us," wrote Boston sportswriter Harold Kaese, "it was more fun losing with Stengel than winning with a hundred other managers. Unfortunately, the Boston fans did not have the benefit of Stengel's company." In his six years in Beantown, Stengel's Braves finished fifth, seventh, seventh, seventh, seventh, and sixth. When he was accidentally struck by a cab in the spring of 1943, breaking his leg and missing the first two months of the season, a vicious *Boston Record* writer named Dave Egan voted the cabdriver "the man who did the most for Boston in 1943." At the end of the year, Stengel was released, traveling to Milwaukee, where he won the American Association pennant in 1944, to Kansas City, where he impressed Yankee owner Del Webb, and to Oakland, where he was to win the Pacific Coast League pennant in 1948.

When the eighteen-year-old Martin met Stengel for the first time in the spring of 1946, Martin was not awed. It wasn't the case of a kid meeting a legend. Stengel's major league teams had fared poorly all his career. And if Stengel *had* been a legend, Martin wouldn't have cared.

Billy Martin was a pragmatist. He had a goal, and in order for him to meet that goal, he would do whatever it was he had to do. In this case Martin knew only that Casey Stengel was the Oakland Oaks manager, and for him to make the Oaks, this was the guy he would have to impress.

When Billy met Casey, it was literally love at first sight. Martin had no way of knowing it, but Casey Stengel was one of those managers who built teams on pitching and defense. Stengel liked the hitters, but he *loved* the fielders. His philosophy always was that you won games by not losing them, by not giving them away, by not making the mental mistakes that John McGraw had loathed so deeply. Fundamentals were everything to Stengel, and part of fundamentals was making the plays on defense. For his infielders to make those plays, he wanted them to take dozens and dozens of ground balls. Until age caught up with him, Stengel's fondest activity as a manager was hitting ground balls to his infielders.

When Stengel first saw Martin come out onto the field to work out, he demanded a fungo bat in order to hit him grounders.

"Kid, get this one," Stengel barked. He whapped a hard-hit ball to Martin's right.

Martin fielded it cleanly and nonchalantly threw it in. He mouthed off to Stengel, "Is that the best you got?"

Stengel, who used to sass the great McGraw, saw a kid who reminded him of himself in his youth. Stengel liked his players to be cocky, liked them to talk big, to hold their heads high, to play with utmost confidence. Players like that, Stengel knew, would be very hard to defeat.

Stengel, who had been a tough kid himself, loved Martin's show of arrogance and sass. Stengel continued to slash one hard grounder after another. It became like a ballet, the constant movement of the bat and the reaction by the slick fielder, the accurate throw back to the old man with the bat. All the while Billy accompanied his throws with wisecracks and taunts as he sought to make a contest of what was ordinarily a practice exercise.

When he was done, Stengel was heard to say, "The kid's got it." It's safe to say that if Stengel hadn't felt that way, Billy Martin would have spent his life bartending or driving a truck or fighting house fires with most of his friends and relatives.

Both remembered that first meeting very clearly.

"It was Red Adams who would keep telling Casey about me," said Billy. "They wouldn't let me hit, but I'd go out into the field, and Casey would hit grounders to me, and Red would keep telling Casey, 'How'd you like him? See that kid out there? He's going to make it.' Casey would say, 'That skinny kid?' Red'd say, 'You watch, Casey.' Well, Casey kept hitting me grounders. I bet he hit between eighty and a hundred grounders, and I'd catch most of them, but some would bounce up and hit me, and I'd just throw them back ready for some more.

"Casey told Red, 'That little son of a gun. I've hit him so many grounders, I think he's trying to wear me out. He doesn't catch them all, but he doesn't back off from any, either.' "

Stengel also remembered that first meeting years later. "I remember the first time I saw that fresh kid quite well. Red Adams had some of our bonus boys out early this spring day. They were dressed up fit to kill. Then out on the diamond comes this skinny kid. If he hadn't been moving, I'd have thought him a scarecrow. He wore his own tattered uniform and silly-looking cap. Red put him in at shortstop. After practice I told Adams his second baseman looked pretty good.

" 'No, you're wrong,' Adams told me. 'The best player on the field was the shortstop.'

" 'You mean the ragamuffin?'

" 'Yep, that's the one. He'll be back tomorrow. Take another look at him.' "

Stengel did. In one afternoon the two men, the punk kid and the old-time ballplayer, would develop a bond that would not be broken for a decade. Binding them was their deep love for the game of baseball.

Casey Stengel's wife, Edna, a former silent-movie actress, said about her husband, "He doesn't talk about anything else. He has only one life, and that's baseball. That way he's happy, and I'm happy for him."

Stengel had stayed in the game all those years because he loved it dearly. And because he loved it so, as a manager he was a purist. He wanted his players to love the game as much as he did, to study it, learn every aspect, the ins and outs, the minute strategic nuances that for him made the game the greatest in the world. If a player did that, Stengel would be solidly in his corner, teaching him, encouraging him, protecting him, feeding him those tips and instructing him in the lore of the game that made it so endlessly fascinating.

Over the years Stengel had had players like that. But it was not until "the ragamuffin" came along that spring of 1946 that Stengel found a soul mate, a protégé, in time an adopted son.

Stengel proclaimed that he was sold on Billy Martin, and the Oaks offered him a contract. Eddie Leashman had scouted Billy for two years and also had recommended him. Billy was offered two hundred dollars a month and assigned to the Oaks' minor league team in Idaho Falls, Idaho.

Jimmy Hull, a scout for the Oaks, came over to Billy's house. He wanted to know if Billy wanted to go to Idaho Falls.

Billy told me, "Of course I wanted to go. I was eighteen years old, and I had worked in a slaughterhouse, worked in a pickle factory, done all sorts of odd jobs. My whole life I had wanted to be a baseball player. Did I want to go? Is the Pope Catholic?"

Hull wanted to know if Billy had any clothes for his trip.

"Just what I'm wearing," Billy told him.

"Where's your high school graduation suit?" he was asked.

"My uncle died. They took my suit from me and buried him in it."

"You got a suitcase?"

"Nope." Billy said he had never taken a trip before.

Hull handed Billy six fifty-dollar bills and told him to buy himself a new suit, some shirts, ties, and a suitcase. He said he could keep the rest for spending money.

"Can your dad drive you to the train station?" Billy was asked.

"He can't," he said. "He's working."

"How about your mother?"

"Can't. She don't drive. Besides that, we don't own a car."

Hull volunteered to pick him up and drive him to the train. The night before, Billy's family gathered at the house to give him a send-off. The next day he was off to Salt Lake City, where he was to meet his Idaho Falls teammates.

For an eighteen-year-old kid right out of high school, talent isn't always enough. The question always is whether the kid wants to play badly enough to survive the homesickness that inevitably comes during that first season away from home.

After Billy signed with the Oaks, he convinced scout Jimmy Hull to give a tryout to a group of his baseball-playing buddies. After the tryout the Oaks signed Babe Firman, Ruben DeAlba, and Howard Noble, an excellent outfielder with a strong arm who had not wanted to play on the Berkeley High School team.

Firman reached the Oaks after playing in the minors, but Howard Noble and a badly homesick Ruben DeAlba quit their first year.

Billy Martin didn't have such problems. On the baseball field he showed incredible confidence. At Idaho Falls he played third base. He didn't get into any fights, and he hit .254 and made sixteen errors.

The next spring he trained with the Oaks. In 1947, Billy fully expected to make the Oaks team when Stengel sent him down to Phoenix. Billy told him, "You sure blew one, Casey."

In his first exhibition game with Phoenix, Billy had six hits. The next day he had four hits and drove in five runs. On opening day of the exhibition season Billy batted eighth. By the start of the regular season, he was batting sixth, and then it was fifth, and when catcher Clint Courtney broke his arm, he was moved up to fourth.

He finished the season hitting .393 with an incredible 173 RBIs, and that season he showed excellent baserunning ability, stealing 31 bases.

After his year at Phoenix, Martin badgered Stengel to promote him to the Oaks. Billy had spent the final month of the 1947 season in Oakland, but he wanted to make sure he was going to stay there. They met several times at Bay Area banquets during the winter after the 1947 season, and they would sit and talk baseball. Stengel would tell Billy he didn't have a position open for him to play. "Find one," Billy would tell him.

"I knew I would have the damndest time keeping him off my team," said Stengel. "He wanted it so bad."

In 1948, Stengel put Billy on the Oaks team even though he didn't have a spot for him. The Oaks of 1948 were composed of some talented major league veterans, including Ernie Lombardi at catcher, first baseman Nick Etten, short-stop Dario Lodigiani, third baseman Cookie Lavagetto, and outfielder Les Scarsella.

When Billy arrived in training camp, he made it clear to the veterans that he was there to take someone's job.

During spring training Stengel put him at third, and right away Billy began playing just as hard as he could, fielding like it was the regular season and showing off his powerful arm. "The kid's trying to take your job away," the vets said to Lavagetto. There was resentment against the kid for trying to show them up.

Said Billy about it later, "Though they were getting mad at me, I really didn't care. I was there to win a job."

Stengel roomed Billy with Lavagetto, who the year before had attained immortality in the 1947 World Series with the Brooklyn Dodgers, hitting the double that broke up Bill Bevens's no-hitter and beating the Yankees in Game 4. Despite his heroics, the Dodgers released Lavagetto. Brick Laws signed the thirty-six-year old Oakland native to play for the Oaks.

Lavagetto, who later would manage in the majors for five years with the Washington Senators and the Minnesota Twins, said of Billy, "He wanted to learn everything I knew. He wanted me to replay every big-league game I was ever in. He was so interested, so determined to succeed, you had to admire him."

What Lavagetto remembered best about the young Martin was that when the kid asked him about the hit that had broken up Bevens's no-hitter, he didn't ask, "How did it feel?" as most reporters and fans did, but rather he asked, "What kind of pitch did you hit? Why didn't you pull the ball? Where were the outfielders playing you?" To Billy, the veteran quickly saw, baseball was like a game of chess, intricate and complex, and the kid wanted to master the details.

Stengel and Martin attached themselves to each other like a novice karate student with his Sensei. But Billy didn't treat Stengel reverentially. Rather, during his apprenticeship he was always sassing Stengel.

The other players never ceased to wonder how Billy got away with the way he talked to Stengel. One day Casey halted a workout and walked over to Billy. He asked Billy to show him how he made the double play.

Billy took the throws with both toes on the bag, whirled, turned, and threw. He did it several times.

"Yeah," said Stengel, "that's right." But Stengel wanted less movement, less of what he called "fancy Dan."

"Look, kid, you ain't just out there jitterbugging. Let me show you how to make the double play properly."

Stengel demonstrated. Martin considered what Stengel was telling him and said, "I'll do it your way, but I don't see what's wrong with my way. I got quick hands and feet."

"You ain't on the dance floor jitterbugging," Stengel said.

"If you can't do it, Case, don't knock it," Billy told him. "My way is good enough."

The other players expected Stengel to send Billy to the clubhouse. Instead, he just walked away, hiding a grin with his hand. With Stengel, Billy Martin could do no wrong. The boy loved the game as much as he did. The Old Man couldn't ask any more than that.

There were times that Martin got too mouthy, and Stengel always let the kid know who the boss was by pinch-hitting for him or lecturing him. Stengel was as good with the needle as Martin was.

During most of training camp in 1948, Billy sat on the bench because he didn't have a position to play. During one game Casey yelled, "Martin get over here." Billy eagerly grabbed his glove.

Stengel said, "Stick around, kid. I may need you to umpire."

If Stengel felt the opposing pitcher was too tough for the kid, he'd keep him on the bench and spend the game sitting next to him and talking to him about that pitcher, asking what he was throwing and where. He also talked to him about strategy, and Billy quickly began to appreciate Stengel's encyclopedic mind. He saw that Casey always was two or three steps ahead of the opposing manager.

Billy finally got to play shortstop when Dario Lodigiani got hurt. When Lodigiani returned, Billy replaced Lavagetto at third. When Lavagetto played third, Billy played shortstop.

When Billy finally broke into the lineup, Stengel batted him eighth. One day Billy questioned him about it.

"That's my lineup," Stengel said. "And that's where you're supposed to hit."

Billy said, "Well, what do you think I am, the groundskeeper? I shouldn't be hitting eighth. I hit .393 last year."

Billy hit .277 in 1948, and with the Oaks changing from the Nine Old Men, a reference to the makeup of the United States Supreme Court at the time, to the Eight Old Men Plus the Kid, Oakland finished 114–74, Casey Stengel's best managerial record ever. It was Oakland's first Pacific Coast League win in twenty-one years.

Billy Martin may not have had the talent of some of the other players, but he had something burning inside him the others didn't have. Billy hated to lose so badly that he played with an intensity and a dedication that anyone playing with him had to admire and anyone playing against him had to despise. For Billy to keep up, he had to work harder. He was more driven than others because he didn't have their ability. A smart manager who has a player like Billy Martin lets him lead. Casey Stengel was a very smart manager.

At the time of his signing with the Oaks in the spring of 1946, Stengel had told owner Brick Laws, "It will take me a year to learn the league, another year to develop and buy players to compete, and then with a little luck I can win it in the third." Which is exactly the way it happened.

It was during the 1948 season that Billy had an inkling he was going to achieve his dream of playing for the Yankees.

The Oaks had played the New York Giants in a couple of exhibition games, and Billy had started and executed a couple of hit-and-run plays, and afterward Horace Stoneham, the owner of the Giants, tried to buy Martin's contract. The Giants would have been a perfect place for Billy to play. The combustible Leo Durocher was the Giants' manager, and the two would have gotten along famously—or killed each other.

But Stengel, though only the Oaks' manager, had been given final say over who played, who was sent down, and who was traded. Stengel told Stoneham, "Next year I'm going to the Yankees, and eventually the kid is going to go with me."

While Casey Stengel was managing the New York Yankees to a pennant in 1949, Billy was left behind with the Oaks for one more year of seasoning.

"Billy was very upset when Casey didn't take him that first year," said childhood friend Ken Irvine. "He was hoping to go, but he realized he didn't have enough experience."

When Stengel took over control of the New York Yankees in 1949 he talked plenty about the kid. When Martin finally arrived on the team in 1950, the senior Yankees, some of whom had never met him, had a nickname for him. They called him Billy Stengel.

# YANKEE
# DOODLE DANDY

When Billy returned for the 1949 season with the Oaks, Casey Stengel was gone, headed for the Yankee manager's job in New York. The man who replaced him, Charlie Dressen, had managed the Cincinnati Reds from 1934 through 1937. His teams had been second-division losers, but Dressen was another one of those baseball men who had made a study of the game, knew it inside and out, and as he proved with the Brooklyn Dodgers in the 1950s, could win when he had the horses.

When Charlie Dressen arrived for the Oaks' spring training in 1949, he announced that no job was safe. Dressen initially was wary of Billy because of Billy's outspoken loyalty to Stengel, but it didn't take long for Dressen to embrace the youngster.

Billy knew how to ingratiate himself with a manager. From the start of spring training, he made himself indispensable. He volunteered to pitch batting practice, worked with the infielders, hit ground balls, and helped the hitters in slumps. When it came to baseball, he was tireless, and Dressen noticed.

Two days before the season was to start, Billy played in a Sunday morning exhibition game, hitting a single and a triple, stealing a base, and turning two double plays. After the game he went to Dressen and asked if he could drive the sixty miles east to Stockton to play in the B game.

"Do you want to make the drive to Stockton?" Dressen asked.

"Sure do. Cookie may need me."

"Go."

Billy contributed a hit to help win that game, too.

The next day Dressen told him, "You're my second baseman. Anybody who wants to play ball that bad belongs on my team."

Dressen fell in love with Billy's passion for the game, much as Stengel had done. Dressen would yell at Billy, "Take charge. Don't let those other guys bully you. Talk back to them. Holler at them."

Billy appreciated Dressen's aggressive style and his knowledge of the game.

Martin played hard for Dressen, and in 1949 he had an excellent year, hitting .286 with 12 homers and 92 RBIs, and he showed that despite his skinny frame, he was resilient, batting 623 times during a grueling 172-game Pacific Coast League schedule.

On October 13, 1949, Casey Stengel made good on his promise to Billy. New York Yankee GM George Weiss announced that the Yankees had purchased the contracts of Oaks players Billy Martin and Jackie Jensen.

Jensen had played high school baseball at Piedmont High School before going on to the University of California, Berkeley, where he became an all-American football player. He starred in the Rose Bowl for UCal and was a true Bay Area hero.

When Jensen signed with the Oaks, his college stardom enabled him to make more money in salary than most of the veterans on the team.

Jensen was a rich kid, a college kid, a Goat, but his status as a teammate overrode any prejudice Billy might have had about him. Billy's sister Pat, however, thought Jensen a terrible snob and rooted against him, much to Billy's chagrin.

"I always admired my brother, because no matter how tired he was, he'd always sign autographs for little kids. At Oakland, kids would come up to Jensen, and he'd walk away from them. I didn't like it," she said.

"I'd go to the park and boo him, and it was such an intimate park you could hear each fan. Billy knew I was doing it, and he said, 'Pat, you can't come to the park and boo him. He's a teammate of mine. He's a nice guy.'

"I'd say, 'No, he's not a nice guy.'

"After I did it a second time, Billy said, 'You don't have to like him, just don't insult him out there.' And I didn't do it anymore."

When the Yankees announced the purchase of Jensen and Martin to the Yankees, the press wrote glowingly about the nationally known Jensen. Stengel talked about Martin.

"Is he a good player?" asked John Drebinger of *The New York Times.*

"Yeah," said Stengel, "and he's got a big mouth—just like me."

Stengel was asked what kind of player Billy was. "He's a hard-nosed, big-nosed player," Stengel said.

He told Arthur Daley, the columnist for the *Times,* "There ain't nothin' this kid don't think he can do."

Billy was ecstatic about his sale to the Yankees until he learned that the Yankees had paid Jensen $60,000 to sign, a huge sum in those days. But Jensen had had options. He could have played pro football, and he could have used his college degree to get a high-paying job. Billy Martin had no options. When Brick Laws sold him to the Yankees, Billy got a plane ticket, nothing more. He also had to take a $1,500 pay cut from his $9,000-a-year Oaks salary to $7,500. His treatment was an omen of how the Yankees would deal with him for the rest of his career in New York.

When Billy arrived in St. Petersburg, Florida, for spring training in 1950, his reputation had preceded him. Casey Stengel had seen to that. Besides calling him Billy Stengel, the players, a tough bunch of grizzled vets, called him Casey's Bobo, the Dead End Kid, and Billy the Brat, a reference to New York Giants second baseman Eddie Stanky, who was referred to as the Brat.

The Yankee veterans noticed from the start that Stengel and the kid rookie had a special relationship. Before he even arrived, Stengel told reporters, "That fresh punk, how I love him."

"The funniest thing," said Phil Rizzuto, "was watching him and Stengel together. They really got on each other. Most of the other players never talked back to Casey. Billy always did. In a loud voice, too.

"Billy always talked back to Casey, always kidded him, and always fought with him. Casey made one thing clear to the rest of us very early. He was a Billy Martin fan."

When Billy arrived to play for the Yankees, he was no longer Billy the Horn. After the 1949 Oaks season, he had had surgery done on his nose.

One of the first notions Billy had to rid the writers of was that his name was Alfred Martin.

"The name's Billy Martin," he told Milton Gross of the *New York Post.* "Billy Martin. Now don't forget it."

When he arrived in spring training camp in 1950, Billy told Stengel, the World Series–winning manager the previous autumn, "Now we'll get this team going."

On the depth chart Billy was third in line behind flashy Jerry Coleman and aging veteran George "Snuffy" Stirnweiss. On the 1950 Yankees, Billy wasn't going to play much. Ordinarily bench warmers are over-the-hill veterans who are happy to still be in the game. Young kids usually are sent to the minors for seasoning. But Stengel wanted Billy with him, and he had the clout to put Billy on the team. After leading the Yankees to win the American League pennant and the World Series against the Dodgers in 1949, Casey Stengel had become a genius overnight.

When Stengel took over the team in the spring of 1949, experts predicted the Yankees would finish third at best. Stengel half-joked, "Third ain't so bad. I never finished third before."

At the start of the season his star player, Joe DiMaggio, had painful bone spurs, outfielder Charlie Keller was out with a painful back, and except for Phil Rizzuto at shortstop, the rest of the team was made up of players with limited experience like Yogi Berra, Jerry Coleman, Hank Bauer, and Gene Woodling. The pitching was strong, but the lineup unsettled.

The 1949 Yankees needed to win the last two games of the season against the Boston Red Sox to win the pennant. They did. Casey Stengel's reign had begun.

When Stengel opened spring training in 1950, he was no longer Casey the clown. He was Stengel, Manager of the Year. This camp was different from the year before. The uncertainty was gone. Confidence was exuded by everyone. The pitching was still strong, the double-play combination of Jerry Coleman and Phil Rizzuto was as good as they came. The only major problem Stengel faced was what to do with the fading Joe DiMaggio. The Yankees looked like a powerhouse.

The Yankees never won many of their exhibition games because Stengel was preoccupied with experimenting with his minor league prospects and second-line arms. Winning in spring training meant nothing to Stengel. In fact, as Stengel knew, the teams that won the most games in spring training often did poorly in the regular season. Those teams played to win in spring training so an owner, knowing his team was suspect, could gull his fans and sell advance tickets before the real season began. Stengel had no such mandate and used the exhibition season to get all his vets work and at the same time to evaluate his young talent.

From the start Billy knew he was under Stengel's protective umbrella, which gave him license to be as fresh and sassy as he could be. As had been the case when Billy first came up to the Oakland Oaks in 1948, Stengel had no position for him to play. Billy concentrated on making himself as useful and noticeable as he could.

One day during spring training Billy wasn't getting much work at second, so he went to the mound to throw batting practice. Stengel's pitching coach, Jim Turner, ordered him off the mound. He told Billy he wanted his pitchers throwing BP.

Turner had been the manager of the Portland team in the Pacific Coast League when Billy played for the Oaks, and he had mercilessly ridden Martin, calling him Big Nose over and over. Billy hadn't forgotten.

"Who the hell are you?" Billy said. "Are you the manager of this club? I thought Casey was the manager. When you're managing this club then you can tell me what to do."

Another time former Yankee shortstop Frankie Crosetti, who was Stengel's third-base coach, tried to show Billy how to make the double play. Billy told him, "Bullshit, I got a better way."

The veterans noticed.

Just as he had done in 1948 when he first came up to the Oaks, Billy made it clear he was angling for a starting job.

According to Billy's sister Pat, "In 1950 Coleman said to Billy, 'You'll never get this job.' Billy told him, 'Watch me.' "

When Billy first came up, shortstop Phil Rizzuto was cool to him, and Jerry Coleman "hated him," Pat said.

Billy's behavior wasn't designed to make friends among the competition. During practice Billy would get territorial whenever anyone else tried to play second base. He acted like he was a veteran, refusing to observe the rookie code of obsequiousness. In his first spring training he was assigned an upper berth on train trips. He complained to road secretary Bill McCorry, who told him the lowers were for regulars.

Said Martin, "And what the hell makes you think I'm not a regular?"

The veterans got a kick out the kid's brashness, and they almost fell off their locker room benches one day when the great Joe DiMaggio walked by and said to Billy, "Would you like to go out to dinner with me tonight?" DiMaggio ordinarily was a loner who kept separate from his teammates away from the ballpark.

Billy was surprised, but his teammates were flabbergasted.

Johnny Lindell and Cliff Mapes, two veteran outfielders, had played with DiMaggio for several years and had never gone out with the Dago. Why the kid? they wanted to know.

Billy, who unlike most rookies was a prolific self-promoter, told them, "Do you know why he's taking me out?"

"No, why?"

"Because he likes to go out with people who have class. That's why he isn't taking you bums with him."

DiMaggio genuinely liked Martin, then only twenty-two, for the same reasons Stengel did. The kid embodied everything he admired—dedication, enthusiasm, confidence, ambition—and Joltin' Joe loved Billy's winning personality, which enabled him to get away with being cocky and brash.

"Hi, Dago."

"Hi, kid, how you doing?"

DiMaggio wanted Billy as a companion because he wasn't suspicious of him as with most people. Like many famous people, DiMaggio always felt that people wanted a piece of him. Often they did. DiMaggio abhorred the press, whom he distrusted for its prying. Early in his career the press had sided with GM George Weiss in DiMaggio's salary disputes with the Yankees, and he never forgot or forgave. DiMag trusted Billy implicitly not to tell stories about him to the writers; he saw that Billy distrusted the writers as much as he did. To Billy the writers were like the Goats, better educated but not as street-smart as he was. He felt they were parasites because they had the power to pass judgment on him and the other players even though they had never played the game. Billy disliked anyone who dared second-guess or criticize him. The writers did that almost every day.

As the years went on, Billy's feelings toward the Fourth Estate turned from disdain to hatred and loathing. Billy would tell anyone who asked that the writers didn't know what they were talking about, had too much freedom in what they wrote, and could invade the clubhouse and his privacy whenever they wished, even going so far as spying in the urinals for quotes. Billy feared the power of the press. Joe D knew he didn't have to worry about Billy becoming buddy-buddy with any sportswriter.

DiMaggio and Billy came from the same background—from fishermen. They were both Italians, blue-collar men with limited educations. When DiMaggio first came up to the big leagues and was asked by a reporter for a quote, he didn't know how to respond. He didn't know what a "quote" was. Billy, likewise, wasn't a philosopher about anything except baseball and girls, which were the only subjects either of them cared about. The Big Dago and the Little Dago were quintessential jocks.

Both loved the company of young women, especially blondes. Later, DiMaggio, who had married and divorced actress Dorothy Arnold, would marry film star Marilyn Monroe. Billy's women weren't that famous, but they were just as numerous, and some of them were just as sexy.

Not only did Billy spend evenings with DiMaggio eating dinner in his hotel room, but Billy would even play practical jokes on DiMaggio.

One day DiMaggio came into the locker room, and Billy asked Joe if he would sign an autograph on a baseball. DiMaggio was glad to oblige. Billy then shot a squirt of blue ink all over DiMaggio's expensive shirt and suit.

"I just couldn't believe that Billy would squirt ink all over Joe's nice-looking gray suit," said Whitey Ford, another rookie.

It was disappearing ink, but DiMaggio didn't know it.

Billy told me, "He gave me such a dirty look that if there was a way I could have run out of the clubhouse, I would have."

Billy kept telling DiMaggio, "It'll disappear, Joe. It'll disappear."

Said Whitey Ford, "Billy would say to me, 'He's just like anyone else. All you have to do is open up when you're around him.'

"I'd tell him, 'I can't do that.' "

There were days when DiMaggio would come strolling into the clubhouse, and Billy would be walking right behind him, imitating his every move. Their lockers were adjacent, and when DiMaggio would take his pants off, Billy would remove his. When DiMaggio would ask for half a cup of coffee, Billy did the same. Joe would spit into a spittoon, but Billy, who never learned the art, always missed, spitting tobacco juice all over the place.

"You fresh little bastard," DiMaggio would say to him.

The veteran players saw a brash kid, but Billy Martin's brashness was a mask. His entire playing career, he told me one time, from the day he put on the Yankee uniform to the day he was dealt away, was plagued by insecurity. "Every day I played," Billy told me, "I woke up fearful that I was not going to measure up." It was a fear that stayed with him all his life.

Billy once talked to author Maury Allen about how he felt when he first joined the Yankees. His brashness, Billy told Allen, was "an act. I was scared shitless. I didn't know if I was as good as those guys. I had to convince myself before I could convince anybody else. To me the Oakland club was the big leagues. These were guys I had heard about for years, and now I was with them."

When he came to the Yankees, Billy Martin learned immediately what it meant to have Yankee pride. There was a code of behavior that the Yankee players followed. Before the game the players displayed an air of confidence. They were supposed to win. During the game the players executed and didn't make fundamental mistakes. If they made a mistake, they didn't make excuses. And if it happened that the Yankees did lose, players were solemn in the clubhouse and on the team bus. Above all, the individual took a backseat to the welfare of the team.

Explained pitcher Eddie Lopat: "We were a twenty-five-man unit. Hell, I didn't give a damn if [Vic] Raschi won 40 games or [Allie] Reynolds won 50. I didn't give a damn *who* won just as long as New York won. We had an esprit de corps on that ball club. There wasn't one jealous bone on that whole ball club. That's what amazed Stengel, too. He never saw that before. Also, the older players used to reprimand the younger ones for lack of hustle. If they didn't put out, we'd say, 'Hey, you're playing on this club, and you'd better put out because that's the way we play ball here.' You know a player can fool a manager or even a coach, and a lot of guys burn the candle at both ends six nights a week, especially the younger ones, but you can't fool your teammates. We'd corral them and say, 'Hey, we're going into Cleveland or Chicago, and you'd better get your ass in bed because you're taking money out of my pocket.' Mickey Mantle and Whitey Ford used to say that they thought we were the meanest men they ever knew.

"I can remember one incident in 1948," Lopat continued, "when we were playing Detroit in the stadium. It was the seventh inning and we were behind 3–2, and Yogi Berra, he was the first man up, he hit a short pop fly to right center between the second baseman and right fielder, and the ball dropped in. Well, Yogi thought the ball was going to be caught, and he trotted down to first, and had he been running, it would have been a double. The next man hit a grounder that forced him at second, but if he had been at second, he would have been able to run to third, and then there was a fly ball that would have scored him with the tying run. We lost the game 3–2. When he came in, and this is what shocked me, he was sitting there putting on his catching stuff, and Charlie Keller walked up, not vicious or malicious, and Charlie said, 'You feeling all right, Yoge?' He said, 'Yeah, fine.' And Keller said, 'Then why the hell didn't you run the ball out? You cost us a run.' Well, he couldn't argue, because before Keller got through, the other guys, [Johnny] Lindell, [Tommy] Henrich, Billy Johnson, jumped on him, too. They all told him, 'Bust your ass when you're in there, buddy. That's the way we play.' DiMag never said anything. He just looked at him with a stern look. But he was steaming. So anyway, from then on, when Yogi hit a pop fly, oh boy, he ran."

Billy Martin learned Yankee pride. It became a part of him. He saw its impact on the team. He saw what happened to opposing teams when every man played for himself. They lost. The Yankees won.

Billy didn't play much in 1950 and 1951 because second baseman Jerry Coleman was playing so well, but for those two years Martin made a strong impression during a frustrating time.

On Opening Day of 1950 the Yankees were losing to Mel Parnell of the Red Sox 9–0 when Billy pinch-hit with two men on. He doubled off the left-field wall, the Yankees batted around, and when he came up again, the bases were loaded. Billy singled in another run, and the Yankees won the game 15–10. Stengel danced around the clubhouse like he had just won another pennant, and the players hugged each other in glee.

Then Billy sat for two weeks. Stengel had him sit right beside him much of the season.

"Billy sat next to Casey and picked his brains," said Phil Rizzuto. " 'Why did you do that, why did you do this?' He was always thinking baseball, learning, struggling to improve."

"You could see Billy had a special relationship with Casey," said Whitey Ford. "He would drive Casey nuts on the bench on the days he wasn't playing. Even when he was playing, he would be all over him, asking him about different plays. He took over the infield on every play. He had a good professional and personal relationship with Phil Rizzuto, and even though Phil was a veteran, it was Billy who we all heard and listened to on the field."

Stengel talked to Martin about the American League hitters and pitchers, told him stories from his career, ordered him to sit with him in hotel coffee shops or lobbies, always talking baseball, thinking about the game, sharing their passion.

In a column dated May 1, 1950, Billy Martin asked columnist Jimmy Cannon, "Do you think I can manage? I have all the credentials, you know. I can really run a game, run a team. I'll do it some day, you'll see." This from a rookie bench warmer.

On May 14, Stengel sent Billy to Kansas City, the Triple A farm team. He explained that the Yankees were trying to sell George Stirnweiss, so they didn't want to send the veteran down.

"We'll keep you down for three weeks," Casey told him, "sell Stirnweiss for $25,000, and then bring you back."

It worked out just that way. But according to Billy's sister Pat, Billy suffered so badly emotionally when the Yankees sent him down that he called her on the phone and told her he wanted to come home. After he thought about it more, he stayed.

When Billy returned in mid-June, he continued to sit on the bench behind Jerry Coleman despite his favored status with the manager.

"It was obvious Casey had a warm feeling for Billy," said Jerry Coleman, "but I can say this in all honesty: Casey never let his heart rule his head. He played the best nine men he could find every day. Nobody ever thought Billy played a day or an inning when he wasn't the best choice for that day against that pitcher, for whatever reason Casey decided."

Billy may have been good, but at the time Coleman was better. Stengel looked at it this way: "Coleman's the best," said Casey, "but that fresh kid makes [the double play] better than any of them others," meaning better than anyone in the league except Coleman.

As a player Stengel had been a vicious bench jockey, and he employed Billy in the same role. Before one game with Cleveland, Stengel told him, "I got a job for you today. Get on Al Rosen. Ride him."

Stengel had Billy do the same to Jackie Robinson during a midseason exhibition game. Billy showed no respect. He was vicious. Billy yelled at the Dodger star, "If I was in your league, I'd have your job, Fatso."

Billy all the while persisted in pushing Stengel to play him ahead of Jerry Coleman.

"He's a nice guy and all that," Martin kept telling Stengel about Coleman, "but I can play second base better than he can."

DiMaggio was the one calming influence on Billy during those two difficult years.

"Be patient," DiMaggio would tell him. "Your time will come."

Beside suffering through his own inactivity, Billy spent the 1950 season consoling DiMaggio, who was playing in his next-to-last season. In the spring DiMaggio had begun to court his former wife, Dorothy Arnold. When the season started, she was with him on the road, but their romance wilted somewhere along the way, and in the spring the throwing arm of the Great DiMaggio lost its power to the ravages of arthritis. As his various nagging injuries accumulated, he slowed markedly in the field. At bat, balls he normally would have pulled into the seats were now looping weakly to right field. His athletic deterioration created tension in the clubhouse.

In the first week in July it reached a head when Stengel removed DiMaggio from a ball game at the start of the second inning after he had misplayed a hit the inning before. Joe had already taken his position in center field, and when Jackie Jensen trotted out to inform him that he had been replaced, a humiliated DiMaggio had to trot off the field in full view of the Yankee Stadium spectators. He became sullen and morose.

After the game Joe snapped to reporters, "There is nothing wrong with my legs or anything else. I was taken out, and if you want to know any more about it, ask Stengel."

DiMaggio stopped communicating with anyone, pulling himself into a shell of pride and loneliness. Through August he was hitting in the .260s.

In early August, Stengel wanted to bench DiMaggio, but he knew Joe's teammates might resent him for doing it. On the other hand, Stengel knew the team would suffer if he did not do it.

As always Stengel did what was best for the team, and on August 12, Stengel announced that DiMaggio would take a week's rest.

"I know some people say I am through," said DiMaggio with bitterness, "but those are the same people who said the same thing in 1946."

After resting a week, Stengel returned DiMaggio to the number-four spot in the batting order. On the first day back against Philadelphia, DiMaggio hit a long home run to win the game. In the next eleven games DiMaggio hit .450. The Yankees won ten of those games.

By mid-September the Yankees and the Detroit Tigers were neck and neck for the pennant. The Yankees had brought up a young pitcher, Whitey Ford, a twenty-one-year-old blond kid who looked fourteen. Ford, like Billy, was young and cocky. The year before, while with Class AA Binghamton, Ford had telephoned Stengel, saying he could help him win the pennant.

"I've learned everything I can learn in the minor leagues," he told him. Stengel rejected Ford's offer but many years later confided that he should have listened to the kid.

"I'll bet he would have done just what he said he would do," Stengel said.

When the Yankees recalled Ford, the player the young pitcher contacted when he met the team in Boston was Billy. They had been teammates at Kansas City. It was early in the morning, and Whitey woke him up, but Billy was glad to hear from him.

Billy said, "I've got two girls who are going to have breakfast with us."

"Sure enough," said Ford, "when we went downstairs, there were these two girls in the lobby. One of them had been living near Billy in New Jersey, and she knew some of the ballplayers. But it looked pretty funny, a couple of rookies walking into the Kenmore Hotel dining room at breakfast with two blondes. We took a bit of heat from the rest of the players for that little entrance."

Ford and Billy became close friends. They were similar in nature, fierce competitors who would fight to the death rather than lose. Ford became very popular because he was cherubic and handsome, while Billy, angular and seemingly sinister, was seen as the Black Bart of the team. Both had an important attribute: Each knew how to win.

On the mound Ford had poise and savvy. When he came up in 1950, Stengel handpicked Ford's opponents, all second-division teams, as the kid went 6–0 and kept the team in the pennant race. For a crucial September game against the Tigers, Stengel tapped Ford to start.

After the anthem, veteran shortstop Phil Rizzuto visited with the young pitcher. Solicitously Rizzuto put his arm around Ford's neck and said, "Eddie, just take it slow and easy, and you'll beat these guys. Just go out and pitch your game."

"Scooter," Ford replied, "all I gotta do is throw my glove out there, and I can beat these guys. Don't be worrying about me."

Ford allowed one run. He was pitching a 1–1 game into the ninth inning when the Yankees scored eight runs and broke the game wide open.

As for the pennant, starting pitchers Vic Raschi, Allie Reynolds, and Eddie Lopat did the rest, and Stengel had his second straight league championship.

Jerry Coleman was the star of the 1950 World Series against the Philadelphia Phillies. After the Yankees swept the Phils in four straight, Hall of Fame second baseman Frankie Frisch proclaimed that Coleman surely would be a Hall of Famer. Unfortunately for Coleman, though, 1950 would be the apex of his career. After slumping in 1951 because of a serious injury, Coleman was drafted into the army for two years, giving Billy his break.

Billy himself had been drafted at the end of the 1950 season, but after serving five and a half months in the Army, he got a discharge. Billy had gotten married in October 1950 to his high school sweetheart, Lois Berndt, and he told the Army he was supporting a wife, his parents, and his three younger siblings. The Army bought his story, and he was released in time to play for the 1951 season.

Stengel had lost Whitey Ford to the Army for 1951, but he had a fine crop of young rookie candidates, including Gil McDougald, Andy Carey, Tom Sturdivant, Bill Skowron, Bob Cerv, and a nineteen-year-old shortstop named Mickey Mantle.

Mantle's sprinter speed and prodigious hitting became the talk of the 1951 spring training camp. Mantles, as Stengel called him, was a switch-hitter who hit long home runs from either side of the plate, and though very husky, he could run from home to first in just over three seconds.

Through the rookie camp Stengel played Mantle at both short and third. His throwing was strong but erratic. He was unpolished but very talented.

Stengel, who was childless, had already adopted one son in Billy. When Mantle came up to the Yankees, he adopted another one. He saw in Mantle the making of another Casey Stengel, and to prevent Mantle from having to return to the minors to learn the complexities of infield play, Stengel switched him to the outfield and decided to teach the boy how to play the position himself. He also retained Yankee star Tommy Henrich to coach him.

Mantle, who came from a small Oklahoma town where five hundred people was a huge crowd, was overwhelmed by the throngs coming to the Yankees' spring training games. He was awkward and spoke with a slow Western twang that increased his self-consciousness. He was also scared—of people and of failure. Before his first exhibition game Mantle was so frightened he could barely raise his arms high enough to catch a baseball.

But Mantle hit .402 in exhibition play and was being touted as the most exciting young player since Jackie Robinson.

In the spring of 1951 the Yankees swapped training sites with the New York Giants and trained in Phoenix. Before returning to New York they played a series of exhibitions in California, where both co-owner Del Webb and manager Casey Stengel lived.

In San Francisco in a game against the Seals, Stengel started a full lineup of Californians: Fenton Mole at first, Jerry Coleman at second, Billy Martin at short, Gil McDougald at third, and an outfield of Joe DiMaggio, Jackie Jensen, and Gene Woodling. Californian Charlie Silvera caught, and twenty-year-old rookie Tom Morgan pitched.

On Opening Day 1951, Stengel started rookies Mantle and Jackie Jensen in the outfield and Gil McDougald at third. Morgan, who had pitched twenty-five consecutive scoreless innings during the spring, was given the Opening Day start.

"I wish I didn't have so many green peas," Stengel said, "but I can't win with my old men. We have to rebuild."

In the spring Mantle hit long home runs, but he was striking out a lot. In one game he failed to get a proper jump on a fly ball because he was still moping about having struck out. After the inning Eddie Lopat cornered him in the dugout.

"You want to play?" Lopat yelled at him. "If not, get your ass the hell out of here. We don't need guys like you. We want to win."

In mid-July Stengel sent Mantle to the Yankees' minor league farm team in Kansas City to calm him down and get him untracked. When he returned several weeks later, he would resume a long, productive career that lasted until 1968 and won him election to the Hall of Fame.

When Mantle returned from the minors to the Yankees, the player he hooked up with was Billy Martin. They were soul mates. Though one was from a big city and the other from a small Oklahoma mining town, they were two bookends. More than anything else they liked mischief and fun. They went to the movies, fished, played golf, and hunted wild game and wilder women, even though both had married. They were young and Yankees, and Stengel did what he could to get the two kids into their hotel rooms on time, with only limited success.

One night Billy and Casey Stengel went to a banquet. During the evening Billy introduced himself to a very pretty girl and arranged to meet her afterward. When the banquet ended, Billy tried to make his getaway, but Casey grabbed him by the arm and wouldn't let go. "Stay here with me and listen. You might learn something." Billy periodically tried to pull away, but Casey refused to let go, and he held him there until twelve-thirty, at which time Casey said, "You can go and see that girl now if you want to."

Said Billy, "The bastard had heard us arranging our meeting, and he was making sure I'd get in bed on time for the next day's game."

Mickey, who came from Commerce, Oklahoma, taught Billy about country-and-western music and attire. Billy taught Mickey about bar life.

Mantle was nineteen, Billy twenty-three.

"Everyone thought that because we were major leaguers that we were mature adults," Billy once told me.

One of their favorite pastimes was wrestling. When the Yankees traveled, they went by train, and the two would room together. Mantle would get on his knees and let Billy take his best hold, and then Mantle would do his best to shake him off. Mantle, who was as strong as a blacksmith, would throw Billy against the wall, but Billy, who loved competition more than anything, would always come back for more. One time Billy, determined not to get thrown off, grabbed hold of Mantle's gums with his fingers and held on for dear life.

"He couldn't eat for two days," Billy said.

They shared a two-bedroom apartment at the Concourse Plaza. They enjoyed trying to sneak into each other's bedroom in the middle of the night to watch the other making love to his wife.

They brought water guns to the clubhouse and squirted each other. They bought the newfangled Polaroid camera and took great glee snapping pictures of teammates sitting on the toilet with their shorts around their ankles. They threw darts against the wall of the clubhouse. They went to bars at night and found eager women and sometimes picked the wrong ones and got Billy in fights, but they were protected because back then the sportswriters wrote only about the games and because the two of them could do pretty much whatever they wanted to do and get away with it under Casey Stengel's protective umbrella.

Billy played in only 34 games in 1950 and in 51 games in 1951, but the time spent was not wasted as he continued his education under Stengel. In those games when Stengel put him in, Billy did whatever Stengel asked of him. He broke up double plays. He got hit by pitches. He hit-and-ran. He didn't play all that much, but opposing fans were quick to pick up on his arrogance and his pugnaciousness, and he became a favorite target for a good booing. First of all, he was a Yankee. Second, he was an aggressive Yankee. Third, he was angular and scrawny, and he scowled a lot, and he looked to be exactly what he was: the sort of guy who would slug you if he didn't like your looks.

One time, infield star Phil Rizzuto received a death threat. Stengel ordered Rizzuto to switch uniforms with Martin. Such was his loyalty to Stengel that Billy agreed without hesitation. Here was a player who would put his life on the line for his manager.

During the infield drill, Billy was wearing Rizzuto's number 10. He didn't stop moving. During the game he was a man in perpetual motion, darting this way and that, listening for the whine of a bullet.

Rizzuto wore Billy's number 1, and after the game Rizzuto demanded back his uniform. Every time he went to the plate he would be booed so loudly that he decided the booing was worse than the threat of getting shot.

One aspect of Billy's personality that impressed Stengel was that he seemed totally fearless. Billy was afraid of no man. When the bench-jockeying from the other team became fierce, Stengel would shout across the diamond, "You SOBs better watch out. That Martin will get you." And he would.

Billy finally got his chance to start for the Yankees in the summer of 1951 when Jerry Coleman sustained a serious injury and began to slump. Stengel finally benched the slick-fielding second baseman and started Martin. He had Martin batting eighth, prompting a familiar refrain.

"Why am I batting eighth?" Billy screamed at Stengel. "Why the hell don't you play the batboy over me?"

"Where do you think you should be hitting, Mr. Martin? Fourth?"

"And why not?"

Billy Martin played 23 games at second and 6 games at shortstop. Toward the end of the 1951 season Stengel put the veteran Coleman back into the starting lineup as the Yankees made their pennant run.

With twelve games to go in the 1951 season, the Yankees led Cleveland by one game. When Indians starters Bob Feller, Bob Lemon, and Mike Garcia folded down the stretch, the Yankees were champions for a third year in a row.

Stengel played Jerry Coleman and rookie Gil McDougald at second base against the Giants in the 1951 World Series, which the Yankees won in six games.

The victory, however, was not without its cost. In Game 2, New York Giants rookie phenom Willie Mays lifted a routine fly ball out toward center field. As Joe DiMaggio waited under the routine fly ball, Mantle came racing over from right field to back him up. Unexpectedly the youngster fell in a heap and lay motionless on the green lawn of the Yankee Stadium outfield.

Mantle had been watching the downward flight of the ball, and when DiMaggio hollered, "I got it," Mantle had stopped suddenly and caught the back cleat of his right shoe on a rubber drain cover in right center. Mantle had to be carried off on a stretcher, to the horror of his parents, who had traveled from Commerce, Oklahoma, to see him play. Mantle did not play again in the series. His injury was the first of a series of crippling injuries that hampered his long, illustrious career.

When Billy Martin came to spring training in 1952, it was with the knowledge that he was going to be the starting second baseman. Jerry Coleman had been a World War II pilot who had flown in the South Pacific and early in the year was drafted back into the armed services. Stengel moved Gil McDougald over to third base, leaving the second-base job for Billy.

There are certain people who seem to make trouble for themselves. Billy was that way. Billy was fearless, and he had a devil-may-care attitude. He didn't believe anything could happen to him, no matter what the activity.

In the early spring of 1952, Billy almost cost himself his starting job with the Yankees because he put himself in a position to hurt himself, which he proceeded to do. It was a chance to earn a hundred dollars, which was a lot of money then, but the downside could have cost him his career.

Joe DiMaggio had a pregame television show. His sponsor was Buitoni macaroni. For one of the Buitoni commercials, Joe needed a teammate to demonstrate the technique of sliding in slow motion.

In the commercial Martin was supposed to slide into second base while Phil Rizzuto leaped over him. Billy shot the scene, no problem. The next day he got a call. Could they shoot it one more time?

That day he wore a new pair of spikes. They were not broken in, and when he hit the bag, the new spikes caught, and everyone in the park could hear the *crack, crack* sounds from his ankle.

"You could hear that popping noise," said Phil Rizzuto. "It rebounded all over the park. It was awful. I'll never forget that look on Billy's face."

Rizzuto said, "Get up." Billy couldn't. The ankle was broken. As the young infielder lay on the ground grimacing in pain, both Martin and DiMaggio wondered how the hell they were going to explain to Stengel what had happened.

The Yankee doctor, Sidney Gaynor, whom the players universally distrusted, tried to say it was only a sprain. Mantle, who was there with Billy when it happened, insisted it was broken, and he and Dr. Gaynor almost got into a fight.

When Martin arrived at the hospital, Mickey's diagnosis had been correct. Billy's ankle was busted in two places.

Gaynor, who was famous among the players for screwing up, put a cast on Billy before the ankle finished swelling, and in the evening Billy's leg hurt so much that Gaynor had to come back and cut the cast off.

Martin was out from March 12 to May 12. Stengel never held it against him, but Billy worried so much about his future that he lost thirty pounds. Stengel, who was genuinely concerned, would tell Billy, "Worry is something which never does a fella any good. It'll take weight off you which you can't afford." Billy worried anyway. It was his nature.

The day Billy returned, the players saw that his brash attitude hadn't changed. He came to the park that day and threw his gear into the locker vacated by the retired Joe DiMaggio.

"Better me in Joe's locker than some rookie he doesn't know," Billy said.

A few days after Billy returned, he injured his right knee after a headfirst slide. He missed a few more games. Billy began to wonder whether he was injury-prone.

Billy told Al Stump of the *Saturday Evening Post,* "I was frightened. I couldn't sleep, thinking about all the guys who washed out with bad legs. I couldn't eat. I vomited everything."

Around the time Billy took over at second base, Mickey Mantle, who had been recuperating from his serious knee injury suffered during the World Series, was rounding into shape.

When the Yankees bought the contracts of Billy and Jackie Jensen from the Oakland Oaks, Stengel had predicted that Jensen would be the next great center fielder after DiMaggio, but GM George Weiss, who favored kids who came up through the channels of his Yankee farm system, in 1951 traded Jensen to the Washington Senators for veteran outfielder Irv Noren. It was a terrible trade, as Jensen, a robust hitter, went on to become the all-star Stengel had predicted him to be. In 1958, Jensen, then with the Boston Red Sox, was voted Most Valuable Player in the American League.

With Jensen gone, Stengel gave the job to another of his phenoms. Though Mantle had never played the position before, just as soon as his knee was strong enough, Stengel sat Irv Noren and stationed the powerful youngster in center field.

By the middle of the 1952 season, on a team with famous veteran players, Casey Stengel had placed his two adopted sons on the green grass of Yankee Stadium. An eye for talent was part of Casey's genius. He had plucked Martin from his "ragamuffin" existence in Oakland and tutored him, and he had spotted the "hayseed" Okie from Class C, took him under his wing, and taught him what he needed to know.

On the field stood Stengel's legacy, Mutt and Jeff, Billy Martin and Mickey Mantle, two kids who were soon to be the heart and soul of the world champion New York Yankees.

Since he was a youngster Billy Martin had told anyone who cared to listen that one day he would be an infielder for the Yankees. No one *really* believed him—except the one man who mattered most, Casey Stengel.

# THE MOCK
# ATHLETE

**H**enry Steinbrenner, George's father, as a youth was a talented track star. He had set an American Athletic Union record in the 220-yard high hurdles while running for MIT in 1927, and in 1928 his time was good enough to make the U.S. Olympic track team. Frank Treadway, a childhood friend of George's, remembered one Halloween when as a young boy he and a friend decided to play a prank and throw wads of wet toilet paper against the windows of the Steinbrenner house. In the middle of their mischief Henry Steinbrenner spotted them. Quickly the small boys ran off the property. In a panic they climbed a wooden fence, shinnying over it in their desperation to escape their friend's fearsome father.

Henry tore off after them. When he got to the fence he didn't stop, but gracefully hurdled over it. Soon thereafter Henry caught the petrified pranksters. "I had no idea he could run like that," said Treadway.

As a boy, George loved sports. He idolized the local Cleveland teams, the Indians in baseball, the Browns in football, the Barons in hockey. Like so many boys, he dreamed of being a professional athlete. Unfortunately, the gods did not give him the skill to reach his goal.

At Culver Military Academy, George ran track and played on the football team. He also enjoyed playing basketball but wasn't good enough to make the Culver varsity. He was a forward on the band intramural team with an uncanny off-balance shot from the corner. He did not play baseball, which overlapped with the outdoor track season.

Every classmate at Culver who talked about George's track prowess remembered that George ran track as a way to please his father. When they discussed it, it was always in the context of his wanting to prove himself to Henry.

"His father came to school and pushed him quite a bit," remembered classmate Jim Beardsley, who was part of a track team that didn't lose a meet in four years at Culver.

"I had a feeling he was definitely competing with his father's record in the athletic world," said another classmate, Lee Robinson.

"He certainly wanted to prove himself in track because of his father," said Ket Barber.

But his father had been national collegiate championship-level. George didn't have his father's talent. When you compete with your father and don't measure up, the burden is enormous, and your self-esteem suffers terribly.

According to Coke Smith, George's track coach at Culver, George was one of the top runners in the school. While at Culver, said Smith, he was able to run the 120-yard high hurdles in 15.2 seconds, "good, according to Indiana standards."

Teammate George Steiner recalled that the best hurdler on the team was named Atkinson, a boy who ran the hurdles in 14.9.

"It won't win state tournaments," said Steiner. "It's medium quality, not real great, and George was a couple tenths behind him."

Track coach Smith noted that he thought George could have been a better hurdler had he worked harder at it but that football was his greater love.

George was an end on the Culver football team. He played a little his junior year, then started his senior year. Barber, who played on that Culver team, remembered that George played hard, didn't accept defeat well, and was tough on himself.

"He would say, 'We should have done this, I should have done that.' He'd slam a locker or two. That kind of approach, as opposed to the kind of guy who would look at his shoes and go in a corner and hide."

Classmates recalled that George and quarterback F. Harris Magruder were an effective combination, that George had "pretty good hands," the quickness to get open, and that George was particularly anxious to score a touchdown.

Classmate Paul Hensil remembered that in one game George caught a pass in the open, was headed for the end zone, but "fell flat on his face somewhere short of it." George had tried too hard, tripping himself up in his rush to score. Later in the season he did catch a "touchdown or two," according to team members.

That George started at end caused some bad feelings among the boys who knew him best.

"Most of my close friends felt there were better-qualified people who didn't get to play because of George," said Lee Robinson. "When George wanted an extra rank or wanted to be on the football team, he arranged to have his father's money used to further that goal."

In his own mind, being a starter on the school football team was not a high enough achievement for George, who wanted history to remember him as being better than that. Once when I interviewed him, he proudly told me that at Culver he had won the Callahan Award, given to "the best football player on the team."

When I told Lee Robinson that George said he had won the Callahan, he said, "Yes, he won it, but there were obviously better *musicians* in the band than George."

I was taken aback and asked him what the Callahan Award was given for.

"For the best band musician," said Robinson, who noted that the only reason George got it was that his father was close to Colonel Payson, the band director.

"His father would come through all the time and spend hours with Colonel Payson," said Robinson.

George entered Williams College in the fall of 1948 and made the freshman track team. He was good enough to make the varsity as a sophomore. If George had given a less-than-best effort in high school, when he got to college he attacked track with a singular dedication.

Dr. Jack Brody, a sprinter who trained with George at Williams, remembers him as someone who was "dead serious" about the sport. Said Brody, "He would get up and do a morning workout as well as an afternoon session, going through a full workout. He really meant to get the most out of himself. He was really determined. There was no fooling around."

The irony was that despite his efforts, he never improved on his best high school time of 15.2. Said Brody, "That was about it. Even with great coaching and his dedication and hard work, that's as good as he was. He did not have great talent. He had real guts."

Brody's sense was that George never gave up because either he had an unrealistic belief in how good he was or he was looking for a miracle. Or there was a third possibility.

According to Brody, George talked about his father as if he was a powerful tyrant. George talked about him "an awful lot," and the other runners would refer to him as the Baron, a scary, imposing man. But, said Brody, when Henry Steinbrenner came to visit George, he was always "affable and pleasant, and very nice." It was George who was scared of him, and it was his fear that he was communicating to the others.

Said Brody, "He had a great need to be loved by this person who he was afraid of. He felt that if he worked hard enough it would really happen, and his father would love him. The rest of it was not a rational commitment."

Even though his times were more than a second and a half behind the top hurdlers, George entered major tournaments such as the Knights of Columbus meet in Cleveland.

His friend Frank Treadway came to see him run that night. "I felt sorry for him," said Treadway, "because there was no race at all. Here was this rich, white college kid trying to beat the black hurdlers, and there was no race. What impressed me was that he had the push and gumption to go down there and do it."

George didn't go out for football his freshman or sophomore years. George told me he couldn't play because he had dislocated his shoulder at Culver his senior year. Observers at Williams say that what George lacked was talent.

He tried out for the football team his junior year. Steve Blasky, who was on the school newspaper, was there when George went out for the team.

"I remember him trying to catch pitchouts, and he just couldn't catch it. And Pete DeLisser, the quarterback, was in hysterics," Blasky said. "George wanted so badly to be a running back, but he had stone hands. After two days of tryouts, George was cut."

Other members of the football team say George's other problem was that he didn't have the heart for the game physically.

"He was not a gutsy guy. That's one thing about that game: You either love the contact or you don't. You can either take a hit or you can't, and George couldn't take a hit," said Peter Callahan, a member of that team. "George was much more with the mental aspect of the game."

During his junior year, George was the assistant sports editor of the Williams campus newspaper. "He figured himself as something of a Red Smith," said Callahan. That year George cemented a relationship with football coach Len Waters by becoming his unofficial PR man.

"Waters wanted a spokesman, and George was his spokesman," said Callahan. "Waters was using George as badly as George was using him."

By his senior year he and Waters had forged a friendship.

Said Callahan, "Waters kept George on the team senior year because George had cultivated him through his newspaper activity."

Said Blasky, "He wrote these glowing stories about Waters and ingratiated himself with him, and George made the football team his senior year."

He did not, however, play. No matter. George had learned an important lesson: If you position yourself with the right people, you can get wherever you want to go even if you don't deserve to be there.

Even though he wasn't a football player, the people George enjoyed spending time with were the football players. If he couldn't be a good athlete, he could derive some self-esteem from hanging out with the fellows who were good.

"George was in a box," said Dr. Brody. "If a father makes you feel lousy as a son, the son can only try to emulate and be better, but George couldn't be better. And that's his self-image. He couldn't be as good as he was supposed to be, so he was cut off—he had to get his praise from the outside. But deep down he's failed."

His need to hang around these athletes was strong. It became important that these men be his friends. But athletes often welcome only other athletes. Pretenders are quickly rejected or become the butt of their humor.

George took his fair share of abuse from the other trackmen on the team.

"He trained harder than anyone else, and the other track guys would make fun of him for doing that," said Dr. Brody. "I used to think, Don't they recognize how hard he's trying? He just doesn't have a great deal of talent.

"He'd be pushy, trying to crack the clique of veterans, members of the mile relay, and they were pretty rotten to George. They didn't like him and would make remarks about him, or remark about the Baron, which is what they called his father. He'd find rejection. To his face, they'd tell him, 'Beat it.' He'd get very red, and come right back. He was remarkably thick-skinned about it. Nothing would stop him from doing it.

"People are cruel. They saw George the Freshman as an immature jerk, and it stuck with him. They would say to him, 'Knock it off. Why are you trying so hard?' And he was the sort of guy who just wouldn't go away. None of them really had the affection for George that I thought he deserved. I saw him as a sweet guy trying very hard. George was good company. Those guys saw him as an asshole.

"And by the time we were juniors and seniors, the younger kids were really wretched to him, 'cause they were being supercool and wouldn't want to train, and they could beat him, and they would tease him because he worked so hard and still wasn't getting anywhere. I remember a quarter-miler named Jones, who was a year behind us. Jones ragged George. What infuriated George was that Jones didn't train very hard, and he was on the mile relay team, and George trained very hard, and he couldn't make it. To his face Jones would call him 'the fat ass from Cleveland,' because he knew it drove George crazy."

It was the same way with the football players. George as a freshman joined the Delta Kappa Epsilon fraternity, which was the house of choice of many of the top football players at Williams.

"George was attracted to the Dekes," said Dr. Brody, " 'cause he liked being with the athletic crowd. He liked being around athletes, and he was respectful, almost obsequious. They used to tease the bejesus out of him, but that didn't bother him."

"It wasn't just that he hung around jocks," said Steve Blasky. "It was that the jocks made *fun* of him because around them he was trying so hard. George was a joke to the real football players."

Said Dr. Brody, "I always had the feeling that George's father had in some way fucked him up, made George believe his father thought he was no good. In some way, his father said, 'George has got to be the best,' and George wasn't the best—he felt insignificant next to the Baron, so he started to hang around with the jocks.

"But they weren't the best. They were sort of tin best."

Said Charlie Glass, who was a Deke one year behind George, "George was an exaggerated version of the stereotypical freshman. He was overeager, and his enthusiasm was unseemly for that time. He was something of a joke among a lot of people. They talked behind his back, made fun of him. They thought he was a jerk."

Said Dr. Brody, "George was a terrible, *terrible* judge of character. He didn't know his friends from his enemies. He had no knowledge of what friendship among men would be. He had no sense of loyalty. What was important to George was adoration. He wanted to be as big a man as his father. And he can never make it."

The athlete George looked up to most was a fierce, at times vicious, football player by the name of Chuck Salmon.

Salmon, a fellow Deke, was captain of the Williams football team. He was a Golden Gloves amateur boxer whom classmates say was one mean son of a bitch when he was drunk. He was also a real hero to George.

Said Steve Blasky, "George was a big hero-worshiper, and Salmon was real easygoing. So George hung out around him. He was a real jock sniffer."

Salmon tended to befriend people who were not part of the "in" group. One of those Salmon took in was George. They roomed together their junior year. Their classmates remember sports arguments the two would have. Salmon was a great Yankees fan, arguing the merits of the team's young stars, Mickey Mantle and Billy Martin. George took the side of the Cleveland Indians, arguing the merits of Bob Feller, Bob Lemon, and Al Rosen.

After the class graduated from Williams in June 1952, Salmon gained recognition in a *Time* magazine article that described how against orders he had chased a Korean MiG back across the Yaloo River two days after the armistice was signed.

After the war Salmon became a member of the famed Thunderbirds precision-flying stunt team. On May 12, 1959, Chuck Salmon was killed flying his F-100C during practice over Nellis Air Force Base in Reno, Nevada. He and another plane touched, he lost control, and when he ejected, he struck his head against the canopy, knocking himself out. As a result he wasn't able to pull the rip cord of his parachute, and his body was crushed on the desert floor below.

George has appropriated for himself Chuck Salmon's tough-guy persona, and also his football credentials. In one interview with the *Cleveland Plain Dealer*, George told a reporter he had been captain of the Williams football team. This raised eyebrows among the group that knew and loved Chuck Salmon.

"It was the worst thing George ever did," said Peter Callahan. "I screamed about that."

Commented Steve Blasky, "George always had a big pair of balls. Anyone who has the nerve to create the athletic background for himself that George did—well, you've got to have a lot of chutzpah, and that's what George always had."

George created his background because he evidently didn't feel others would respect him enough for who he really was. It must have been painful to be who he was, and so he concocted a version of George Steinbrenner and gave himself an invented past.

George didn't want others to know the truth: that he had been a competent high school football player and a decent college runner. A less-troubled individual might well have been proud of those achievements. But to George being competent and decent on that low level was unacceptable.

The bottom line: George Steinbrenner felt like a failure as an athlete.

What George would take from college would be the memory of all those athletes who had made fun of him, who had shunned him, who had made him feel like an outsider. One day he would show all the athletes who was boss. One day he would make the real athletes feel the humiliation and lack of appreciation they once had made him feel. One day they would work for him, and he would get even.

# STARDOM

The year George Steinbrenner graduated from Williams College—1952—began with both Billy Martin and his buddy Mickey Mantle hobbling, Mickey from knee surgery and Billy from a broken ankle. Mantle suffered heartbreak in the spring when his father, Mutt, died of cancer. With his father's death, Mantle became the sole support of his new bride, Merlyn, plus his mother, two brothers, and a sister.

Billy and his wife Lois, and Mickey and his wife Merlyn, were living together in a two-bedroom apartment in the Concourse Plaza Hotel in the Bronx, not far from Yankee Stadium. The two kids would be famous by the end of the year.

In mid-May both began playing regularly. Stengel unleashed Martin. He told him he would pay him twenty-five dollars every time he got hit by a pitched ball. He encouraged him to defend himself and his teammates from opposing bullies.

"He's got it here in the heart where it counts," Stengel often would say about him.

Almost immediately, following Stengel's direction as well as his own inclinations, Billy got involved in a series of fights on the field, setting his reputation in cement.

Against the Red Sox in Fenway Park before one game, Boston rookie Jimmy Piersall, who soon would be institutionalized as a schizophrenic, started agitating Billy. "Hey, Pinocchio," Piersall kept shouting at Martin, calling attention to

Martin's smaller but still Roman nose, "what's with the schnozz?"—a reference to Jimmy Durante, a show business personality famous for his own large nose. Finally, Piersall said, "I dare you to fight me."

It was the sort of invitation Billy relished. "I'll meet you under the stands, big shot," Martin shouted back. Each went into his respective dugout and circled under the stands behind home plate, with Yankee coach Bill Dickey in hot pursuit of Martin.

Billy got to Piersall, however, and with two short, vicious rights to Piersall's face, Martin slugged the Red Sox shortstop to his knees, leaving him bloodied. Boston pitcher Ellis Kinder and Dickey broke up the fight before Billy could inflict further damage.

Casey Stengel could not hide his approval of Billy's fierce combative nature. "It should wake the other tigers up," Stengel said, beaming. "It's about time they realize they gotta fight harder this year. I just hope that some of the kid's fire spreads to some of the others.

"Another thing," Stengel said, still crowing, bragging like the kid was his own son, "I'll have to ask him to confine the fighting to his opponents." Billy had knocked Bill Dickey's cap off and nearly spiked him trying to get at Piersall again.

"I don't want to lose any of my coaches," Stengel said, giving a broad, all-encompassing wink. Stengel had had his leader all along. Now he had his leadership.

After Piersall was hospitalized for a mental disorder and Billy was criticized for beating up a sick man, Billy tried to give the incident the right spin. He told reporters he hadn't known of Piersall's mental problems. "I was ready for the guys with the white coats myself."

But privately he bragged to Mantle, "You think I can't punch? Hell, I knocked that guy crazy."

In July he became involved in another fistfight, when St. Louis Browns catcher and bully Clint Courtney brazenly slid into Billy with spikes high. Martin, enraged, forcefully tagged the bespectacled Courtney right between the eyes to end the inning. The dust cleared, and as Martin walked back to his dugout, Courtney followed on his heels. This was the perfect scenario for a Billy sucker punch, the scent of possible danger combined with a take-no-prisoners philosophy.

Discerning the unfriendly footsteps, Martin stopped brusquely, wheeled around, and landed a couple of sharp rights to the jaw of a surprised Courtney. Billy also knocked over two umpires who tried to intervene. To add insult to Courtney's injured jaw, the umpires threw Courtney out of the game and allowed Martin to continue. Billy was, however, fined by American League president Will Harridge.

After the first Courtney fight, Billy bragged, "Look at all the money Rocky Marciano gets for knocking guys out. I didn't make nothing and put on a better fight. On top of which, I got fined!"

A year later Billy was involved with Courtney in another brawl. Teammate

Gil McDougald was trying to score from second on an infield single. The throw home had him beat by ten feet, but the aggressive Yankee third baseman bowled over Courtney, separating the catcher and the ball for the go-ahead run.

Courtney led off the bottom of the inning. When he came to bat, he told Yankee catcher Yogi Berra that "someone is going to pay." Courtney singled sharply to right, and as he made his turn at first, he swore loudly and continued toward shortstop Phil Rizzuto covering second. He had no chance to arrive safely. He didn't care. His goal was mayhem.

As Courtney approached Rizzuto, pitcher Allie Reynolds, first baseman Joe Collins, right fielder Hank Bauer, third baseman Gil McDougald, and of course, Billy, all charged toward the second-base bag.

Courtney jumped feetfirst at Rizzuto, catching the Yankee shortstop's right leg, bloodying it in two places.

In retaliation the Yankees mugged Courtney. After both Collins and Mc-Dougald swung at him, Reynolds pinned Courtney's arms, and Billy wound up and coldcocked him, bloodying his face and knocking off his glasses. Outfielder Bob Cerv then stamped the lenses into splinters.

Billy had been waiting to attack Courtney since they had played together in the minor leagues.

"It started a long time ago when we were in Phoenix," said Billy. "He spiked a kid by the name of Eddie Lanee. Eddie was a neighbor of mine in Berkeley. He got killed in Korea. We played high school ball together. All that year I only missed one game, and that was the game. Eddie was playing third base, and he's got Courtney out by twenty feet, and Courtney jumps up and rips his right leg open. That day I couldn't get him. I was in the stands. But from that day on, every time I got a chance I punched him. Every time."

It was this second Courtney fight that branded Billy as a fighter. For the rest of his life he had to fend off or punch out a series of challengers, on and off the field.

When it came to his gunslinger reputation, Billy clearly had mixed feelings. On one hand he knew it made him a target. Not long after the second Courtney fight, Billy said, "They gave me a reputation as a fighter, and now every guy and his brother is trying to make me earn it.

"I don't know what it is. Maybe it is my face. Maybe it's because I am such a skinny little guy. But somebody always wants to take a crack at me. I don't go around looking for fights, but neither do I back away from one. The good Lord hates a coward."

But while he tried to play down his tough-guy reputation, he would do things like go to an old-timers' banquet where Ty Cobb shared the dais with him and say to the gathering, "I have a lot of respect for the old players. But I'll tell you this, Mr. Cobb. If I'd been playing when you were playing, you'd only have to come into second high on me once. After that you wouldn't have had any teeth."

Stengel, who loved a good brawl back when he was a player, had no second thoughts about Billy's pugilistic tendencies. Casey actively encouraged Billy's fighting, at least on the field. Stengel knew the value of starting a fight: It brought the team together, and it tended to unsettle the other team.

While Billy was making a name for himself with his fists, by July 1952 Mickey Mantle was making fans forget that Joe DiMaggio had left the team and retired. In a game in Cleveland, Yankee first baseman Joe Collins hit a long drive into the upper deck in right-center field. The ball traveled 475 feet. Mantle was on deck, and as Collins trotted home, he said to the youngster, "Go chase that."

The next pitch Mantle hit about twenty-five feet to the left of where Collins had hit his homer and about fourteen feet farther back. Mantle circled the bases, came into the dugout, and went over to the drinking fountain where Collins was standing. Mickey took a drink and, without looking up, said, "What did you say, Joe?"

"Go shit in your hat," Collins replied, walking away from the grinning Mantle.

In 1952, only his second full season in the majors, Mickey batted .311, hit 23 homers, drove in 87 runs, and finished third in the Most Valuable Player balloting.

With Billy captaining the infield with his chatter, talking to the pitchers, keeping everyone alert, he became like a second manager on the field.

Late in 1952, Billy pulled a muscle and had to miss a game. John Drebinger of *The New York Times* asked Casey Stengel why he wasn't in the lineup. Stengel, dripping with sarcasm, told him, " 'Cause I don't wanna win. I only use him if I wanna win."

The Yankees led the Indians by two and a half games with eleven to play and won eight of their next nine games, losing only to 24-game-winner Bobby Shantz of Philadelphia. Every victory was important, because the Indians won nine of ten. Stengel won his fourth straight pennant with what the critics were calling his worst team since his arrival in 1949.

It was Billy Martin who clinched the 1952 pennant in the final few days of the season with a bases-loaded single with two outs in the twelfth inning.

In the clubhouse after the game Stengel posed for pictures, holding up four fingers—for four pennants in a row. Talking about Martin, he said, "He done it, didn't he? A lot of them don't like him, but he wins for ya and why wouldn't ya like him if you had him?"

The Yankees played the 1952 World Series against the Brooklyn Dodgers. The series opened in Ebbets Field, where Stengel had played several years as a Dodger. The Yankee manager personally took young Mantle out to the tricky right-center-field wall to teach him how to play the intricate caroms.

"You mean *you* once played here?" Mantle asked.

Stengel commented later, "The kid thinks I was sixty years old when I was born."

The Yankees and Dodgers split the first six games of the series. In Game 7 the Yankees led 4–2 going into the Dodger seventh. The day before, Stengel had relieved Vic Raschi with Allie Reynolds, who had pitched seven and two-thirds innings. In Game 7 Reynolds was not up to it. Carl Furillo walked, Rocky Nelson popped out, Billy Cox singled, and Pee Wee Reese walked. With the bases loaded, Stengel removed Reynolds. Vic Raschi came in and got an out. Stengel returned to the mound.

He called into the game number 21, a blond-headed left-hander named Bob Kuzava.

"He's bringing in a lefty in Ebbets Field?" the fans wondered. "He must be crazy."

When he was manager, Casey Stengel ran the team. He dominated that team. No one, not the owners, not the general manager, no one, told him what to do or how to do it. Mickey Mantle or Yogi Berra may have been the hitting star and Whitey Ford may have been the best pitcher, but the number-one personality was always Casey Stengel. The players knew he was the boss, knew he made all the decisions on the field. He was the one they had to answer to. His authority was unquestioned. And because of this he could manage without fear of criticism or of being second-guessed.

If Casey Stengel had a reason for picking Bob Kuzava—and he always had a good reason for whatever he did—the players would have to live with it. Kuzava had to face Duke Snider and Jackie Robinson, two heavyweights, the right-handed power of the Dodger lineup. As he was making the long stroll to the mound, Kuzava was thinking to himself, "This guy must be crazy to bring me in here." Kuzava turned his head to look back at Ebbets Field's frighteningly short left-field fence.

But Kuzava felt confident against Snider. Against him in the International League he had had good success.

Snider popped up. Two outs.

Jackie Robinson was next. Stengel ordered Kuzava to keep Robinson off balance by changing speeds on him. Kuzava complied. On an off-speed pitch Robinson, too, popped the ball up, this one to the first-base side of the pitcher's mound. As there were two outs, all three base runners were speeding around the bases toward home just as soon as the ball left the bat and started skyward. Kuzava gave way for one of the fielders to catch the ball.

Catcher Yogi Berra yelled for first baseman Joe Collins to make the catch. Collins, however, lost it in the afternoon sun. He didn't move an inch. As it began its downward path, runners Carl Furillo and Billy Cox had already crossed the plate, and Pee Wee Reese was rounding third with the potential winning run.

Billy Martin, at second, saw the glare on Collins's sunglasses and realized he was blinded. Quickly he assessed the situation and saw that none of the other fielders was going after the ball.

Martin, who had no business being involved in the play, started after it. As the wind carried the ball away from him Martin raced to the side of the mound, where on the run he bent low to catch the ball and save the game.

Stengel, his heart palpitating, showed no sympathy for Collins. "Wake up out there," he yelled.

In the Yankee field box GM George Weiss showed no appreciation for Martin's heroics. "Little show-off," said Weiss. "He made an easy play look hard."

Martin himself had not thought very much of the catch until he saw it on film and realized how far he had run.

Kuzava held the Dodgers at bay the rest of the way to preserve the World Series victory, the Yankees' fourth in a row.

Fifteen years later Jackie Robinson would call Stengel a "lousy manager, over the hill." When asked by columnist Jim Murray to comment on Jackie's evaluation, Stengel responded, "I would have to say Mr. Robason shouldn't think he was the only man who was brought in the big leagues who was a wizard. Why, he hit the lousiest pop-up I ever seen in a World Series. I brought in this left-hander and they say, 'My goodness, you shouldn't bring in a left-hander as Brooklyn was built with left-handers in mind,' and this left-hander Gazzara [Kuzava], I said to him, 'Why wouldn't you change speeds on this amazing wizard?' and this wizard Mr. Robason hit the ball clear to the pitcher's mound and Mr. Billy Martin catches it and we beat Mr. Robason's team for the fourth time in five, and the time they beat us [1955] he wasn't in the lineup, he took the day off in the seventh game, you could look it up, so it's possible a college education doesn't always help you if you can't hit a left-handed change-up as far as the shortstop, but I'm not bragging, you understand, as I don't have a clear notion myself about atomics or physics or a clear idea where China is in relation to Mobile."

The next year, 1953, Edward "Whitey" Ford returned from the service to join Martin, Mantle, and the Yankees. Ford and Billy Martin had played together at Kansas City in 1950, and had become close friends, and while Whitey was in the Army, Billy and Mickey became friends. When Ford rejoined the team in 1953, this troika of Yankees banded together.

Ford, a hard-boiled competitor, was guileful and slick. He had outstanding control over his assortment of pitches and over his emotions. He took wins and losses with equal casualness. Anger was never a part of his makeup.

Whenever Casey Stengel needed a win in a crucial situation, all he had to do was call on Whitey Ford. He was one of the smartest, classiest, most successful pitchers in the history of the game.

In a way he was a Yankee symbol. Though a witty man off the field, on it in front of the public he was serious, almost arrogant, exuding a confidence in himself that suggested infallibility. For sixteen years happiness was rooting for the New York Yankees when Whitey Ford was the starting pitcher.

With Ford's return to the team, the year 1953 marked the high-water mark for the wild trio of young stars. On the way north from spring training in Florida, the team played exhibition games at Cincinnati and then in Pittsburgh at Forbes Field. After the Cincinnati game Mickey, Whitey, and Billy went to Covington, Kentucky, which at that time had a notorious reputation for nightlife. The train for Pittsburgh was to leave at ten that night.

They missed the train. What to do?

They decided to catch a plane in the morning.

The next morning it was snowing, hard, in Cincinnati. All flights were canceled. What now?

Whitey, the ringleader and idea man of the trio, said, "No problem." They hailed a cab and drove to Pittsburgh. It cost them five hundred dollars.

They arrived during batting practice. Billy and Mickey, badly hung over, hoped Casey wouldn't notice. As Billy headed for the bathroom, Casey put his hand on Mickey's shoulder.

Stengel said, "I don't know where you assholes have been. I don't know what you've done, but I wanta know. . . ."

Stengel saw Mantle's condition and figured Billy was in the same state. "Where's the other little bastard?" asked Casey.

Stengel told Mantle that both he and Billy would be playing the entire exhibition game as punishment.

On Mantle's first at bat he hit the longest home run in the history of Forbes Field.

In the dugout Casey said, "Nice hit, Mickey. Take the rest of the day off."

As Mickey walked past Billy, Martin started chanting, "Teacher's pet. Teacher's pet."

Said Mantle, "We were boys then."

Talented boys. Recalled Mantle, "We were young and determined. We had the feeling that nothing could stop us. We were going to be the best damned ballplayers in the world."

It's often said that the team that is loosest and most relaxed has the best chance of winning, and the 1953 Yankees were certainly loose and relaxed. And they rarely lost.

In 1953 the Yankees won 99 games, finishing eight and a half games ahead of the powerful Cleveland Indians. Whitey Ford finished the year 18–6 with an earned run average of 3.00.

Mantle, twenty-one, batted .412 during spring training. During the season he hit .295 with 21 homers and 92 RBIs. Billy Martin was the second baseman and acknowledged team leader. In 1953, Billy hit 15 home runs and drove in 75 runs, outstanding numbers for an infielder. Catcher Yogi Berra hit .296 with 27 homers and 108 RBIs.

Casey Stengel would tell anyone who asked that the 1953 Yankees were the best team he ever managed.

He said, "We got the best shortstop in Phil Rizzuto, and the best second baseman in Billy Martin, we got Yogi Berra, the best catcher, and Mickey Mantle, the best center fielder. The outfield is swell and the pitching is tremendous."

The Yankees won eleven of their first fourteen games, forged a lead, and never gave it up. Aided by an eighteen-game winning streak, by early June they had a ten-game lead over the Cleveland Indians.

During that three-week, eighteen-game winning streak in May and June, Stengel became a tyrant. He called team meetings and chewed out players for the smallest imperfections in their play. The longer the streak, the rougher he became. Stengel knew that as long as the team won, the players could and would take it.

The Yankees could have clinched sooner than they did, but in the last week of June the Yankees lost nine home games in a row, allowing their lead to shrink to five games. Stengel became physically ill as a result of his anxiety. He openly feuded with the press, who chastised him for playing Mickey Mantle with a swollen and painful right knee. After the eighth consecutive loss, he banned all reporters from the clubhouse. After the ninth loss, the reporters boycotted Stengel.

Through the losing streak Stengel said little to the players. The losing streak was broken on a single by Billy Martin, and the next day Stengel held his meeting and chewed into the players for forty minutes, accusing them of lax play and complacency.

Once the Yankee ship righted itself, Stengel returned to his more congenial ways. He made peace with the press as the Yankees glided to an easy pennant. Martin, who loved to tease, one day chose Casey as his target.

"There was this one game in Washington," recalled pitcher Eddie Lopat. "The Old Man had had a bad night. You know, his eyes were all bloodshot, his head was down on his chest, he wasn't saying a word. Billy went up to hit and popped up. He came back to the bench steaming and smashed his bat against the bat rack. A lot of those bats flew all over the dugout, and Casey was really jarred. He grabbed Billy and told him to watch that stuff.

"We were winning big, so the Old Man fell off again. Now Billy was at bat for a second time. This time he took a called third strike, and he was really mean coming back to the bench. He smashed his bat against the top step of the dugout, and the old man was jolted awake. He reached over into the bat rack, picked up a fungo stick, and started chasing Billy with it. When I last saw them Casey was running up that ramp, Billy was only a couple of steps in front of him, and he was screaming, 'No, Casey . . .' "

The Yankees clinched against the Indians on September 13, when Billy drove in four runs against Early Wynn and two relievers. The pennant-clinching, Stengel's and Billy's fifth in a row (four with the Yankees, one with the Oakland Oaks), was expected and taken with aplomb by all the Yankees.

The Yankees' opponent for the World Series in 1953 was the Brooklyn Dodgers again. The Yankees won three of the first five games. The sixth game was played at Yankee Stadium.

Whitey Ford led Carl Erskine 3–1 in the eighth inning. Stengel brought in Allie Reynolds in relief. The Superchief did fine in the eighth, but in the ninth he walked Duke Snider, and then Carl Furillo pulled a fastball over the fence to tie the game.

Clem Labine, the Dodgers' star reliever, opened the bottom of the ninth by walking Hank Bauer. After Mantle bounced a high chopper between third and the mound that Billy Cox was unable to handle cleanly, both runners were safe.

With one out Billy Martin was the batter. The hero of the 1952 Series repeated his heroics when he stroked a fastball on a line over second base to score Bauer with the winning run. It was his twelfth hit in the six-game series. It earned the Yankees their fifth straight world championship and their sixteenth World Series triumph in twenty tries.

After the game the ebullient Martin told reporters, "The Dodgers are the Dodgers. If they had eight Babe Ruths they couldn't beat us."

Billy Martin had batted 12 for 24, the second-most productive batting performance in Series history behind Babe Ruth's 10 for 16, .625 in 1928. His eight RBIs was second only to Lou Gehrig's nine RBIs in 1928. Martin won the Babe Ruth Award as the most valuable player in the 1953 World Series.

"That's the worst thing that coulda happened to Martin," Stengel said. "I ain't gonna be able to live with that little son of a bitch next year."

Billy was particularly pleased that he had outplayed the more renowned Dodger star, Jackie Robinson.

"See, there was a black lawyer by the name of Walter Gordon out in California that helped my mother when I was a kid," said Billy. "He had also helped Jackie, so when we played against Jackie in the series, I always wanted to show that I was a better second baseman. That was my real challenge. And I always outhit him, and I always outplayed him. Every series we played in."

Martin was also awarded the Hickock Award in October as the outstanding pro athlete. He beat out jockey Willie Shoemaker and middleweight fighter Bobo Olson.

Stengel was virtually crowing over Martin's performance.

"There has been a tendency to underrate Martin," said Stengel, "because he is scrawny, is no beauty with that big schnozz of his, and looks like he was underfed and weighs only 135 pounds. But he has been a strong factor in every club for which he has played since he asked me for a chance in that Oakland park in 1946. I defy anyone to knock Martin down as a great ballplayer. Can he make double plays? Will he fight, especially against big odds? Will he come through when coming through means most? You have to say yes to all three questions. They say I have been biased in favor of Martin because I gave him his first chance and nursed him along to be sold to the Yankees. Well, if liking a kid who will never let you down in the clutch is favoritism, then I plead guilty."

# LOIS

**B**illy Martin was a national hero. Two years in a row he had been instrumental in helping the New York Yankees to World Series victories. But with Billy Martin, as with most famous men and women, the public saw only the performance and the kudos. It had no knowledge of Billy Martin's misery.

Shortly after Billy's great triumph in the series, the fifth World Series victory in a row for the Yankees, in the fall of 1953, Billy's wife Lois won her struggle to divorce him.

It was the official end to a three-year marriage that had begun poorly and went downhill from there. Billy, only twenty-two, was leading the itinerant, carefree life of a major league ballplayer. He spent half the season on the road, and when the Yankees were at home, he didn't stay home. He went out after the games, coming home late after sojourns in bars.

Lois had left him in the summer of 1952, only a few months after she learned she was pregnant, repeating the pattern that began when Billy's father left Billy's mother when she was pregnant.

After Lois served him with papers, for more than a year Billy pleaded with her to call off the divorce. It was too late. Billy, basking in his newfound fame and comfortably ensconced in the egocentric jock society, had paid scant attention to her during their two years of life together, and she was the sort of person who had enough self-esteem that she would not abide being treated badly. Once she made up her mind to leave him, there was no changing her mind. All during Billy's glorious 1953 season, he was in a deep depression over losing Lois and their baby girl, Kelly.

Billy had started going steady with Lois Berndt when he was playing in the Oakland Oaks farm system. He was nineteen. Lois was a student at Berkeley High School.

"Lois was a doll," Billy said. "She was a really pretty girl."

Billy had met her through his best friend, Howard Noble, who was dating a girl named Mary Ann Nelson. Lois and Mary Ann were best friends, and Howard would prod Billy to take Lois out. At the time Lois was dating a boy named Ricky Navarro. Billy enjoyed the challenge of getting girls with steady boys to go out with him, and he put the rush on Lois. Billy was, after all, a famous local baseball player, and who could compete with that?

During Billy's two years with the Oaks the two were a steady item.

"Through her junior and senior years, they were locked together," said Sam Curtain, who had been Billy's childhood friend and who married Lois after Billy and Lois were divorced. "As far as women are concerned, I can't remember Billy being with anybody but Lois. I used to see him in the clubs but never with anyone else."

Lois Berndt, who is now Lois Curtain, said she met Billy through Howard and Mary Ann and remembered Billy as being a fun person to be with.

"He had a lot of energy," she said. "Why do any two people drift together? I guess after going around together for such a long time, it was inevitable that we would someday marry."

When Billy went to New York to play his rookie season with the Yankees, Lois remained behind in Oakland. It was during this period that rather than sequester herself alone at home, she went out some, going to parties with Ricky Navarro and a couple of her high school friends. There was nothing improper about it. Billy and Lois weren't even engaged.

Billy's sister Pat went to school with Lois, and she noticed that Lois wasn't staying home. Pat and Lois didn't like each other, adding an element of discord to Billy's life. Pat made sure Billy, who was a violently jealous person, knew Lois was going to parties.

"I went through junior high and high school with Lois," said Pat. "I didn't like her. I told him not to marry her, that while he was in New York, she was running around on him. But Billy may have liked Lois *because* she was running around on him. He once said to me, 'If they are good, they won't be after me.'

"I tried to stop the marriage. I really tried. I said, 'Don't waste your time marrying her, Bill.' When they were planning the wedding, I told him, 'You'd better think about this real good, because she's going out on you, and you're getting married.'

"He said, 'Patsy, are you sure?'

"I said, 'Yeah, Billy. You think I'm gonna lie to you? Why don't you ask Ricky Navarro?'

"Billy didn't want to believe this, and she would tell him, 'Your sister doesn't like me,' which was true."

When Billy returned to West Berkeley after playing for the Yankees in 1950, he and Lois decided to marry.

The wedding took place in October 1950, just an hour after Billy had finished playing in an exhibition game for Casey Stengel's All-Stars in the Oakland ballpark. After the wedding Billy traveled to Hawaii for an All-Star game. He didn't take Lois with him. There was no honeymoon.

Billy's story was that he married her because she had been lonely during the season and he had felt sorry for her, so he married her. Billy's friends say he was crazy about Lois.

According to Sam Curtain, "Billy wanted to marry Lois. He was in love with Lois, because Lois is a classy lady. She still is. She had a little bit more than most of the girls he was running around with. She made him look good. It made him feel good that everyone in his age bracket liked her and that she had stability."

Pat remembered Lois without fondness. "They got married at St. Ambrose Church. She would never show us the wedding pictures."

The night before their wedding, the Berndt family held a reception. Billy had asked Pat to be in the wedding party, and she agreed. But according to Pat, Lois didn't invite Billy's parents to the dinner.

"Lois didn't want them there," said Pat. "Lois didn't like my mother, even though I was the one who was talking against her."

No sooner did they marry than Billy was drafted into the Army. Billy was shipped to Fort Ord as a private. He told Lois not to come, that he was too busy trying to become a soldier.

Highly agitated that the Army took him from the Yankees so soon after he had made the team, Billy, who had no connections, sought his own way out. He arranged with his stepfather, Jack Downey, for Downey to quit his job driving for Juilliard Liquors so that Billy could claim he was supporting his entire family and get a hardship deferment.

Said Pat, "Billy talked my dad into staying off work. He even paid him for a while. Billy told my mother, 'Tell Dad to quit his job.' So to help Billy, Dad quit his job."

Asked Pat, "Do you know how my dad suffered inside to be out of work? He had supported the family, not Billy. He was doing it to do the kid a favor. And Billy ended up back in the service anyhow."

While Billy was in the service arguing for his discharge he was sending Lois checks to pay his stepfather. When Lois didn't deliver the check one week, Billy sent Pat over to get it from her.

Pat knocked on the door. Lois answered. When Pat asked for the check, according to Pat, Lois refused to give it to her. Pat explained why Billy was sending the checks, that her father was staying out of work so Billy could get out of the army.

"Just give me the check, and I'll leave," Pat told Lois.

One word led to another, and Pat slugged Lois.

"It wasn't a fight," Pat said. "I punched her out."

Pat told her, "I want you to get on the phone and tell him I hit you. Then I want you to tell him who you're going out with now." Pat was aware that Lois continued seeing her own friends. "I haven't said anything about this guy, but I will," she said.

According to Pat, Lois finally handed over the check.

Billy eventually found out what had happened. After a time, he said to Pat, "I have to ask you a question. Just tell me the truth. Did you hit Lois?"

Pat said, "I sure did, right in your apartment." Billy asked her why, and she told her story. Pat told him, "I'm sorry I didn't hit her twice, but once was good enough for her."

Says Pat today, "I did hit her, and that was the end of it. She should have known better with me. All during her school days I never wanted her with my brother."

Billy managed to convince the Army to let him out on a hardship five and a half months after going in. Had he stayed in two more weeks his obligation would have been over. But because he didn't serve the minimum six months, he was subject to recall as though he had never been in.

Billy's ruse to get out of the Army didn't sit well with his close friend Ruben DeAlba. Ruben's older brother, whom he idolized, was killed in Korea, and it bothered Ruben that Billy had shirked his duty. One evening, Ruben began taunting Billy. Without warning, Billy started punching, and before he was done, Billy had almost killed his friend.

When Billy returned to the Yankees in 1951, he took Lois with him to New York. They lived at the Concourse Plaza Hotel in the Bronx, about a mile from Yankee Stadium, sharing a two-bedroom apartment with Mickey Mantle and his bride, Merlyn.

Lois recalls the friendships she made with Yogi and Carmen Berra and Charlie and Rose Silvera. She remembers the chuckles everyone got when Yogi, who had starred with the Yankees since 1947, compared his far larger paycheck with Billy's, who was making just $7,500 that year. Not only did Billy have to pay for their room in the Concourse Plaza, but they were paying for their apartment in Albany, California, as well. They weren't wealthy, but Lois never complained.

"We didn't need that much money back then," said Lois. "We always had enough money."

Lois remembered that the relationship between Billy and Mickey excluded her and Merlyn Mantle.

"Billy and Mickey would cut up, but they were not cutting up for our benefit. It was ballplayers cutting up for other ballplayers. That was the fun. They didn't include the wives in something like that. And what they would think was funny, we didn't have any interest in."

While in New York, it bothered Lois that Billy seemed animated around his teammates but sullen around her.

Mostly what Lois remembered was loneliness.

"Merlyn and I were young and newlyweds, and we were new to the baseball element. I liked it, but I didn't like to be alone so much. That's very difficult for a young person. You get married and you think you're going to be spending some of your time together, but Billy was always busy doing something. At Oakland he and his teammate Mel Duezabou worked in the afternoons in the Morrell meat-packing plant. In the off-season they worked at Rogers Men's Clothier pushing clothes to customers. It was beneficial for the owners to say, 'I got a couple of Oaks working for me,' or 'I got a Yankee player working here.'

"I guess I just tired of being alone so much. And one can only take so much of baseball. When he was with the Yankees, I always went to the games. What else was there to do? You went to the games.

"It's hard being a baseball wife. At a time like that you don't want to be left alone."

She remembered Billy going on barnstorming trips to Hawaii and Japan without taking her.

"That hurt," she said. "I wanted to go. I guess he didn't want to take me. Maybe there was something better over there than there was at home. If you have the opportunity, why have the wife along?"

During the summer of 1952, she discovered she was pregnant.

"I was only twenty," said Lois. "I know at that time I didn't really want children because I thought that Billy was still a child himself, and then I would have two kids."

When Lois learned she was pregnant, she told Billy she was going back home to California. Their apartment in the Bronx was hot and humid, and as she began to grow big, she became more and more uncomfortable. Since she was left alone a lot, she decided it would be better to return home to stay with her parents.

"In '52 Merlyn Mantle and I were both pregnant, and we were both feeling neglected, and we said that we were leaving, going home, and when neither Billy nor Mickey put up a fuss for us to stay, we left."

According to Billy's sister Pat and her husband, Ken Irvine, when Lois left Billy to go back to Albany, California, she resumed her relationship with a man named Bill Smith.

"Bill Smith was a West Berkeley guy," said Ken Irvine. "They called him Joker. He was a motorcycle rider who wore a leather jacket and a ducktail."

"Lois tried to dress him up," said Pat. "There was a very nice men's clothing store, where Billy used to buy his clothes. I'd go in there once in a while if I had to buy a present for Billy or Tudo, pick up something for my mother.

"One day I got a phone call from one of the owners, and I was asked to come up to the shop. He wanted to talk to me.

"I said to my mother, 'I wonder what he wants. I hope he isn't going to offer me a job in a men's shop.'

"I got up there, and we went into the back, and he said, 'I have to talk to you and tell you something. I don't know if I should tell Billy or not. We were debating it, but rather than get him all riled up, we thought we better talk to you first.'

"He said, 'Lois is coming in here and spending hundreds of dollars on men's clothes that are not Billy's sizes. They are for a large man, six foot, six foot one.' He knew the guy, but he didn't tell me his name at the time. He said, 'She's spent hundreds of dollars on this guy. She dresses him completely. We don't know what to do. We don't want Billy getting mad at us. What should we do?' ''

"This was the type of temper Billy had," said Ken Irvine. "He had the old Roman temper, kill the messenger. If the store owner had told him, he'd have blown his stack right there in the store. And he didn't want that."

Pat told the store owner, "I'll tell him."

"I waited till Billy called," said Pat, "and I told him what was going on. Well, he was home in no time flat and confronted her with this. The shop had all the bills, so she couldn't lie out of it. And there were a lot of incidents between Billy and this Bill Smith, a lot of problems. Then Billy went back to New York, and that was the end of it.

"One time I went with a girlfriend somewhere, and there was Joker with a bunch of guys, and I don't know how we even got into it. But I said to him, 'You have a lot of nerve having Billy's wife buying all your clothes. No wonder you look so nice. My brother's buying your clothes for you.'

"He got up to hit me. I said, 'Go ahead, and when you do, not only my one brother will come, all three of them will come.'

"Four or five of the other guys grabbed him and held him. They said to me, 'The guy is goofy. Don't say any more to him.'

"But Billy felt betrayed. He said he was giving her a good life, what she wanted. He didn't deny her anything, and he just felt betrayed.

"After the Bill Smith stuff, it all disintegrated. Even after Kelly was born, Lois would not allow any of us, including my mother, to see the baby.

"We saw her one time in a car. I went over to see the baby, and she rolled up the window, and I said a few things."

When Billy came home after the 1952 season, he rarely stayed home, going to banquets or bars.

"It has always been difficult for me to sit in one place," said Billy. "I had to be on the go, and I just couldn't sit home. I had to get out."

Their daughter, Kelly Ann, was born in the fall of 1952. Billy noticed that when Lois came home from the hospital, she despised him.

"I could see that she hated even to see me," Billy said. "She hated everything about me."

Shortly after Billy returned to Lois from playing ball, there was a knock on the door of her parents' home, where they were living.

"Here," a man said. He presented Billy with a summons and complaint for divorce. It was the first he knew of his wife's plans.

"What's this?" Billy asked Lois.

"I don't love you anymore," she answered.

According to Sam Curtain, her husband of forty years, Lois is the type of person who once she makes up her mind, doesn't change it.

"Lois cut Billy off because Billy was a big player with women," said Curtain.

"He was still very young at the time, and he didn't know how tough she could be. She's a very fair person. What she gives, she wants back in return. And Billy couldn't do that. He was insecure, and he just liked to play around.

"When he had a wife, he always had to have a girlfriend in case the wife dumped him. That's the insecurity, and so she just cut him off," he said. "That's the way she is. When she makes up her mind, that's it, and there's no two ways about it. That life with Billy was over for her."

Said Billy, "I loved Lois, probably more than I realized, and I wanted her back and I wanted to be able to be with my baby, and I could not accept the reality of her wanting a divorce. I wouldn't give her the divorce right away. I held back quite a while because I was praying she'd change her mind. I guess I should have realized there was no way I was ever going to get her back."

Said Sam Curtain, "For many years, Billy wanted her back. After Billy, she went with Bill Smith, who Billy hated and I hated. Then she went with a guy named Don Strong, and then I started taking her out. This was two years after her divorce from Billy.

"One summer Billy came back to Berkeley, and I ran into him at Hogarty's bar. He said, 'I never thought you'd be a wife stealer.' I said, 'I'm not a wife stealer. She's been divorced for two years.'

"He was still wishing the hell he could get her back. We almost had a beef in the place that night, but luckily cooler heads prevailed. It was good he was living back East, because I'm sure something would have happened if we had seen each other more often. Billy was so insecure."

Throughout the 1953 season Billy couldn't stand the thought that Lois was divorcing him, and he was close to a nervous breakdown.

Said Mickey Mantle, "One particular day when he realized there was no longer any hope for a reconciliation, he wrecked our hotel room. I mean, he literally tore it apart."

Billy fell into a state of deep depression. He had trouble eating and sleeping, and he was on tranquilizers. Each day when the Yankees played at home, he traveled to St. Patrick's Cathedral to pray and ask for strength.

One morning after Mass, a man stopped him. "Are you Billy Martin?"

Martin nodded pleasantly.

"If you're a member of this parish, I'm going to quit."

Only his friendship with Mickey Mantle saved him from going over the edge mentally.

"He'd see me call and try to talk to my wife and daughter on the phone," said Billy, "and she'd hang up on me, and I'd be upset, and he thought one day that I was going to tear up the whole hotel room."

Through 1953, Lois's lawyers pressed him for the divorce. The fans read about his troubles in the papers. One afternoon a fan threw a baby bottle at his feet.

"Go home and feed your family, you no-good bum," the fan shouted. A local newspaper maliciously said that he was neglecting his family at home.

Billy was tense and unhappy all through 1953. His only relief from his personal hell was playing ball. On the field during 1953 he played the best ball of his career.

Off it he was a mess.

"The guys who are happy playing ball are those who can adjust to the nuthouse they have to live in," Billy said. "I've never been able to get a good, steady grip on myself in this racket."

Anxiety gripped him as the 1953 World Series was getting under way. "I was about to crack up mentally before the Series," he confided.

In the 1953 World Series he went 12 for 24, drove in the winning run of the final game, and was named the Babe Ruth Award winner as the most valuable player of the Series.

Mickey Mantle, who as a rule didn't analyze what was going on around him, said of Billy, "There are athletes who are at their best when they are angry because their anger is always directed at their opponents. Billy was like that."

After the 1953 Series Billy went home and spent a week in bed in his mother's house. He kept up his attempt to reconcile with Lois, to no avail. He then flew to Oklahoma and stayed the winter with Mickey and Merlyn.

One night in Commerce while visiting Mickey, Billy went by himself to a local bar called the 400 Club. When Mickey finally arrived, Billy was inviting two guys to step outside with him. They were taunting him, and he had had enough. He was ready to fight.

According to Mickey, no one challenged him after that.

While in Commerce, Billy had his pick of women in town. According to Mickey, Billy loved everybody, "even one of my best friends' wife."

That winter, according to Mickey, he and Billy would tell Merlyn they were going fishing, but instead they would head for a bar in Joplin to have a few drinks. "Before I knew it I was drunk," said Mickey. "I wouldn't even think about going home."

By 1954, Mantle had become a prolific drinker. So had Billy, who had used the booze to help him get through the toughest year of his life.

"If I could get through that year," Billy once told me, "I knew I could get through anything. I knew after that experience that I could take anything, that nothing could defeat me. Nothing or no one."

# THE MOCK AIRMAN

The difference between how the armed services treated Billy Martin and how they treated George Steinbrenner says something about the advantages of fame and fortune. Billy was twice drafted into the service, but he was kept in the States safe from harm because he was a famous baseball player.

George Steinbrenner joined ROTC at Williams College as a means of escaping military service while he attended college. Unfortunately for him and the rest of the ROTC units nationwide, the Korean War continued to rage after George's graduation in June 1952, making George, a low-ranking officer, prime fodder to perform frontline duty in Korea.

War is often a test of a person's political connections. The sons of the rich rarely end up getting shot at unless they opt to do so. George Steinbrenner's arrangement within the confines of a rigid system during his two years in the Air Force allowed him a freedom unthinkable to the average airman.

While his hero, Chuck Salmon, went off to fly combat against Korean MiGs, George got a position as cushy and as far from danger as was possible. He was appointed the special services director of Lockbourne Air Force Base, eleven miles south of Columbus, Ohio, a several-hour drive to his Bay Village home, safe from danger. His job was to run the athletic program at Lockbourne, which today is called Rickenbacker Air Force Base.

No one from Lockbourne went to Korea. It was the height of the Cold War, and the airmen from the Lockbourne SAC base went to England to fly reconnaissance against the Soviet Union.

According to those on the base, George's mother, Rita Steinbrenner, had been the one who wanted George shipped close to home in Columbus after his basic training at Lackland Air Force Base in Houston.

Recalled Jeanette Montgomery, the secretary to Charlie Eisenhardt, the deputy commander, "At the time we had a Colonel Esmay in charge of personnel, and I suggested a shipment out might be in order for Lieutenant Steinbrenner, 'cause he was a pain in the neck, and Colonel Esmay came back and said that George was sent to Lockbourne, that a Congressman had done it on account of George's mother wanted Georgie close to home.

"I don't know exactly how they worked it, but they worked it through Washington."

And according to those who were at Lockbourne at the time, Henry Steinbrenner had also used his influence with another powerful friend, Charlie Edward Wilson, President Truman's Secretary of Defense, to get George placed there.

Henry Steinbrenner and Wilson had worked closely together during World War II. Henry, the owner of a fleet of ships on the Great Lakes, had had a significant military role as a transporter of goods and supplies. Wilson ran the supply effort. He was a very powerful, important man in Harry Truman's administration.

That George was out of harm's way was not in itself so unusual. What was incredible was the arrangement Henry had forged to allow his son to remain free of all service rules and regulations. It was like Culver all over again, but this was no private school. This was the United States Air Force. Henry knew how to use his power to get whatever he desired and struck a deal with the Lockbourne base commander, Colonel Charles B. "Bo" Dougher. George was made an aide to Dougher, answerable *only* to Dougher. Dougher saw to it he would take care of George. In exchange Dougher would get his first general's star.

Dougher had been a colonel since February 19, 1943. After that he went no higher until August 25, 1953, when he received his star. It was an arrangement that causes George's immediate superior officer to gnash his teeth even to this day.

Major William Smith was that officer. Recalled Smith (his last name is a pseudonym at his request), "I had been close to Colonel Dougher. I had served under him in World War II, and when I was back in his command in 1952, I was surprised to find he was still a colonel.

"Dougher went from colonel to one star to two stars with the help of the Steinbrenners. Dougher was close to retirement, so the Steinbrenners were just what he needed.

"I can remember before George arrived on the base, Dougher called me down to the office to tell me there was a special problem coming up, and as he knew me all those years, he knew I would be able to handle it. He said that George was a very special young man, so I was to look out for him. He didn't tell me what the problem was.

"The usual young man gets transferred to a station, and he takes care of himself. It's very rare to have the commanding officer worry about just another second lieutenant.''

When George arrived, Major Smith discovered that George had been given immunity from having to obey the rules—any rules—including showing up on the base every morning.

"Most of the junior officers were jealous because he didn't have to come in and be in formation at eight o'clock," said Smith. "He could party all night and sleep all day. George didn't go out of his way to be nice to junior officers. He went out of his way to be nice to colonels. Among his peers he had a reputation of sucking up, polishing apples with the brass.

"At times George was inaccessible to anybody for three or four days at a time," said Smith. "There were times we had to send somebody to wherever George was staying, not to mention make many telephone calls with no answer, only to find out he was home up in Cleveland.

"Periodically when we had a parade, everyone had to show up, and George wouldn't, or he would be late. Any other officer would get court-martialed for that. He was excused. Dougher would say, 'He's young, and he has to be handled carefully. He's a special case.' "

Said Colonel Jerry Adams, another young officer under Dougher, "I was aware Dougher was protecting George. I was also aware of Bill's frustration. He never got at odds with Dougher at all. Everyone fairly knew that Dougher was George's patron, and that was the way it was. Bill just swallowed and steamed."

Said Smith, "I frequently tried to stop George from getting his way when I saw what he was doing, but I never was successful. If he did something and I caught him, George would say, 'Yes, I will do better,' but it didn't last very long because doing it his way was important to him. He just wasn't used to having people stand in his way."

Some of the fast ones George pulled have become part of the legend of the former Lockbourne Air Force Base. Though George caused some major consternation, he was never punished.

One time George hired his own band for a dance, paying for it out of his own pocket without consulting anyone. It was a magnanimous gesture, but it infuriated the musicians' union, which threatened never to allow its musicians play at Lockbourne again.

Another time, according to Smith, George requested money from the Welfare Fund Board to put up lights for the Lockbourne baseball field. Several times he was turned down. Major Smith was the secretary of the board, and after he came back from a short vacation he discovered that George had erected the lights anyway behind his back.

George had told the contractor he would pay for them if the Air Force wouldn't. The cost: $20,000.

When the request went back to the Welfare Board, this time Dougher asked the board to reverse itself and vote to rescue George from having to pay for the lights. It did.

"He wanted his own way," said Smith, "and he wasn't used to having anyone say no to him."

Another time, said Smith, professional ringers played for George's Lockbourne baseball team when it competed in a tournament in Japan.

"George was a very good coach," said Major Smith, "but winning was more important than how he won. Winning was more important than winning according to the rules. The rules never meant much to George."

When Smith heard about it, "Our feeling was it couldn't happen to a more deserving character. He's finally gotten in a situation where he's going to get his just reward," said Smith.

But whatever he thought the ramifications were going to be, nothing happened to George. The feeling was that once again Dougher had used his influence to make George's problem go away.

But it was not individual incidents that bothered the brass above and the officers below so much as it was George's arrogance about his special position and his lack of consideration for anyone else.

According to Smith, George flaunted his arrangement, even bragging about it to some of the girls he dated.

Said Smith, "The gals would say to each other, 'He's the lieutenant who has the base commander in his pocket.' "

Said Jeanette Montgomery, "I don't even like to talk about the guy. He was someone who said, 'This is what I want, and this is what I'm going to do. I'm going to get what I want to get, and the rules don't apply to me. I'm going to do it my way.'

"And it frustrated everyone, because you couldn't do anything to him. He was not considerate of other people. It was only what he wanted to do. He was a wheeler-dealer. He was pushy. He had to get his way.

"No matter what he wanted to do, he wanted to win."

Said Major Smith, "His theory was, if you win, it doesn't make any difference who you step on. And from what I gather, that's very true, even today. He was much more mellow than he is today. He had spurts of ruthlessness then, but it was mostly submerged. His character was always there."

While he was at Lockbourne, George worked hard at getting his name in the local newspapers. Arranging publicity for himself has been one of his main goals in life. Early on, George figured out how to win over the press.

George was able to do that because he was the Lockbourne athletic director and its basketball and baseball coach. He provided both the *Columbus Dispatch* and the *Columbus Citizen-Journal* with newspaper articles about himself and his team.

"He wined and dined those covering sports because he was very interested in getting his name in the paper," said Smith. "You would find more about him than the commanding general in the local papers. His picture would show up in the *Dispatch,* and the commanding general's wouldn't. And he was loaded in the base newspaper. You'll find lots and lots of press on George."

Tom Keyes, who was the sports editor of the *Dispatch* at the time, was a great admirer of George's. And why not? George did all his work for him. He handed in stories ready to run. ''George Steinbrenner's Lockbourne Skyhawks yesterday defeated the . . .''

''He made us aware of the athletic program down there,'' said Keyes. ''I think he did a better job of bringing it to the public that anybody prior or since. He would camp in my office and say, 'Here it is,' and you got the message pretty quick.

''In a lot of situations, with amateur-type teams, they are willing to tell you what's going to happen, but when they lose, they don't give you the results. That never happened with him. He was so thorough and complete. We got information daily. It was like him covering the base team almost like we covered Ohio State.''

George worked to keep his name in front of the sporting public by supplying stories and doing Keyes favors, such as giving him boxes of baseballs for an elementary-school team Keyes was coaching.

''This wasn't GI issue,'' said Keyes. ''This was coming out of George's pocket. I know, because he wasn't the type to take it from the Air Force.''

George was very active in athletics all over the Columbus area. While at Lockbourne, George continued his practice of hanging around the best athletes he could find in an area. The star player on the Ohio State team was a halfback by the name of Howard ''Hopalong'' Cassady, the winner of the Heisman Trophy in 1955 as the best college football player in America. George and Hoppy became good friends.

George was also a presence at area high schools, attending sports banquets around the city, presenting various schools with footballs and basketballs signed by all the team members.

After George left Lockbourne in June 1954, it was discovered that the footballs and basketballs to be used for base recreation were gone. From floor to ceiling, all that remained in the storeroom were empty boxes.

The base inspectors were perplexed. Why would anyone steal dozens of footballs and basketballs? The base officers were about to skewer the warrant officer in charge of the athletic equipment when they recalled how George had attended all those banquets, giving away all those balls to the schools. George had been the last officer in charge of the supply room, but by this time he was gone from the service, beyond anyone's reach.

Said Jeanette Montgomery, ''I didn't care whether George took the footballs and the basketballs. Only thing was, some poor little warrant officer would have gotten stuck if Commander Adams hadn't interfered and got him off the hook.''

After leaving the service, Major Smith worked with Presidents John Kennedy and Richard Nixon and later became a professor of sociology at a New York City college.

''I think George is one of the most interesting characters I ever met,'' he said. ''I read about him in the papers, and he hasn't changed. The blacks get blacker and the whites get whiter.

''He is not of the twentieth century. He fits in better with the nineteenth, the last of the robber barons.''

# THE SPARK PLUG

As a result of Billy's renown, which stemmed from his superb performance during the 1953 World Series, his local draft board ordered him back into the Army just before spring training of 1954.

Billy had been drafted in 1950, and after serving five months, the Army had discharged him on a dependency deferment because he convinced them he was the sole support of his parents, wife, and daughter.

By the end of 1953 Martin's wife had divorced him, and at the age of twenty-five, four months before he would have been ineligible for being too old, the Army ruled his parents were no longer in need of his support, and he was reclassified 1-A and drafted. Bitterly Martin fought the ruling and lost.

In April 1954 he again applied for a hardship deferment. He drove to the hearing in a baby blue Cadillac.

"How broke can he be?" the Army brass reasoned, and turned down his application. He was told, "You're a big star, and you have made a lot of money. We believe you're in a position to serve your country."

Once inducted into the Army, which was being accused of coddling athletes, Billy was made an example of when he was forbidden from playing on the Fort Ord baseball team. The Army refused to give him credit for the five months he had served earlier. It also gave him fewer passes than his fellow GIs.

Things improved during the eighteen months he spent at Fort Carson, near Colorado Springs, where he was player-manager on the post team. One consolation was that finally he was on a team on which he could bat anywhere in the lineup he wished.

With Martin in the service in 1954, the Yankees did not win the American League pennant. The champion that year was the Cleveland Indians, led by manager Al Lopez and a pitching staff led by iron-man pitchers Early Wynn, Bob Lemon, Mike Garcia, and an aging Bob Feller. Third baseman Al Rosen and outfielder Larry Doby provided much of the Indians' power.

Mickey Mantle had had two operations on his left knee after the 1953 season, but because he did not heed his doctors' instructions to exercise during the off-season, when he arrived for spring training the surrounding muscles were weak, and it was not until the final days of the training period that he was able to run. Hampered by a bulky leather-and-metal brace, Mantle was unable to bat left-handed and had to be platooned with Irv Noren. Through the spring months Stengel expressed his frustration and disgust with Mantle's physical condition.

"If he did what he was told after the first operation," Stengel said when he saw that Mantle would be unable to play in the exhibition games, "he would be able to play now. This kid—you can't ever teach him nothing in the spring because he's always hurt. You want to work with him batting left-handed and you can't. You want to do something for him and he don't let you. What's the good of telling him what to do? No matter what you tell him, he'll do what he wants." Casey touched his arm and his body. "He's got it here and here." Casey then tapped himself on the side of the head. "But he ain't got it here."

Mantle recovered by June, and by midsummer was the most productive hitter in the league, a threat to win the Triple Crown. The Yankees won a lot of games, but they were still unable to catch the Indians, who finished the season with 111 wins and only 43 losses. Early Wynn and Bob Lemon each won 23 games. The Yankees finished with 103 wins, eight games back.

When the Indians won the pennant Stengel told reporters, "I was surprised that I lost it. Until after those last two games in Cleveland I didn't expect to lose it. The fault was carelessness in all parts including myself. I kept saying, 'We'll catch them next week.' "

With Billy still in the service, 1955 didn't look any brighter for the Yankees. On September 1 the White Sox took over first place from the Yankees. A few days later the Cleveland Indians took the lead. Stengel was not optimistic about the Yankees' chances of winning.

Young Andy Carey had slumped for the Yankees at third base, in large part because he insisted on pulling everything pitched to him, and his long drives to left were just long outs in cavernous Yankee Stadium. Also, Jerry Coleman at second and Phil Rizzuto at short were not hitting, and the infield seemed to lack leadership and direction.

And then, unexpectedly, the Army returned Billy Martin to the Yankees. He was discharged from the service in August 1955. He had been promoted to corporal, given an honorable discharge, and awarded the Good Conduct medal.

The Yankees were in second place behind the Cleveland Indians when Stengel learned that Billy might become available for the final month of the 1955 season.

Stengel told GM George Weiss, "Get him here quick. He's my good-luck charm."

Weiss, who had never been a fan of Billy's, replied, "He won't be in shape."

Stengel ordered Weiss, "Get him here. He's always in shape to play for me."

When Billy got out of the Army, he told reporters, "It's tough on a baseball player. Right now I'm twenty-seven years old, and I've got nothing in the world but my name and my daughter."

When Billy returned, Stengel benched Andy Carey, moved Gil McDougald from second to third, and started Billy at second.

"Until I arrived here in Chicago a few hours ago," wrote sportswriter Bill Corum, "I felt that, farfetched as it seemed, the perennial bridesmaids of the American League, the White Sox, might become bride. Now I know better. Because I picked up the paper and the headline said that Billy Martin had rejoined the Yankees. That, of course, just about settled the pennant race in the junior league. The Indians have pitching, the local Sox have a pretty good club, and the Bosox of Boston are belligerent. But you don't beat Stengel when he's got Billy Martin."

Stengel rejoiced when Martin came back. He was getting back an infielder, and also a son. "That fresh little bastard," Stengel would say. "How I love him."

Upon his return Martin said to Stengel, "Case, when we were bushers out in the Coast League and then when we came to New York, you and I never played on anything but winners. So take my word for it, there is nothing to worry about. We'll take the league apart before the end of the season."

When Martin returned from the Army to the Yankees in September 1955, Stengel immediately inserted him into the lineup. Martin, despite the layoff, hit .300 and gave the team the spark and inspiration it was lacking.

Into the second week in September the Yankees trailed the Indians by two games as the White Sox faded. During a team meeting Martin spoke. He was angry. He told his teammates, "I had three cars when I went into the Army, and now I don't even have one. I'm broke, and you're playing as though you're trying to lose. We gotta get into the Series. We gotta."

With eleven games left in the season, the Yankees trailed the Indians by half a game. When the Yankees beat the Red Sox in the ninth inning on homers by Hank Bauer and Yogi Berra, they took over first place and never lost it. The Indians had printed World Series tickets but never got to use them.

After the Yankees charged into first place, Stengel rhapsodized about Martin. He told reporters, "That fella can shame others into winning. He never went to college but he's smart. He doesn't even have to think two seconds to do the right thing at the time. He can play three positions and hits when it counts. Let's say he is a valuable fella, one who makes the manager's job easy."

Though Billy had played in only 20 games in 1955, the other players voted him a full World Series share, a singular honor. Ballplayers don't readily give money away. They knew that without him they wouldn't have been in the Series.

"I was happy and proud when I heard about it," Billy said.

When the Yankees won the 1955 pennant, Casey Stengel was on the cover of *Time* magazine.

Going into the 1955 Series the Yankees were hampered by serious injuries to Mickey Mantle and first baseman Bill Skowron. Mantle had a torn thigh muscle. Bill Skowron had a broken toe.

The Yankees and Dodgers again staged a memorable duel. Yankee pitcher Don Larsen was a partyer on a team of serious imbibers. One night he hit a light pole at five in the morning during spring training. Stengel, who saw only Larsen's great arm, found that amusing. By the end of the year Stengel's faith in his bon vivant pitcher had paid off.

The Series was tied after the first six games. In the finale Dodger left-hander Johnny Podres beat the Yankees 2–0. Outfielder Sandy Amoros's catch of Yogi Berra's fly ball in the eighth inning ended the Yankees' chances of victory as Podres, who sported an effective change-up, finished strongly, challenging the Yankee hitters in the twilight with fastball after fastball.

When the final out was completed, Billy Martin burst into uncontrollable sobbing, and when he entered the locker room he pounded on the lockers with his fists, lacerating his hands. Martin hid in the trainer's room so his teammates wouldn't see his tears. An hour passed before Martin, who hit .320 in the Series, was able to control his emotions.

Stengel sat naked in his office, a towel draped over his lap, talking to two reporters, including Howard Cosell. To Stengel defeat was part of the game. In the past he had won and he had lost.

As Martin sat slumped in front of his locker, his eyes welled with tears as he said to Cosell, "A man like that shouldn't have to lose." Defeat to Martin was like dying. Martin never accepted any defeat. He certainly couldn't accept this one.

Billy blamed himself for the loss. He told reporters, "Podres had been throwing me change-ups all day. But I should have known he'd throw me fastballs when the light started getting bad. I didn't think."

After the World Series in 1955 the Yankees flew to Japan for a twenty-four-game exhibition series.

Before the team played its first game Stengel assembled his players for a short talk.

"Fellas," said the Yankee manager. "We're going on this trip to show the Japanese how to play this game. We're going to show them what this game is all about. And you fellows are going to perform one hundred percent because your jobs next year will depend on how well you do. Your jobs are at stake. So you'll be hustling. You'll be winning. You'll be trying to earn a job for next year."

When the tour ended, the Yankees were 23–0–1. Though a pleasure trip, Stengel's primary consideration was winning. That was the only way Stengel knew how to play.

Stengel wanted the Yankees to be ready for the 1956 season, and when the bell rang the Yankees ran away with it. On May 16 the Yankees defeated Cleveland and for the rest of the season were never out of first place.

In 1956 Mickey Mantle was *the* star. The Commerce Comet finally began to realize his full potential despite his leg ailments, and by the end of May he had 60 hits, 20 of them home runs, including one off Washington Senators pitcher Pedro Ramos that missed by eighteen inches going all the way out of Yankee Stadium. Mantle was on the cover of *Time* magazine in late May 1956.

This was one of those magical years of Yankee domination, like the 1927 Yankees of Ruth and Gehrig, which went 110–44, and the 1936 Yankees of Gehrig and DiMaggio, which went 102–51. The 1956 Yankees won 97 games, lost 57 and finished nine games ahead of the Cleveland Indians.

It was a year for Stengel when most everything went right, and very little went wrong.

During a game against the Red Sox, Stengel called time out. Third baseman Andy Carey was the batter. Stengel beckoned to Billy, the on-deck batter, to come back to the dugout.

"Run out there," Stengel said to Martin, "and tell that guy to swing at a good pitch and hit a home run."

"What did you say?" Martin asked.

"I said to tell that son of a bitch to swing at a good pitch and hit a home run."

Martin ran out to relay the message to Carey. Red Sox catcher Sammy White overheard and said, "You guys have to be kidding."

On the very next pitch Carey lashed out at a high, inside fastball and pulled the ball over the left-field fence for the game-winning home run. As Carey rounded third White said to Martin, "You know, that's the funniest thing I've ever seen in my life."

Replied Martin, "When the Old Man tells us to do something, we do it."

After the 1956 season, which featured excellent performances by rookie pitchers Johnny Kucks (18–9) and Tom Sturdivant (16–8), GM George Weiss was asked where the Yankees would have been without them had they not produced so spectacularly.

"We would have come up with somebody else," Weiss answered with an arrogance that made fans around the country come to hate the Yankees.

That year Whitey Ford won 19 games, and Mickey Mantle won every award known to sports, including the Triple Crown, Most Valuable Player, and the Hickock Award.

Mantle was awesome. He beat out Ted Williams in hitting, .353 to .345; Al Kaline in RBIs 130 to 128; and Vic Wertz in home runs, 52 to 32. He led all major leaguers in total bases with 376, runs scored with 132, and slugging with a .705 percentage. He was a unanimous choice as Most Valuable Player.

After Mantle won the MVP Award, Billy badgered him into making an acceptance speech. Mickey told him, "I've got news for you, pal. I wrote a speech. Here it is. 'Thanks a lot.' "

Part of Stengel's genius was that though everyone knew he had his favorites, his favorites still had to play hard for him. No one was coddled. No one was given the star treatment.

Even after Mantle won the MVP in 1956, Stengel still found a way to tell Mantle he better not get a swelled head. At the end of the season a reporter asked Stengel who was greater, DiMaggio or Mantle.

Stengel responded, "I'd have to say DiMaggio because he played right-handed and the park wasn't built for him and he didn't need a manager."

It's doubtful Stengel was being totally sincere, but Stengel wanted Mantle to know there were still future goals to be sought. He didn't want his star to become complacent. The kid had just won the Triple Crown. Now Stengel was putting up to him a greater goal: to become the greatest center fielder in Yankee history. Stengel, a genius at motivation, was challenging Mantle and slapping him down at the same time.

Billy didn't have a bad year in 1956. He hit .264 with 9 homers and 49 RBIs, and again it was his leadership that was his most important contribution.

When Stengel introduced some of his players to Dwight Eisenhower before the start of the first game of the 1956 World Series, he said, "This is my fresh kid, and this is the big fella; this one is my professional, Mr. President, and this fella may blow a train but never a signal."

Stengel was talking about Billy Martin, Mickey Mantle, Whitey Ford, and Don Larsen, his erratic pitcher whose antics caused him to miss an appointment every once in a while.

The Yankees led the 1956 Series three games to two over the Brooklyn Dodgers. Stengel resorted to his practice of playing veterans over kids in crucial games when in Game 6 he played Joe Collins at first base instead of youngster Billy Skowron and longtime St. Louis Cardinal outfielder Enos Slaughter in left field instead of the less experienced Elston Howard.

Bob Turley was pitching a shutout for the Yankees, but the team had been unable to score, and in the tenth inning Jackie Robinson hit a ball over the head of the aging Slaughter, who had been playing shallow to prevent the winning run. When Slaughter misplayed the ball the Dodgers won the ball game.

After the game Stengel told Turley, "I suffered more with you in this game than any game I've ever seen."

On the team bus going from Ebbets Field back to the stadium Billy Martin was in a foul mood. Like many of the Yankee veterans, Billy was furious that Stengel had played Collins and Slaughter instead of the more talented younger players. But no one had the audacity to complain to Stengel except Billy.

"If you're going to keep playing that fucking National League bobo out there, we're going to blow the Series," Billy told him.

"Who would you play?" Stengel asked.

"You better put Elston out there, and you better get Skowron's ass back on first base."

A writer who had overheard the conversation cornered Martin afterward. "You think you know the Old Man that well?"

"I'll pick the lineup for you tomorrow," Martin replied. "Here it is." Billy's lineup included Howard in left and Skowron on first. The next day, so did Stengel's.

The Yankees won Game 7 9–0 behind rookie Johnny Kucks's three-hit shutout, two home runs by Yogi Berra, a homer by Howard, and a grand slam by Skowron.

In the clubhouse after the game Stengel sought out Martin, and noting the home runs by Howard and Skowron, Stengel said, "You're a smart little bastard, aren't you?" The two men hugged each other warmly.

Stengel would say about Martin, "There ain't nothing he don't think he can do. He thinks he knows more about baseball than anyone else, and it wouldn't surprise me if he was right."

Casey Stengel and Billy Martin were together for six seasons. The Yankees won pennants all six years and won the Series five out of six. At the end of the 1956 season *Sports Illustrated* magazine named Billy Martin as one of the four mainstays of the Yankees, along with Mantle, Yogi Berra, and Whitey Ford.

Considering what Mantle had done that year, *Sports Illustrated* paid Billy a remarkable compliment when it wrote, ". . . it is difficult not to conclude that he is the most valuable as well as the damndest Yankee now extant."

# THE COACH

When George Steinbrenner arrived at Lockbourne Air Force Base he told anyone he wanted to impress that he had tried out with the Cleveland Browns professional football team.

The people at Lockbourne Air Force Base had no one with whom to check. When George said he had played pro football they saw a six-foot 185-pounder, and putting that together with his position as special services officer in charge of the athletic program, they believed him. Their belief that he had played pro football helped him win over his players when he became coach of the Lockbourne air base basketball and baseball teams.

According to those on the base, George put together winning teams. When he coached the base basketball team, no one was sure how he did it, but he managed to recruit a six-foot-seven center named Bill McCauley by getting him transferred to the base. Led by McCauley, George's basketball team played Big Ten quality ball and became all-service champions.

While at Lockbourne, George's great passion was coaching. The base did not have a football team because the Air Force didn't want its flyboys getting injured, and so George went outside the base to coach high school football teams. He became an unpaid assistant to head football coach John Montgomery at Lynden McKinley High School in Columbus. John was the husband of Jeanette Montgomery, the secretary who had disliked George so much at Lockbourne. Working with Coach Montgomery, George did some scouting, and he also helped with strategy. George may not have played the sport, but he showed a special aptitude for coaching football. He was a forceful leader, someone the players looked up to, and he showed a real flair for and understanding of the game.

John LeCorte was the star player at Lynden McKinley. In LeCorte's opinion, George's coaching contribution played an important role in the school winning the city championship that year. LeCorte recalled the game against Columbus Central as one of the highlights of the undefeated season.

"We knew Central would have a powerhouse," LeCorte said. "Central was rated in the top ten in the state of Ohio. We had a team picked as also-rans. We were picked as three-to-four-touchdown underdogs.

"George scouted them, and after he watched them play he came in with a whole new concept of defense, which was called a New York Giants–Eagle defense, a man-to-man defense. This defense proved to be very successful. We stopped their offense, and we beat them 7–6.

"I have to say George Steinbrenner's Eagle defense was what did it. Because Central's Coach Parks had never seen it before."

While George was based at Lockbourne he connected with the jocktocracy at Ohio State University. He hung out at the Wigwag Club, the OSU social club, and he made friends with many of the local OSU alumni boosters.

One of the Ohio State University alums who befriended George was a former all-American basketball player at State named Jimmy Hull. Dr. Hull, an orthodontist in Columbus, officiated high school basketball games around Columbus, and one night after a game at Aquinas High School the head of the school, Father Taylor, told Dr. Hull he was looking for a combination basketball coach, football coach, and athletic director.

Hull recommended George. After he was released from his Air Force duties in the summer of 1954, he was hired by Aquinas with the understanding that he would get his master's degree in physical education at OSU. Dr. Hull also arranged for George's enrollment into the Ohio State phys-ed master's program.

Tony DeSabito, voted the best football player in the state of Ohio in 1955, was the star player on that Aquinas team. To DeSabito, George was a great man, a savior. He took a team that had no facilities, worked on the program, helped the kids get into college, and took no salary as a reward. DeSabito remembers the galvanizing influence George had on the school when he came there.

"He was a great person, a good coach, loved kids, did a lot for everybody," said DeSabito. "He didn't have to come there, but he did, and he helped us a lot.

"Before he came to us, he had coached basketball at Lockbourne and had a terrific season with them. They were well known. He always had write-ups in the papers, 'Steinbrenner's Lockbourne Air Force Base team did this, did that.'

"I remember reading about him all the time, and we were so glad he was coming to us.

"We didn't have a locker room. He made us one. He had a carpenter come in and make one out of chicken wire. We never had a jockstrap to use, and he made sure we had a clean one every day.

"Everybody loved him. We all thought he was a man from heaven coming down.

"When you're a kid and you don't have anything, when you come from a very poor family . . . He didn't have to do that. He came on his own will. I don't think he even got paid. He did it because he liked doing it.

"He made us turn out to have a winning season. We played in the toughest city league, and it was one of the best seasons we had in football. He coached in basketball, too. He did both.

"He was very good, wanted to make sure we were behaved, didn't do anything wrong at night, made sure we didn't stay out late, that nobody drank, nobody smoked cigarettes. He was a very strong disciplinarian, just like he is with the Yankees.

"We minded him. We knew we had to play right. You didn't get to play if you were smoking or out at night. And he stuck by his rules. The priests would give in. But he stuck by them. That's why Father Taylor let him come in and run it the two years he was there. Not too many outsiders could do that, but he was strong, and the kids loved him.

"His drills were unreal. He made you be in shape. We had to run around the track before practice, and if you were pussyfooting around, not doing your job, you had to run around more.

"George was trying to make us good. He would do anything to have us have a winning season. There was nothing he wouldn't do."

Tom Keyes, the former sports editor of the *Columbus Dispatch,* remembers the lengths to which George went to gain an advantage for his Aquinas team.

Said Keyes, "Aquinas was opening the season with Steubenville Central Catholic, which was 140 miles east of here, so he went to Father Taylor, who was the principal of the school, and he said, 'What are we going to do about scouting?'

"Father Taylor said, 'We don't have any money for scouting.'

"That didn't satisfy George. He hired a couple of former Cleveland Browns friends, flew them into the Pittsburgh airport, put them up overnight there, paid all their expenses, paid them to scout the team, so he got a full scouting report on Steubenville Central."

George Steinbrenner is a complicated man. On one hand he is ruthless and relentless, on the other, all his life he has picked out youngsters, chosen them as his protégés, and helped them in important ways. When you played for George, the one given was that, like with Svengali, the boys under his tutelage always had to submit totally to the man.

John LeCorte was one of George's first protégés. A year before George helped with the football program at Lynden McKinley, he anointed LeCorte during a track meet.

It was a meeting that changed LeCorte's life.

"I'm from a little town in the southern part of Ohio called Gloucester, population a few hundred," said LeCorte. "It's a coal-mining town.

"My junior year in high school I was running in an indoor track meet at Denison University. I had won the 55-meter and the 200-meter that day and was a member of the 880-yard relay. An individual approached me at this time, walked up to me, and he said, 'You have to be one of the worst track runners I've ever seen in my life. You have a poor start . . . etcetera.''

"I was seventeen. In my mind, I thought, Who are you to say? But I didn't. I said, 'I appreciate that.' He said, 'I can really help you. My name is George Steinbrenner.'

"I thought, Who is George Steinbrenner? Also, I wondered, How can you criticize the city champion for two years? I was Columbus champion for four years in track and field.

"I usually won three out of four events, and in some meets I won four, because I was also good in the broad jump. I said, 'Mr. Steinbrenner, see the gentleman across the track? That is Mr. White.' That was our track coach.

"I explained to Mr. Steinbrenner that I didn't want to insult Mr. White. Plus you just don't take up with strangers, right? When you first meet George Steinbrenner, a sensational feeling you don't get.

"The next evening, Monday night, the track team was doing stretching and calisthenics, and Steinbrenner drove over to Lynden McKinley High School from Lockbourne Air Force Base, and he had his first-lieutenant uniform on, and he had a '53 Pontiac convertible, plush red, white top, and of course, that stood out in my mind. I wondered, Who is this guy?

"He walked up to me and said, 'I talked to Mr. White and he said I could coach you and help you along after you have your regular track practice.'

"At track practice I would run a couple of 220s, a couple of broad jumps, and I was done. George handed me a book on track and field, and then he gave me a log of the types of foods I should eat, and then he gave me a schedule that I was going to start from that day on.

"He said, 'Are you ready to go to work?' I said, 'I'm ready to go in for a shower.' He said, 'No, John, you haven't started yet.' I thought, The man is taking his own time to come out here, so I guess I should cooperate. I said, 'What do you want me to do, George?' He said, 'The first thing we're going to do, we're going to go to the starting block.' And he changed my starting form completely. Normally my right foot was up and left foot was back. He changed it to left foot up, right foot back.

"He said, 'You're going to come out of the starting block like a shotgun.' I said, 'I'm very uncomfortable.' It was very awkward. There was no way. I said, 'How can you criticize me on my start when no one has beaten me yet? I'm the city champion.'

"He said, 'John, I'm telling you. You have the worst start in the world. This is what you've got to do to improve if you're going to be halfway decent in track and field.'

"I said, 'What is ''halfway decent'' supposed to mean?'

"From there, we went to 120-yard dashes, 220s, 330s, 440s, a 660. Then, for some strange reason, he felt I had talent for the 180 low hurdles. I said, 'I never ran this in my life.' I knocked down three hurdles, and my right kneecap was nothing but a mass of blood and cinders. I still have them in there.

"It was, 'Let's get back up and do it again. You have to get the two and a half steps in between the hurdles, let's go. Get your timing down. Cut your movements down. Cut your legs down.'

"I said, 'George, I cannot run the 180-yard low hurdles.'

"He said, 'Don't argue about it. This is the way it's got to be done.'

"I had had a football coach, a basketball coach, and I had a track coach, but I had never had a coach talk to me like this. Why was I taking it from him?

"I said, 'George, tell you what. I'll do the 100, 220, 440, long jump, but forget the 180-yard hurdles.'

"He said, 'John, you're running the 180-yard hurdles.'

"Within seven days we went to Columbus Central High School, and we had a dual track meet. Paul Schooly was the city champion in the 180-yard low hurdles. Paul and I ran against one another in other events. He went to Everett Junior High. We ran against each other.

"I beat Paul by two and a half hurdles, which was totally amazing.

"I became a product like an owner who owned a horse. I had a timetable. I didn't eat at home. I lived with my brother and sister-in-law. My parents were gone. I had to go to a particular restaurant in Lynden, and my menus were set up by George Steinbrenner. If I needed spending money or needed to borrow his car, he was there. But I was like a colt. I ran seven days a week.

"George know who my opponents were, their strong points. He studied them. There was a Cleveland magazine that had the times of all the runners. We went to the Mansfield Relays, one of the biggest relays in the state of Ohio. You had Indiana, Michigan, and West Virginia in the track meet. It is one of the best. Many Olympic champions came out of it.

"He told me I had to run a 23.5 in the first 220 if I was going to win the Mansfield Relays. I said, 'George, this is not my race.' He clocked me, and I did win the Mansfield Relays the one year with George Steinbrenner.

"Keep in mind you're not talking to a human being. You're talking to a horse. Because mentally I was a horse, because this was the type of program he had me under.

"We went to a Worthington relays, north of Clements, and George could not attend, and it was raining so bad that day, but they didn't call it off. They had twelve teams, Lynden McKinley, Ridgewood, Worthington. I set a record in the 100-yard dash that night. We had to run through water. I set a record in the 440, won the 220, and I took one jump in the broad jump, and the next day in the *Citizen-Journal*, the paper's headline said, LE CORTE CRACKS THREE, WINS FOUR FIRST PLACES.

"I was in study hall. We had a principal by the name of W. C. Dyer, one of the toughest principals you ever wanted to be associated with, and anytime he called you into his office was for a problem. I was called to the office. I wondered, What did I do wrong? I knew I hadn't skipped school, knew my grades were all right.

"I arrived at his office. He asked me to come in. He said, 'You have a personal telephone call.' I picked it up, and it was George. He said, 'LeCorte, what in the hell happened to you last night?' I said, 'What?' He said, 'Jesus, I saw those times. I could have run those times backwards.'

"I said, 'George, did you read the newspaper? I broke three records last night.' He said, 'That's not good enough. I'll see you at Lynden McKinley tonight.' Normally that would be a night off.

"He came back that night.

"You can give 120 percent, but that's not good enough for George Steinbrenner. You are going to be the best, whatever it takes.

"This guy was so dynamic. He could be a great coach at marbles. Sometime in life George Steinbrenner studied the various aspects of sports, because I don't think another human being has the knowledge in every sport that George Steinbrenner has.

"George Steinbrenner, if he could go down on the field and coach that team, would be successful.

"He tried to break me up. My wife and I went together three years in high school. George would say, 'Look, LeCorte, practice track and football, girls are secondary. You're spending too much time with her.'

"He wanted me to go to college and get a degree. He wanted me to find out what life was all about.

"George took me from my home in June 1954, took me to Ohio University. I did not want to go to college. I told him, 'I'm not going.' 'Yes, you are.' Zoom, we go down south on Route 33 to Ohio University. Next thing I know, I'm living in the best dorm, best hall at Ohio University, and everything was paid for, by George Steinbrenner.

"He gave me exposure to our society and showed me what life is all about. And he asked nothing of me, not a thing. Nothing. How do you repay a guy like this?

"I'm a little guy. I'm a nobody, but George Steinbrenner has a heart of gold, and I'm blessed to know him. I can't say enough about him. I can talk about him day and night."

Coaching provided the ideal milieu to fit George's personality. George was a person who was emotionally unable to trust others on any level. He made acquaintances with those who could either help him or submit to him. He didn't make friends. He needed a society in which he could be king, in which he could make all the decisions and force all his subjects to bend to his will and in the end even thank him for his tyranny. Coaching was the perfect environment.

One year later George was coaching in the college ranks. In 1956, George became freshman end coach at Northwestern University. The head coach, Lou Saban, had been an acquaintance of George's back in Cleveland, and George was able to convince Saban that he had enough of a coaching background for the job. That year Northwestern tied one game and lost all the rest.

Ben Froelich was one of the ends George coached at Northwestern. Like the others who played for him, Froelich has fond memories of playing under George.

"We had a bunch of ragtag ends, and George was all proud of us, though we weren't that good," said Froelich. "They used to have contact scrimmages, and he'd take us out of the scrimmage, call us the End Club. 'The End Club is going to meet over here while other guys bat heads, get damaged.'

" 'End Club, let's have a meeting,' and we'd stand around and talk to George. He was protecting us. He was one of the boys.

"There was another guy who played end, who was an outstanding athlete, Stillwell, Stilly we called him. He flunked out of school the next year, but he was really great, a high school all-American out of New Trier High School, and George used to lock Stillwell up in his room to get him to study. Stillwell would put the radio on so it sounded like someone was in the room, and he'd sneak out the fire escape.

"I always wondered how much George knew about playing end. I don't think he ever played football. I didn't think he did, but he was a friend of Lou Saban's somehow.

"Steinbrenner was in grad school, getting a degree while he was coaching, and he didn't know a whole lot about coaching ends, and I think it showed because we tied somebody and lost the rest of our games. And then Saban and the rest of his staff was gone. Bam. That was it. Stillwell didn't make it the next year. And neither did George.

"George was fun to work with, a very, very nice guy who wasn't that much older than we were, and one of the boys, a real friend to everyone and not a real disciplinarian by any means. Saban was also really friendly and nice and having a lot of fun.

"When Ara Parseghian came in the next year, it became a business. Parseghian said, 'First thirty-three keep their scholarships,' and 'We're going to start winning football games,' which he did. He proved it could be done at Northwestern. And nobody has done that since."

After that 0–8–1 record George moved over to Purdue University under coach Jack Mollenkoph. Again he was end coach. According to the Purdue quarterback, Len Dawson, George was involved in the passing game along with quarterback coach Bob DeMoss, who later became head coach at Purdue.

According to Dawson, who went on to have a spectacular Hall of Fame career in the NFL, George Steinbrenner taught him an important lesson (albeit a cliché) about football: When the going gets tough, the tough get going.

Said Dawson, "My senior year I had injured my shoulder, a bone bruise. George and I were having coffee, and he said, 'The other coaches are really concerned that you're not playing.' Apparently they felt that even though it might be painful, I could play.

"I knew the expression 'play with pain,' but until you really experience it, go through it, you don't know whether you can or not. And George did a number on me and convinced me—whether he got me irritated enough or got me thinking about myself—at the time I was thinking about the NFL draft—and he got me motivated to where I said, 'Damn it, I'm going to play.' And I did, and didn't have any problem, and it taught me a lesson, really helped me in professional football, because there were many, many times there were aches and pains I had to endure in order to play.

"He taught me a lesson that I used all the way through. That's where it started. George was the one who did it.

"I know when I left after our conversation that I was determined to play. He used psychology on me, hit at my pride. He did it.

"He definitely made an impression with me."

What was most notable about George's coaching career was how far he was able to progress despite his never having played the game. And he did it without any help from his father. Football coaching gave George Steinbrenner his self-esteem. He had boys who would do exactly what he told them, without questioning him. He had boys who looked up to him, even loved him. He had power to change their lives.

He had parlayed his charm, his ability to position himself, and his skill at taking advantage of his connections to become a coach not at one but at *two* Big Ten colleges.

The sad irony was that George Steinbrenner never got to find out just how great a coach he could have been. Just as he was beginning to learn the college game, the only person with power and control over him, Henry Steinbrenner, short-circuited his dreams by ordering him home to help run Kinsman Transit, which like all Great Lake shipping companies was in financial difficulty.

George's friends say that Henry Steinbrenner gave George a choice: He could either stay in coaching, in which case he would never be allowed to join him in the business, or he could "come home now." Henry told him, "Decide."

Once again Henry wasn't trusting George enough to make a *real* choice. Henry wanted what he wanted: George to come home and work with him.

George knew his father well enough to know he wasn't bluffing. If he returned to Cleveland, one day he would own the company. The alternative was risky: to do what he loved, but the risk of forfeiting the money and power was too great. George agreed to come back to Bay Village and help run Kinsman.

All his life George regretted that he had been forced to abandon his dream.

Said George, "If I had stayed in coaching, I think I could have been a head coach at a big school."

Later, when he owned sports teams, he resumed his coaching career on an unofficial basis, much to the chagrin of the many managers, coaches, and players hired to work under him.

# THE BETRAYAL

**B**illy Martin's value as a player for the New York Yankees was appreciated best by the men who played alongside him. At bat he didn't have gaudy numbers, and on defense he looked awkward in the field, even though he made the plays. In 1955 and 1956 it had been his leadership, even more than his play on the field, that had sparked the team. Billy had become a de facto player-coach for Casey Stengel. In fact, it was a gross injustice that the Yankees had not recognized Billy Martin's contributions by officially naming him captain of the team. Billy's special value, recognized by everyone in that Yankee clubhouse, was that he was an inspirational leader who knew what to do to win ball games.

"It was 1955, my first season with the Yankees, and somebody hit a pop-up between first base and home plate," recalled pitcher Bob Turley. "Moose Skowron was playing first, and Yogi was catching. My job was to run over to call the play. I called, 'Yogi, Yogi,' and the ball came down and Yogi dropped it. Nobody said anything, but when the inning ended Billy got all over me in the dugout, calling me a dumb so-and-so and saying, 'How long you been in this game? Don't you know any ball a first baseman can reach he catches it, because he has a better glove?' I never really thought about that, but Billy had. I never made that mistake again."

And it was Billy who had noticed that Bob Turley was excellent at picking off the other pitcher's signs. Turley would see what kind of pitch the opponent was throwing and whistle when a fastball was coming. Mickey Mantle particularly enjoyed having Turley call the pitches. When he knew what was coming he could really tee off on a pitch.

Part of the reason Billy didn't get his share of the credit was that he was snappish with the press. Another reason was that Yankee GM George Weiss strongly disliked him. Weiss was jealous of manager Casey Stengel, and Billy was Stengel's boy. Weiss, a reclusive man, felt he deserved the credit for the Yankee dynasty. Stengel, who was outgoing, received more credit than Weiss felt he deserved. Billy was the man in the middle.

All his career Casey Stengel had pushed Billy to be fiery and combative.

Said Stengel, "Every time we were asleep, I would make Billy start a fight to wake them up. It worked good. A club that's asleep don't win."

But George Weiss felt such behavior was antithetical to being a Yankee. Martin, caught in the power struggle, was no politician. Rather, he was an idealist who put the team first. He believed in Stengel, knew that Casey was privy to the secrets to winning games. Intimidation was part of Casey's formula, and Martin was his intimidator. Knowing Weiss disapproved didn't stop him, and so Weiss saw Billy as Stengel's player, not one of his own.

Weiss also held a strong class prejudice against Billy. Weiss, an elitist who lived in tony Greenwich, Connecticut, preferred his players to be blond and blue-eyed. During Weiss's rein with the Yankees, which ended in 1960, the team had only one black player, Elston Howard, and Howard came to the Yankees after being held back in the minor leagues three or four years longer than he would have been had he been white.

Weiss hadn't liked Billy from the time the young second baseman came up to the Yankees in 1950 and dared to criticize him for sending him down to the minors.

"I won't forget this," Weiss told him. He never did.

Weiss didn't like Billy's boyhood friends, his penchant for spending time after games in bars, or his fighting ways.

Weiss, who kept close tabs on the personal lives of his players, had long feared that Martin's pugnaciousness would hurt the Yankees' reputation someday. Weiss was aware that when Billy was a player with the Oakland Oaks, he was in the practice of going to bars after his Oaks ball games, preferring the company of male friends in a surrounding of convivial drinking to any other form of entertainment.

Even as a teen, Billy was known in the neighborhood as someone to avoid when he was drinking with his friends, including members of the West Berkeley Boys, whom he had not abandoned after becoming a professional ballplayer.

Sam Pedone, a childhood friend of Billy's, had played baseball for San Pedro Park in games when Billy was playing for James Kenney Park. After Pedone graduated from high school, he became a bartender at the 58 Club across from the Heinz factory in Richmond, a town not far from Berkeley.

Pedone remembers that during the period when Billy was playing for the Oakland Oaks, he and a group of his friends would come into the bar evenings after Oaks games. Billy's group included some rough characters, including Tony "the Hog" Gaugino, who was a roofer, Howard Noble, his best childhood friend, and Jesse Garcia, a tough kid who used to play ball with Billy. Howard and Jesse were truck drivers. With them was another roofer, Henry "the Spoon" Silva, a witty kid who always seemed to have money in his pocket from selling newspapers on the corner of University Avenue and San Pablo on weekends. At times one or two others would join their group.

According to Pedone, they came well-dressed and were noticed immediately by everyone in the club when they arrived. They would congregate at the end of the bar, looking for trouble.

"They tried to act like Mafia goons, and Tony, who was only about five foot six but several years older than Billy, was the leader of the group," said Pedone. "They could make trouble."

Pedone said that whenever they walked into the bar, he got nervous.

"Every time I saw them, I knew they were going to start something," he said. "So you had to keep an eye on them. The hope was that they would stay for a certain time, nothing would happen, and they would move on to another bar. At that time there were about ten bars they would go to, one after the other. I can remember some of them. There was the Six Bells, the It Club, and the Leap Club.

Billy liked to drink scotch and water. The others mostly drank beer. "They didn't stand at the bar long enough to talk," Pedone said. "They came to drink. If there were women there, they had nothing to do with them.

"They weren't loud, but everyone noticed them. The people in Berkeley knew these people Billy hung around with, knew they were not good drinkers, that if they did drink, they couldn't hold it, and that when they started drinking, they'd become involved with other people, trying to start something.

"Billy was a good drinker. He could hold his liquor, but Billy was a Sunday puncher. Billy didn't ask any questions. He'd just haul off and smash someone. Billy liked to take a Sunday on anybody, and if he was with a group, the rest of them were the same way. That's how it was.

"Billy didn't start fights because he was drinking. The drinking never affected his mood. Billy would hit someone because he felt like it. He liked hitting people. I don't know if he wanted to make a name for himself or what. He was hard to figure out. People would recognize him because he played for the Oaks, and they'd come over and ask for autographs, but Billy was the type of person who thought people were against him, for what reason I don't know. He always had a chip on his shoulder. Why? Who knows?

"So this was not a group I wanted in the bar. You'd see them come in, and you knew something was going to happen. And if it looked like they were going to start something with a person, I would have to tell them, 'Take a hike,' and they'd leave. I've been here at the 58 Club for forty years, and we never had a big ruckus. They never gave me a hard time because they respected me."

Weiss's knowledge of Billy's love of alcohol and penchant for throwing his lethal right hand kept Weiss in a constant state of nervousness about Stengel's favorite player. For the entire time Billy was a Yankee, Weiss looked for a way to trade him.

By the fall of 1956, Billy's fielding skills had seriously eroded. Playing at Denver, the team's top farm team, was a twenty-one-year-old second baseman with all-star potential named Bobby Richardson. Billy was becoming expendable.

Billy, a shrewd judge of talent, was quite aware his skills were fading. After Billy had left the service in September 1955, he saw he no longer was the same player he had been during his glory years of 1952 and 1953.

His bat was still there, but in the field he lacked his old quickness. He didn't know whether it was a result of getting older or his inactivity, but he was not playing with confidence, and he was afraid for his future. Baseball continued to be an emotional struggle for him.

"Baseball has to be played instinctively," said Billy. "It's a game of reflex, of touch, of feel. Everything has to be automatic. That's why you practice, so things are done smoothly, automatically in the game. It no longer was automatic."

Billy resumed the melancholia, depression, and hypertension that had plagued him in 1952 and 1953 during the period of his marital problems with Lois. At times he was finding it difficult to overcome his depression.

"I was never able to get a handle on myself in this game," Martin said.

Making his turmoil worse was his full realization that he was sinking deeper and deeper into George Weiss's doghouse.

Weiss had made contract negotiations very difficult during the spring of 1956. Weiss had offered him a contract calling for a salary of $16,000. Billy returned it unsigned.

Billy told Weiss he needed money to start a fund for his daughter Kelly's education and to help send his sister Joan to college.

"Maybe an expensive Eastern school. When I see her graduate I'll know baseball paid off," Billy said.

But Weiss wasn't sympathetic and wouldn't budge from his original offer, and while the Yankees were working hard in St. Petersburg, Billy was forced to sit at home in his room at the Edison Hotel in New York waiting for Weiss to raise the ante.

The other players wondered why Weiss was being so tough on him, considering how important he had been to the team.

Weiss finally went up to $20,000. Reluctantly, bitterly, Billy signed it.

On May 22, 1956, Martin was involved in a shouting match on the field in Kansas City. Yankee pitcher Don Larsen brushed back outfielder Harry Simpson of the A's. In the eighth inning A's pitcher Tom Lasorda brushed back Hank Bauer. The next pitch went at Bauer's head.

Martin started to run from the dugout onto the field when three Yankees held him back. Martin was swearing at Lasorda, threatening him. With Mantle at bat, Martin made another threat. Lasorda walked over to the Yankee dugout. "Come on," Lasorda yelled at Martin.

The umpires kept them apart.

Later Billy had to be restrained from going after some hostile fans who were baiting him.

All the while the new kid Bobby Richardson was working his way through the farm system to the Yankees. In 1956, Billy was worried that his days as a Yankee were numbered. He knew that there would be no loyalty, no thank-yous. He knew that it would come down to money.

Youngster Richardson was a budding star who would cost the Yankees far less in salary. That Billy loved the game and had given his all for the Yankees didn't cut it with Weiss, who could get rid of an irritant and at the same time save fifteen thousand dollars in salary without losing anything in the field or at bat.

On August 25, 1956, Weiss had dropped Phil Rizzuto, once the longtime Yankee veteran had slowed. Rizzuto, who had been a Yankee regular since 1941, was enjoying the Old-Timers' Day festivities with the rest of the players. The thirty-seven-year-old All-Star was snapping pictures of Joe DiMaggio and the other former Yankees when he received a call that Weiss and Stengel wanted to see him in Stengel's office.

Weiss said to him, "We're going over the roster. Norm Siebern and Irv Noren are hurt, and we need another left-handed hitting outfielder for the World Series. We want to go over this list with you and determine the most logical player we can let go."

Rizzuto, flattered that Weiss and Stengel thought so highly of his opinion, readily agreed. Phil went down the list and suggested Charlie Silvera be released because the bullpen catcher never played. Weiss rejected the idea. Rizzuto suggested Mickey McDermott, who didn't pitch much. Weiss said no. He then suggested pitcher Rip Coleman, and Weiss said no. Slowly it started to dawn on Phil what Weiss was aiming toward.

Weiss said, "Let's go over the list again." Again Rizzuto enumerated the players he thought expendable. Again Weiss said no to all his suggestions. Finally Weiss summoned the nerve to tell Rizzuto what he had in mind all along. It was Rizzuto who was going to be released. Gil McDougald, Jerry Coleman, and Billy Martin were available to play shortstop, and Rizzuto was clearly over the hill. Rizzuto's career was over.

Martin now knew that he was in the same spot Rizzuto had been in. Weiss was just looking for an excuse to get rid of him.

Only Casey Stengel was standing in his way. After the 1956 World Series, Martin had attempted some goodwill by walking over to Weiss to shake his hand. According to writer Joe Archibald, Weiss seemed "embarrassed."

By the end of August 1956, Mantle was challenging Babe Ruth's record of sixty home runs for a season. Mantle slumped badly in September. There were articles, perhaps spread by Weiss, perhaps even believed by him, that Martin was a bad influence on Mantle, that he was keeping Mantle out late and spoiling his chances to top Ruth.

Martin had reveled in New York City's nightlife, and Weiss sent word he wanted Martin to move out of the Edison Hotel in Manhattan and move to the Bronx into the Concourse Plaza Hotel near Yankee Stadium. Billy refused. One night as Billy got out of a cab in front of his hotel, he discovered that Weiss was having him followed by private detectives.

Billy felt betrayed. He felt that Weiss should have appreciated all he had done to help the Yankees win their many pennants. Instead he had toiled for not that much money, only to be told by Weiss he wasn't the sort of guy who was a real Yankee.

Martin bitterly told Joe Archibald, "Maybe if I'd gone into the used-car business or opened a scallopini restaurant when I was eighteen I'd be better off than I am now."

During the 1956 World Series, Billy told Mantle that he was hearing rumors that Stengel and Weiss were arguing over him, that Weiss wanted to trade him.

Billy started watching Stengel as a barometer of his future. Once during the 1956 Series, Billy teased Stengel about his oil wells and bank holdings, something he did every once in a while. This time Stengel got huffy. Martin noticed.

In the third game of the 1956 Series the Yankees led 5–3. In the top of the ninth Carl Furillo hit a ball deep to right field. Furillo rounded second, outfielder Hank Bauer threw the relay to Martin, and Martin fired to Andy Carey at third, a perfect throw that beat Furillo by a foot.

After the play Martin glared up at Weiss in the owner's box.

Said Stengel to reporters afterward, "That throw of Billy's, his quick thinking, saved Ford's game. It could've saved the Series. Supposin' that Furillo got to third, then scored on any kind of a hit. That means there's only one out and they're only a run behind. With them home-run hitters they got, it could have easily been tied up."

That was then. By spring training of 1957, Casey Stengel was touting his kids, Bobby Richardson and shortstop Tony Kubek, as the Yankees' infield combination for the future.

By 1957 it looked like Richardson might win a place on the Yankee roster. Martin, to his credit, never blamed Richardson for his troubles. Billy enjoyed teasing the clean-cut youngster who read the Bible during his downtime.

"What are you doing here?" Billy would ask Richardson with a straight face.

"What do you mean?"

"It's just that I put something in your milk last night, and you shouldn't be here today. Didn't you drink it?"

Or Billy would tell him, "I wrote to your draft board today. You'll be hearing from them soon."

Billy, quick to feel slighted, was certain that Stengel's affection for him had cooled. Once that happened, he analyzed correctly, Weiss would soon get his way.

Billy was on his best behavior during spring training, but one day, with no warning, Weiss called him into his St. Petersburg office. Billy couldn't figure out why he was being summoned.

Weiss told him, "I hate to tell you this, Martin, but you get into any trouble and we'll do something drastic."

Billy, seething, held his tongue. "You have nothing to worry about, Mr. Weiss. Trouble is the last thing I'm looking for."

"You've been warned, Martin," said Weiss, who dismissed him.

Billy went directly to Casey Stengel's room at the Soreno Hotel for an explanation. "I've done everything but lick his boots," said Martin. Stengel had no satisfactory answer.

The 1957 season began. The Chicago White Sox took an early lead. Stengel, grumpier than before, threatened that some of the players would be shipped out.

Martin was asked by reporters, "We still hear they're going to break you and Mantle up."

Martin was peeved. "I hear they're getting ready to fly to the moon." He paused and got serious. "They do that and Mick and me will just keep two other guys out late," he said.

The beginning of the end for Billy came when, in early May, third baseman Andy Carey severely sprained an ankle. Stengel moved Billy from second to third and gave the youngster Bobby Richardson an opportunity to show his stuff at second.

The kid played like a star. Billy saw himself as George Weiss's excess baggage.

Weiss, the Yankee GM, was a bottom-line man. Casey Stengel had won five world championships in a row but in 1954 had finished second to the Cleveland Indians while winning 103 games. Stengel, who turned sixty-five at the end of the '54 season, had been unsure whether Weiss would ask him back in 1955.

Weiss had hired Stengel in 1949 primarily because Stengel could work with young kids, was an excellent teacher, handled players well, and knew and loved the game. But Weiss was the sort of person who knew no loyalty. If there was someone out there who could do a better job, Stengel realized, whatever he did for Weiss in the past would become irrelevant.

Weiss *never* allowed sentiment to get in the way of his personnel decisions. He was ruthless and cold-blooded, but his decisions always were the right ones in terms of whether they benefited the Yankees.

Mickey Mantle learned firsthand the sort of hardball that Weiss could play when cornered. Like Billy, Mantle was a Stengel protégé, which didn't sit well with Weiss, who didn't like his players protected from him by anyone, including the manager.

After the 1956 season, when Mantle hit for the Triple Crown and won the MVP, he demanded his salary be doubled from $32,500 to $65,000.

Weiss tried several tacts to defeat his twenty-five-year-old superstar. First, he tried blackmailing Mantle, threatening to tell his wife about some of the extracurricular escapades Weiss's detectives knew about.

"It can hurt your image, Mickey," Weiss told him.

Mantle told him he would quit baseball, go home and run his businesses.

Said Weiss, "Go ahead, stay in Dallas." And then he said, "While you're down there, I might just trade you for Rocky Colavito and Herb Score."

Two days later Mickey got a call from co-owner Del Webb. Mickey told Webb that Weiss had threatened to trade him to Cleveland.

"Absurd," said Webb. "We wouldn't consider such a thing." Webb told Mickey that if he came to camp, Webb would take care of the contract. In St.

Petersburg, Mickey presented his case to Webb, and he got his $65,000, which was still far below the salaries of peers such as Ted Williams and Stan Musial, who were making $100,000.

Outsiders were under the impression that Weiss and Stengel were friends. They weren't. George Weiss didn't have time for friends. His entire life revolved around running the Yankees. Stengel, who was both wealthy and tightfisted with money, told reporters the best thing he had to say about Weiss was that in the minors Weiss paid on time and his checks never bounced.

To Weiss, Stengel was an employee, and over the years Weiss resented Stengel's occasional intrusions into his business.

One of those intrusions was Casey Stengel's insistence on keeping Billy Martin on the Yankee team. The two had locked horns as early as Billy's freshman season back in 1950.

On May 15, 1950, one day before Billy's twenty-second birthday, the Yankees sent him down to Kansas City, their Triple A farm club until 1955, when the Philadelphia A's moved there. Martin was furious, and he went to Stengel about it.

Stengel told him, "I gotta send you down. We have this tight roster problem, and George Weiss wants . . ."

"Goddamn it, don't I deserve to be on this club? Ain't I proved I could play? What the hell is this? What do you have to do to make this club?"

"You mad?" asked Stengel.

"Sure, I'm mad."

"Then go see Weiss."

Stengel didn't want Martin sent down either.

The argument between Martin and Weiss began the feud between them. Martin barged into Weiss's office. The rookie told the Yankee boss, "I took a cut coming from Oakland to come to the Yanks. A three-thousand-dollar cut. It isn't fair your sending me to Kansas City. Somebody's going to be sorry."

"You talk fresh," Weiss said.

"I'm only fighting for my rights, Mr. Weiss. Make me a free agent. Other big-league clubs would be glad to get me."

"There is such a thing as a reserve clause, Martin. And you have quite an opinion of yourself."

"I just know I'm a good ballplayer."

Weiss never forgave Martin for his lack of respect.

All those years with the Yankees, Weiss had wanted to trade Billy. Later in his career Martin told a reporter that Weiss had wanted to trade him to Washington in 1951 along with Jackie Jensen, but Stengel made him call off the deal. When Billy broke his ankle doing the commercial for Joe DiMaggio in the spring of 1952, rumors again surfaced that Weiss was going to trade him.

As much as Weiss disliked Billy, Billy loathed Weiss, who once had called him "Casey's pet" to his face. No matter how friendly Martin tried to be, Weiss would act that much more distant and aloof. Martin would make fun of Weiss, mocking his diffidence and his stinginess. Billy resented that Weiss had never given Billy credit for his on-field heroics.

Billy Martin was a man who hated to be controlled or told what to do. His attitude was that no one would ever control his life, not an employer or a wife. It was one reason he had so many jobs and wives over the course of his life. What made Weiss's stewardship so galling was that his ideas of hearth and propriety seemed so old-fashioned to Billy.

Weiss didn't like Billy's fights on the field and also disliked Billy's demeanor, the swagger, the conceit, and his manner, including his love of bars, drinking, and women.

One time Weiss received a letter from the mother of a girl Billy had taken to a nightclub.

"I didn't know big-league players were allowed to go to nightclubs," she wrote. When Weiss read the letter to Martin, Billy laughed in his face.

"You've got to be kidding," Martin said. "I'm single. Divorced. I like girls. What's wrong with a single guy liking girls?"

Even when Billy and his teammates were just fooling around, Weiss saw their antics as something more serious. Weiss had not been amused when, after the Yankees clinched the 1952 pennant, a group of the players had dinner at the Latin Quarter nightclub and signed Yankee co-owner Dan Topping's name to the check.

Billy, Mickey Mantle, Whitey Ford, Hank Bauer, Gil McDougald, Andy Carey, and Gus Triandos had driven to the Latin Quarter for dinner and a show. All ordered large dinners and a few drinks. The bill came to about $250. When the waiter brought the check, Billy, who was carrying cash, offered to pay for it. Mickey Mantle said, "Naw, let's all chip in. We can handle it."

Whitey Ford, who had had a few drinks, had his devilish mind working. He expressed the opinion that it might be a clever idea to sign Yankee owner Dan Topping's name to the bill and let him pay for it.

"He's got a million bucks," said Whitey.

What the players didn't know was that Topping was dining at another table around the corner, out of their sight. When the waiter brought Topping the bill, the self-important playboy financier didn't find it funny.

The next morning George Weiss called Mickey and Billy on the phone and ordered them to be at the Squibb Building on Fifth Avenue in fifteen minutes. Billy and Mickey sat like two truants in grade school, waiting to see the principal.

Weiss told them, "I have a full report here. What do you think? We're stupid? We know everything. So I'm fining you five hundred each for what's been going on all year. That's for openers. And now . . ."

He buzzed his secretary. "Tell Mr. Topping the boys are ready to see him."

Topping had made them wait an hour. When they walked into his office, he threw the Latin Quarter bill at them.

"What is this?"

Mickey confessed. He said, "Yes, we signed the tab. We wanted to have a good time. The party at the stadium ended too soon. We were only . . ."

Topping said, "I can have you all sent to jail for forgery."

Billy said, "Mr. Topping, it's a mistake. Please, I'll take the blame."

A few weeks later, after the Yankees beat the Dodgers in the Series, Topping returned the fines at the victory party. Billy and Mantle went to Topping and got their money. They told Whitey to do the same. Ford, however, was annoyed he had been fined at all.

"Tell him," Whitey said, "to shove it up his ass."

But it had been Billy who had offered to take the blame for the incident, and Weiss was more than willing to oblige.

"Billy was a great roommate," said Mickey Mantle with his tongue in his cheek. "Whenever anything bad ever happened, they would blame it on Billy."

Mantle and Martin roomed together from 1951 through 1957. When they were kids, their pranks seemed harmless.

But as Martin and Mantle got a little older, drinking colored their off-field activities. When Mantle's father died in the spring of 1953 at age forty, it marked a string of deaths in the Mantle clan. Most of the Mantle males had worked in the mines, and the mine dust had given them cancer and killed them off at an early age. When Mickey's father died, Mickey was firmly convinced he would not reach age forty himself, and he embarked on a course of wine, women, and song that would have killed men of half his strength and endurance. Billy, trying to put his divorce from Lois behind him, kept up with Mickey drink for drink until even Stengel, who could sit at a bar all night long, began to be concerned.

One time Casey held a clubhouse meeting with the whole club during which he said, "Damn it, some of you guys are drinking so much you're getting whiskey-slick."

Said Mantle, "I didn't know what the hell he was talking about, but I knew who he was talking *to*."

That Yankee team of the 1950s had an inordinately high percentage of heavy drinkers, including Casey Stengel himself. Stengel loved to drink and talk baseball with the sportswriters and anyone else who cared to keep up with him.

Stengel was one of those managers who didn't care about character. Talent was all that mattered to him. What a player did off the field didn't concern Stengel in the least. If Mantle and Martin were caught drunk at three in the morning, Casey would wink, as if to say, "Those are my boys."

One time in spring training, pitcher Don Larsen crashed his car about four in the morning. Stengel told reporters he "must have been mailing a letter." Stengel made Larsen run extra wind sprints that day in practice but otherwise didn't punish him.

Among the outfielders, Mickey Mantle and Hank Bauer could really hoist them, and in the infield the stars at the bar were Joe Collins and Billy, who at the time was an amateur compared with some of the others. It was a wild and woolly group on the road. Hangovers were commonplace. Mantle played hung over more than he cared to admit.

Stengel himself had played for a drinking manager, John McGraw. McGraw liked his players to be grizzled fighters. He didn't want gentlemen. Stengel, behind the clownish face and the Stengelese jargon, was one tough customer. He had been a cutthroat player who on the base paths could slice up a fielder with his spikes if he wanted to. When he became manager, Stengel went so far as to tell reporters he preferred drinkers to players who didn't drink.

When clean-living Bob Turley was in a slump, Casey said about him, "Look at him. He don't smoke, he don't drink, he don't chase women, and he don't win."

He derisively referred to two of his young players, infielders Bobby Richardson and Tony Kubek, as his "teetotalers," preferring the rowdier social habits of one of his other youngsters, Clete Boyer. But there were limits that had to be set.

On those who drank too much, Casey cautioned, "No ballplayer should get into the habit where he has a few drinks before a ball game, which is what began to happen after night ball came in. When I had one of those boys I said, 'Well, this man is limited. If he don't want to change, why, disappear him.' "

When asked about the players who stayed up chasing women, Stengel said, "It ain't gettin' it that hurts them, it's staying up all night looking for it." He added, "They gotta learn that if you don't get it by midnight, you ain't gonna get it, and if you do, it ain't worth it."

Weiss was aware of how much drinking and running around players did, and he didn't like it. Weiss sent private detectives to investigate Martin, Mantle, and pitcher Whitey Ford. The merry trio would take the sleuths on wild-goose chases.

"Mickey and I used to tease Billy that he was leading us astray," said Whitey Ford, "but that wasn't the case 'cause Billy really didn't drink *that* much. He wasn't what you would call a real big drinker. But he'd go out with us. I don't believe any one of us led the others astray. The three of us just got along real good together.

"George Weiss didn't believe in any fooling around. He didn't go in for that nightlife that we went in for. He didn't believe in *any* fooling around. But I think our nightlife was overrated. We went out, sure. But you just can't sit in your room night after night. We picked our spots, like if there was a day off the next day, especially them two because they had to play every day. I pitched every fourth or fifth day. I *really* could pick my spots.

"One time we were in Chicago, and we went to a Polynesian restaurant. The waiter said he would only give us two Zombies each, so naturally we decided to have three. And we convinced him to give us the third one. I think there were seven ounces of rum in each one of them. And after we finished the third one, we looked at our watches, and it was late, and we had to catch the train to the next city.

"We must have run about five blocks to the train station. It was a real hot night, and when we got there we were soaking wet. And then Mickey and Billy got into a wrestling match. The two of them, they used to wrestle all the time. And we got on the train, and the next thing you know the two of them are throwing up all over the train."

Weiss always insisted that Martin was the bad influence on Mantle, though it was clear to everyone who knew him that Mantle had the ability to get in plenty of trouble by himself.

What especially bothered Weiss was that Mickey Mantle's name began appearing in gossip columns. Weiss blamed Martin for whatever Mantle was accused of doing.

Mantle and Martin had missed a few trains and buses, and a couple of times Mantle had injured himself while he and Billy were fooling around.

In the spring of 1957, Mantle and Billy went out to play a round of golf. They had each rented an electric golf cart to take them from shot to shot. At first they raced, but after a while they sought a contest more exciting, and they began ramming each other, trying to tip the other over.

Going toward the seventh green, Martin faked a turn to the right and then quickly turned back left, catching Mantle's cart broadside, rolling the Yankee star and the cart. When Mantle, the league's MVP, toppled off, the tumbling cart rolled over him. He sprained ligaments in his left foot and needed crutches for a short while.

The press was told that Mantle had hurt himself stepping in a hole during fielding practice. When he finally did play in late April, he limped when he ran.

Martin suffered from a stiff neck and shoulders, an injury that had resulted from a late-night wrestling match between himself and Mantle, and later in training in 1957, Billy injured his foot, developed tonsillitis and a high fever, and then was struck on the head by a pitched ball. While Billy recuperated, Bobby Richardson played second and did it spectacularly, displaying a quickness in the field that Martin no longer had.

There was one other aspect to Billy's life that Weiss had become aware of: Billy was becoming more prone to fights in bars. Since his marital problems with Lois and the subsequent divorce, Billy's alcoholism was becoming more of a problem. He was going to bars more often and drinking more heavily than ever before. The more Billy drank, moreover, the more bellicose he would become. Even Mickey Mantle noticed it.

"If somebody would say something in a bar," said Mantle, "Billy would have to know why and what they said it for, and it would lead to an argument."

As far back as July 1953, Billy Martin began to spout his favorite defense that he had never started a fight in his life. "They gave me a reputation as a fighter," he said back then, "and now every guy and his brother is trying to make me earn it." But Billy always insisted it was his right to drink at bars. He would get his back up when someone in a conversation said something he felt offensive. And as soon as the other party took offense at his reply, Billy would come out swinging.

Billy's close childhood friend Lewis Figone witnessed one such fight at the Stocksman Hotel in Elko, Nevada, during the winter of 1953. Fegoni and Billy had gone deer hunting, and they stopped overnight in Elko.

Figone and Billy were sitting in a bar in the Stocksman, and they were watching the bar show. The performers were two brothers, Wayne and Jerry Newton. A few months later they appeared on "The Ed Sullivan Show." (Wayne Newton then dumped Jerry and leapfrogged to stardom.)

At the bar Billy was talking to the man on the adjacent stool about golf, and this person, who was also drinking, said to Billy, "You may be able to play baseball, but I bet I can take you at golf."

When Billy drank, any challenge became an affront. Billy made a nasty reply, and before the melee ended, Lewis Figone suffered cuts bad enough to leave scars.

"It just started over nothing," said Figone. "I was turning the other way, and the next thing I know, the guys were swinging."

Stengel, for one, didn't care whether Billy drank *or* fought or drank *and* fought. Casey had been a drinker and a brawler, and he felt that his athletes who enjoyed a good drink and a good fight were more valuable to him than the less aggressive teetotalers. During clubhouse harangues Stengel often would finish by saying, "Some of you milk-shake drinkers ain't doin' so hot either."

Said Mantle, "After all those years of traveling around himself, I guess he knew that nothing can screw up a ballplayer like too many rich, heavy, thick milk shakes."

There was nothing funny about Billy's behavior to George Weiss, who was afraid Billy might get in a fight and kill someone. What would *that* do to the reputation of the Yankees?

The noose was tightening. By early June 1957, Billy had become more and more uptight over the prospect of getting traded. His drinking intensified, and Mantle, fighting his own demons, kept up with him. Both were terrified and miserable over the real possibility that Billy might get traded.

In early May 1957 the Yankees took over first place from the Chicago White Sox, whose fortunes dimmed considerably when on May 7 Gil McDougald struck young pitching sensation Herb Score in the face with a line drive off his bat. Score had won sixteen games as a rookie in 1955 and added twenty more in 1956. The incident was the beginning of the end of the careers of both Score and McDougald, the latter a sensitive man who lost his special zest for the game on that fateful day.

A week later a group of Yankees including Billy, Whitey Ford, Mickey Mantle, Hank Bauer, Yogi Berra, and Johnny Kucks and their wives went out on the town in New York to celebrate the birthdays of Yogi Berra (thirty-two) and Billy, who had turned twenty-nine.

Originally the next day had been an off day, but because of a rainout, a game was scheduled. The players should have told manager Stengel they were going to be out late. They didn't. It was a mistake.

The evening began at Danny's Hideaway, where they had dinner. Afterward, at the suggestion of Yogi Berra's wife, Carmen, they went to see the show at the Waldorf-Astoria, featuring singer Johnnie Ray, whose songs "Just Walking in the Rain" and "Cry" were high on the hit parade.

After watching Ray they then went to the famed Copacabana for the two A.M. show starring the multitalented Sammy Davis, Jr. The Yankees had a special up-front table. At the next table was a group of seventeen Bronx bowlers and their wives. They were celebrating a championship with a lot of liquor.

Sammy Davis, Jr., was singing, dancing, entertaining in his usual high-energy style. Everyone was enjoying the celebration for Berra and Martin when one of the bowlers stood up in the middle of one of Davis's songs and called out to him, "You jungle bunny." Davis, flustered, ordered the band to stop. He walked toward the edge of the stage and said to the man, "I want to thank you very much for that remark. I'll remember it."

Hank Bauer, who was seated close to the drunk, hated it when people screamed such epithets at Ellie Howard. He ordered the drunk to "shut the hell up."

"Make me shut up," the drunk challenged.

One of the drunk's buddies said to Bauer, "Don't test your luck tonight, Yankee."

For the next half hour the bowlers ignored Sammy Davis and heckled the Yankee players.

Billy, his beautiful evening in ruin, finally lost his patience. He told the tor-mentors, "We're here to enjoy ourselves. You've been spouting off all night. If you want to talk about this somewhere else, we can get away from the table and settle it outside so the rest of the people can enjoy themselves."

"Let's go," said the fat drunk.

Billy, with Mantle on his heels, quickly left the table. When Hank Bauer got up, his wife Charlene tried to stop him. "It's none of your business," she said. He went off anyway.

When the bowlers and the Yankees started to leave their seats, a mass of tuxedo-clad people rushed to keep the two factions apart. Cooler heads started to prevail. Martin and the brother of the obnoxious drunk agreed to keep the main instigator away from the other Yankees, but when they entered the spa-cious men's room to break up any slugfest, they found Yogi Berra and Whitey Ford restraining Hank Bauer by the arms. The fat drunk was out cold on the floor with a broken nose and other head injuries.

The scene incriminated Bauer, who denied having hit the guy. He told in-vestigators he had wanted to but didn't have the opportunity because two Copa bouncers severely beat him first.

The players' first reaction was to find the quickest exit. They were escorted out the kitchen, a passageway leading to the lobby and the street, but before they were safely away, an entertainment columnist for the *New York Post* named Leonard Lyons saw them.

After they left he began asking questions, and because he was able to get only one side, that of the drunk bowler who accused Bauer of punching him, the next day's headlines blared BAUER IN BRAWL IN COPA.

The next day Bob Fishel, the Yankee public relations director, informed the players that the drunk was suing them for a million dollars. In fact, he never did.

George Weiss was livid. His prejudice convinced him that Billy had hit the man, no matter what the story was reported to be. When Weiss interviewed each player, no one admitted hitting the drunk. Weiss was convinced everyone was covering up to protect Billy.

"The way I heard it," said Ed Sapir, Billy's longtime attorney and friend, "Billy was in the bathroom being the peacemaker, and Mantle had too much to drink, and when everyone got in a big pile, Mickey couldn't locate Billy, so he was screaming, 'Billy, Billy, Billy,' and all the Filipinos in the kitchen heard was 'Billy, Billy, Billy,' and when the police came, they asked the Filipinos who did it, and they said, 'Billy, Billy, Billy.'

Said Sapir, "Billy told me, 'That's how I was the culprit at the Copacabana.' "

The likelihood is that if any Yankee hit the drunk, it was Hank Bauer, though Bauer has publicly denied having hit the guy, contending that the Copacabana bouncers were the ones who did it. He has, however, admitted to friends that he was the one who coldcocked the man.

To Billy's credit, never in all the years he lived did he squeal on Bauer, and he was highly respected by his teammates for that.

"He took the fall," said Bill Kane, the Yankees' longtime traveling secretary, who was a close friend of Billy's.

The Yankees testified before a grand jury, and within an hour the district attorney threw out the case for insufficient evidence.

As a punishment for their being out that late, Stengel benched some of the players. Stengel was miffed because the players had not asked his permission to stay out late the night before a ball game. Had they done so, he said later, "it would have been all right. But when you don't get permission from the manager, you're going at your own risk."

According to Stengel, the Yankee owners and GM George Weiss chastised Stengel after the Copa incident, saying "that the manager wasn't handling the players right."

Stengel took action. He didn't start Whitey Ford, but he was suffering from arm trouble anyway. Yogi Berra was benched, but Berra was in the middle of a slump. Billy didn't play the next day, but he had lost his starting job a week before when Carey returned to third. Stengel was playing Richardson at second.

An angry Dan Topping levied $1,000 fines on Mantle, Martin, Bauer, Berra, and Ford, and Kucks was hit with a $500 fine.

The players and some teammates were furious that Topping had fined them *before* the grand jury hearing. The fines served little purpose but to create resentment.

When Billy leaked the amount of the fines to the press, more animosity was created.

The Copa incident gave George Weiss the excuse he needed to trade Billy.

The deadline for making trades was June 15. If Billy could get through that day, he was safe for another year. But if the Copa wasn't enough of a reason for Weiss to trade him, on June 13, in a game against Chicago, Billy attacked White Sox outfielder Larry Doby.

It started when Yankee pitcher Art Ditmar knocked Doby down with a fastball. Doby sprawled to the ground. The pitch was so wild it got past catcher Ellie Howard and rolled to the backstop. Ditmar covered home to keep the runner at second from scoring. When he reached the vicinity of the plate, Doby said to Ditmar, "If you ever do that again, I'll stick a knife in your back."

"Go fuck yourself," Ditmar answered.

Doby swung with a punch that just missed Ditmar's face, knocking off the pitcher's hat. Both benches cleared. It took police thirty minutes to restore order.

With the participants milling around, Billy walked over to Ditmar to ask him what Doby had said.

"He said he was going to stick a knife in me," Ditmar told him.

Billy ran toward the unsuspecting Doby and pounded him with blows.

The Yankees won the game. It could have been argued that the melee was what prompted a nine-game Yankee winning streak. Billy, as always, was doing what Stengel had asked him to do, protect his pitchers and stir up his men.

The next day Billy was fined $150 for his role in the fight. The day after that he was traded.

Weiss and Stengel had an agreement that Weiss would consult Stengel on all trades. According to Stengel, Weiss had tried to trade Billy "three or four times," but Casey had always stopped him. This time, says Stengel, "I gave in only when they arranged to get me a left-handed hitter, Harry Simpson, who I thought would help us in Yankee Stadium. And we had Bobby Richardson coming along to play second base for us."

Before the game on the 15th, Stengel suspected that Weiss would trade Martin before the end of the day. Billy ran into Stengel in the early afternoon in the Muehlebach Hotel in Kansas City. Stengel told him, "Looks like you're gone. I don't know. You were the smartest little player I ever had. You did everything I ever asked."

The Yankees played Kansas City that night. Billy was not in the lineup. The trade deadline was only hours away. Billy had had his gear packed since the Copa incident. Infielder Jerry Coleman was convinced he was the one who was going.

In the clubhouse before the game Billy said to Coleman, "There is only one way to find out. Go and look at the lineup. If your name is on it, you're not gone. I'm gone. If my name is on it, you're gone."

Coleman went and looked and came back and said to Billy, "You're not on it." For the first time Billy sat in the bullpen during a game. He figured that if he hid, the Turk with the ax wouldn't be able to find him. No such luck.

Lee MacPhail was the Yankee official who delivered the news of the trade to Kansas City to Stengel. In the middle of the sixth inning Stengel sent for him. He said to Billy, "We want to talk to you." Billy went to the clubhouse. Stengel told him, "We traded you to Kansas City, and I told them guys that you're the greatest player."

Billy said to Casey, "I don't want you to tell them nothing."

The owner of the Kansas City A's, Arnold Johnson, came over, and Casey started to brag to him about Billy.

Billy said, "You don't have to tell him nothin'. I'll play for you, Mr. Johnson. You don't have to worry."

When the writers asked him about the trade, Billy said, "I have nothing to say. Ask Stengel. He has all the answers."

But of course Billy had plenty to say. He was asked about Weiss's charge that he was a bad influence on the team.

"How can you be a bad influence on six pennant winners?" he said. "In three seasons I roomed with Rizzuto [1950], Berra [1951], and Mantle [1956], and at the end of the three years each won the MVP. If I ever led anyone astray, it was myself. I'm no drinker. I can nurse one drink so long that bartenders have said to me, 'Do you want me to put that in a container so you can take it home?' I roomed with Mantle and he won everything that year. How bad an influence could I have been? I busted my ass for that team, and Weiss acted like I didn't care."

After Billy was traded, Jackie Robinson, who Billy had taunted mercilessly in the past, defended him. Robinson, the first black player in the game, was sensitive to prejudicial treatment. He realized that Weiss had traded Billy for reasons other than his skills.

Said Robinson, "Billy is not a Dead End Kid or any of the other things he has been called. He is a smart player, always thinking, always daring, always looking for a way to win. A player like that gets to be a pain in the neck to some people, I presume, but it has nothing to do with the man. He has always played up to the fullest the times I played against him."

Weiss traded Billy and three prospects—Woodie Held, Bob Martyn, and Ralph Terry—to the A's for outfielder Harry Simpson and relief pitcher Ryne Duren.

Though he had given his approval, Stengel showed his displeasure with the trade. When a reporter asked if Simpson would be the new left fielder, Stengel barked, "I'll play who I want."

One irony was that the other player Weiss had traded Billy for, Ryne Duren, was a terrible alcoholic with a penchant for fighting.

Ralph Terry remembered when Casey called him into the office to tell him of the trade.

"He said it would be a terrific trade for me because I would get a chance to pitch there and would really learn," said Terry.

"I asked him, 'Who else is in the trade?' Then he started talking by saying, 'We gave up a helluva lot, we gave up Billy Martin, he's one helluva player, one of the best I'd ever had and you could look it up,' and then he just went on and on about Billy for ten or fifteen minutes. I just sat there in his office, not saying a word. I was really upset about my own career and he was talking about Billy. I finally looked up at him, and he had tears in his eyes, he was really in bad shape, and he said, 'You're just lucky you're going over there with Martin.' "

Mickey Mantle and Whitey Ford also cried unashamedly when they learned Billy had been traded away.

"It's like losing a brother," Mantle said. "He was the best friend I ever had."

For a man who had difficulty abiding even the smallest criticism, getting traded by the Yankees was a blow Billy would never get over. A large part of the hurt was his conviction that his lower-class background was a big reason George Weiss didn't like him. It was a continuation of the West Berkeley Boys versus the Goats feud, with the rich snubbing and then casting out the boys from West Berkeley. Billy had tried to make Weiss like him. Billy could charm just about anyone when he wanted to. But Weiss was immune.

To Billy, George Weiss, the autocratic German from Greenwich, was the King Goat.

Adding to his misery was his knowledge that Casey Stengel, who knew the importance of being on the right side of a political issue, never uttered a word in Billy's defense after it became clear that Weiss was going to trade him. Casey didn't defend Billy by saying that Billy hadn't hit anyone at the Copa. He never spoke of his years of valuable service. He didn't say a word. Stengel may have loved Martin, but Stengel, an astute judge of talent and another bottom-line man, was getting the left-handed hitter he had asked for, and also he knew that Bobby Richardson, the twenty-one-year-old potential all-star, was a better player. Standing in Weiss's way wasn't good baseball.

That's what galled Billy so badly, his well-founded suspicion that Casey may have known he was going to be sent away and that he let Weiss trade him with his blessing. Even if that weren't so, Billy thought that Stengel let Weiss trade him because it was in Casey's own best interest not to get George Weiss angry at him by defending Billy.

"That's what hurt me all those years," said Billy.

Said Martin on October 9, 1957, "I was caught in the middle between the field manager and the general manager. What worries me now is that I might have been used [by Stengel].

"I never wanted to get caught in a political setup."

After Billy's final game as a Yankee, Whitey, Mickey, and Billy sat in a bar drinking. Whitey left at about one in the morning. He had to pitch the next day. Mickey and Billy stayed long after the bar had closed.

Billy told Mickey he would never speak to Casey again. What hurt most about his getting traded, he said, was that the relationship he had with the Old Man was over.

"I don't want to hear his name mentioned anymore," Billy said.

Mickey said, "Billy, you shouldn't blame Casey. It's not his fault. He just works for the club. He can't control everything that Weiss sets out to do."

Billy wouldn't hear it.

Billy told me, "I didn't talk to Casey for seven years after that. I felt he let me down. It was worse than just a manager doing that. It was like a father letting me down. 'Cause the one person I never thought would let me go was him. I always knew Weiss was trying to get rid of me, but I figured Casey would hold on to me and tell Weiss that I wasn't that bad."

For many years the bitterness of his trade from the Yankees haunted Martin.

"I needed Stengel only one time in my life, and he let me down," Billy would say about Stengel. "I'm not mad at him. I just don't want to have anything to do with him."

Even though Billy stiffly kept up his decision not to talk to Casey, his words softened in time.

One time when he was playing for the Detroit Tigers in 1958, he was riding Charlie Maxwell and Al Kaline for not hustling. Maxwell, trying to strike a nerve, sarcastically asked Billy what he had heard from Stengel.

Billy replied heatedly, "He had to do what he did or Weiss would have fired him, too."

Finally, at the winter meetings in Houston in 1964, Billy gave up the boycott. Billy went over to Casey and spoke to him. Stengel acted like nothing bad had ever happened between them.

Billy never stopped talking about Casey Stengel. When he was Yankee manager, Billy would take friends into the bar next to the Plaza Hotel in New York and show them where Casey used to sit. Billy would tell them, "This is where Casey first came up with his famed expression, 'You can look it up.' There was a big record book at the bar, and Casey used to say, 'He hit so-and-so in 1910, and you can look it up.'"

When Casey Stengel died in 1975, only one member of the Yankee dynasty attended his funeral. That was Billy Martin. The night before Stengel's funeral, Billy slept in his bed.

"He was the greatest influence on me in the game," said Billy. "I'll always love the Old Man."

Martin's abrupt dismissal from the Yankees left a scar that haunted him his entire life. His two running mates, Mantle and Ford, were his equal in the night-life department, and yet the Yankees had allowed them to continue their escapades while playing out long, productive careers. Their uniform numbers were retired. They were given days and feted with gifts. But Billy, whom Stengel and some teammates felt had been just as important a force on the Stengel Yankees, was dumped, thrown out, discarded without as much as a thank-you.

Billy may not have believed in sticking to the rules, but he did believe in a strict code of fairness in which a person was supposed to be rewarded commensurately with his performance. Billy had played on Yankee pennant winners in 1950, 1951, 1952, 1953, 1955, and 1956. The Yankees had won six pennants and five world championships. Everyone knew he had been as responsible as anyone. Where was the justice? Where was the praise?

It didn't come from the reporters. By the time he had been traded away, he had alienated them so badly none sprang to his defense or rushed in with words of praise.

In a few days he was playing in a Kansas City uniform. With Bobby Richardson continuing his excellent play, Billy Martin quickly was forgotten in New York. His days as a homeless ballplayer were about to begin. To fill the void, Billy turned to booze.

"I'll tell you when his drinking *really* started," said Billy's sister Pat. "As a kid he was fun loving. When he got to the Oaks, he was still happy-go-lucky. When he got to the Yankees, they made him feel like a bum, like he wasn't any good. He hadn't come from wealth. He didn't have a college education. So it was, You're just a nobody. And that was George Weiss who made him feel like that.

"After a while you have to get a thick shell. 'Cause if you don't, they're going to keep kicking you. And who in the hell is anybody to kick anybody? whether you have no money or a lot of money. That doesn't make you any better. Billy would talk about this all the time.

"I can remember Billy got a phone call one time. It was from Weiss, telling him when he came back to New York, he wanted him to get rid of all his friends in West Berkeley. He wanted him to eliminate all his friends, including Howard, Deutch, and everybody, and Billy was arguing back and forth and said he would never give up his friends.

"He told Weiss, 'My home is West Berkeley, and I will never give up my friends.' Weiss was giving him a bad time.

"I was standing right there listening to him. When Billy hung up, he was so upset, he was yelling and screaming and saying all kinds of stuff about how Weiss was trying to run his life and make him something that he wasn't, that he was giving all he could to baseball, and that should be enough.

"He said, 'Why should I give up my friends? They're working, making money. They aren't in prison. They hold good jobs. But this isn't good enough for the Yankee front office.'

"Billy could not take getting fired by the Yankees, when the Copa wasn't his fault, which he was blamed for. It was after that when the drinking started.

"When Weiss traded him to Kansas City, he was so hurt it was just like taking both his legs off. I can't tell you how hurt he was. It was terrible. He was bitterly emotional. And he carried it with him. Then he was happy he was going back to the Yankees as manager, and then the abuse started again.''

# HENRY AND
# GEORGE

In 1960, at the age of thirty, George Steinbrenner joined his father in an attempt to save the foundering shipping company. His father gave him the title of treasurer but never for a minute let him forget who was in charge.

Kinsman Transit in the early days had pinned its salvation on the grain trade and stuck with it, and it managed to survive while the shipping companies that specialized in carrying iron ore went under. Kinsman always had enough grain around to keep busy, though the supply was dwindling.

The grain usually started out in Duluth, from which farmers shipped wheat and corn over the water to Buffalo. Before the St. Lawrence Seaway opened in 1958, that was a tremendous amount of business. After the seaway opened, there was much less grain to carry into Buffalo, hence Henry's siren call for George.

All through college George had told horror stories about his father's autocratic, tyrannical behavior, but when his father twisted his arm to return home to work with him, George came.

Joe Bennett, a close friend of George's, recalled those days.

"When George returned to Cleveland to work for his father," said Bennett, "he was pretty much a dispatcher, and I don't think a 'dispatcher' is a term most people would recognize. A dispatcher is a pretty important person. He kept track of the boats.

"I can remember being at George's house at a party when the captain would call him, 'I'm at the Soo, and I'm on the way down.'

"A boat would show up at Duluth and have so many hours to load the boat, and hours were money, and George kept track of how many hours it took the guy to get loaded.

"If a boat was on its way to Pontiac, Michigan, and there were too many boats in the harbor, he could unload someplace else. George would have to tell him where.

"George was also a salesman. He sold contracts to Republic Steel and some of the other companies. He was a much more personable person than his dad was.

"His dad gave him a lot of responsibility."

Another childhood friend, Frank Treadway, recalled the nights when George would suddenly have to leave home on business.

"Many was a time when George would get a telephone call just when he was ready to go out on a Saturday night," said Treadway. "A sailor had been arrested up in the Soo off one of Henry's boats and thrown in the pokey for disorderly conduct. George would drive or fly up there, give up what he was doing for the weekend, and get this guy out of trouble."

What bystanders and friends remember most about the relationship between Henry Steinbrenner and his son George was that they fought, often and loudly. This was a trait passed down from generation to generation.

Bill Crippen, who worked next door to the Kinsman offices, remembered the fighting.

"I met the Steinbrenners after World War II in 1947," said Crippen. "When I went to work in Cleveland, my company and Kinsman Transit were on the same floor in the Rockefeller Building at East Sixth Street and Superior in Cleveland. When I started, we could hear Henry's father, George, yelling at young Henry through the walls.

"It was before the days of air-conditioning, and in the summertime everyone left their doors and windows open. You could hear them bellowing back and forth. The nature of the beast. Once that door closed, they became tigers. Outside, there were no two finer gentlemen you ever met in your life.

"As time progressed and old George died, it became old Henry yelling at young George."

Some of the fighting stemmed from a difference in philosophy. Henry was a fiscal conservative who was satisfied with the status quo. By comparison George was a gambler who was never satisfied with what he had.

Recalled Frank Treadway: "I'm not sure Henry ever took an awful lot of money out of the corporation. George used to say, 'Kinsman Transit has a couple million in cash, and what I can do if I could only lay my hands on that money.'

"George understood what twenty percent down and borrowing eighty percent from a bank meant. Henry wouldn't do that. He had a nice home in Bay Village that was bought many many years ago, and hadn't cost that much. He drove inexpensive cars. He might have belonged to Westwood Country Club, but he certainly didn't spend a lot of money out there. There were no fancy vacations taken, no three months on the south coast of France. Here was a tight old German guy who didn't spend any money.

"I can remember George one time snuck down into the basement during work hours to get his hair cut. The phone rang in George's office, and when George didn't answer it, Henry realized that George had gone. Henry was goddamned if he was going to go down into the barbershop, and so he began banging on the old steam pipes that he knew ran through the barbershop down to the boiler room below, and this was George's message, and when George didn't come back up, the old man came storming down. They were eyeball to eyeball. Henry said, 'Goddamn it, George, what are you doing getting your hair cut on company time?' George hollered back at him, 'It grows on company time. I'm going to have it cut on company time.' "

According to Treadway, George at times was scared of Henry, who was a big man, the controller of the checkbook, and who had a penchant for firing employees, including George. Henry, it seemed, was not adverse to making him look foolish in front of his friends.

Said Treadway: "George would be on a freighter trip with friends, and he'd get off the boat, and his father would come down the docks and fire him! He'd embarrass him in front of his friends. George's sisters never got married until they were into their thirties, and the thinking there was they had seen so much fighting with the father and the son that they thought all men were bastards."

Patsy Stecher, another of George's childhood friends, recalled one of those times when Henry fired George. Perhaps *firing* is too strong a word. It was a game Henry and George were playing, with Henry using whatever ammunition at his disposal to keep his son under his control.

"We went on a trip on the *Finley* with George," said Stecher. "The *Finley* was a lake freighter. We rode from Buffalo to Sandusky, Ohio. As we were pulling in, George looked off in the distance, and he saw this tiny figure standing on the dock, and he knew it was his father. He was no bigger than two inches tall, and he said, 'My father is mad.'

"The boat smashed into the dock. And the father got on board. George was working for the Kinsman Company at the time, and George had taken disciplinary action into his own hands—his father had fired someone, and George had kept the guy on or, the reverse, that his father didn't want the guy fired, and George fired him. It had to do with a seaman on one of the ships. But he had gone against his father's wishes.

"The father came on board, took him into a room, gave him holy hell, and fired George.

"George was determined to get up real early the next morning and clean out his office so that Monday morning when his father went in, the office would be all cleaned out, and he'd have a one-upsman on his father.

"What happened, that night there was a knock at their apartment door. He was living in Rocky River at the time. George went to the door. It was his father. His father was carrying all the contents of his office desk and dumped it on their living room floor and left.

"His father beat him to it."

Said Joe Bennett, "Henry was a very straitlaced person. Henry had no sense of humor, for crissakes. Henry had respect for George, but Henry was aloof.

Henry was not affectionate. I never saw Henry hug George, and he *certainly* would not have kissed him.

"On the surface Henry would fire George every once in a while, but in his case I think the word *fire* is kind of silly because he was giving him stock in the company and firing him at the same time."

But according to his friends, George would be unnerved by the "firings." They made him feel powerless. The psychological impact on George was great. A person who feels powerless tends to project their own insecurities and believe that everyone is out to control him. As a protection against that belief, he reacts to others by trying to get an advantage over them from the start. If you are such a person, you don't trust anyone. You don't make close friendships. If you are always calling the shots, you have the power. If you fire people periodically, you maintain your power.

Henry Steinbrenner was a tyrant who made everyone under him, including George, cower. When George went out into the world, he wanted to make sure no one would make him feel powerless again. He would make all the decisions. He would set the rules. He would be the boss. He would rule. If anyone sought to challenge him, he would squash him like a grape. Whatever it took, whoever took on George Steinbrenner would end up the loser.

No one would ever again tell George Steinbrenner what to do.

And when George went home to his own wife and children, he didn't act any differently. He was the boss. His wife did what he said or else. For a while she considered divorce. His constant yelling and bullying was ruining her self-esteem. But somewhere along the line she decided that her status in the community was as important to her as the legitimacy of the marriage was to him. She stayed married, but the two led separate, parallel lives.

George had met his wife, the former Elizabeth Joan Zieg, while at the Lockbourne Air Force Base in Columbus. They were introduced by a former Ohio State basketball star, Jimmy Hull, the man who had gotten George into coaching and made him welcome by the OSU alumni family.

Dr. Hull knew Joan Zieg, who was eighteen at the time, because she was a patient of his dental practice. Her father, Harold Zieg, was another fervent Ohio State Buckeye follower. When President Fossett retired from OSU, Zieg, a very successful real-estate mogul, presented him with a new Cadillac.

When George asked Dr. Hull if he knew any eligible young ladies, Hull mentioned Joan. When it was time for the next adjustment of her braces, Dr. Hull sent a duplicate appointment card to George. They met in the summer of 1955.

"She was a beauty," said Dr. Hull, "and still is. I'm sure George saw some pretty girls, but he never saw one any prettier than Joan. George went for her in a big way. He knew he had a jewel when he met her."

On Christmas Eve 1955, George proposed. When they married in 1956, Dr. Hull was the best man. Henry Steinbrenner insisted on tails and black tie. Everyone wore tails and black tie.

As the organist struck up "Here Comes the Bride," George said to Dr. Hull,

"Get me out of here." Replied the dentist, "As usual, George, you have talked too much. I'll get you out of here. You're going down that aisle to marry Joan."

The night of the wedding the families got together for a bash at the University Club. At nine sharp, Henry Steinbrenner got to his feet, and he said, "Good night, everybody. I've enjoyed it." He thanked Dr. Hull, and he went home. Nothing, not even George's wedding, was going to disrupt Henry's rigid schedule.

According to George's childhood friend Joe Bennett, George's father-in-law at the beginning didn't much like George, who at the time was into his football coaching career.

Said Bennett: "At the beginning her dad was anti-George pretty much. Harold was a real-estate guy in central Ohio. He had made a lot of money, and he thought George was a hair-brained type, kind of weird because here was this young guy, running around doing things like coaching.

"I can remember Harold Zieg telling my father, 'Jesus Christ, the next time George calls up, I'm never going to loan him any money.'

"At that time George didn't have all that much money. There were strings to the money, and Henry wouldn't give George a nickel if he didn't know where it was going."

George took Henry's abuse and always came back for more. In a dysfunctional relationship the one who is abused begins to look upon the abuse as a substitute for the abuser's love. The worst part of an abusive relationship is that it tends to continue from generation to generation as children of abusers tend to abuse the ones they love. So it was with George.

After he married Joan Zieg, say his Cleveland friends, George didn't make his wife bathe in the cellar after eight o'clock like his father had done to his mother, but he dominated Joan in other ways.

Frank Treadway remembered how George could reduce his wife to tears by humiliating her in front of their friends.

Said Treadway: "George didn't know how to have fun. He had a hell of a time relaxing, though in his younger days, there would be four to six couples at a neighborhood party, and he could kick off his shoes and have a good time.

"I remember one time we had a party at Clifton Beach, and slacks for women were just beginning to come in. It was a cold September day, and the wind was blowing, and George came out from town from work, while his wife came down to the party with my wife. She wore slacks, and she looked great because she was a young, trim, beautiful woman.

"When George arrived at the party and saw her wearing slacks, he told her, 'If you won't take your pants off, don't bother coming back to the party.' George forced her to go home and change.

"He only thought he was doing what was right. He was proud of her and felt she shouldn't show off her cute little rear end.

"We lived four doors down from the Steinbrenners, and she would come over, sit on our back porch, and cry her eyes out.

"At the time Joan thought he was womanizing. He'd go away with a pair of pajamas and come home without his bottoms. Joan would read into it. I never thought George was chasing skirts.

"But Joan came from a family where people loved each other, and she finally got her bellyful of George hollering at her and telling her what to do.

"Joan would come over, and we'd hear her stories, and there would be tears, and finally she went back to Columbus, and there was a trial separation.

"He was a dictator. He treated her as he treated his kids and the way Henry treated him and his sisters and his mother. Mrs. Steinbrenner, Sr., lived in terror of her husband at times. And Joan had to become tough, tough, tough.

"There was a small organization in Bay Village called the Lake Erie Junior Nature Science Center, and this was something my mother and father lived next to. It was like a petting circus for kids. In order to survive and feed the animals and buy the real estate, build the buildings, my father became active and became president of it and would go out and raise money from Dr. Stecher and Vernon Stouffer and the Smythes, and Treadway Union Commerce Bank gave some money.

"Well, Joan was in charge of decorations for a banquet, and my father was beginning to age, and he didn't see or speak real well, and though he was trying to thank everyone for this lovely evening, damn if he didn't forget Joan's name. She stormed out of there, swearing and cursing like a sailor. It was unbelievable.

"I thought, My God, Joan, how you've changed.

"This happened around 1964. To me she had to get just as tough as he was in order to live with this guy. She just became hard as nails.

"She had adopted some of George's mannerisms, and she was swearing like a trooper. My father tried for a week afterward to call and say he was sorry and apologize, and she would have none of it. But this was not the girl that George married. And I make the summation that she had to become tough, tough, tough in order to stay with the guy.''

Appearance has always meant everything to George. How things were was not as important as how things looked to others. To most of his friends, he and Joan appeared to be the average young couple. Behind the facade there was trouble from the start.

As family men, Henry and George were not the same. Henry was rough on his wife in some ways, but his loyalty came to her and their children before anything. George was not only rough on his family, but he compounded the problem by allowing his other interests to come first.

During his early years back in Cleveland, in addition to his responsibilities running Kinsman Transit, George was involved with the local professional sports teams, the Browns, the Indians, and the Barons, but especially the Browns, becoming close friends with Browns quarterbacks Otto Graham and Cliff Lewis.

George was civic-minded as well, starting a football program for junior high school kids in Bay Village. He was involved in the Knights of Columbus track meet. He started an organization called the Junior Olympics that gave youngsters a chance to run in track meets. In 1960 he chaired Cleveland's March of Dimes drive and was named Cleveland Junior Chamber of Commerce Man of the Year *and* Ohio Jaycee Man of the Year.

Increasingly he would leave home and not tell Joan where he was going. Once he left for several days unannounced, and Joan began calling around, frantic for word from him. He surfaced in Southern California. The friend who found him told her he was attempting to sell the screen rights to the Sam Sheppard murder case.

Joan was no mouse, and in time, when George screamed at her, she began yelling back. One time a neighbor walked into the Steinbrenner kitchen just as she was hurling a frying pan during a fight with George.

On July 7, 1962, Joan sued George for divorce, charging "gross neglect of duty." She sought alimony and custody of their two children.

Two months later she dropped the suit. According to friends, she and George had reached an unusual arrangement. They would stay married, because it suited George to have the social legitimacy of being married, but they would lead separate lives when they were apart, which is much of the time. At public functions they would appear together as husband and wife.

Said Frank Treadway, "He wants to maintain the image of marriage. I've been divorced, and divorce for a lot of people is very painful and an admission of defeat whether it's your fault or her fault. She became a figurehead. I think they were in love to begin with, and they may have some kind of love left today."

Explained Patsy Stecher, another member of the young couple's circle of friends, "Joan and I were good friends, and we were always having babies about the same time. We had kids about the same age. She makes no bones about it: Living with George Steinbrenner is very difficult.

"One time she said something amusing to me. She said, 'I don't know why I married George, because anyone who you go out with on the first date who talks three hours about himself, I should have known.' She has a sense of humor about it.

"But they don't live together that much, so life isn't *that* difficult. As far as where they are coming from, I don't know. I do know his lifestyle is very difficult on her.

"Joan has her own interests in Tampa. She has her own hotel on the water in Tampa, and she has her own greyhound racing dogs, so she's busy.

"I can say that George prefers to run the New York Yankees pretty much alone. He doesn't like to mix Joan in with his business. She is a very, very beautiful woman, and it's my guess he wants to be in the limelight, and if the cameras come on and she's too much around him, they are going to shoot the camera on *her* and not on him. That's my own observation.

"I once asked her why she was never on television, and she said, 'It's not as plain as the nose on your face, but it's pretty obvious why.' George does not want her on."

Said Joe Bennett: "George and Joan have had a stormy marriage. It was continuously stormy. There are people who like to fight."

When George moved to Tampa after leaving Cleveland in disgrace over his involvement in the Watergate scandal, he purchased a neocolonial home in the most exclusive part of the city. The house, which looks like a plantation with its big white pillars holding up the front portico, was built with one wing. After he bought the house, he had a matching wing built on the other side. George lives in the old wing, and Joan lives in the new wing. Except when they appear together, the arrangement allows them to lead separate lives.

When George built the new wing for Joan, she didn't like the bathroom George had put in, and in 1992 she demanded a different bathroom. George said no, but because she has wealth independent of George, she had the means to do as she pleased, and so she called the contractor to take out George's bathroom and put in the one she wanted.

The contractor, who was unquestionably loyal to George, informed her that he would not work for her, that George had exclusive right to his services.

Taking a page from a Dominick Dunne novel of the quirkily rich and famous, the contractor figured out a way to accommodate Joan and not lose the business with George. To oversee the construction of Joan's bathroom, he called his father out of retirement.

It was the perfect solution. The contractor kept the business in the family, Mrs. Steinbrenner got her bathroom, and George was able to say he had gotten his way after all.

# THE ITINERANT

For the next four and a half years after Billy Martin was traded by the Yankees in June 1957, he traveled from team to team, as general managers and old friends attempted to capture the Yankee magic through Billy and have it transferred to their clubs. After playing a desultory half year at Kansas City, Billy would play for Detroit in 1958, Cleveland in 1959, Cincinnati in 1960, and Milwaukee and Minnesota in 1961.

For Billy to be at his most effective as a team leader he needed a manager like Casey Stengel who respected him, wasn't jealous of his attempt to motivate the other players, and could give him reassurance and stability. But no manager could have given Billy what Stengel had given him, and because his skills were deteriorating—mediocre ballplayers don't command sufficient respect from the other players—his leadership skills also faded. These were difficult years for Billy.

Billy came to the ballpark the day after his trade from the Yankees without getting any sleep. After returning from his night of drinking with Mickey Mantle, he had gone back to his hotel room and sobbed for a couple of hours until daylight.

The next day the Yankees were facing his Kansas City Athletics at the stadium. With Whitey Ford on the mound, Billy was facing a friend. His first time up, the bases were empty, and Whitey signaled to Billy he was throwing a slow curve. Billy singled off the wall in left. Later, ahead by a comfortable margin, Whitey led him know he was throwing another slow curve, and Billy hit a home run.

"It was the funniest feeling in the world," said Billy. "I was running around the bases, and I wasn't even happy."

After the game Kansas City manager Lou Boudreau was talking to the players, telling them how happy he was that Martin was on the A's.

Billy, hurt and alone among strangers, was contemptuous of Boudreau. "He was giving them a bullshitting pep talk." Billy told me, "I couldn't believe it. Players don't pay attention to that stuff. They never did, never will. I was so unhappy not being a Yankee anymore."

Billy admitted that after he was traded he was no longer the same player. "I tried and tried, but I couldn't get my heart into it. It felt like my heart was broken."

Billy hated playing for Kansas City. There was no expectation of winning, and most of the players were interested in their own statistics first, the team's welfare second. Boudreau, though he admired Billy, was distant. Billy's disdain for Boudreau was fueled by a feeling that on this second-division team the manager didn't care all that much either.

At Kansas City Billy concentrated on the nightlife. He lived at the Berkeley Hotel, where the stewardesses all stayed. Billy continued his drinking, sitting at the hotel bar for many hours, trying to medicate his hurt feelings.

His stay in Kansas City brought Billy one benefit—a steady relationship. The woman was Gretchen Winkler, twenty-four, one of the stewardesses he had met. They married two years later on October 8, 1959, at Wilbur Clark's Desert Inn in Las Vegas.

In midseason of 1957, Kansas City manager Lou Boudreau was replaced by Harry Craft, who wanted his own players. That was fine with Billy. Kansas City was a team for losers, he felt, and he wanted out of there.

In November 1957, Detroit GM John McHale acquired Billy from K.C. in a thirteen-player trade. Tigers manager Jack Tighe had always loved the way Billy played, and he was thrilled with the acquisition.

Billy spent the winter in Kansas City selling used cars. He needed the money. Even though he had played through June 15 with the Yankees, this time when the Yankee players voted World Series shares, he got nothing.

When Billy got to Detroit, McHale told Billy the players didn't play as a team. He asked Billy to fire them up in spring training. Billy talked so much about the pennant, he got to believe it himself.

The Tiger brass that spring bragged about the effect Billy would have on the team, but when the season began, the Tigers started slowly, and Martin took a lot of abuse from the fans, many of whom had despised him when he was a Yankee.

Manager Jack Tighe had moved Harvey Kuenn, who had slowed, from short-stop to centerfield and installed Billy at shortstop. Billy defensively was barely adequate at second, a position that required far less range. Billy also didn't have quick enough hands for shortstop, and once the season began he was shifted over to second.

"We needed a shortstop," said Al Kaline, "and they played Billy there, and he couldn't do it. He tried, but he couldn't cover the ground, he couldn't make the throws, he just wasn't a major league shortstop."

The Tigers, a .500 ball club, were mediocre at best, and Billy found playing for them frustrating and not much fun.

Billy's frustration came mostly from what he considered to be a lack of motivation from the other Tigers players. Billy got into arguments with some of the Tigers players when he accused them of lax play. He had the audacity to yell at Tigers star Al Kaline, whom he didn't think always hustled as hard as he could have.

Tighe was fired and Bill Norman hired. The team collapsed in late July. The fans booed Martin hard.

In late August, Billy collided with Earl Battey, the White Sox catcher, and cracked some ribs.

At the end of the 1958 season, Martin told Bob Greene of the *Detroit News*, "Tell 'em I'm sorry I did not win the pennant for them. Tell 'em that, for I really am."

After the 1958 season the next general manager to trade for him was Frank "Trader" Lane of the Cleveland Indians. Lane sent two quality pitchers, Ray Narleski and Don Mossi, in the deal for Billy.

After he was traded, Billy took a verbal punch at his former team. He called the Tigers players "a bunch of spoiled babies."

"The trouble with them," Billy said, "is they got too much publicity, too much money, and not enough spirit."

Al Kaline, for one, told reporters he was glad not to have Billy on the team. Kaline said it made him angry always listening to Billy talk about how the Tigers were going to win the pennant.

Billy blasted Kaline after leaving Detroit for Cleveland.

"I say if you don't talk about winning a pennant and think it all the time, you don't belong in baseball," said Billy. "A leader can't lead that club, because they won't let you."

In 1959 the Indians finished second behind the Chicago White Sox, five games back. The Yankees finished third, which gave Billy a tiny bit of satisfaction. But it was a hard year for Billy, because his manager, Joe Gordon, despised him. Billy had been making the double play his way since he began with Casey Stengel, and Gordon wanted him to make it another way. Billy rebuffed him. Gordon complained to reporters about the large number of errors Billy committed. In retaliation Billy had someone in the Cleveland PR department look up Gordon's fielding record, and he revealed Gordon's 260 errors in eleven years as compared with Billy's 45 errors in seven years.

The season was also difficult for Billy because his physical problems were mounting. He separated his throwing shoulder fielding a bunt. His left knee would give out on him. He was still the best second baseman on the team.

Billy always contended that if Gordon had used him right, the Indians would have won the 1959 pennant. At times—Billy thought the wrong times—Gordon would pinch-hit for him.

Gordon tried to bench Billy, but GM Frank Lane, who valued Billy for the spirit he infused into a team, ordered Gordon to keep him in the lineup. Gordon naturally resented Billy for this, too.

"We really had a winner for sure," said Billy. "But Gordon blew it. Gordon didn't like me, but when he gave me the works, it cost him the pennant. He took me out of the lineup when we were moving and put me back too late. He let his personal feelings hurt the team."

The Indians were in first place in August, when Billy was almost killed by a pitch thrown by Washington Senators pitcher Tex Clevenger. These were the days before batting helmets were mandatory. Billy didn't wear one. Clevenger's fastball broke his jaw and cracked his eye socket bone and cheekbone. He was unconscious when placed on a stretcher, and operated on.

"I had seven broken bones, cracked my eye. Knocked the cheekbone loose, and I was fed from my arms," Billy said.

The next day he couldn't see out of his eyes, the swelling was so bad. Clevenger came to the hospital to visit, and when he saw Billy, he started crying.

The beaning by Clevenger would lead to one of the more publicized incidents in Billy's career, his attack one year later on pitcher Jim Brewer.

At the end of 1959, Gordon got his wish. Billy was traded, this time to the Cincinnati Reds in the National League, along with pitcher Cal McLish. Cleveland received over-the-hill infielder Johnny Temple. Without Billy the next year, Joe Gordon's Indians slipped farther down the ladder, and Gordon was fired.

At Cincinnati, Billy played for tough-guy manager Freddie Hutchinson. They had similar personalities. Freddie wanted Billy to inject some needed ability and fight into his players.

The ability was gone, but the fight remained. After one spring training work-out, Billy and outfielder Lee Walls hit the Tampa bars. It was the middle of the day, and the bar they chose was empty but for one customer who was slumped over a beer.

When the bartender saw Billy and his Cincinnati teammate, he bought them each a beer. The drinker at the bar immediately became offended. No one had bought him a beer.

"Who the hell are Billy Martin and Lee Walls anyway?" the customer asked.

Billy, who when sober often tried to be a peacemaker, sent over a beer to calm the customer down. The customer, really furious, took the beer and threw it in Billy's face.

With one punch Billy laid him out cold on the floor.

Billy respected ol' Hutch, but when he arrived for spring training Billy found he couldn't play well in the field—his legs didn't work anymore—and at the plate he was gun-shy. For the first time he was afraid. In batter's terms, when the pitcher let fly, his ass pulled away from the plate.

Billy tried to fight his fear. He put on four warm-up jackets, and he had Reds pitchers Joe Nuxhall and Cal McLish deliberately throw baseballs at him. It didn't work. His hitting fell off dramatically. That year he hit but .246, with 3 home runs and just 16 RBIs.

In 1960, Billy played in fear that his career was at an end. His skills weren't there, though he fought just as hard as always. In one game Reds pitcher Raul Sanchez hit three Philadelphia Phillies in a row. When Phils manager Gene Mauch ran out to complain, Billy came running in from second to intercept him, fearing he was going for Sanchez. As Billy went for Mauch, he was blindsided and knocked to the ground. When Billy jumped up and learned that six-foot-eight Gene Conley was the one who leveled him, he punched the tall pitcher in the neck. Conley, an old pro, didn't take it personally. They shook hands, and nothing more was said.

On August 5, 1960, Billy was involved in another fight, and this one had far greater consequences. The Reds were playing the Chicago Cubs, led by Billy's former manager, Lou Boudreau, and Cubs rookie left-hander Jim Brewer threw Billy a pitch that was two inches behind his head. Billy got his arm up, and it hit him on the elbow. The umpire ruled the pitch had hit his bat and called it a strike, which angered Billy further.

Said Billy later, "I had promised in the papers that anyone who threw at me would be sorry, and I kept my promise."

Billy told himself, "I'll fix him," meaning Brewer.

On the next pitch, which was wide outside, Martin swung and flung the bat toward the mound at Brewer, trying to pretend it had slipped out of his grip. Billy had wanted Brewer to "skip rope," but his aim was off, and the bat went twirling down the first-base line.

Billy waited at home for someone to go out and get the bat. No one did, so Billy had to retrieve it.

"I had been hit by Clevenger the year before," said Billy. "I wasn't about to let anybody get another shot at me. If he wanted to hit me, let him do it with his fists. I walked out there to give him his chance."

As for the events leading up to Billy punching Brewer, Billy's account goes about as it usually did: He could see Brewer out of the corner of his eye; Brewer was yelling something nasty at him; and then he could see Brewer's clenched fist.

"I could see that he was going to punch me" was the way Billy usually described the action before the first blow, which always was Billy's.

Billy punched him in the jaw, and Brewer went down.

According to Brewer, he asked Martin, "Do you want to fight?"

Billy said, "No, kid, I just came after the bat."

And then, Brewer said, Billy bent over as if to pick up the bat and then sucker-punched him to the left side of his jaw. That's what really happened.

If nothing more had transpired, Brewer would not have had his face crushed, and Billy's reputation would not have been sullied as badly as it was. Unfortunately for Brewer and Billy, whose names would be twinned in baseball annals forever, the melee would continue.

As players milled about, Billy's teammate and friend Cal McLish was kicked in the stomach. In retaliation McLish punched Brewer five or six times to the right side of Brewer's face, caving it in. Brewer was taken to Wesley Memorial Hospital for surgery.

Billy, true to his personal code of honor, never said that McLish was involved. He figured the fight was over and would be forgotten. First Billy was fined $500 and suspended five days. He could live with that.

But then, after years went by and Billy had become a coach, he was served papers saying the Cubs and Brewer were suing him for $1,040,000. That was when Billy, who had little money at the time, issued his great line, "How do they want it, cash or check?"

Six years later the case went to trial without Billy's knowledge. When the defense did not appear, a jury awarded Brewer $100,000. Two years later, after Billy cried foul, the judgment was cut to $35,000 in the Illinois Appellate Court, and then Billy was given a new trial.

On January 29, 1969, after six days of testimony and three and a half hours of deliberation, Brewer had to settle for $10,000 in addition to $12,000 in legal fees. Losing that money kept Billy in debt for several years afterward.

Gabe Paul was an executive with the Reds the year of the melee. Gabe backed Billy throughout.

"Billy was not the one who hit Jim Brewer," said Paul. "One of our pitchers, Cal McLish, hit him.

"Brewer's face was smashed on the right side, and if Billy hit Brewer, he'd have had to hit him with a right hand on the right side, which is almost impossible to do.

"The thing about Billy, if a guy had his jaw broken, he never would admit he *didn't* do it. So he took the lawsuits and everything else."

Paul says that Cubs owner Phil Wrigley was the one who got Brewer to sue. He also says he blames Reds owner Bill DeWitt for not protecting Billy.

"DeWitt was negligent," said Paul. "He didn't care whether Billy had to pay. He just didn't care. That was Bill's nature. He didn't care about the players. He didn't care about anyone but DeWitt. If DeWitt had followed up on it, Billy would have been all right. But Billy was not the type of person who took care of details. He'd have beaten it if DeWitt had gone about it the right way.

"I remember calling Billy's home to talk to him about the case. I talked to Billy's sister and told her how much they were suing for. His sister said, 'Why, that little son of a bitch, he can't rub two nickels together.' "

After the Brewer fight, Billy's career had only another year to run. On December 4, 1960, Billy was sold to the Milwaukee Braves for $40,000. John McHale, who had moved over to the Braves, thought enough of Billy to deal for him a second time. Making things more cozy for Billy was a reunion with his former Oaks manager Charlie Dressen.

"Don't think he won't help us," Dressen told *The Sporting News*. "They warned me against buying him because he has ambitions to be a manager, but I don't care. I got him because I think we can use him."

But just before the season, the Braves acquired Frank Bolling from the Tigers. Bolling, who had taken Billy's job at second base with the Tigers, became the regular. Billy pinch-hit six times without a hit.

After sitting on the bench through May, he was traded to the Twins to play for his former Oaks roommate Cookie Lavagetto. It was the situation he enjoyed most after leaving the Yankees. Billy genuinely liked playing for Lavagetto, but then Calvin Griffith decided to go in a new direction, and he fired Lavagetto midway through the season and at the end of the year decided Billy was no longer part of his plans.

Sam Mele, who took over for Lavagetto, was a paisan of Billy's from way back, but when in spring training Mele sent a young kid named Bernie Allen to pinch-hit for him, Billy became angry.

"Damn it, Sam, I can hit this guy. I've hit him all my life. I can hit him better than the guy you're sending up there."

"I'm managing this club."

"That's what you think. I'd give up if I couldn't do a better job."

"That will cost you a hundred."

But Twins owner Calvin Griffith, a shrewd judge of talent, could see that Billy's range at second base had dropped so considerably that he had become a liability in the field. The Twins wanted Allen to take his job.

Billy tried to hang on as a utility player, but Griffith wanted Billy to retire and become a scout. Billy, like most ballplayers, was reluctant for his career to end.

Sam Mele put his arm around Billy and told him, "Calvin and I got together, and we think maybe your career has been a great one but it's time . . . Look, you have to go."

Billy started to cry. "I can help you," Billy said. Mele also began to cry.

"Every good thing has to come to an end," Mele said.

Billy had one final hope when former teammate Hank Bauer called to see if he would agree to be a utility player on the A's. Billy was willing, but two days later Bauer called back to say that A's owner Charlie Finley had changed his mind about it.

Billy received a $105,000, three-year offer to play in Japan for the Chunichi Dragons, but Billy still hadn't forgiven the Japanese for Pearl Harbor, and he turned the offer down. Also, Billy's paranoia told him that if he became exiled in Japan, American baseball would forget about him, and he would never get back in.

When Billy turned down the lucrative offer from Japan, Griffith understood just how much Martin cared about the game.

On April 2, 1962, Martin signed a contract to be a scout for the Twins. He was not yet thirty-four years old. His playing career, which had begun in 1934, when he was six, was over.

"It's like dying almost," said Billy, "because playing was something I had been wanting to do since I was a child, and subconsciously on some level you know you're not going to be able to do it much longer. You never, ever admit to yourself that one of these days you're going to have to quit. You never think you're going to be through. You feel you'll be able to play forever. You don't want to admit you're losing it. You just don't want to. That's the toughest thing in the world for a player to do.''

Billy was released by the Twins during spring training of 1962. He was convinced he could find another team. He discovered he was wrong.

"All of a sudden I was no longer playing baseball, which I loved so much," said Billy. "My whole childhood, baseball was all I did. Girls weren't the name of the game. Baseball was. So when the day came that I had to turn in my uniform, I was devastated. For days and days I couldn't get over it.

"I went down to the Twins camp in Melbourne, Florida, to scout the minor leagues, and the whole time I felt terrible. I felt like the whole world had come to an end. I was depressed, despondent.

"All I had wanted to be all my life was a baseball player, and here it was the end. No other club had contacted me, and I certainly wouldn't call them. I wouldn't beg for water if my heart was on fire.''

# THE CLEVELAND
# PIPERS

**G**eorge Steinbrenner, the young man about town, loved sports. As a football coach he had been involved. Away from the game working for his father at Kinsman Transit, he connected himself to the Cleveland pro sports teams as best he could through his friendship with some of the players, and he added to his interest by betting large sums of money on sporting events.

George particularly enjoyed betting on Big Ten and Notre Dame football games, sometimes laying down as much as four thousand dollars on one game. George's betting infuriated his father.

Recalled his friend Joe Bennett, "Sports was George's main interest. All sports. He was a real sports nut. We all were. George was a heavy better, and the old man didn't like that. Not at all. George bet football and baseball and bet a lot on basketball, and he bet a lot of money. He might bet four thousand dollars on Notre Dame–Navy."

George also continued his obsession with generating publicity for himself. Said Bennett, "George would go out of his way to meet PR people like Marsh Samuels. He wanted to get his name in the papers. He hung around sports personalities, just liked being around them. Each town has its own sportswriters. He cultivated them. If he was at the opera, he made sure his picture got taken."

In March 1961, George took the opportunity to once again become a participant in the sports arena. He hadn't been good enough to play, and his father kept him from coaching. George took a third avenue of involvement. With the financial assistance of some of his closest friends, George became a team owner, purchasing Ed Sweeney's Pipers, an excellent semipro team in the National Industrial Basketball League. Sweeney, the owner of the team, was going bust. It was George's plan to rescue the Pipers from oblivion. At the same time it was an opportunity to generate publicity for himself.

Recalled his friend Bob Stecher: "George always wanted to own a professional football team. He told me that once when we were boys. He was always more interested in football than baseball. George always loved sports. Let's face it, he always wanted to be in the limelight, and you don't get in the limelight just making money as you do in professional sports. And I also suspect, though I shouldn't say this, he was interested in sports primarily because it is a glamorous business. I don't know that he cares *that* much about home runs or the strategy—but if he's interested in those things, his main interest is the entertainment aspect of it. And I think it's true of most owners of professional sports teams."

In two years George Steinbrenner took this bankrupt amateur team and almost got it into the National Basketball Association.

What he did was both amazing and at the same time profoundly disturbing to those few who were outraged by George's absence of decency in his actions.

In March 1961, George began calling his closest friends, attempting to get them to invest with him in the Pipers, a basketball team that was in the process of winning the championship of the top industrial league in the country. All it would cost, he said, would be $25,000 in past debts, plus enough money for the 1961–62 season. The operation would be low-budget because the salaries of the Pipers, which ran about $4,000 a man, were paid in part by the team and in part by local companies who hired them to work.

George needed his friends because his father, who had tried hard to dissuade George from buying the team, wouldn't give him a cent toward its purchase. Henry Steinbrenner wanted George concentrating on Kinsman business. In fact, Henry made it as hard as possible for George to run the basketball team from his desk at Kinsman Transit. He didn't want George discussing basketball business on company time, and when someone called him about the team, Henry would become furious. Several times he walked over in the middle of one of George's conversations and pushed the disconnect button.

To frustrate his father, George installed a secret telephone in a drawer of his desk. When he was away from his desk, he kept the drawer locked. Henry at times would complain about hearing the faint ringing of a phone somewhere in the office.

Days after George took ownership of the Pipers, the team was invited to play a series of exhibition games in the Soviet Union. Immediately George got into a serious argument with the coach of the team, John McClendon, a talented and highly respected winning coach. McClendon, who was loyal to his Pipers players, wanted to take the entire squad. But George wasn't satisfied with the players he had. He wanted a team with stars, and he composed a squad that featured the five starting Pipers and a group of college all-stars. Among the college stars was Jerry Lucas, the Ohio State center, who led the team to an 8–0 record on the tour.

George also fought with the State Department, which wanted the team to be billed as a United States all-star amateur team. George wanted the team to be called the Cleveland Pipers. The State Department, which was footing the bill, wouldn't give in.

This was one of the earliest times when George Steinbrenner did not get his way, and it's interesting to see how he reacted: vengefully.

George countered by saying that if he didn't get his way—if the State Department insisted on this squad being an amateur team—well then, he wouldn't pay *any* of the players, including his own Pipers players. To stop him, Coach John McClendon called the *Cleveland Plain Dealer* and revealed what George was trying to do.

No matter. The State Department wouldn't let him call the team the Cleveland Pipers, so George didn't pay. While they were in Russia, Pipers players Jack Adams, Dan Swartz, and Roger Taylor complained to George and to the papers about George not paying them. After the incident appeared in the papers, George finally paid them.

The players, who had worked for him only a short time, saw clearly that their new owner was a spoiled, spiteful person.

Said team captain Jack Adams, "George is very vindictive. If you don't do exactly what he wants, he'll go to any extreme to get even with you."

When the players returned from Russia, they knew enough about him to realize that he would hold their complaining about his behavior against them. The talk among themselves was that this new owner was the type of person who would fire their coach and eventually trade them away just to get even.

"When he traded the three of us, it was an attempt to get back at us for spilling the beans about our not getting paid for the Russia trip," said Adams. "I knew sooner or later he was going to get me. As long as he needed me, I'd be okay. As soon as he could find someone to take my place, I'd be gone."

Toward the end of the summer, as the Pipers were preparing for their first season in the fledgling American Basketball League, George was lobbying to get rid of Coach McClendon. When the board of directors voted on who should be coach, the vote was 16–1 in favor of McClendon. According to board members, George was the one vote against.

Even though the vote was tilted against him, George tried different ways to get rid of Coach McClendon all season long. What occurred between John McClendon and George would forecast the way George would treat many of his baseball managers.

Usually an owner fires a coach because he isn't winning. But in this case McClendon won everything there was to win. Still, George wanted to get rid of McClendon. The Pipers' coach had reacted negatively to something lousy George was trying to pull and had tried to stop George from doing it. He had stood up for his players and refused to let George interfere with his rightful leadership.

George would have fired McClendon before the season had started if he felt he could have gotten away with it. New to ownership, George was unsure what firing McClendon would do to the morale of the team because the Pipers players loved him. Until he could find a coach with a stronger name recognition—giving George a more plausible excuse for his discharge—McClendon would stay. But McClendon would have to pay the price. Until then, George would spend half the season badmouthing and harassing him until McClendon was so revolted by George's amoral behavior toward him and his players that he finally quit.

When the Pipers returned from their tour of Russia, stories appeared in the Cleveland papers that McClendon wasn't the right coach for the Pipers because he didn't live in Cleveland during the off-season. The articles mentioned that "the owners" wanted a coach who lived near the players all year round. The articles did not name who those "owners" were.

McClendon countered by taking a job during the summer working for the Cleveland recreation department.

"I knew what George was up to," said McClendon, who says he viewed George as a "spoiled brat of a millionaire's son."

What was so ludicrous about George's campaign to get rid of John McClendon was the fact that he was a *great* coach. His Pipers team had defeated the 1960 U.S. Olympic basketball team led by Jerry Lucas, Oscar Robertson, and Jerry West in a game in Canton, Ohio. Under his leadership it won the NIBL championship.

That should have told George to leave well enough alone. But George didn't give McClendon a minute's peace, and it wasn't any better for the players once the season started, as George meddled and badgered them and caused resentment that worked against the best interests of the Pipers.

"I always thought the coach should be the coach of the team and everybody else was supposed to stay out," said McClendon. But McClendon was dealing with an unusual young man. George's ego came first, the Pipers second.

The Pipers began their 1961–62 season in October, and it wasn't three months before the press was writing about Steinbrenner's abnormal behavior.

A column by Jack Clowser, a longtime columnist for the *Cleveland Press,* praised Coach McClendon and the Pipers players for their hustle, desire, and drive, and at the same time made a scathing indictment of George's actions.

Clowser described how Steinbrenner charged into the Pipers' dressing room after the Pipers blew a ten-point lead and lost the game by a point.

"John, I don't want to tell you how to run your team, but . . . " Clowser quoted Steinbrenner as telling McClendon.

Clowser described how Steinbrenner then proceeded to do exactly what he said he didn't want McClendon to do. Steinbrenner railed about lack of team effort, blasting some of the players by name, even charging that some of them were more interested in going out on dates than playing basketball.

Clowser accused Steinbrenner of undermining Coach McClendon and of hurting team morale. He praised McClendon for keeping the team together despite a rash of injuries and praised the healthy players for working hard to take up the slack.

"For this," wrote Clowser, "they should be receiving front-office plaudits instead of criticism."

The players stood by McClendon steadfastly while George tried to undercut the coach and get him to quit. Said McClendon, "Players are used to people who are with you, up *or* down. George was not like that."

The players became furious when George planted stories in the papers criticizing them, and their anger grew when George used his news reporter background in an attempt to fuel fan interest by planting made-up stories about feuds his players were having with players on other teams. One story had the Pipers' Dick Brott planning revenge on Connie Hawkins, the league's top player. Brott was mortified.

"It's hard enough to play the game without him stirring Connie up," said Brott.

According to McClendon and many of his players, George did not understand the game of basketball. They complained that he was always pushing injured players to return before they were ready. They bristled when George came and sat on the bench during games and made a spectacle of himself.

"It wasn't very comfortable," said McClendon. "The fellows didn't like it." Neither did McClendon.

According to Frank Treadway, when a player made a bad pass or missed a shot, George would stand up and wave his arms and yell at McClendon, "Take that son of a gun out of there. Put him on the bench." Said Treadway, "We had a terrible time sitting on him."

One night George became so infuriated with one of the officials that he ran out onto the court and stood nose-to-nose with him until he had to be dragged off the floor in full view of the hundreds of fans who stomped and cheered and hollered as loudly as if the team had won the championship. It was pure theater, something not seen at a basketball game in Cleveland before or since. McClendon and the players were not amused.

One time the Pipers drove from Cleveland to Pittsburgh in two station wagons. On the way McClendon's vehicle had a blowout. McClendon instructed his captain, Jack Adams, to take the starters in the other car and go ahead, that he'd be there as soon as he could.

McClendon and the remaining players fixed the tire, and they arrived about ten minutes before halftime. The Pipers were leading by fourteen points. Captain Adams called time-out.

McClendon told his players, "I don't have anything to say. Whatever you're doing, keep on doing it."

A few minutes before the half, the Pipers again called time-out, and during the time-out Adams knelt on the floor and diagramed a play with white chalk. McClendon looked on approvingly.

At halftime in the locker room, with the Pipers still way ahead, McClendon was talking to his players when George opened the door suddenly and entered. In a loud voice he began shouting, "Who am I paying to coach this team, you or Adams?"

McClendon, ordinarily a mild-mannered gentleman, had great difficulty controlling his temper. He told George, "I don't allow anybody in my dressing room. You'll have to leave. And I don't allow anyone to talk to me like that in front of my players.

"Besides that, what do you care *who's* coaching the team as long as we come out of here with the victory?"

According to McClendon, George's uncontrolled, erratic behavior and his attacks on them in the papers hurt the performances of several of his players.

The Pipers' center was Dick Brott. Under McClendon's system, Brott's job was to feed the ball to the scorers and to rebound. He managed the flow of play and set up others. Brott was also a fine defensive player. The legendary Connie Hawkins averaged more than 40 points a game in the ABL, but Brott held him to only 17 a game. George apparently didn't understand the concept of players' roles, and he constantly yelled at Brott to score more.

According to McClendon, Brott withered under George's constant criticism. "He was a fighter, and I loved him," said McClendon, "but Dick couldn't take what George was doing to him. George worried Brott."

Said Brott, "As far as I knew, nobody liked Steinbrenner. He would do things like call you into the office and tell you you were a loser. Imagine, he told me I was a loser! I didn't say a word.

"When he signed me, he had asked me to stop smoking cigarettes, and I did, and after he called me into his office, I started smoking again. I figured, I had given up all that, why not do something that I enjoyed?"

George ignored McClendon's system when he went out and signed "name" players for the Pipers in a futile attempt to draw bigger crowds to the Cleveland Arena.

Two of the players George signed were Bill Spivey, the former Kentucky all-American, and Bevo Francis, onetime superstar of college basketball.

At seven feet, Spivey was a large presence, but he wasn't in good enough shape to run with McClendon's other players. Unable to run, he held little value to McClendon, who kept him on the bench. George had promised Spivey a lot of money. He had even moved his family from Lexington, Kentucky. When George traded him three months later, Spivey was furious.

"You were a chess piece," said Jack Adams. "That's strictly all you were. You had a feeling all the time that he was using you."

Bevo Francis had once scored 113 points in a game for Rio Grande (Ohio) College, and he too was a basketball legend. But Francis was "way out of shape," according to McClendon, and though he played only when the team was far ahead or behind, he did win one game with a last-second heave at the buzzer.

In 1961–62, coach John McClendon led the Pipers to the first-half championship of the Eastern Division of the league. Their opponents were the Kansas City Steers, run by general manager Mike Cleary, an astute judge of talent and an excellent administrator.

Cleary had started the season as GM of the Pipers but George had fired him.

Cleary, who ranks in sports history as the first executive ever fired by George Steinbrenner, knew basketball. In fact, the last thing Cleary did for the Pipers before George fired him was to lure Dick Barnett, a high-profile shooting guard sitting on the bench of the Syracuse Nats, to play for the Pipers. Barnett had played for McClendon as a college player at Tennessee State. Cleary promised Barnett if he came to Cleveland, McClendon would design an offense around him. Barnett, an all-American, made the jump.

George then made a deal with the *Cleveland Press* for an "exclusive." George was big on exclusives. He liked them because he could control the flow of information, giving him a role of great importance with his sources, and he liked them because with them he could barter with one newspaper against another to get bigger headlines and more space for the story.

When George learned the Pipers had acquired Dick Barnett from an NBA team, he knew he had a national story. This would be big news in Cleveland. But George wanted it to be a front-page story, so he made a deal with the *Cleveland Press* that the *Press* would put the story on the front page the next day if he gave the paper an exclusive. George did this without telling Cleary.

Mike Cleary sent out the press announcement with a warning that the information was not to be revealed until six the next morning. Not everyone heeds such warnings, and when a radio sportscaster aired the story on his late-night show, news of it spread quickly, and it was picked up in the *Cleveland Plain Dealer* early enough so that it had the story as well as the *Press*.

The *Press* killed the big front-page scoop.

Furious, George blamed Cleary. George's logic was that the general manager was in charge of the entire operation and therefore the leak was the general manager's fault. Cleary tried to explain that things like that sometimes occur.

"It's not anyone's fault," Cleary told George. "It just happens."

"Nothing just happens," George replied, and he fired him. A week later Cleary, who had built the Pipers team for Ed Sweeney, was hired by the Kansas City Steers. After the ABL folded a year later, twelve of Cleary's players signed with the NBA. Those from the Pipers included Barnett, John Barnhill, Connie Dierking, and Larry Siegfried. If Steinbrenner could fire a quality judge of talent such as Cleary, no one would ever be safe from his rages.

It was a pattern of behavior George would exhibit over and over with the New York Yankees. According to psychiatrist Dr. Irving Kolin, who is a clinical associate professor at the University of Florida, director of Glen Beigh Hospital in Orlando, and an expert in interpersonal behavior, the arbitrary firing of competent employees is common in companies run by tyrants with low self-esteem.

According to Dr. Kolin, the heads of the most successful companies give employees power and the ability to make decisions, but when a tyrant runs a company, he won't do that because his ego suffers when others make decisions. He must be the king, and the king must rule. And when an employee challenges him or wants to do something in a different way, he sees it as a challenge to his authority and may even fire him.

According to Dr. Kolin, the executive-as-tyrant feels he is always right, so whenever something negative happens to him, regardless of the reason, heads roll because it's never the King's fault, and *someone* has to take the blame.

Said Dr. Kolin, "If you are a king who rules the kingdom, other people threaten you. If you don't have the traits healthy personalities have growing up, such as basic trust in others and self-esteem, if someone makes a mistake rather than work with the person and try to understand what happened, you get rid of him. You cut off his head.

"The Saddam Husseins of this world, very insecure men, kill their subordinates rather than have to worry about whether they are trying to take over. They create chaos in their organizations to keep their power.

"Fearful tyrants who run companies tend to like to create chaos and change by firing people. That way, they create fear in everyone else, and they see that as a way of maintaining power.

"Tyrannical behavior is often self-destructive. Creating chaos often hurts the kingdom, and the king eventually loses his power."

So it was with King George and the Cleveland Pipers.

After George fired Cleary, he then topped himself for destructive, unsportsmanlike behavior. He proved himself emotionally unsuited to own a sports franchise.

After the final game of the Kansas City Steers' victory over the Pipers to win the first-half league championship, George stormed into the Pipers locker room and announced that "heads would roll."

And because the Pipers had lost, he refused to pay them—not only their share of the playoff money but their regular salary as well. When the players went to the Pipers office to get their paychecks, they were turned away.

"Guys played their hearts out, and when we got home they didn't get paid," said John McClendon. "Here was a bad sports attitude. The guy couldn't take it. And here we had another half season to go. And when he wouldn't pay the players, I resigned to bring it to the attention of the public, 'cause all these guys had families, kids, they were up against it, and they needed the money. I figured they'd get paid if I told everybody."

It's no wonder that when the team began the second half of the season playing in Los Angeles and Hawaii, they played poorly. Their record was 1–8, and when they returned to Cleveland, they still hadn't been paid.

The players complained to the Cleveland papers on January 16, 1962, of their bitterness toward George.

Steinbrenner called a meeting of the players and demanded they sign a retraction denying their demand or else he would fold the team and not pay anyone.

McClendon was faced with a serious moral dilemma. On the one hand, he couldn't ask his players to sign George's lies and be a part of unethical extortion. On the other, he knew if he didn't, George would make his players suffer financially and emotionally.

Reluctantly he asked his players to sign the retraction, which stated that there had been no ultimatum, that no one resented George as the article had stated.

His statement said that "Mr. Steinbrenner has our unquestioned support. We feel we have let him down by possibly not coming to you sooner with a true picture in this matter. . . . We are behind him 100 percent."

The last line of George's prepared statement said, "Somewhere your reporters got some unreliable information and we hope that all this can be set straight so we can get down to the business of trying for that championship."

Joseph Goebbels had nothing on the propagandic wizardry of young George. After making bald-faced lies and then coercing his players to utter them, George was lucky the league didn't fine or suspend him. It was a practice George would employ again ten years later on a national scale. That time, it would almost land him in jail.

After George blackmailed his players to sign his "retraction," he delivered the document to the papers. On January 29, 1962, a story that included George's fictional version of events made page 1 of the *Cleveland Press*. So did the players' reaction to his tactics.

In the article John McClendon announced his resignation and said in a statement:

"I am and have been able to withstand personal attacks but I cannot stand by and see a good group of young athletes intimidated into a position which has seriously affected their personal attitudes and performance. Furthermore, I cannot be a party to any act which tends to put a player of mine in an untenable position. This position on my part as coach destroys all their respect for me and confidence in me."

McClendon went on to describe the players' seething resentment toward George and said that he felt bitter about the owner's underhanded treatment of them.

The next day, after the front-page article written by Bob Sudyk, George phoned the *Press* reporter and screamed at him that he would never get another newspaper job in this country, that he would see to it that Sudyk would be "blackballed for life."

In response to McClendon's charges, George denied having coerced the players into making their statement.

Said George, "The players don't hate me as he would have everyone believe. McClendon can't resign. He must give me sixty days' notice, according to the contract." Curiously, here was George using McClendon's contract to force him to stay when he had been trying to discard him for months.

In the end George "let" McClendon resign. At the same time he traded away the three players who had complained about not getting paid during the Russian trip: Adams, Swartz, and Taylor.

When Adams returned to Cleveland to pack his things, he found a call waiting from Steinbrenner, who informed him that if he would agree to take over for McClendon as coach, George would renege on the trade and keep him in Cleveland. Adams turned him down, knowing that what George really wanted was a coach with a big name and that if he took the job, it wouldn't be long before he would be fired also.

It was the last time Adams ever talked to George. When Adams returned to Eastern Kentucky as a professor, he called George because he felt George could help him recruit basketball players in the Cleveland area. But, said Adams, "he would never return my calls. He was through with me."

When Dan Swartz was traded, he met with George for a final time. During the conversation, he grabbed George by the lapels, pulled him across the desk toward him, and spat a gob of chewing tobacco in his face.

After McClendon resigned, George paid the players and signed the "name" coach he was seeking. Bill Sharman, the legendary Boston Celtic, had been the coach of the ABL's Los Angeles Jets, a team that folded because of financial problems. George hired Sharman to take over the Pipers.

With the hiring of Bill Sharman, George's interference virtually stopped as he spent the rest of the season in a valiant effort to keep the team afloat financially.

As a postscript to the McClendon affair, three days after he hired Bill Sharman as coach, George did something unheard of in sports. He rehired John McClendon and made him Pipers vice president. George had a reason for re-signing McClendon, of course, though he would never admit it.

The outcry against George's treatment of McClendon had been so shrill that George felt he had to do something to ease the backlash. And so he hired McClendon as team vice president. McClendon, who always sought to protect his players, took the job to help them through the transition to a new coach.

Few were fooled by what George wrote in his press release announcing the rehiring of McClendon. Said his release, "Needless to say, we are delighted and proud that Mac is back with us. In his new position he will be better afforded the opportunity to accomplish what he does best and enjoys most—this is meeting the public and telling them about his greatest love—basketball and the Pipers."

It was claptrap. McClendon was a great coach. What he enjoyed best was coaching. None of the PR blatherings could hide what George had done to McClendon.

McClendon, ever the gentleman and diplomat, supported the Pipers' new coach, Bill Sharman, working to close any rift caused by the way he had been treated. At the end of the season McClendon was asked to go to Southeast Asia to teach basketball. He traveled to Malaya and Indonesia, continuing to spread goodwill, as he did wherever he went. Afterward he spent a year coaching back at Tennessee State and then coached at Kentucky State.

Years later John McClendon was asked whether George had disliked him because he was black. He laughed. "I've been asked that forty times," he said. "I could never say George's attitude was racial, because he treats everybody the same. He isn't anti-black. He's anti-human."

At the end of that first and only full ABL season, the Pipers played the Kansas City Steers for the championship. After splitting the first four games, the Pipers beat the Steers in the finale. Ben Fleiger, the Pipers general manager who had replaced Mike Cleary, accepted the trophy for the team, and after the ceremony, he gave it not to Sharman but to John McClendon.

\*   \*   \*

By January 1962, George's problems with his players paled compared with a more serious concern: With three months left in the season, the team had run out of money. George had started with $50,000 in capital. Half of it went to Ed Sweeney to buy the team. His plan was to bring star players to the team, even if they cost more, and begin drawing fans. George had excellent players. To attract them he paid inordinately high salaries by NBA standards. When many players were making $3,500 in the NBA, Steinbrenner was paying Dick Brott, a six-foot-eight defensive wizard, $7,500 guaranteed. He was paying $17,000 for Dick Barnett and $13,000 for Ohio State star Larry Siegfried, who had been the Boston Celtics' top draft pick. George figured his stars would draw enough fans to cover their higher pay.

George had made one miscalculation. He hadn't counted on the incompetence of the management of the American Basketball League. Abe Saperstein, the owner of the Harlem Globetrotters and the league's founder, had no experience running a league. He had awarded one franchise to Hawaii. The cost of air travel was astronomical.

There were few star players in the league. The best player, Connie Hawkins, had been accused in the 1960 college point-shaving scandals. The league was very hard to sell to the fans, and without a television contract, it was doomed. George couldn't even interest a local Cleveland station to televise the Pipers games.

George tried building interest in the team by spreading the story that the Pipers and the Syracuse Nats of the NBA were having merger talks.

In February, George began acting as though the league office didn't exist and began making his own rules. On February 18, 1962, the other league owners petitioned to throw George and his Pipers out of the league for not paying its owed share of gate receipts and the playoff money.

When the Los Angeles Jets folded, George decided he wasn't going to fly out to the West Coast to play only one team, and he canceled his games with the San Francisco Saints, leaving the Saints owner in a more precarious financial position.

When the Saints were scheduled to play the Pipers in Newcastle, Pennsylvania, the Saints were no-shows, and the Pipers had to conduct a scrimmage game to entertain the fans. General manager Ben Flieger and vice president John McClendon walked around the stands with cigar boxes collecting contributions.

One night the team ran out of game balls when a fan grabbed the last one and ran out of the arena. The players finished with a practice ball. Another night the team hadn't paid the cleaning bill, and players couldn't get their uniforms. For that game each player wore a different-looking uniform.

Before some games there wasn't enough money to pay maintenance workers, and Flieger would have to lay duct tape to make the three-point field goal circle. Flieger himself was only paid periodically, and he and his family suffered during his employment with the Pipers.

It got so bad that George was kicked out of the office that he had rented from the Western Reserve Life Insurance Company, a firm George recently had started with some of his friends, and one day when Bill Sharman, John Mc-Clendon, and Ben Flieger came to work at the Cleveland Arena, they discovered padlocks on the doors. They had been evicted for nonpayment of rent.

George spent hours on the phone calling new investors, but the problem he faced was that his embarrassing behavior too often had been reported in the papers, and even though they were a fine basketball team, the Pipers were becoming a laughingstock around town. George was nervous and upset, but he continued to be upbeat that it would all work out.

"There were a lot of if-comes on the table," said Piper director Bob Ferry. "There were all kinds of people who were supposed to come forward. George would say, 'I talked to so-and-so, and he's going to come in on this.' A lot of those people never materialized." Still, says Ferry, "it always amazed me that George had the guts and tenacity to keep approaching people for money."

George managed a $50,000 investment from Detroit trucking magnate Ralph Wilson, but it was hardly enough to stem the tide of red ink.

George held a meeting with General Manager Ben Flieger and Art Modell, the owner of the Cleveland Browns. Modell wanted to help.

"Tell me what the situation is," he said. When Modell learned how bad it was, he backed out. Before the meeting ended, he asked Flieger whether he had been paid of late. Flieger told him the truth, that he hadn't been paid in weeks.

A week later Modell called Flieger and offered him a job with the Browns.

One thing about George: he wasn't a quitter. Like Captain Ahab on the *Pequod* facing the specter of the white whale, George stood at the deck of the Pipers' listing freighter confident he would ultimately prevail. All he had to do was finish out the season, and he knew he would make it. George had grand plans.

Finding fresh capital for the Pipers became George's obsession. He was hitting up his old investors for money. The Western Reserve Life Insurance Company had a modest office in the Union Commerce Building in Cleveland, and on Saturdays George would meet with the directors. Sitting behind a big desk, George would take out his checkbook and say, "Now, we had a little trouble in Kansas City last week. We weren't able to pay our airfare home, and we haven't paid the cleaning company for the towels and uniforms, and the players need to be paid, and so we need $15,000." And George would get the ball rolling by writing out a check for $5,000. He'd turn to Jim Stouffer or Dick Lezius or Louis Mitchell, or any of the other directors, and he'd ask for the rest of the money.

Frank Treadway sat in on these meetings, and not long after the demise of the Pipers, he paid a social call to the team accountant. They went to lunch.

Treadway recalled how each week George had always written out a large check, and to satisfy his curiosity, Treadway asked the accountant, "You know, I'd be interested in something. How much do you think George lost in all of this?"

According to Treadway, the accountant replied, "He didn't lose any more than you did." Treadway was stunned, as he had lost only his original investment of $4,000.

"How can that be?" he asked incredulously.

Explained the accountant to Treadway, "When George handed in the directors' checks the next Monday morning, he never gave me any of his checks."

Treadway was a good friend of another Pipers director, Louis Mitchell. During the heyday of the Pipers, Treadway and Mitchell would have lunch together because both were in the stock market. Treadway would get upset with Mitchell because Treadway didn't trust George, and no one else seemed to have the same concerns about him that he did.

Treadway would say, "Lou, for God's sake, don't you see what this guy is doing to you? You're writing a check out to him every week." Mitchell didn't care. To this day Mitchell swears by George and insists that he loved every minute of being a Pipers owner.

Pipers director Bob Ferry felt the same way.

"I went in with my eyes open," said Ferry. "There's a famous last line from *The Last Hurrah*, 'Thanks for the laughs.' That's the way it was for me."

Said Treadway, "It was like being in love with a prostitute. You know it's wrong, but you can't help yourself. Giving money to George became an obsession with some of these people."

Before he was through, George's win-at-all-costs methods almost ended his marriage and cost him the friendship of one of his closest and dearest friends. At the same time it ended any hope George had of ever owning the Cleveland Indians baseball team.

As the season went into the winter of 1962, George was spending more and more time trying to raise money for the Pipers and less and less time at home. Finally, his wife, Joan, couldn't stand it any longer, and they separated. George moved into the YMCA in downtown Cleveland. Then Joan discovered that George had sold some of her stocks and her stamp collection without asking her.

The stock transaction was completed after a series of lies and evasions. Frank Treadway brokered the deal. George called Treadway to sell one thousand shares of Western Reserve Life Insurance stock.

Treadway wanted to know: Was the stock restricted? If it was, George as a company insider could not sell the stock after acquiring it until a minimum period of time set by law. George swore to Treadway that the stock was not restricted.

Treadway asked George, "Is the stock yours?" George swore it was.

"I understand all the rules," George told him.

Treadway made the sale on the phone and told George to bring him the stock certificates within five days. When he brought it, Treadway was horrified to see that not only was the stock restricted, but it didn't even belong to him. It was his wife's.

Immediately Treadway sent George upstairs to speak to the bank directors. Never at a loss for words, George told them he wanted the money to buy Joan a surprise Christmas present, that he was getting her a new car.

"He sweet-talked them into paying him the eight thousand dollars," said Treadway, "when they should have known better."

When his wife found out that George had sold the stock and spent the money, she was furious, say friends. So was her father, who at first threatened to call the police to have George arrested. After cooler heads prevailed, he backed down. "The securities company was petrified that she or her parents would complain to the SEC," said Treadway.

But she never did. She did, however, sue George for divorce. A reconciliation followed.

George and Jim Stouffer had been friends since childhood. Jim was the son of Vernon Stouffer, the frozen-foods magnate. Their mothers were both Christian Scientists who traveled together to England. The families were as close as could be. When George started the Pipers, Jim enthusiastically invested several thousand dollars. Before the end, Jim finally began saying no.

According to several of the men who were there when it happened, George and Jim had a falling-out over money. Jim was closemouthed about the details but he was clearly infuriated by George's conduct.

Said Frank Treadway, "When you believe in yourself to where the important thing isn't how I do it, the important thing is that the basketball team gets its jock straps out of the laundry and gets to the finals. How I get there is immaterial. Everyone will forgive me for my transgressions if I can win the American League pennant. Everyone will forgive me if I win the World Series. Everyone will forgive me if I can get out of this industrial league and get into the ABL, and they will all forgive me if I get out of this ABL mess and get into the NBA.

"I don't think George meant anything harmful," said Treadway. "It was fairly hush-hush. Jim went to his parents, and Vernon went to Henry, and there were some hot words there. A very distinct coolness fell between the two families. George was never forgiven by the Stouffers. After a year of not talking to George, Jim Stouffer finally forgave him. If you have enough money, maybe those things don't mean that much."

Said Ben Flieger, "Dick Lezius and Jim Stouffer were bitter about George after the Pipers."

Added Bob Ferry, "The relationship with George and Jim had deteriorated badly, and that was too bad because they were great, great friends, the best upfront friends."

With the team $240,000 in the red, the season ended as an artistic success. Under Bill Sharman, the Pipers rebounded from their slow second-half start to win the American Basketball League championship. The players were hoping for playoff money. After the playoffs, they learned the winner's share was the same as the loser's: zero.

At season's end everyone was discouraged and depressed over the finances. All had given up hope—except George. At the ABL draft of college players, George chose as the Pipers' first-round selection Jerry Lucas from Ohio State, the most highly sought-after collegiate player in the country. Lucas was coveted by the National Basketball Association because he was a white talent in a league dominated by black stars such as Bill Russell, Wilt Chamberlain, Oscar Robertson, and Elgin Baylor. Lucas was so good, Steinbrenner believed, that if he could sign him to a contract, he could get the Pipers into the NBA.

First he had to sign Lucas, who was also drafted by the Cincinnati Royals. George had a few things going for him: Lucas didn't really want to play pro ball, he wanted to go to graduate school; and Lucas had played with the Pipers on the trip to Russia. Also, there is no better salesman on earth than George.

George romanced Jerry Lucas as he later would Reggie Jackson. He offered him money to complete his education. He gave him a personal tour of Cleveland, taking him and his wife, Treva, to the Union Club and the University Club.

George convinced Lucas he would be not only his boss but his friend. He offered Lucas a stock portfolio and money for his education worth $45,000. The Royals were offering him only $30,000, take it or leave it. Lucas signed a personal service contract for 1962–63 to work for George. News of the signing sent shock waves through professional basketball.

It also shocked the Pipers' board of directors because the Pipers were $300,000 in debt. George was asked, "How can we sign Lucas when we have no money?"

His response: "Don't worry about it. Stop worrying about things. I'll take care of it."

George was gambling that with Bill Sharman and Jerry Lucas, the NBA wouldn't dare pass up the Pipers, a gamble he won when in early July 1962 the Pipers were invited to become the tenth NBA franchise.

Director Bob Ferry remembered the day George called him from New York to tell him the good news. According to Ferry, George was sitting with NBA commissioner Maurice Podoloff, and he said, "Bob, I have great news. We're in the NBA."

Ferry said, "That is absolutely fantastic. Tell me about it."

George said, "All we need to do is raise $250,000. Get on the phone, Robert, and raise $250,000, and get back to me as soon as you can."

But there were no more sources left from which to borrow money.

With a July 30 deadline running out, George almost made a deal with George McKeon, the owner of the ABL's San Francisco Saints. McKeon was to give George $150,000 for a half-interest in the team. As part of the deal, George was to step down as president. Ken Kreuger, who headed the Kansas City Steers, would run it, with Mike Cleary returning as GM. But McKeon was in *only* if the ABL folded.

When Abe Saperstein announced the ABL was to begin play in 1962, McKeon announced he would remain loyal to the ABL. George had no money and no time left.

When George walked into the July 30 meeting with the NBA at the Roosevelt Hotel in New York City, he was whistling through his teeth. He had raised almost half the needed amount, but it wasn't enough. The NBA board of governors wanted cold cash, not promises—no notes, no future considerations.

The final phone call was placed by George to Louis Mitchell, a man who had backed George generously all the way through. George tried one more appeal for Mitchell to invest the $100,000 he needed.

When George called, Mitchell added up in his head the value of his stocks and bonds. It amounted to $87,000. He could have come up with the money had he wanted to.

With George waiting at the other end of the phone, Louis Mitchell mulled whether he wanted to go further.

"I kind of thought for a minute whether I wanted to blow my wad," said Mitchell, "and I decided not to."

And with that, the Pipers were done.

George ended up paying Jerry Lucas to finish his degree, and a year later he joined the NBA with the Cincinnati Royals, beginning a respected career that culminated in the New York Knicks' championship of 1973.

After the NBA turned down the Pipers, columnist Gordon Cobbledick wrote in the *Cleveland Press* on August 1, 1962, "We find basketball an unseasonable topic of conversation wherever Clevelanders gather, and it seems to me the only conclusion possible is that next to winning a baseball pennant or a football championship, the surest way to get yourself and your year talked about is to foul things up beyond recognition."

On the same day, an editorial was written on the Pipers in the *Press*. It said, "If the future of professional basketball in Cleveland—and the interest in it— hasn't been wrecked by now, it has moved perilously close to it.

"Instead of a pro basketball season involving the top teams and the best players, Cleveland may have none.

"This sorry spectacle can be traced directly to one man, George Steinbrenner, owner of the Pipers.

"Steinbrenner, who seems congenitally unsuited to be in the sporting world, has been more of a hindrance than a help to the ball team from the time of the first whistle.

"He has engaged in unsportsmanlike conduct, in and out of the gymnasium.

"Steinbrenner has hurt the whole range of professional sports in this sports-minded town.

"He should get out of pro basketball and stay out."

# SURVIVAL

After Billy was released as a player in the spring of 1962, Minnesota Twins owner Calvin Griffith hired him as a scout and a troubleshooter. Billy's salary was $10,000. He took the job because it was the only one offered. The crafty Mr. Griffith was the only owner willing to take a chance on a drinker with a reputation as an uncontrollable wild man who enjoyed punching people and who couldn't get along with others.

Baseball has always been a family-run or conservative corporate enterprise. Team owners want get-along company men, not renegades such as Billy, to be their general managers, farm directors, managers, and coaches. Baseball owners are more comfortable with less talented get-along guys than with more talented lone rangers. As qualifications for a baseball job went, there couldn't have been a less likely candidate for a managerial job than Billy Martin. Except for one attribute: Everyone who knew him understood that he possessed one of the most brilliant baseball minds in the game. The trouble was his body, including the elbows that settled at the bar and the fists that swung when provoked.

Calvin Griffith, many of whose top people were relatives and friends, put Billy to the test. Could he overcome his reputation? Could he work with others?

Griffith hired Billy as a scout whose job it was to evaluate talent in the Twins organization. He gave Billy a cubicle in the office, a secretary, and an expense account. Billy also went to all the Twins' home games, sat in the stands, and evaluated the opposition. When the Twins wanted to make a trade, Billy was consulted.

Billy occasionally scouted top high school prospects. He recommended paying kid pitcher Jim Palmer the $50,000 he was asking, but Calvin wouldn't pay it. Palmer became a star with the Baltimore Orioles.

This was to be the pivotal job in Martin's career. His survival in baseball was at stake. Martin, who was a genius at survival, played this game to perfection. He did his job well, kept his drinking under control, and was cordial to the other team executives and to the members of the local press. He made a rare ally among the media, befriending *Minneapolis Tribune* columnist Sid Hartman.

As a bonus for the Twins, Billy became a one-man public relations bonanza. To make ends meet, he took a job in public relations for the Grain Belt Brewery. Between the Twins and the brewery, he met a lot of people. Billy spoke at many banquets, making a raft of friends in Minnesota for himself and the Twins. Working for the brewery, he made the round of local bars, buying drinks and talking about the Twins.

"Every bar in Minnesota knew him," said Calvin Griffith.

Martin worked as a Twin scout for three years, and then in 1965, Griffith and manager Sam Mele hired Johnny Sain to be the team's pitching coach and Billy to be the third-base coach.

Billy could work as hard as anyone when faced with a challenge, and during the 1965 season, Billy proved his value. He tutored the infielders, stressing fundamentals, which impressed Mele. Billy began working with minor leaguer Rod Carew before anyone else recognized his great talent. He taught Bernie Allen to play the infield.

Frank Crosetti had taught Billy that when he was the middle man on the double play, he had to "get to the bag as quick as possible and anticipate the bad throw," and Billy drilled it into his charges over and over.

The Twins had a number of very talented Latino players on the team, including two Cubans, shortstop Zoilo Versalles and outfielder Tony Oliva. Among the Twins' talented young prospects were infielder Rod Carew from Panama, and outfielder Cesar Tovar from Venezuela.

But Latino players were trouble for American managers and coaches. They didn't know the language, and American coaches and managers didn't think it was their job to learn Spanish so they could communicate with them. Latino players, many who came to this country as impressionable teenagers, thus lived in their own little baseball ghetto, without instruction and without guidance like the American players got.

Latino players as a group also had a reputation: They were sensitive and didn't hustle all the time. They didn't play for the team. They were moody. They were easily intimidated if thrown at.

Billy Martin had an advantage over other coaches. He had grown up with his buddies Ruben DeAlba and Jesse Garcia and other Mexican immigrants in West Berkeley, and he liked them, understood them. When he was handed the coaching job with the Twins, it was the Latino players he gravitated to because, while the white power hitters such as Harmon Killebrew, Bob Allison, and Don Mincher may have liked him, the Latino players, who had been ignored for so long, needed and *loved* him. Billy knew enough Spanish to communicate with them, and he knew how to challenge them without hurting their feelings so badly they would stop playing hard.

Billy adopted as his personal project Zoilo Versalles, and in 1965 the young shortstop scored 126 runs, hit 19 homers, drove in 77 runs, and played an exciting game at shortstop, helping to lead the Twins to the pennant and winning the Most Valuable Player award in the American League.

If Versalles got down on himself, Billy would boost his morale, or he'd have Oliva or another infielder, Sandy Valdespino, talk to him.

There were ten teams in the American League in 1965. Billy's former team, the New York Yankees, finished sixth. The next year they would finish in the cellar.

A lion's share of the credit for the 1965 pennant went to Billy. Sam Mele, who respected and liked Billy, gave him his full support. Mele showed a lot of class, because from the very first day of spring training, the press started writing that Billy was out to take his job. Mele never let it affect his feelings for Billy. The two would fish together often, and their respect for each other never dimmed.

The year was not without its bumps and obstacles. Mele asked Billy to help develop the Twins' running game, and Billy told Mele he was going to be very aggressive during spring training. Several times Billy sent runners home, only to see them get thrown out. But Billy was doing it for a reason, preparing the Twins for a more daring, more exciting brand of offense.

One of Calvin Griffith's brothers, Bill Robertson, became upset that runners were getting thrown out, and according to Billy, went to Mele to try to get him replaced. Mele rebuffed him.

At the end of the season, when Calvin Griffith went to Mele and asked him who had taught the players to steal and run the bases, Mele told Griffith the truth: "Billy taught them."

From his first job as a coach, Billy showed his brilliance as a teacher and at the same time demonstrated no facility for baseball politics. Billy's coaching was instinctual. He did it naturally, without effort. But he did it as though he were working in a vacuum. While he worked hard for Mele, he ignored the other coaches, working separate and apart from them and earning their enmity. The other coaches, Jim Lemon, Hal Naragon, and Johnny Sain, resented that Billy never showed up on time for coaches meetings and that Mele never said anything to him about it. Billy, in turn, disliked Naragon and Sain, believing they were out to get Mele fired and Naragon hired.

Billy particularly disliked pitching coach Johnny Sain, who had been a teammate with the Yankees. Sain sometimes exempted his pitchers from workouts, infuriating Billy, who felt Sain gave special treatment to the pitchers. Billy believed the team came before any player or group of players.

Sain believed in the positive approach, telling a pitcher how good he was no matter how he performed. Billy believed in honest evaluation. "You're horse-shit" was not part of Sain's vocabulary—like it was Billy's.

Billy and Sain would glare at each other when their paths crossed.

The Twins won the pennant but lost to the Los Angeles Dodgers in seven games in the 1965 World Series. Billy blamed Sain and Naragon for losing the Series, contending that when the two set up the pitching rotation with manager Mele, they deliberately didn't consult him because they knew he didn't agree with them.

Billy thought pitcher Jim Merritt should have started Game 3. Billy felt that Merritt threw harder than Camilo Pascual, who was the choice of Sain and Naragon, and that Merritt had been the best pitcher on the staff the final month of the season.

The Dodgers, moreover, featured the fleet Maury Wills, and Billy knew that Wills would go wild on the base paths against Pascual, who featured a high leg kick.

Pascual pitched and lost, and the Twins lost in seven games.

"They cost us the World Series, and we really should have won," Billy told me.

In 1966 the Twins finished second to the Baltimore Orioles. The irony for Billy was that two of the Orioles' star pitchers were Jim Palmer, whom Billy had wanted the Twins to sign, and Wally Bunker, whom Billy had scouted and dismissed because he experimented too much with his pitches.

According to Billy, in 1966 Naragon and Sain were undermining Mele more than ever. Rumors began that Mele's job was in jeopardy. Billy felt they were responsible.

On the last day of the season the Twins beat Baltimore, assuring the Twins a second-place finish, a game ahead of Detroit.

Billy went up to Mele and hugged him.

"What are you so happy about?" Mele asked. "We didn't win the pennant."

"We finished second, Sam," Billy said, "and now they can't fire you."


During the 1966 season Billy undid all his good work with one punch, something he would do several times during his career.

This incident occurred in July 1966. Billy was involved in a fistfight with the Twins' traveling secretary, Howard Fox.

The problem started when Fox invited the New York Yankees to travel with the Twins on a charter flight to Washington, D.C., where the Twins were scheduled to play the expansion Senators. He arranged for the plane to fly from D.C. to New York, where the Yankees were to disembark.

The flight, a charter originating from Norway, was three and a half hours late arriving, giving the Yankee players, including Mickey Mantle, Whitey Ford, Roger Maris, Clete Boyer, Hal Reniff, and Billy, who was with them, plenty of time to drink at the airport bar. When the flight finally was announced, some Yankee players attempted to carry Styrofoam cups of liquor onto the plane.

The Norwegian crew did not know that the men entering their plane were

American baseball heroes. One of the Norwegian flight attendants, a law-and-order type, systematically confiscated the booze as the Yankee players entered the cabin.

The steward informed them that carrying liquor on board was against the rules and that he was just following orders.

Roger Maris and Clete Boyer, two men who could get nasty and abusive when drinking, were particularly incensed.

After the plane took off and was on its way, Maris asked the steward for another drink. The steward curtly told the Yankee star he was busy.

Maris finally was able to get one from a stewardess. The steward, who apparently felt Maris had had enough to drink, ordered Maris to give it back.

Yankee pitcher Hal Reniff screamed at the steward, "Get the fuck out of here."

"Don't talk to me like that," said the steward.

Clete Boyer told him, "I'll knock you on your ass if you don't get away from us."

The pilot came out of the cockpit to see who was causing the trouble with his steward. He walked over to Ralph Houk and Sam Mele, the two managers, who were seated next to each other in the front of the plane. Houk was asleep, so the pilot said to Mele, "You better straighten those guys out or I'm going to set the plane down and kick them off."

Howard Fox, seeing Houk was asleep, began wagging his finger in front of Billy's face, infuriating Billy. Fox, college-educated and well-to-do, didn't like Billy, especially when Billy was drinking. In this case it was Billy's old pals who were drinking and acting up, and Fox wanted Billy to talk to them. Fox said, "Can't you get your pals to shut up?" Billy became enraged that Fox would ask him to do such a thing.

Billy snapped, "That's none of my business."

Fox bristled at Billy's tone as much as the substance of the response.

About that time Ralph Houk woke up and interceded. The unpleasantness ended for a while.

Later on the flight Billy, who tended to let his anger build silently, yelled at Howard Fox, "Kiss ass, Howard." Fox didn't answer. Billy yelled it again. Fox didn't answer, so Billy yelled it again, without response.

When the Twins got to the Statler Hilton Hotel in Washington, Fox continued to discuss with Billy the boorish behavior of the Yankee players. Fox was of the opinion that Billy cared more about protecting the members of his former team than in doing what he had asked. That Billy could have gotten the Yankee players to modify their behavior was questionable, but Billy had a way of antagonizing people who didn't like him, and such was the case with Howard Fox.

Fox handed out the room keys, one by one, to the players, deliberately making Billy wait to the very end, when he threw Billy's key in his face. Billy, who as coach should have gotten his keys before the players, reacted to Fox's hostility.

"Did you have to wait till last to give me my key?" Billy asked. "You do that again, and I'm going to beat the living hell out of you."

Fox took off his glasses and placed them on the counter of the check-in desk. He said, "All right, you loudmouthed bastard, you want me, how about here and now."

Martin hit Fox, who was ten years older, in the face. Players intervened, and after order was restored, Fox took a page from Billy's book by racing over to Billy and landing a sneak punch to Billy's face.

Billy would spend several more seasons in the Twins organization, but during the whole time, Howard Fox was an enemy in a game in which even one naysayer can get you fired. If it did nothing else, the fight slowed his advancement to Twins manager.

In 1966 the Twins had finished second. In 1967 the team started poorly. There were two candidates to replace Mele: Martin and Cal Ermer, who was managing Denver. Billy campaigned for the job through columnist Sid Hartman.

Cal Griffith publicly said Billy wasn't ready. The fight with Fox in the back of his mind, Griffith didn't trust Billy not to be involved in other such embarrassments.

Griffith called Billy in for a meeting. Martin expected to be named the new Twins manager. Instead Griffith told him that Cal Ermer was getting the job and offered Billy the manager's post in Denver, the Twins' top minor league team. Billy's initial reaction was that Howard Fox or someone else in the organization was trying to bury him in the minors.

"What kind of team do you have in Denver?" Billy asked the Twins owner.

"Not too good."

"Got any pitching?"

"No."

"Any hitting?"

"No."

"Any fielding?"

"No."

"Well, why do you want me to go down there?"

Griffith said, "Jim Burris, the Denver general manager, asked for you, but if you don't want to go, you don't have to." Griffith told him that if he wasn't happy managing Denver, he could have his old job back as Twins third-base coach.

Billy, who didn't trust many people, was convinced Griffith was trying to get rid of him. He asked around for advice.

Sherry Robertson, Griffith's brother, told him to go to Denver. Cal Ermer advised him to go. Even Billy's wife Gretchen told him to trust Calvin and go.

"Take it," she said. "You'll never be happy unless you see if you can do it."

"If I go down to the minors, they'll forget me up here. I'll never get a big-league shot," Billy said to her.

"Nobody will ever forget you," she said.

That night Billy couldn't sleep. It was an important decision, a major cross-roads, and Billy feared he was making the wrong move, whatever that move was. He was so agitated, he even vomited.

With the coming of daybreak, Billy told Gretchen, "I'm going to take the job." Billy told her he didn't know why he had decided it that way. Ultimately Billy's internal logic won out.

"If they don't want me to stick around, why should I?" He went to the ballpark and told a surprised Calvin Griffith he would take the job.

Billy took over the Denver Bears on May 27, 1968. Their record was 8–22, last in the division, the worst record in the American Association.

Billy went to visit Denver GM Jim Burris in his office overlooking the field. Burris was in the habit of making his manager play tape-recorded speeches to his players. Burris's first words to Billy were: "This is my domain. This is where I watch and do all the second-guessing."

Billy told him right off, "I don't want you coming into my clubhouse. You come only when you're invited."

Burris, who respected Billy from his playing days with the Yankees, reluctantly agreed. He didn't interfere with Billy once. They became good friends and worked very well together.

"I didn't know he could manage," said Jim Burris, explaining why he had hired him. "I just knew he was fun to be with, that he was quick, and that he had been a very good ballplayer under pressure with the Yankees. That stuck in my mind more than anything else. I always had the feeling that middle infielders and catchers were the best manager material.

"We needed a new manager, and it just came to me that this guy could do something with our ball club. So it wasn't any great piece of genius that caused me to approach Billy or any conviction that I was really right."

The first night after Billy arrived in Denver, he sat at a local bar with one of the older players, pitcher Art Fowler, and they went over the team. Fowler had liked manager Johnny Goryl and was resentful that the Bears had fired him. That afternoon Art was cold to Billy, so Billy was determined to win over the veteran pitcher.

Over beers Billy asked Fowler about the team. Fowler told him that several of the players, Graig Nettles, Bob Oliver, Pat Kelly, and Ron Theobald, had a lot of talent. They talked pitching. Both, it turned out, had the same theory: that winning games was mostly in the mind, that pitchers can win if they are taught *how* to win, that they can win if they throw strikes.

Billy and Art began a relationship that would last until Billy's death. As managing became more and more stressful, Billy would need someone to be a buffer between him and his pitchers. For many years that buffer was Art Fowler.

Denver lost the first game it played under Billy, 11–1. The next day Billy got a telegram. "Nice going, Billy." It was signed "Mickey Mantle."

As a manager, Billy Martin had one great talent that few other managers in the history of the game possessed: more than any other quality, he could make players believe in themselves. This, more than his tactics or his intimidation, was the secret to Billy's success. Billy knew what it took to win ball games, and he could instill that knowledge into his players. Once they learned his secrets, they also learned other—negative—things about Billy, and those negatives usually would serve to bring him down, but for the honeymoon period, usually the first full season, the players were so grateful for Billy's leadership that they would endure whatever indignities he would heap upon them for the opportunity to be winners.

Winning, the players soon learned, was all Billy cared about. To win, players had to execute, hustle, and put the team first. For many players it wasn't as easy as it sounds. You had to be a certain kind of player, thick-skinned and tough, to play for Billy Martin. You had to be willing to kneel at Billy's feet and give your allegiance to him. You had to let Billy know you trusted him and would be loyal to him. If you could do all that, and most of the smart players could and would, then playing for Billy became a joy and a wonderful experience. If you could not, playing for him could be a living hell.

Graig Nettles was one of the young players at Denver when Billy arrived there. Before Billy came, Graig once told me, he didn't think he had the talent to make it to the big leagues, that mostly he was having fun, but once Billy got to Denver and began to teach him, and after hearing from Billy how good he was, Graig figured he could do it, that he would make it as a ballplayer.

"The first month or so I didn't like Billy," said Nettles. "To be more precise, I hated him. He didn't think much of me on the field, and he would take me out for defense. He jumped all over me. He would yell and scream at me. He yelled and screamed whenever a player made a mistake. He'd scream right in the dugout in front of the other players after you came in from the field. 'Goddamn it, why didn't you take the extra base? Jesus Christ, can't you tell the guy in right field has a weak arm? What the hell is wrong with your brain? Are you a dummy?' I never had a manager do that.

"The first couple of weeks our manager had been John Goryl, a mild-mannered guy. We were in last place. Then Billy took over. Billy didn't think much of college guys. He held us in contempt, the same way he holds National League players in contempt. He felt we thought too much, that we hadn't scuffled around enough in life, that we had it too easy all our lives, that we weren't hungry enough. And so what he did, he put us through hell, the same way the Army puts you through boot camp to toughen you up, and after about a month I began to understand that the reason Billy did all that screaming and yelling was so you wouldn't make the same mistake again. He forced you to think while you were out on the field, made you aware of what was going on in the other club, who could throw, who could run, the right thing to do in every situation. Ordinarily they don't teach you this in the minors. Billy wanted us to always be thinking. He drilled it into my head: 'Figure out how fast the batter is so you'll know what to do when the ball is hit to you. If he's slow, you have plenty of time. If he's fast, you can't waste time. If there's a runner on second and a ball is hit to left, if the runner is fast, cut the throw. If he's slow, let it go through.' These are the things he taught me that I use to this day.

"One time he took me out of a game in my hometown of San Diego, which embarrassed the hell out of me. He waited until I was on the field, then he called time, and then he sent someone else out there to replace me. He was letting me know that he was going to be the boss of the ball club, that the players were not going to run the team, that *he* was. And I have since learned that for a ball club to win, the manager has to have the respect of the players, and the manager has to be boss. The manager has got to be the leader, not the players, and this was the message Billy was giving us. Things had to be done his way.

"And when we did them his way, we started to win. We played Billy Martin baseball. We stole bases, used the squeeze play, bunted men around, and played exciting, heads-up baseball, the hard-nosed way he plays the game. He took that team, which was in last place, and he made us into winners.

"When I saw the results, I stopped hating Billy Martin, and I began to see him for what he was: an extraordinary leader. Billy has always said that if you follow him, he will lead you to victory. The problem Billy has is that it isn't always easy for major league players to make that leap of faith. Some players will not respect the manager, no matter who he is. Reggie Jackson is one of those players.

"And the next year, when Billy began managing in the majors at Minnesota, he wasn't any different, except that he didn't yell at the veterans. The veterans knew him and respected him, and he turned them around and taught them how to win. And it isn't any different today. On a Billy Martin team, there is only one boss: Billy Martin. And if you do it his way, you'll win."

The Denver Bears started winning games. They were unpredictable. Bob Oliver, the team's other slugger besides Nettles, stole home twice. Billy had them double steal, hit-and-run, squeeze, and sacrifice. Once they tied a game on a steal of home.

They were intimidating. Billy got thrown out of games eight times by the umpires. One time he was fined and suspended, and he and Jim Burris rigged up a walkie-talkie system, with phones that went from Billy in the office to the dugout and the bullpen. With the team losing by a wide margin in the seventh inning, a seething Billy threw down his walkie-talkie and sullenly went and sat in the stands for the rest of the game.

Billy would do things for players that would amaze them. He sent one player home in the middle of the game after determining he was having marital problems. He told the player to patch it up with his wife and come back the next day. He did.

He caught another player, a pitcher, coming to the park with liquor on his breath. Billy sent that player home with his uniform on. He wouldn't let him change clothes. He told him not to do it again. The pitcher's season turned around after that.

He forced players to stop alibiing. He benched five of his college-educated players to show them who was the real brains of the team.

Losing became anathema, and by the end of the season the Denver Bears were the best team in the league. They won twenty-six of their last thirty-five games to finish in fourth place.

"If we had had one more week, we would have won the pennant," said Billy.

Under his leadership, the team went 65–50. Billy had performed a miracle, one that he would repeat over and over again.

Calvin Griffith noticed that not only had the club improved dramatically under Billy, but there was a by-product to his managing: Attendance at Denver rose by more than 100,000 fans.

Still, Griffith hesitated to hire Billy to manage the Twins. He wanted Billy's results. How could he overlook them? He just didn't want Billy and his white-trash behavior.

Griffith was aware that Billy and Art Fowler, whom Billy had named his pitching coach, liked to drink a lot. Griffith didn't mind that Billy drank. Griffith himself liked a drink.

What troubled Griffith was Billy's behavior. Griffith didn't like the way Billy mistreated umpires, and when word came back to Griffith from some of the disenchanted Bears players, especially some of the less talented pitchers, of his rough language and even tougher treatment of them, the Twins owner paused.

Griffith ran his team like a scion on a Southern plantation. Even though he paid them peanuts in comparison to other owners, he was paternalistic to his players.

Griffith feared promoting Billy, whose unpredictable nature made the Twins owner *very* nervous. Billy was a battler, but Griffith suspected he couldn't always control *who* Billy would be battling.

Despite his misgivings, Calvin Griffith decided he had to give Billy the chance, and on October 11, 1968, he hired Billy Martin to manage the Minnesota Twins for the 1969 season. Billy signed a one-year contract.

When he was hired, Billy demanded Griffith hire Art Fowler to be pitching coach. Art Fowler had pitched in the minors from 1944 until 1954 before he made the majors with the Cincinnati Reds. Fowler had been the pitching coach for the Los Angeles Angels in 1964, and then he went to Denver as a pitcher at the age of forty-five.

When Billy became the manager of the Bears, he told Fowler, "If I go back up there, you're going with me."

Griffith wanted as pitching coach Early Wynn, a twenty-three-year veteran who had retired in 1963 after winning 300 games. Wynn had led both the Indians in 1954 and the White Sox in 1959 to pennants.

Griffith and Billy compromised: In 1969 the Twins would have *two* pitching coaches, Fowler and Wynn. The arrangement would prove difficult for everyone.

When he signed, Billy assured everyone that the Twins would win the pennant. He guaranteed Griffith that attendance would increase, and he promised exciting, hustling baseball.

For his part, after Billy signed his name to the contract, Twins owner Calvin Griffith crossed his fingers and held his breath. After the news conference, Griffith told a reporter he felt as if he were "sitting on a keg of dynamite."

# WE WIN—YOU'RE
# FIRED

Clark Griffith, Calvin's uncle, was one of baseball's founding fathers. As a pitcher, he won 240 games over a twenty-one-year pitching career that began in 1891 in what was then the American Association and ended in 1914, with Washington in the American League. Along with Ban Johnson and Charles Comiskey, Clark Griffith helped start the American League. The Old Fox, as he was called, was elected into the Hall of Fame in 1946.

Clark Griffith owned the Washington Senators from 1912 until his death in 1955. Griffith had bought ten percent of the stock in the club for $27,000 in 1912. At the same time he signed a three-year contract to earn $7,500 a year as team manager. In 1919 he borrowed $87,000 from Washington's Metropolitan National Bank to buy the majority of the stock.

Winning wasn't the first priority to Clark Griffith. Staying in business, being part of the game, and observing all conventions were more important to Mr. Griffith. He started out pinching pennies to pay off his debt. If a player wasn't cheap, he refused to buy him.

He didn't buy Hall of Fame third baseman Pie Traynor because his asking price was $10,000. He did buy shortstop Bucky Harris—he was cheap at $2,000, and it was Harris who led the Senators to pennants in 1924 and 1925.

Once Griffith bought a player, he paid that player less than other clubs paid. The reserve clause was in effect, binding a player to his team indefinitely, so a player was forced to accept the meager money Griffith paid him. His alternative was to quit the game entirely.

The Senators had a handful of stars in addition to pitcher Walter Johnson, who was the best player in the history of the franchise. There was Sam Rice, Goose Goslin, and Joe Cronin—Griffith's son-in-law, whom he sold to Boston for $250,000 in 1934.

It was only when the best players were at war in 1945 that Washington again had a winning team. A fluke. Other than that, nothing more.

From 1946, when the wartime players returned, to Griffith's death in 1955, the Senators had one hitting star, Roy Sievers, and a group of pitchers including Latino stars Camilo Pascual and Pedro Ramos, the sort of players Griffith preferred because they were pretty damn good for cheap.

By the 1950s the Washington Senators year after year were among the league's doormats. The team's unofficial motto read: First in War, First in Peace, and Last in the American League.

Clark Griffith appointed his nephew Calvin to the post of executive vice president in 1954. Calvin was forty-one. Calvin had been the team's bat boy, bullpen catcher, business manager at Chattanooga, farm-team manager at Charlotte, then vice president of the Senators in charge of player salaries and radio-television contracts.

Calvin Griffith had always scorned the farm systems favored by the richer clubs, choosing to buy players cheap and pay low salaries. When Calvin took over when his uncle died in 1955, he continued the practice of seeking Latino players.

Calvin transferred the team from Washington to Minneapolis in 1961, renaming it the Twins. Tony Oliva and Zoilo Versalles won him the pennant in 1965, and with Billy as manager in 1969, Oliva, Leo Cardenas, Cesar Tovar, and Rod Carew helped the Twins to the division title.

But like it had been with his uncle, winning pennants wasn't what was most important. Aside from making the money to keep the team going, what was most important to Calvin Griffith was enjoying the ownership of his team without turmoil, without aggravation. It was important to Calvin that everything run smoothly.

With Billy Martin at the helm, calm seas were rare.

The most important thing to understand about Billy Martin is that no one—not any of the owners who hired him during his career, including George Steinbrenner—was the bottom-line man that Billy Martin was. Billy's bottom line was winning. Billy knew what it took to win. He knew that to win he needed to have the owner's complete support, that any sign of an owner undercutting him would be seen as a sign of weakness by the players.

Billy knew that to win, sometimes he had to fight for his players to keep their respect, even if the person he was fighting was in the front office.

He knew that to win there was only one way for the team to do things—*his* way, even if it meant angering or alienating a player or two or ten.

Billy's bottom line was that if the players played the game his way—and some players wouldn't because his way often was brutal and unsportsmanlike—they would win.

Billy was willing to pay the price for being a bottom-line guy because winning to Billy Martin was *all that mattered.*

To the owners, doing it Billy's way became too great a price to pay, even when the team won. Billy would raise the tension level so high that he would take all the fun out of the game. Worse for him, he would personally offend his bosses, and in the end winning became less important to them than firing him. So it was at Minnesota, his first managerial job in the major leagues.

When Billy took the Minnesota job, he took it on a twenty-four-hour-a-day basis. Billy's intensity and singleness of purpose was evident from the start. He told his players that the team would return to his style of play when he had been third-base coach—hitting-and-running, stealing, heads-up baseball. He told his team it would win the pennant.

Billy took the Minnesota job with the goal not only to win but also to bring people into the ballpark. He believed in earning his pay, and he was determined to do the job for the owner. No one worked harder than Billy Martin.

Throughout spring training he stressed fundamentals. During the spring games he had them practice, practice, practice, at times angering the opposition by the intensity of play during a series of games that were supposed to be exhibitions.

The great controversy of the Twins' spring was Billy's feud with another rookie manager, former Red Sox superstar Ted Williams.

In a game against the Washington Senators, a new franchise that had replaced the departed team and was managed by Williams, the Twins had the bases loaded in the seventh inning with two outs. Martin called for a squeeze. It worked.

Said Billy, "You should have seen Ted Williams and some of the Senators. You'd have thought I committed murder. They were calling me everything. While this was going on, our runner on third stole home. Williams was blowing his stack by now. I don't know what he was thinking or saying. I didn't care. I wasn't trying to show him up. I wanted those two runs. I wanted to win the game."

Billy said to reporters about Williams after the game, "He was the greatest hitter I ever saw, but as a second baseman I didn't have any respect for him, because he never slid into me. On a double play he'd go out of the baselines. It's nothing personal."

Nothing personal? Billy was calling the great Ted Williams a pansy.

Billy's attack on Williams got Billy plenty of attention, and it warned the fans in advance that Billy Martin's team was going to be a fighting, spirited, exciting ball club. Attendance improved for the team from the first home stand.

The major problem Billy had—with the Twins and everyone else who hired him—was that rightly or wrongly he thought of himself as the most important cog in the organization.

All his life he had detested authority, and on a ball team the owner was the supreme authority. Billy could not get through a season without offending the owner one way or another.

His makeup was such that Billy would not perform tasks that he felt demeaned him. One of those tasks, one that is demanded in almost every organization, is meeting daily with the general manager or the owner. When Billy was hired, Griffith had asked him to meet with him every day.

"Come before four o'clock in the afternoon because I take a nap from four to five," Griffith told him.

Billy despised meetings. Early on, Billy found reason not to go.

"Calvin Griffith wanted me to go up to his office every day and tell him what I was doing on the field," Billy said. "The first day I went up he was on the phone and couldn't see me. The second day his secretary told me he was taking a nap. That was it. There was no third day."

The first major maelstrom blew in May. Billy was the instigator. One of the targets was Griffith's brother Sherry Robertson. The background of the blowup was Billy's frustration after the Twins had lost four games in a row.

The issue, as far as Billy was concerned, was that two of Griffith's farm systems executives had stabbed him in the back and made him look bad to his players. To Griffith and the executives, Billy's reaction to what they had done was the behavior of an unstable man.

They were both right.

The blowup arose when the Twins front office decided to send Twin pitcher Charley Walters to the minor leagues. Billy was told by Calvin Griffith that Walters was going to Triple A Denver, and that's what he told the kid.

When it turned out that farm director Sherry Robertson and Robertson's assistant George Brophy sent Walters instead to Double A Charlotte, Billy became furious. Billy felt Walters deserved to play at Denver, and he felt that Robertson and Brophy had embarrassed him by deceiving him, making Billy look like a liar to Walters.

Billy didn't have the emotional makeup to let a transgressor go unpunished. Billy felt compelled to respond to his feelings of embarrassment by dishing out a barrage of words to guarantee that his provoker feel just as or more humiliated.

Billy had forged a relationship with *Minneapolis Tribune* columnist Sid Hartman, and he chose Hartman's column as the forum to vent his anger.

Billy didn't believe in blind quotes or couching his language, such as having Hartman say, "A source close to Billy Martin said . . ." If Billy had something to say, he wanted to say it, wanted it known he had said it, made it known he was angry. Confrontation was Billy's style, even in his use of the press. Billy was constitutionally unable to let the smallest slight pass. He would take no shit from anyone, as his mother always counseled, even if his behavior was self-destructive.

Billy, through Sid Hartman, blasted Robertson and Brophy in the most unkind terms.

"Those guys don't know anything about players. Why didn't they ask me?" he said.

Billy said about Brophy, "He gets all kinds of alibis and lies. These are my players. I didn't sign them. I inherited them. But I'm going to fight for them.

This manager is no figurehead. If we're going to lose, it will be my way and nobody else's. I know managers get fired, but let me die my way.''

Sherry Robertson, who was dumbfounded by Billy's stridency, responded that Billy was way out of line.

The next day Calvin Griffith called a meeting with Martin, Robertson, and Brophy.

Having stirred up this commotion, Billy now had to face the consequences. Always it was only afterward that he would realize how self-destructive his actions had been, and he would be forced to apologize—to Billy it was "groveling"—saying he was sorry not because he meant it but because he knew if he failed to do so, he faced dire consequences.

And so after the meeting, Billy apologized to Robertson and Brophy.

"I hope it's forgotten," Billy said.

This was the sort of talk Billy always used to try to save his ass afterward. Often after these situations, he would let others know how he *really* was feeling.

Later he said to a reporter about Brophy, "If he'd been a younger man, I'd have punched his lights out."

The next thing Billy did to offend Calvin Griffith was to issue an edict saying that anyone who didn't belong would be barred from *his* clubhouse. Billy set himself up as the one who would decide whether the person would be barred.

Two of the people Billy subsequently booted from the Twin dressing room were Calvin Griffith's grown son, whom Billy felt was undermining his authority by his presence, and the legendary Minnesota politician (and LBJ's Vice President) Hubert Humphrey, who had gone down to the clubhouse at the request of Calvin Griffith to have his picture taken with a few of the players. But on that day the Twins had lost a game they shouldn't have, and Billy was in a foul mood, and when Humphrey tried to have his picture taken, Billy had him ejected.

According to Billy, Humphrey understood completely.

"I told him, 'Mr. Vice President, I'm trying to teach these guys that losing is a hard thing to take, and I just don't want you to go around shaking hands and having them smile, because they're taking the loss hard, and that's the way it should be.' "

Humphrey may have understood, but Calvin Griffith was both deeply embarrassed and furious.

Later, when Griffith asked Billy about it, Billy told him, "I don't care who he is. No picture taking in *my* clubhouse."

Billy's next run-in was with one of Calvin's favorite players, pitcher Jim Kaat, a bright, articulate man who had been a fan of pitching coach Johnny Sain. Billy had hated Sain, and Kaat resented Billy for it. When Sam Mele was manager and Billy the third-base coach, Kaat had made a mild comment in the papers that he didn't feel Sain was being fully utilized. Billy hadn't forgotten. Billy could hold a grudge with the best of them.

When Billy took over as manager, Billy saw Kaat as someone who hadn't been loyal to Mele and had the potential to not be loyal to him. Billy was on his guard. He told Kaat, "If you ever cut me in the papers like you did Mele, I'm going to fine you $5,000. Pitch for me and keep your mouth shut."

When this exchange of words was printed in the paper on July 4 by writer Dave Nightingale, Martin set off his own fireworks, swearing at Nightingale in front of everyone in the clubhouse for meddling in the team's business.

The next altercation, this time with another of the pitchers, Dave Boswell, came on August 6 and put Billy in the history books as one of only a handful of managers ever to KO one of his players.

The team was in Detroit, and several of the players, as well as Billy and Art Fowler, were drinking at the Lindell A.C., Billy's favorite watering hole. The Lindell A.C., owned by Jimmy Butsicaris, who was Billy's best man at his wedding to Gretchen, was renowned by players all around the league as the best sports bar in Detroit.

The incident began when Art Fowler came into the Lindell A.C. and sat down next to Billy and outfielder Bob Allison, who had come to drink together.

Billy said, "Art, how did the running go today?"

Billy required his pitchers to run twenty laps every day. Art told Billy that pitcher Dave Boswell had refused to run.

"He defied me," Art told Billy.

Billy told Art, "You go on back to the hotel, and I'll handle Boswell tomorrow at the ballpark."

When Boswell saw Art leave, he came over to Billy and said, "Art told you about my not running, didn't he?"

Billy said, "That's his job. He's a good pitching coach. It's his job."

Boswell, who had been drinking, said, "Well, I'm going back to the hotel to kick his butt."

Billy said, "Bozzy, you're not going to do anything like that. Number one, Art only has one eye, and number two, you're not going to kick his butt."

Boswell said, "Yes, I am," and he started out the door.

According to Billy, Bob Allison, a close friend of Boswell's, ran out to stop him, but Boswell would not be deterred.

Allison, a large man, provoked the fight when he said, "If you're going to be tough about this, why don't you hit me?"

Allison said he was standing with his hands in his pockets when Boswell hit him and dropped him to the ground.

Billy says that Boswell threatened him and hit Allison three times in the head, had him groggy.

The denouement was pure Billy. "Boswell was wearing a great big chain around his neck," Billy said. "And I had learned as a kid fighting in the streets that when you're fighting a bigger guy, it's best to get close in rather than stand away, so I grabbed hold of the chain, got in real close, and I started punching him in the stomach as hard and as fast as I could. I just kept pounding him in the stomach with my right hand, must have hit him forty times until I heard him grunt, and I thought I had him.

"Right then I backed off, and I punched him three or four times to the face, and he bounced off the wall, I hit him again, and when he hit the ground he was out.

"When he fell to the ground I was about to pull him up and let him have it again when Jimmy Butsicaris grabbed hold of me and said, 'Billy, he's out.' "

As Billy looked down at Boswell's bruised and bloodied body, he said to himself, How in the world did this happen? Nobody's going to believe it. How the hell do I get myself in these situations?

Later in the hospital a doctor asked Boswell if someone had hit him with a pipe.

In his own defense Billy said Boswell had swung at him first, which was not true.

Boswell later called Billy a liar.

According to Billy, he and Boswell had made up in the hospital, and they arranged for Boswell to go home for a few days so the swelling on his face would go down. There hadn't been any reporters around to witness the fight, so Billy felt confident the incident would stay private. But when Boswell went home and the pitcher's father saw his face, Papa Boswell was so horrified he called the newspapers to talk about what Billy had done to his son.

Calvin Griffith was equally horrified that his manager would attack one of his players, and when the team returned from the road, Griffith and Billy's nemesis Howard Fox met with him. According to Billy, Griffith and Fox said they had been told that three players had held Boswell while Billy hit him. Though it had been Boswell who started the altercation, they first talked of suspending Billy.

Even after Billy told his side of the story, Griffith wanted to know, "Why did you hit him so many times?"

Billy had to explain the strategy of fighting a bigger man.

According to Billy, Howard Fox still wanted to fine and suspend him.

Billy said to Fox, "Maybe you would have preferred if I had lost the fight? Would that have made you happy?"

Billy told me, "It probably would have."

Calvin Griffith really didn't care *who* won the fight. That wasn't the issue. What bothered him was that the fight took place at all. He felt it had happened because Billy had been in the same bar with the players. The fight was why baseball had set down the stricture that a manager was never supposed to drink with his players. But Billy enjoyed sitting at the bar and drinking with his favorite players. To Billy it was a silly rule.

The Twins moved on to New York to meet the Yankees. Gerald Eskenazi was covering the Yankees for *The New York Times* their first day into New York, and he gingerly explored the aftermath of the fight.

"What's your relationship with Boswell now?" asked Eskenazi.

"Everything is fine," Billy said.

"What happened after you punched him?" Eskenazi asked, wanting to know how the fight had affected their relationship.

Billy's answer: "Well, when he came off the wall, I hit him again."

Said Eskenazi later, "That's the way Billy saw things."

There was only one thing that kept Griffith from firing Billy right then and there: The team was fighting for a pennant, and Griffith wanted that pennant more than he wanted to be rid of Billy.

That year the Twins finished 97–65, nine games ahead of the Oakland A's. Harmon Killebrew was the league's Most Valuable Player. Cesar Tovar and Rod Carew, strong backers of Billy's, had outstanding seasons.

Even Jim Kaat, who didn't like the man, had praise for his leadership ability. "That year," Kaat said, "we never played a game we didn't think we would win."

One great irony was that Dave Boswell ended up winning 20 games that season. He would credit Billy with making him successful. After the final pitch of win number 20, he ran into the dugout and kissed Billy on the forehead.

When the Twins won the Western Division title, the writers credited Martin, as they should have. The team had been mediocre before him. He had transformed them. But neither Griffith and his relatives nor the players liked reading all that praise for Billy. Each group wanted a share of the credit.

The year 1969 was the first year of division play, and the Twins had to face the Baltimore Orioles for the American League pennant.

The first game was a tough 4–3 loss in twelve innings. The second game was another tough loss, 1–0 in eleven innings.

In Game 3, Billy decided to start Bob Miller instead of Jim Kaat, who was a close personal friend of Calvin Griffith's.

After the Orioles won Game 3 by 11–2, Griffith stood at the bar at Metropolitan Stadium and kept muttering, "Why Bob Miller?"

Not even the press backed Billy on that one. Fans voted ten to one that he should have started Kaat.

After the playoffs Calvin Griffith called Billy in for a meeting. Calvin asked Billy the same question: "Why Miller?"

"Because I'm the manager." It was the same answer he had given reporters. It was also the answer that sealed his fate in Minnesota, where too many people in the Twins organization—Sherry Robertson, George Brophy, Howard Fox—hated him.

Billy and Cal Griffith had a meeting. Billy told Griffith he wanted a two-year contract and a clearer line of authority.

Griffith said, "I just can't make up my mind about anything."

Billy says he immediately knew Griffith was going to fire him.

"I want to spell out one thing before I leave the room," said Billy. "Did I do everything I said I was going to do?"

"Yes."

"Did I make them hustle?"

"Yes."

"Did they win?"

"Yes."

Billy then asked Griffith about Howard Fox, who Billy knew was criticizing him to his players as well as to Griffith and the other members of the front office.

"Did you stop Mr. Fox from talking about me to the players like he did?"

"I told him," said Griffith.

"You didn't stop him," said Billy. "I did my end. You didn't do yours. You do whatever you want to. And I still have the utmost respect for you."

On October 13, 1969, Martin was fired.

Billy heard of his firing on a local radio station a few days later.

Griffith told one reporter that he had fired Billy because he played cards with his players.

Replied Billy, "They've been doing it for a hundred years. The way I looked at it was, how was Calvin finding these things out? Howard Fox is telling him. If he's going to fire me, fire me. Don't come up with pettiness. Little childish things. If it wasn't playing cards, I might have taken a cold shower. Didn't shower in my room, showered with the players. And that's too much communication. I was fired for overcommunicating, and other managers have been fired for undercommunicating. Whatever the excuse, they're going to be looking for it. Who's kidding who?"

Calvin Griffith tried to explain to the public why he did what he did. It wasn't easy. Billy had made this team special. Now he was gone.

"I thought there were problems all summer long," Griffith obfuscated. "The team played interesting baseball, but I didn't like certain things."

When Griffith explained why he was firing Billy, he talked about Billy's inability to follow "policy and guidelines."

If Griffith had been honest, he would have said, "He may be a great manager, but I really hate the guy, and I don't want to have him around me anymore."

Billy was convinced that Howard Fox was the one who pushed Calvin Griffith to fire him. He pondered how different Twins history would have been had he not made an enemy of Fox.

"After the incident with the room key, it was over as far as I was concerned," Billy said, "but apparently in Howard's mind it wasn't, and he carried it with him all those years. And the shame of it was that by pushing Calvin to fire me, he cost Calvin perhaps five million dollars. We had a sound, aggressive ball club, and I was convinced we could have won the pennant five years in a row."

When Billy was fired, he returned to clean out his locker. Among the items in his footlocker was a pack of love letters from Calvin Griffith's granddaughter. She was a student at the University of Michigan, and Billy had surreptitiously dated her all through the season.

After the firing, Billy showed the love letters to friends.

"Boy," said Billy, "the old man would sure be pissed off if he knew."

# HIGH AND TIGHT

When his firing by the Twins was announced, there was an emotional outpouring by the fans of grief and disgust with Calvin Griffith and the Twins management. Given a choice between Billy, or Griffith, Robertson, Brophy, and all the rest of Griffith's family, the fans would have preferred Billy that stay and they go. Attendance had risen by 200,000 over the year before, and the next year it would fall by 100,000. Billy, not his players, had been putting those people in the seats. At an average of seven dollars a seat, Billy himself was bringing in between one and two million a year just by his presence.

But companies do not always make important decisions based on profit and loss. Personality and emotion can be factors, especially in a family-run business like Griffith's in which rule number one is: The boss is always right. Rule number two: See rule number one.

After he was fired, Billy appeared as a host on two morning radio shows in Minneapolis, and he worked as a special assistant to the head of the station. He continued his work for the Grain Belt Brewery in the public relations department, speaking at clinics and luncheons. He worked on the campaign of Bob Short, a candidate for governor of Minnesota.

During spring training in 1970, Billy toured the baseball camps. A reporter asked him if he would manage again.

Said Billy, "Nobody will hire me. I tell the truth. Owners don't want guys who tell the truth. Besides, I'm out of baseball now. I have a good job with the brewery and the radio station. I don't need baseball anymore."

Later Billy would say, "The year I was out was the loneliest year of my life."

Halfway through the 1970 season, Billy got a nibble. The call came from Charlie Finley, the owner of the Oakland A's. Finley called Bob Short to ask whether Billy would be interested in managing his team. Billy flew to Chicago to talk with him. They met on a Sunday and talked for five hours. Finley told him that manager John McNamara was going to be fired.

"Will you take over the team Tuesday in Washington?" Finley asked Billy.

Billy told Finley he'd take the job if McNamara stayed as his third-base coach.

The next day Finley called back and said he was going to hold off firing McNamara but that Billy should do some player evaluation of the A's team, then take over later in the season. Finley assured Billy that he would be available to take Billy's phone calls anytime Billy wanted to reach him.

According to Billy, the next day the A's started on a winning streak. The first time Billy tried to call, Finley didn't take his call.

Charlie Finley has a different version. Said Finley, "I hired Martin to manage my club for two years, 1971 and 1972. We agreed to a very fine salary—the same figure Dick Williams signed for later.

"This was about two months before the end of the 1970 season. Then with a month to go, he told me he wanted to take over the club right then.

"But I had given John McNamara my word that he would finish out the season and I wouldn't go against my word. Two weeks later, Detroit offers Martin $10,000 more than what I offered him and he asks if I'll release him from my agreement."

According to Billy, Finley told this story to make him look like the bad guy. In response Billy called Finley a "liar." He said he considered suing him for his remarks, then added, "But there's an old saying: Never get into a pissfight with a skunk."

Calvin Griffith later admitted trying to talk Finley out of hiring Billy. Billy had won a division championship and made Griffith millions, but battling Billy had scarred him.

"Don't do it," Griffith told Finley. "You'll be taking a terrible chance."

With Finley so warned, Billy didn't get to manage the A's until nine years later. Instead he signed a two-year contract to manage the Detroit Tigers, for whom he had played in 1958.

The Tigers had been world champions in 1968, behind the hitting of Jim Northrup, Al Kaline, Willie Horton, and Bill Freehan. Denny McLain had won 31 games and Mickey Lolich 17.

In 1969 McLain again was a star, winning 24 games, but his private life was falling down around him, and would bring the Tigers a long way down in 1970, as the Tigers fell under .500, twenty-nine games behind the Baltimore Orioles.

Jim Campbell, who had been GM since 1960, knew he needed to do something to change the chemistry of the team. On October 2, 1970, he offered Billy the Detroit job and gave him a two-year contract at $65,000 a year.

As Billy did with every team he took over, he predicted a pennant. Detroit's fans, blue collar, hardworking, many hard drinking, saw Martin as one of their own and celebrated their good fortune.

In the off-season Billy sought out the players, talking to them about pride and hustling. Billy established early in spring training that he was to be the leader. He let them know he was a very, very bad loser. The club had been cliquish under manager Mayo Smith, and Billy rode the players hard because "they were bickering or complaining or alibiing like a bunch of babies."

One player Billy screamed at all season long was outfielder Jim Northrup. Billy was convinced Northrup, a left-handed hitter, had the power to be a home-run hitter, and he was always goading Northrup to pull the ball. But Northrup preferred going the other way, and he would send Billy into a fury.

"He just hated my guts," said Billy, "but I didn't care because I wanted him to do what was right, and he was pigheaded and wouldn't."

By mid-June the Tigers were battling for the lead. One of the critical games came against the Indians, when Detroit pitcher Bill Denehy hit Cleveland catcher Ray Fosse in the ribs with a pitch. There was a donnybrook. The year before there had been many cliques within the team. This year there was one team with everyone fighting as one. As late as mid-September, the Tigers were within five games of Baltimore. Billy had worked his magic once again.

If you look at the statistics of pitcher Bill Denehy in *The Baseball Encyclopedia*, it doesn't tell you that he could throw a ball at ninety-five miles per hour. All it says is that in 1971 Denehy was 0–3 with a 4.22 ERA. But on Billy Martin's pitching staff, Bill Denehy was a *big* man. He filled an important role on the staff. Whenever Billy needed an assassin to throw at or hit an opposing batter, the man Billy called on was Bill Denehy.

Denehy, who like Billy was a pretty good drinker, saw both sides of playing for Billy. He saw Billy's ruthlessness, but he was the sort of competitor who, like Billy, would do absolutely anything he was asked in order to win, including injuring an opponent purposefully. He accepted Billy's philosophy of anything goes, watching Billy and pitching coach Art Fowler teach the staff to throw the illegal spitball, since Billy's philosophy was to win any way you could, whether by fair means or foul.

He was also a participant in the nightlife and the high jinks, the wonderful childishness that usually accompanied being part of a Billy Martin team.

As you listen to Denehy talk about his season with the Tigers, you can also see why the more humanitarian players, both opponents and his own players, came to hate Billy's style of play. *All* his opponents hated to see his team on the other side of the field because Billy transformed baseball from a game to something akin to war. Playing against Billy took away a lot of the fun and added an element of danger. At the same time he forced the opposition to play the game his way. Since few teams could match Billy in ruthlessness or managerial skill, at the end of the game Billy usually ended up the winner. It was so throughout his whole career.

\*    \*    \*

"I was brought up from the minors two weeks into the '71 season," said Bill Denehy, "and just a few hours after I joined the Tigers, I met Billy in the Grand Hotel bar in Anaheim, California. When I arrived I looked for people I knew. I found Tom Timmerman and Kevin Collins, whom I had played with on the Mets, and I was sitting at the bar with them, and it got to be one-thirty in the morning when Billy walked into the bar.

"My first thought was, I don't want to meet my new manager smashed. I was pretty well under the weather by that time.

"He came over and I introduced myself, and I apologized for my condition. He put his hand on my shoulder, and he said, 'Look, let's get things straight right now. I'm not your fucking baby-sitter, I'm your manager. I don't care what you do off the field as long as you do the job on the field.' That was the key that unlocked the door. From then, my attitude became, 'You tell me what you want done, and I'll do it.'

"He told me how important it was for me to do the job in the bullpen, even though I had never been a reliever before. He kept talking about winning the pennant, what we had to do.

" 'If we have to knock somebody down, we'll do it,' he said.

"The next day in the clubhouse we were going over the California Angels hitters. One of the Angels, Tony Conigliaro, had been beaned a few years prior to that and had disclosed he was having trouble seeing the fastball.

"We brought this up at the meeting. Billy was sitting back in the corner. He came forward and said, 'Gentlemen, we can't worry about this hitter not being able to see the ball. That's his problem. Our problem is to go out and win this ball game, and we have to win it any way we can.'

"He said, 'The first time up I want you to knock him down right on his can. If he can't see the baseball, then he doesn't belong in the game. We're not going to baby-sit him and not going to lay down for him, because he may be lying to us.'

"Billy had contempt for pitchers who wouldn't throw at hitters. We had a pitcher by the name of Jim Hannan who Billy ordered to knock the first hitter down. Jim, a very religious person, a very good person, said, 'I can't do that.' The next day Jim was traded to Milwaukee. Could have been in the works, could have been a coincidence.

"We had another pitcher named Daryl Patterson. Billy told Patterson to hit somebody the first pitch, the start of an inning. The first pitch was a called strike.

"After the game was over, Billy went after him in the clubhouse, called him 'gutless' and a few other things, and the next day he was sent to the minor leagues.

"A week or so later, we had played the first weekend against Cleveland and bombed them, beat them four straight, and badly. We went into Cleveland the first night, and it was the same thing. We beat them bad.

"On Friday night Sam McDowell was pitching against us. McDowell hit two of our players and knocked down a few more. Martin put me in the game. I got the call. Charlie Silvera was the bullpen coach, and he said, 'Chris Chambliss is the second hitter.' Chambliss had come up the week before and was 11 for 17 at that point. [Silvera] said, 'Billy wants you to knock him down.'

"The first hitter was Ray Fosse, a big right-handed hitter. He liked the ball out so he could extend his hands, so we pitched him inside. I hadn't pitched in five or six days.

"Even when I was sharp, I was a little wild. The first pitch was an inside fastball, and I threw it, and it ran, and I hit Fosse in the back. He charged the mound.

"What do you do? There is no book to tell you. I reacted. I had never had anyone charge the mound before in my whole career. As he came in to football-block me, I jumped up in the air and kicked him. He ended up with seventeen stitches from his ear down to his neck. While he was rolling on the ground, somebody stepped on his hand and broke it.

"I got dragged off by Sam McDowell, who was kind of laughing, 'Take it easy. Take it easy, Irish. Take it easy.' I said, 'I'm okay, Sam. You can let me go.' He let me go, and I ran back into the pile. By this time a trainer had put a towel over Fosse's neck. I jumped up in the air to hit him again, to take a cold shot at him, and at that time Bill Freehan walked right in front of him. I knocked out Bill Freehan cold, then got dragged off, tossed out of the game.

"Willie Horton hit an Indians pitcher with one punch—he broke his cheek-bone, jaw, and nose with one punch. Ike Brown hit a guy—they put three guys on the disabled list after that fight.

"The funny thing about that incident, after the game was over—this was supposedly the bloodiest fight ever—we ended up going to a bar, and I was sitting down there, and the next thing I know, four drinks hit my table. I looked. 'Where was this from?' I asked. The bartender said, 'It's from the group in the corner.'

"I looked in the corner, and there were Ike Brown, Willie Horton, Gates Brown, and Tony Taylor, our four black players.

"I walked over to them and said, 'Thanks, guys, but what's this for?' Willie came out of his seat and put his arm around me, and he said, 'I want to tell you something. If you ever get into a fight again, you don't have to worry about a thing. I'll always protect you. But I want to tell you, from all the times I've been with the Tiger organization, this was the first time a white guy hit a white guy.' Until this day, he doesn't know that I hit the *wrong* guy! Billy had wanted me to hit Chambliss, who is black.

"After the big fight, Billy publicly said he deplored fighting, deplored knock-down pitchers, but privately he told us he was proud of how we stuck together and fought together and how we faced up to the Indians' challenge.

"That brought our club together. It was one of the closest-knit clubs I had ever played with during my ten years of professional baseball.

"On another occasion I was pitching a game in Detroit, and the Red Sox were killing us. Billy had me warm up. I took eight warm-up pitches in the bullpen. I wasn't even breaking into a sweat yet. He put me into the ball game.

The bases were loaded, there were two outs, the top of the ninth inning, and Jimmy Lonborg was the hitter.

"Billy said, 'This guy used to knock down all my hitters when I was with the Twins. I want you to knock him down the first pitch.' Well, I was going out to dinner with Lonborg after the ball game. He and I had played together in Puerto Rico, and we were good friends.

"Billy started walking off the mound, and I made the sign underneath my chin to Jimmy that the first pitch was going to be up and in, and he nodded to me.

"I made my warm-up pitches, and I took my windup, and I just about got to the point where I was coming over my head and was raising my leg, and he hit the ground!

"Quickly I had to hurry my motion, and I threw one in his vicinity. Christ, he was laying on the ground, for God's sake.

"Everyone was looking around, like 'What's going on?'

"After the ball game I said to Jimmy, 'Did you get my sign?' He said, 'Yeah.' I said, 'Why did you go down so early?' He said, 'Because I didn't trust you, you bastard.'

"Knocking down or hitting batters was my job, and toward the end of the season I came into the clubhouse one day in Detroit, and in place of where I kept my glove, somebody—Gates Brown or Mickey Stanley—had replaced it with an Everlast boxing glove. And the reason it was either Mickey or Gates was that the two of them came up to me when I was looking for my glove, and they said, 'What did you do, get a new glove contract?'

"I was a team player, and I would do anything to win, so I fit in very well with Billy, because he wanted everyone to do his part, and I'm sure if he said to me, 'I want you to go in there and shoot somebody,' if I could have done it without going to jail, I'd have probably shot somebody.

"We had players who didn't like his ruthlessness. They also didn't like him because he was too hard on them, some of the veterans especially. Our second baseman, Dick McAuliffe, didn't like him. I know deep down, Al Kaline didn't like him.

"I remember a game in Minnesota, we lost a doubleheader, Billy's first trip back into Minnesota, and after the game was over, we attacked the spread in the clubhouse there. Billy walked in and saw all the guys eating, and he came in and tipped over all the tables and the food, picked up a chair, started cussing, saying, 'You guys are a bunch of losers. All you're interested in is filling your face.' He took a chair, and whipped [it] right over Al Kaline's head and into his locker. Al just kind of looked back over his shoulder and then looked into his locker.

"Billy said something one time. He said, 'On a ball club, there are ten guys who would do anything for you, ten guys who hate your guts, and five guys who are undecided. The good managers get the five guys who were undecided on their side.'

"Overall, as far as learning the game, running the bases, how to bunt, how to look at situations of what the other team might do, when they might bunt or steal or suicide squeeze, the running of the ball game, Billy was better than anyone I was ever around in baseball. He was uncanny.

"I learned more about the total game of baseball from Billy than from anybody. Billy never missed a trick, never let anything get past him. He was like a hawk, circling around a farm field looking for mice for dinner. He could be talking to a writer, but at the same time he would be watching his catcher in infield practice to see whether his throws to second were accurate. He'd watch his outfielders to see whether their arms were strong, whether they hit the cutoff man consistently. He'd watch to see whether his third baseman was fielding the ball cleanly, watch his second baseman and shortstop to see whether they were making the pivot smoothly.

"During the game he'd watch the pitcher, always scouting. He always did consider himself the best scout.

"What Billy did more than anything else was talk about aggressiveness. It was like in a fistfight. If you get that first shot in, you have the best chance to win. That's what he preached. He wanted you to score the first run. He wanted you to scratch and crawl and always create something, get the pitcher to balk in a run, a double steal, get the opposing team to throw the ball away. *Anything* to cause the other team to make a mistake to get your run.

"He was always talking about taking the extra base, going from first to third, challenging the arms of the outfielders, knocking the second baseman down, knocking the shortstop down, not being afraid to lean over the plate with the bases loaded and get hit by a pitch, to do *something* for the team.

"Billy would get to a point in the game where he would say to a batter, 'Go up to the plate and get hit by a pitch.' He would say, 'We got the bases loaded. Forget hitting a fly ball. Get on top of the plate and take one for the team.'

"Billy had done it. He never would ask you to do anything he wouldn't do. And if you did those things, he was tremendously loyal to you. I'm sure the way I pitched that year, I didn't have a good year, but he kept me around all year round because I had a role. And I knew that, and because I was struggling and still had a bad arm, I knew this was what I had to do to stay in the big leagues. And so I did it.

"Billy would do absolutely anything to win a ball game. Through pitching coach Art Fowler, Billy taught the pitchers how to throw spitballs. The way he taught us, he would take the crotch of the uniform, turn it inside out, and wet it, and then we would take white soap when we were at home and gray soap when we were on the road, do it before a ball game, then turn the pants right-side out and let them dry. What would happen, as you began to perspire, you'd get the slick stuff. If you wanted to throw a spitball, all you had to do was grab your crotch.

"The thing that was so inventive, when an umpire came to the mound, an umpire can check you. He'll check for Vaseline behind your ears, but Billy was smart enough to know that an umpire isn't going to come out there in front of all those people and grab you by the crotch. And that's where we kept the stuff.

"The thing Billy hated the most was having another team show him up. He would always talk about never allowing ourselves to be intimidated. And to keep from being intimidated, Billy played with a ferociousness unmatched in baseball.

"One way Billy tried to intimidate you was by talking to you. He could do it subtly, before a ball game, say to an opposing hitter, 'I noticed your swing yesterday, and it looks like you're a little slow with the bat.' Or 'I notice you're looping your swing a little bit. You didn't do that the last time we played.'

"Or he'd say to a pitcher, 'Geez, you look like you're dragging your arm as you're coming through.' All he was trying to do was get them thinking about anything except the job they had to do on the field.

"He could also do it loudly. Billy would yell a lot of things to certain hitters during the game. 'You're a cunt.' 'You're an asshole.' 'I'm going to stick one in your ear.' Anything to agitate a guy, try to get his mind off the game.

"When Billy started playing his intimidation games with the batters, he knew the other team wouldn't go out on the field. They'd be crazy to. We had large people, Bill Freehan, Willie Horton, Mickey Stanley, Jim Northrup, Norm Cash, and Gates Brown.

"Billy always will be a Yankee. Everything else he did was just something in between his career with the Yankees. Our bullpen coach, Charlie Silvera, told me that. Charlie was the Yankee third-string catcher when Billy was with the Yankees, and Charlie had story after story about Billy Martin.

"Charlie had stories about Billy's reputation and what he was looking for and how to get along with him. I found it easy. I didn't have to be told. I thought there was good chemistry between us from the start. Billy could be the greatest guy. He was great with fans, always told the players to go out and sign autographs. He was very good at that himself.

"But when he put a uniform on, he went from Dr. Jekyll to Mr. Hyde. He transformed into this fierce, animalistic, caustic person who would win at any cost. It went from a baseball game to a battle. Instead of taking the bunker, you had to win the game. At any cost.

"And if you lost—I never saw anybody take a loss harder than him—it destroyed him. There were four or five days in a row he wouldn't eat anything. He'd drink at night, and that didn't help his spirits any.

"Drinking was a part of what Billy Martin was all about. It was his release, what he did after a ball game to ease the pressures.

"I can honestly say that if he had been drinking the night before, by the time the players got to the clubhouse he was sober. Never was he not sober prior to the players coming into the clubhouse. He was *always* ready to manage, because that's what he expected of you.

"He would say, 'I don't care what you do off the field. When you get to the ballpark, I want you ready to play.' There was no such thing as a hangover. You didn't get hangovers. You took coffee or aspirin. And you didn't have nagging injuries. You didn't have them. It wasn't said, but those were things you read between the lines.

"I enjoyed playing for Billy. I enjoyed his camaraderie. I enjoyed his friend-ship. His two confidants were Art Fowler, the pitching coach, and Charlie Sil-vera, our bullpen coach.

"Art Fowler was Billy's right-hand guy. He was Billy's guy between him and the pitchers, to calm things down. Art Fowler was a great person, as good a positive person as you could find. His idea of teaching you was for him to get on the mound, and he'd pitch, and he'd say, 'Watch this.' And he would throw his sliders or curveballs.

"As far as I was concerned, he did nothing to help me with pitching. In fact, about the only two positive things I can remember him doing was one time he came out and said, 'If you want to pitch better, you have to throw more strikes.'

" 'Thanks, Art.'

"The second time, I was getting hit pretty hard, and he came out to the mound, and he said, 'Billy's getting pissed and the Budweiser is getting warm, so if you know how to cheat, now is a good time.' He walked off the mound.

"I remember another time I had not been pitching well, and I was a little down on myself, frustrated, and during batting practice Art walked out to the outfield where I was standing, and he put a paper bag over his head with the two eyes cut out. He came over to me. I was standing with Mickey Lolich, and we started laughing. I said, 'Art, what the hell you got the bag on your head for?' He said, 'Everybody in the front office and the fans here in Detroit and a lot of media people really think you stink, and I don't want to be seen spending any time with you, so I thought I'd come out and talk to you with the bag on my head, because I still love ya.'

"That type of stuff got you loose.

"I was famous on the team for giving hotfoots, and in Baltimore the bullpen benches were raised. Tom Timmerman was the last guy on the bench, and I snuck under five or six guys on my chest, crawling, and I put four matches into his shoe, and I had ethylchloride that I sprayed on his shoe and then sprayed a trail back to me.

"I was six players away from Timmermann, and I dropped a match at my feet, and it went boom, right under the bench down to him, lit his foot up, and it was smoking. Turns out, Tom had had an injury when he was a kid, and he had no nerves in his right foot. It burned a hole right through his shoe, blistered him badly. He couldn't pitch that night.

"What was Charlie Silvera going to do? You can't say, 'Denehy gave Tim-merman a hotfoot and he can't pitch tonight.' Charlie would have got fired, and God only knows what would have happened to me. So Charlie called back in and said, 'Timmerman has a blister, and I don't think he can pitch tonight.' So he covered for me.

"With Billy, there was kid stuff going on all the time. Like with the hotfoots. I tried to get him during a game when I was on the bench. I knew I wouldn't pitch that night. I crawled under the bench, and I was going to give him a hotfoot. I had the matches in his foot when I must have pushed in too hard.

"He looked down at me and he said, 'If that thing ever gets lit, you know you're in serious trouble.' Then he walked away. Never brought it up again. And I'm sure, if I had given him a hotfoot, he would have gotten a kick out of it.

"We had a big stainless steel whirlpool in the clubhouse, and after a lot of games, three or four of the guys would hop in it, and Billy would have a couple beers, one in each hand, and he would jump in there. Sometimes he would somersault into it and sit there and pour beer on the guys if it was a good game.

"When we won, he was the greatest guy in the world to be around.

"Billy told me that when he first got into baseball, somewhere in his childhood, he associated winning with winners and losing with losers. And he wanted to be a winner, and he never wanted to be a loser. And that's why he always fought and did everything he could to win a ball game.

"Billy taught you how to be a winner. When you played for Billy Martin, he taught you how to accept the challenge. He taught you how to fight for what your right is. He taught you to stand up for what you believe in.

"More than anything else, he taught you that if you want something, you have to go and get it.''

# A TIGER TITLE

For the first two years, Billy was happy in Detroit. He made the acquaintance of John Fetzer, the owner of the Tigers, and he worked well with Jim Campbell, the general manager.

Said Billy, "There is nobody sticking the knife in my back here. I don't have to look over my shoulder. I don't have petty problems here. It is the way it should be—the manager is the boss of the players."

Unlike in Minnesota, where he had some speedsters, the Tiger lineup was lumbering and mediocre. Al Kaline, on the decline, couldn't run, and neither could first baseman Norm Cash. Bill Freehan was a leadfoot behind the plate, and so was Willie Horton in left.

Billy decided that he would fashion a team based on pitching and defense. Up the middle, catcher Freehan, the double-play combination of Dick McAuliffe and Eddie Brinkman, and center fielder Mickey Stanley were exceptional. So was the fielding of third baseman Aurelio Rodriguez. It was hard to get a ball through the left side.

On the mound he had his two favorites—Mickey Lolich, and Joe Coleman, who hated Billy's guts. "He just hated everything about me because I used to get on him so bad," said Billy. "He'd want to throw his horseshit slider, and I'd make him throw his fastball."

After Lolich and Coleman were mediocre pitchers like Joe Niekro, who hadn't yet developed his knuckleball, and Dean Chance, who was over the hill, along with a group of hopefuls including Chuck Seelbach and Bill Slayback. Billy screamed at Tommy Timmerman and Mike Kilkenny frequently. Billy wanted Kilkenny especially to be more aggressive.

During the off-season Billy asked GM Jim Campbell to trade Jim Northrup and infielder Dick McAuliffe, as well as Joe Niekro, pitcher Les Cain, and Mike Kilkenny. Billy wanted Campbell to acquire another solid starter in exchange for Northrup.

But Campbell had been farm director for many years, and these were among his hopefuls.

"He didn't feel he could get rid of them," said Billy, who as always had to do the best he could with what he was given.

The Baltimore Orioles once again were favored to win the pennant in 1972.

As he had done in Minnesota, Billy continued his philosophy of intimidation, and why not, with brutes to back him up such as Cash, Horton, Northrup, Freehan, Gates Brown, and Mickey Stanley. His pitchers threw at heads, and all through the season the team played great defense and heads-up ball.

The fighting style of the Tigers was exemplified in a game on August 22 against the Western Division champions, the Oakland A's.

Catfish Hunter had defeated the Tigers in the series opener. The next evening, with Oakland leading by four runs in the seventh, Tiger pitcher Bill Slayback threw a fastball at Bert Campaneris's head. Billy was convinced that if you threw a ball at a Latino batter, he could be easily intimidated. Campaneris, Billy felt, was especially vulnerable. Billy saw that Campaneris liked to get out of the way of runners coming into second. One of the names he had for him was "pussy." As a result, Billy had his pitchers throw at Campaneris often.

This time Campy ducked, and the ball sailed past catcher Bill Freehan. Moments later, responding to a signal from Martin in the dugout, Slayback threw a pitch behind the head of another Latino player, Angel Mangual, who had homered earlier. Mangual, a small but powerful man, charged the mound and knocked down Slayback with one flying punch. Both benches cleared.

Detroit fans littered the field with rubbish.

It was a year during which the farm system didn't add any new blood to the roster, but the Tigers caught a break when pitcher Woodie Fryman was released by the Philadelphia Phillies. Fryman, who was from Kentucky, was a tough hombre who fit in perfectly with Billy's way of play. Billy and Art Fowler constantly worked to make Fryman throw strikes more consistently, and he helped make a division championship possible by winning ten games down the homestretch.

At the end of the year the Tigers traveled to Boston for a three-game series. The Tigers needed to win two out of three for the title.

The Tigers had played the Red Sox Opening Day, and during the game Red Sox shortstop Luis Aparicio got on base, stole second, and tried to score on a hit by Tommy Harper. But Aparicio slipped going around third, didn't score, and the Tigers won the game by a run.

Mickey Lolich started the first game of the critical series for the Tigers.

Losing by a run, Aparicio was on second when Carl Yastrzemski singled. Aparicio was fast, and everyone figured he would tie the score, except that he tripped over third base and fell—again. Yaz, running hard, also ended up on third. One of them was out, the Sox didn't score, and the Tigers were victors.

The next day Woodie Fryman shut the door on the Red Sox, and Billy and the Tigers were division-title winners.

By the end of 1972, Billy had lost a great deal of weight. He had virtually stopped eating. For the first time Billy acknowledged the terrible toll managing took on him, the first time he publicly admitted he had to drink to settle himself down.

"Being a baseball manager is a terrible job," Billy said. "You have to be father, mother, baby-sitter, and policeman to twenty-five guys. Things got so bad I had to take a drink all the time to settle my nerves. It's a hell of a thing to go home and say hello to your kid and wobble."

As a reward for his work, Billy's contract was extended through the 1974 season at a salary of $60,000 a year.

The series opener of the American League Championship Series was held in Oakland. The Tigers lost the first game when Jim Northrup missed Billy's sign for a suicide squeeze against Rollie Fingers in the ninth. There were runners on first and third and one out. The Tigers needed a run. Billy gave Northrup the squeeze sign. Northrup missed the sign. Instead he swung and hit into a double play.

"We should have won," said Martin, who was never convinced that Northrup didn't see the sign.

"I don't know whether he did or didn't," Billy said.

John "Blue Moon" Odom shut out the Tigers in the second game. In the first inning Bert Campaneris singled, stole second, and scored. The A's led 3–0 in the fifth when Campy singled and, after feinting a dash to home, scored on a wild pitch.

With two runners on base Billy called for left-hander Fred Scherman and ordered him to throw at slugger Reggie Jackson, another of the A's players whom Billy often targeted during his managerial career. Scherman's first pitch was a sidearm fastball, high and tight, that sent Jackson into the dirt. His next pitch was identical. Jackson went down again.

Scherman let fly again, and this time Jackson doubled into the alley in left center for two more runs and a 5–0 lead.

Billy wasn't done. If he couldn't win, he wanted revenge of sorts. In the dugout he conferred with pitcher Lerrin LaGrow, a tall rookie who was to be his next pitcher.

Campaneris led off the seventh. He knew what Martin wanted to do. LaGrow's first pitch was an inside fastball that hit Campy in the left ankle as he tried to spin away.

Billy had pushed Campaneris to the limit. When Campy finished his cartwheel, he regained his balance, grabbed his bat tightly, swung it around, and fired it at LaGrow's head. LaGrow hit the ground as the lethal bat whirred inches above him.

The Tigers' Ike Brown led the charge to the mound, picked up the bat, and smashed it. Three umpires had to restrain Billy from attacking Campaneris.

Campaneris and LaGrow both were kicked out of the game. Campaneris was suspended for the remainder of the playoffs. Billy had incited Campy, and he had taken the bait, and it got him where Billy wanted him, out of combat.

After the game Billy railed at the A's star.

"The man has no guts. He should be suspended. There shouldn't be a place in baseball for anybody dumb enough to throw a bat. The man's an idiot. . . . If he had come out and taken a punch at my pitcher, I could respect him. But a bat? The next thing he ought to do is carry a knife. Or does he fight with his feet?"

Reggie Jackson said of Billy, "I hate Martin because he plays tough. But if I played for him, I'd probably love him."

In Game 3, Joe Coleman struck out fourteen A's in a 3–0 shutout.

In Game 4, it was Catfish Hunter against Mickey Lolich. The score was 1–1 going into the seventh. Rollie Fingers and Vida Blue held the Tigers, while the A's scored twice in the tenth.

The Tigers didn't quit. In the Tigers' tenth, A's pitcher Bob Locker gave up two singles. Dick Williams brought in Joe Horlen, who threw a wild pitch, then walked Gates Brown to load the bases.

Bill Freehan grounded to third. Sal Bando threw to Gene Tenace, who was playing second. As Tenace waited for the ball, Gates Brown slid into him hard. The ball glanced off Tenace's glove as a run scored. Everyone was safe.

The Tigers still trailed by one, but there were no outs and the bases were loaded. Forty thousand Tiger fans were behind their team. How could the Tigers not come back?

Dick Williams brought in pitcher Dave Hamilton, who walked Norm Cash to tie the game. Jim Northrup then hit a long, high fly to right. Matty Alou, playing shallow, just looked at it. Gates Brown scored as the Tigers won 4–3 to tie the series.

After the game A's owner Charles Finley was in a fury. He began railing against Billy. Finley discussed Billy's personality defects, recounted the time he punched out Howard Fox of the Twins, and began raving that league president Joe Cronin wouldn't even let Campaneris sit in the dugout.

After Billy heard about Finley's remarks about him, he remarked, "Tell Charlie that if something like this happens again, he may wake up some morning and find his mule's head in his bed."

In the deciding Game 5, Woodie Fryman, the Phillie castoff, faced the A's Blue Moon Odom. The Tigers scored a run in the first inning, but it was all Odom allowed. After complaining of nausea from the tension, Odom was replaced in the sixth inning by Vida Blue. Blue, not given the start because of a feud with Charlie Finley, shut the Tigers down over the final four innings.

Meanwhile, the A's scored a run in the second on a double steal. Reggie

Jackson, who ruptured his hamstring muscle on the dash home, staggered the final few feet but slid in safely under the throw.

George Hendrick replaced him in center. In the fourth inning there were two outs and Hendrick was on first after beating out an infield hit. He went to second and scored on a single by Gene Tenace, just ahead of left fielder Duke Sims's bouncing throw. It was the winning run. The rest of the game was scoreless as the A's won 2–1.

After the game GM Jim Campbell second-guessed Billy for putting Sims into the game in left.

Billy would spend all of 1973 arguing with Campbell.

The rap always leveled at Billy Martin was: He will self-destruct. But the why and wherefore of his self-destruction has to be viewed in its context: With the Tigers, as with the Twins, once again the premise was that peace and tranquillity within the corporation was more important to Organization Men than success.

Winning was Billy Martin's bottom line. Everything else, Billy believed, including his personal behavior on and off the field, should have been irrelevant.

It was a clash of cultures, the same battle Billy couldn't fight and win as a kid in Berkeley, one he was to lose over and over as an adult in baseball. It was a question of form over substance. The men with power believed in form above all else. Billy went for substance and blithely ignored the form.

In Detroit, Billy drank and slept around at night, and on the field he attacked umpires, his own players, and sometimes even the front office verbally. When Billy went after umpires and players, the men in the front office ignored it. When he transferred those tactics to his treatment of the front office, they resented him deeply, and rather than ignore Billy's intemperate behavior and listen to what he was screaming about, the Tigers fired him.

After winning the division title in 1972 and losing to Oakland in the playoffs, Billy in 1973 saw that he had a team that was rapidly aging, and he was becoming frustrated that the front office didn't have young players to replace them.

Billy's bottom line was winning the World Series, and Billy saw that without some help coming from the minors, he wasn't going to be able to reach his goal. For that, he placed the blame squarely on the shoulders of the Tiger front office, headed by Jim Campbell. Billy wanted Campbell to do something to help him. But Campbell was insisting that their stars on the farm weren't ready and needed more seasoning when Billy knew the truth: The Tigers' minor league cupboard at the time was bare.

''I looked at our prospects, and it was my opinion that none of them would make it. I knew their shortcomings, and I told Campbell he was wrong. I said, 'These guys are not going to make it, and you're strapping me into a position where our club is getting so old we're just going to be out of it. We can't depend on these young guys. They're not that good.' ''

But Campbell insisted that kids like Ike Blessit and Marvin Lane would be stars. None of them turned out that way.

In 1972, Campbell had disgusted Billy when he wouldn't listen to his advice about signing Phillie slugger Deron Johnson. Billy had found out from Woodie Fryman that Johnson was available, and he advised Campbell to buy him. Johnson would have been cheap and would have added another solid bat.

Campbell said no, that his scouts had seen Johnson hit and said he was washed up. Johnson eventually signed with Oakland and in 1973 hit 19 home runs and drove in 81 runs for Dick Williams.

"If we had signed him, we would have won the pennant in '73 and not the A's," said Billy.

This is where the niceties of being a good company man come into play. Campbell told Billy he couldn't overrule his scouts and side with Billy because it might have upset the corporate climate and hurt morale among his scouts and minor leaguers.

Billy told him, "I'm looking to win a pennant, not win popularity contests. The hell with the feelings of the kids on the farm. What about the guys on the Tigers?"

Billy pleaded with Campbell to sign Johnson. He wouldn't do it. Billy resorted to yelling and screaming, to no avail.

By the middle of 1973, Billy saw that the situation wasn't getting any better, that the team would fall on hard times shortly unless Campbell did something, and it was clear to Billy that he wasn't about to do anything.

Billy reacted to what he perceived to be Campbell's incompetence. He decided to try his hand at corporate intrigue, not realizing it was a game he was incapable of winning in whatever organization he was in. Like the Latinos and blacks who had been part of his world as a kid, Billy didn't have the proper birthright or breeding to play the corporate game. It was the same sort of thing when Babe Ruth wanted to be a manager. No one thought the crass Babe had enough self-control to manage, so no one gave him a chance.

Billy could be the manager—he proved he could do that, but for many years no one thought him to have sufficient breeding to be general manager. By the time Oakland gave him the chance in 1980 to be general manager, his private life had sunk into such chaos that there was no way he could succeed.

Before that it was a question of caste and class. Billy loathed college guys. He hated the white-wine crowd, preferring scotch or gin. Billy's education prepared him to drive a truck or be a fireman, but he lacked polish. He was uncomfortable in a shirt and tie. He was poor at small talk. He was also incapable of sucking up, an important corporate asset.

In other words, Billy was out of his element trying to play the corporate game in his attempt to outmaneuver general manager Jim Campbell.

He had spent time with owner John Fetzer, who made his fortune owning television and radio stations. Billy would call Fetzer at his office, discuss the club with him, schmooze him, go to Fetzer's farm and visit with him.

It was a strategy he pursued wherever he went. Billy liked to deal with the owner and ignore the top officials like the general manager and the farm director. Billy may have hated it when players climbed the ladder to go over his head, but it was a game he enjoyed and practiced.

And so Billy mounted a campaign to force Fetzer to choose between the urbane Jim Campbell and himself, believing Fetzer would choose Billy over his general manager because of the way he had brought the Tigers a division title, because of what he could do for the Tigers versus what Campbell could do.

What Billy didn't understand was that to John Fetzer and most of the men he worked for, Billy was an uneducated, uncouth man from the slums whom they didn't want to be around because he drank too hard and fought too much. On one level they were afraid of him. Billy got invited into their world because he was renowned. Had he not been the manager, Billy would have come in through the servants' entrance.

Billy was kidding himself to think that Fetzer would ever pick him over the general manager with whom Fetzer worked closely. To Fetzer, Jim Campbell was far more important to that organization than Billy was—even if Billy could make the team win and Campbell couldn't. Once again it was form over substance.

While Billy was looking only at the team's bottom line, the Organization Men were looking at such things as Billy's conduct, which they found reprehensible. Organization Men drank and maybe they fooled around, but they were never open about it. Organization Men bitched and moaned, but they didn't air dirty linen in public as Billy did when he was upset about something.

To them Billy was a very loose cannon, so they were afraid of Billy Martin and what he might do or say. Rather than try to live with his gaucheries, the Tigers fired him with one year left on his contract.

The Tigers' serious reservations about Billy began in late March 1973 when Billy and pitching coach Art Fowler were drinking in a bar in Lakeland, Florida, during spring training. As with the incident with pitcher Dave Boswell in Minnesota, Billy got in trouble because one of his players, Ike Blessit, was drinking in the same bar he was drinking in. Blessit, who is black, was one of the Tigers' young prospects. Ike was one of the more colorful characters that the staid Tigers ever had. Unfortunately for the Tigers, he turned out to be a star mostly in his own mind.

The first day the Tigers brought Ike to the big leagues, Al Kaline was taking batting practice. The Tiger star was on the downward slide, and he was fouling off pitch after pitch. Ike told him, "Get out of there and let the blessed one show you how to do it."

Ike, a rookie, should never have been drinking at the bar where Billy and Art were, but it was his air of superiority that convinced him that he had just as much right to drink there as the big-leaguers. On this night the Blessed One had a little too much to drink, and he got into an argument with a white patron over a girl, who was white. This didn't sit too well with the bartender, who called the police.

When Billy went over and told Blessit he should leave, the player told him, "I'm a big leaguer. Why can't I be here, too?"

Billy told him, "Son, get the fuck out of here."

The two had left the bar and were talking together outside when the police pulled up. A policeman told Blessit he was under arrest. Billy told him, "He hasn't done anything."

Billy began raging at the cop.

"Okay, you're under arrest, too," the policeman told him. Billy was charged with swearing in public and was fined thirty-two dollars.

Blessit ended up playing in four games in 1972. It comprised his entire major league career.

The next public disturbance, shortly after the Blessit incident, was created by Billy over what he perceived to be interference by GM Jim Campbell with one of his players.

Outfielder Willie Horton was upset with Billy. The year before Horton had been hit in the eye with a pitch, was out a week, and after he returned he asked Billy to take him out of the lineup a couple of times, which infuriated Billy. In Cleveland the two got into a shouting match in the Tiger dugout, and the players had to pull Billy away because Horton was too strong to move and they were afraid someone was going to kill someone if they didn't do something.

The next spring Billy began platooning him, and Horton felt that at age twenty-nine he shouldn't have to be a platoon player, and he complained to the press, which was a no-no with Billy. It was a matter of time before Billy retaliated, and true to form, Billy charged that Horton wasn't hustling during· an exhibition game and kept Horton out of the lineup the next day.

Horton walked out of the Lakeland ballpark in the sixth inning and went to see Campbell.

After the game Billy met with Horton and Campbell, who asked the two to bury the hatchet.

After the meeting Billy announced he was quitting as manager. He said he didn't feel he was getting sufficient backing from his general manager. He felt Horton had defied him, and he wanted his moody slugger fined and suspended. Campbell didn't want to do that.

"I've had it. I resign," Billy said.

Ten hours later Martin was still missing. When asked by a reporter if Billy was serious about quitting, Campbell said, "I can't understand Billy Martin. Can you?"

After drinking all night at the local Holiday Inn, Billy called Campbell at his home at five-thirty in the morning and woke him up. He apologized and was forgiven. Afterward Billy said, "Campbell promised me that no player would go to him without going through me."

The Tigers were in the hunt through 1973, sitting in first place in early summer. Contributing to the Tigers' success was Billy's resurrection of relief pitcher John Hiller.

Hiller had undergone heart surgery, and few in the Tigers organization wanted to risk the chance he might drop dead on the mound. Hiller had a meeting with Billy at the Coach House. He said he wanted a chance.

"What did the doctor say?" Billy asked.

"He said I was going to die of something," Hiller replied.

Billy had Art Fowler check out his stuff in the bullpen. In the bar that night Fowler told Billy, "He can throw the fucking ball through a wall. And it moves!"

Billy went to Campbell, who said it was too great a risk. Billy told Campbell, "The kid is going to die of something. This is what he loves to do."

Hiller got his chance, and in 1973 under Billy and Art, John Hiller had 10 wins, 38 saves, and a 1.44 ERA. The next year he won 17 games. Again Billy had seen the talent.

But as the days wore on, the toll the long season had on the older players began to be felt, and the team slipped behind the youthful Baltimore Orioles.

As it often did in the latter part of a pennant race, the pressure began to get to Billy, his drinking increased, and his behavior become more erratic.

He feuded openly with outfielder Jim Northrup, a starter under Billy in 1972 but a platoon player this year. Then Billy skipped a charter flight from Oakland to Chicago in order to meet Patty Stark, his steady girlfriend who lived in Kansas City. Billy showed up for the White Sox game forty minutes late.

General manager Jim Campbell knew Billy was married to Gretchen. He wasn't happy that Billy was running around on her, that this relationship was causing him to shirk his duties to the team.

Said Campbell, "There were times he would go fishing or would show up late at the park without an explanation. When I questioned him about it, he would say, 'I'm here for the game, ain't I?' It was hard for Billy Martin to understand his obligations as a manager. I thought he would learn. He never did."

Then when the Tigers lost a doubleheader to the White Sox, Billy publicly voiced what had been troubling him all season long by criticizing Tigers minor-league-development executives Eddie Katalinas and Hoot Evers for failing to provide him with young players to buttress his team.

Billy was riding his players very hard, and he was becoming harder to live with. His fuse was short, and on the last day of August, after a game with the Cleveland Indians, Billy created an embarrassing situation for the Tigers when he told reporters he had ordered his pitchers to throw spitballs because Indian pitcher Gaylord Perry was throwing them and the umpires had refused to stop him. Billy said he had ordered Joe Coleman to throw spitters in the eighth inning and Fred Scherman to do so in the ninth.

If American League president Joe Cronin and commissioner Bowie Kuhn didn't stop Perry, Billy said, his pitchers would continue to throw the illegal spitball. Billy added to everyone's discomfort by calling Cronin and Kuhn "gutless."

Jim Campbell, deeply embarrassed at such a breach of corporate etiquette, ordered Billy to keep quiet. It didn't matter whether Billy was right or wrong in what he was saying. What was important was *how* he was saying it. Campbell might have tolerated a memo, but not a public airing of such an issue. Campbell was piqued that Martin had spoken out against the commissioner, the league president, Tiger executives, *and* the players in their minor league system.

Said Campbell, "You just can't have that sort of thing. It breaks down the efficiency of your whole organization."

The next day, instead of heeding what Billy was saying about Perry, who admitted throwing a spitter years later in his autobiography, *Me and the Spitter*, Cronin suspended Billy for three days.

Said Cronin, "Your blatant action and your endorsement of such tactics cannot be tolerated."

On the third day of his suspension, Jim Campbell fired Billy for not playing by the "policy and guidelines" of the organization. Campbell called Martin into his office on September 2, 1973, and told him he was fired "for the good of the organization."

"Didn't I do what was good for the organization?" Billy asked. "Didn't I win and draw people?"

But once again, winning and drawing people weren't what was called for. The Tigers, like the Twins, would have preferred a less independent manager who paid more attention to the needs of the team executives.

According to Campbell, Billy's outbursts had "destroyed" the morale of the front office. More to the point, Billy's outbursts had been an accurate appraisal of the Detroit farm system at the time, which caused Campbell deep personal embarrassment. Campbell let coach Joe Schultz finish out the last nineteen games and then hired Billy's former Yankee teammate Ralph Houk. However, in talking about Billy's limitations, the manager he compared him to was Cincinnati's Sparky Anderson, who would later manage the Tigers.

Said Campbell, "Sparky Anderson understands the different parts of a baseball team. I don't think Billy ever did."

Billy was as shocked at being fired by the Tigers as he had been in Minnesota. Said Billy, "Did I or did I not do a job for them? When they needed me, I came in and did the job. Didn't I give them a winner? I'm going to bow out gracefully. I'll let Jim Campbell explain to the whole world why he fired me. If I had it to do all over again, I wouldn't do anything differently.

"Apparently winning and drawing people to the park aren't enough. I've done it twice and been fired both times."

When Billy departed, the Tigers were 71–65.

Coach Joe Schultz finished the rest of the season 14–12. The next year under Houk the Tigers finished 72–90, last in the Eastern Division of the American League. The next year they were last again, and the year after that they were fifth.

Said Billy, "When you think about what I had been telling Campbell, who do you think was right about the Tigers being too old and too slow?"

# BILL REEDY

Away from Tiger Stadium, Billy had worked out a living arrangement that suited his lifestyle perfectly. He lived with his wife Gretchen and their son Billy Joe in Birmingham, Michigan, a car ride from Detroit in the suburbs, and he would meet various girlfriends or one-nighters at Art Fowler's apartment downtown, or he would go with Art to either the Lindell A.C., owned by his longtime friend Jimmy Butsicaris, or to Russell's Steak House or Eastman's Gaslight with Art's good friends Bill and Carol Reedy.

Art Fowler had met Bill Reedy on an airplane flight in 1962. Reedy had been in the service at the time, and Art was still pitching for the California Angels. It was the All-Star break, and the two men were sitting together on the plane, and they had a few drinks together and became friendly.

For years Art would call Bill Reedy to tell him how things were going. While at Denver, Art told Bill how Billy Martin had offered him a pitching coach's job if Billy ever made it to the majors. "But you know how that shit goes," Fowler said to Reedy.

When Billy did hire Art to be his pitching coach with the Twins in 1969, the three men became a barhopping triumvirate whenever the Twins came to Detroit.

After Billy was fired by the Twins, Billy and Art were away from the junior circuit in 1970, but at the end of the year Bill Reedy got a call from Art.

Reedy was working as a printer at the *Detroit News* at the time, and the phone rang late one night. It was Art, who was drinking, calling from his home in

Spartanburg, South Carolina. He said, "Guess where we're coming, big boy?" He told Reedy that Billy had just called him to say he had just cut a deal to manage the Tigers.

And for the better part of three years, Billy Martin, Art Fowler, and Bill Reedy were together constantly on weekends and sometimes after home games.

With Bill Reedy, Billy Martin felt comfortable. In the years before Bill Reedy met Art Fowler, Reedy went to local Detroit bars with a pool-hustling friend of his, walked in freshly shaven around midnight and left with the good-looking women. As a result, Reedy and his friend got into fistfights often. Reedy, who had boxed in the Army, loved to fight.

One night in 1968 at the Anchor Bar, Reedy and four of his friends beat up eighteen people, including some writers from the *Detroit Free-Press*. The only one identified in the fight was Reedy, and after the police came and arrested him at his job, he refused to name names. He spent three days in jail and had to pay $22,000 in costs.

When Art Fowler came to Detroit in 1969, Reedy stopped going to the country-and-western bars and began hanging out in the less troubled hotel bars. Because he didn't want to get Art in trouble, he also stopped fighting.

Although both Billy and Bill Reedy enjoyed a good fight, that was not the reason for their friendship.

Hard drinking was one bond. Because Billy was an alcoholic, many of his closest friends, including most of the coaches closest to him, were drinkers. They shared a lifestyle that they enjoyed, the camaraderie of men who loved to sit at a bar and drink. Bill Reedy could hoist them with the best. So could Art Fowler. When Bill Reedy opened his first bar, the Hummer, in Detroit in 1984, it became Billy's primary watering hole in town.

But that wasn't the most important factor either. Billy liked Bill Reedy because he was a good listener. Bill Reedy was the one person to whom Martin could open his heart.

"What's the matter, Billy?"

"Aw, nothing," and then Billy would spend the next two or three hours talking about it.

Bar talk provided an outlet for Billy that others reserved for their wives or for psychiatrists, neither of whom Billy fully trusted.

"We would meet in a place called the Coach House, which was two blocks from the Lindell A.C.," said Reedy. "It was a very small bar, not a lot of people went in it, no one knew Billy would be in there. I would show up an hour and a half after the game. That gave Billy and Art a half hour to shower, and at the park they could talk baseball for forty-five minutes. Because when we were together, we didn't talk baseball. We talked about hunting and fishing, and business. Just anything that was going on, boxing. We didn't talk baseball. He never asked my opinion about the team or his managing. I don't think he asked my opinion six times in twenty years. It wasn't my business.

"We talked politics because he knew I was involved in that, and we talked about women.

"And sometimes Billy would come down to the Coach House and see my wife, Carol, and my son, Billy, and he would leave an open check. He would go home, drive up to Birmingham, which was outside Detroit, and Art and I would finish out until two in the morning, and I would get up and go to work the next morning. It was killing me those two and a half years he was in Detroit. I was glad when they went out on the road."

When he wasn't involved in one-night stands, Billy often would call Bill Reedy and ask to meet him alone, or to travel to another city like Chicago, Cleveland, sometimes New York, to be with him. They'd sit together in a bar and drink, two buddies passing the time. Sometimes Billy wanted to talk. Sometimes he didn't. Rarely was the conversation very heavy or philosophical. It wasn't too long before Billy's routine on Sunday would include going to noon mass and calling Bill Reedy.

Along with his other attributes, Billy saw that Bill Reedy was a person who accepted him without criticism or comment. Billy *hated* criticism. Bill Reedy adopted a nonjudgmental attitude toward Billy. Reedy's thinking was that whatever Billy did was his own business.

It wasn't long before their bond became so close that Billy trusted Reedy and his wife with his most complicated affairs: his active sex life.

If Billy needed someone to squire one of his girlfriends on the road, he'd have Bill and Carol Reedy meet him, and Carol would do the chaperoning.

"Sometimes," said Bill Reedy, "Billy would ask me to go to Chicago and bring Carol and Billy, and Carol became the buffer. She would entertain whoever Billy wanted her to entertain. And we'd meet him in Chicago, and he'd fly in one girlfriend or whoever."

Carol, who also tried not to be judgmental about Billy's sybaritic lifestyle, for many years was amazed at Billy's appetite for young girls.

"Art had an apartment in Detroit," said Carol Reedy, "and Billy was always bugging him about letting him use the apartment. Arthur used to say, 'Billy wants to use that apartment, and I don't want him staying there.'

"One day Art said he was coming home, and there was this young girl out in the hallway, and she's banging on the door, saying, 'Where is my girlfriend? You bring her out here or I'm going to call the police.' Arthur said, 'Oh no, don't do that. I'll get her.' He went in. There was Billy with this little girl who was about sixteen years old, and Art said, 'Billy, God, there is going to be trouble.' Billy said, 'Get her ass out of here. She's ugly anyway.' But she had big boobs.

"Arthur told me, 'They are going to kick me out of there.'

"One day I was at my doctor's office, my gynecologist, and he began to tell how the daughter of his minister—she was seventeen—had gone down to Tiger Stadium and she somehow got to Billy Martin, and he told me how Billy invited her, and she went up to the hotel room with him.

"I wondered, What was she doing at Tiger Stadium without an adult? I said, 'I don't feel sorry for these seventeen-year-old girls. I'm not proud of Billy doing that, but that's his business, and I don't get into his business. But I'd like to kick her father's fanny, minister or no, for not knowing where that kid is. If it was my daughter, I'd know.' But people are like that. These groupies would hang around and show off this and show that, and don't wear this or that. Billy loved the young girls.''

Said Bill Reedy, ''Gretchen and Billy Joe were with him in Detroit, and he was relatively happy then. As happy as Billy Martin could be, because he always had that roving eye.

''Billy and Gretchen lasted more than ten years, but it was only a matter of time before she gave up. Again it was a case of a wife neglected after too many years who finally decided to have a life of her own.''

Bill Reedy understood why Gretchen wanted it to end. ''Whatever she did, I'd say she was justified. I've only talked to Gretchen a few times on the phone, and I found her to be a nice lady.''

While Bill and Carol were aiding Billy in his love life, at the same time they were passing the friendship test of the always-suspicious Billy Martin.

Part of the reason Billy and Bill Reedy got along so well was that Bill Reedy accepted Billy on his terms. Bill Reedy overlooked Billy's faults and saw only the friendship that Billy radiated toward him. Bill Reedy provided Billy an ear twenty-four hours a day, and he provided a safe haven whenever Billy needed to escape from the pressures bearing down on him. And when they were together, Bill Reedy, like many of Billy's close friends, acted as a bodyguard, fending off potential combatants in bars or, when need be, beating them up. And every once in a while, when Billy was able to avoid their defenses and punch someone, Reedy would take the rap, saying he had been the one who had thrown the punch.

Over the years Billy Martin saw time and again that Bill Reedy was a true friend. Bill Reedy, Billy knew, was someone he could count on without reservation.

# THE LONE RANGER

After two tours of duty as manager, Billy Martin had won two division championships with teams that had no business being there. He also was fired twice and both times was blasted by team administrators for not being a team player. Who would hire Billy knowing what they knew about him?

A friend or a desperate man.

Bob Short, Billy's next employer, was both. After Billy was fired by the Twins at the end of the 1969 season, Billy did some campaigning for Short, who was then running in the Democratic primary for governor of Minnesota.

Short was a trucking magnate, the head of Short Line trucking. Through his connections with the Teamsters, he had borrowed $10,000, and with other investors he bought the Washington Senators, which he moved to Texas beginning in the 1972 season. Short's problem was that he was undercapitalized. Short desperately needed an attraction if he was going to hold on to his team. Billy was the perfect answer for a terrible team that was drawing only flies.

Just as soon as Short heard that Billy had been fired by the Tigers, he immediately fired his manager, Whitey Herzog, whom he had called the best young manager in baseball only four days before, and hired Billy. Short said he didn't want to lose Martin to another team.

Billy, who had a contract with Detroit and could have continued to sit out for another year, was reluctant to get back into managing so quickly.

But Short would not allow Martin to say no. He gave him a three-year contract at $65,000 a year, a new house, and the use of a new car for the next three years. Most important, Short gave Billy last say over the twenty-five-man roster. Billy could pick any minor leaguers he wanted, and he could veto trades.

Bill Reedy remembered just how smooth the transition had been. "After the Tigers fired Billy and Art, Art stayed a week in Detroit," said Reedy. "We partied for a week, and Art and I stayed close. Art took it like he always did: 'Who gives a shit? I'll go back South.' Budweiser was seventy cents a bottle back then in Spartanburg. Art didn't give a shit about anything.

"So he left my brother's gas station, and three hours later I hear, 'Bob Short fired Whitey Herzog and hired Billy Martin.' And they said, 'You would fire Whitey Herzog?' Short said, 'I would fire my mother if I had a chance to hire Billy Martin.'

"By the time Art got home, there was a phone call. 'Call Billy.' He got on an airplane and flew to where he had to fly to meet Billy. They were going back to work in Texas."

When Billy took over in Texas, the Rangers were a chronic second-division club.

Since the move from Washington in 1972, the Rangers had been perhaps the sorriest franchise in all of baseball. Management had treated its players arbitrarily and shabbily. Most anyone who has played for the Rangers has horror stories about how management manipulated and hurt their careers, not to benefit the team, but to save nickels and dimes. Until recently Texas has been considered the graveyard of the American League, except during the two and a half years when Billy Martin was managing. Those years, most players who were there will tell you, the Rangers had it together. And Billy Martin was the reason why.

In his first appearance as manager of the Rangers, Billy raised eyebrows when he announced that the Rangers were going to win the pennant. Now.

"If I didn't think I could win, I wouldn't be here today," he said. Those listening didn't believe even Billy Martin could make the Rangers competitive. Few realized just what a baseball genius he was.

Bob Short had pulled a major coup in 1969 when he hired Ted Williams to manage his Washington Senators. Williams, a fabulous personality, was not a particularly good manager. He had trouble understanding why his players couldn't hit as well as he had, and the team struggled to the point where Williams couldn't stand the losing anymore and quit after the 1972 season. That year the Rangers were 54–100.

Short chose outfielder Whitey Herzog to manage in 1973. It was Herzog's first stint as manager. The team didn't do any better under Herzog. When Short fired him, the Rangers were 47–91, last in the American League West. The Rangers went 9–14 as Billy spent the last few weeks observing, judging, and biding his time until the spring. The team's final record was 57–105.

That spring Short and Billy worked together to rebuild the team. They drank together, palled around together. It was the relationship Billy had always dreamed about and would never again have with a team owner. Bob Short recalled one evening when they were drinking together, Billy was reminiscing about his playing days with the Yankees when suddenly Billy said to him, "I'm a Yankee. No matter what my uniform shirt says, I'm a Yankee. Don't you ever forget it."

Short, who had been a fan of those Yankee teams, allowed Billy to do whatever he wanted to do. Billy turned the club upside down, bringing in new blood from the Rangers' farm system. When asked if the Rangers would be contenders, Billy said, "I not only believe it, I'm staking my reputation on it, and my baseball reputation means a lot to me."

Lenny Randle, the team's all-purpose infielder and a sensitive, intelligent man, remembered what the Ranger organization was like in 1973 before Billy came, and what a difference Billy's presence meant to the team.

"I couldn't understand some of the things that were going on," said Randle. "I felt baseball wasn't a fair business to be in at that point. Part of it was what was happening in general, the Curt Flood incident, the Andy Messersmith incident, and it bothered me the Rangers were trading good guys and were not giving guys who deserved to play a chance.

"I was at Spokane in '73. Del Wilber was the manager. I was going to quit baseball, and Del talked me out of quitting. He said, 'You're my second baseman, I shoot from the hip, I won't mess with you,' and he encouraged me to have fun and enjoy the game. He told that to everyone, and everyone produced, we had an all-star team, and we won the Pacific Coast League title. And everyone on that Spokane club went to the big leagues, Bill Madlock, Ron Pruitt, Bobby Jones, Don Stanhouse. But Whitey Herzog couldn't see that at the time. He saw his way.

"We didn't want to go up to the Rangers. We wanted to stay in Triple A with Del. Money didn't mean anything. There was more to life than what was going on up there. The Rangers were a joke. We were having more fun doing what we were doing, winning, enjoying life and playing, getting more value out of that as human beings than we would have had we gone to the Rangers.

"And when Bob Short got rid of Herzog and hired Billy, that was the smartest move they ever made. It was the greatest move for the state of Texas and for baseball, period.

"Billy Martin knew talent. He came to spring training in '74, and he said, 'I don't know what they didn't see in the past, but I see a pennant.' They probably thought he was crazy. But we knew we had good players. The Rangers had never promoted them, never given them a chance.

"Billy took Mike Hargrove from A ball, and he hit .325. He took Jim Sundberg from A ball and made him a major league catcher. Nobody else could have done that. They would have let him bury himself for four or five years and then given him a shot, where Billy saw he was ready right away. Billy gave me a chance, and I hit .302. He moved Dave Nelson from third base and teamed him with Toby Harrah to be our double-play combination. Billy saw Roy Howell's talent and brought him up. He took Jeff Burroughs, who had done nothing, and Jeff became a hitting star and the Most Valuable Player in the league [in 1974].

"Billy sent Bill Madlock in a trade to the Cubs for Fergie Jenkins, and Fergie won twenty-five games. Fergie was so good he could move the infielders and the outfielders to the exact spot where the batter was going to hit the ball. That's how much confidence he had out on the mound. Even though it was his first year in the American League. He was phenomenal.

"Billy Martin knew talent, respected players, and knew how to get the most out of each guy, and if a guy didn't do it, Billy would send him elsewhere. If a guy did it, Billy would go to bat for you contractwise, salarywise, moneywise. He'd say, 'Give me a hundred percent, and I'm your man.' There was *no one* who didn't want to play for him. Sure, he kept twelve guys happy, and ten were up in the air, and the rest hated him. Maybe he *was* General Patton, but he won. And at the end of the year *everyone* was happy with the checks we got or with the contracts they negotiated the next year.

"Playing for Billy was the most fun I ever had in baseball. It was terrific. I remember squeezing in three games. There was a man on third, get him in, bunt. Billyball. He knew I could bunt. I could bunt for a hit almost at will, so I would bunt to second base for a hit and get the run in. That's what made me make the team.

"You did the little things to win games. You'd steal a base or hit-and-run, or you'd steal a sign from the catcher while you were on base and pass it to the hitter. 'A fastball is coming inside.' And boom, there it goes. Billy taught us strategy, the scientific approach to baseball. A lot of managers don't teach that, and it's the difference between winning and showing up. All the students of Billy's had good, long careers. Some guys couldn't do it because they felt there was too much pressure. 'I'm a power hitter, why am I bunting? I want to go deep.' And he'd pop up. A lot of guys weren't students of the game before Billy came along, and when they became that, that was the difference between being a winner and a loser."

The Rangers improved dramatically in 1974. The team hustled, hit-and-ran, bunted, squeezed, and stole bases and games.

Early in the season a pitcher failed to cover first base. The next day Billy had the whole staff practicing the play. Billy never said a word. For the rest of the season, no one ever messed up the play.

The first game the Rangers played against his old club, the Detroit Tigers, was a triumph for Billy. The Tigers had brought up Ron LeFlore, whom Billy had recommended to GM Jim Campbell even though LeFlore had spent hard time at Jackson State Penitentiary in Michigan. LeFlore twice was on second base for the Tigers, and twice Billy's pitchers picked him off second. And then Billy had a player steal home on them to prove a point that the Rangers were for real and also that the Tiger brass never should have let him go.

Billy always preached loyalty to the team, and he couldn't have been prouder during a game the Rangers played in Cleveland against the Indians. It was Ten-Cent Beer Night, and toward the end of the game some of the fans had become so drunk and rowdy that they ran out onto the field to attack Ranger outfielder Jeff Burroughs. The other players ran out to rescue him.

Cleveland had to forfeit. Martin was proud of the all-for-one attitude displayed out there.

Short and Billy had a marriage made in heaven. As late as July 30, the Rangers were in a tie for second place, and attendance was up by 200,000 fans.

Billy's Texas honeymoon ended when Short, out of money, sold the team in midsummer to Brad Corbett, the president of the Robintech Corporation. Corbett's main line of business was PVC pipe.

Billy was under the impression that his role on the team would remain unchanged.

"The new owners have given me the full control of the team," he announced. "There's no middleman bothering me. It's beautiful."

And so it was during Corbett's first season, when the Rangers almost won the American League West. The team that kept Billy from a third division title was the powerful Oakland A's, managed by Dick Williams and led by an all-star cast.

Billy's Rangers played hard and tough and gave the A's a fight. In one game against the A's, Billy's new glamour boy, Jeff Burroughs, hit a three-run homer off A's ace Vida Blue in the first inning en route to a 10–3 win. The A's Gene Tenace had hit two homers for the A's, and late in the game Ranger pitcher Jim Bibby hit Tenace between the shoulder blades with a fastball.

One of the players who terrorized the Rangers was A's slugger Reggie Jackson. On Easter Sunday, Texas led the A's in the eighth inning, 2–1. The one A's run was a Reggie Jackson home run. In the eighth Jackson got up to face pitcher Steve Hargan. There were runners on second and third. Most managers would have walked Jackson intentionally. Martin opted to pitch to Jackson, who homered to win the game.

Mused Jackson, "I don't know whether they don't respect me or whether they don't think I'm that good."

On September 6, Texas played in Oakland. The day before, during a 3–0 Catfish Hunter victory, the scoreboard gloated, "Good Night, Billy Boy."

Texas won the next three games of the series. Ferguson Jenkins won the finale. Texas was only five and a half games out, and then on September 13 and 14 the Rangers beat the A's twice and were only four games out. It was the closest the Rangers would come, as the pitchers began to tire and fail. Oakland won the finale of that series, with Rollie Fingers pitching five spectacular innings of relief.

Roy Howell, who was brought up from the minors for the Rangers' September homestretch, has his own theory about what turned the tide against the Rangers.

"We had the A's," said Howell, "and then Billy made a comment about the California Angels right before we had to play them in a series. Billy said, 'They can take batting practice in the hotel and not break anything.' That was Billy's way of telling the Angels to go piss up a rope. He didn't like their style of baseball. He didn't like the way they played the game—a ping, a dive, a duck. They didn't have anyone who could hit the ball out of the park. Mickey Rivers was their star player.

"Billy thought by doing that it would jump our engine and maybe piss them off enough to take them out of their game plan, but it didn't. They chinked us to death. They came and kicked our ass three straight games.

"That took care of that year."

The legendary A's finished five games ahead of Billy's no-name Rangers. At the end of the year Billy was voted Manager of the Year by the Associated Press.

"If we had had just one more consistent pitcher, we would have won it," said Billy.

Billy attributed his success in Texas to a lack of interference from the front office.

Said Billy, "Because of Short, I was able to bring us Sundberg and Hargrove and get Jenkins, and I was able to promote Lenny Randle from the minors.

"It's so much easier not to have to fight with other members of an organization to get the players I want. If I hadn't had the say-so at Texas, no way I would have gotten Sundberg and Hargrove. The farm director or the general manager would have complained. They'd be yelling at me, 'Are you trying to tell us how to do our job?' Typical red-tape crap, instead of just giving me who I want and helping me and the team.

"I've gone from player to scout to third-base coach to minor league manager to major league manager, and along the way I've picked up many years of knowledge and experience. But when I sit and talk to personnel directors, they fight me. 'Are you trying to tell me who to bring up?' they say. It's ridiculous. You'd think we were from different organizations."

The Rangers were picked as the team most likely to win the pennant in 1975. Said Martin, "We will win the American League."

It had been a great year for Billy. It was perhaps the finest job of managing since Casey Stengel rebuilt the fading Yankees in 1949. Perhaps it was even greater.

Said Billy, "I have a real foundation here. I think I'll stay here the rest of my career."

# STABBED

# IN THE BACK

W hen Billy arrived for spring training for the 1975 season, it was with the expectation that the Texas Rangers would win the American League pennant. In 1975 the team started slowly with pitching problems. Pitcher Fergie Jenkins went from 25 wins in 1974 to 17 wins. Jim Bibby, who had won 19 games in 1974, had arm problems, and Billy traded him to Cleveland for Gaylord Perry. Jim Sundberg played every game but didn't hit even .200. The Rangers were a .500 team, but they were still playing good ball.

Roy Howell played third base for Billy in 1975. Howell, just twenty-two, was one of those players who dove for every ball, hustled on every play, didn't mind getting his uniform dirty—in short, Billy's kind of ballplayer. Howell, like Lenny Randle and Toby Harrah and most of the starters except catcher Jim Sundberg, who Billy tormented beyond reason, loved to play for Billy.

"I had heard all the stories about Billy, how he was tough on young players, how he expected the game to be played the way he played it, which I had no problem with," said Howell. "I'm a dirtbag, and I enjoy playing the game that way. I make up my own judgments based on how people treat me, so I went there with an open mind.

"Billy did not like young ballplayers. He wanted players with experience and knowledge, but the guys from the Ranger farm system, Mike Hargrove, Jim Sundberg, Mike Cubbage, and myself, we knew how to play the game. He didn't have to teach us, and that took away the youth bullshit that Billy had trouble with.

"We went in open, and he gave us a chance to play; a new generation was coming. Every ten years the generation rolls over. With the Texas ball club it was rollover time.

"Billy was tough on you if you let him be tough on you," said Howell. "My whole thing with Billy was, 'You can go so far, but there are boundaries.' And we went face-to-face more than once, but the thing with Billy, he wanted to know whether you'd stand and run or whether you'd stand and fight. Billy wanted you to stand and fight. When I got to the big leagues, they gave me uniform number 27. I had been wearing 13 in the minor leagues. I walked up to him at the batting cage in spring training and told him I wanted to wear 13. Billy said, 'Nobody wears 13 on my ball club.'

"I looked him straight in the eye and said, 'Why, are you scared?' He turned around and looked at me, and he started laughing. 'Go get the fucking number,' he said. 'I don't care.'

"That showed me he respected me. And so I wore 13.

"Billy would test you. With Billy, Billy has a love-hate relationship with his players. Either you love him or you hate him. He builds you up to be the biggest thing since bubble gum, and then he tears you down to see how you react. Today you're the best; tomorrow, you're the lowest piece of shit on earth.

"The biggest thing, Billy was unpredictable when and why and how he would do something. You'd be on a hitting streak, and with no explanation, you'd be on the bench for a week. And the next time you played, you'd be hitting against Sparky Lyle in the ninth.

" 'What kind of balls you got, kid?'

"How do you handle that? You handle it by going out on a daily basis and doing your job and going on from there.

"Billy was especially hard on Jim Sundberg. It tore Sunny up a lot. Sunny was very impressionable, came out of Iowa, had exactly three-quarters of a season at A ball when Bill Fahey broke his nose and Billy made him the starting catcher in '74.

"Billy pounded him hard. Billy called a lot of the pitches, and if Billy called a pitch, the pitcher threw it, and the batter hit it, to Billy it was still Sunny's fault. Or the pitcher's fault. If an opposing batter got a hit on an 0–2 count, the pitcher got fined five hundred dollars, and so did Sunny.

"Even if you did what the boss said, if it didn't turn out that way, it would still be your fault, and that would upset guys. They were the ones who got their ass ripped. That was the hardest thing for the guys. And you couldn't let it get to you. Of course, if you're human, it did. Sunny got white hair real quick, and he started drinking scotch.

"During the game Billy was a good tactician. He knew what to do. Most of the times he made the moves that were supposed to be made. If he moved a defense or if he made a move to bring in a left-hander, and we gave it up, then Billy would snap. Nobody was safe when Billy would snap. He would start at one end of the bench and go to the other end, saying anything that came up from the last month. And then when the team came off the field, he'd go up and down on us.

"Billy motivated by fear. 'Either you do it this way, or I have the power to get rid of you.' Even with the veteran players, he tried to keep that edge of motivation with fear, though with our ball club the veterans weren't going to let Billy, or anyone, manipulate them that way.

"I had a good lesson by watching the veterans and seeing how they handled things. They shut him off. It's like your mom and dad, it goes in one ear and out the other. If you know what to do, you go out and do it and you get to the point where you don't listen anymore. If you can do that, you'd be okay. If you took it personally, then Billy would get you. You *could not* take it personally. I never did.

"The thing was, Billy was the best there was at showing you ways to beat somebody.''

The two players Billy rarely confronted were pitchers Fergie Jenkins and Gaylord Perry, who was now throwing his spitter for him rather than against him.

Ron Pruitt, a catcher behind the indestructible Sundberg, recalled one game when he was caught in the crossfire between Billy and the cantankerous Gaylord Perry.

"This was the very first game I played in the field," said Pruitt. "Sundberg got thrown out of the game, and I had to come in. Gaylord Perry was pitching.

"Gaylord would always call his pitches. He didn't want anybody calling his pitches. He had a wipe system with his glove, where you put down a finger, and he'd wipe up or wipe down, and you'd have to count. I really did not know what he was throwing, any pitch he threw. I was just concentrating on catching the ball—I don't know how I caught them—I must have been so psyched. I wasn't going to let anything by me, whether it hit me in the arm or whatever.

"That was in '75, when Gaylord was at the top of his game. I came out to the mound, and he said, 'I'm the only one who knows when I'm going to throw a spitball. Don't call a spitball. I'll let you know. I'll wipe.'

"And then I went into the dugout, and Billy said, 'Look, I'm calling the pitches. Look over to me after every pitch.'

"The guys told me it was a hundred-dollar fine if I missed a sign from Billy.

"So I'm thinking, Aw, no.

"Whatever Billy would call, I would put that finger down, and then Gaylord would wipe to it anyway. It sounded simple enough, but I couldn't keep track of the signs, and so I really didn't know what he was throwing.

"The game went on, and it was the eighth inning, and we were playing Minnesota, a tight situation, runners on second and third, and Billy hadn't given a spitball sign the whole time.

"I looked over, and Billy was licking his fingers, big, like it was so obvious. I thought, Oh no. So I gave Gaylord a spitball sign, and he looked at me like, What, are you crazy? And he wiped it off and threw a curveball, and Dan Ford hit it off the wall for a double to put Minnesota ahead.

"Billy came out. He said to me, 'What the hell? I told you what to throw. What sign did I give you?' I said, 'A spitball.' And Gaylord said, 'I'm the only one to call a spitball,' and they got into a big argument.

"And I'm thinking, What the heck did I do?

"Gaylord came to my defense. He said to me, 'Don't worry about it.'

"That was the first time I played in the field in the big leagues, and I thought, Oh man, if this is what I have to look forward to . . . If this is the way it's going to be, this is one tough league."

The one buffer between Billy and the players was pitching coach Art Fowler. Roy Howell, the third baseman, remembers Art's visits to the mound.

"It didn't matter who it was," said Howell, "Art would walk out there, look you straight in the eye if he could, 'cause his eyes were always cockeyed, and he'd say, 'Billy asked me to come out here, and I got one thing to say to you: If you can't get this guy out, I'll kiss your ass.' And he would turn around and go back. That's all Art would ever say.

"He didn't say much to Fergie or Gaylord, 'cause what are you gonna tell them? He was only out there because Billy got the ass about something."

Lenny Randle, the second baseman, especially enjoyed it when Billy sent Art out to talk to Fergie Jenkins.

"It was great," said Randle. "Art would say, 'God dang, Fergie, I don't know what the hell I'm doing out here, I'd rather be shooting quail. But Billy sent me out to talk to you. You're getting ready to go into the gall-dang Hall of Fame. What the fuck am I doing out here? I'm just stalling, I guess. What do you want to do, talk, or do you want to get this guy out?'

"Fergie would laugh. 'I know, Art. I need a breather. I'll get him out.'

"We'd crack up. It would relieve the tension. Art was a tension reliever for the whole team. He was the kind of guy you could be loose with every day, joke with, and he'd keep the stress off you. A lot of people didn't realize what a catalyst he was for every team.

"Sure Art drank with Billy, but we didn't care. In Texas it was good old boys having fun. There was no controversy about it. No one had cared what Babe Ruth did when he played. Then it became, 'Inquiring minds want to know.' But it had nothing to do with what went on on the field."

Billy's relationship with Brad Corbett, team president Bobby Brown, and GM Dan O'Brien was also "off the field," but it had everything to do with Billy's future in Texas. Since the day Bob Short sold the team to Corbett, Billy resented the new owners. He had been expecting to have the same control over the team that he had had under Short, and Corbett began treating him as Campbell had done and Griffith before him, as an underling rather than as the key decision maker. In 1975, Billy created issues concerning personnel that raged throughout the spring and summer.

Billy's major beef with the new GM, Danny O'Brien, concerned the teenage sensation Short had signed in 1973 out of high school, David Clyde.

Billy knew the kid wasn't anywhere near ready for the majors, but since Short was running out of money, Billy kept him on the team and pitched him in a few games in an attempt to boost the gate.

Once the wealthy Brad Corbett bought the team, Billy saw no further need to use the kid as a gate attraction. He wanted to send him down to the minors. Billy had no intention of pitching him, and Billy saw he was beginning to get into some major league drinking habits on the road.

"He was way over his head," Billy told me. "I wanted to get him away from there before he hurt himself too badly."

None of the new management, not owner Corbett, president Bobby Brown, or GM Danny O'Brien, would do it. Corbett hadn't told Billy that the arrangement had changed, but it was over David Clyde that Billy learned he no longer had final say over personnel.

Billy protested vehemently about keeping Clyde, as he should have. One who fought Billy on the issue was team president Bobby Brown, the heart surgeon who had been Billy's teammate with the Yankees.

According to Billy, Brown told him, "Billy, we can't send the kid down. It'll hurt his feelings."

Billy began screaming at his former teammate.

"We really got into it," Billy said. "It was the beginning of the end for me in Texas."

Billy hadn't been happy about keeping the eighteen-year-old on the squad when Short owned the team. He knew that the last pitcher to make it big from high school to the majors had been Bob Feller, but that was in the thirties, and it probably had been foolhardy for the Indians to have done that. The worst thing you can do to a kid, Billy knew, is start him out in a situation where he is overmatched. Billy even threatened to quit if Brown kept the kid up, but he backed down.

Brad Corbett, who in 1974 was an expert on piping, in 1975 became a self-proclaimed expert on baseball. He decided that this year he was going to have a hand in the decisions concerning trades and players. Corbett overruled Billy and sided with O'Brien on Clyde.

Clyde, who hurt his arm and never did have the career expected of him, places the blame on Billy when the men he should have condemned were Short and Corbett, people who wanted to use him as a drawing card.

"I was a pawn in Billy Martin's life," said Clyde. "All of that had a tremendous effect on me. I lost all confidence in my pitching ability. I started to drink. My marriage fell apart. I didn't know what I was doing half the time. I was miserable.

"Billy Martin hurt my career. I don't know if I will ever recover from those early years."

If the Ranger front office had followed Billy's advice, had sent Clyde down to the minors, and had let him pitch against kids of his own age and skill, Clyde might have developed. He couldn't have done any worse the way the Rangers handled him.

Another decision Corbett made over Billy's wishes was the acquisition of Willie Davis, a favorite player of Corbett's when Davis had been in his prime with the Dodgers. Unfortunately, he no longer was in his prime, and Billy was furious that the Rangers had given up young Don Stanhouse to get him.

There were a couple of incidents that also got Billy in further trouble with Brown, a genteel man with high moral standards. Brown had trouble abiding Billy's chronic drinking and his habit of bringing his girlfriend Patty Stark on the charter flights with the team.

Always fearful that his wife Gretchen would leave him or cheat on him, Billy protected himself from a surprise like the one given to him by his first wife, Lois, by always having a girlfriend in the wings. It was a pattern that Billy would continue over the next decade.

The odd aspect of this behavior was that everyone, especially the players, knew the girl he brought along wasn't his wife. But Billy was a person who took a lot of pleasure being escorted by young, beautiful girls. He wanted others to view him as being a stud. Billy was forty-seven. Patty Stark was a United Airlines stewardess in her early twenties. The girlfriend, later Billy's wife, who took Patty's place a couple years later would be in her mid-teens.

Some of the players who sat on the fence about how they felt about Billy were turned off by his constant flaunting of an active sex life with someone who was not his wife. The handful of ballplayers who respected their own wives enough not to participate in adulterous activity were repulsed.

On more than one occasion Billy bumped one of his players from the first-class section to coach so Patty could sit with him. Everyone on the charter flight took notice, but no one dared say anything.

One incident that hurt Billy in Bobby Brown's eyes occurred on just such a flight, when Billy slapped the team's elderly traveling secretary, Bert Hawkins, across the face. Hawkins's wife had asked if she could form a wives' club. Billy vetoed the idea of it. Billy always felt the wives should be kept separated so they couldn't compare salaries and couldn't share stories, an added protection for any philandering ballplayer. Billy felt the gossip of the wives served only to threaten morale. And since he had his girlfriend along with him on the road, Billy certainly didn't want *his* wife involved in any such club.

On a charter flight, both Billy and Hawkins had been doing some drinking, and when Hawkins spoke to Billy about his wife's plans for the wives' club, the two began arguing. When Hawkins raised his voice in anger, Billy slapped him. He later apologized, but the Texas front office had one more black mark to place against his name. Bobby Brown put Billy "on probation."

The other incident took place in the clubhouse after a game.

Under Billy's system, his catcher took the brunt of his merciless pressure. Just about anything that went wrong between the pitcher and catcher would be the catcher's fault. Texas catcher Jim Sundberg had taken Billy's abuse for one and a half seasons, and unlike some of the other players, the pressure from Billy made him ill. He was having heart palpitations and feared a heart attack. Mentally he feared he was going to have a nervous breakdown. He was in a no-win situation with Billy, and he couldn't take Billy's constant second-guessing and criticism.

Billy had a rule that if the game was tied or if men were in scoring position, Sundberg had to call a breaking ball. Fergie Jenkins was pitching, the bases were loaded, and Jenkins insisted on throwing a fastball, which the batter hit into center field for two runs.

Billy began screaming at Sundberg, who told him, "I didn't throw it, he did, why don't you go talk to him?" It was the first time the young catcher had stood up to him.

Billy yanked Sundberg from the game and demanded that Rangers president Bobby Brown send him to the minors. Brown, who was in the clubhouse after the game, refused.

Two days later Billy had forgotten the incident, telling Sundberg he was "the greatest catcher since Bill Dickey," but both Sundberg and Brown were turned off by Billy's behavior. Again it was form over substance. Brown thought Billy was being too tough on his players, and his view was confirmed when his players would complain to him about Billy.

Billy, for his part, felt that the front office was sabotaging him. He didn't want Corbett inviting players to dinner. He didn't want Brown talking to the players, listening to their complaints. He wanted complete support, knowing well that if a player was *allowed* to complain about the manager to the front office, he would, and Billy would lose control.

Billy was aware that his third-base coach, Frank Lucchesi, had formed an alliance with Corbett and was constantly criticizing Billy behind his back, telling Corbett what was wrong with the club. Billy was also aware that catcher Jim Sundberg, who Billy was driving to the brink of insanity, was siding with Lucchesi. Given a choice between siding with the man who was making him sick and driving him to drink, or anyone else, Sundberg chose to end his misery and go with Lucchesi.

Billy protested Corbett's open-door policy.

"A manager isn't trying to win a popularity contest," Billy always preached. "When the owner or the general manager opens his office to the players and sits and listens to their complaints, what do you think that does to the manager's authority? It cuts the balls right off the manager. And I tried to tell Corbett and Brown that."

The Ranger executives didn't like Billy, so they didn't listen. They continued to allow the players access. By the summer, Billy was complaining to reporters that Corbett and O'Brien were ruining his team because they didn't back him and because they had stopped listening to him with regard to player moves.

Billy told the press, "I can't win with the players Brad is forcing on me." Billy was correct about that, but the focus no longer was on winning or losing. To Brad Corbett, Billy was being "disloyal."

The final incident came when the California Angels released backup catcher Tom Egan. Billy wanted O'Brien to buy him to back up Sundberg. O'Brien refused. Billy flew into a tirade. He smashed his five-hundred-dollar wristwatch against the wall of his office. The watch had been a Christmas present from Brad Corbett.

The day after their argument, the Rangers held an Old-Timers' Day. Billy refused to participate. He was so disgusted, he wouldn't leave his office in the clubhouse.

Said Billy, "I had taken over the job the year before, and we had improved dramatically, and here I was in the middle of the same old bullshit again. Short had sold the ball club, and I was left all alone. It was apparent Corbett wanted to take over and do everything, and I didn't agree with him, so the handwriting was on the wall."

Newspaper stories began appearing in the local papers expressing Billy's frustration. The combination of the booze and Billy's sense of what was right for the team and what was wrong about it got the best of him. As in the case of most alcoholics whose judgment is impaired by the disease, Billy's actions could not have been more self-defeating. Emboldened by the booze, he committed employment suicide.

In the evenings, after he had a few drinks in him, Billy's anger grew and grew until he could no longer hold it in, and if a newspaperman happened along, Billy would unload his innermost feelings. Billy *wanted* the issues out in the open, hoping to talk sense into his bosses, but as the one in the subservient position, such candor rarely helped him; indeed, it almost always hurt him.

Billy was also blunt to Corbett's face. Billy asked him if the rumors of his impending firing were true.

"They might be," said Corbett.

"Is it because I don't come up to the front office every day like Frank Lucchesi?"

He said, "That might be the reason."

Replied Billy, "If that's the reason, you go right ahead and do it if you think it's right."

On the morning of July 21, the day of his firing, Billy went on his daily radio show and said about Brad Corbett, "Everybody has their ego, and sometimes their ego is not very smart." He added, "[Corbett] wants to call the shots. One year in baseball and all of a sudden he's a genius." Billy predicted Corbett was going to fire him.

Billy told Frank Lucchesi, "You're crazy if you take this job, Frank."

According to Billy, Lucchesi told him, "I haven't talked to anybody about taking the job, Billy."

Said Billy later, "I didn't believe that for a minute."

When Lucchesi replaced Billy as manager, the Rangers were fourteen and a half games out of first place.

Billy always harbored bitterness about his firing at Texas, especially against Jim Sundberg, whom he felt he had rescued from oblivion in the minors and given a big league job.

One of Billy's confidants, Matt Keough, who pitched with him in Oakland and in New York, recalled: "Whenever Billy talked about players being disloyal to him, the player he and the coaches talked about was Jim Sundberg, who Billy managed at Texas.

"Sunny was a Texas guy, an outstanding defensive catcher, but evidently Jim was relaying what was going on in the clubhouse, the airplanes, and the hotels to the front-office guys. Billy found out about it more after he was fired. The Texas front office knew things they could only know about if some player told them. And Billy found out it was Sundberg, who Billy's coaches referred to as the Pipeline. That's a universal expression for guys taking it upstairs. In baseball there is an age-old axiom: 'What you hear, see, and do in that clubhouse stays there.' If it leaves there, you are breaking the cardinal rule of trust.

"Billy would not have managed Sunny again under any circumstance. You cross him on that level, you can forget it."

Lenny Randle remembers the deep disappointment he felt at Billy's firing. He recalled the difference between the successful year in 1974 and the discord of 1975.

"In '75," said Randle, "Billy wanted to control the field, and other people wanted to control the field *and* Billy. I don't know why. It happens. It's ego, like Toys 'R' Us. 'It's my toy, and now I want to play with it. I want the PR.' Corbett got involved. He was a pipe magnate, owned Robintech, and after one year he was a baseball expert, and he interfered.

"Billy was right up front with him. He would say, 'I don't tell you how to run your pipe business. You don't have to tell me how to run the baseball team. I'm trying to help you win. You can have all the champagne and glory. At least let me run the club.'

"That chemistry didn't get on, and people he had on his staff began to undermine him, backstabbing him, running up to the office, trying to pick our brains—'Do you think Billy should stay? You think David Clyde should go to the minors? Was he a gate attraction?' We weren't into that. We just wanted to play and win.

"As a result Billy started seeing part of the club going one way and the rest going the other as other staff members tried to take his job. The loyal players stuck with Billy, and the players who thought they might get a better deal with the other staff members went with them.

"Billy saw this happening.

"Billy had taken players who no one else would give a shot to. Or a coach no one would let coach, and he'd let him coach. Or someone buried in the minors, he'd make him play well and become a winner. You can look at Billy like an Al Davis kind of guy, a man who builds winners. He knew talent, and knew what to tell a player.

"He made me believe I could play third, short, second every day of the week, center field and catch if I had to. And I'd still get five hundred at bats in a season and it wouldn't faze me. I knew I could do it. And it didn't bother me, because I knew I was going to play every day. Some guys would say to me, 'Let's look at the Ouija board. Fregosi has a bad back. You're at third today!' Or 'Tovar has a bad hammy, you're in center.' 'Nelson pulled a muscle, you're at second.' 'Fahey is sick. You're catching.' I even caught.

"Mickey Mantle one time said to me, 'Goddamn, Lenny, Billy said he didn't know what the hell he'd do if it wasn't for you. Good thing you have multiple personalities.'

"I remember right before Billy was fired, the morale was good. We were in

Kansas City, and about fifteen of us went frog hunting at night, with Billy and Mickey. You go out in the swamp with a flashlight, and when you see the eyes of the frog light up, you grab him and catch him and make frogs legs and eat him the next day.

"About fifteen guys were there, from Duke Sims, Fregosi, [Paul] Lindblad, Jim Merritt, Spencer, Tovar, a whole bunch, and it was something fun to do. We ate the frogs the next day. It wasn't finger-licking good. You wanted to think it was like chicken.

"So maybe they thought we were too loose or he lost control. I have no idea what the thought was. We were still playing good ball. And they just fired him, let him go, and we were shocked. Shocked. A very morbid feeling, because we had had so much.

"I just knew the third-base coach would end up being the manager, and it was bizarre. How can this guy, with seventeen years in the minor leagues, all of a sudden be managing? What was the deal? And everybody starting thinking back and saying, 'I remember, he was always up there talking to Corbett.'

"And when Lucchesi came in, it was a different chemistry. Something was missing. They started trading people. They used people to motivate or to degrade or humiliate, whipping boys, in order to enhance his discipline, an Edward G. Robinson approach. It was, 'I'm going to be tough, and this is how we're going to do it.'

"We had won without the tough-guy approach. That drastic a change wasn't necessary. We all knew what our roles were under Billy. Billy told each of us what he expected of us, and then the new manager wasn't wise enough to know. It was like amnesia, and it just changed the morale of the team."

Roy Howell remembered how traumatic it was for Billy.

"Because of the way it happened," said Howell, "the feeling was of back-stabbing by Lucchesi to Martin. In that aspect, baseball is a cruel game. I always confront the bull straight on. If I don't like somebody, I don't go in any other direction but straight at him. Billy respected me for that.

"Lucchesi went around the back door, and that's what he had been doing, chirping on Billy, 'Billy was doing this or that,' to Danny O'Brien, who was the GM. 'He's the whole problem.' So what were they going to do? They can't fire the whole ball club, so they fired the manager.

"In '76, Frank was still there, and Lenny and I had trouble with him, and that's a whole other story. It came to a head in '77 when Lenny punched Frank.

"But when Billy was fired, we knew we were in trouble. The players didn't have the confidence in Frank. He was a good third-base coach, but we didn't know what he would do on the field. He had managed in the minors, but Frank managed with his feelings instead of managing with his knowledge, and Billy did both.

"When Billy said, 'I believe this is going to happen,' it was an educated situation. Frank would say, 'This is going to happen, I know it is,' and he would make a move that way. Baseball is its own monster, and if you do it in the right form or fashion—everything is predictable. On 2–1, 3–1, you're going to hit-and-run, pitch out—Frank would manage more away from that, a feeling.

"One time I was swinging the bat good against a left-hander. I had gotten three or four hits, and comes the ninth, the ballgame was tied, man on second base, two out, first pitch, I took a good swing and fouled it off, second pitch, fouled it off, and Frank called time out and sent Gene Clines up for me. Because he had a feeling. I went berserk. I came in screaming, hollering at him. 'What the hell is going on?' To me that was showing me up. You just don't do that. Geno came in, and on the first pitch he hit a ball four inches above the hands, the ball landed behind the pitcher's mound, a hand grenade, the second baseman stopped it, the run scored, and we won the ball game. And Frank was running around yelling that he was a genius.

"Well, by the time he got in his office, he didn't shut the door. I shut the door. We went round and round and round.

"That type of managing didn't sit with the guys very well. Guys didn't have confidence in him that way."

With Billy gone, Texas returned to its old ways, ruining young players, jerking players around, becoming the graveyard of baseball. Frank Lucchesi finished out the 1975 season, finished tied for fourth in 1976, and he was fired in 1977, after he harassed Lenny Randle, taunting him, until Randle KO'd him with one punch during spring training.

Lucchesi sued Randle. During the trial, such luminaries as the Reverend Jesse Jackson, Hank Aaron, and Curt Flood showed up to support Randle, but Lucchesi's case was lost when Billy Martin showed up to vouch for Lenny's character and to testify as to how Lucchesi had taken the manager's job from him.

# THE
# STEINBRENNER
# YANKEES

**I**n the early fall of 1971 frozen-foods magnate Vernon Stouffer decided to sell the Cleveland Indians. Vernon and his brother Gordon in 1924 had opened a restaurant, Stouffer Lunch, in the Schofield Building on East Ninth Street in Cleveland. Their idea had been to serve food like his mother had cooked. They wanted the service to be quick. Ten years later they owned eleven restaurants throughout the East. The chain then grew to forty-five restaurants and five motels, and when frozen foods became possible, Vernon Stouffer became a pioneer and a very wealthy man.

George Steinbrenner by 1971 had become a shipping force. After taking over Kinsman Transit from his father, a number of his smaller competitors were forced out of business and then in 1967 he bought the giant American Shipping Company. With the benefit of valuable government contracts gained through his many contacts in Washington, AmShip prospered.

At the same time, George had made connections with a number of wealthy Clevelanders. Unlike the investors in the Pipers, this time when he went after the Cleveland Indians he didn't involve small-timers in the venture. This time only the really rich needed apply.

With plenty of financial backing, George sought to buy the Indians from Vernon Stouffer. George had been an Indians fan since he was a little boy, and as a freshman at Williams he kept a statue of an Indian on the mantle above the fireplace of his dorm room. One evening he told freshman-year roommate Don Martin, "I'm going to own the Indians one day."

Vernon Stouffer had bought the team for $8 million in 1966 and had run it into the ground. When George's friend Jim Stouffer informed him that his father wanted to sell the team, George asked Jim to put together the deal. George and his group of investors offered to pay Vernon $8.6 million cash.

Steinbrenner, certain he had a deal, contacted his friend, Gabe Paul, the Indians' president, and Gabe agreed to run the team for him.

Working for Vernon Stouffer had been difficult for Paul. In July 1969, Vernon decided that Alvin Dark, his manager, should be in charge of player personnel, and over Gabe's objection, Dark made decisions that hurt the team badly. By 1971 the Indians were in last place, Dark had been fired, and Gabe was back in charge. When Steinbrenner asked Paul if he would work with him to rebuild the Indians, Gabe was ecstatic.

When Stouffer told George he wanted more money for the team, George upped the offer to an even $9 million. Vernon was on the verge of accepting the offer when George shot himself in the foot and cost himself the Indians. Vernon was a man who hated to feel he was being taken advantage of or manipulated. He had not forgotten George's falling-out with his son Jim over the Cleveland Pipers.

Nevertheless, Jim had seen fit to forgive George, and so Vernon was considering George's deal when George made the tactical mistake of leaking news of the transaction to the *Cleveland Plain Dealer*.

STOUFFER WEIGHS $9 MILLION OFFER, the headline said in the *Cleveland Plain Dealer* on October 2, 1971.

Several days later former Indians third baseman Al Rosen called sportswriter Bob August of the *Cleveland Press* and told him to hang around for a big story.

With Al Rosen and Gabe Paul at his side, George called Vernon Stouffer in Scottsdale, Arizona, to finalize the deal. When Vernon answered, he was drunk, and George was surprised and disappointed when Stouffer told him he would not accept the deal.

When the *Cleveland Press* called Vernon Stouffer to find out what was happening, Stouffer unloaded on George, accusing him of trying to steal the team out from under him.

The deal was dead.

Gabe Paul said that as soon as George got the cold shoulder from Vernon in Scottsdale, he knew the newspaper leak had been a mistake.

"When George called Vernon, Vernon never alluded to the fact that Jim Stouffer had structured the deal," said Paul, who was in the office with George and Al Rosen during George's fateful call. "It was Jim's deal. And the thing fell apart on the phone that day, with Vernon loaded. I was listening. I know. And George was going to pay cash.

"When Stouffer sold it to Nick Mileti, instead of taking cash from George he got Green Stamps. He didn't get paid off for a long time."

George's childhood friend Frank Treadway is convinced that Vernon wouldn't sell the Indians to George because he never forgave George for what he did to his son Jim with the Pipers.

Said Treadway, who was close with both families, "I don't think Vernon wanted to see George with the team."

George was forced to look elsewhere. He told Gabe Paul that Jim Nederlander, the theater producer, and John DeLorean, the car magnate, were interested in going in with him on a deal to buy the Detroit Tigers.

Gabe Paul called around to check whether the Tigers were for sale. Among the calls he made, Gabe called Mike Burke, the man who ran the Yankees for the Columbia Broadcasting System. Burke told Gabe that he was planning to head a syndicate to buy the Yankees from CBS. Did Gabe know anyone who might be interested in investing with him?

Gabe certainly did.

Mike Burke had symbolized the Yankees since a gullible CBS bought a shell of a team from Dan Topping and Del Webb in 1964. Burke, white-haired, elegant, part of the horsey set, had been a war hero. Working for the OSS, he had sneaked into Italy and blown up bridges. He won a Silver Star for going behind enemy lines and bringing a defecting Italian admiral back alive just before the Allied invasion of Salerno. Gary Cooper, who also played Lou Gehrig in *Pride of the Yankees*, had played Burke in the movie *Cloak and Dagger*.

During the Cold War Burke had worked for Allen Dulles to overthrow the government of Albania. He headed the CIA in Germany. After finishing his government service, he ran the Ringling Brothers Circus. After Teamster boss Jimmy Hoffa closed the circus down, Burke went to work for CBS, rising quickly in the company, in part through his friendship with headman William S. Paley.

It was Burke who suggested that CBS buy the Yankees from Topping and Webb. Among the CBS executives, Burke had shown the most passionate interest in the team, and Paley figured if Burke could deal with the talent in the record business, he would do well running their baseball team. In September 1965, Mike Burke was officially named president and chairman of the board of the New York Yankees, Inc.

The Yankees had lost $11 million in 1972, and CBS badly wanted to dump them. The Columbia Broadcasting System was a multimillion-dollar conglomerate, and it was the feeling among the execs at Black Rock that the Yankees were a flyspeck of an investment that was bringing them neither prestige nor financial gain. CBS czar William Paley liked Mike Burke, and he informed Burke that CBS wanted to sell the Yankees and if he wanted to be the buyer, he had better act quickly before word of CBS's intentions became public.

Paley set an asking price of $10 million. The price was a steal considering that the Yankees were the premier franchise in baseball and in 1970 the sad-sack Seattle Pilots were sold for $12.2 million. The franchise was worth closer to $25 million. The Yankees were a contender with a strong farm system. Thurman Munson, Roy White, Fritz Peterson, John Ellis, Ron Blomberg, and Steve Kline were all farm system products.

The team had been in first place in September 1972 only to fold down the stretch to Billy Martin's Detroit Tigers. The farm system boasted many more bright prospects. Lee MacPhail had traded four of them for Graig Nettles, but there were plenty left.

(On the historical criticism of the way CBS ran the Yankees, Mike Burke said, "People don't recall history very accurately. They don't know what the hell they are talking about.")

In September 1972, Mike Burke met Gabe Paul for breakfast at the Plaza Hotel on Fifth Avenue. Paley had given Burke the exclusive right to broker the deal to buy or sell the Yankees. What Burke needed to do was find someone who would supply the money to buy the team and at the same time allow Burke to continue to run it.

Mike Burke was hoping that Gabe and his investor friends would fill the bill. If he could raise the money, even if it came from Attila the Hun, he would become rich. Burke had confidence he could figure out a way to work with his new partner, whoever he was.

The next time Gabe and Mike met, Gabe brought George. The deal was that George would put up the money and Mike Burke would get five percent of the stock as a reward for putting together the deal. George assured Mike he would stay in the background and allow Burke to continue running the team. He told Burke that Lee MacPhail would keep his job as general manager. Gabe stressed that he and Lee were close and that he wouldn't do anything to hurt Lee.

When the meeting was over, it was agreed that Mike Burke and George Steinbrenner would go to CBS and buy the Yankees.

In mid-December the two met with William S. Paley and Arthur Taylor, who was in charge of the legal work. Burke offered the $10 million. Two days later Paley called him back and accepted.

The switchboard operators at Yankee Stadium became aware of George Steinbrenner in December 1972 because he would be on the other end of the line and in a gruff, demanding voice would treat them rudely. This was something new to the Yankees. Under the courtly Mike Burke, nobody was rude to anybody.

The purchase of the Yankees from CBS by general partners Mike Burke and George Steinbrenner was announced on January 3, 1973. In its profile of Mike Burke, *The New York Times* stressed his flair for fashionable clothing, his love of the game, and how his ability to measure beauty by "watching the shadows move out toward the pitcher's mound" helped reshape the reputation of the Yankees at a time when their on-the-field record needed help.

There was also a feature on Burke's partner. Said the partner, "The Yankees are baseball. They're as American as apple pie. There are still great things about the past that are worth going back to and grabbing into the present."

When asked about his involvement in the Yankees, the partner said, "I won't be active in the day-to-day operations of the club at all. I can't spread myself so thin. I've got enough headaches with my shipping company."

It was the last peaceful moment Mike Burke would have until the day he surrendered to George and quit the Yankees three months later.

The question is whether George and Gabe deliberately sandbagged and then blindsided Mike Burke. Gabe Paul says that as part of the deal, Mike Burke had agreed to step down as head of the Yankees but reneged at the initial press conference. Mike Burke said that he had been caught unaware when it turned out that Gabe Paul was going to run the team for George.

Mike Burke had wanted to run the Yankees, but in the end he discovered that George Steinbrenner was pathologically incapable of working with other human beings and constitutionally unable to allow another person to make decisions. Burke learned that one's reward for getting in bed with George Steinbrenner was systematic harassment, a barrage of criticism, and ultimately, terror tactics, which forced Burke to resign. Burke would sell his stock, take his millions, and retire in luxury to a huge farm in Ireland, where he died.

With a new season and some fresh capital, Mike Burke prepared for spring training as though nothing had changed. Before the sale papers with CBS were signed by him and Steinbrenner, Burke negotiated a contract with outfield star Bobby Murcer that made Murcer the first $100,000 Yankee player since Mickey Mantle retired in 1968.

When Steinbrenner, who was in Florida, read about the contract, he called Burke on the phone, and according to George's lawyer, Tom Evans, who was with George at the time, "he gave Burke a tongue-lashing like he was a two-year-old child."

Evans waved frantically at George because the sale papers hadn't been signed. Evans was afraid that Burke would realize George's true nature and scuttle the deal. Evans did not realize how badly Mike Burke needed George.

Said Evans, "George kept ranting about Burke's stupidity in paying Murcer so much money, and Burke just listened and took everything George had to give." At that point Evans knew that if there was to be a confrontation between the two men, it was clear who would emerge the victor.

From this first interaction, it was also clear that George had no intention of doing what he had publicly said: let Burke run the Yankees.

If Burke didn't understand the full import of George's tantrum that day, once he and George signed the sale agreement he *knew* he had trouble. *Nothing* Burke did was satisfactory to George, and nothing the former CBS employees did was good enough for Gabe Paul, who had moved into an office at Yankee Stadium, ostensibly to keep an eye on George's interests.

The patterns of meetings between Burke and Steinbrenner rarely varied. No matter what Mike Burke wanted to do, George disagreed with him. There was an elevator shaft adjacent to Burke's second-floor office, and employees would stand at the bottom of the shaft and listen as George and Burke screamed at each other at the top of their lungs. Said Fred Bachman, the Yankee Stadium manager, "That it never came to blows was nothing short of miraculous."

To Steinbrenner, Mike Burke's traditions meant nothing. Burke would say, "I've been doing it this way." George would say, "Screw you, that's not the way it's going to be done anymore."

Two weeks after the deal was completed it was announced at a press conference at the "21" Club that Gabe Paul would be one of the sixteen limited partners. The announcement raised eyebrows with the former CBS employees. Gabe had been the general manager at Cincinnati and Cleveland. Were Gabe and Lee MacPhail going to be able to work together any better than Mike and George?

Gabe quickly made it clear that he was going to be second-in-command to George, and as second-in-command, he was going to be George's henchman. Anytime Howard Berk, Mike Burke's right-hand man, wanted to do something, he would talk to Gabe Paul about it. Gabe would sit and listen, his glasses sitting high on the edge of his nose. When Howard finished talking, Gabe's answer rarely varied: no. When a furious Howard Berk complained to Mike, Mike then fought with Steinbrenner, who backed Gabe and browbeat Burke until he capitulated. This caused Howard to be reversed on almost every decision and made Mike Burke look like a weak stooge, which in fact he had become.

The Yankees had been a family under Mike Burke. With George's people infiltrating the organization, no one trusted anyone anymore. Employees would whisper around the coffee machine, talk quietly in the dining room, all the while looking around to see who was listening to their conversation. In the bathroom no one talked until they checked the adjacent stalls. The employees made jokes about the place being bugged.

Under Mike Burke the pay was poor but working at Yankee Stadium was a joy. When George and Gabe Paul arrived, the fun stopped.

One of the ways the Steinbrenner people got rid of the Burke people was to give them new assignments in jobs they didn't want to do. Fred Bachman, the stadium manager, was made head of season-ticket sales. Bachman demurred. Gabe Paul told him to switch or quit.

Said Bachman about Gabe Paul, "He made it miserable for everybody. He had no tact, and no matter what it cost him in terms of personal pride, he would espouse the Steinbrenner line. If Steinbrenner said to go around and call everyone a cocksucker, he'd go around and call everyone a cocksucker until you got fed up and quit."

George and Gabe could justify their behavior because from a financial perspective, Mike Burke was a lousy businessman. After George and Gabe took over, they upped the team's take of the concessions from twenty-three to thirty-five percent. The Yankees' radio and TV deals netted the Yankees only $60,000 and $200,000 in 1972, and George blamed Burke.

In February and March, though George spent most of his time in Cleveland running AmShip, he bombarded Burke with letters and phone calls. In April, when George returned for Opening Day, they had their first major blowup.

Burke, who was urbane and sophisticated, loved the artsy set. One year he had poet Marianne Moore throw out the first ball. This year Burke invited his personal friends to Opening Day, including artists and performers from Lincoln Center. George told him, "It's a waste of money giving those tickets to those people. I don't like the people you are inviting." George demanded that Burke sell the tickets to the public. Burke refused.

Before the start of the opener, an angry Steinbrenner said to Burke in front of about forty of his friends, "We'll see how your $100,000 ballplayer does today."

When Murcer struck out with the winning run on base to end the game, George stormed into his office and said, "There's your $100,000 ballplayer for you."

Said Mike Burke, "That tore it. I knew I couldn't work with him."

When George began to annoy the players and to meddle and harass manager Ralph Houk, Burke sat by helplessly and watched.

George and Mike made a final attempt to define Mike Burke's role with the Yankees. They told public relations man Bob Fishel to set up a press conference at which the two men would announce their respective duties. But when they sat down to define them, the first thing they had to decide was which one would do the talking for the Yankees. Burke said he thought he should be the one. George disagreed. A shouting match ensued with some vicious name-calling on both sides. The press conference was never held.

In the end Burke capitulated. The Saturday in late April when he announced his decision to quit, Burke was seething in his private box at the stadium. George had hired baseball clown Max Patkin to perform during the game. For twenty years Patkin had toured major and minor league parks mimicking players, doing pantomime, and taking pratfalls. Burke didn't want him in Yankee Stadium. Clowning, Burke felt, was *not* part of the Yankee tradition. It lacked class. George felt that since the team wasn't very entertaining, he would add some color to the proceedings.

When Patkin held up the game to make a couple of playful pitches from the mound, Burke kept saying, "That's awful, awful."

On April 29, Mike Burke made it official. He was quitting.

Sitting side by side with Steinbrenner in what had been his office, Burke told reporters that they had discovered they couldn't work together. He said he hated to give up his position. He read from a William Butler Yeats poem: "I balanced all, brought all to mind."

Burke left with a rich consulting contract and his five-percent share in the team and was hired to be president of the Madison Square Garden Corporation, where he proceeded to run the Knicks and the Rangers into the ground.

With Mike Burke gone, the former CBS employees left in large numbers. By the end of 1973, Lee MacPhail left to become president of the American League; Bob Fishel joined him. Howard Berk went back to CBS, and Fred Bachman quit when his nervous stomach no longer enabled him to digest his food and he could no longer sleep at night.

The final argument occurred as Bachman and Gabe discussed the Yankees' planned two-year move to Shea Stadium during the renovation of Yankee Stadium. Bachman felt that the Mets' stadium was filthy, their promotions inadequate, their group sales department a shadow of his own. Gabe began telling him what a great job the Mets were doing.

Said Bachman, "To Gabe, everything the Mets did was gospel, and everything I was doing was garbage."

They argued, and Bachman's head began to throb. When he walked out the door at the end of the day a nervous, unstable person, Bachman decided to look for work elsewhere. After a sleepless night, he resigned the next morning.

After seven years of loyal service to the Yankees, Bachman told Gabe he was quitting.

"If that's how you feel, then good-bye," said Gabe.

Yankee manager Ralph Houk also quit. On the final day of the season Houk called his players together. He told them that he had to get away from George, that he couldn't work for him and maintain his self-respect. Houk told them that no manager would ever be able to have any authority with Steinbrenner around and that he couldn't work that way.

By the end of 1973 the Burke regime had been routed. Firmly in control was George M. Steinbrenner III.

# AN ADMITTED
# FELON

Some felonies are more acceptable to society than others. It all depends who is doing the committing. *Who* you are often determines the punishment. In America justice is not blind. The rich and powerful know how to make the law work for them. Just as George Steinbrenner stayed out of Korea, so he was able to stay out of jail.

George had spent years cultivating his power base in both Cleveland and Washington. For years he donated to charities and gave sporting equipment to kids. When George needed backing to keep him out of jail, he called on every single recipient of his largesse he could think of, every powerful man he knew to vouch for him. A blanket of character references followed, and in the end, the judge balanced his good works against the wrong he had perpetrated and decided that George wasn't such a bad guy after all.

The man prosecuting the case, Thomas McBride, was dumbfounded and deeply disappointed when the judge fined George a paltry $20,000 and let him go free. According to one story, McBride threw his briefcase halfway across the courtroom when he learned of the decision.

The crimes George committed were against the democratic process. He broke laws that were supposed to prevent illegal campaign contributions. He ordered his employees to break those laws, and then when he got caught, he ordered them to lie about his role to the FBI. He obstructed justice by directing them to fake records to back his story. He headed a conspiracy of criminal behavior, but because George Steinbrenner had powerful friends who said he was a good guy, he didn't spend one minute in jail.

George used all the weapons in his considerable arsenal to escape his just punishment. He used his connections and money to hire Edward Bennett Williams, one of the best legal defenders in America. He used his connections with the most powerful people in Cleveland to vouch for him with the judge. He used his status to sway the judge to give him probation instead of jail time.

His actions after he took his slap on the wrist were the most dastardly of all. Even though he admitted his crime in court, George Steinbrenner proved unwilling to take responsibility for his actions. Though he knew fully what the law was and deliberately broke it to suit his goals, George refused to admit to having done anything wrong.

After he got off he used his media connections to institute a public relations campaign in which he painted himself as the unwilling victim of scheming men. To make certain his cover story looked credible, he did something so vile as to be almost unthinkable. He accused his Williams classmate Tom Evans of precipitating his problems by introducing him to Nixon's fund-raisers. Then he foisted the blame onto another of his friends and college classmates, his lawyer, Jack Melcher, a man who trusted him. All to salve his damaged ego. For the rest of his life, trying to ruin the reputation of others would become one of George's pursuits.

Henry Steinbrenner had taught George the rudiments of influence peddling early. At Culver, Henry got George promoted using his clout with the head of the school. After Williams, Henry got him a secure post at Lockbourne using his influence with a congressman and a Secretary of Defense.

George inherited a large trust fund left by his grandfather when he turned thirty, and he became rich. He saw that the rich were able to use their money to buy friendship and, if those friends were in high places, to buy immense power.

While working in Cleveland with his father, George had devoted hours to civic causes, making powerful friends locally, maneuvering for political power. George, a true robber baron, loved monopolies. He enjoyed being able to go in the back door and broker a contract. Why fight an opponent for a contract in the free market when you can make an inside deal?

He had given money to the campaign of Cleveland mayor Carl Stokes, but switched allegiances to Stokes' bitter political opponent, James Stanton, then the city council president.

It is perfectly consistent that a man with no morals has no political philosophy. The only thing that is important is practical politics.

*Who* George backed didn't matter as long as the person who took his money ended up doing his bidding.

On the gubernatorial level George backed Democrat John Gilligan, whose chief fund-raiser was one of George's closest associates, Sheldon Guren. Gilligan knew how to play the game.

When Gilligan had to decide where to build a new state office tower in Cleveland, the site he chose was near land owned by Guren's company.

After George bought out his father at Kinsman Transit and took over the American Shipping Company, he set a course that would connect him to the most powerful movers and shakers in America.

When George became involved in shipbuilding on a large scale, he saw quickly that the business was largely dependent on the U.S. government, which was influenced greatly by the powerful maritime lobby. Without the maritime lobby and government contracts, the industry long ago would have gone under. George wanted to become an important player with that lobby.

To do that, in 1967 George sought a connection to Washington. The man he hired to be AmShip's lobbyist was Neal Roach, who had been campaign manager for the Democratic Party in 1944, 1948, and 1952. In 1965, Roach was appointed public relations director of the Democratic campaign committee, and in 1968 he served as chief fund-raiser for Presidential candidate Hubert Humphrey.

Roach became George's entrée to the Democratic Party. Roach would say later, "George just kept pestering the life out of me to get him involved in fund-raising." According to Roach, George would say to him over and over, "When are you going to get me introduced to these people?"

Roach finally introduced George to Senator Daniel Inouye of Hawaii, who appointed George as the fund-raiser for the annual Democratic dinner. The Democrats, in disarray after the defeat of Hubert Humphrey, were millions in debt. George used all his powers of persuasion to sell more than $800,000 in tickets to the dinner. The next year he again was given the dinner chairmanship, and this time he raised $1.2 million. While in the job, George cemented connections with Massachusetts Congressman Thomas "Tip" O'Neill, Massachusetts Senator Ted Kennedy, and Inouye.

While chairman of the dinner committee, George learned the ins and outs of fund-raising. His tutor: Neal Roach. According to Roach, he taught George that there was one cardinal rule to fund-raising: Never accept corporate checks. They were illegal.

Said Roach, "You look at a corporate check, and that's it. You have to turn it back in. You can't fool around faking it."

Roach said that he made sure George returned all the corporate checks he received for the Democratic fund-raising dinners.

Whenever George was asked how he came to get the dinner chairmanship job, he would make it sound as though he had been somehow chosen to save the Democratic Party. He'd tell people that five men had turned down the job and, after reading about all his achievements, that party leaders had turned to him.

He would omit one important player in the story: Neal Roach. The truth was that the Democrats weren't chasing after George. The truth was that George was chasing after the Democrats.

And at the same time he was also forging ties with the Republicans.

Around the time George was taking over AmShip, legislation was being considered by the powerful House Merchant Marine and Fisheries Committee, which would appropriate $300 million for new shipbuilding. George enthusiastically lobbied for passage of the bill. Richard Nixon, who was President, initially opposed it but was swayed to change his position by an ally of George's, Republican Congressman Charles Mosher. The legislation became law in 1970.

George chose as his contact within the GOP a Williams classmate of his, Thomas Evans, a Wall Street lawyer with the firm of Mudge, Rose, Guthrie, and Alexander, the former and future law firm of President Richard Nixon and Attorney General John Mitchell.

Evans had known George in passing at Williams and had not seen him since graduation in 1952, and then one day in early 1970, soon after President Nixon took office, George called Evans on the phone and invited him to see the new play he and Jimmy Nederlander were producing, called *Applause*.

George cemented his connection with Evans by appointing him to the board of directors of AmShip and hiring his law firm as East Coast counsel at an annual fee of $25,000. When George later bought the Yankees, he gave Evans the legal business and allowed Evans to buy a two-percent interest in the team.

Evans says he was not fooled by the tickets and the directorship. Evans, who had worked closely with Richard Nixon in the law firm and had been active in the 1968 campaign, when he was named general counsel to the Presidential campaign, said he knew all along George was interested in him for his connections to Richard Nixon.

Tom Evans remembered that in his initial conversations with George, George extolled Nixon's virtues and told Evans how grateful George had been when Nixon changed his mind on the Great Lakes legislation.

Evans knew George wanted something, exactly what, he didn't know. Said Evans, "I didn't feel there was anything specific that George had in mind, though I did have the feeling that I was being massaged, and George does that very well."

George's subsequent actions would show that he was seeking the path to power in Washington to solve certain problems AmShip was having with the U.S. government.

One problem was a contract AmShip had entered into with the Commerce Department to build an oceanographic survey ship, the *Researcher*. The project was ninety-nine weeks late, and George was facing steep penalties for late delivery. Worse for George, cost overruns had totaled $5.4 million. George didn't want to have to pay it.

George also had problems with the Labor Department. In 1971, a ship AmShip was building in its Lorain, Ohio, shipyard caught fire, and four men were killed. Investigators for the Labor Department charged AmShip with poor safety controls and fined the company $10,000. George didn't want to have to pay that, either.

The Justice Department was also a concern. George, who truly had the spirit of the nineteenth-century robber barons, worked toward monopoly.

Robert Sauvey was working for the Gartland Steamship Company when George asked him to go to work for Kinsman Transit. At dinner George told Sauvey, "You might as well go to work for us, because I'm going to run Gartland out of business anyway."

Said Sauvey, "And he did in 1967." Sauvey ended up working for Kinsman and George.

George wanted to buy two major competitors, Great Lakes Towing and Wilson Marine, but the Justice Department indicated if he did so, they would charge Kinsman Transit with antitrust violations.

This was what was at stake when George approached Tom Evans, who had just been appointed deputy finance chairman of the now-infamous Committee to Re-elect the President (CREEP).

George told Evans he wanted to make a big contribution. Who could he talk to? Evans put him in touch with Herbert W. Kalmbach, who handled the large contributors.

In George's version of what happened, he contends that Evans and Kalmbach approached him for the money. It's an important link in George's version of a chain of events that "proves" his innocence. George charged that Herb Kalmbach had "twisted his arm" for money and that he gave it because he feared the wrath of Richard Nixon and his henchmen.

Years later, when I told both Evans and Kalmbach what George had said, they disputed his account.

"George spoke to me initially about his interest in making a donation," said Evans. "It was George's idea, and George set it in motion."

Said Kalmbach, "Arm twisting? People who know me know I would never do that."

When asked whether Kalmbach had been twisting George's arm, even special prosecutor Tom McBride believed it had been a story made up by George.

"That was a bunch of baloney," said McBride. "The Republicans were a little heavy-handed in getting campaign contributions, saying the White House doors would be open to those who supported the President. That was standard fund-raising tactics. But beyond that—anything approaching extortion—there was no evidence of it."

George met with Herb Kalmbach at his office in Washington. They talked sports awhile and then talked numbers. George initially had wanted to donate $50,000. Kalmbach asked him for $100,000. George said he would come up with the money. He did not tell Kalmbach *how* he was going to come up with the money.

The scheme George intended to employ to raise AmShip funds for CREEP was an illegal ruse he had concocted two years earlier and had been using to raise money for other pet politicians.

As always, George ensured himself deniability.

In the fall of 1970, George called Robert Bartlome, the secretary of American Ship, and Stanley Lepkowski, its treasurer, and explained to them that he wanted them to round up some loyal workers through whom he wanted to funnel some contributions to the various congressmen and senators important to maritime legislation.

The way George explained it to Bartlome and Lepkowski, each of the employees who agreed to be a part of the plan would receive a $5,000 "bonus" check. After deducting taxes the employee was then to write a personal check for $3,000. The few hundred dollars that remained was to be returned to AmShip as petty cash. The reason the checks were made out for exactly $3,000 was that any contribution larger than that was subject to being reported.

The checks, sent out in the fall of 1970, included donations to U.S. Republican Representatives Charles Mosher and Frank Bow, Democratic Senators Dan Inouye and Vance Hartke, who were both on the Senate Commerce Committee, and Ohio gubernatorial candidate John Gilligan.

At the time, George had complained to AmShip's lawyer, Jack Melcher, a classmate at Williams along with Tom Evans, that the campaign laws were unfair. Melcher warned George that corporate contributions were illegal. George did not reveal his bonus scheme to Melcher, who as corporate attorney owed a higher duty to the stockholders.

Stanley Lepkowski, like all of George's loyal employees, was reticent about challenging him, fearing his wrath. Nevertheless, Lepkowski expressed his reservations. George told him not to worry, assuring Lepkowski that it was a common practice among large corporations.

In 1971, George used this arrangement to funnel more money to various politicians.

By 1972, George had his mechanism for big-time campaign contribution law breaking. In order to donate $100,000 without having to report it, George had to make a total of thirty-three donations of $3,000 apiece, plus one donation of $1,000.

At their meeting Kalmbach gave George a list of dozens of Republican campaign committees. One was the Loyal Americans for Government Reform, another the Stable Society Council. Committees such as these were used to keep campaign contributions a secret. The law required that a candidate had to report only funding made directly to him. But if the funds were donated to a campaign committee, no reporting was required. The myriad campaign committees allowed large donors to split up their gifts into $3,000 chunks, avoiding disclosure.

George had one major stumbling block. Congress had passed a new campaign law that would take effect three weeks from his meeting with Kalmbach. After that, all contributions, either direct or through a committee, would have to be reported.

George had a time problem. His bonus system required time to carry out because of the paperwork. To raise the $100,000, George decided to use his scheme to siphon off $25,000 from AmShip and to pay the Republicans the remaining $75,000 himself.

Steinbrenner told Bartlome to go to his men with their bonus checks, instructing him how they should make out the checks for their "personal" contributions. George then put those checks together with his twenty-five checks for $3,000 each, and he gave it to Ron Slater, a former high school football coach working for George, who—not knowing what the satchel contained—took it to Washington, where the checks sat in a huge pile of such envelopes, including $70,000 from Roy Winchester of Pennzoil and $250,000 from fugitive financier Robert Vesco.

George's expectations fell far short of the reality with Nixon's White House. Less than a week after his donation, the Justice Department announced it intended to block AmShip's purchase of Great Lakes Towing. Three weeks later George settled with the Commerce Department to pay $230,000 in late fees on the *Researcher*. He still had to pay the $5.4 million in cost overruns.

When, in August, Kinsman completed the purchase of Wilson Marine, making it the second-largest fleet on the Great Lakes and giving it a powerful hold on grain shipping, the Justice Department brought an antitrust suit.

When the suit was brought, George charged the Justice Department with harassment, saying it was positive proof Nixon was out to get him.

Tom Evans, who handled the case for George, expressed skepticism at George's charge.

"George had eighty percent of the grain shipping on the Great Lakes, and his acquisition brought him up to something like ninety percent. It seemed to me a perfectly legitimate antitrust case, and we handled it as such."

Evans ended up settling the case. George could keep Wilson Marine, but he had to sell off ten of his boats over time. George ended up with the grain-hauling monopoly he had sought after all.

After Richard Nixon was reelected in November 1972, George went to Washington for a quid pro quo on his money. He wanted his brother-in-law, Jacob Kamm, appointed as an ambassador. He didn't get it or any other consideration for his $100,000. All he got, in the end, was trouble.

Bob Woodward and Carl Bernstein were the initial troublemakers. The scandal they uncovered was to be known as Watergate, the break-in of Democratic headquarters that occurred on June 17, 1972.

Investigating the campaign contribution scandal for NBC television was Jim Polk, who would win a Pulitzer Prize for his reporting. Polk had heard rumors, started by George, that Kalmbach had twisted his arm for contributions from AmShip. Polk went to see George, who denied giving CREEP any money.

Three months later, in January 1973, Polk began examining the bank records of the various committees. Two of the checks given were for $3,500. Why $3,500? Polk wondered. Because George's loyal men had made a major screwup, that's why.

Instead of making thirty-three checks at $3,000 each and one check for $1,000, George's lackeys, rather than going to the trouble to write the last important $1,000 check, took a shortcut and made up the extra grand by writing out two checks for $3,500. And the eagle-eyed Jim Polk caught them. The two $3,500 checks were made out by Roy Walker and Daniel A. Kissel.

Polk could not find where Roy Walker worked, but he did track down Kissel, who was listed as a treasurer of an AmShip subsidiary. Polk made a call to AmShip and learned that Walker was a security officer.

Polk went to see Walker at home. Walker lived in an expensive neighborhood. Walker told him the contributions were personal. Polk had no reason not to believe him.

He then went to see Kissel, who lived in a lower-middle-class neighborhood. When Polk saw where Kissel lived, he knew something was fishy about the contributions.

Said Polk, "He's not making the kind of money where he can write a $3,500 check for a campaign."

Kissel would not comment when Polk asked him about the contributions.

Polk then went to see Robert Bartlome at his AmShip office. Bartlome fed Polk a story about how a group of his employees had been talking about their loyalty to President Nixon, how they wanted to help him out, and how they had all written out checks. Polk didn't believe a word Bartlome was saying.

Polk let the story drop for a while and took up the trail of fugitive Robert Vesco, another friend of Nixon's.

Meanwhile, George had bought the Yankees in January 1973. Two months later Polk met George at the "21" Club in New York. The reason Polk hadn't dropped the story, which was a small one compared with the one concerning Vesco, was Polk's ego. He knew he was being conned by George. He wondered why.

At their meeting George denied everything. When Polk asked a question, George changed the subject. When the questioning became too intense, George began telling Polk that family members were ill and it was a bad time for him.

A waiter called George to the phone. When he returned, he told Polk his son had been in a pickup truck accident in Florida.

"I'm sure the kid will walk again, but he'll never run well enough to play football again," George told Polk. George told Polk his boy was recuperating at Massachusetts General Hospital.

The next day Polk called Mass General. He was told that no patient named Steinbrenner was registered there. Polk called Mass General several times over the next couple of weeks. Each time he got the same reply. Polk concluded that George had lied to him.

Three months later, while Polk was investigating Kalmbach, he was told by a source that there had been no quid pro quo, and that George had given CREEP $100,000.

The next day Polk flew to Cleveland and met with George at the Pewter Mug restaurant. George admitted to the $75,000 donation, insisting it was his own money. George told Polk the reason he had given it.

"I felt that Cleveland needed an input to the White House," he said. George denied any knowledge of the illegal $25,000.

In the middle of this conversation, George began talking about his wife, saying she had a terrible illness, that she faced an uncertain future.

"A story like this would upset her," George told the reporter. Polk did not tell George he had checked out his other story about his kid's truck accident. Said Polk about George's tug for sympathy, "He kept going over that refrain, but by that time I was tired of hearing George's refrains."

In Washington, Watergate prosecutor Archibald Cox appointed a young prosecutor named Thomas McBride to go after campaign finance abuses. Polk called McBride and in a subsequent meeting told McBride everything he had learned about George and AmShip.

Said Polk, "McBride was not investigating AmShip when I walked in that door; when I walked out of there, he was."

George had one thing going for him more than anything else: The men involved in the illegal scheme would not squeal on George unless a force more powerful than even George was brought to bear.

George liked to hire loyal men, those whom other companies might not be so quick to hire: alcoholics, down-on-their-luck ex-jocks, men who would owe George their lives and show him loyalty and obeisance no matter how badly he treated them.

The eight employees who had participated in George's illegal scheme were scared to death of him and his power to hire and fire them. That's why they went along with the check-writing scheme when George asked them to do it. They stood to gain nothing from writing the checks. But they did it merely because he had asked them to.

George's childhood friend Frank Treadway knew two of the eight men involved in the AmShip contribution scheme, Bob Dibble and Matt Clark.

"When I was a kid and lived in Lakewood," said Treadway, "my first recollection of Bob Dibble, I was probably twelve years old, and Bob was maybe eighteen, and I was out skipping around my grandmother's backyard on a Sunday morning making too much noise, and Dibble was home from college and had had a hard night on Saturday night, and he opened up the window and hollered out at me, 'Frank, for God's sake, it's the middle of the night.' It was ten o'clock Sunday morning, and I had been up for three hours.

"Years later we moved out to Bay Village, and who was living across the street from me but Bob Dibble. He had inherited an insurance business from his father, and it was a pretty good business, but as the years went by, the clients went, and Bob was not a real aggressive person, so new accounts were hard coming in.

"I moved a second time in Bay Village, and Steinbrenner lived between Dibble and myself. Bob married a lovely Danish girl who he had met in World War II as an aircraft artillery man up in Greenland. They wanted to go back to either Denmark or Greenland and be part of the U.S. government and slip into retirement. Well, that didn't work out. This was years ago. Somehow Dibble's plight had come to George's attention, and first thing I know, Dibble is working for George.

"One day I'm getting on the airplane to fly to New York, and here's Dibble tucking Joan Steinbrenner into her airplane seat. I said, 'Bob, are you going to New York?' He said, 'Oh no, but it's up to me to see that Joan is on the plane and comfortable and all her needs are being met.'

"It was like the Queen of Sheba being escorted on this United Airline plane.

This is what he had allowed himself to be reduced to, taking George's wife, putting her on the plane, tucking the blanket around her.

"Matthew Clark was another story. Matt was a young man very much interested in Little League football. The Bay Village people over the years have won a lot of football games when they shouldn't have, and one of the reasons was before seventh-grade football attained any kind of formal standing in the community, guys like Matt Clark were giving up their Saturdays to teach these kids, and when it would come time to raise money, who can we go to? Let's go to George. So somewhere along the line Matt Clark fell into George's web, and he went to work for George.

"I'm sure these people acted in fear of their jobs. I'm sure they acted that way because George assured them there was nothing wrong with what they were doing. And I'm sure it was George's money and not their money."

Proving it—that was the hard part.

George had concocted an authentic bonus plan to cover up the illegal scheme. In March 1973, George had called Lepkowski and had ordered him to bring the records of the check-writing scheme. George then destroyed them.

In June 1973, Archibald Cox issued an ultimatum to those who had made illegal campaign contributions: Confess or be prosecuted. George called AmShip's general council, Jack Melcher.

George told Melcher that some of his employees had made campaign contributions to Nixon's campaign, insisting they were voluntary. Even so, George told Melcher, someone should go see Archibald Cox. Jack Melcher had been a student of Cox's at Harvard Law School. George was looking for a connection to Cox.

"What do you want to see him about?" Melcher asked him.

"I want you to tell Archie that these contributions are perfectly legal but that the employees did make the contributions," said George.

"He's looking for sinners, not saints," said Melcher.

"Are you sure we shouldn't do that?" said George.

"It's ridiculous," said Melcher. "Absolutely ridiculous."

For weeks George talked to Melcher about Cox, without revealing that he had instigated the check-writing scheme.

All was quiet until AmShip's auditors, Arthur Anderson, came upon the check Stan Lepkowski had written to one of the political action committees. The auditor asked Lepkowski about the bonus. Lepkowski told him the truth, that it wasn't a bonus but a campaign contribution.

The auditor was now placed in the awkward position of having to certify corporate books that weren't entirely accurate. The accountant told Melcher he had better take action.

Melcher talked to Lepkowski and some of the other men involved in the scheme. All told Melcher what George wanted them to say. Melcher suspected that they were lying. To appease the auditors he wrote an affidavit for the men to sign under oath that their contributions had been voluntary.

In August 1973, the FBI interviewed the eight men. Melcher, who didn't know what the truth was—that George had been behind the scheme all along—advised them to tell the truth. What Melcher didn't know what that George was meeting the men behind closed doors, refreshing their memories with the story he wanted the men to keep repeating: The contributions were voluntary and had nothing to do with pressure from George, that all George did was supply the list of committees.

On August 31, 1973, Watergate prosecutor Tom McBride subpoenaed The Eight to testify. They went to George for advice. One of George's qualities was that his men thought him to be invincible, capable of overcoming anything that might come his way. They were in awe of his powers. George told Clark and the other men he was doing all he could to keep them from having to testify.

According to Jack Melcher, from the start of the investigation George stonewalled the feds while at the same time telling the employees charged with being part of the conspiracy that he would make sure they didn't have to testify.

Said Melcher, "George was constantly saying, 'I want the best for you, and I want you to be totally straight,' and all along George conveyed the impression he was going to meet with the Watergate prosecutor and short-circuit their appearance.

"Publicly he felt terribly about these poor guys being put through this ringer, that he was going to take some extraordinary steps so that these fellows never would have to appear before the grand jury.

"All along, George kept saying, 'Don't worry about it, guys. I'll take care of it. Talk to your lawyers. I'm going to talk to McBride.'

"He was saying he was going to come clean when he knew he wasn't. He knew perfectly well he wasn't, but he was giving them confidence, reassurance."

Two days before the appearance date both Bartlome and Lepkowski told George they would tell the truth at the Watergate hearings.

George, determined to put off the hearings, sent Melcher and another lawyer, Tim McMahon, to see prosecutor Tom McBride. McBride told the lawyers that until George came forward and told the truth, there would be no postponement.

When the lawyers returned from Washington, they met George at the airport. On the ride back to AmShip's headquarters in Lorain, Ohio, George sat in the backseat. Melcher said to him, "What the hell is all of this? Let us in on your secret. At least you can be straight with us."

George told Melcher, "Jack, I don't know what's going on. They're persecuting me. They're persecuting me in Washington, the Republicans. They know I've been active with the Democrats. The Republicans are persecuting me."

George and the lawyers arrived at AmShip, where George met alone with Bartlome and Lepkowski. According to Bartlome, George again attempted to tell him what to say in front of the grand jury. This time, Bartlome said, he again told George he intended to tell the truth.

George laid his head on the table and began sobbing.

"I'm ruined," he cried. "The company is ruined. I must find a bridge to jump off."

\* \* \*

On September 14, 1973, George's eight employees testified in front of special prosecutor Thomas McBride. They were given immunity. Until they walked in McBride's door, they had fully expected that George would get them out of having to talk. Over the weekend he had repeatedly told them, "Don't worry about it, guys. I'll take care of it. You talk to your lawyers, but I'm going down to talk to McBride."

According to Jack Melcher, the night before George and his employees were scheduled to appear before the committee, he was told by Steinbrenner to stay in his hotel room and wait for his call.

Said Melcher, "I sat there and sat there and nothing happened until early in the evening, when George called and said, 'I really want to go in and see McBride and tell him everything,' but 'the lawyers' wouldn't let him do it, [but] he was still going to work on it.

"Very late he called and said he had been with the lawyers all evening, and it hadn't been worked out yet. He gave me the impression that his new lawyer, Edward Bennett Williams, was working on an arrangement with McBride.

"The employees were to appear about nine-fifteen the following morning. George had built himself up in the eyes of the people in the company as being one of the more powerful people in the United States. They felt George could do anything.

"There was incredulity that he couldn't handle this, get it stopped. Also, there was great unhappiness about his unwillingness to do anything.

"I started getting calls from some of these guys. The phone started ringing about six in the morning.

" 'What in the hell is the matter with him? He's told us all along he's going to go in and talk to McBride. I don't want to go in and say these things. I don't want to tell this story. But I have to. My lawyer says I have to tell the truth. I don't want to do this. Can't you do something with him, Jack?' At that point I could do no more with him than with the President of the United States.

"See, these guys were holding down $15,000-a-year jobs, and they were afraid for their jobs.

"He could have walked in to the prosecutor and said, 'Yes, I did it,' and he would have escaped with just a fine. The problem is that George Steinbrenner never does *anything* wrong. It's *always* somebody else's fault. It's ego.

"It goes back to what his basic character . . . that if anything goes wrong, it's always somebody else's responsibility. He's going to stick somebody. George always has somebody who has badly advised him, who did something he didn't know about.

"He makes grandstand comments about how he's the leader of the group, and he's got the ultimate responsibility, but that's nonsense.

"He always has someone who's going to take the fall."

Melcher didn't discover his own scapegoat role until well after the Watergate hearings.

*   *   *

After sitting in his hotel room in Washington all afternoon waiting for George to call, Jack Melcher finally got the call. During the conversation, George informed Melcher that he had been meeting with his new lawyer, Edward Bennett Williams.

"I wanted to go to McBride," George told Melcher, "but he wouldn't let me." George told Melcher he'd get back to him.

Williams was one of the most powerful trial attorneys in America, a lawyer who had gained an acquittal for Teamster boss Jimmy Hoffa, the defender of the rich and famous including mobster Sam Giancana, red-baiter Joseph McCarthy, and Congressman Adam Clayton Powell, who was accused of stealing money from his campaign. Edward Bennett Williams knew how to win hard cases.

To keep from having to go to trial, Edward Bennett Williams and George continued stonewalling. In the meantime reporters dug up stories about how George had funneled illegal contributions to local politicians. The contribution to Congressman Charles Mosher was an embarrassment. It was revealed that the donations had been corporate contributions.

George, the Great Compromiser, used his connections and influence to do what he could to make things easier for his employees before the Senate Watergate Committee. Just a month before his employees were to appear, George made a $5,650 donation to Senator Dan Inouye, who was a member of that committee.

(That donation, which Inouye returned, was made public in February 1974, when it appeared in a Senate campaign report. Inouye told reporters, "I still look upon George Steinbrenner as a friend. Just because he has been indicted, I'm not going to shun him.")

On the day Robert Bartlome and Matt Clark appeared before the committee, Inouye said little, except toward the end of the day. He had two questions for Clark.

The first question established that George had never asked Clark directly for a contribution. Clark told the truth there. Bartlome had been the go-between.

The second one helped George establish Melcher as the strawman.

Asked Inouye of Clark, "Why didn't George go to the special prosecutor? Who advised him not to?"

Replied Clark, "Well, most of the time when Mr. Steinbrenner made this statement, he would say his attorneys, although I do think on one occasion he did mention . . . Mr. Melcher."

Says Jack Melcher, "Matt Clark made a reference to my conversations with him and the other guys. My mission, as outlined by George, had been to tell these guys before they met with the FBI that they should tell the FBI what happened, and to hold their hand and tell them everything would be all right.

"I went over the facts of this thing as I knew it, as they had been told to me by George, and also I had these fellows sign affidavits, and that's where I got myself in trouble, because I was accused of telling these fellows what they should be testifying to, although that was not intended at all."

When prosecutor Thomas McBride indicted George, he had to decide where to hold the hearings and the trial—Washington, where the campaign contributions were delivered, or Cleveland, where the obstruction of justice and the cover-up took place.

McBride chose Cleveland, George's backyard. On April 5, 1974, George was indicted on fourteen criminal counts. Five counts were for illegal contributions, two for encouraging false statements to FBI agents, four for obstructing justice, and two for obstructing a criminal investigation. George and AmShip were charged with conspiracy, and the company was charged with making illegal campaign contributions.

George called the press. He was furious, not about the indictments, but because they were made on April 5, Opening Day. He would have to miss it.

George never went to trial for what he did. Edward Bennett Williams and prosecutor Tom McBride made a plea bargain. Williams took advantage of the fact that McBride was severely understaffed and didn't want to have to go to trial.

On August 23, 1974, George went before Judge Leroy Contie and changed his plea from innocent to guilty on two counts, a felony on the campaign contributions and a misdemeanor on the obstruction.

Commented Jack Melcher, "I couldn't believe that Steinbrenner pleaded guilty, because up until then, he had been making these public statements, protestations of his innocence. He had stood on the courthouse steps and told the world he would ultimately be vindicated and that he had done nothing wrong."

Prosecutor McBride was confident George was going to jail. But he miscalculated. In the interim week, George's co-defense counsel, Robert J. Rotatori, called every one of George's powerful friends in Cleveland and asked them to write George a letter attesting to his charitable work and good character.

Seventy-one letters to the probation department, which was charged with deciding whether George should go to jail, came in an avalanche, from mayors, congressmen, school and college officials, Cleveland's anticrime program, the Catholic Youth Organization, lawyers, union officials, bank officials, and executives from companies such as Lorainglass Company, Buckeye Sheet Metal Company, and Toledo, Lorain, and Fairport Company.

Apparently the probation department weighed George's charitable contributions and decided that they outweighed the severity of what he had done, so the probation department recommended George be let off with a $20,000 fine. Judge Contie went along with the recommendation.

Not only did Edward Bennett Williams get George off with a slap on the wrist, but George was freed without ever having to testify under oath as to what he had done. Few others, including Richard Nixon, were afforded that luxury.

George was now free to tell his version of the Watergate saga, safe in the knowledge that there was little on the record except the testimony of Robert Bartlome and Matt Clark, his loyal employees, to contradict him. He could now place the blame squarely where he felt it belonged: on the shoulders of his two Williams classmates, Tom Evans and Jack Melcher.

In George's version, Evans talked him into giving the contributions, and Melcher did the rest.

Said Evans, "The thing I resent about George is that he lied about me. He seemed to indicate I tried to get a contribution from him and that there was a suggestion of a quid pro quo. That is a lie.''

Evans got away easy. George couldn't pin the bonus scheme on him or else George would have gone after his law license.

''If it hadn't been that George had set up that scheme in 1970 before he was back in touch with me, when he was giving money to the Democrats,'' said Evans, ''there's no doubt in my mind that George would have blamed it on me.''

Jack Melcher ended up taking the fall for George. Melcher didn't know it, but after George got finished with his PR manipulation, it would soon be promulgated that Melcher, not George, was the real villain of the AmShip campaign contribution scandal. According to George, the scheming Jack Melcher had told babe-in-the-woods George how to do it, and Jack Melcher had instructed the eight employees as well. Jack Melcher was the real brains behind the operation, and he, George Steinbrenner, who didn't know anything about campaign contributions and how they worked, was merely a patsy.

There are some who believe Melcher did aid in the cover-up, among them Thomas McBride, who felt that if Melcher didn't know somewhere along the way that George was lying to him about what he had done, he should have known. In April 1974, Melcher pleaded guilty to being an accessory to the obstruction. In other words, at worst, he was part of the cover-up, not the original plan.

Said Melcher, ''I pled guilty to a misdemeanor, being an accessory after the fact to Steinbrenner's contributions. I appeared before the court, and I was fined.

''I admitted I had had conversations, and that I had doubt as to the bona fides of what had happened. The truth was, I didn't know and didn't want to know. When you're working with Steinbrenner, he's the guy pulling the strings. You go along.''

Melcher took the plea, he said, because at the time he was facing heart surgery and was in no shape to face a long trial.

At George's sentencing, Edward Bennett Williams used Melcher as the fall guy. Williams told the judge that George had been misguided by perhaps the worst legal counsel he had ever seen. He was talking about Jack Melcher.

Tom McBride told the judge that George had tried to pin the blame on Evans, Kalmbach, and now Melcher.

Said the prosecutor, ''The devising of this scheme can be laid solely and properly at the door of Mr. Steinbrenner.'' He added, ''Mr. Steinbrenner concealed the true facts surrounding these contributions from his counsel, and without commenting on the competence or incompetence of Mr. Melcher, I know no lawyer who can give proper advice if a full and adequate disclosure of the facts is not made to him by his client.''

After George avoided jail, he went after Melcher with a vengeance. At first Melcher was only the butt of his stories. One was that before the grand-jury hearing was to take place, Melcher advised George to ''get out of the country for a few months until this Watergate mess blows over.'' According to Steinbrenner, he told Melcher, "I'm not a fugitive, and I'm not leaving. You must be nuts."

Melcher's first inkling that more trouble was brewing came in a little article in the local Lorain, Ohio, newspaper, an editorial suggesting Melcher should be disbarred.

In May 1974, Melcher was asked to take a leave of absence from AmShip. He returned to work in September, and in October he was told George wanted him to resign. Melcher refused. George then fired him.

An investigation by the Cleveland Bar Association ensued. By Christmas 1974, he was cleared.

Said Melcher, "When my guilty plea appeared in the newspaper, I got a letter from the Cleveland Bar Association saying they were going to investigate this. Right before Christmas 1974 the lawyer I had helping me called and said the committee had met and decided there was no grounds for any action. It was kind of a nice Christmas present.

"In late January, there came a notice from the Ohio State Bar Association saying they were going to go after me, and would I give the Cleveland Bar Association authority to turn over to them any information they had.

"At this point, I was beginning to start having heart problems. I began getting very serious chest pains. We were going to go through another one of these hearings, in Cleveland, and they were going to bring the commissioners, and finally I said to myself, 'The hell with it. I've had it. I'm not going to go through with it anymore.'

On December 12, 1975, Jack Melcher permanently resigned from the Ohio Bar.

Said Melcher of George, "I thought I knew him, and I trusted him. I'm not sure how I survived the thing. You never get over it."

Several weeks after his sentencing, George called the *Cleveland Press*, offering to give his complete cooperation in what would be a long feature on what *really* happened. The only catch: the paper could not quote him directly.

The story was given to the paper's top investigative reporters, Roy Meyers and Tony Tucci, who were eager to do it because during the whole episode George uncharacteristically had kept away from the press.

Two days later Meyers and Tucci spent an entire day interviewing George, who had convinced them he had been "screwed, blued, and tattooed," as Meyers put it.

Quickly the reporters discovered that George's story was a smokescreen.

"When we began checking out his story," said Meyers, "within two weeks we were very impressed with what a liar he was."

After some digging, they came to the conclusion that it had been George's scheme, that he had coerced his employees to lie, and that he was no innocent victim, as he contended.

Now George tried to stop them from writing their story. George put pressure on his friend, executive editor Herb Kamm, who told his reporters to return to

Cleveland. Over the phone Kamm informed them of George's hidden catch: Kamm had agreed that George could see the story before the paper printed it. Meyers and Tucci were shocked.

Instead of returning home, they went to see federal prosecutors Leon Jaworski and Tom McBride. They listened as McBride complained that Judge Contie hadn't given George jail time.

Meyers and Tucci returned to Cleveland to write their story. It was a four-parter, and it refuted George's claim that he was an innocent victim. As promised, the story was sent to George prior to publication.

George asked for a meeting with Kamm, Meyers, Tucci, and a couple other editors. George opened by telling them, "It's a shame my friends won't back me up." George wanted a favor. It seemed that baseball commissioner Bowie Kuhn was about to decide whether he was going to suspend George after his conviction. George asked the editors to hold the story until Kuhn made his decision.

At one point Roy Meyers thought George was about to cry. George told them his wife Joan was in Cedars of Lebanon Hospital in New York. "We don't know what it is." George paused for effect. "They tell me it might be stomach cancer, and she's worried and depressed, and if this story came out, it might kill her."

The editors agreed to hold the story until Bowie Kuhn made his decision. Too bad none of them had spoken with Jim Polk or bothered to check with Cedars of Lebanon Hospital.

The story didn't run for more than two months because the *Press* went on strike. Meyers went to Alaska during the strike. Tucci found a temporary job. When they returned, they learned that George had awarded "fellowships" to a select list of out-of-work *Press* reporters to lecture in the city schools. Included were reporters of sports, labor, and fashion.

If anyone thought his Watergate conviction had cured George of influence peddling, they were sadly mistaken.

Roy Meyers said to editor Bill Tanner, "The guy is unbelievable. At least he was smart enough not to offer it to Tony and me."

Tanner laughed.

"But he did," said Tanner.

The boys ran their story, all right, but George ended up compromising it in a clever way. He demanded that he be given the opportunity to rebut their story, and so the *Press* ran a fifth part. It was a question-and-answer piece. George wrote the questions *and* the answers. George had the effrontery to demand that the paper put the names of the two reporters on the piece he had written. It refused.

Just before the series was to run, Roy Meyers finally called Jim Polk. Asked Polk, "Did he pull the Tiny Tim bit on you?"

Meyers asked what he meant. Polk then told him about George's sob story about his wife's unnamed illness and that he had told him his son had been in a truck crash and was in Mass General. Polk told Meyers that when he checked it out, it turned out George had made up the Mass General story.

Young turks: Mickey Mantle and Billy Martin. (Marvin E. Newman)

*Standing left to right:* brother Frank Pisani, Billy, sister Pat Irvine, sister Joan Holland, brother Jack Downey, Jr. Seated, mother Jennie, father Jack Downey. (Courtesy Patricia Irvine)

Two sides of managing: arguing with an umpire, and a rare moment of relaxation with slugger Reggie Jackson, whose relationship with Billy was tempestuous. (Richard Pilling, top; UPI, bottom)

Billy and George Steinbrenner: Each man envied what the other had, Billy coveting George's wealth and power, George—the ultimate jock wannabe—coveting Billy's Yankee insider status. (UPI/Bettman)

Bill Reedy, Art Fowler, and Billy celebrate Billy Martin Day.
(Courtesy Bill Reedy)

Four close friends on the day of Billy's marriage to Jill Guiver:
Eddie and Peggy Sapir, Carol and Bill Reedy. (Courtesy Bill Reedy)

The day after the wedding: Billy, Jill, and Mickey. (Courtesy Bill Reedy)

Billy's truck, photographed at the garage where it was taken after the accident. (Photograph reprinted by permission of William C. Fischer, Fischer Bureau of Investigation, Endicott, New York)

The ditch that Billy drove into, and the drainage pipe he hit, just before the entrance to his driveway. (Courtesy Bill Reedy)

Inscription on Billy's tombstone. (Courtesy Bill Reedy)

Meyers then told Polk that George had sobbed to him that his wife, Joan, was in Cedars of Lebanon Hospital with cancer. Polk chuckled.

After he hung up, Meyers fumed. He should have checked out George's story and called the hospital, and he didn't.

In the end George, the master manipulator, accomplished his goal: He kept the story out of the paper until after Bowie Kuhn made his decision.

On November 27, 1974, Commissioner Kuhn suspended George for two years and pronounced him "ineligible and incompetent [to engage] in any association whatsoever with any major league club or its personnel."

As with Judge Contie's decision, it was a gentle slap on the wrist. In practical terms, George could not show up at the stadium for two years. Otherwise, say Yankee employees, he carried on as though nothing had changed, conducting business as usual.

It was while George was under suspension that he fired Bill Virdon and hired Billy Martin for the first time. Billy himself told me that the deal was completed with a phone call from George.

When Billy went to work for the Yankees, he didn't realize that he was about to lock horns with a man more talented at controlling people than he was. Billy demanded absolute loyalty from his players. He insisted they do things his way because he knew that if they did, they would win. When others did things Billy's way, success followed. He had proved it over and over.

His new boss, George Steinbrenner, also insisted that people do things his way, not because his way was better, but because he was a rich, insecure man who needed to control others as a way of feeling good about himself and feeling important. Billy didn't know it, but he had been one of George's childhood heroes, and that qualified Billy to become one of George's punching bags, as the failed athlete from Cleveland would destroy Billy's self-confidence and ruin his reputation in a long campaign to make him submit to his authority.

The pattern would be repeated over and over again, as George would seek to "rehabilitate" and at the same time abuse former heroes of his, including Lou Saban, Al Rosen, Gabe Paul, and Bob Lemon. Only former Browns quarterback Otto Graham managed to escape George's grasp when Graham took the job coaching football at the Coast Guard Academy.

Howard "Hopalong" Cassady had been one of George's heroes and close friends while at Ohio State in 1955. A few years after George took over the Yankees, Steve Blasky, who had gone to Williams with George, was invited to sit with him in his private box at Yankee Stadium for a game. Waiting on them was a man Blasky thought looked vaguely familiar.

Said Blasky, "The man wasn't much younger than me, a very nice looking man. He was acting like a waiter, and George treated him like one. In fact, George was treating him like shit. He told him, 'Come on, move your ass. Get the drinks.'

"I said to this guy, 'Are you Mr. Cassady?' He said, 'Yeah, I'm Hopalong Cassady.' After the man left, I said, 'George, that's Hopalong Cassady. He won the Heisman Trophy. He was one of my heroes.'

''George said, 'Well, he works for me.'

''I said, 'How can you treat this guy that way? He's a hero of mine.'

''He said, 'Well, he's working for me.' ''

And now Billy Martin, another of George Steinbrenner's heroes, was working for him. George Steinbrenner used Billy's love for the Yankees as the sword he held over a man too hooked on liquor to break away from George and the Yankees. If Billy didn't do exactly what George wanted him to do, or if Billy threatened George's ego by becoming too popular, or if Billy talked back to him or made fun of him, it was off with his head. Five separate times.

Intermittently over the next ten years George Steinbrenner would contribute to the death of Billy Martin by driving him crazy, taking away his self-respect, wrecking his morale, and ruining his reputation, with the effect of exacerbating his drinking problem.

Experts in alcoholism argue that some people control others by keeping them so upset and roiled up that they continue to drink in great quantity. If Billy had been sober, chances are he would have left George after the first go-round and never returned, rather than take the abuse George heaped upon him all those years. But because Billy was an alcoholic, his thinking was that he had to keep proving he was the right man for the Yankee managerial job no matter what obstacles he encountered.

If Billy had only known how George had treated John McClendon and the Cleveland Piper players. If Billy had only known that George Steinbrenner was the sort of man who would deliberately break campaign contribution rules and then, when he got caught, blame others. If Billy had only understood that George was a pathological liar who had a strong need to control people working for him in order to make him feel like a man. If Billy had only understood the truly evil actions surrounding George's illegal campaign contributions to President Nixon's Committee to Re-elect the President, maybe Billy could have been saved from having to work for him.

But Billy didn't know, and if he had known he probably wouldn't have cared. Because Billy had his own ego problems. Billy had been cast aside by the Yankees years earlier, and here was his chance to return and show everyone that George Weiss had made a big mistake by trading him away. And as far as Billy was concerned, there was no situation he couldn't handle, no man he couldn't master. No matter who it was. Even George Steinbrenner.

# BACK TO THE

# BRONX

**G**abe Paul, president of the New York Yankees, happened to be visiting Bob Short in July 1975 when Texas owner Brad Corbett called Short's Minneapolis office to say he had fired Billy. The Yankees were in town for a series with the Twins.

According to Short, when Paul heard that Martin had been fired, Gabe said, "That's the end of Billy Martin. He's been fired by the Twins, Tigers, and Rangers, and no one else will hire him now."

Short said, "You got to be kidding. There will always be someone in this game to hire a manager like Martin."

Gabe insisted no one else would hire him. Short said he would bet Gabe five hundred dollars.

"He'll be hired within ten days," Short predicted, adding that if Gabe wished to make another bet, Short would tell him which team Billy would go to.

"Tell me," said Gabe.

"The Yankees." Billy's Yankees.

"You're crazy," Gabe told him. "I know Steinbrenner better than you do, and George would *never* hire him."

Short proposed a bet at ten-to-one odds. "Five hundred to five thousand that Martin will be the new Yankee manager."

According to Short, Gabe accepted the bet. According to Gabe, no such bet was ever made.

Whether there was a bet or not, Short was right that the new owner of the Yankees, George Steinbrenner, wanted Billy as manager. Short knew it because Steinbrenner had asked his help in getting Billy to sign with the Yankees.

Steinbrenner, who had been suspended by baseball commissioner Bowie Kuhn for two years in November 1974, had been barred from running the Yankees. In his ruling, Kuhn forbade Steinbrenner from having any association whatsoever with any major league club or its personnel.

George removed himself from the Yankees physically, but his telephone was rarely more than an arm's length away, and he kept in constant contact with Gabe Paul.

The same day Steinbrenner talked to Bob Short, he said to Gabe Paul about Billy, "That man is a fiery manager. Let's get him."

"I think you'll be making a mistake, George."

"I want him. Let's get him."

Little was publicly known about George Steinbrenner at the time. He had come from Cleveland. He owned ships. He got rid of the old, staid CBS regime, which the fans saw as a positive. Even though Kuhn had barred him from contact with the other Yankee executives, on New Year's Eve 1974, he spent a large sum of money to buy free agent Catfish Hunter for the Yankees. In 1975, Hunter finished the season 23–14 and returned the Yankees to respectability.

Yankee fans looked forward to a return of Yankee hegemony under the new ownership. When you're a kid and your team wins fourteen pennants in sixteen years, and then, all of a sudden, the glory fades, you miss that dearly. Here was an owner who was going to bring back the Yankees in all their glory.

After Billy was fired by Texas, he took off to go fishing on a secluded lake in Colorado, somewhere near Grand Junction. He wanted absolute privacy, wanted to cleanse himself from the layer of disgust that had covered him in Texas. Billy knew the firing would make Corbett, Brown, and O'Brien happy but would cause his players and the Rangers fans to be losers, which bothered him deeply. He swore he would never put himself in such a subservient position again.

At the same time the new owner of the New York Yankees, George Steinbrenner, spoke to his GM, Gabe Paul. Steinbrenner had decided that Billy Martin would be *his* new manager. Bill Virdon was a good technician, but to Steinbrenner, who had a theatrical bent, Virdon lacked excitement or flair. He didn't put asses in the seats, a favorite Steinbrenner test. The Yankees were boring under Virdon, and George Steinbrenner was looking for pizzazz, show business, box office boffo. He wanted a manager and a team that would make things happen.

Gabe's response, "We have to be able to control him."

Gabe Paul swore he would not allow Billy the leeway that Bob Short had given him at Texas.

Gabe told me, "I didn't think a manager should have anything to do with the farm system. They don't have time, and they don't know all the details of agreements you have with players and why you move some fellows around."

Gabe worried that Billy would start second-guessing his player moves. He worried that Billy wouldn't be a team management player, wouldn't meet or consult with him. In short he worried that Billy would be Billy.

Steinbrenner's worries were moral concerns, which was pretty ironic considering he was under suspension for his own illegal acts at the time. He knew Billy's reputation and feared that Billy would get drunk and punch somebody, embarrassing the Yankees.

Gabe sent his trusted assistant, Birdie Tebbetts, to negotiate a contract with Billy. At the same time Gabe called Billy's home and left a message with Gretchen Martin's father for Billy to meet Tebbetts in Denver.

When his father-in-law called, he told Billy, "Birdie Tebbetts said the contract would be 'very lucrative.' "

Billy said his intentions were not to sign with the Yankees or anyone else but to sit out the rest of the season, collect the rest of the money owed him on his $72,000-a-year contract, and, as he put it, "let time heal my wounds."

At their first meeting Birdie showed Billy a contract. Billy was miffed. It wasn't lucrative, as Tebbetts had told his father-in-law, but rather was for the same $72,000 he was getting at Texas. And there were clauses in the contract that upset Billy from the start.

One said he had to "personally conduct yourself at all times so as to represent the best interest of the New York Yankees and to adhere to all club policies." Another clause prohibited him from criticizing management. A third provided that he had to keep himself available to management to consult with them. If he didn't comply, he could be fired without pay.

Billy told Birdie he wasn't interested.

Birdie and Gabe then played good cop, bad cop on Billy. From the first, Birdie was the good guy. At that initial meeting he blamed Gabe for the clauses. He was soothing Billy, telling him to sign the contract despite the clauses. Even as Billy was saying no, Birdie was keeping Billy on the line, asking him not to be precipitous. Birdie then lied to Billy, telling Billy he wanted to call Gabe in New York.

Gabe wasn't in New York. He was in the next room of the hotel listening in on their conversation.

Gabe called Birdie's room and asked if Billy would meet with him the next day. Billy agreed.

The next day Billy again declined to sign the contract. He repeated to Gabe that he didn't like the money or the clauses.

"It smelled," Billy told me. "I was putting myself in a position where this George Steinbrenner, the Yankee owner, could handcuff me, and I didn't know him very well. I really didn't know anything about him."

"No, Gabe, I don't want to do it," Billy told Gabe.

Gabe told Billy not to be too hasty.

"Why don't you talk to George?" Gabe suggested. Gabe called him and put him on the phone.

"Billy, I would like to have you as our manager," Steinbrenner told him.

"I'd like to be manager of the Yankees," Billy said, but he spelled out the reasons he didn't like the offer.

George's first reaction was to threaten him. "If you don't take this offer now, you will never get it again. C'mon, Billy, be the manager. Here is your big chance to manage the Yankees, something you've wanted to do."

Steinbrenner had done his homework. He knew Billy's weak spot, and he was pushing all the right buttons to get him to sign a contract that the Yankee owner later would use as a war club against him.

Billy said he would go home and think about it.

Billy could not have known it, but the man at the other end of the phone was a master manipulator who *always* got his way. He wanted Billy to be manager. He wanted the clauses in his contract. He knew that Billy's weakness was his soft spot for the Yankees. If Steinbrenner couldn't get what he wanted one way, he would take another tack and get it a different way.

Steinbrenner had Billy's confidant, Bob Short, call Billy and tell him to take the job. Billy told Short of his reservations.

Short said, "It'll work out. If the man wants you that badly, it'll work out."

Unfortunately for Billy, Short couldn't conceive that anyone could be as controlling and monstrous to work for as George Steinbrenner would prove to be.

Short asked Billy if he could talk to Gretchen, and they talked for an hour. Billy asked Gretchen what he should do. She recommended he take the job.

That night Billy mulled over what to do. He trusted that he could work with Gabe Paul. But he didn't know how long Gabe would be with the Yankees. Gabe had been in baseball forever, and he was nearing retirement. Billy, who had a sharp, analytical mind, wondered what would happen to him after Gabe left. His experience signing with Bob Short and getting dumped by Brad Corbett had left him shaken.

Billy had "bad vibes" about Steinbrenner. He didn't like the clauses, the way George had threatened him to sign the contract, and the way he had gotten Bob Short to call him.

"My every instinct argued against signing this contract," Billy said.

The next morning he went to a meeting with Gabe and Birdie intending to say no. Inexplicably, even to himself, he said yes.

Gabe, for one, *knew* Billy would sign all along.

"I thought then, and I still think now," Gabe said, "he was going for it right from the start. Because the Yankees meant a lot to him, and the opportunity to manage the Yankees certainly was vindication about having been fired by them. Down in his heart, I knew Billy wanted to manage the Yankees."

George and Gabe had gotten their way. Billy signed the contract with the behavior clauses in the contract. Gabe, for one, was glad they were there. "I thought it would help keep him in line," he said, "and it did, to a certain extent. Sure, it did. It helped. Not entirely, but it helped some. All the time he would refer to them. He'd say, 'Take those clauses out.' Which showed he was thinking about them. He talked about them all the time."

As one indication of how much he wanted the job, Billy signed to manage the Yankees even though Gabe refused to let him bring Art Fowler with him as pitching coach. Art had played for Gabe in Cincinnati, and Gabe didn't like him back then.

"He drinks too much," Gabe told him. His pitching coach would be former Cleveland pitching star Bob Lemon.

"What a joke," said Billy later. "They wouldn't let me have Fowler, but they let me have Bob Lemon. He drinks more than Fowler."

Thirteen days after he was fired at Texas, Billy became the manager of the New York Yankees, replacing Bill Virdon, who had been named Manager of the Year in 1974 by the UPI.

Lee MacPhail, the general manager under Mike Burke and CBS, had hired Virdon, and when George Steinbrenner and Gabe Paul took over the Yankees, MacPhail and Virdon became part of the mass exodus of former CBS employees. MacPhail, a highly respected baseball executive, left to become American League president. With George Steinbrenner and Gabe Paul in control, it was out with the old and in with the new, including a new manager, Billy.

August 14, 1975, was Old-Timers' Day at Shea Stadium, where the Yankees were playing while august, hallowed Yankee Stadium was being refurbished into a neomodern, ugly hunk of concrete. Hank Bauer, one of the Yankee old-timers, said about Virdon, "How could a guy be Manager of the Year and supposedly get so bad over the winter?" The same could have been said of Billy.

On Old-Timers' Day, Billy the Kid upstaged all the old-timers, including Joe DiMaggio and his Hall of Fame buddies, Whitey Ford and Mickey Mantle. Billy was embarrassed to be introduced after the great stars, and he asked Steinbrenner, "Can I go out in another spot?"

"No," Steinbrenner ordered, "you go out last."

Waiting there for his first introduction as Yankee manager, it was just as Gabe Paul had said, a final vindication after eighteen years of homelessness. Billy had started under Casey Stengel, and here he was filling his mentor's shoes.

When asked how he felt about that, Billy became emotional. Tears began to form. He gasped for breath.

"The only job," he said. "The Yankee job. This is the only job I ever wanted."

Back in Glendale, California, Casey Stengel, eighty-five years old, was dying of cancer. He had severe pain and was slipping away.

Stengel's housekeeper, June Bowlin, was watching television when she saw the news.

"Casey, Casey," she said, "Billy is the new manager of the Yankees."

The wizened old man smiled and began to cry.

Said Bowlin, "He loved that boy so."

When public address announcer Bob Sheppard intoned over the loudspeaker, "Number one, the new manager of the Yankees . . . Billy Martin," Billy ran onto the field wearing a cowboy jacket, pants, and boots, and was greeted by a standing ovation. There were a few boos, and it was just like Billy to hear the boos over the din of adulation.

Billy told himself, "They're booing right now, but before I'm through everyone will be cheering."

Billy the Kid was back in pinstripes, eighteen years and two months after that June day in 1957 when Yankee GM George Weiss traded him to Kansas City.

"Every time I'm fired," Billy told reporters, "I get a better job."

Billy spent the remainder of the 1975 season observing his players, looking to weed out the bad apples, the chronic complainers, the backstabbers, the malcontents, the clubhouse lawyers. Billy saw he had the best catcher in Thurman Munson and the best relief pitcher in Sparky Lyle. Roy White was a hustler and a pro, as was Lou Piniella. Chris Chambliss and Graig Nettles on the corners were also solid professionals. Catfish Hunter was as good as they came.

Billy spent that period trying to get to know the players. He drank with them, celebrated victories with them, charmed fans, and began a long-running feud with the men he viewed as enemies of himself and of his players: the sportswriters. Occasionally he lost his temper, as he did late in September after a game the Yankees lost. On the bus from the ballpark to the hotel, a couple of the players in the back of the bus were talking about the big college football games the next day. When Billy heard players talking about football, he began screaming. He said, "Maybe you guys are in the wrong sport."

Only about half the players were on the bus, and nothing more was said, but it was an indication that in 1976 things were going to be different. Baseball would become a serious, all-encompassing pursuit.

Billy and Gabe discussed who he wanted traded away. Billy respected Gabe, who had started in baseball back in 1935 as a batboy in the minor leagues for the Rochester Red Wings. He moved on to Cincinnati, where he became traveling secretary and then general manager. He is credited with building the Reds team that won the 1961 pennant. After running the Houston Astros and the Cleveland Indians, he came to the Yankees as an owner with George Steinbrenner in 1973.

Billy and Gabe worked closely together. At Billy's urging, Gabe traded pitchers Pat Dobson and Doc Medich and outfielder Bobby Bonds. Gabe sent Dobson to Cleveland for Oscar Gamble. On December 11, Gabe sent Bonds to California for Mickey Rivers and pitcher Ed Figueroa. An hour later he sent Medich to Pittsburgh for young second baseman Willie Randolph, pitcher Ken Brett, and one of the great personalities of baseball, pitcher Dock Ellis.

In Rivers and Randolph the Yankees were adding real speed to the top of the lineup. Said Gabe Paul, "Speed is a real necessity, especially with Billy as the manager. Usually you tailor a manager to a team. But this was an attempt to tailor a team to a manager."

Not all managers know how to or are willing to handle trouble. Three of the incoming players—Rivers, Gamble, and Ellis—had reputations for being rebellious and hardheaded. Billy didn't care about that. Neither did Gabe Paul. Billy's favorite line was that he would play Hitler, Mussolini, and Stalin if they had ability. Said Gabe, concurring, ''I believe there is no substitute for talent. It's the manager's job to handle talent. I'd rather have a louse who hits .300 than a nice guy who hits .200.''

As 1976 began, Billy and Gabe were working together to help build the Yankees, which hadn't won a pennant since 1964, into a powerhouse. At the beginning of spring training, Billy wrote a letter to each of his players saying that the days of Yankee mediocrity were over. He stressed pride, desire, and the will to win. ''I have never been with a loser, and I'm not going to start now.''

# A YANKEE FLAG

Under the terms of baseball commissioner Bowie Kuhn's two-year ban, which kept George Steinbrenner from running the Yankees, the Yankees' owner wasn't scheduled to return from exile until the fall of 1976, which meant he would have missed being part of the Yankees during America's bicentennial year, and he would have had to stay away during the dedication of the new Yankee Stadium.

But on March 1, 1976, baseball commissioner Bowie Kuhn announced he had shortened Steinbrenner's ban and allowed him to return as head of the Yankees. The lifting of the ban came eight months after Steinbrenner had saved Kuhn's job as commissioner. There had been a "Dump Bowie" movement among the owners, which was eventually going to succeed, but Kuhn gave Steinbrenner dispensation to attend a meeting of the major league owners during the summer of 1975, and at that meeting Steinbrenner spoke out and voted against the infidels who wanted the inept Kuhn fired. As a result, Kuhn got a new seven-year contract.

Both Kuhn and Steinbrenner denied any deal, but why would Steinbrenner have voted for Kuhn, whom he despised for his pompous, narrow mien as well as his shortsighted, stupid decisions, unless he was hoping for a commuted sentence? And why would Kuhn have commuted his ban except out of gratitude?

Red Smith, the late columnist for *The New York Times,* despised both Kuhn and Steinbrenner. Wrote Smith sarcastically, "By granting a parole to George

M. Steinbrenner III, Bowie Kuhn has shown once again what scholars knew all along—that baseball's supreme being is not only all-wise but also all-merciful.''

Steinbrenner might have been away in body for almost eighteen months, but his presence never stopped being felt. During spring training of 1975, manager Bill Virdon, always a good soldier, came into the Yankee clubhouse carrying a cassette recorder. He said, "Okay, guys, you gotta listen to this." It was a recording made by Steinbrenner, giving the players a pep talk, advising them that they had to give a hundred percent, that they had to do themselves proud, that they had better remember Yankee pride and tradition.

Said Graig Nettles, in our book *Balls*, "He probably thought we were going to take that seriously, as though he were Knute Rockne giving his players a pep talk. We were sitting there at our lockers, laughing at him. Damn, that was funny.

"No one could look anyone else in the face. We all turned toward our lockers to keep from breaking up laughing. We couldn't believe it! We had never heard anything like this! It was so strange. Virdon stood there with his stone face, trying to keep from being disrespectful, while we all sat in our lockers howling with laughter.''

When the players heard Steinbrenner had been cleared to resume ownership of the team, they braced themselves for an onslaught of what they called "George's petty shit," but during spring training of 1976, George rarely interfered with Billy or his players. Part of the reason may have been that Steinbrenner didn't think he had a very good team and felt he would hurt his reputation by being involved with it.

Before the 1976 season, George even bet Billy a tugboat that the Yankees would not win the pennant.

During the winter Billy, Mickey Mantle, Whitey Ford, Yogi Berra, and Elston Howard had all gone with Steinbrenner to Curaçao to conduct a baseball clinic. It was evening, and Billy and George were in the gambling casino. George had given each former player five hundred dollars in cash. Whitey and Ellie had lost all their money. Billy had won a thousand.

According to Billy, George came over and gave Whitey and Ellie another five hundred dollars.

"Where's my five hundred?" asked Billy.

"You're winning," George said.

Billy asked him, "You mean to say that you're going to penalize me for winning?"

Later that evening Billy and George sat down to discuss the coming season. Billy said, "George, don't worry about it. We're going to win the pennant."

George said, "You know, we have a lot of holes." He thought about what Billy had said and added, "You are, like heck."

Billy, feeling flush, asked him, "What do you want to bet?"

Steinbrenner said, "Tell you what. I own some tugboats. If you win the pennant, I'll give you a tugboat."

Billy said, "A tugboat is worth $300,000, right?"

George said, "You win, you got it."

* * *

Though Billy was excited about the coming season, in his private life he was feeling sad and lost. Though his wife Gretchen had been instrumental in helping him decide to take the Yankee job, when Billy moved from Arlington, Texas, to New York, she refused to go with him. They had been married sixteen years. She had heard the rumors. She had been left behind long enough. She wanted a divorce. Their eleven-year-old son, Billy Joe, remained with her.

Around the same time Billy's first child, Kelly Ann, twenty-two, was arrested on drug charges in Barranquilla, Colombia. She was detained at the airport as she was about to board a plane for Miami. A pound of cocaine was found strapped to her thighs with elastic bands.

Kelly was convicted of drug smuggling and sentenced to three years in prison.

Kelly desperately needed to have her father in her life, but Billy rarely seemed to have time for her. Children did not fit into Billy's lifestyle. Even when she was a young adult, Kelly, like all children, looked to her father for assistance. Billy would make promises but rarely would keep them.

Kelly had been in a car wreck, and her bills were piling up. Kelly knew that asking Billy for help was fruitless, so she decided to take a walk on the wild side, accepting a payment of $10,000 for smuggling drugs back into the States.

On November 17, 1975, she was arrested. It cost her two years of her life in a Colombian prison. Throughout those years, Billy was under enormous pressure to get her out of jail as he called upon influential friends and paid tens of thousands of dollars to Colombian officials and various lawyers.

When Billy talked about the incident he told me, ''The guy who set her up has two broken legs.'' But years later when I asked Kelly, she said she had seen the man a couple years ago, and he was walking just fine.

When Kelly finally got out of prison, she told Billy, ''Hey, Dad, I needed the money, and I couldn't depend on you. I couldn't depend on anybody but myself.''

During that spring a group of about thirty Yankee employees gathered for a meeting to discuss the state of the team. Some of the employees wondered why everyone was invited, since George, Gabe, and Billy could have just as easily held it in private. At the meeting they went over the team position by position.

Roy White was to be in left, Mickey Rivers in center, and Oscar Gamble and Lou Piniella platooning in right. Thurman Munson was the catcher. The infielders—Chris Chambliss at first, Willie Randolph at second, and Graig Nettles at third—were set, but when they got to shortstop, George said, ''Jim Mason.''

Billy divided his players into three groups. One group was ''his players.'' A second group were players who were not ''his players'' but who otherwise could play. The third group were players Billy felt were not good enough to play for him. Billy had no interest in those players whatsoever. Jim Mason belonged to the third group.

Billy said, ''Release him. He's no good. I won't play him.''

Gabe replied, ''Billy, I paid Texas $100,000 for Mason.''

Billy said, "I know you did. I was the manager at Texas when I sold him to you. He couldn't play then. I couldn't believe you paid $100,000 for him."

"Then what should I do with him?" Gabe asked.

"I wouldn't care if he steps off a curb and gets hit by a car," said Billy.

"But I paid $100,000 for him."

"I don't give a fuck. Get rid of him."

Gabe said, "Tell you what I'll do, Billy. I'll showcase him for a few weeks, and then we'll trade him."

Billy said, "You'll showcase him, and he'll show everyone he can't play, and then you'll stick me with him, and I'll have to play him."

Mason ended up playing ninety-three games at shortstop in 1976. He hit .180. Fred "Chicken" Stanley, who was one of "Billy's players," eventually became the Yankee shortstop that year. The next year Gabe Paul traded away Oscar Gamble to the White Sox to get All-Star shortstop Bucky Dent.

Another player Billy traded away was left-handed pitcher Larry Gura. Billy had been sitting in the lobby of the hotel in Cleveland when Gura walked in with outfielder Rich Coggins. Both were carrying tennis rackets.

One of Billy's rules was that there not be any tennis playing on the day of a game. Billy fined them both, leading to an ugly confrontation with Coggins in the dugout before the game. In May the Yankees traded Gura to Kansas City for catcher Fran Healy.

Later Billy admitted he had made a mistake with Gura. The kid could pitch. For nine seasons Gura was a starter on the staff of the Kansas City Royals.

Billy ran the team, setting the tone during spring training. When George asked if he could play one of his tape recordings in the clubhouse, Billy turned him down.

The one annoyance Billy had was Gabe's insistence that the two meet every afternoon per the contract. Billy bitched about it, but he went to the meetings.

On the field and in the dugout, Billy was clearly in charge. With Mickey Rivers and Willie Randolph at the top of his lineup, the Yankees began winning games in a very un-Yankee-like way, playing inside baseball, hitting-and-running, stealing bases, outhustling the opposition. Only Graig Nettles, who would lead the league in home runs in 1976 with 32, was a long-ball threat.

On Opening Day in Milwaukee, Billy called a team meeting. Billy told his players, "You know, we're going to win this thing this year. You're all good enough to win. The only way you won't win is if you don't listen to me and do what I tell you. Anybody who doesn't want to do it my way can leave now, but I'm *guaranteeing* you right now, if you do what I tell you, you'll win this thing—easy.

"Anyone who doesn't think so can leave now, no hard feelings. I might be rough, but I'm going to treat you like men until you act different. I'm not a guy checking curfews; just be ready when the bell rings."

The players, who normally aren't impressed easily, were moved by what Billy had to say. After losing the first game of the season to Milwaukee, the Yankees were ahead by three runs in the ninth inning of the second game when a Brewer hit a grand-slam home run. After the Brewer crossed the plate, Billy called time and went running out to talk to the umpires. It turned out that one of the other umpires had called time. Billy got him to admit it, and the home run didn't count. The Yankees went on to win the game.

That night on the plane, Billy turned to Bill Kane, the Yankees' traveling secretary, and said, "I got these guys now. They'll do whatever I tell them." He said, "We'll win this easy. You watch. We'll win it *easy*. They will do everything I tell them."

Four games into the season the Yankees took the lead and never lost it. They had tight pitching, led by Catfish Hunter, Ed Figueroa, and Dock Ellis, solid defense, and they hustled and intimidated the opposition as only a Billy Martin team could.

On May 20, Yankee outfielder Lou Piniella, trying to score, crashed into Red Sox catcher Carlton Fisk. When Graig Nettles rushed in to make sure Lou was okay, Bill Lee started yelling at Graig, who picked the outspoken pitcher up and slammed him to the ground, dislocating his shoulder. Instead of feeling sorry for Lee, Billy opined that Lee should have kept his mouth shut.

By July 25 the Yankees led second-place Baltimore by fourteen and a half games. Two days later, against the Orioles, pitcher Dock Ellis hit Reggie Jackson in the face with a fastball. Over the years Billy's pitchers often had hit Reggie. He was one of those hitters Billy felt a need to try to intimidate. In retaliation Oriole pitcher Jim Palmer hit Mickey Rivers with a pitch in the ninth inning.

After the game Billy belittled Oriole manager Earl Weaver and pitcher Jim Palmer. Billy said, "That was about the weakest knockdown I ever saw in my life. It belongs in the Hall of Shame. Knowing Jim, I'm sure he was directed to hit Rivers. He's not that type of guy. I'll deck Earl at home plate the next time one of our guys is deliberately thrown at."

In June, Steinbrenner called Billy to tell him of the two blockbuster deals he had just made. The first was the purchase of superstar pitcher Vida Blue from Charlie Finley's A's. The cost was $1.5 million, an incredible sum at the time.

The second deal was made over the strong objection of Gabe Paul. It was inspired by Steinbrenner's son Hank, then thirteen, who told his father that the pitcher he ought to acquire was All-Star pitcher Kenny Holtzman. George proceeded to do so, receiving Holtzman and three lesser players from the Baltimore Orioles for veteran left-hander Rudy May and three very talented youngsters.

Blue would have been a stellar pickup for the team, but commissioner Bowie Kuhn, overlooking a hundred years of baseball history, voided the sale, along with the sale of Rollie Fingers and Joe Rudi to the Boston Red Sox for a million each, as being "against the best interests of baseball."

As for the Holtzman deal, Billy was sorry Kuhn couldn't void that one as well. When Billy saw who the Yankees had given up—Rudy May *and* Tippy Martinez *and* Scott McGregor *and* Rick Dempsey—he was horrified. Steinbrenner was an impatient man who overvalued marquee players and far undervalued the worth of his farm system players. It became a game for competing general managers to see who could fleece the Yankees of their best prospects.

In this trade the Yankees gave up most of their left-handed pitching talent, a commodity needed to tame the short right-field porch in Yankee Stadium, and even *with* Rick Dempsey, Billy felt the Yankees didn't have enough catching.

As it turned out, Holtzman, the former Oakland pitching star who had won 21, 19, and 18 games over the last three years, went 9–7 for the Yankees in 1976, assuring them the pennant. The next year he came down with a sore arm. At the same time Scott McGregor became an anchor of the Orioles staff, finishing in double figures in wins for nine years in a row, including a 20-win season in 1980. Dempsey became an All-Star catcher. May won 18 games for Baltimore in 1977, and for ten years Martinez was a relief star for the Birds.

In 1976 the Holtzman trade was one instance when Steinbrenner overruled his brain trust, but the disastrous results wouldn't make themselves felt for a few years. Ken Holtzman came to the Yankees and fit right in. As the team rolled on, everyone was happy, with a minimum of dissension or interference from George. In the minds of the ballplayers, there was no question who was running the team: Billy. Doyle Alexander had come to the team in the Holtzman trade, and in his first few starts with the Yankees, after starting strong he would fade around the seventh inning.

On Old-Timers' Day against the Orioles, Alexander gave up four runs and seven hits in four innings. Billy came out to the mound and pulled him.

Alexander was angry. He said, "Those were horseshit hits. My arm's as good as the last time."

Billy told him, "I decide how your arm is, not you."

Furious, Alexander went into the clubhouse.

After the game Billy held a team meeting. He told the team, "A player *never* talks back to the manager, not in front of the other players. I have an office with a door for that." He added, "If anyone does that again, I will kick the crap out of him right there in front of the team."

The night before Doyle Alexander's next start, he came to Billy and apologized for his actions.

It was a very happy ball club. Nettles, Lyle, and Munson, three critical but smart ballplayers, all admitted that they had never played for a manager who knew how to win like Billy did. In his autobiography, the usually grumpy and surly Munson said, "We have fun together. We like each other. In the past there were factions, cliques, a division on the team. But this ball club is fun. This ball club is together."

On September 25, they clinched the division title.

Pitcher Dock Ellis was instrumental in the Yankee success that year. After coming over from the Pittsburgh Pirates, Dock posted a 17–8 record with a 3.18 ERA, and he did it while under the influence or either drugs or alcohol the entire year he was there. Dock *thrived* playing under the high-octane pressure generated by Billy Martin. Dock, a man who was particularly sensitive to racial discrimination, saw no signs of it on Billy's Yankees. A man who enjoyed intimidating others with the best of them, Dock reveled in the way Martin ran the Yankees.

One time Billy skipped Dock in the rotation, and he and Billy had a set-to about it. The fallout didn't last long. The two had a mutual admiration society.

Billy would say to him with a grin, "Dock, pitchers are like coconuts on a tree. If I want another one, all I have to do is shake the tree."

It was, said Dock Ellis, the most fun he ever had in baseball.

"I spent eight years with the Pittsburgh Pirates before I came over to the Yankees in '76," said Ellis, "and in all those years on the Pirates, not one of those teams had the camaraderie that the Yankees had in the one year.

"The difference was that on the Yankees, the white boys knew how to party. In white man's terms, to party means to do everything, you name it. We would diss each other. They didn't care. It was kick ass and take names, led by Billy Martin.

"Billy would say to us, 'Do whatever the fuck you want to do, but give me one hundred and twenty-five percent.'

"I can remember in spring training, it was hard for me because I was trying to fool the players. I was doing dope, getting high, but I didn't want them to know it, because they were all new to me, and I had to have my time to check them out, because what they were telling me was, 'We're cool. We're all cool. We know you're cool. We found out about you. Come on.'

"And I was saying, 'No, I don't do that.' Because in my head I was saying to myself, I don't know you guys.

"It was opening night, we were in Milwaukee, first night of the season. I can remember Lou Piniella and Rick Dempsey were fighting with each other. I said, 'What's wrong with these crazy motherfuckers? What are they doing? Why are they fighting?' I wouldn't even go in there. Who knows what they were fighting about. On that team guys were always arguing, 'You should have caught that ball.' 'You shouldn't have called that pitch.' But they talked baseball all the time.

"And after the game the guys came and got me. The partying was on!

"I used to tease Billy Martin. We'd get drunk all the time, and I'd say, 'You don't run this fucking team. Catfish Hunter runs the fucking team.'

" 'What do you mean?'

"I'd say, 'Everyone respects Catfish. Everyone don't respect you.' I used to fuck with him all the time. He'd say, 'I run this fucking team.'

"One time Billy ran out of a bar. I yelled at him, 'Don't forget, Catfish runs this fucking team. If it wasn't for Catfish, you wouldn't be where you are today.'

"Billy got to the door. He said, 'I run this fucking team.' And he took off. Billy was cool.

"I saw Billy win five games the year I was there. He won five fucking games just intimidating the umpires. Where they owed him a call. Even if the ball was down the cock, they called it a ball, and on the next pitch our hitter would hit a home run, and we'd win the game. I remember him saying a lot, 'You owe me, motherfucker.' Even after he got kicked out of a game, he would scream back, 'You owe me, you motherfucker.'

"And they remembered. You could tell. Why would the umpire call a ball down the middle a ball? Damn. And over in the dugout, Billy would be going, 'See that, hee-hee-hee-hee-hee-hee. See that, hee-hee-hee-hee-hee-hee.'

"Billy believed in intimidation. And that's what he wanted the team to do, to intimidate the other team. We were coming to town, and we were coming to kick your ass. Here come the fucking badass Yankees. They're coming to kick your ass. And Billy wanted to be in charge.''

With the Yankees safely in front throughout the spring and summer, George Steinbrenner kept his counsel. There were some things he wanted Billy to do, but Gabe Paul made sure there was very little friction. Gabe Paul, the man the players called "the Smiling Cobra," was a bottom-line man like Billy. Billy won games, and that was all Gabe cared about. Billy's drinking, his womanizing, his umpire baiting, even his spats with the front office—Gabe could handle that. Gabe could also handle George. Steinbrenner dished out verbal abuse to all his employees. Gabe's way of dealing with George's critical tirades was to sit silent and take it, get red in the back of his neck, and when George ran out of steam, he would reason with him. Usually Gabe was able to talk him out of doing or saying something stupid.

Commented journalist Ed Linn, "Gabe has a way of remaining so unnaturally calm in the face of dissension, turmoil, and omens of doom that he has been moved to wonder himself whether there isn't a missing gene somewhere in his makeup.''

The one blowup Gabe had with Billy came in August, when Billy demanded that Gabe bring up reserve catcher Ellie Hendricks to back up Thurman Munson and Fran Healy. It was a reprise of the issue Billy had make such a stink over in Texas.

The difference this time was Gabe's attitude toward Billy. Gabe ignored the words and told Billy no. The clause in Billy's contract, Gabe knew, would keep Billy from making a public protest. Whatever Billy said to him, no matter how profane or antagonistic, washed off him like dirty dishwater—as would George's words.

To Gabe, what was most important was that Billy manage *his way*—without interference from anyone, especially George. In 1976, Gabe did everything he could to make sure George stayed out of Billy's way.

"George used to want me to talk to him after each game," said Gabe, "talk about the conduct of the game. And I never believed in that. I'd say to George, 'I'll talk to him tomorrow,' which I felt you did with a manager. You didn't talk to him *after* the game, but the next day.

"And George would say, 'No, I want you to talk to him tonight.' So I'd see Billy in the pressroom after the game and say hi, so if George said to me, 'Did you talk to him?' I could say, 'Yes, I talked to him.'

"I used to tell Billy, 'Manage the way you want to manage. If you manage the way someone else wants you to manage, you're not yourself.' I don't think a fella can manage that way. If you're thinking about what someone else is thinking, when you make a decision, there's no way you can do it. No way.

"And Billy was great. He appreciated that. For me, it was no big deal. I was just doing the right thing.

"George and I used to have breakfast a lot. I lived on 69th Street in Manhattan, and he lived around the corner from me on 71st or 72nd and Third Avenue. There was a little delicatessen we used to go to. As long as we were talking one-to-one you could take issue with him, and he would be reasonable.

"There were times when George wanted me to do something that wasn't right, when I was supposed to go and tell Billy to make a lineup change, or try to tell Billy when to hit or bunt, which any fan would. George was a fan. He would have enjoyed managing.

"Sometimes I told Billy what George wanted, and sometimes if Billy didn't think it was the right move, he wouldn't do it, and sometimes I wouldn't tell him. Because I knew what the result would be. I'd make up an excuse to tell George.

"It wasn't that tough. What's right is right. I have my own ideas about managing, and one of them is that you can't have a guy wondering what he is supposed to do, thinking about what someone else thinks he should do. He has to manage on what he thinks. So many decisions are snap judgments, and he has to make them quickly, and if his mind is wandering, he's not going to make good decisions.

"I used to tell George that. He would say he understood, but sometimes his ideas and my ideas were different."

On September 9, 1976, Billy signed a three-year contract extension. Everything was still peachy. The honeymoon was holding despite a flap the month before when Steinbrenner decided to flex his muscles with Billy a little by inviting out-of-work manager Dick Williams to sit with him in his box during a game. This was during his contract negotiations with Billy, and George insisted that Williams was "just a friend," but Billy knew better.

"It didn't intimidate me," Billy said, "but it sure made me madder than hell."

Graig Nettles remembered the incident in *Balls*. Said Nettles, "It had to unsettle Billy just for him to see Williams looking down on him like that.

"Just the fact that Williams was out of a job put pressure on all the other managers, including Billy. And Billy wasn't the most secure person in the world, not after having been fired at Minnesota, Detroit, and Texas."

At the announcement of Billy's new contract, Steinbrenner told reporters, "Billy and I have a rapport that few people in sports have. I've seen him go to Minnesota and Detroit and Texas and do a hell of a job and get fired. I don't think that will happen here, because I know Billy. I know how to get along with him. We joke with each other—I tell him he's number one and a half and I'm number one—but he knows he has to go along with the system."

He added, "In a winning organization, no one is indispensable, and it goes for me, too, and I think Billy understands that now."

A couple weeks later the Yankees lost several games in a row. Graig Nettles noticed that George was getting edgy. Said Nettles, "Our lead was cut from ten to seven games. For a few days there he started to panic, and he was screaming and threatening to fire Billy, but we began winning again and he quieted down.''

Billy and George were still getting along very well—until it became clear that the Yankees *were* going to win the pennant. Then Billy noticed something odd about George: The Yankee owner was unhappy that Billy was getting so much credit.

Since Steinbrenner had hired him to manage the Yankees, Billy had had two goals: The first was to win the pennant, but the second, almost as important to him as the first, was to become George Steinbrenner's friend. Billy wanted to be George's buddy, to go to lunch with him, spend time with him, be part of George's circle. Billy wanted the status that went with being the friend of a rich, powerful man. He wanted to be able to go places with George and be seen with him and to get to know the people George knew, such as Barbara Walters and Donald Trump.

He should have known better. Billy had had the same yearning to join the Goats back in Berkeley, but despite his success on the ball field in high school, he could never crack their society. Even his Goat teammates had shunned him. George, Billy discovered early, would no more accept Billy as a friend than the Goats would. The irony was that all his life George had been a jock sniffer. At Williams the real jocks had spurned him. In this case Billy Martin, the most famous manager in the game, wanted to be George's friend; yet George spurned Billy because Billy was a white-trash guy from the slums, a drinker, a brawler, a womanizer, and George was both offended by and afraid of him.

But Billy would not stop trying to win his friendship, not until Billy came to fully understand just how flawed George was as a person. Billy both envied and truly despised George, yet he coveted a close relationship with him.

Billy had thought that winning a pennant would seal their friendship. He was bitterly disappointed to find out it wasn't to be.

"At that point," recalled Billy in his autobiography *Number 1,* "I began to feel that George was acting jealous of me. He seemed to resent that he didn't have a big enough hand in it, seemed to feel that he wasn't going to get enough of the credit, and it bothered him that I was getting so much publicity.

"The Yankees were supreme again. That was the real glory, and he should have been happy and let it go at that."

What bothered Billy most of all was that no matter hard Billy tried, and he tried hard, he couldn't get George to like him as a person.

"He had no reason to be jealous of me," said Billy. "We should have been best of friends."

But Billy didn't know George Steinbrenner. George *was* jealous that Billy was getting so much credit. George did resent Billy for it. He resented Gabe Paul for it as well. He did not have enough self-esteem to allow Billy and Gabe their glory. Instead George began bragging about how he had personally rescued the Yankees from oblivion.

Said Billy, "They asked me to do a job, and I did it. What more did the man want of me? But ego creeps in, unfortunately, and like other owners, the man likes to read his name in the papers, and he feels it necessary to tell people he was responsible for the success of the Yankees. Not the twenty-five players or the coaches or the manager, mind you. But him.''

The playoff series against the Kansas City Royals started with bitter feuding. Larry Gura, whom Billy had traded to the Royals, and hitting star George Brett, whose brother Ken had been a disappointment to Billy on the Yankees, both called Billy names.

The Yankee players responded by hounding Brett, calling him names, and his error in the first game helped the Yankees win. Billy screamed at Gura, the starting pitcher, trying to rattle him.

Royals left-hander Paul Splittorff (relieving starter Dennis Leonard in the third inning) won Game 2 and Dock Ellis came back strong in Game 3. Billy skipped Ken Holtzman in favor of pitching Catfish Hunter with three days' rest, but Hunter wasn't sharp, and the series went to a fifth and deciding game.

Before the final game, Billy was feeling nervous, and he decided to work off some of his excess energy by getting into a pissing match with the reporters, whom he often treated with disdain. He ordered that a rope be placed around the batting cage to keep all the newspaper writers away from the Yankee players while they were taking batting practice.

Veteran writer Dick Young objected. Billy grimly told him the rope was there to protect the writers from foul balls.

Said Young, "Why don't you tell the fans to go home, too?"

"I'm the boss here," said Billy. "I don't tell you how to run your newspaper."

Young kicked the barrier down. One of the Yankee security guards put it back up.

The Royals got off to a 2–0 lead in the top of the first, but the Yankees came back with six runs to lead by three after six innings.

In the top of the eighth George Brett, who continued screaming back and forth with Billy, hit a three-run home run to tie the game.

The Royals took the field for the bottom of the ninth. The boisterous Yankee fans threw garbage down on Royals outfielder Hal McRae. One run would win it for the Yankees.

Mark Littell, a left-handed reliever, completed his warm-up pitches. Yankee first baseman Chris Chambliss was the first batter. Littell attempted to throw Chambliss a fastball inside, but he didn't come in enough. The pitch was waist-high, and the muscular first baseman pulled the ball on a line toward the low right-field stands. Fair or foul? Chambliss stood there watching, and when the ball cleared the fence fair, Chambliss leaped into the air, and the packed Yankee Stadium crowd went into ecstasy.

After the game Billy and George embraced. Billy said, "I got to thank George and Gabe." The duplicity at Texas was still on his mind. He said, "There was no backdooring, no one going behind my back to them."

He wiped champagne and tears from his eyes. He thought of Casey Stengel, who had died the year before. Casey would have been so proud.

Said Billy, "I wish Casey was here to see it. This was his pennant."

Billy should have ended his comments right there. Those kind words would have completed the circle that had been left broken since 1957, when Weiss traded him away. But Billy's demons controlled him, and he had to add a coda: "Hey, who's that guy [Pete Franklin] on that late-night Cleveland show who's always riding me? I got a message for him—I want you to print it. Tell him to kiss my dago ass.

"Those guys who didn't think this team could do it, who picked against us, who said I'd never win one, where are they now? Now they can kiss my dago ass. I won it. The Yankees are back where they belong, on top."

Spoken like a true Yankee.

The Yankees flew that day to Cincinnati, where they were to play the next evening. Having to play so soon after a tough series put a fatal strain on the Yankee pitching staff.

In 1976, Steinbrenner didn't do anything to infuriate the players until the World Series, when they discovered he had commandeered all the tickets for his Cleveland cohorts and left his players holding an empty bag. Minutes before the national anthem of the first game, some of the players still were scrambling to find tickets for their family and friends.

Said Graig Nettles in his book, "There was a lot of screaming and yelling. Everyone was upset. Thurman was furious. It was like George was telling us that he got us to the Series all by himself and screw the players.

"Five minutes before the national anthem, we got the tickets."

Billy started Doyle Alexander against Don Gullett in the opener. Gullett was unbeatable. When the Yankees lost the second game on an error by Chicken Stanley, Steinbrenner gave Billy a window into the future. George showed his true colors when he told Billy, "If you play Stanley at shortstop again, I'll get rid of him." According to Billy, the best he could do was convince George to allow Stanley to be a utility player in 1977.

Dock Ellis got knocked out early in Game 3, and the Reds won in a sweep when in the finale Reds catcher Johnny Bench hit two home runs, one off Ed Figueroa, the other off reliever Dick Tidrow.

After losing the final game, Billy was feeling low. He was sitting on the floor of the trainer's room when Steinbrenner came in. Said Billy, "He looked at me, and if daggers could have come out of the man's eyes, they would have. He was looking at me like, 'How can you do this to me?' as if I had lost the Series in four straight on purpose, like he was embarrassed. Who the hell wasn't embarrassed? The Reds outplayed us.

"George," said Billy, "was really going to get into things, because he wasn't going to be embarrassed like that again."

What Billy didn't understand, however, was that George Steinbrenner was not like other owners. He insisted the team win, but if the team didn't win, his response would not be made in terms of sound baseball decisions. For most owners, just being in the World Series would have been a terrific achievement. But George Steinbrenner grew up with the constitution of a spoiled child. Rather than exult in the joy of having been the American League pennant winner, his response was a measure of punishing retribution that would bring a great deal of pain and embarrassment to both Billy and his players.

What Billy would soon learn was that George Steinbrenner was under the delusion that only *he* could succeed and that everyone else could only fail. From his father, Steinbrenner had learned how to dominate and manipulate. He had proved it by his actions at American Ship, and he continued his practice of terrorizing his hirelings on the New York Yankees.

The one thing Steinbrenner couldn't do, and has never learned how to do to this day—perhaps never really cared enough about—was build a baseball team. Gabe Paul had built this team. Billy had rounded it into a winning unit. When the team failed to win the World Series, in George's mind punishment was in order. He would make both Billy and Gabe pay.

Right now he needed Gabe Paul and he needed Billy. One day, he knew, he wouldn't need them. One day he wouldn't need anyone.

# REGGIE

In 1973, in his first year as owner of the Yankees, George Steinbrenner invited Williams College classmates Peter Callahan and Pete DeLisser to sit with him in his private box. The game was against the Oakland A's, and on this day Reggie Jackson hit a home run and led his team to a lopsided victory.

Callahan remembered that all through the game Steinbrenner was picking up his phone, calling manager Ralph Houk "every other minute." Callahan, who was prescient, whispered to DeLisser about the Steinbrenner-Houk relationship, "This is never going to last."

Before the game ended, Steinbrenner turned to Callahan and told him, "Pete, I got to tell you, I'm going to get Jackson, and I'm going to get Billy Martin."

Said Callahan, "He was embarrassed, and he was going to do something about it."

George was "able to do something about it" during the fall of 1976 because a Los Angeles Dodger pitcher named Andy Messersmith and a Montral Expos pitcher named Dave McNally had turned the economics of baseball upside down the year before. In 1974 Messersmith had had a 20–6 record and a 2.59 ERA with the Dodgers. Messersmith had been among the league leaders in games started, earned run average, and strikeouts, and he felt he deserved a modest raise and a no-trade clause in his contract.

The Dodgers were owned by Walter O'Malley, the richest and most powerful of the baseball owners, an arrogant tightwad who treated his players like they were lucky to have a job. O'Malley offered Messersmith less than what he wanted and refused him his no-trade clause.

In response, the pitcher told the Dodgers he would play out the season without a contract, file a grievance, and then ask an arbitrator to determine whether he was free of his contractual obligation. This was an extremely risky thing for Messersmith to do. Were he to hurt his arm, he would be a *big* loser.

But Messersmith, who ought to have his own *room* in the baseball Hall of Fame (who was more influential in the history of the game than he?), had principles. And he had talent. Playing without a contract, Messersmith in 1975 won nineteen games with an ERA of 2.29. By the end of the year the Dodgers, running scared (what if he won in arbitration?), began softening their stand. A resolute, angry Messersmith held firm.

At the time, a player's contract contained what was known as the reserve clause. It said that the club had the right to automatically renew the contract from year to year. In effect, if you signed with one team, because of the reserve clause, that team owned you in perpetuity; for as soon as the term of one year ran out, the reserve clause would kick in, and the contract would take effect for the next year.

Messersmith argued that if a player signed for a year and the contract ran out, the year was over and so was the contract, and the player then would be free to sign with whomever he chose. To baseball owners, free agency was as scary a concept as communism was to American citizens in the 1950s. Chaos would reign. Baseball would be ruined. There'd be pestilence in the land.

If the arrogant Dodgers had paid Messersmith his crummy thirty grand, who knows how history might have been changed?

At the end of the year independent arbitrator Peter Seitz ruled that the reserve clause was *not* renewable and did not bind a player indefinitely and that Messersmith was free to sign with anyone he wished at the end of 1976.

End of reserve clause. End of low salaries.

When Seitz made his ruling, few understood its far-reaching import. But as a result of the ruling, the first free-agent draft was held during the winter of 1976. Some of the traditional general managers skipped this opportunity to add major talent. Some picked only a couple players as a public relations move to look good to their fans, having no intention of making decent offers to any of them.

Several teams saw it as an opportunity to improve dramatically. Gene Autry and his California Angels were drooling, as was the new Atlanta Braves owner, Ted Turner. George Steinbrenner, the man who revered stars, was, too. Among the players he drafted were second baseman Bobby Grich, shortstop Bert Campaneris, and outfielders Don Baylor, Gary Matthews, and Reggie Jackson.

The Yankees' great need, as George, Gabe, and Billy all agreed, was at shortstop. The player Gabe wanted was Bucky Dent of the Chicago White Sox. The White Sox, and gremlin owner Bill Veeck, didn't want to pay Dent what he was worth. Chicago GM Roland Hemond agreed to trade him to the Yankees for Oscar Gamble, but he also wanted a couple of the Yankees' prize minor league pitchers, among them Gil Patterson, LaMarr Hoyt, and Ron Guidry.

Gabe agreed to give him Gamble and Hoyt. Hemond wanted one more—Guidry. Paul refused. An impatient Steinbrenner told him, "Do it." Gabe steadfastly refused. The deal hung in the air without resolution.

And so, going into the free-agent draft, the Yankees still desired a shortstop. Gabe Paul thought Bert Campaneris had slowed too much, and Billy didn't like the way he played, didn't think he had much courage.

Gabe felt that if the Yankees could sign Bobby Grich, they could move him to short, and he would be terrific. Baltimore had played him at second only because they had a spectacular shortstop in Mark Belanger. Grich was a strong hitter as well.

Billy Martin coveted A's outfielder Joe Rudi. The Yankee lineup featured left-handed batters Mickey Rivers, Chris Chambliss, Graig Nettles, and Oscar Gamble. Billy wanted a another righty bat to go along with them. Rudi, a great fielder with an excellent arm, was a professional hitter. But at age thirty, Rudi lacked speed, Gabe felt. The Yankees hadn't even put Rudi on the list of players with whom they wished to negotiate. Billy had no say in the matter. There was a clause in his contract that said so.

The Yankees wanted to sign one more hitter, in this order of preference: Grich, Baylor, who had right-handed power, and Gary Matthews, another strong righty. Left-handed slugger Reggie Jackson, a home-run hitter but a notoriously mediocre fielder, was little more than an added name as a sop to the fans.

After the Yankees drafted the players eligible for signing, Steinbrenner told the press, "Grich, Gullett, Baylor, and Jackson are the players we're most interested in."

At the time George had set his sights on his first two names, Grich and pitcher Don Gullett. He was so sure he was going to get Grich that he didn't even begin talking to Don Baylor's agent until it was too late.

The signings around the country came in a flurry. Baylor signed on November 16 with Autry and California. The next day it was announced that Rudi had signed with California, Campaneris with the Texas Rangers, Dave Cash to Montreal, and Don Gullett with the Yankees.

Atlanta had a handshake with Matthews, and Cleveland signed Wayne Garland. Six Yankee choices were gone.

The Yankee push was on to sign Grich, who was taking a leisurely drive from Baltimore to his home in Long Beach, California. Grich was taking the southern route, and he had reached New Mexico, where he was exploring Indian ruins.

When Grich heard that his former roomie, Don Baylor, had signed with the Angels, he called his agent, Jerry Kapstein, and told him he wanted to play with Baylor. It didn't hurt that Anaheim was close to his home. Another factor was that the man who had initially signed him to a contract in baseball was Harry Dalton, the Angels' general manager.

Grich told Dalton that if the Angels made a fair offer, he would accept it and not get into a bidding war.

Gene Autry told Dalton, "Any ballplayer who wants to play for us that badly, let's go get him."

In the meantime George and Gabe went to see Kapstein and Grich, who finally had arrived home. They used all their charm and persuasion, arguing the bottom line, that Grich would *guarantee* them a world championship.

They almost got the fine second baseman to bite.

When Grich hesitated, George lost it. His ego took over. He attacked Gene Autry and Harry Dalton. He began by saying he didn't think it right that the Angels were signing three players. He said he was going to the commissioner's office to stop them from doing so. He threatened an investigation.

George had removed the mask of civility and allowed his real personality to come through. And Bobby Grich didn't like it.

When Grich met with Harry Dalton, he asked Dalton whether Steinbrenner's threats had any substance. Dalton rightly assured him that they did not. Quickly Grich wrapped up a deal with the Angels.

Having lost Grich, the player he really wanted, George moved into face-saving mode. As quickly as possible he began leaking stories that it hadn't been Grich the Yankees were craving, but Reggie Jackson.

Steinbrenner, through his experiences at Lockbourne and with the Pipers in Cleveland, continued his practice of giving newspaper reporters exclusives, knowing it was likely the reporter would be so happy to have the story, he would print what George had to say verbatim without checking to see if he was lying, without asking follow-up questions. Such is the importance of a "scoop."

Steinbrenner called Murray Chass of the most prestigious paper in the city, *The New York Times*, and told him that the Yankees were wavering about Grich because they weren't sure he could make the switch from second to short. He added that Gabe Paul was also turning toward Jackson.

The George touch: Chass could have the story only on the condition that he not be quoted. Chass had to say it was coming from "a source."

No journalist likes to print a quote by an unnamed source, but sometimes you have to do it to get your scoop, and so the next day Murray Chass wrote his story, just as Steinbrenner knew he would. George's "source" ploy was one he would use hundreds of times in the next fifteen years to pursue his own agenda and throw dirt on his players.

From the moment George learned he had lost Grich, he went after Reggie Jackson very hard. Jackson certainly had his positives. With the bat, he was a Hall of Famer, on a par with the giants, such as Mickey Mantle, Harmon Killebrew, and Mike Schmidt. Reggie was a winner. Every year, it seemed, his team was in the playoffs and the World Series. But that wasn't the main reason Steinbrenner wanted him. Keeping himself from looking bad in public was the primary reason. Winning was the by-product. Reggie was the only impact player left, and if George didn't sign Jackson, he would be humiliated after all his talk in the press. That's why he insisted on signing him.

Gabe Paul didn't want Reggie. Billy Martin *certainly* didn't want Reggie. Gabe, who didn't care about personalities, didn't want him simply because he was a mediocre fielder. Also, Reggie was a left-handed batter, when the crying need was another righty bat. Furthermore, Gabe knew, if George paid Reggie more than his own veterans—Munson, Nettles, Piniella, and Chambliss—he'd have to handle the bitterness that was sure to follow.

Billy, who built his teams around pitching and defense, didn't want Jackson because of his fielding, but also rejected him because Billy didn't like prima donnas. Billy wanted each of his players to put the team first. He also wanted his players to put *him* first. Billy was the boss. Subservience by his players was very important to Billy. And Reggie had never taken a backseat to anybody.

Also, Billy was satisfied with his right-field platoon of Oscar Gamble and Lou Piniella, two of his favorite players. They had helped him win a pennant, and Billy didn't feel the team needed Reggie to come in and screw up the chemistry. He felt the addition of Don Gullett would be enough to push them over the top.

Reggie, Billy knew, would be tougher to handle than a bull at a rodeo. Reggie had the reputation for being a most unsettling force on a baseball team. He had a reputation to make any manager grimace. On the field Reggie was a shameless self-promoter, one of the reasons Billy often had his pitchers throw at Reggie. Off the field Reggie had a way of turning all the media attention in his direction. With Reggie on the team, it was as though everyone else was invisible. Not only was he a shit stirrer, but he was a genius with words, as good as the best televangelist. After hitting a home run, he once told reporters, "It was as if all the power of the earth and the sky and the sands and the waters were in these hands."

Reggie loved the media attention because he had a superstar's ego. He was savvy enough to figure out that the more press you get, the bigger the star you become, and the more attractive you are to sponsors and television interviewers. It was a spiral that spun higher and faster until Reggie was on the cover of *Time* magazine on June 3, 1974.

Most players hated the drudgery of having to talk to reporters and didn't mind that Reggie had cornered the quote market, but Reggie wasn't the only player with an ego. Some A's players resented him deeply for trying so hard to eclipse them.

His A's teammates who bothered to analyze him were convinced that Reggie had a character flaw. At a young age Reggie had been abandoned by his mother. One day she lined up the children to say good-bye, selected a couple of his sisters and a brother to take with her, and left Reggie behind with his father. Reggie was always trying to come to grips with his abandonment. Teammates saw that those who tried hardest to befriend Reggie often received the harshest treatment in return. Teammates also said that when they walked into the clubhouse, they didn't know whether Reggie would be friendly, as he could be, or rude and antisocial, as he often was. Or boastful and manic.

Said teammate Rick Monday, "Reggie Jackson is at least three different people. One of them I have always liked and admired and respected very much. The other two I can't stand. The trouble with being with Reggie is you never know which one of him you get."

Reggie *had* to be the center of attention. He was part of an Oakland A's team that won world championships in 1972, 1973, and 1974. Reggie was the captain. He *craved* being the leader, a title other players adamantly refused to acknowledge because he *wanted* it *so* badly.

Said teammate Bill North, "He was caught up in his own insecurities, that whole leadership bullshit."

He was a terribly insecure man. A's teammate Gene Tenace asserted, "He was insecure, sensitive, easily hurt. This game does that to you." But for a man supposedly so sensitive, Reggie had an easy way of insulting others. Teammates discovered that the biggest mistake they could make when it came to dealing with Reggie was to show him kindness. Always he would react with an ugly demeanor.

Reggie constantly abused autograph seekers and people who wished to take his photograph.

Teammate Don Baylor recalled in his autobiography that Reggie constantly insulted waiters and fans when they came up to him while he was eating dinner.

Said Baylor, "No one likes being insulted by a jerk, being in the company of a jerk. I just don't believe he ever knew how to handle the attention."

Reggie was always doing things that infuriated his teammates. Since first signing with the A's, Reggie had invested his money wisely in real estate. No question, he was a very smart man when it came to business. But he liked to flaunt his wealth. His teammates were fascinated and turned off when he would sit in the clubhouse, take out his wallet, and count the stack of bills in front of them.

Catfish Hunter quipped, "He'd give you the shirt off his back; of course, he'd call a press conference to announce it."

He was uncomfortable in public, but at the same time no one tried harder to make himself a god in the eyes of the public. Teammates tired of hearing him orate constantly in front of the press. Their resentment caused some of them to undervalue his great talent. Some of his teammates hated having him on the team. Not his bat, which was powerful and could win games all by itself. Him. Reginald Martinez Jackson.

Gabe Paul warned George, "He will be a destructive force."

George didn't care. He wanted to sign someone *big*, and never mind the consequences.

George went after Reggie as he had gone after Jerry Lucas with the Pipers. He wined and dined Reggie at the prestigious "21" Club. Billy was living in New Jersey at the time, and he read in the paper of their dinner. Billy, sensitive to slights by the rich since his childhood, had led George's team to a pennant, and George had never taken him to the "21" Club. In fact, George had never taken him *anywhere*. Billy reacted like a jilted lover.

On Thanksgiving Day 1976, when other men were sitting down and having holiday turkey with their families, George Steinbrenner was out signing his new marquee player to a five-year contract for $3.75 million plus a Rolls-Royce.

After the ink dried, Reggie noted that the way George had come after him, it was "like trying to hustle a girl in a bar." Reggie didn't know it, but the "girl" George really had wanted had gotten away, and he, Reggie, was only sloppy seconds.

When Reggie arrived for spring training in 1977, he and George held a press conference. Billy had not been invited. Reggie was holding his black bat. He told the reporters, "You see this? This is the Dues Collector. This now helps the Yankees intimidate every other team in baseball. That's what I do just by walking into this clubhouse. Nobody will embarrass the Yankees in the World Series as long as I am carrying the Dues Collector."

When Reggie showed up for spring training, he had a large contract and a bad elbow, the first sore arm he had suffered in his career. His insecurity mounted daily as he had to face the awesome reality of having to live up to the preseason publicity brought on by that contract. A loner, he was lonely. Making him feel uneasy was the standoffishness of some of the other players, especially Thurman Munson, Graig Nettles, Lou Piniella, and Sparky Lyle, who resented his presence and his contract. His manager, Billy Martin, made it known he had wanted Joe Rudi.

Staring the possibility of failure in the face, Reggie Jackson was scared shitless.

It was during this time that Robert Ward, a freelance writer hired by *Sport* magazine, approached Reggie at the Banana Boat Bar in Ft. Lauderdale. Ward offered Reggie a sympathetic ear. They sat over beers. Ward several times asked Reggie for an interview. Finally Reggie agreed.

When Reggie let loose a torrent of words explaining what he was feeling in his heart and soul, Robert Ward captured it. Ward walked away from their meeting with a story that when it was published toward the end of May, would create as much angst on a team as has ever been created in the history of the game of baseball.

Reggie was facing the prospect of having to take a backseat to catcher Thurman Munson. Reggie knew what Thurman meant to the fans. He knew how much Billy loved him. One of the things Reggie wanted Ward to understand was that he could not play second fiddle to anyone, even someone as beloved as Thurman Munson.

Like George, when Reggie felt insecure, he attacked the object of his insecurity. And so Reggie Jackson, using the entire arsenal in his very large vocabulary, picked out for his most scathing criticism the popular Thurman Munson.

Reggie in *Sport* magazine: "You know, this team . . . it all flows from me. I've got to keep it all going. I'm the straw that stirs the drink. It all comes back to me. Maybe I should say me and Munson . . . but really, he doesn't enter into it. He's being so damned insecure about the whole thing."

Ward asked him why he didn't just talk it out with Munson. Reggie told him, "No, he's not ready for it yet. He doesn't even know he feels that way. . . . He'd try to cover up, but he ought to know he can't cover up anything from me. Man, there is no way. I can read these guys. No, I'll wait, and eventually he'll be whipped. There will come that moment when he really knows I won, and he'll want to hear everything is all right, and then I'll go to him and we will get it right."

Ward, astounded, said to Reggie, "Do you want this printed?"

Reggie told him, "Print it."

Reggie continued. "The way the Yankees were humiliated by the Reds, you think that doesn't bother Billy Martin? He's no fool. He's smart. Very smart. And he's a winner. Munson's tough, too. He is a winner, but there is just nobody who can do for a club what I can do. That's just the way it is. Munson thinks he can be the straw that stirs the drink, but he can only stir it bad."

Again Ward said to him, "Are you *sure* you want me to print this?"

Reggie told him, "Yes, print it. I *want* to see that in print. I want to *read* it."

On May 23, Reggie, and the rest of the sports world, got to read it.

Said Graig Nettles in his book, "The crazy times really began after Reggie announced he was 'the straw that stirred the drink,' and of course, Billy right away wanted Reggie to know that he, Billy, was the straw. And all the while, there was George, sitting in his office thinking *he* was stirring the drinks. I'll tell you, for a couple of years there, there was an awful lot of stirring going on. Something crazy was going on every single day."

That the Yankees were still able to win a world championship in 1977 was a tribute to Billy and the players, including Jackson, who despite everything that went on during that tumultuous season turned out to be the ultimate show-man.

# WHAT
# REGGIE WROTH

With Reggie Jackson on the team, the veteran players now had *two* people to hate. The first was Steinbrenner, of course. He had been looked at by the players as a wacko since that first year in 1973, when on Opening Day he wrote down the uniform numbers of the players whose hair he felt was too long.

That day Ralph Houk called a team meeting, and he read a letter from Steinbrenner. Said Houk, "The following players have to get haircuts." And he proceeded to read off uniform numbers: "Number 19, number 28, number 41." The players began to laugh. So did Houk. For George it was just like back at Williams College when the real athletes were laughing at him. And once again he kept coming back for more.

The funniest thing he did happened in Texas. Gene Michael, who has a deep fear of bugs, was playing shortstop. On this day someone took a hot dog and stuffed it into the finger of Michael's glove. Gene ran out to take ground balls before an inning in the game, put his fingers in, felt the hot dog, and threw his glove about fifty feet in the air.

Steinbrenner was sitting in a box seat near the dugout, and in a rage he ordered the batboy to find out what had happened. He demanded the hot dog be brought to him, and after the game he went to manager Ralph Houk and demanded Houk find out who did it.

Said Sparky Lyle, "Ralph couldn't believe it. Neither could we. We called it The Great Wiener Caper."

After that, little about George was funny to Houk or the players. Houk, a major who had fought the Japanese during World War II, was as tough as they come. George felt a need to dominate Houk, to make him bend to his will. George hounded his manager, called him day and night, leaving messages for him wherever he went, even calling him during games. Houk had been in baseball for forty years. Who was George Steinbrenner to be telling him what to do? George had no previous experience in baseball. What did he know about running a baseball team?

By the end of the year Ralph Houk decided he was not going to take the abuse a day longer than his contract mandated. He quit on the final day of the season, joining the exodus begun by GM Lee MacPhail and George's partner, Mike Burke.

The players remembered Houk's farewell on the final day of the season. He told the players, "I have to quit before I punch the guy. I don't want to leave the game of baseball by punching an owner. But if he keeps on bothering me like he does, I'll end up hitting him."

The next manager was Bill Virdon. He was the perfect manager for Steinbrenner. He carried out orders no matter how ridiculous. Virdon took George's calls, went to his meetings, held his tongue, and still he almost won the division title in 1974, losing out with two days left in the season.

On the final day of the season Steinbrenner came into the clubhouse and gave a bizarre speech to his players. The Yankees had barely lost the division title to the Baltimore Orioles. Everyone in the clubhouse thought that a superb accomplishment. When George spoke to them, he made it clear that they had lost the title, not because Baltimore had been a better team and had deserved to win, but because of Ralph Houk, now managing the Detroit Tigers. Houk, George told them, had started his young pitchers against the Orioles so the Orioles would win and the Yankees would lose.

To the players George sounded like Humphrey Bogart playing Captain Queeg in *The Caine Mutiny* as he sought to place blame on the stewards for the disappearance of the strawberries.

Instead of congratulating his players on a fine year, he told them they had better win the season finale. "You have to show the people of New York that you can go out a winner."

The players were now convinced he was a crackpot. What did the fans care whether the team lost the final game? they wondered. Said Nettles, "The fans are a lot smarter than he ever gives them credit for."

When Bowie Kuhn suspended Steinbrenner for his illegal campaign contributions at the end of 1974, the players sighed in relief. When Virdon came to spring training in 1975 and played a recording of a pep talk by George, the players once again laughed at this blustery pretender with no credentials trying to talk to them like a Pop Warner football coach.

When George returned in 1976, the team broke in front early and won, so he was relatively quiet. That the team had started in first place almost from Opening Day and went wire to wire to a pennant was a big factor in what had turned out to be a relatively tranquil season. George tended to panic and run his mouth when things seemed to be going wrong, but little went wrong that year, so George kept a low profile.

In 1977 his large profile would loom over everyone. Things would be different. After a pennant in 1976, the Yankees were back in the limelight, and beginning in 1977, George wanted that spotlight to shine on him. Billy had observed that George was feeling slighted because he hadn't gotten his share of the credit for the pennant victory. In the year 1977, George would make sure the public knew to whom the credit belonged. The man who had said he was going to run his ship business and leave the Yankees to the professionals was going to be a hands-on owner.

George's new acquisition, Reggie Jackson, also would make a difference in team morale in 1977. Because of this one player, the closest-knit, loosest team in the league would become one of the most deeply divided teams in baseball history.

Billy hated the new pairing of George and Reggie because it was the type of relationship Billy disliked most, a player with ties to the owner. A relationship like that—Carl Yastrzemski had such a relationship with Boston owner Tom Yawkey, and Al Kaline had had it with John Fetzer of the Tigers—created all sorts of problems by rendering the manager powerless and making him feel impotent. And Billy was a guy who *hated* not feeling in control.

Said Graig Nettles at the time, "To Billy, Reggie's being there isn't all that different from George being there, and everyone knows how Billy feels when George tries to tell him how to run the team."

When the Yankee players came to camp, they were ready to mutiny. They had won the pennant for the Yankees in 1976, made the owner a small fortune, and what was their reward? The owner was doling out a king's ransom to a player they didn't want on the team in the first place.

No one had complained when Steinbrenner paid millions to Catfish Hunter. No one said anything about Don Gullett's contract, either. The players liked Hunter and Gullett, two gifted pitchers who kept their mouths shut and let their statistics speak for their brilliance.

When Reggie Jackson got his millions, the Yankee players protested openly. Pitcher Dock Ellis wanted more money, as did Graig Nettles, Sparky Lyle, Mickey Rivers, and Thurman Munson.

Said Lyle in his book *The Bronx Zoo*, "George told us to be loyal to him and he would be good to us. His loyalty went out the window. We helped him to win." Sparky threatened not to pitch in spring training until George gave him an equitable contract.

George had promised Munson, the Yankee captain, that he would always be the highest-paid Yankee. But when he made that promise, George hadn't anticipated the huge jump in salaries made possible by the Peter Seitz arbitration ruling. Munson was named American League MVP in 1976. He wanted his contract rewritten. George, faced with the choice of keeping his word and having to pay millions more than he wanted to pay, kept stalling him.

According to Munson, George had also promised to renegotiate if the Yankees won the pennant. George said the promise applied only if they won the World Series. "Obviously one of us heard the wrong thing," said Munson. "I don't think it was me."

It was like the bet with Billy that the Yankees would win the pennant in 1976. George had bet him a tugboat. When the Yankees won the pennant, George said they had bet the Yankees had to win the World Series. He refused to pay up.

All during the winter Munson made speeches at banquets, asking to be traded. George was stung so badly, he tried another of his famous ploys—he called Munson up at one in the morning during a poker game and said he wanted Munson to lie and sign a press release retracting his charges. Munson refused. What could George do, trade him? That's what Munson wanted him to do.

The prideful Munson kept saying, "He lied to me. He made a fool of me."

Reggie, in his *Sport* magazine diatribe, described himself as "the straw that stirs the drink." He was the stirrer all right, but it wasn't a drink he was stirring. For the rest of the season Billy Martin would have to spend the majority of his time worrying about the egos of George Steinbrenner and Reggie Jackson rather than concentrating on managing his team. His biggest headache would be George's pet player. Billy knew what he had to do to control Reggie Jackson, but he was impotent to do it as long as George Steinbrenner protected Jackson. Billy began to feel about Reggie the same way Lockbourne's Major Jones had felt about George: angry, frustrated, and agitated.

As the season progressed, George Steinbrenner continued to meddle and tighten the screws around Billy, who drank like never before. His rages became greater and occurred more often. His health worsened as he stopped eating toward the end of the season.

As he did everywhere he went, George Steinbrenner took away all the fun for Billy, the players, and everyone else involved with the Yankees. Because of Steinbrenner's insistence that he be the center of attention, that he make the important decisions, that everyone bend to his will, no matter whether his edicts made sense or not, Billy and many of his players suffered severe emotional trauma during a season at the end of which the Yankees won the world championship. What galled them was that even though they had won despite his interference and stupidity, Steinbrenner tried to take all the credit.

Dock Ellis was the first one to come to Billy's defense. As Ed Linn reported in *Steinbrenner's Yankees*, early in spring training the outspoken pitcher declared that in the future Steinbrenner should stay out of the clubhouse.

"We don't need him riding in here like the Lone Ranger," Dock said. "Steinbrenner had better stay off Billy Martin's back, because the players are in Billy's corner."

The owner's response was predictable. When George is angry with someone he will say anything to defend himself or he will attack his target.

In response to Ellis's comments, George told reporters, "If anybody says I've been on Billy Martin's butt, he's a liar. I've had no conversations with Billy Martin about the ball club since spring training."

Everyone knew that George had met with Billy every day during spring training, second-guessing him, making stupid suggestions, interfering to the extent that even Gabe Paul was powerless to stop him. Billy, his players knew, wanted to kill him.

The first major interference from George concerned Reggie. Around the third day of spring training, Billy called Reggie in for a talk. Billy had overheard Reggie telling reporters he was going to be the big man on the team. Billy told him, "A real leader does his leading on the field, not in the clubhouse. If you do your job, nobody will bother you." Billy added, "I hope you and Thurman will get along." Reggie didn't tell him about his diatribe delivered to Robert Ward.

The first salvo in the Billy-Reggie-George wars came in the middle of spring training when Billy batted Reggie somewhere other than fourth, which was where a superstar slugger was supposed to hit.

Billy, who resented Jackson's presence from the moment he arrived in camp, was testing Jackson, as he did every player. He wanted to know if Jackson would be a team player. Quickly he saw he would not.

Reggie went to see George, demanding he bat fourth.

Billy's resentment against Reggie's whole being, especially Jackson's love of being the center of attention with the writers, galled Billy every day he came to the clubhouse.

Before a game in Milwaukee in April, in response to a question, Reggie told reporters his arm was still hurting. Reggie didn't think he had said anything so terrible, and in fact, he hadn't, but Billy didn't like that he was being so open with the writers, and as a punishment the next night Billy kept Reggie out of the lineup.

In front of a couple of writers, Billy stood next to Reggie so he would hear, and he said, "Reggie's arm must be bothering him. That's what he told the press, anyway. A couple of days off will probably do him a world of good." Billy paused. "Isn't that right, Mr. Jackson?"

Reggie, clearly embarrassed, said, "Right."

When the Yankees went to Oakland, where Reggie's stardom had blossomed, Reggie invited friends and relatives. Billy sat him in a game against left-handed pitching star Vida Blue. He didn't even pinch-hit. Billy played Dell Alston, just up from the minors. Again Reggie felt embarrassed.

Six weeks into the season Reggie Jackson was feeling alone and unwanted.

According to Reggie's autobiography, when he signed with the Yankees, George told him that if he ever was unhappy, he could leave the Yankees any time he wanted. Reggie said he asked George to put it in writing, but George told him it was "unnecessary."

Reggie claimed George told him, "Anybody who doesn't want to be here, I don't want here."

Commented Reggie, "The amazing thing is that I believed him. I made that mistake a lot with old George."

Reggie went to see Gabe Paul and demanded to be traded, but Gabe calmed him down. "You can't just look at the hole in the doughnut," said Gabe. "You have to consider the whole doughnut."

Into May Billy continued to bat Reggie fifth in the order, behind Chris Chambliss. Billy said he wanted Chambliss there because he struck out less often. In truth, Billy disliked Reggie so much he would have batted him ninth if he thought he could have gotten away with it.

Every day some reporter would ask Reggie about it. Reggie would say, "I guess I'm just an overpaid, mediocre ballplayer like everybody says I am."

Billy wanted Jackson to bend until he broke down and admitted this was Martin's team, not Reggie Jackson's team.

He didn't *have* to do that, of course. He could have done what Casey Stengel did with Joe DiMaggio—recognized his greatness and just let him play, ignoring the insecure but immensely talented DiMaggio's occasional snide criticism.

But Billy refused to do that. Not only would he *not* acknowledge Reggie's great talent and his impressive statistics, he did everything he could to show up Jackson in a deliberate attempt to force Reggie to heel to the team. In the press, Billy would say just that.

"He's not a team player."

Billy wasn't the only one who resented Reggie's cushy inroad with George. Because of the players' coolness to Reggie, Thurman Munson found himself in a funny position. The Yankees had started slowly early in the season, and according to Munson, Steinbrenner blamed the disharmony on the team on him. He threatened Munson that if he didn't get along better with Reggie, he'd fire his man Billy.

George told Thurman, "You better start getting along with Reggie or Billy will be in a lot of trouble."

Commented Munson in his book, "Imagine that! I was suddenly put in the middle and made responsible for Billy's job."

Except for Fran Healy, the gentle catcher who liked and felt sorry for Jackson, not a single Yankee ballplayer tried to make Jackson feel wanted on the team, not even Catfish Hunter or Kenny Holtzman, his former A's teammates.

That was Reggie's position on the team *before* his remarks to Robert Ward in *Sport* magazine became public. On May 23, 1977, the day the magazine hit the newsstands and everyone on the team read what he had said about Thurman, no one, not even the players in the lockers next to his, would come anywhere near him.

Catcher Fran Healy, who was a conciliator, said to Munson, "Maybe he was quoted out of context."

Said Munson, "For three fucking pages?"

Munson was truly mystified when he read what Reggie had said about him being able only to "stir the team bad." Sitting in the trainer's room, he said to first baseman Ron Blomberg, "I just go out every day and play. I helped the Yankees win the pennant. I was MVP. What's so bad about that?"

In the game that day Reggie hit a home run off Red Sox pitcher Bill Lee. When he crossed home plate, the other players were waiting for him with their hands extended. Reggie, having felt their hostility before the game, made a sharp turn and headed for the other end of the dugout without shaking anybody's hands.

Said Reggie later, "I was an outcast. Fine, I at least wanted them all to know that I didn't have to have a picture drawn for me anymore."

A reporter asked Reggie why he didn't shake their hands.

"My hand hurt," he said.

"Fucking liar," said Munson when he heard that.

The next day Reggie attempted to apologize to Munson. Munson refused to hear it and walked away.

A day later Carlos May and Mickey Rivers moved their lockers away from Reggie's.

Two days later, on the back of Reggie's uniform, someone left a note reading, "Suck my ass."

As Ed Linn reported in *Steinbrenner's Yankees,* Fran Healy was finally able to join Reggie and Munson over dinner. Thurman remained hostile. He said to Reggie, "Tell me one thing you have that I'd want. I have three beautiful children and a lovely wife. I have a happy home life. What do you have? You have nothing."

As the Yankees began a three-game series in Boston in mid-June, what was truly amazing was that despite all the distractions caused by Reggie's divisive personality and George's meddling, the Yankees were in first place, a half a game ahead of the Red Sox.

The era of bad feeling, however, was just beginning. Before the first game in Boston, Billy sat on the bench, talking to shortstop Bucky Dent, explaining why he had asked him to bunt early in the game the day before. Billy knew that Bucky's confidence was sagging, and he was trying to make Bucky feel better.

In his autobiography, Reggie recalled what happened next. In the middle of the conversation, Billy turned to Reggie, who was sitting there on the bench, and asked, "It was the right move at the time, wasn't it, Reggie?"

Reggie could have done the political thing and agreed. Perhaps all that followed would have been avoided. But Reggie didn't like Billy any more than Billy liked him. He chose not to.

Reggie said, "Skip, if you're asking me for my honest opinion, I wouldn't have had him bunt. It's only June. It was early in the game when you had him do it. Something like that might affect Bucky's confidence later in the year when you'll probably have him hitting away in that situation. You're going to need him then. It's too early in the pennant race for that kind of stuff. So, anyway, no, I wouldn't have bunted him."

Billy's neck went red. To Billy, Reggie was showing him up in front of another player. Later Billy would tell reporters that Reggie had been second-guessing him for weeks in front of other players.

In the middle of the game, with the Red Sox ahead by six runs, Boston outfielder Jim Rice hit a bloop to right. Reggie was very tentative, slow to get to it. When Reggie was feeling low, the first aspect of his game to suffer was his fielding, and so he made extra sure the ball didn't get past him by taking his time getting in front of it.

Rice, seeing Reggie's hesitation, turned the corner and hustled into second.

Billy came out to the mound to replace pitcher Mike Torrez. He told the pitcher, "I'm going to get that son of a bitch for not hustling."

It's rare when a manager takes a player out of the game in the middle of an inning. There is no more humiliating move a manager can make. Billy sent Paul Blair out to replace Reggie.

Reggie had shown Billy up in front of Dent, and this was Billy's revenge, demonstrated in front of the world.

"What the fuck do you think you're doing out there?" Reggie said that Billy yelled at him in the dugout.

"What do you mean? What are you talking about?"

"You know what the fuck I'm talking about. You want to show me up by loafing on me? Fine. Then I'm going to show your ass up. Anyone who doesn't hustle doesn't play for me."

"I wasn't loafing, Billy. But I'm sure that doesn't matter to you. You never wanted me on this team in the first place. You don't want me now. Why don't you just admit it?"

"I ought to kick your fucking ass."

"You're an old man."

Billy, snarling, came after Reggie.

"You're forty-nine years old and you weigh 160. I'm thirty and weigh 210. Let me tell you something: You aren't going to do shit. What you are is plain crazy."

Coach Yogi Berra held Billy in a bear hug. Reggie later said that it was lucky for Billy. But who knows?

Reggie walked into the clubhouse. As he waited for the game to end, he was hoping for a chance to fight it out with Billy. Fran Healy and pitcher Mike Torrez talked him out of it. At the same time Bucky Dent was in the locker room preparing to undress and leave the team in the middle of the game. Healy, a hero on this day, talked the shortstop out of that, too.

If Reggie had wanted to cool tensions, the thing he should have done was duck reporters and keep his mouth shut. Or he could have apologized for loafing, even if he didn't think he had done that.

But Reggie Jackson had been a star for too long to apologize. Reggie didn't think he had loafed (many others didn't, either) and it wasn't in his character to eat humble pie when he felt it wasn't deserved. Ego. It's one reason stars become stars: They consider their own best interests first.

Reggie called reporters Steve Jacobson of *Newsday*, Phil Pepe of the *Daily News*, and Paul Montgomery of the *The New York Times* and spent the evening telling them about the difficulty of being Reggie Jackson. He told them that to his teammates he was just a "rich nigger," that they would never accept a black man making the money he was making. Which, of course, was utterly ridiculous. Reggie had precipitated the rift with his teammates because of his insistence on thrusting himself into the limelight, and because he had insulted Thurman Munson in the worst possible terms. But Reggie could never admit when he was wrong, so he was blaming Billy and his teammates for feeling unloved and unwanted.

Reggie spoke about how his close relationship with Steinbrenner made Billy and the other Yankees jealous. He told them he didn't care about their feelings anymore.

His one conciliary remark was, "I'm going to play the best I can for the rest of the year, help this team win if I can, and then I'm going to get my ass out of here."

After the game, which George Steinbrenner had watched on television, the Yankee owner acted as though Billy had attacked *him* rather than Reggie. Ed Linn reported that George called Gabe Paul and demanded he fire Billy.

Said George, "Did you see him? He was ready to kill him. What kind of example is that to set for American youth?" One of George's favorite reasons for firing someone is that person's effect on "America's youth." Of course, if George was acting nasty or underhanded, America's youth *never* was affected.

Gabe knew better than to fire Billy. He knew that to do so would make it seem that Reggie was in charge of the team.

George, through his "source close to the Yankees" gambit, floated a trial balloon through Milt Richman of the Associated Press that Billy would be fired and Yogi Berra would replace him.

During the next day George met with Reggie, who told him not to fire Billy. Reggie knew the ramifications. He didn't want to have to face the wrath of the fans and his teammates. Thurman Munson told George that if he fired Billy, he and Graig Nettles would quit the team.

After the Richman story came out, howls of protest were raised by Yankee fans.

George couldn't fire Billy, but he felt he had to do something to punish him. George and Gabe called Billy into a conference. Their response was not to back Billy, as they should have done since he was the manager, but to crack down on him. They reiterated the effect of the clauses in his contract. They ordered him to meet with them more, get to the park earlier than was his custom, and to study charts and statistics that Steinbrenner prepared for him on a daily basis.

They warned him about badmouthing the front office, and they ordered him to be more flexible in how he used Reggie.

The issue wasn't the bottom line, because the Yankees were ahead. The issue was George's ego. Billy wasn't doing his bidding, wasn't treating his new star with the deference he felt was proper, even after all those terrible things Reggie had said. In this battle of wills, baseball was irrelevant. Only one thing counted: that Billy knuckle under.

George told Billy he wasn't going to fire him at this time, but he warned, "It's in Gabe's hands now."

**30**

# GEORGE VS. GABE

In spring training of 1977, Gabe Paul told Billy he wanted him to live in Ft. Lauderdale with the rest of the players rather than live the bachelor's life with Mickey Mantle in Boca Raton. Sometimes Billy would show up with a young woman. Other times he'd be late and hung over. Gabe wanted him taking the bus with the team.

Billy did what a kid does when he asks one parent and gets an answer he doesn't like. He goes to another parent. Billy went to George and asked him if he could stay in Boca. George said he could.

Spring training had a week to run when Steinbrenner lost it. When the Yankees were negotiating with the Mets to spend two years at Shea Stadium while Yankee Stadium was being renovated, the Mets had driven a hard bargain. Part of the reason was that Mets management was afraid the city would not fund the renovation and would stick the Mets with the Yankees as co-tenants on a permanent basis. There was even a clause that if the stadium wasn't completed after two years, the Yankees had to leave anyway and play at Roosevelt Field in Jersey City or some other site, and so George disliked the Mets. Steinbrenner also believed that if the Yankees beat the Mets, baseball fans would be more apt to buy Yankee tickets and not Mets tickets. A Yankee loss to the Mets during an exhibition game could cause him to go into punishment mode against his team members.

In this game, when the Mets won 6–0, the person Steinbrenner chose to punish was Billy.

He ordered Billy to take the team bus and to show up on time. He ordered him to play Reggie.

Billy, angry that George cared so much about the result of an exhibition game, showed his displeasure and didn't take the bus. He drove in his rental car. When George discovered that Billy had not followed orders, George began to scream at Billy in front of his players.

As Ed Linn recounted the exchange in his book, Billy said, "You fat bastard, I don't give a shit what you say. I'm going to do it my way."

"You lied to me. You told me you were going to ride the bus," George said.

"Fuck you, I'm not riding on no fucking buses. Get the fuck out of here."

Gabe Paul got between them.

"Don't talk to him like that," Gabe said.

"Then *you* can tell that fat bastard to go fuck himself. Hear me? He can go fuck himself."

George screamed at Billy not to *ever* talk that *way* to him *again*.

"I'll talk to anybody like that," said Billy, heading for the trainer's room. George and Gabe followed on his heels.

George yelled that Billy had lied to him. Then he verbalized what was *really* bothering him.

"You promised to play the starting team the entire game," an angry George hollered.

Billy yelled back, "Don't tell me how to manage my ball team, you lying son of a bitch. I'm the manager, and I'll manage how I want to manage. It was an *ex-hi-bi-tion* game. This is not a game where you leave your blood and guts on the field to win. It's a game where you try things, to get ready for the season. There are things I have to find out *now*."

"You should have already found them out," George yelled. "The season begins in a week, and you aren't ready."

Billy, who was aware of George's football background, shouted that in baseball you don't prepare for a 162-game season like you do for a 10-game season in football. Billy slammed his fist into the ice bucket, with cubes and water splashing all over a sputtering George.

"I ought to fire you," he screamed.

"You want to fire me, fire me. But leave me the fuck alone."

George sent for Yogi Berra and told him he was the manager.

Yogi, who had the reputation of being a master of funny malapropisms, was a sane, sensible, calming influence. Yogi told him, "Now take it easy, George. Billy's a good manager. You don't want to go doing anything because you're mad now."

"The job is yours," George yelled.

When Billy left, he believed he had been fired.

The next day, when Billy met with George and Gabe, he had his job back. And from that day, he rode the bus and never yelled at George in public again.

Billy believed the way to deal with George when he was in one of his irrational states was to scream and swear at him. General manager Gabe Paul, on the other hand, had his own way of dealing with Steinbrenner's vituperations.

According to Pearl Davis, who was Gabe's loyal secretary, George would curse at Gabe unmercifully.

"He'd barge right into his office and curse him out for different things," said Davis. " 'Why the fuck did you do this or do that?' 'Bastard.' Sometimes I would hear this, and I would go in to make sure Gabe was all right. Steinbrenner would say, 'What the fuck do you want?' I'd say, 'I came in to see if my boss is all right.' It didn't matter if the issue was tiddlywinks. If George didn't like something, you heard about it."

Gabe's way of handling George was to take it until George was finished yelling and keep his mouth shut. If you worked for George for a lengthy period of time, which was unlikely because of his penchant for firing employees on a whim, you ended up either an alcoholic or with health problems, or both.

Gabe Paul was suffering from ill health when he came to spring training in 1977. Soon after camp opened, Gabe collapsed. First reports were that he had suffered a mild stroke.

Had he died, leaving George Steinbrenner at the helm, the Yankees probably would not have won titles the next two years and been as competitive as they were in the years after that.

While Gabe was in the hospital, Oakland A's owner Charlie Finley, an owner with a really keen eye for talent, almost stole minor league prospect Ron Guidry from the Yankees.

Every time Guidry pitched in spring training, it seemed, the lefty reliever was hit hard. Had he been merely decent, Steinbrenner would have tried to trade Sparky Lyle, who also had not been pitching well. But because Guidry was totally ineffective, Lyle had to be kept. And Gabe wouldn't let him trade Guidry.

With Gabe in the hospital, Finley, smart but rapacious, moved in on Steinbrenner. He offered pitcher Mike Torrez for Dock Ellis, whom Steinbrenner wanted desperately to dump for a number of reasons, but Finley wanted "a little extra." He wanted minor league infielder Mickey Klutts and Guidry.

Fortunately for the Yankees, Gabe didn't die. Gabe could still talk, and he was able to talk Steinbrenner out of including Guidry in the deal.

"Where do you find an arm like that? Nowhere," Gabe told George.

George made the trade for Torrez without including Guidry. It was the trade that won the pennant for the Yankees because, when Torrez reported too late to pitch the next game, Billy needed a starter and gave Guidry the opportunity to show his greatness.

"All I want from you is five innings," he said.

Guidry loaded the bases in the first inning with one out. He then struck out the next two hitters on hard sliders. He was pitching a shutout going into the ninth inning when Lyle relieved for him.

Ron Guidry posted a record of 16–7 with a 2.82 ERA in 1977. The slim lefthander would win twenty games for the Yankees three times. In the pen that year, Lyle went on to win the Cy Young Award, given to the best pitcher in the league, the first American League relief pitcher to be so honored.

On April 5, Gabe finally was able to land shortstop Bucky Dent from the

Chicago White Sox. He gave up Oscar Gamble, LaMarr Hoyt, who in 1983 won the Cy Young Award with the White Sox, and minor league pitcher Bob Polinski.

As the 1977 trading deadline approached, the Yankees still needed a powerful right-handed bat. The team was 25–11 against righties but 10–15 against lefties. The hitter Gabe was able to acquire was Cliff Johnson from the Houston Astros. Cliff, a bad fielder, was born to DH.

Gabe got him from Houston for three minor league prospects, Dave Bergman, Mike Fischlin, and Randy Niemann. It was another outstanding trade. Cliff Johnson helped the Yankees to two world championships. Dave Bergman went on to a solid if unremarkable career; the others didn't do much in the majors. But it was a deal Steinbrenner—who said he hadn't wanted to lose Bergman—tried to nullify for almost a year after it was made, even *after* Johnson had proved his value.

In addition to trading the Yankees to respectability, Gabe Paul in 1977 continued to be the buffer between George and Billy Martin, and between Billy and Reggie.

Gabe understood why Billy disliked Reggie so, but he wasn't sympathetic. Gabe was pleased to have acquired Reggie's bat. He would tell Billy, "It's the manager's job to handle the players I give you. There is no substitute for talent. He may be a troublemaker, but he hits home runs."

When Billy and Reggie had their confrontation in Boston on national television, Gabe shrugged the whole thing off. He figured it would all blow over and be forgotten.

When Steinbrenner started talking about firing Billy, Gabe again stepped in to provide the voice of reason. When Gabe finally convinced George not to fire him, George told Billy his fate was "in Gabe's hands now."

Two days later Steinbrenner's addiction to self-aggrandizement began to kick in. George knew he needed Gabe, but it killed him that he did. To reporters he verbalized his preferred, reconstructed, "George Steinbrenner as all-powerful decisive leader" scenario.

He told reporters that he, George Steinbrenner, was the one who had made the decision not to fire Billy.

He boasted how he had threatened Martin as well as Reggie, how he had chastised Thurman Munson, and how players had told him his pep talk to the team had given the team a lift.

Privately, George was telling reporters, the tension on the team was beyond Gabe's understanding, that Gabe would call him no matter how small the problem.

George made Gabe Paul, the man who had built the new Yankees, look like a bumbling, addled gofer.

When reporters told Gabe what George had said, he caught the first flight out of La Guardia Airport to his home in Tampa. Gabe could stand taking the abuse in private, but this was too much.

That night George caught another plane to go and bring him back. George, who knew who the *real* brains of the operation was, begged and scraped and pleaded for Gabe to come back. Steinbrenner promised it would never happen again.

George stopped making fun of Gabe to reporters. But in front of strangers, George would say, "Gabe isn't what he used to be. He's not well. He can't make decisions."

Oh, did Steinbrenner wish he didn't need Gabe.

# A WORLD
# CHAMPIONSHIP

After the blowup in Boston, the tug-of-war between Billy and Gabe on one side and George and Reggie on the other continued unabated. The anger in Billy built.

In early July 1977, Billy spoke about the tension to Thurman Munson. Billy expressed concern that Steinbrenner was dictating lineup changes to him, that George's lineup was inferior to his own. He said he was worried about getting fired and not getting paid because of the bad-boy clauses in his contract.

"As we spoke," wrote Munson, who respected Billy and admired him greatly, "tears welled up in his eyes. To avoid having anybody see him so upset, we took a walk around the block until he could clear the air a little. I felt very close to Billy that day."

With the Yankees only percentage points out of first place, on July 10 Thurman defended his manager. He told Murray Chass of *The New York Times* and Steve Jacobson of *Newsday* that Steinbrenner was dictating the lineup to Billy.

Munson, who had learned from Steinbrenner the way to do it, insisted he be identified only as "a prominent Yankee." He was quoted as saying, "George doesn't care about anybody's feelings. He treats everybody like that. He's done something to everybody. He's destroyed Billy. He's made him nothing. Not a single guy on the club is happy, except Willie Randolph." (Willie, a quiet man, avoided controversy at all costs.)

Thurman's complaint was that George was making Billy bat Randolph leadoff while keeping Mickey Rivers on the bench. Munson wanted Mickey leading off and Randolph second, the Yankees' best combination.

When the "prominent Yankee's" charges were made, George jumped into denial mode. "It's a lie," he said, which was a lie. "And any player who says it isn't is a liar." He added, "Billy hasn't had one iota of pressure from me about the lineup."

George did something else that infuriated Munson. He publicly blamed Carlos May for the quotes from the unnamed prominent Yankee. Munson did the honorable thing. He went to Steinbrenner and told him he had said those things, not May. He then told his teammates what he had done.

When the team got to Kansas City, Steinbrenner held a clubhouse meeting in which he lectured, threatened, and criticized "anonymous players who leak things to the press," acting at the meeting as though he didn't know it was Munson who had made the statements.

Munson was mortified.

Said Munson, "Here I had gone to the man on my own and told him I had made the statements. My teammates knew I had done that to get Carlos off the hook, and now, right in front of me and all my teammates, he was making me look like a liar—as though no one had confessed to the quotes! I was stunned."

Thurman also was getting tired of Billy's vindictive behavior toward Reggie. Thurman wasn't stupid. He knew all along that Jackson should have been batting fourth. Billy was arguing that Reggie struck out too much, so Chambliss was batting fourth and Reggie fifth. The offense was sputtering, and Munson, the captain, took the lead in telling both Steinbrenner and Billy to do what was best for the team.

When attacked, one of George's conditioned responses was to order others to lie for him to prove he hadn't lied in the first place. George did that in this case by ordering Billy to call a press conference to say that the charges that George was interfering with him were completely untrue. Steinbrenner dictated a statement, handed it to Billy, and Billy dutifully read it. Under questioning, Billy denied that Steinbrenner had dictated the statement.

As orchestrated by Steinbrenner, it was a perfect lose-lose scenario for Billy. If Billy had refused to do this, who knows whether he would have kept his job. But by agreeing to it, Billy lost self-respect for doing it when he knew the whole thing was a charade, and Billy also lost some respect from his players, who could only sit by and watch as Steinbrenner cut his balls off in public.

The night of Billy's public humiliation, July 14, Thurman Munson and Lou Piniella went to see Steinbrenner. The likelihood was that Steinbrenner had asked Piniella, who didn't hate him, to bring along Munson, who did. Piniella later said he had come "as a favor" to George.

Munson, backing Billy all the way, found the pressure placed on Billy unbearable, and in defense of Billy, he told the owner to fire him now or leave him alone.

He told Steinbrenner, "You've got to get off Billy's back. You're driving him crazy. If you're going to fire him, then fire him. If you're not, leave him alone and let him manage."

Munson said, "Nobody can live with the kind of pressure you're putting on him." Piniella, also backing Billy, told George to take the restrictive clauses out of his contract. "If not, fire him," Piniella said. He, too, was worried for Billy's health.

It was two in the morning. After drinking in the hotel bar, Billy returned to his room, which was down the hall from George's. He heard a conversation among Steinbrenner and the two players and immediately suspected that everyone was plotting against him.

George's first response when he opened the door was to tell Billy no one else was there. But when Billy barged in, he found the two players hiding in the bathroom.

"You're plotting against me," he said. George ordered him to sit down.

"Take your goddamn job," Billy said.

The four men talked for another four or five hours about the team. At the end of the meeting, Billy was swayed by what Thurman Munson had to say about Jackson, and he agreed to bat him fourth, let Piniella be the permanent DH, and go to a four-man rotation. In return, Steinbrenner agreed to guarantee Billy's salary despite the bad-boy clauses and publicly state that he would finish out the year as manager.

Said Munson in his book, "If nothing else, Billy could relax about his security. He might be fired tomorrow, but he would be paid for three full seasons."

Reason and civility seemed to rule. The adversaries put away their guns and ammunition. When the team moved on to Kansas City, Reggie was batting fourth.

The team lost. Martin went back to his old lineup with Chambliss batting fourth and Reggie fifth. Billy was going to do it *his* way.

At the All-Star break George fully intended to fire Billy. Steinbrenner called Munson and told him that in his opinion there was no way the team could win with Billy as manager. By this time Munson was sick of the whole issue.

Munson told him, "It's up to you. Do what you want." Munson told him that all the players were pros, that who the manager was was no big deal, that no player would quit if Billy was to be fired.

George was still telling the press it was up to Gabe Paul. George called Walter Alston, former manager of the Dodgers, to see if he wanted to take the job. Alston turned him down. Gabe Paul told George not to bring in an outsider. George suggested Gene Michael, the Yankees' third-base coach. Gabe preferred Dick Howser. Gabe called Howser and left a message. He also called Howard Cosell and told him to wait for a big story. But Howser refused the job. Howser told Gabe that Billy wasn't the problem, George was. Gabe called Cosell back to tell him the story was off.

At the park the next day Billy made a tearful speech about Yankee pride. Ron Guidry pitched a shutout as the team won.

The next day Billy came to the park but didn't put on his uniform. He expected to be fired. "I feel like those guys on death row. I need a reprieve from the governor."

Gabe called Billy on the phone and told him to come up to see him. Figuring the ax was about to fall, Billy kept Gabe waiting a full half hour while he talked with reporters about George and his interference and lies.

Billy then went to see Gabe.

"Am I fired?"

"You're here, aren't you?"

"But what about tomorrow, next month?"

"You'll still be here. You're the manager."

But Gabe warned Billy about criticizing George. "If you stir shit, it stinks," Gabe told him. Billy had just stirred shit for a full half hour with the media.

Two days later George, stung by Billy's comments, called a press conference. Everything Billy said about him was a lie, he said. George bellowed, "We have come to a time when for his own good we must demand an accountability of what Martin does and says."

He reiterated an old line: "Billy's fate is in Gabe's hands."

As he had with John McClendon, George badly wanted Billy gone, not because of Billy's managing, for the Yankees were right near the top of the heap, but because Billy continually made George look bad in the press. And now George had put himself in a box. He couldn't fire Billy without Gabe's permission unless he wanted to look like a total liar and humiliate Gabe again. And the one person acceptable to Gabe to replace Billy, Dick Howser, wouldn't take the job.

The stories about Billy getting fired made Billy more of a hero in New York City than ever before. The fans knew why the Yankees were winning—it was Billy and the way he managed—and they rallied behind him.

So George couldn't fire him. He could certainly do the next best thing—he could harass and humiliate him, and he did just that. You'd have thought his experience with the Pipers might have taught him something, but George's personality hadn't changed since his Cleveland Piper days. His weak ego needed to feel massaged, and the way he did that was to make those who threatened him take his abuse.

Steinbrenner called reporters together to give them a list of the seven qualifications that he said Gabe had drawn up for judging a manager.

The list read:

1. Won–lost record.
2. Does he work hard enough?
3. Is he emotionally equipped to lead the men under him?
4. Is he organized?
5. Is he prepared?
6. Does he understand human nature?
7. Is he honorable?

Lying is an art. If you combine a little bit of the truth with a lie, your lie doesn't seem to be a lie. The truth was that the first six items had been on a list drawn up by Gabe three years earlier when the Yankees were looking to replace Ralph Houk. Using it, they hired Bill Virdon.

Steinbrenner had added item 7 to make the list applicable to Billy.

Gabe was appalled that Steinbrenner was using his list in this manner.

George would have been okay with the public if the list had been only items 1 through 6. But by asking, "Is he honorable?" George had set himself up for ridicule. It was he, after all, who had been suspended from running the Yankees for two years for being an admitted felon. It was he who had obstructed justice. It was he who had cheated the system.

Observers didn't particularly care that George might have been humiliating himself, but they certainly noticed that he was able to humiliate Billy.

Said Thurman Munson about the list, "I couldn't believe Billy would stand for it. But his love for the Yankees was deep and genuine, and he was determined not to buckle under."

Next came an article built around Steinbrenner's disinformation. He had given Phil Pepe of the *Daily News* the story of how Munson and Piniella had come to his hotel room on the night of July 14. But the version that Steinbrenner told Pepe was that the players had come on their own to plead with George to fire Billy. Piniella and Munson learned a lesson many had learned before them and many would learn since: George was shameless when it came to twisting a story to fit his own purposes. Either his mind was warped in the way he processed his experiences or he was a pathological liar. Either way, Piniella was furious when he read what Steinbrenner had said, and he told him off in no uncertain terms. Munson also was livid but kept quiet.

When Munson hit his 100th career home run against Baltimore on July 28, a magnum of champagne was sent to the clubhouse for him after the game. Munson believed it had been sent by Steinbrenner and that George had sent it because he knew Munson was angered by the Pepe story.

Said Munson, "He even called and denied having talked with Phil at all."

Even though he was having another MVP year, Munson had difficulty coping with the mayhem in the Yankees.

Commented Munson in his book, "Suddenly everything seemed to be falling apart at once." Pitcher Ken Holtzman called Steinbrenner a fool for giving him a rich contract and then allowing him to languish in the bullpen all year. Reggie whispered about an escape clause that would let him skip town after the season, a reference to George's promise that he could leave if he were ever unhappy.

Catfish had a bad arm and a hernia. Don Gullett and Ed Figueroa had arm problems.

And worst of all, a fiercely proud Munson felt that Steinbrenner's behavior made the Yankees look like a laughingstock. Munson didn't know it, but George was used to being a laughingstock. It didn't bother him. But it made Munson's blood boil. When George gave walkie-talkies to the manager and to Gene Michael in the press box so Michael could tell Billy where to position the fielders, Bill Veeck of the White Sox hired a clown to stand beside Michael and ridicule him for the walkie-talkies. Munson didn't want to be part of a team others were making fun of.

The pressure seemed to be getting to everyone. When the Yankees lost two straight in Seattle, Billy, crying, asked the writers to leave. Piniella was furious after the Seattle losses, confronting those players who had asked to be traded. In another incident, Reggie was charged with assault on a kid in the stadium parking lot after the All-Star Game. (He was later cleared.)

Steinbrenner offered a public apology to the people of New York for the team's poor play. Gabe Paul was more blunt, telling the players to cut the crap and start playing good baseball.

Catfish Hunter and Mike Torrez sniped at Billy on an Oakland radio show, criticizing his pitching rotation, which Billy had tinkered with all year.

Through it all, the Yankees kept winning. Against Baltimore, Reggie hit a home run in the tenth inning to win, and the Yankees won five of six to ease the tension some.

When the team went West, Billy benched Reggie against Ken Brett of California. When Reggie talked of leaving this time, Billy finally got some support in the front office. Gabe told him to shut up and play. The next night he hit the 300th home run of his career.

Steinbrenner has never understood that having fun at what they do is equally important to the players as winning. The constant strain of playing on a team riddled with dissension finally got to Thurman Munson, who wanted out. He wanted to be traded to Cleveland so he could be nearer his family.

In defiance of one of Steinbrenner's idiotic rules and demands, Thurman Munson grew a beard.

"Petty shit," Billy said to the writers. And then he broke down, began to cry, and went running back into his office and locked himself in.

On the way back to New York, the team stopped in Syracuse. The mutiny against Steinbrenner continued. George did not believe in giving his players an off day. On some off days he ordered them to practice. On others he scheduled exhibition games such as the one against their top farm club in Syracuse. Sparky Lyle and Mickey Rivers threatened not to go.

Billy paid Rivers some money, as he did periodically, and Mickey went. Lyle didn't go and was fined five hundred dollars. In Syracuse Gabe made a personal plea to Munson to shave the beard.

Gabe asked, "Goddamn it, Thurman, what the hell is all this stuff?"

"Goddamn it, he isn't going to tell me what to do."

Gabe said, "All you're making is a lot of turmoil for everybody. For me and Billy, would you do me a favor and get your goddamn beard cut off?"

Thurman said, "I'll do it for you. But I ain't gonna do it for anyone else."

In Syracuse Thurman phoned his wife, Diana, who began to cry. The negative stories about her husband had gotten to her. Thurman shaved off the beard. Two writers saw him buying razor blades at the hotel lobby store, and they knocked on the door asking if they could watch him shave. Munson refused, and starting that day, whenever he was asked a question, his standard answer to a reporter was, "I'm just happy to be here."

Gabe gave Munson permission to leave the exhibition game early so he could fly home to Canton. Mickey Rivers, angry that Munson was getting special treatment after Mickey had been denied the right not to come at all, refused to come out of the clubhouse after a rain delay.

At Syracuse Gabe Paul said to Billy, "Why don't you end all this horseshit and bat Jackson fourth?"

Billy told him he had been considering doing that himself.

"Why don't you do it today?" Gabe asked him.

Billy said he would.

He did. Syracuse won, 14–5.

When the Yankees came back home, Steinbrenner, on August 10, gave Billy one more chance—bat Reggie fourth or else. He also wanted Billy to bat Piniella every day.

Billy wanted something from George—Art Fowler.

Said Billy, "George, if you want to get the whole thing turned around, get me Art Fowler. There is no one better to work with the pitchers."

George brought up Art's drinking. Billy told him Bob Lemon drank more.

"I need a guy who is loyal to me first and the pitchers second, someone whom I can work with. Give me Art, and it'll straighten itself out," said Billy.

George agreed to let Billy have Fowler if he batted Reggie fourth. George did something else that seemed to be part of his character. After threatening to fire him and nearly driving Billy to the brink of a nervous breakdown, Steinbrenner gave Billy a new two-year contract. He didn't take the bad-boy clauses out, but he raised his salary.

At this meeting Billy and George talked civilly, each praising the other. "Billy, you're doing a great job," George told him. When asked how much of a raise he wanted from his $72,000 salary, Billy said, "I told him he could fill in the numbers. I knew he'd be fair and generous, and he *was* generous. He wrote in $90,000 for each of the two years, which was really flattering."

Who knows why, but out of the blue George forged a détente with Billy.

Around this time Steinbrenner and Billy shocked Madison Avenue when they agreed to film a Miller Lite beer commercial together. Marty Blackman, the man responsible for the pairing, had approached Billy and George during spring training about doing the ad, in which one was to argue that Miller beer "tasted great" and the other was to say it was "less filling."

When Blackman was approached by the advertising firm of Backer and Spielvogel to ask them, he responded by saying the odds of getting them to say yes were 1,000 to 1.

Blackman flew to Ft. Lauderdale to ask Billy. His reply was, "Are you fucking nuts? If there was a coffin, I'd put the last nail in it."

Blackman told the agency what he had said. They told him to "keep trying."

When Blackman called Steinbrenner, he said he liked the idea. George told Blackman, "If I don't fire him by the All-Star break, I'll be glad to do it." He said he would give his share of the money to charity. Blackman remembered no acrimony on Steinbrenner's part.

In early July, several weeks before his self-appointed date, Steinbrenner called Blackman.

"I'm keeping him," he said. "Let's do it."

Blackman called Doug Newton, Billy's agent at the time. Newton told Blackman, "Marty, this is a love-hate relationship. We have to get Billy on a day it is love."

"When?"

"Marty, you have to trust me."

Blackman told the agency that Newton was working on it. "When he says yes," Blackman told the agency, "you have to shoot the next day." Blackman was assured they would be ready.

Ten days later Doug Newton called to say Billy would do it.

Within a week it was arranged, and Blackman was tense because with Steinbrenner and Martin there was always the possibility one of them would walk out.

Steinbrenner arrived on time. Billy kept everyone waiting an hour.

"George did a controlled burn," said Blackman, who suspected that Billy was making Steinbrenner wait on purpose, something Steinbrenner often did to others. As time passed, Blackman's anxiety increased. Everyone worried that Steinbrenner would storm out.

Blackman recalled, "Once Billy arrived on the shoot, you'd have thought they were lovers. There was no clue of acrimony. You'd have thought they were Hansel and Gretel."

Some reporters came to watch the proceedings, and afterward George and Billy held a press conference.

Anticipating an evening of rancor from the two public adversaries, Blackman thought to himself, I guess you learn something every day.

With Billy and Art Fowler working together once again, the pitching was superb the rest of the way. Fowler was there five weeks, and at the end of the season the players voted him $6,500 as his World Series share. With Fowler in charge, Ron Guidry won seven games in a row, including three shutouts, and Mike Torrez pitched seven complete games in a row.

With Reggie batting fourth and Piniella playing every day, the hitting straightened out as well.

The Yankees finished the season 40–10. In these last fifty games, Reggie had 49 RBIs. Thurman Munson was 27 for 54 at the end to finish at .308. The Red Sox, as was their history, folded in the stretch, ending up tied with Baltimore, two and a half games back.

The division clincher featured a shutout by Don Gullett and a grand slam by Jackson. The home run gave Reggie 110 RBIs, more than any Yankee since Mickey Mantle's 111 in 1964.

Billy won the division title in 1977 virtually with a team of nineteen players. Carlos May was sold in September, leaving the team with twenty-four players. Dave Kingman and Dell Alston were ineffective, and Billy wouldn't play five others: Ken Holtzman, Fran Healy, Ken Clay, George Zeber, and Mickey Klutts.

Said Thurman Munson, "After 162 games, we were just too good to be denied."

The Yankees had clinched a tie for the pennant with four games left in the season and won it outright on October 1, when Boston lost to Baltimore.

Reggie walked into Billy's office and offered him some champagne.

"I will if you will," Billy told him. They toasted each other. Billy told him, "You had a helluva year, big guy. I love you." Reggie took another slug of champagne.

Reggie and Billy got along the rest of the year, even though each hated the other passionately.

Munson and Jackson also got along, even though Munson hated Jackson just as passionately.

Meanwhile, Steinbrenner was doing all he could to discredit the accomplishments of the man who in two years had won him two pennants. Steinbrenner's actions toward Billy and Reggie had brought the team to the edge of mutiny, and only the intercession by Gabe Paul kept it intact.

Billy was right when he said, "We had won against all odds. George had done everything he could to keep us from winning, but he had failed."

After the Yankees clinched, George was asked whether Billy would be fired after the playoffs and the World Series. His answer: "We'll have to wait and see."

Said Billy, "I thought to myself, In two years we've come in first two times. How much better could I possibly do? What does this man want from me?"

For a second year in a row the Yankees had to face the Kansas City Royals for the pennant. Kansas City won two of the first three. The Yankees had to win two in a row in Kansas City, a tough task, to win it. The Yankees just did win Game 4, 6–4. For Game 5, it was the battle of two tough left-handers, Ron Guidry against Paul Splittorff.

Billy Martin, always playing on the edge, raised eyebrows when he decided to bench Reggie in the final game against Splittorff. Billy said that Catfish Hunter and Ken Holtzman had told him Reggie hadn't had much success against Splittorff while he was playing for the A's.

The statistics backed them up. Reggie had been 2 for 15 lifetime against Splittorff. And Billy didn't want Reggie out there playing defense on Kansas City's unforgiving AstroTurf.

Paul Blair, a right-handed hitter, was batting over .400 against Splittorff. The important determinant was that in a crucial situation, pitching and defense were what Billy relied on most. Billy figured if the Yankees could knock the starter out and replace him with a righty, then Reggie could come into the game at that point.

It was an arguable strategy, even though Reggie Jackson was *the* dominant slugger in the league. The one negative was that if the Yankees lost the game, Steinbrenner surely would fire Billy.

In the clubhouse Billy told Steinbrenner what he intended to do. As they were talking, Catfish Hunter walked by. Billy asked him, "Can Reggie hit Split-torff?"

"Not with a fucking paddle," Hunter replied.

Said Steinbrenner, "You do it, but if it doesn't work, you're going to have to suffer the consequences."

Billy said, "Fine, as long as if it works, I get the credit."

Fat chance.

No one wanted the Yankees to win more than Reggie, who feared a backlash if the team lost. He knew critics would say they won it the year before without him and lost it this year with him.

"Everybody will say it's my fault," he said, "and Steinbrenner will look like a fool."

Guidry was pitching with only two days' rest. The Royals scored twice in the first inning. Each team scored in the third. Guidry's arm was tired, and Billy brought in Mike Torrez in relief. Torrez pitched shutout ball through the eighth inning. He was a savior.

Splittorff got the hook, and Royals manager Whitey Herzog, whom Billy had replaced at Texas, brought in righty Doug Bird. Said Billy about the move, "We shall always be grateful."

With the score 3–1 in favor of the Royals and men on the corners, Billy sent Reggie up to pinch-hit. The pressure was on.

Throughout the game Reggie had acted with class. He cheered his teammates. He sat beside Billy, and they chatted. Billy even told him how pleased he was with his attitude and told him if the Yankees won, he would play him in all the World Series games no matter who was pitching.

Reggie, an incredible clutch hitter, came through with a single, putting the Yankees down by one.

The Yankees scored three in the ninth off Dennis Leonard and Larry Gura. Paul Blair, Roy White, and Mickey Rivers got the key hits. Willie Randolph's sacrifice fly won it.

Sparky Lyle came in and shut the door on the Royals, and for the second year in a row the Yankees had gone to the final inning of the season and won.

After the game Mickey Mantle called Billy in his office to congratulate him. Billy told Mantle, "He can't hurt me anymore. He can't touch me now."

The two antagonists, Billy and George, embraced. Billy even poured champagne on his head.

"That's for trying to fire me," Billy said.

Steinbrenner's reply, "What do you mean 'try'? If I want to fire you, I'll fire you."

Pondered Billy, "I wonder whether another manager going into his second straight World Series was still fighting for his job."

The Yankees defeated the L.A. Dodgers in six games. After winning Game 1 in twelve innings, Billy started Catfish Hunter in Game 2. The Cat was going on two days' rest, but Billy hoped he could go five innings. If he could, it would set up the rest of the rotation. Hunter was bombed by the Dodgers.

Before Game 3 in Los Angeles, Reggie held court. He put the blast on Billy. He told the writers, "How could the son of a bitch pitch the man? How could they embarrass him like that?"

Reggie was talking from emotion, not knowledge. Billy knew exactly what he was doing. Replied Billy, "Let him worry about playing right field, and I'll do the managing. Where the hell does he come off saying something like that?"

Though Catfish had lost, the pitching *was* set the rest of the Series. The Yankees swept the final three games.

It was during this World Series that Jackson was labeled "Mr. October." Though Reggie hadn't done much up to that point in the Series, it hadn't stopped him from being openly critical of Billy. Thurman Munson, whose dislike for Jackson hadn't waned, harshly responded to Reggie's criticism.

During batting practice before Game 3 Munson was being sarcastic when he said, "Billy probably just doesn't realize Reggie is Mr. October. If I was hitting .167, I wouldn't be second-guessing the goddamn manager. And I'm going to stop talking because the more I talk, the madder I get."

That's how Reggie got his famous nickname, Mr. October.

Reggie Jackson was the hitting star. He went out and earned the nickname Munson had tagged him with. He hit a home run in Game 4, another in Game 5, and three home runs in the final game against three pitchers on three pitches. Only the great Babe Ruth had ever hit three home runs in a World Series game. Reggie had hit four on four consecutive swings, and five home runs in a six-game Series, which no one had ever done.

In the winter after his triumphant Series, a reporter asked Reggie about the coming season. Reggie was realistic. "The man hates me," he said about Billy. "He'll be out to get me again. One of us has to go. Which one?"

# "ONE'S A BORN LIAR, AND THE OTHER'S CONVICTED"

After the Yankees won the World Series, Billy sat at his desk in his office. He was exhausted. He had fought the other teams in the league, fought his star player, and fought his owner, who respected no man.

"It was tearing me up," said Billy in his autobiography, "making me sick, and it was a miracle I didn't have a stroke or a nervous breakdown. If I had been an older man or if I hadn't had a strong constitution, I might have had one, because of all the hassle and bullshit from him, petty bullshit, harassment. Not every once in a while. Constant harassment. Every day, whether or not he was in town, he'd call and cause problems. Petty shit, every day, every single day."

Billy went to the Sheraton Hotel in Hasbrouck Heights, New Jersey, where he was living, for a party. His now-estranged wife Gretchen and his son, Billy Joe, came up for the party. Friends and fans were there, shoving, hassling, and periodically one of Billy's girlfriends would come over for a kiss and Gretchen would want to know who it was. Finally, Billy smashed his drinking glass against the floor, and he walked out. He drove to a nearby bar where no one could bother him.

He was happy for Gabe Paul. In all his years in baseball Gabe had never won a World Series. "He had been so good to me in many ways," Billy said, and Gabe had. But now Gabe was moving on. He had intended to retire, but one of Gabe's closest friends, Steve O'Neil, had bought the Cleveland Indians, and

O'Neil told Gabe he would not make the deal unless Gabe agreed to run the team for him. Gabe took the challenge.

Yet when Billy returned for spring training in 1978, he was telling reporters how much trouble Gabe Paul had been. In one sense he had been trouble. Gabe took Billy's guff and deflected it. Billy couldn't put anything over on Gabe. Billy told reporters how much he was looking forward to working with George's new general manager, Al Rosen, the former Cleveland Indians hitting star.

Said Billy, "Gabe just got in the way. I won't have any problems with George anymore because I can deal with Al Rosen. He's a baseball man. He understands me. Gabe didn't understand me."

This time Billy was dead wrong. Gabe had protected him from George far more than he realized. And Gabe had overlooked Billy's drinking and his womanizing. Gabe's bottom line had nothing to do with personality, conduct, or politics. It was one reason he worked with Steinbrenner so easily. George could say the rottenest, most hurtful things about Gabe to his face, and Gabe would stare him down, ignore the words, and concentrate on helping the Yankees win.

Gabe Paul felt Billy was the best manager in the game no matter what he said or what he did in bars or bedrooms. Gabe would take the grief and see that Billy kept his job.

If Gabe Paul had stayed with the Yankees, there's no telling how many pennants Billy Martin would have won with the team. Casey Stengel had won five in a row. Billy was looking to equal his mark. That was Billy's goal: five in a row. He was at two pennants and counting, with a team as strong as the last one.

Just before he left the Yankees, Gabe Paul made two decisions that would help the Yankees to yet another title. He advised Steinbrenner to let Mike Torrez become a free agent and to sign super reliever Rich "Goose" Gossage. He did so, but as soon as Gabe was gone and Goose showed how good he could be, Steinbrenner did all he could to let everyone know that he, George Steinbrenner, and not Gabe, had been the team's trading mastermind.

It is George Steinbrenner's sickness that he cannot praise others but must denigrate their accomplishments to make him feel like the strong leader. An article written by George Vecsey is a case in point.

In *The New York Times*, Vecsey wrote that while president, Gabe had been crying in his office from the strain George had put him under.

When asked to comment, George didn't deny that Gabe had cried. He also didn't deny that he had made him cry. His conclusion was, Big deal, Gabe hadn't been that important anyway.

"I don't mind Gabe leaving with his image intact," said Steinbrenner. "But he was in business for forty years, twenty-five as general manager, and did he ever win a pennant before? You think he made all those moves with this team himself? You think all of a sudden he got brilliant?"

Gabe *had* been brilliant, and now with some money behind him, he had won. Gabe and Billy had won it, not George. What had George done except undermine both men? Steinbrenner made it sound like the Yankees had won despite Gabe.

The man who replaced Gabe, former Cleveland Indians star Al Rosen, was someone beholden to George. They had been friends back in Cleveland—Rosen had been chairman of Group 66, a community group that Steinbrenner had been involved with, and they had remained friends through some years of heartbreak for Rosen.

In 1971 Rosen's wife, Terry, who had filed for divorce, committed suicide by jumping out of the nineteenth floor of the Hotel Warwick in Philadelphia. Months later, Rosen's stepson was killed in a fall from his apartment building at Case Western Reserve University.

Then, in 1975, Rosen's name made headlines in connection with a scandal surrounding the sale of apartment house projects as tax shelters by Hill Properties. Rosen and a partner had syndicated one Hill Properties investment deal. In 1974 Hill Properties went into bankruptcy. Investors lost millions.

Rosen, who had been a security broker for Bache and Company before starting his management firm, was never charged with any wrongdoing. Because of the Hill Properties bankruptcy, Rosen left Cleveland for Las Vegas, where he took a job as director of branch operations for Caesar's Palace.

When George called Rosen and offered him the Yankee executive vice-president's job, Rosen was thrilled. The offer came out of the blue. He had never expected to be back in baseball.

And so he was beholden, a primary prerequisite for a Steinbrenner executive.

George constantly had been thwarted by Gabe Paul, who had effectively sheltered Billy from George's goofier ideas. Al Rosen hadn't been hired as a buffer. He had been hired as a puppet, a messenger of counterproductive edicts from Steinbrenner to Billy, the vice president in charge of explanations.

For two years Al Rosen, a decent, capable baseball executive, was caught in a tug-of-war between Billy and George. With Rosen there instead of Gabe, Billy began 1978 on a seat hotter than he had left it at the end of 1977—when the Yankees had won the world championship.

Al Rosen was a moralist. He believed in family, friendship, and treating people right. Honor and integrity were important values to Al Rosen.

Rosen didn't like Billy. Years earlier, in one of his many brawls, Billy had tried to sucker-punch him when Rosen was playing for San Diego in the Pacific Coast League.

Billy didn't like Rosen. Rosen had power over Billy and no experience in his job. Billy believed he knew how to perform Rosen's job better than Rosen.

By the end of the spring Billy and Rosen were fighting. Rosen had brought up catcher Mike Heath from the minors without consulting Billy. Billy found out about it from the writers before an exhibition game. Then the phone rang in his office. It was Rosen with the information.

To Billy's mind, Rosen had shown him up in front of the writers. With biting sarcasm Billy said to Rosen, ''Thanks, Al, I know about it. The press told me. Thanks.'' And he hung up the phone.

By late May, Billy was attacking George in the papers. Rosen wouldn't be coming to his defense. This time there was no one to protect Billy from George.

Billy's anger stemmed from Steinbrenner signing two expensive free-agent pitchers, Andy Messersmith and Rawley Eastwick. The year before, Gabe Paul had conferred with Billy because he had respected Billy's opinion. Even if Gabe disagreed with Billy, he at least gave Billy the courtesy of getting his input.

Steinbrenner and Rosen worked together and didn't bother consulting with Billy at all. Billy, who felt he knew talent better than either of them, didn't like Messersmith or Eastwick, and he felt contempt that George would spend a lot of money for what Billy felt was damaged goods.

Billy turned out to be right, too. Messersmith was 0 3 for the Yankees, won two games for the Dodgers in 1979, and retired. Eastwick pitched eight games for the Yankees, winning two. He was peddled to Philadelphia in midseason. He won five games the next three and a half seasons and then retired.

Billy, showing his contempt for George's inability to judge talent, referred to Messersmith and Eastwick in the papers as "George's boys."

Steinbrenner, of course, retaliated in kind. He revealed to the writers a letter from AL president Lee MacPhail criticizing Billy for giving the finger to a heckler in the stands.

There was something else George wanted to talk to Billy about. Billy was dating an underage girl, and George wasn't happy. Over and over George warned Billy to break it off, that if he didn't, he would end up in the kind of trouble that would disgrace the Yankees.

Billy was still married to Gretchen, who was living in Texas. He had a live-in relationship with Patty Stark, a woman in her mid twenties. When Billy came to New York from Texas, he moved Patty from Kansas City to live with him.

Patty Stark was liked by all who knew her, including Billy's sisters and his daughter, Kelly. Everyone who knew Patty said that they wished Billy had married her. Perhaps, they said, everything might have turned out differently.

"I liked Patty," said Kelly Martin. "She was very nice. And Dad and Patty got along really good. Matter of fact, she was the one who would send me Western Union telegrams when Dad would promise he was going to send money, and then it would never come, never come, never come. I'd have to call back and say, 'They're kicking me out now. Do you think maybe you could send me child support?' She would be the one who signed the telegrams 'Love, your dad.' And then down below, where it says who sent it, it was 'Patty Stark.'

"When Dad managed the Yankees, he lived in New Jersey, and when he'd call, a lot of times she'd be there. He'd say, 'Here, I want you to talk to Patty.' He always wanted me to talk to his girlfriends. 'Here, get to know my daughter, be friends with my daughter.' "

But Billy's custom was not to take his wife—or in this case, his steady girl-friend, Patty Stark—on the road with him. As he had demonstrated to Bert Hawkins, the Rangers' traveling secretary, when he was managing Texas, he didn't like wives on the road. They could see too much, squeal on a player or two, perhaps squeal on him. If he had a girlfriend on the road with him, she had no standing to say anything to anyone. It was safer that way.

The girl on the road in 1978 was Heather Ervolino. She was sixteen at the time, short but curvy. She oozed sexuality and had a large bust and a great ass, everything Billy wanted in a relationship.

The first time the two had met, earlier the year before, Heather, her younger brother, and her girlfriend, Samora Landreano, had walked the block from her South Bronx home to Yankee Stadium to meet players and get autographs after a game. Her younger brother had been a big fan of Billy Martin's, and they had made a point of meeting Billy.

Heather's outstanding physical attributes, combined with a childlike innocence, wowed Billy. He became smitten with her and went into pursuit mode. For Billy the chase was always the best part of a relationship. The problems always came after the roping and tying up.

During that first meeting Billy signed his autograph and wrote down his phone number for her. She didn't call, but she didn't stop coming to the players' gate, either.

Billy left the young girl tickets. Once she took the bait, she was his.

For several months Billy took great pains to keep Heather's existence secret from Patty Stark. Patty had been with Billy since 1973, when Billy managed the Texas Rangers. Billy had separated from his second wife, Gretchen, to keep company with Patty.

Said Billy's sister Pat, "That's the girl he should have married, 'cause she would never have given him any trouble. She was a very nice girl, and she did love him."

By all accounts, once Billy met Heather and became focused on her youthful sexuality, Patty was on her way out.

Billy talked Patty into hiring Heather to clean their apartment a couple days a week. Of course, Billy didn't tell Patty he had the hots for Heather. Rather, he told her that he felt sorry for her because she came from the slums of the Bronx and that she needed the money. After one look at that body, Patty should have realized that Billy wanted her for more than floors and windows.

Patty hired Heather to clean house, and soon the two women began attending ball games together. It wasn't long before Billy told Patty they were through, and in 1978, Heather moved in with him. Billy was fifty, Heather sixteen.

A sobbing Patty Stark told Pat Irvine, Billy's sister, "I never should have let that girl into this place. I should have known better."

Pat thought, This is very wrong of my brother.

Billy first introduced Heather to his close friends Bill and Carol Reedy in 1978. The Reedys were waiting for Billy at one of Billy's favorite steak houses in New Jersey when he walked in with Heather. She was a teenager who considered Billy's friends to be "old people." Carol Reedy remembered Heather as being "scared to death."

Carol Reedy felt sorry for the girl. She was too young for Billy, Carol felt. "I wanted to choke Billy," she said years later.

Eventually Carol came to like Heather very much. The two women both came from the Bronx, and Billy got a kick out of that. Billy would say to Bill Reedy, "We'll leave the two Bronx Bombers, and we'll go." Even though Heather was twenty years younger than Carol, their common roots gave them something to talk about, and it put Heather at ease.

But to George Steinbrenner, all he could see were the headlines if Heather's mother decided to charge Billy with the Mann Act or with statutory rape.

When George confronted Billy about Heather, Billy's paranoia acted up. He could not understand how George possibly could have known about her unless one of his coaches or players had ratted on him. When a telephone operator warned Billy that George had been tape-recording his phone conversations—as absurd as that may be—Billy was paranoid enough to believe it. Billy wondered what sort of man he was working for. (George has consistently denied recording Billy's calls.)

The Yankees went to the West Coast for a road trip. When Billy came back, he made all his personal calls from a pay phone outside Yankee Stadium.

By mid-June 1978, Steinbrenner was showing up at the clubhouse screaming that the team was embarrassing him and the city of New York. He threatened to clean house, to bring up the minor leaguers if the Yankees didn't start producing.

Steinbrenner rattled every player on his team after a game in which rookie pitcher Jim Beattie was hit hard by the league-leading Boston Red Sox.

To the reporters he said, "He was scared stiff. What the hell was he doing out there?"

Before the end of the game, Steinbrenner warned coach Gene Michael that Beattie better be out of his sight before he got down there. The next day Steinbrenner shipped Beattie to Columbus, the Yankees' Triple A Club.

His vindictive mad-hatter behavior was undermining Billy and also shaking the confidence of the players, upping the pressure on everybody. No one could relax. When asked about Martin's status as manager, Steinbrenner used the same ruse he had employed the year before with Gabe Paul. He told reporters, "Al Rosen will decide."

When the reporters rushed to call Rosen, he said Billy was manager and would continue to be so.

By doing that, Steinbrenner was creating headlines when no story actually existed. It was a pattern that would remain through Billy's five stints as Yankee manager, a daily question-and-answer as to whether Billy Martin would continue to be the manager. It made interesting reading—BILLY STILL MANAGER—even if it was a nonstory, but this constant wondering about Billy's fate made him jumpy and turned his mood even more sour than usual.

"In two years I won a pennant and a world championship," said Billy. "I'm sick and tired of hearing about being fired. I give George Steinbrenner one hundred percent loyalty, and I expect it in return."

He was expecting the impossible. The nonstories about whether Billy would be fired were getting Steinbrenner's name in the newspapers every day, and George was getting off on it. These stories were making Steinbrenner seem as important to the Yankee fans as were Billy and the players. As long as reporters would call him and ask about it, George would keep everyone guessing and in limbo.

The players became disillusioned and downhearted. Said outfielder Lou Piniella, "If I was rich, I'd quit. I used to love playing baseball. Now I hate it. I just hate everything about it. I especially hate the garbage that goes with it."

On June 26, Steinbrenner called Billy into his office and told him his job was on the line. The Yankees were eight games out of first and losing. The pitching staff was in disarray. The way Billy saw it, with Hunter, Gullett, Tidrow, Holtzman, and Ken Clay all suffering from injuries, he felt he and Fowler were doing a great job keeping the Yankees as close as they were.

George's irrational response was that if the pitchers are hurt, that's the fault of the pitching coach.

Two days later Al Rosen told Billy that Clyde King would replace Art Fowler as pitching coach. To Billy it was madness; it was like firing Billy. He told all the coaches that he was going to fight for Fowler, and he called Rosen's bluff.

Rosen, caught in the middle, decided to pass the decision over to George, which may have been George's plan all along. When Billy and George met, George made a proposal: Billy could keep Art Fowler, but George would bring in Clyde King to work with the young pitchers. Billy was forced to agree even though he hated King, whom he felt was a spy for Steinbrenner.

George made Billy cave in to one other demand as well: Billy would have to abide by George's lineups and follow his suggestions.

Two days later in Milwaukee, Billy Martin decided he was going to quit. He knew he was the best manager in the game, but Steinbrenner made him feel like a failure. He wondered whether he could get another job if he resigned.

Billy was sitting in the bar of the Pfister Hotel with Art Fowler. Fowler left to meet with old friends, leaving Billy by himself. Feeling terribly depressed and alone, Billy returned to his room.

At two A.M. Billy knocked on the door of Maury Allen, the columnist for the *New York Post*. Unlike most of the writers, who made no bones about hating Billy, Maury Allen is a gentle man who has never hated anyone in his life. Billy needed to talk to someone. He asked Allen to come to his room a couple doors down.

Billy told him, "Why should I have to take all this shit? I'm a Yankee. I've been a Yankee all my life. What's he been? Rich. He's not a Yankee. I'm a Yankee. I don't have to take this. I can leave the team now. I'll live. I don't have to listen to this crap, take his phone calls, ruin my life and health. What for? I'm a Yankee."

In front of Allen, Martin began sobbing, his entire body shaking, his arms flailing, his head in his chest, his hands squeezing his legs. He kept repeating, "I'm a Yankee. I'm a Yankee."

Allen saw that Billy was close to a nervous breakdown.

After a few minutes Billy regained his composure.

"We'll win it, you watch," Billy said. "We'll win it."

By July, as the Boston Red Sox began pulling away from the Yankees, George's intrusion on his life had made Billy's life a nightmare.

George made it clear to the players that *he* was taking over. He told them he was doing it for Billy's good, which was as diabolical an explanation as he could concoct.

Here he was driving Billy crazy, making him physically ill with his meddling, and now he was justifying his taking over Billy's authority as manager because of Billy's health.

Billy was managing this team to the best of his considerable abilities, and all he was getting in return from the owner was severe criticism and warnings of an imminent firing. By July, Billy was beginning to crack up. He knew Steinbrenner's lineup was inferior to what he should be putting out there. The Yankees lost three of four games using the lineup.

Said Reggie Jackson in his autobiography, "It became obvious that he was putting a lot of pressure on Billy, who when under pressure usually did three things: (1) Got mad. (2) Went to the bar. (3) Went after me.

"By July he was showing up later and later at the ballpark, looking shakier and shakier when he did, wearing his sunglasses more and more often for the afternoon games.

"As the Red Sox began to pull away from us, it was nothing for Billy to show up at twelve-thirty for a two o'clock game and for us not to have a batting order posted as late as one o'clock.

"When he did show up, sunglasses on, he wouldn't go near anybody."

If Billy wanted out, so did Reggie. How the Billy-Reggie-George triangle would end would depend on who could commit the more outrageous act of defiance.

Reggie's came first. On July 17, with the team fourteen games behind the Red Sox, Billy continued to post a lineup dictated by George that had Reggie at DH, which was the way Billy preferred using Reggie, but George had inserted catcher Thurman Munson into right field because of his bad knees. Mike Heath was given the catching assignment.

It would have made a lot more sense to play Reggie in right, as it was his natural position, and DH Munson. Billy swallowed hard but felt he had no choice but to go along even though the Yankees had lost three of four with George's lineup.

Before the game on July 17, as he recalled in his book, Reggie met with George, Al Rosen, and Yankee executive Cedric Tallis. Reggie told George he wanted to play right field every day. This time George switched allegiances and told Reggie that he was siding with Billy. He cited Reggie's fielding deficiencies. For the first time Reggie discovered that his "friend" was no longer an ally.

Reggie demanded a trade.

George told him, "You better get your head on straight, boy."

"Who the hell do you think you're talking about?"

"I'm talking to you."

"Well, let me tell you something," said Reggie. "Don't you ever talk to me like that again as long as you live."

Reggie and George stared at each other. Reggie addressed Rosen. He said, "Al, you're Jewish. How would you interpret the part about 'boy'?"

Rosen told him he didn't think George was saying it the way he was interpreting it.

"I think you should both cool down," Rosen said.

Steinbrenner said, "Cool down, hell. Reggie, you get the hell out of my office."

"I don't feel like leaving. I kind of like it here. I'm staying."

So Steinbrenner stormed out.

When Reggie returned to the field, he was in a foul fury. Steinbrenner's treatment of Reggie then caused Reggie to direct his anger toward Billy. George set the whole thing up and then watched as Billy and Reggie went at each other.

That evening in Kansas City, Billy had Reggie batting cleanup. The game was tied in the tenth inning when, with Thurman Munson on first, Billy asked Reggie to bunt. It was a one-pitch strategy designed to decoy the Royals. Billy wanted Reggie to show the bunt, so the Royals infielders would play farther in, giving Reggie a better chance to hit the next pitch through the infield. It was the type of move Billy was known for.

But Reggie was too upset and angry with George to appreciate Billy's finer points of baseball. When Billy gave Reggie the bunt sign, Reggie came to an erroneous conclusion: Billy was making him bunt to make him look bad. The game before, Billy had benched him against lefty Larry Gura. Now this. And after the way George had treated him, Reggie Jackson was not going to take any of Billy's shit. Not on this day. No sir.

Reggie squared to bunt and took ball one. The infielders moved in a couple steps. As intended, Billy then signaled for Reggie to hit away.

Except that Reggie was determined to make his Last Stand. When Reggie saw the first bunt sign, he decided he was going to pay Billy back for taking him out of the game against Boston the year before.

Reggie defied Billy. He refused to hit away. He again squared to bunt. He missed.

Third-base coach Dick Howser walked over to Reggie and told him Billy wanted him to hit away.

"I was told to bunt. I'm bunting," said Reggie.

Howser was stunned. "He wants you to hit away."

Reggie said, "Listen, Dick, nothing against you, but when I left the dugout he told me to bunt, and I'm going to bunt. I'm gonna get the runner over, and Piniella will come up and knock the run in, and we'll win. I'm a real team guy, right?"

"I hope you know what you're doing," Howser said.

Reggie later admitted to being so sick of the situation he was in, he really didn't know what he was doing. Angry, tired, and whipped, he was reacting rather than thinking.

Twice more Reggie tried to bunt, missing and striking out.

\* \* \*

In the end the stink over Reggie's defiance of Billy—an act that was prompted by George Steinbrenner's attempt to bully and humiliate Reggie—was the incident that led to Billy's resignation. Billy hadn't known of the meeting, didn't know *why* Reggie had done it. He assumed automatically that Reggie's actions were directed at him and him alone.

After Reggie struck out, he waited in the dugout, hoping for a chance to duke it out with Billy. Then he went to the clubhouse.

The Yankees lost in the eleventh, which made a bad situation terrible. When Billy came into the clubhouse, he avoided Reggie. He went into his office and began throwing things.

During that same game, relief pitcher Sparky Lyle, who had lost his closer role to Goose Gossage, was asked by Billy to pitch the third and fourth innings. He refused and, in protest, left the game and went home.

Reggie had pushed Billy over the edge. Here Billy had been forced to do things Steinbrenner's way, things that he knew hurt him in the eyes of his players, and here was a player defying him, which might have hurt him just as badly.

"I don't disobey orders," Billy said. "Tell me what to do and I'll do it."

Billy wanted Reggie suspended for the rest of the season. Reggie was hoping to be suspended for thirty days. Steinbrenner suspended him for five games. As for Lyle, no one said a word about his defiance of Billy. Lyle was one of Billy's favorites.

Reggie flew home to San Francisco and spent a week hiding at the home of a girlfriend.

The Yankees won four straight without Reggie, and Billy was feeling more at ease than at any other time during the season because he didn't have to worry about George second-guessing where he batted Reggie.

In Chicago, a day before Reggie's return, Billy learned of something Steinbrenner had done that set him off on a course of self-destruction.

Billy and Bill Veeck, the owner of the White Sox, were drinking in the Bard Room of Comiskey Park after a Yankee victory when Veeck told Billy that earlier in the spring Steinbrenner had proposed a trade of managers, Billy for Bob Lemon, whom Veeck ended up firing.

Apparently Steinbrenner had suggested this to Lee MacPhail, the American League president, and MacPhail had called Veeck. Veeck said he was waiting to hear from Steinbrenner.

One wonders whether Veeck, who hated Steinbrenner and the Yankees passionately, was purposefully roiling the already-muddy waters. Veeck was an iconoclast. If his intention was to stir up trouble, this time he would succeed in a big way.

Billy was incredulous that Steinbrenner would have even considered such a trade. Billy for Bob Lemon? Billy would have been deeply insulted if George had offered Billy for Earl Weaver. Billy's anger, at both Steinbrenner and Jackson, intensified.

The next day the bus was ready to leave the hotel for the ballpark. Reggie was expected but hadn't arrived. Billy ordered the driver to leave without him. Reggie took a cab and got to Comiskey Park fifteen minutes after the team.

In the cab on the way to the park, Reggie decided he would make a public apology for his defiant at-bat as soon as he got to the ballpark.

Naturally it was one of the first things the reporters asked him. Had Reggie said, "I'm sorry. I was angry, and it was my fault," perhaps what followed would not have occurred. But George, Reggie, and Billy all had one thing in common: None were able to admit fault.

Said Reggie, "For the way they interpret the offense, I guess an apology is in order. The way I interpret it, I haven't done anything wrong."

Nothing wrong? He had bunted with two strikes against the express orders of the third-base coach *and* the manager. *Nobody* in his right mind bunts on the third strike unless specifically ordered to do so.

Because of Reggie's many interviews, he didn't take batting practice. That made some teammates angry.

Said Graig Nettles in his book, "Instead of going out and taking batting practice, he held a press conference in the clubhouse. And that's the thing that pissed Billy off the most. Billy felt that Reggie had been away for five days and was rusty, and he should have been out on the field before the game getting ready. All the players knew Reggie should have been out there, and perhaps somebody should have said something to him, but he was standing in the clubhouse in front of all those reporters, and something like that would have just made more headlines, so none of us did."

Billy sent Dick Howser to tell Reggie he wasn't playing. Having won four in a row, Billy wanted to keep the same lineup. When the Yankees won their fifth straight, the Red Sox lead had dropped from fourteen to ten games.

After the game Billy again joined Bill Veeck to drink some more. Jack Lang of the *Daily News* came into the bar, and Billy asked Lang what Reggie had said about what he had done.

Lang showed him Reggie's quote about his not doing "anything wrong."

"Ick," said Billy.

"Is that a comment on my story?" asked Lang.

"No," said Billy. "On him."

Billy told Lang that if Reggie didn't keep his mouth shut, he wasn't going to play him, and this time he didn't care what George wanted.

Billy, who had stopped eating, had a couple more drinks with Veeck, and when it was time to leave, he carried his scotch onto the bus in a paper cup. As the bus was pulling into the airport, he asked reporter Murray Chass if he could talk to him in the terminal for a few minutes.

After the game Reggie dressed and got on the bus with the rest of the team for the drive to O'Hare Airport. At the airport Reggie and Fran Healy went to an ice-cream stand and bought milk shakes.

At the same time, Billy went to the airport bar to continue his drinking. Chass found Billy at the bar.

Fueled by the scotch, his defenses lowered by alcohol, Billy decided to vent his anger to a person who not only despised him but had the means to destroy him by publishing his words.

On some level Billy knew exactly what he was doing. He decided he could not take the battering any longer and that he had to get out of an intolerable situation. The vehicle for his exit from hell was *New York Times* reporter Murray Chass.

Billy asked Chass, "Jackson's refusal to admit he was wrong, is that conduct detrimental to the Yankees?" It was a reference to the bad-boy clause in his own contract. A brooding Billy thought it unfair that he be bound by one set of rules when Reggie was not so bound. He was also furious with George and hurt and angry that George had even considered trading him to the White Sox for Bob Lemon.

Billy continued talking. He said, "I'm saying shut up, Reggie Jackson. If he doesn't shut up, he won't play. I don't care what George says. He can replace me right now."

Chass asked if it was off the record.

"No sir," said Billy, "it's on."

To Billy, Reggie *was* Steinbrenner. They were the same—his enemy, disruptive to his team, agitating his friends, destroying his authority and his life. Billy Martin could not stand the status quo any longer. He needed to step away from the situation before he died. He wasn't eating, and he was taking pills for his liver, on which doctors had discovered a spot.

Chass headed for a pay phone to call his editor at *The New York Times*. Henry Hecht of the *New York Post* was with him. The *Post* was an afternoon paper. Chass knew his scoop was safe.

Chass returned, but Billy wasn't finished. He spoke of the special treatment George had afforded Reggie, letting him "drive across Florida in spring training in that damned Rolls," allowing him to skip batting practice, allowing him to report late. As he spoke he became more and more incensed at the perceived injustice, the difference between the way George coddled Jackson and constantly berated Billy. After all he had done for the man.

Chass and Hecht left Billy to wait for the plane to be called. While he waited, Billy brooded. For two years Billy had felt the pain caused by Steinbrenner's constant attacks, his constant push for Martin to do more and more and more and be better, better, better, both as a manager and a person. But to Billy, what George wanted him to do was "Mickey Mouse." To Billy, George was the high school principal whose office he had to visit every day for the purpose of enduring constant criticism, a rat-a-tat-tat beating against his frail ego.

At that moment Billy Martin hated George Steinbrenner as much as he had hated any person in his life. And Reggie Jackson was the constant reminder of George's power and that George enjoyed using that power against him.

Pain and jealousy mixed with hatred.

As the flight to Kansas City was being announced, Chass and Hecht walked toward the entrance gate. Billy came by.

"Did you get that in the paper?" Billy wanted to know. Chass said he had.

"I ran him out today," said Billy about Reggie, "and he'll get the same thing tomorrow."

Billy then mentioned Reggie's response to the bunt incident. He also noted that Reggie earlier had told reporters he hadn't talked to Billy in a year and a half. Billy wanted the reporters to know that Reggie was a "liar."

Billy had heard Graig Nettles first utter the phrase that he felt perfectly captured the essence of Reggie and George. He repeated it to Chass.

Without mentioning Steinbrenner by name, Billy said the magic words that will link the three men in baseball history forever.

"One's a born liar, and the other's convicted."

Chass again asked Billy if he wanted the line printed.

"Print it," Billy said.

Perhaps if Steinbrenner hadn't called Reggie "boy" on July 17, and if Steinbrenner hadn't proposed his trade with Bill Veeck, and if Steinbrenner hadn't pushed Billy over the edge, none of this would have happened.

But in George's race to see which man—Billy or Reggie—he would drive over the edge first, Billy crossed the line that day at O'Hare Airport ahead of Reggie.

When Chass went to Reggie to ask for a comment, his answer was, "No comment."

Said Reggie later, "For the first time in my career, I'd bitten my tongue and shut up."

The next day in Kansas City, a tearful Billy resigned.

# GONE AND BACK

**B**illy suffered from bad timing. Two weeks after Billy blew up, the New York newspapers all went on strike and stayed out the rest of the season. Had the incident happened during the strike, his immortal line would never have been printed. Murray Chass and Henry Hecht would have been home, not on Billy's heels.

Chass may not have been out to get Billy fired, but he certainly made all the right moves to ensure Billy's demise. After the plane landed in Kansas City and Chass got to his hotel room, his first call was to Steinbrenner to tell him exactly what Billy had said about him.

"Was he drinking?" George wanted to know.

Chass would have been telling the truth had he said, "Billy was as drunk as a skunk," but instead Chass's response was more precise. He told George he hadn't *seen* Billy drinking.

George told Chass, "I've got to believe no boss in his right mind would take that."

Henry Hecht was the object of hatred and contempt by many of the Yankee players and especially by Billy, because Hecht, the players felt, seemed to enjoy criticizing them. They hated him because they knew he would hurt them with his words if he could. They hated him because he stirred up trouble. They hated him because he had influence with the public, this little, nerdy, arrogant, unathletic guy with glasses who used his power to hurt them. Much like George.

Hecht, who criticized but was thin-skinned when he was criticized, hated Billy with a passion. When Hecht heard Billy say, "One's a born liar, and the other's convicted," Hecht knew it meant Billy's demise. On the flight from Chicago to Kansas City, Hecht told Paul Blair, "I can't tell you what he said, but Billy's gone."

Hecht, too, called Steinbrenner immediately. George kept asking him, "Did he really say it?"

If Murray Chass and Henry Hecht had not printed what Billy had said, Billy would not have quit the next day. But in this case Billy knew he had given the two reporters a great quote, and on some level he was sure what the results of his actions would be.

Some of Billy's allies blamed Chass, others blamed Hecht.

Bill Kane, the Yankee traveling secretary, is convinced that despite stories to the contrary, Chass was the only one who heard the key line.

Said Kane, "Murray didn't have the guts to go with it himself, so he told Hecht, knowing Henry would print it because he hated Billy so much.

"Then," said Kane, "Murray made sure Billy would get fired. He called George to tell him what Billy had said."

Third baseman Graig Nettles, who himself hated Henry Hecht, placed the ultimate blame on the *Post* reporter.

Said Nettles in *Balls*, "Billy's problem was that Billy had the attention of the nation on him, and he would leave himself open to guys like Henry Hecht. It was bound to happen that sooner or later Henry would nail Billy, because when Billy was feeling the pressure, sometimes he would have a pop or two and say things he shouldn't. That's what happened when he said, 'One's a born liar, and the other's convicted.' It was Billy's fault that he said it. But those two guys, Hecht, and Murray Chass of the *Times*, never should have printed it. And the only reason Chass printed it was that he knew Hecht certainly would run it, and he would look bad if Hecht printed it and he didn't. Billy never should have been fired. Never. But he was, because the writers didn't like him, and they allowed Billy to sandbag himself. And I will never, ever forgive them for it."

In the light of day, with the effects of his heavy drinking having worn off, Billy decided he didn't want to be fired, but it was too late by then.

Steinbrenner called Al Rosen, who called Cedric Tallis, who was with the team in Kansas City. Billy was drinking in his room with his coaches when Tallis came into the room.

"Did you say it?"

"No."

Later he denied it to Rosen and to Steinbrenner.

Steinbrenner knew it would look better if Billy quit rather than if he fired him. He called Billy's agent, Doug Newton, and told him that if Billy wanted to get paid, he had to resign.

Billy scribbled his resignation speech on six pieces of Crown Center Hotel stationery. Mickey Morabito, Billy's good friend and drinking companion, was the Yankees' public relations man, and Mickey suggested Billy wait a few minutes while he typed out the speech. Billy agreed.

Morabito went back to his room, which was next to Al Rosen's. Morabito told Rosen of the resignation. He typed the notes and returned them to Billy.

Rosen went to see Billy.

"Keep in touch," Rosen told him.

As the reality of the situation finally began to sink in, Billy's eyes filled with tears. Billy, accompanied by his friend Bob Brown, took the elevator to the mezzanine, where a mob of reporters awaited him.

Billy held an unlit cigar in his left hand, his notes in his right. Choking on the words, he announced he would read his statement but would not answer any questions.

"That means now and forever," Billy said, "because I am a Yankee and Yankees do not talk or throw rocks."

Billy, shaken, held his dark glasses against his face. His legs barely supported him. In a thin, high-pitched voice he talked about how he didn't want to hurt the team's chances for the pennant with any more undue publicity. He said the team had a real shot at the pennant and said he hoped it would win. Steinbrenner had told Doug Newton that to get paid, Billy had to say he was resigning because of his health, and Billy said that, and then he apologized to Steinbrenner, as he had been ordered to do. Billy also threw in a gratuitous line about not having said the magic words.

Tears began to flow, and his body shook.

"I'd like to thank the Yankee management, the press and news media, my coaches, my players . . . and most of all . . . the fans."

He began to blubber. Sobs came, loud gasps, which embarrassed everyone around him. George Steinbrenner, the Boss, had reduced the great Billy Martin to a blubbering mass of jelly.

Phil Rizzuto, who had never been close to Billy, had been his teammate many, many years ago. Phil put his arm around Billy, and the two former Yankee greats walked alone down the hotel corridor toward the exit.

The Yankee players watched Billy's departure on television. Said Reggie Jackson about Billy's performance, in which he talked about Yankee pinstripes and extolled the Yankee tradition, "I wanted to laugh. I didn't know, of course, that George and all Yankee fans everywhere were eating that shit up like it was ice cream."

The response to Billy's firing was a hysterical outpouring of anger by Yankee fans. Thousands of calls came into the stadium switchboard, some making threats on Steinbrenner's life.

The day after Billy was fired, Arthur Richman, who was in charge of promotions for the New York Mets, called the head of the Mets, Larinda De Roullet, the club owner, and told her, "I guarantee you forty to fifty thousand for the next two nights if you do one thing: Hire Billy Martin."

Richman, an old friend of Billy's, had called Billy at his home in New Jersey and told him about the Mets job. Richman made sure it was in the papers that Billy was negotiating with the Mets.

Now Billy had George in a box. It was Steinbrenner's worst nightmare: the one man who could put fannies in the seats at Shea Stadium and take the media play away from the Yankees. Even more upsetting, what if Billy were hired by the Mets and led them to a World Series?

George witnessed firsthand the hold Billy had over New Yorkers. Everyone loved him: cabdrivers, business executives, women. Everyone. Billy was Everyman. To fans, George represented the evil Military-Industrial Complex squashing Everyman.

The fans' fury moved and scared George. And there was something else about Steinbrenner's relationship to Billy. He certainly didn't like him. He never invited him even to have dinner with him. He treated him shamefully. But on some level it fed Steinbrenner's ego to have the best manager in baseball, Billy Martin, managing the Yankees.

Billy was out on July 25. In one of the strangest turns of events in sports history, two days after Steinbrenner forced him to resign, he began negotiating for Billy's return to the Yankees (just as he had done after his public excoriation when he fired Cleveland Pipers basketball coach John McClendon).

Steinbrenner was at home in Tampa visiting the home of *Tampa Tribune* columnist Tom McEwen. After dinner they watched the Yankee game on TV. Dick Howser was managing the team as it awaited the arrival of Bob Lemon from the West Coast. Steinbrenner began talking about Billy.

"Billy's health couldn't have taken much more of this pressure," Steinbrenner told McEwen. It was as though George had had nothing to do with "this pressure." As the cameras panned to Howser on the bench, Steinbrenner said, "That's Billy's job." He picked up the phone and called Doug Newton, Billy's agent.

He said to Newton, "Tell Billy I'll talk to him in the Carlyle tomorrow. Tell him to call me when he gets in. I'll send a car for him. Tell him I want to see him tomorrow night."

When Billy heard George wanted to talk to him, he said, "He should have thought about that the last six months. If he'd have treated me right, I'd have still been the manager."

The next day Newton called Billy to say several teams had called about hiring Billy to manage. Billy said no. He was hooked on the idea of coming back to work for Steinbrenner, though he was unsure whether Steinbrenner was serious or whether he was just being polite.

"George is just crazy enough to be serious," Newton told him. Billy opined that he didn't think he could work with him but that it wouldn't hurt to meet with him.

Billy flew to New York to meet with Newton and Steinbrenner on July 27, two days after leaving the Yankees. In Newton's office Billy started talking about how strange it was not to be the manager, and then he broke down and cried.

"Do you really think George is sincere?" Billy asked.

Billy and Newton went to see George at his suite in the Carlyle Hotel. George asked if Billy would consider returning as manager in 1979.

"If things were very different, I would," Billy said. According to Billy, George admitted that he liked to have his nose in everything. George said Billy's weakness was that he didn't manage with statistics. (Translated, he was saying that Billy's problem was that he didn't pay attention to *George's* statistics.)

"If both of us could give a little, I don't think we'll have any problem at all," George said.

"You're right, George, because you're really not a bad guy."

"Actually, you're not, either."

Both of them were lying up a storm.

Billy said, "One of the problems is that you and I didn't talk to each other." George agreed. People who can't stand each other don't talk much. Billy said he was upset that certain players could go and talk to him, "and that's not good."

George said, "If you promise to do a couple of things and if I promise to do a couple of things, I don't think we have a problem."

Said Billy, "If we both keep our word, we won't have a problem." It was a big *If.*

According to Billy, he told George he didn't know squat about running a baseball team and wanted him to leave him alone, and he wanted the restrictive clauses taken out of his contract.

George agreed, according to Billy. He would get $100,000 per year for 1979 and 1980, with no restrictions.

In exchange George wanted Billy to teach him the game of baseball. Billy said he would be glad to. Billy asked George to teach him more about the business side of baseball. Said George, "Sure I will."

They agreed to stay in close contact. Billy said he would work with Al Rosen and Cedric Tallis but asked George to call him directly if there was a problem.

In talking about why he rehired Billy, this man with a felony conviction on his record cited Jesus, as people who screw up badly often do afterward.

Said George, "What kind of man would I be if I let a guy go for saying something about me that was true? I'm the leader of this team. I had to be able to take the heat. I knew he said it. I also knew it was true. He had made a mistake. I had made a mistake. The only guy who had never made a mistake was the guy with long hair, the guy who walked on water. I kept thinking about that all night long."

George told reporter Maury Allen, "I just couldn't live with myself if I didn't do something to help him, if I didn't give him another chance."

George told Billy the perfect day for the Yankees to make the announcement would be July 29, Old-Timers' Day. Bob Lemon, whom close friend Al Rosen had favored to replace Billy, would manage the rest of the year, and Billy would come back in the spring.

Billy commented, "I felt that maybe I was getting the respect from George I felt I deserved."

George said he first had to tell Rosen and Lemon. "We're ninety-five percent there,'' George said. ''Now, whatever you do, don't say anything to anybody about this conversation.''

As an indication of how much George and Billy trusted each other, George called Doug Newton the next day to accuse Billy of leaking the story. This was one day after he had promised Billy to call him directly if there was a problem! So much for promises.

In fact, Billy hadn't even told Bill Reedy or Art Fowler.

Billy got angry at Newton, who made the call back to George. Billy said, ''Tell George he can shove the job up his ass—again.'' He hung up. When Newton tried to call back, Billy wouldn't answer the phone.

The next day was Thursday, July 27, two days before Old-Timers' Day. Billy had cooled off. George told Newton that when Al Rosen found out about Billy coming back in 1979, he threatened to quit if Lemon didn't get a fairer amount of time to manage. George called to say he didn't want to lose Rosen, that Billy could scout in the organization for a year and return in 1980.

Billy thought Lem should get his full year in and agreed.

Newton asked him, ''What if Lem has a terrific year and wins the pennant? Do you think George will renege?''

Billy said he believed George about wanting to bring him back. So did Newton.

Saturday came. The honeymoon was still holding. Billy told no one about the Old-Timers' Day surprise, not even Mickey Mantle.

When Bob Sheppard, the public address announcer, introduced all the former Yankees, finishing with the Big Three—Whitey Ford, Mickey Mantle, and Joe DiMaggio—he then said in his wonderfully stentorian tones, ''. . . the manager for 1980, and hopefully for many years to come . . . Number 1 . . . Billy . . .''

Nothing else could be heard over the clapping and cheering for more than six minutes from the crowd, which rose to its feet to salute him. It was the loudest display of public affection for a Yankee hero since the day the fans said good-bye to Lou Gehrig in 1939. It may have been greater. The fans *liked* Gehrig. They *loved* Billy.

In front of the microphones Billy told the throng, ''I'm happy to be back with the Yankees.''

General Manager Al Rosen, for one, could not understand the intensity of emotion for Billy, whom he despised. Sitting in his seat on the press box level, he said to his wife, ''New York. It must be New York.'' Rosen was grim.

Mike Farber of the *Bergen Record* wrote, ''Billy Martin rose on the fifth day, the greatest return in almost 2,000 years.''

Billy held a press conference after the Old-Timers' activities. George announced there would be no questions. Billy was to make a statement. George had told Doug Newton that Billy was to praise George for giving him another chance, to say that he took him back despite emotional, physical, and drinking problems.

''Doug, he's to say he's getting off the booze, that he had been drinking too much, that he's going to reform. Doug, you tell him to say all those things at the press conference.''

Billy refused, and at the press conference he spoke in his best Stengelese. When he was done, George called Newton aside and said he wanted Billy to add a few written statements to his speech about his bad health and his drinking problem.

Newton refused to be caught in the middle. He told Steinbrenner to ask Billy himself. "I'm not Billy's ghostwriter," Newton told him.

Steinbrenner never asked Billy face-to-face. Said Billy, "He didn't dare."

Was George serious about rehiring Billy? It was a question Billy asked himself over and over during the winter of 1978.

The one player most affected by this surprise announcement was Reggie Jackson. For a few days Reggie had rejoiced over not having to play for his tormenter anymore. His joy was short-lived. Reggie's conclusion: George was choosing Billy over him.

That night Reggie told his father that he would never again trust George Steinbrenner as long as he lived.

Another interested party, Billy's daughter Kelly, was upset when she heard that Billy was returning to manage for Steinbrenner.

"He'd made my dad a nervous wreck," said Kelly. "I hated it every time he went back to the Yankees. My dad loved the Yankees. He started with the Yankees. He liked the concept of Yankee integrity, that you're not just proud to be a ballplayer but proud to be a Yankee, that putting on the Yankee uniform was something special.

"And he was just like me, always hoping that it will be better the next time. He's a glutton for punishment, like me.

"He always went back there hoping maybe George would realize this time that the team was better off with my dad managing instead of George trying to. But every time my dad went back, George tried to dig in a little deeper."

Billy almost didn't get his second chance.

The first thing he did was hold a press conference in which he announced he was going to open a Western-wear shop on Madison Avenue in New York. He said his health was fine and that Reggie was less of a problem on the Yankees than George's meddling.

George called Yankee public relations director Mickey Morabito, who had set up the press conference, to say that if what Billy had said showed up in the newspapers the next day, Morabito would be fired.

Morabito, who knew George wasn't bluffing, was heartbroken. Billy tried to console him. The next day all the New York papers went on strike, and Morabito's job was saved.

Said Billy, "This wasn't the new, understanding George that he had promised he would become. It was the same old George."

Months went by, and Doug Newton was having trouble getting the agreement reduced to writing. George kept stalling, and Billy wondered whether it was all a publicity stunt.

Billy's limbo status continued through November 28, 1978, when Billy gave George a solid excuse not to bring him back. A friend of Billy's from his days as manager in Minnesota, basketball coach Bill Musselman, asked Billy to appear during halftime of a basketball game played by Musselman's Reno Big Horns, a team in the Western Basketball League. Billy said he would go as long as there were no press interviews. Musselman agreed.

Billy was announced at halftime, waved, and walked off. Then he headed for the cocktail lounge to drink with another close friend, Minneapolis restaurateur Howard Wong.

They hadn't taken a sip when a young man wearing a Yankee T-shirt came up to Billy and introduced himself as Ray Hagar. Billy figured he was a fan. They talked about the designated hitter, and then the young man asked Billy to comment on something *New York Daily News* columnist Dick Young had quoted Billy as saying, that Reggie Jackson was not ''a true Yankee.''

Billy realized that he was no fan but a reporter and quickly became inflamed.

Billy blamed the press for getting him fired. He blamed the press for giving Steinbrenner a significant advantage over him. He hated the press for its power to mold opinion. He railed at the questioner over the Young quote.

''Did you hear me say that?'' Billy asked. ''If you didn't hear me say it, don't quote me as saying it.''

Hagar, who had begun taking notes, then asked, ''Aren't reporters honest?''

That's when Howard Wong demanded Hagar's notes.

''I'd like to see you try to get them,'' Hagar said. Wong tried to grab Hagar's notes, and the reporter shoved the elderly Wong. That's when Billy coldcocked him. Later Billy would use one of the telltale signs of Hagar's coming aggression as the excuse. ''When Hagar started to take off his glasses,'' he said, ''I hit him.''

With two hard punches Billy turned Hagar's face into hamburger meat.

This time Billy had hit a reporter.

# JUDGE SAPIR

A way from the ballpark, Billy Martin's friends all sought to protect him from the world and often from himself. Whenever Billy went into a bar late at night, friends such as Lewis Figone and Bill Reedy always kept between him and the public. In Reno his friend Howard Wong had tried to stop Ray Hagar from writing about him, which only got Billy in deeper trouble.

This time Billy needed serious help. When George Steinbrenner read about Billy's attack on Ray Hagar, the Reno reporter, he declared that Billy could come back as Yankee manager only if he were cleared of both civil and criminal charges, a seemingly insurmountable task that led some observers, such as Phil Rizzuto and former Yankee star Bobby Richardson, to wonder whether George had really intended for Billy to come back and manage at all.

Billy was bad at being responsible. All his life Billy had left others to straighten out problems of his making. Learning from the streets taught him some things, but it left him vulnerable to those more sophisticated and politically savvy than he.

When Billy punched out pitcher Jim Brewer, he had counted on the Cincinnati Reds to handle his legal problems. When Reds owner Bill DeWitt didn't keep on top of the case, Billy ended up losing a considerable sum of money.

Billy was facing a worse scenario this time. Ray Hagar had filed assault charges and was talking about civil action, and George Steinbrenner was threatening to end Billy's baseball career.

The facts were clear and indisputable. Billy had smashed in the face of a young man who probably couldn't have hurt Billy if Billy had stood with his hands by his sides.

Who could possibly get him out of a box like that?

Out of the blue he received a phone call from a brilliant young lawyer from New Orleans by the name of Eddie Sapir.

They had first met in December 1968 when Sapir and another New Orleans politician, Bill Connick, the uncle of singer Harry Connick, Jr., flew to baseball's winter meetings to try to find two teams to play in its new domed arena. The plan was to find teams with an open date on their schedules between their spring training games and the start of the regular season.

Sapir approached one major league baseball manager, and after Sapir began his pitch about the Superdome, he asked him to come to his suite so he could show him a miniature of the stadium.

The manager said to him, "What floor is your room on?" He added, "We charge two hundred dollars a floor."

Sapir, appalled, then approached Billy, who was the manager of the Minnesota Twins, to come see his exhibit. Billy corralled Yogi Berra, his former Yankee teammate, and the two went to see it.

Billy, impressed by the Superdome facility and Eddie Sapir, talked the Twins into playing the two games in the dome. Ed Sapir hosted Billy, showing him the town. Martin loved Cajun cooking, especially the boiled seafood.

Later Billy would tell Sapir that if New Orleans ever got a team, to think of him first when hiring a manager. He wanted Sapir to remember his role in arranging the exhibition games.

"Don't forget me," Billy said. "I was the first one in."

Sapir and Martin kept in touch.

First impressions being what they are, Sapir would always remember how Billy had treated him with kindness and respect.

"He was as sweet as he could be to me," said Sapir, "so I really liked him from that day on."

Billy would visit Sapir in New Orleans. Sapir, who managed some pro athletes, never tried to hustle Martin to get him as a client, and as Martin became more comfortable with him, he began to include Sapir more and more. Sapir got to know Billy's friends, including Howard Wong and his wife, Beulah; Billy's wife, Gretchen; her parents, the Winklers; and family friends.

Sapir was elected at a very young age to the Louisiana State House of Representatives. He became one of the seven most powerful officials in New Orleans.

In 1971, just before Pittsburgh played Baltimore in the World Series, Sapir got a call from the wife of a New Orleans doctor saying her little boy had leukemia, was dying, and wanted to see the World Series more than anything in the world. Could Eddie help them get tickets?

Sapir called Martin.

"You got 'em," Billy said. "Whatever they want, they got." Two days later,

Sapir had the tickets on his desk. The boy, Michael Lupin, went to all seven games, traveled to both Baltimore and Pittsburgh, and shortly after the Series, died.

That was the extent of their friendship, except for an occasional note Sapir would send Martin, saying, "Keep up the good work" or "Looking forward to seeing you in spring training."

Said Sapir, "He was good to the city when I needed someone to play in the dome, and he was good to the family of the boy with leukemia. Billy was always there, so I wanted to be there for Billy. And I was."

Shortly after Sapir read about the Ray Hagar mauling, Sapir called Billy.

"What's up, councilman?"

Sapir said, "I don't know who you have handling this for you, Billy, but from reading the papers it doesn't sound like anything's being done for you."

Billy said, "Eddie, I really appreciate you calling. I don't have anybody. Nobody at all. Boy, it's all out there, and George told me if I don't win the trial, it'll cost me my job."

Sapir said, "We gotta win it, man."

Billy said, "What do I have to do?"

Sapir took control. He had Billy, Howard Wong, and Bill Musselman come to New Orleans to plan strategy in order to extricate Billy from his legal snare. The strategy depended upon the cooperation of Musselman, the Big Horn coach.

The way Sapir saw it, it was the Big Horns' fault that Billy had hit Hagar. Billy's one demand when he agreed to come was that there be no press interviews. The Big Horns were negligent in that they allowed Hagar, a reporter, to interview Billy. Therefore, when Billy hit Hagar, it was the Big Horns' fault for allowing Hagar to put Billy in a position of hitting him. Quod erat demonstrandum.

The Big Horns agreed to pay Hagar $8,000 for his medical bills. That settled the civil problem. Sapir then wanted to know what Billy had to do to make Hagar drop the criminal charges.

Hagar told Sapir, "If he apologizes, no problem."

Sapir asked Hagar's lawyers, "What specifically does Ray want Billy to do?"

"Just say he's sorry."

Sapir knew this wasn't going to be easy. Hagar had shoved Howard Wong, who was a father figure to Billy. Wong was someone Billy respected, admired, loved.

Billy told Sapir, "I'm *not* gonna tell that guy I'm sorry."

But Ed Sapir, a master politician, knew how to handle Billy. He told him, "Don't worry about it, Skip. I will handle that, too."

Sapir worked out the details with the Big Horns and Hagar's lawyers, and he and Billy returned to Reno. After an exchange of releases and press statements, Sapir went to the podium to explain the settlement.

He said, "Ladies and gentlemen, the releases we've exchanged will allow you all to understand what we did a lot better. The most important thing is I talked to both of these guys—I talked to Ray, and I talked to Billy—and they are both sorry that the incident occurred." And quoting from *Love Story*, he concluded, "Remember, love is never having to say you're sorry." And Eddie Sapir got off the stage.

Brilliantly he had snatched victory from certain defeat for Billy.

Sapir asked Billy, "Where do you want to make your call to George and have your press conference announcing you are the manager next year?"

Billy said, "I want to visit my dear friend Dan Chandler at Caesar's Palace. I'm gonna get out of Reno."

Sapir called Chandler, who is the son of former baseball commissioner Happy Chandler, and he told Chandler that Billy wanted to come down to his hotel to make the formal announcement that he was going to be manager. Chandler was delighted. In Las Vegas, Billy called George.

Said Steinbrenner, "You're my manager."

Dan Chandler set up a press conference in a large room in Caesar's Palace. Billy announced he was coming back. Again.

## 35

# " EVERY WHORE HAS HIS PRICE "

**B**illy was cleared of assault charges on May 26, 1979. Two weeks later George Steinbrenner fired Bob Lemon as manager and brought Billy back.

Lemon had been a calming influence the year before, when he returned Reggie to right and Thurman Munson to behind the plate. With Catfish Hunter returning to form, the Yankees caught the snakebit Boston Red Sox and won the pennant on Bucky Dent's home run in the divisional playoff game.

But in 1979 the Yankees were flat from the start of spring training. Bob Lemon's son had been killed in a car accident, and suddenly baseball didn't seem all that important to him. When the Yankees lost their first six exhibition games, George ordered a curfew. He stationed a guard on every hotel floor the players were on and warned them of stiff fines.

Thurman Munson, who was on the second floor, thought Steinbrenner's punishment juvenile and unduly punitive—who cared whether the team lost exhibition games? He tied a sheet to the rail of his balcony, and he, Graig Nettles, and three promising phenoms, including pitchers Tim Lollar and Chris Welsh, headed for town. Unfortunately for them, George happened to be eating at a restaurant adjacent to the hotel and he watched them make their escape. (When George traded for outfielder Jerry Mumphrey after the next season, he included Lollar and Welsh, two solid young pitchers, as part of the deal.)

Sixty games into the 1979 season, the Yankees were in trouble because relief ace Goose Gossage had gotten into a silly fight with Cliff Johnson and hurt his pitching hand. George had already traded Sparky Lyle to Texas for telling the truth about him in the book he and I wrote together, *The Bronx Zoo*, and now the Yankees were without a closer.

Reggie had popped a muscle in his calf and missed a month. The Yankees were playing .500 ball.

On June 15 Steinbrenner met Billy at the Columbus, Ohio, home of an old friend, Dr. James Hull, the orthodontist who had introduced George to his wife, Joan. George and Billy sat in chairs by the pool.

"I'm going to make a change. I'm thinking of bringing Gene Michael in until next year."

Billy told him, "I think we can win it. I think I can do the job. I'd like to try it."

George said he would give Billy the job.

He waited for a suitable cover story that would enable him to make the switch with the least amount of criticism.

The play that George used as the excuse to fire Bob Lemon came the next night, June 16, when Mickey Rivers and Roy White let a fly ball fall between them to lose a game. George then witnessed the players joking and kidding around in the clubhouse and on the bus.

"I knew right then and there a change had to be made," George told reporters. George made no mention of the deal he had made with Billy the day before.

The manager George *really* wanted to replace Lemon was Sparky Anderson, who had been fired by the Cincinnati Reds after the 1978 season, but George had promised Al Rosen that Lemon could finish out 1979, and Anderson signed with the Detroit Tigers.

Al Rosen had seen that Steinbrenner was losing patience with Bob Lemon. To make sure Lemon would be well paid for becoming the fall guy, Rosen insisted that Lemon be given a contract as general manager through 1982.

When Steinbrenner told Rosen what he was about to do, Rosen told his friend Lemon, "It's time to pack your bag, Meat."

Rosen was devastated. "Maybe baseball people shouldn't hire their friends," he said.

On June 17, George went with the Yankee team on a road trip to Kansas City, Minnesota, and Texas. On a Friday night George invited Reggie to sit with him during the game. Reggie was on the disabled list.

As Reggie tells it in his autobiography, George, a chronic second-guesser, criticized the players throughout the game, saying they were making too many mental mistakes.

After one play that was followed by a diatribe of criticism and swear words, Reggie said, "George, the guy made a mistake. No big deal. Happens. It's early yet. We'll be all right."

"No, damn it," he replied. "There's something very wrong with this team. There has been from the beginning of the season."

Reggie counseled patience, to wait for Goose's return.

Though he had already made up his mind to do so, George then asked Reggie, "Do you think I should fire Lemon?"

Reggie tried to talk him out of it. "You can't do that. Give him a little more time. We've only played sixty games. Don't panic."

According to Reggie, George never mentioned Billy.

After midnight, reporters called Reggie to tell him Billy had been hired back as Lemon's replacement.

Reggie called Bob Lemon and had a long chat with him. Lem said that George's announcement was that he was being kicked upstairs but that George really was sending him home.

"Every whore has his price, Meat," Lemon said quietly. "I guess I found mine. They're going to keep paying me, so I just take it like a man and keep my mouth shut."

Reggie told Lemon he deserved better.

Reggie went back to his room and called George. It was three in the morning. Reggie didn't care if the call woke the man up. Steinbrenner picked up the receiver.

"Why the hell didn't you tell me?" Reggie said.

"What do you mean?" George asked.

"You know damn well what I mean, George. You sit with me the whole game, you ask me about Lem, and the whole fuckin' time you've got your mind made up to bring Billy back. . . . You had to know what this news would do to me, and you couldn't even give me the courtesy to tell me yourself?"

"I don't need any advice from you on how I run my ball club," George replied.

"Well, let me tell you something," Reggie said. "You better make another move right now. You better trade me because if you don't, I plan to be hurt all year long. 'Cause I've played for that man for the last time."

George told his star hitter, "When I want your advice about how to run my baseball team, I'll ask for it." And he hung up the phone.

Reggie wanted to go home to California, but his advisers convinced him not to.

When George rehired Billy, Al Rosen also took it personally. Billy's return made Rosen's life much harder. Billy knew Rosen didn't like him, and he was suspicious of him. Billy ignored Rosen, the Yankee president, as though he didn't exist. He skipped meetings with him. He didn't return his calls. Instead he dealt with Cedric Tallis.

When Rosen complained to Steinbrenner about Billy, Steinbrenner told him to talk to Tallis and let Tallis talk to Billy.

Rosen suffered inside through the first half of 1979, but he felt he needed the job and kept quiet. Once he told friends he would "pop" Steinbrenner for the way he treated him, but he never did. With the new George-Billy détente, Rosen, like Reggie, felt like the odd man out.

In one incident ABC Television asked Rosen to change the starting date of a game against the California Angels from seven-thirty to five P.M. in order to accommodate the network. Rosen called Billy on the phone a half dozen times to ask his permission to make the change. Billy never returned his calls. Forced to decide himself, Rosen agreed to the change.

The fireballing Nolan Ryan pitched for California and was aided by the lengthening shadows between the pitcher's mound and home plate that were there as a result of the time change.

Billy called Steinbrenner directly to complain about the time change. Steinbrenner called Commissioner Bowie Kuhn to complain about the time change. Kuhn patiently explained that Al Rosen had given his permission for ABC to make the change in order to hit prime time in New York.

Steinbrenner hung up and called Rosen.

"How can you make me look like a damn fool?" he asked.

Rosen explained that Steinbrenner had been busy, that he had tried to call Billy, but Billy hadn't returned his phone calls.

"I made the decision, and it was the right one," Rosen said.

Steinbrenner, who took Rosen's declaration of self-respect as an assault upon him, began berating Rosen.

Rosen hung up. He could stand it no longer. He called friends in Atlantic City, who offered him a job back in the casino industry.

Eighteen months after he quit, Al Rosen needed open-heart surgery.

With Al Rosen out of the picture, Billy was back in control, but the team had too many injuries—Ron Guidry, Goose Gossage, Reggie, Thurman Munson, and Mickey Rivers were all hurt or hurting—and there was too much resentment toward Steinbrenner for Billy to be able to do anything to improve the team's fortunes.

There was also something missing: Billy's aggressive attitude. This time Billy seemed different, a sullen, defeated man.

When George announced Billy's return, he told reporters, "I think Billy knows the conditions. I think he understands the terms. I'm the leader here. I have to make the final decisions. My feeling is he has matured; he finally understands the meaning of responsibility. Billy has changed."

When the reporters asked Billy to comment on what George said, he replied, "The only difference is that now I have a mustache."

But in his power struggle with Billy Martin, George was right about Billy. He *had* changed. His firing had made him see the light. Billy finally understood that if he didn't do what Steinbrenner wanted him to do, no matter how harmful to the team, he would be fired.

Steinbrenner had hired Billy Martin to be his manager, but inside that uniform the Billy Martin he had hired was missing. Instead there was a clone of Billy Martin, like the women in the movie *The Stepford Wives*. Replacing him was George's idea of what Billy Martin should be. The only problem was that George's Billy Martin didn't have the special fighting quality that had made him special, that won him ball games.

Billy did everything George wanted. George wanted him to coach third base the first game back, and he did. Initially George asked Billy to get along with

Reggie, and he did, leaving Reggie alone except to write his name fourth in the lineup every day and play him in right field.

Reggie had resented Billy for the way he had treated him, both when he played against him and for him, but at the same time he recognized Billy's qualities that enabled him to fashion winning teams. Billy and he had feuded for so long, it was almost as though something were missing from Reggie's usual surroundings now that Billy was leaving him alone.

According to Reggie in his book, Billy seemed defeated by George.

Said Reggie in his book, "He was going to let George pull his strings anytime George wanted to, because that's how much Billy wanted to be manager of the Yankees. George played the tune. Billy danced. It will always be that way. In that way, Lem was so right. 'Every whore has his price.' Billy knows that best of all."

Even when Steinbrenner traded away Billy's favorite, Mickey Rivers, Billy said nothing. The multitalented but moody Rivers had lost a lot of money from betting on the horses, and George didn't want to advance him any more money, so he traded him. Perversely George put the reason for the trade on Billy's shoulders.

"We are doing this to help Billy control the club better," said Cedric Tallis.

Billy continued to take George's calls in the dugout without complaint. Billy would say, "That stupid son of a bitch, he still hasn't learned the game," but he always was compliant.

Said Ed Linn in *Steinbrenner's Yankees*, "He took the calls upstairs, downstairs, and in the manager's office. In order to remain the manager of the Yankees, he took more than anyone would have dreamed possible."

Explained Linn, "The first time you allow someone to take your dignity away, it becomes necessary to reshuffle your values. When you keep taking abuse, you have to find excuses for him or yourself."

To excuse George, Billy adopted George's favorite rationalization, and at the time it had validity: George was a winner. He had brought the Yankees back to their former glory.

When Al Rosen quit on July 19, about a month after Billy came back, the writers came to Reggie to ask him about it. Reggie said that Al had wanted to be treated decently, that he was embarrassed about what had happened to his close friend Bob Lemon.

"What George has done to him is terrible," said Reggie. "George just thinks he can buy everybody. Some guys have pride. You can't buy them."

A reporter asked Reggie what would happen when George read his quotes.

Said Reggie, "Nothing can happen to me, because I can hit the ball over the wall. When I can't hit the ball over the wall, they'll get me, too. I know that. He'll get me someday."

When Reggie's comments were printed in the newspapers, George sent Billy to tell Reggie to "cool it."

Reggie told Billy he could not do that any longer.

In 1977 and 1978 George had sided with Reggie in a power play to force

Billy Martin to knuckle under and cry uncle. In 1979 Reggie became George Steinbrenner's target, and so George switched allegiances over to Billy. To George, people were there to serve him, and after their purpose was served, they were discarded. To George Steinbrenner, people were pawns on his chessboard. In 1979 he tried to use Billy as a pawn in his attempt to do all he could to savage Reggie Jackson in the press.

And when George switched his allegiance to Billy against Reggie, something funny happened. Billy stopped hating Reggie, who by 1979 had proved his worth and had won back the grudging respect of Billy and teammates, including Thurman Munson, who no longer hated him and even liked him. No one ever really understood the Reggie Jackson personality, but they saw that underneath the bluster, he wasn't a bad man, and he was a hell of a clutch hitter. As Reggie became tighter with his team, the distance between him and the owner grew.

When Billy returned in 1979, Steinbrenner used the defeated Billy Martin and an undiscerning, divisive press as powerful weapons in his pissing match with Reggie. When Reggie spoke out against the way George had treated Lemon and Rosen, George in a veiled threat told Billy, "If you can't control your ballplayers, I'll find someone who will."

Then he forced Billy to do and say things against Reggie that hurt Billy badly in the eyes of his teammates and, surely, in his own.

Right after Reggie made his comments about Al Rosen, George ordered Billy to attack Reggie for not wanting to play for him, even though Reggie had been playing hard.

Billy complied, just because George had told him to.

"If he doesn't want to come back, I don't think any player should be big enough to dictate who the manager should be," said Billy.

When reporters called Steinbrenner to comment on Billy's remarks, he added, "You can't ask a manager to crawl on his knees."

It was a perfect setup from Steinbrenner's diabolical perspective in that it not only made his target, Reggie, look bad, but it also made Billy look like a weak puppet to his players.

Back in 1973 George had bragged to his Williams classmates that he was going to rebuild the Yankees by bringing Jackson and Martin to work for him. He had done that. And here he was getting his revenge on all those athletes who had ever laughed at him. He, the now-famous George Steinbrenner, owned Jackson and Martin, and he was in control. His father, Henry, would have been very proud.

In his war against Reggie, George made up stories as a basis for criticizing Reggie and even had Billy repeat a couple—even though Billy knew George had invented them.

George concocted the story that Reggie, the player representative, had filed a grievance against the team for being forced to play an exhibition game in Columbus, and George ordered Billy to charge in the papers that Reggie had done that. Billy complied.

It turned out that George had made the whole thing up, that Reggie hadn't filed a grievance at all.

George wanted Billy to tell reporters that Reggie "wasn't a true Yankee." By this time Billy enjoyed having Reggie's bat in his lineup, and he didn't want Reggie to leave, so he refused.

The next volley was a story by writer Dick Young, who had a reputation for siding with team owners, including Walter O'Malley of the Dodgers, M. Donald Grant of the Mets, and Steinbrenner. Young wrote that Reggie was late paying back a $250,000 loan from Steinbrenner. He added that Reggie was rumored to be broke. Young quoted "a source close to Steinbrenner." (Usually, the "source close to Steinbrenner" turned out to be George himself.)

George knew that few reporters could pass up a "scoop" regardless of whether that scoop was true. George also knew that because of his deadline Young would print the story without taking the time to check with Reggie whether it was indeed true. George also knew that no reporter would call him on it after it became obvious that the story was not entirely accurate. No one did.

The story wasn't true on either count. Later it came out that after Reggie's incredible performance in the 1977 Series, George had changed the repayment schedule to benefit Reggie. As per the new agreement, Reggie's payments were current. But the new agreement had not been signed. As Reggie conceded in his own book, he was technically late under the original payment schedule.

Reggie was far from broke. He was a very wealthy young man.

George again ordered Billy to attack Reggie. Billy had no heart for it, so he said, "No player on this team gets special treatment. I'm getting tired of hearing people talk about the owner    "

Later George had other requests for Billy to harp about Reggie. These times Billy took the orders but never said anything.

Billy had agreed that to get the job back, he would do George's bidding, but what Billy didn't understand was that once he compromised his integrity, George would force him to keep doing it over and over and over and over until Billy no longer could live with himself.

Before the end of the year Billy's hatred for George was so great that he decided he just didn't want to be his puppet anymore. When Steinbrenner told Billy he was going to fire Art Fowler because the pitchers were hurt, Billy again stood up to him. It had taken a while, but Billy's conscience no longer could rationalize being involved in such dirty business.

Steinbrenner's campaign against Reggie ended when Reggie's agent, Matt Merola, called Steinbrenner's closest friend, limousine magnate Bill Fugazy, and told him to tell George that if George didn't cut it out, Reggie would start talking to the press about what he had heard George and his friends were doing late at night.

The stories about Reggie stopped.

\*    \*    \*

The chance for the Yankees to make a pennant run ended for Billy and the Yankees on August 2 when Thurman Munson was killed in the crash of his private plane. Munson, whom his teammates called Squatty Body, was one of those great athletes whom all his teammates admired and respected, even though he had an irascible, crabby personality.

Munson enjoyed spitting tobacco on the shoes of reporters, as well as fans trying to get autographs. He relished being difficult. But unlike Reggie, Thurman was warm and supportive of his teammates, who admired, even loved him, for his skill, leadership, and plain old toughness.

They loved to tease him. One time he ordered a gun belt by mail order, and his teammates would keep intercepting the order form and changing the belt size so when it came it would be either much too small or much too large. He never did figure out why the thing never fit him. They enjoyed tacking up photos of fat people in his locker. They enjoyed him.

When he died, a little bit of them died, too.

Munson had taken up flying in 1977 so he could spend more time with his wife, who refused to live in the New York metropolitan area. He began flying home to Canton, Ohio, after night games, sleeping in his own bed, flying back to New York for the next game.

It was a schedule that frazzled his nerves. He grew more and more sarcastic with fans and the press. He was grumpy all the time.

By the summer of 1979, his knees were paining him. Billy played him at first base on August 1. After the game Thurman flew home in his Cessna Citation twin-engine jet, which he had purchased six weeks earlier. It had cost him a million and a half dollars. He arrived home to Canton at three in the morning.

The next day he and two friends, both pilots, took the plane out. Munson took off, circled, and when he approached for a landing, he came in too slowly, and the plane dropped too quickly, about a thousand feet short of the runway. Munson tried to throttle up, but it was too late. The plane hit some trees, crossed a road, and crashed to the ground, catching on fire.

The two passengers were able to escape, but Munson never made a move to get out. He was motionless in his seat. Fighting the smoke from the fire, his friends tried to get to him, but he was strapped in, and after thirty seconds of trying to unhook him, the fuel caught on fire, and there was a conflagration. The friends ran for their lives.

Munson had been conscious for three or four minutes before he died. He had been yelling, "Get me out of here. Please get me out," when the flames engulfed the plane.

Steinbrenner was the one who informed Billy, who was out fishing with his son, Billy Joe.

When Billy heard the news, he began to sob—loud, gasping sobs.

"Call me later," George told him.

The Yankees finished fourth in 1979, thirteen and a half games behind the Baltimore Orioles. The Yankees finished the season with an eight-game winning streak.

Said Billy, "We're going to have a hell of a team next year. We'll win it. Nobody can intimidate the Yankees."

The irony of what happened to Billy Martin is that the man who talked about how he so desperately wanted Billy to stop drinking was also the man who caused him to drink harder than he ever drank in his life.

As part of his agreement to come back and manage the Yankees, Billy made George a promise he could not keep. Both he and George knew that bars were where fights started.

"We just can't have him getting into these things every two months," Steinbrenner said. "It's not good for the Yankee organization."

Though Billy was an alcoholic whose problem was severe, Billy made George a promise he was incapable of keeping: He would avoid bars.

Billy's whole life away from the ballpark revolved around bar life, and he was as addicted to the comforting solace of the bar atmosphere as he was to the booze he drank there.

As an alternative, Billy promised George that if he was confronted in a bar, he would turn the other cheek.

A few weeks after the end of the 1979 season, Billy and his close friend Howard Wong returned to Minneapolis from a hunting trip. Billy had a ticket to fly to Dallas to visit Mickey Mantle, but the trip had taken longer than expected, and Billy missed his plane.

Billy and Howard Wong returned to Wong's restaurant, where they phoned hotels around the Minneapolis suburb of Bloomington, but they couldn't find a room. Hundreds of beauticians had come to town for a convention. All the rooms were booked.

Howard finally found Billy a room at the Hotel de France, the best hotel in the area.

After Billy checked in, Wong told him he would drive him to the airport in the morning. Billy suggested they have a drink or two first.

"Just a couple," said Howard.

They sat in the bar and discussed the fun they had had on the hunting trip. Billy's two scotches became six.

Two men sitting next to Billy and Howard recognized Billy and started talking to him about the Yankees. Howard wanted to leave. Before he could get away, one of the men said the worst possible thing he could have said to a sodden Billy Martin.

"I think Dick Williams did a good job this year. He deserved to be Manager of the Year in the National League. And Earl Weaver deserved it in the American League."

The only thing worse the man could have said to Billy would have been something about his mother.

Billy still disliked Dick Williams for sitting with Steinbrenner in George's box during the 1976 season and making Billy look bad. He had no love for Earl Weaver, either.

"Dick Williams is an asshole," Billy replied. "They're both assholes, and so are you for saying it."

When Billy was drinking, once he became angry, that anger didn't leave him until he could do something physical to relieve his fury. He signed a couple of autographs, and then he asked the man, whose name was Joseph Cooper, what he did for a living.

"I'm a salesman."

"What do you sell?"

"Marshmallows."

Billy chuckled.

"Everybody thinks it's funny, but I make a good living at it."

"You're still an asshole."

Billy pulled out a wad of bills. He laid three hundred-dollar bills on the bar. Billy said, "Here's three hundred dollars to your penny I can knock you on your ass and you won't get up."

Cooper looked at the scrawny Billy and pulled out his penny.

"Let's go."

Howard remained at the bar. Billy told Cooper to meet him in the parking lot. Billy left the bar first, with Cooper on his heels. As the two entered the hotel lobby, Billy resorted to familiar tactics: the sucker punch.

Without warning he turned on Cooper, slugged him in the mouth, and KO'd him. Cooper later had to have twenty stitches to close a split lip.

With Cooper out on the floor, Billy returned to the bar, picked up the three hundred-dollar bills, threw down a five-dollar bill, and said to Howard Wong, "Let's get out of here."

Howard left. Billy went to his room.

When the news hit the Minneapolis newspapers, Billy's first statement was that Cooper had fallen and cut his lip.

Billy called Gene Michael.

"How's George taking it?"

"He's pissed."

"Will he get over it?"

"I don't think so."

By the time Billy called George to tell him the truth—that he had slugged the guy—George had told Eddie Sapir that Billy was fired for lying about the incident.

On October 28, Mickey Morabito read Steinbrenner's statement: "Billy Martin has been relieved of his duties as manager of the New York Yankees and Dick Howser has been named to succeed him effective immediately."

George told Sapir, "He's finished."

In the papers Steinbrenner made a big show of how he was firing Billy to save Billy from himself.

"What happens if a guy pulls a knife and kills Billy?" asked a source "very close to George Steinbrenner." The source was probably so close he could touch himself.

This source said that George felt Billy was "worth saving."

Judge Sapir, when he heard the comments, called George a liar. Sapir knew that Steinbrenner didn't fire Billy because he had hit Cooper, but rather because Billy hadn't debased himself *enough* to suit George's vindictive nature, hadn't attacked Reggie in the newspapers as much as Steinbrenner had wanted him to.

"Minnesota was not the cause of Billy being fired," Sapir said. "George was looking for an opportunity to fire Billy.

"I believe Billy was fired because George found out Billy wouldn't lie for him, because he found out he couldn't control Billy, and because Billy wouldn't be a rubber stamp."

Sapir cited Steinbrenner's request to discredit Reggie Jackson and Billy's refusal to buckle under when George wanted to fire Fowler.

Said Sapir, "Billy refused because that player [Jackson] played his heart out for him and the team. He played hurt and he did everything Billy asked. He and Billy got along fine, and Billy was not going to lie about him." Not anymore, anyway.

When Steinbrenner read what Sapir had said, Steinbrenner blustered that Sapir had "endangered the chances of the Yankees doing anything [for Billy]." Meaning paying Billy on his contract.

It was the first comment in a campaign to avoid having to pay the last two years of Billy's contract.

George's war had turned against Billy, and in this fight Steinbrenner enlisted Commissioner Bowie Kuhn as an ally. Kuhn went on TV and said that he was considering a fine, suspension, or banning Billy from baseball.

Speaking to Howard Cosell on "Monday Night Football," Kuhn used a line previously uttered by George Steinbrenner. Kuhn said, "It has come to my attention that Billy has financial problems and that he has problems when he drinks. We're going to check on this."

On November 9, Ed Sapir and Doug Newton went to meet with Commissioner Kuhn, who failed to show. Representing him was his enforcer, Sandy Haddad, who told them they were investigating "Billy's pattern of behavior," which was another one of Steinbrenner's favorite lines about Billy.

On December 11, Billy spoke at the University of Rhode Island. He told the gathering, "I feel sorry for him. I think the man is sick. I'll be honest with you. I'll only go back if George is gone. I won't even play in the Old-Timers' game. I'll never put on the Yankee uniform as long as he is there."

# BILLYBALL

George continued his vendetta against Billy after he fired him, when he told Billy's advisers he would not pay Billy the $125,000 a year he owed him for the next two years.

George asked Ed Sapir, "Would Billy be interested in a four-year scholarship for his son? Would Billy be interested in an annuity-type insurance plan for his retirement?"

Billy saw that George wanted him to be beholden. Billy wouldn't give George the satisfaction of being able to say he was "taking care" of Billy Martin.

Billy told Sapir, "I want my money with no strings attached. I don't want him to be in a position to tell people he's supporting me. I can take care of myself."

Judge Sapir declined George's offers.

George then suggested Billy come back as color commentator at full salary.

Billy turned the offer down. It didn't make sense. Steinbrenner had just accused him of being a menace to society, and here he was taking him back as a TV commentator?

Billy had his own suggestion.

"Why doesn't George make me his personal adviser?"

This made even less sense. Why work for the guy at all?

Before Ed Sapir could make this suggestion to Steinbrenner, Charlie Finley called to see if Billy would be interested in managing the Oakland A's. Billy was gun-shy. Finley, like Steinbrenner, called his managers up in the middle of the game to make suggestions. Why was it that only the crazies called for Billy? And Finley wanted Steinbrenner to pay most of Billy's salary. Steinbrenner didn't want to pay a nickel of Billy's salary while he was managing the A's.

Eddie Sapir negotiated with Steinbrenner, and Doug Newton negotiated with Finley, and between the two they were able to cut a deal whereby Steinbrenner paid Billy $150,000 as a settlement and Finley paid him $125,000 a year for two years.

Bob Short was the one who convinced Finley. His final argument: "You want to fix George? Pay Billy, and make George pay the hundred and fifty thousand."

Billy became manager of the A's on February 21, 1980. Left to his own devices, Billy Martin took the worst team in baseball to the American League Championship Series and the cover of *Time* magazine.

Back in New York, George Steinbrenner, left to his own devices, sank the Yankees into chaos. The team and the players became of secondary focus while George Steinbrenner day after day became the big story on the New York Yankees. No longer did the fans read about what the players were doing. The man in the headlines most often was George. After two more years of pennant contention, George, in 1982, ran the once-proud Yankees into the ground and turned off a generation of adoring Yankee fans.

While managing the A's, Billy installed his characteristic principles: an aggressive offensive, solid defense, a pitching staff that threw strikes, and a bench that played their defined roles. The press called his style "Billyball."

"The biggest strength Billy had, beside the motivational part of it," said Oakland A's starting pitcher Matt Keough, "was that he knew exactly what his pitching staff needed, and he'd do everything he could to make sure it got it.

"I can remember one spring, Billy brought what must have been a hundred pitchers to spring training, every minor league kid in the organization, for one thing in mind: He was trying to find a short-relief pitcher. We didn't have one.

"He watched each kid throw for about a week, and he found Dave Beard. Once he selected Beard, he said to Art Fowler, his pitching coach, 'Okay, Art, that's the guy. Everyone else can go back to the minors.'

"Billy brought Dave Beard up, and he was a guy who threw as hard as anybody. Billy gave him that short relief role, and in that 1981 playoff against Kansas City, Dave was completely dominating. He was on the verge of becoming a superstar when he hurt his arm.

"Billy could go find talent just like that.

"When Billy took over a team, Billy taught it how to win. He had done it wherever he went. He knew how to do it.

"If you couldn't play defense, you were gonna have a problem with Billy. A pitcher has a very fragile ego. He's out there, and his perception of what's going on most of the time is, 'It's me against the world.' For a pitcher, if your ball club plays poorly behind you on defense, it has a real negative effect on not just that game but the games down the road.

"As a result, Billy would not tolerate guys in the field who could not catch the ball. He knew opposing hitters, and so he ran very different alignments defensively from most managers. He would always talk to the pitcher, center fielder, and middle infielders about how the pitcher was going to pitch to each batter. And he was real big on defense, because if the pitcher makes fewer pitches and he feels confident the fielders are going to catch the ball, he'll be more aggressive, he'll be ahead in the count more, and a lot of positive things will happen.

"There were guys at Oakland who Billy decided could not play for him because they came up short on defense. Second base was a problem for Billy. That was Billy's position when he was a player. Billy knew it best, and if you couldn't turn a double play or if you had trouble on defense, you were going to have hell to pay.

"We had two players in particular who had a hard time with the defensive end of the game—Mike Edwards and Shooty Babitt—both good guys who loved to play, but they had trouble with double plays and ground balls.

"A lot of their problem was because they were nervous. We were in Toronto, and Mike blew a double play. Now, the dugouts in Toronto at that time were right on the field. The inning ended, and Mike was so flustered, he ran into the Toronto dugout. He didn't even know which dugout to go to. And I knew Billy was thinking, The way he's playing defense, that's where the son of a bitch should go.

"That got fixed when we got Davey Lopes and Fred Stanley to play the middle of the infield. They were two veterans, and Billy didn't push the veterans like he did the kids, didn't put that kind of pressure on them. He let them play and pretty much stayed away from them.

"And so Billy had very confident pitchers, because they knew the people behind them were going to catch the ball or else they weren't going to play.

"That fit in with his style, which was not to walk batters. That was Art's big thing, too. You threw the ball over the plate. You pitched ahead.

"Brian Kingman was a pitcher who was very frustrating to Billy because Billy could see he was probably the most talented of the five of us as far as stuff went. Brian was a very intellectual guy. If Brian and Billy had a problem, it was because Brian would not talk to Billy about things that bothered him or about personal things. Brian was introverted, and the misconceptions they had about each other festered.

"Billy would see Brian go out there with that great stuff and get pounded, and he could never figure out why. He knew it had to be some kind of concentration problem or a lack of competitive instinct, and Billy and Brian fought about it back and forth. It frustrated Billy that he couldn't make Brian a winner, made Billy mad at himself for not making Brian the star he thought he should be.

"Billy never did cure it. Brian was not successful on the big-league level.

"The major problem Billy had at Oakland was if we had an injury, there was no talent pool, no one to bring up to fill the gap, and that was very frustrating to him. Once we had injuries, it wasn't the same, and so we were frustrated, and Billy was frustrated, and that led to problems with management.

"Billy's detractors, especially the writers who didn't like him, all talked about how Billy ruined the Oakland pitching staff by pitching them so much, and it's just a bunch of horseshit. The press was so fast to say that about Billy.

"Billy was a high-profile guy. At Oakland we had five pitchers going on five days' rest. We'd pitch very low-pitch games. The five all had nonrelated injuries. To say Billy had anything to do with it was just ludicrous.

"In 1980 Billy had taken a team that lost 108 games, and the next year we won 83 games, and the next year we won the division. The place was rocking and reeling in '80 and '81.

"Billy had it made about that time, and he was having fun. I'll never forget, he used to get the guys up in the bullpen. We'd be saying to ourselves, 'What is he doing getting a left-hander up in the bullpen? He's not going to take Mike Norris out.'

"I'd ask him, 'What are you doing, Billy?'

"He'd say, 'Watch him,' talking about the other manager. 'He'll sit that pinch hitter back down.' And he would. The left-hander would throw for two minutes, you'd see the batter come on deck and see him walk back to the dugout.

"I remember one day we were playing Toronto. Their manager was Roy Hartsfield. I was pitching. Billy came out and said to me, 'Watch me get Hartsfield thrown out of the game.'

"I was on the mound when Billy came out and started talking to the umpire. Before that Hartsfield had been on the umpire for balls and strikes. I wondered, What is Billy doing?

"He started talking to the umpire about something, not even about baseball, just screwing around, and pretty soon Hartsfield came out and wanted to know what was holding up the game. And then Hartsfield said, 'You missed the last pitch. It was low.' That's an automatic ejection. The umpire threw Hartsfield right out of the game.

"I couldn't believe that Hartsfield fell for it. Billy was laughing. Billy was a piece of work.

"Billy had Art Fowler serve as his liaison to the pitching staff. Art was a buffer who could ease the tension with a line like 'You guys read the *Wall Street Journal* and try to make all these fancy investments. I've got all my money invested in houses and lots: whorehouses and lots of beer.'

"One time we bought a dildo and put it in the hotel key box for Art. I told him, 'Art, we got what you wanted.' He said, 'Oh no, if my wife finds this, she'll leave me for it.' He was a very funny man. Did you know that Art had more twenty-game winners who had never won twenty games before than any other pitching coach in the history of the game?

"When Billy went out to the mound, he never allowed a whole lot of conversation. He went out there with very specific ideas, which from a pitcher's point of view was good, because then there was no doubt in your mind. Whenever he sent Art to the mound, it was the same thing. It wasn't a give-and-take discussion. Billy basically went out there with specific instructions, and they were always, 'Don't throw this guy anything to hit' or 'Go ahead and pitch this guy this way, and if he gets a hit, it's on me.'

"Billy had a reputation for being a second-guesser, but if he told you before the game to stay away from a certain pattern, and you went against him, that wasn't second-guessing, it was first-guessing, and if that happened, he'd be really rough on you. The manager who really gets on your nerves is the guy who tells you first, and if you screw up he reminds you about it afterwards. 'Cause you know you were wrong, and then he goes and eats you out about it, and you're *really* frustrated.

"Billy was more apt not to first- or second-guess if I was pitching or Mike Norris or Rick Langford, and later on, Steve McCatty. Because we had proven ourselves to him over the year and a half that we had our own style of pitching and that we could be effective with it.

"There was a short period when Billy would not let Brian Kingman or McCatty throw anything but fastballs after a two-ball count. Which was very frustrating to them. But I think in the end they realized that it was good for them, because it was an incentive not to get to a two-ball count, so they would be more aggressive about getting ahead of the hitters.

"I got to watch Billy in Oakland, and then I was traded over to New York, where he had a strong bullpen of Ron Davis and Goose Gossage, and it was real easy to see why Billy was always so successful, because he could adapt to whatever talent he had. If he had power, he played the power game. If he had speed, he played the speed game. The one thing that usually ran true with all his ball clubs was he was very strict about having good defensive players and having the players in the right alignment.

"He used to frustrate Rod Carew to death because of the way he would set the defense against him. We would pitch to him real soft and play him on the left-field foul line. Billy would have the second baseman almost straight up the middle and have the shortstop over in the hole behind third base. The first baseman and the third baseman would completely take the bunt away from him. The right fielder was over in right center and the center fielder was over in left center, and Rickey Henderson looked like he was standing on the left-field foul line.

"Well, there was just no place for Rod to hit the ball.

"You couldn't have done that to a bad hitter. It had to be a guy with great bat speed.

"In 1980 George Brett would have hit .407 if he hadn't played against our team. Billy basically pitched him like we were playing in Little League. We pitched him real soft, breaking balls, and just showed him fastballs, almost to the point where we threw so softly, it was almost humiliating, and that year he hit .240 against us.

"I can remember a game in September. Kansas City had just clinched the division the day before. Tony Armas, our right fielder, was having a great game. He had seven RBIs, a couple of home runs, and we were winning 7–0. I was the pitcher that day.

"In the top of the ninth we had runners on second and third and two outs, and Armas was up, and Jim Frey, the Kansas City manager, ordered Armas walked intentionally when Tony had a chance at the total-base record for the ball club, and Billy just went crazy.

"Billy always wanted his players to set individual goals because he thought that was very important to being successful. To him it was a gutless play on Frey's part. He snapped in the dugout. He was so stinking mad he couldn't see straight.

"It was the bottom of the ninth. George Brett was the second batter. Before we went back out to the field, Billy called our catcher, Jim Essian, and me over. He said, 'Okay, here's what we're gonna do. Brett's hitting second.' He said to me, 'You get that first son of a bitch out, and I mean it.'

"I said, 'I'm gonna try, Billy.'

"He said, 'No, get the first son of a bitch out. 'Cause this is what we're gonna do. Essian, you're gonna stand up like we're gonna walk George intentionally with one out and nobody on, when we're ahead 7–0, so George can't go over .400, and we'll see how Frey likes that.'

"See, Billy was trying to get Frey, not George. So I got the first batter out, and Brett stepped into the box. The place was packed. Everybody in Kansas City had come to see George hit .400. It was September 24. There was a week to go in the season.

"Essian stood up and held his hand out. Brett looked back, and looked back again. Bill Haller was the umpire.

"I went into the windup, Essian sat back down, and I threw George a slow, slow curve for a strike. I mean, the hot dogs were raining down, the fans were so pissed. And George was pissed.

"George was looking into the dugout at Billy, and Billy was looking over at Frey. Billy didn't even see George, he was so mad. He wanted Frey to pay attention.

"I threw the next pitch, and George hit a little ground ball to the second baseman, and he didn't even run out of the box. He ran straight back to the dugout. He was down to .398.

"You could hear George throwing bats and helmets. He took off up the ramp. You could see Billy go up the other ramp. They met in the middle, and they began arguing, yelling at each other, and I could hear the commotion from the mound. I was still trying to get the last out of the ball game.

"Apparently Billy managed to explain to George why I did what I did. Because the next day I spoke to George's brother, Ken, who was acting as George's caddy at the time, and I said, 'I really didn't want to do that. George will hunt me the rest of my life.'

"Ken said, 'Ah, don't worry about it. George was really pissed at first, but then he realized what Billy was doing.'

"And later on George might well have had a lot to do with Frey getting fired from Kansas City. So, obviously, George didn't forget. And George went on to hit .390. After that at bat, he never got to .400 again.

"It was the damndest thing. No other manager would have ever thought to do that.

"Billy was always one step ahead of everyone else. I remember one game in Oakland. It was early in the game, and Billy got thrown out arguing a call.

"The game was on TV in the clubhouse, and he went up and sat in the office. He called me on the phone in the dugout.

"He said, 'Listen up. I'm going to talk to you on the dugout phone. Then you relay the signs to Clete [Boyer], and I'll run the game from the clubhouse.'

"I said, 'Okay, fine.'

"I stood by the water cooler with the phone in my ear, talking to Billy and relaying his orders to Clete.

"Ken Kaiser, the home-plate umpire, walked over. He said, 'Matt, put the phone down and don't do that anymore.'

"I hung up.

"The phone rang right back. One of the other players picked it up.

"Billy said, 'What the hell happened? Who hung up the fucking phone?' Billy was pissed off.

"The player said, 'You can't put Matt back on the phone. Kaiser came over and warned him.'

"Billy said, 'Put him back on the phone. Fuck Kaiser.'

"I got back on the phone. I had my back to the infield, talking to Billy. All of a sudden I'm standing out on the infield grass, the phone in my hand, the cord dangling. Kaiser had come into the dugout and grabbed me with both hands and pulled me out of the dugout and the phone right out of the wall.

"That was the end of that.

"If you didn't cause trouble and worked your ass off, Billy would usually do something for you that you didn't read about in the papers or hear on the news. You'll never know all the things he did, because he wouldn't talk about them.

"I don't think I ever heard anybody ask Billy for anything where he told them no. Ever. If you went behind his back to do it, there'd be hell to pay. That was one thing he couldn't understand. For someone as generous as he was, to do that to him, he didn't think he could trust you then. And if he thought you were a malingerer, someone trying to bring the club down, or if you weren't happy in your role and you were bitching and moaning about it, Billy didn't like that either and before too long you were probably going to be gone.

"Under Billy we had gone from a terrible ball club to the next year, when we went all the way to the end against the Royals, only to lose out, and then the next year we won 80 games, beat the Royals in the playoffs only to lose to the Yankees. We were *that* close to being in the World Series.

"After '81 we all thought we were just one or two players away from being a dominant team. We had great starting pitchers, a great young outfielder, Rickey

Henderson, who could do everything offensively and defensively, we had a catcher, Mike Heath, with a great arm, a competitor who drove Billy crazy. They fought all the time, back and forth, but Mike was everything you'd want. He could catch, and he could throw.

"During Billy's last year with us he spent most of his time working on the thing we couldn't do because we lacked the talent: scoring runs. As a result we manufactured runs, squeezed, hit-and-ran, did the little things.

"The problem was, we had no depth. We had to remain healthy for us to win. All we had were those three outfielders and the five pitchers. When Billy went to the bullpen, it wasn't successful, so he stopped going to them, and then when some of us got hurt, there weren't any successful young pitchers on the horizon, and it was like we hit a wall, and there was nothing he or anybody could have done about it.

"To have been so close and then to have it all unravel so fast . . . it was very frustrating."

During the late spring of 1982, Steinbrenner's panic about the Yankee decline led him to an inescapable conclusion. He needed the one man who could right his ship, who could bring some semblance of order to this mess of a baseball team. Reggie was not re-signed and three managers, five pitching coaches, and dozens of players shuttled through the team's revolving door.

All during Billy's managership of the Oakland A's, Billy, Judge Sapir, and Steinbrenner had kept in touch. George knew that Billy had a wife in Oakland and a girlfriend in Los Angeles, with whom he fought like cats and dogs. He knew that Billy hadn't stopped drinking. He knew that Billy was just as volatile as ever.

But George was desperate. He *needed* Billy Martin.

Somewhere around June 1982, Steinbrenner told Billy, "If you can get out of your contract with the A's, I'd like to have you back managing the Yankees."

**37**

# BILLY IN LOVE

hen Billy signed with the Oakland A's in 1980, his live-in girl-friend was an eighteen-year-old knockout by the name of Heather Ervolino. They had met in 1978 when Billy was managing the Yankees. He was fifty. She was sixteen.

When Billy moved to Oakland in 1980, he moved Heather, her brother, her mother, and her grandmother with her into Billy's home in Danville, California. They went from a small apartment in the slums of the South Bronx to a home that was so large the bedroom had three ceiling fans.

In a way Billy's new family was a slap in the face of his old family. His sisters, Pat Irvine and Joan Holland, didn't learn of Heather's existence until they went to an A's game and saw her sitting in Billy's box. They were confused because they thought Billy was involved in a steady relationship with a woman named Patty Stark. They liked Patty Stark. Patty had been friendly and nice to them.

Heather, perhaps intimidated by their strong presence, didn't speak to them at the game. From the beginning Billy's sisters, who sat in judgment of Billy and often found his behavior disturbing, felt that Heather was too young for him and that he was too involved with her family.

"Heather was the only girl he ever went out with who he never brought over to the house," said Pat. "Maybe he figured we would get on his tail because she was so young. We felt she should be with her own age-group."

Said Pat, "They came from nothing. Billy pulled them out of the slums of New York.

"Her grandmother was always giving us dirty looks. One time I said, 'Look at the blister.' Then everyone started calling her 'the Blister.' We'd laugh.

"Why Billy never brought Heather over to our house I don't know. We didn't even know her. We'd always say to him, 'Why don't you bring her over?' He never answered."

Peggy Sapir, the wife of Judge Eddie Sapir, Billy's lawyer and financial adviser, liked Heather despite her age, because Heather didn't take advantage of Billy.

"If she had the money to pay the bills, the groceries, and the lights, she was happy," said Peggy Sapir. "She never even used his credit cards. She never took advantage of Billy."

Peggy Sapir remembered the initial satisfaction Billy took from having Heather's family with them.

"At one time Billy got great pleasure out of grandma and mom, Heather and her brother, Heath. [Billy's] family had been dysfunctional, and this allowed him to be the father figure—they had no father, and he really had this personal feeling for them, and he certainly loved her. He did. He loved the whole family. It gave Billy no greater pleasure than to put together this typical American home and family, to give them everything they never had, to take them out of the slums of New York and take them to California.

"Billy hated to be alone. He wanted that sense of family and of being loved. So this arrangement fulfilled a need, but on the other hand there was the side of Billy that couldn't help what he did—all the other women in his life."

Billy Martin took advantage of one perk that his fame gave him. There are women, young and old, who love to love famous sports personalities, if only for a night. One of Billy Martin's missions in life, it seemed, was to reciprocate.

In 1980 Billy's A's were playing the Chicago White Sox, and Bill and Carol Reedy, who lived in Detroit, drove to the Windy City to meet him. That weekend Billy had arranged trysts with three different young women, none of them Heather. One of the trysts was the younger sister of a friend of Heather. This girl lived in New York, but Billy had arranged for her to meet him in Chicago. Bill Reedy, the keeper of Billy's full appointment calendar, knew her story. Bill Reedy made these arrangements for Billy without making moral judgments. Reedy's attitude was, He's my friend. This is what he wants. It will be done.

Said Reedy, "To him, it was mischief. He was getting away with something, and that made it fun. The chase, that's what Billy lived for."

Carol Reedy was amused by Billy's behavior until Billy began putting the moves on *her* younger sister. Carol stopped that cold.

That weekend Billy had given each of his girlfriends money to go shopping while he spent time in his hotel room with one of the others. Shortly after the Reedys arrived in Chicago, Billy asked Bill Reedy if Carol would take one of the young girls shopping.

"Give her something to do," Billy said.

Carol Reedy, who usually was kept in the dark about the details of Billy's sex life, had no idea who the girl was. Carol and Heather were good friends. Had Carol been apprised of her background, she would have refused to play chaperone to Heather's friend's younger sister.

Off they went. The two women didn't talk much about Billy, except that the girl wanted to know how Carol knew Billy.

"Through my husband," Carol told her. Carol knew that this girl was wondering whether Carol and Billy were having an affair as well.

The agenda was for Carol and this girl to go shopping and then go to the ball game and meet Billy in the hotel bar after the game.

The girl told Carol that although Billy allowed her to sit on the barstools, he had forbidden her from sitting at his table or acting like she knew him.

The girl explained this to Carol and added, "If I come into the bar tonight, and I don't say hello, you have to understand that this is what I was told."

Carol and the girl went to the game. They were sitting in the visiting team manager's box near the dugout, and during a break in the action, a camera began to pan in their direction. The girl put her jacket over her head, perplexing Carol.

"Are you a fugitive?" Carol asked her.

"No," she said, "but Heather might see me."

Innocently Carol said, "Heather wouldn't know you from Adam."

"Yes, she would," said the girl. "My sister is her friend. Heather is going to see me and wonder."

Carol thought, Billy, you son of a bitch. She felt the same way about her husband, who knew she was fond of Heather.

The next day Carol was sitting in the hotel lobby with the girl. Bill Reedy told his wife, "Take her back and put her on the bus."

The girl began to cry. She said, "I'm never going to see him again."

Carol said, "Go ahead and cry. You're not."

One of the other two girls who Billy flew into Chicago that weekend was a twenty-four-year-old blonde by the name of Jill Guiver. Billy thought she was the sexiest woman he had ever known.

Billy first laid eyes on Jill Guiver in 1980 before a game against the California Angels. She had a camera on her shoulder. Though she didn't work for any organization, she was telling everyone she was a free-lance photographer. At one time she had dated one of the Yankee players, Reggie Jackson. According to ballplayers who knew her at the time, her photography was her way to get to meet them. The way she looked, an introduction was all she needed. She liked to wear tight-fitting clothes and short shorts. She was *very* sexy.

Jill asked Billy if she could take his picture. Billy asked her if he could take her for a drink after the game. They began dating, which threw a scare into at least four of Billy's players who were also seeing her. These players feared that she would reveal to Billy that they were also going with her and that Billy would take it out on them. They were praying that Billy's relationship with Jill Guiver would soon end, that she was only a phase, in part because they feared Billy's wrath and also because as long as Billy was with her, they couldn't be.

Once Billy met Jill, she became one of Billy's regulars. From the beginning, Bill and Carol Reedy couldn't understand what Billy saw in her, except that she was very sexy. Their relationship was a disturbing mix of jealousy, anger, and a lot of sex. Each made their need for the other obvious. Each wanted the other exclusively. Tension ruled the relationship.

From the start Jill knew just how to push the right buttons to turn a combustive Billy into a raging inferno.

In 1981 Billy had Bill Reedy fly Jill into Detroit for an A's game against the Tigers. Carol Reedy went to Tiger Stadium with Jill, the Reedys' son Billy, and Bob Brown, who was a Teamster friend of Billy's.

When the game began Jill was sitting next to young Billy, and Carol was sitting next to Bob Brown. Carol got up to get some coffee. When she returned, Bob Brown was sitting next to Jill.

Billy went out to the mound. He looked toward his box, and he saw Jill sitting next to Brown, who was his close friend. He began glaring, wondering what Brown and Jill were doing sitting next to each other. It was innocent, but Billy, his ego tied closely to the love of this girl, became irrational.

Carol quickly read the situation. She said to her son, "We're leaving. I'm not staying here for this."

They got up and went back to the bar the Reedys owned, the Hummer.

It was Billy's birthday, May 16, and after the game was over, he returned to the bar. Even though the Reedys were throwing him a birthday party, he was in a foul mood.

As soon as he arrived, Billy started to yell at Jill, and she yelled back. They were loudly calling each other "motherfuckers" and other colorful names, making Carol Reedy and some of the other guests very uncomfortable.

Billy didn't like to sit down and eat a big meal. Rather, he preferred to pick, so whenever he visited the Hummer, Carol Reedy would prepare a tray for him with tomatoes, cheese, and cut salami.

Carol had taken the tray to the basement, went back up for more food, and was coming down again with another tray when she ran into Billy and Jill having this argument.

Carol put the tray down and turned to walk away when Billy grabbed her tightly by the wrist and said, "No, you're not. You're going to stay here and find out what a motherfucking bitch she is and hear how she talks to me and how she deserves to be talked to." Every time Carol Reedy tried to pull away, Billy gripped her arm a little tighter. For fifteen minutes she was forced to watch as they stood and swore at each other.

Billy told Jill, "You are not Billy Martin. I am Billy Martin. When you lay your fucking head on your fucking pillow at night, that's my pillow. I'm number one. You're not number one. You're not anything like number one."

Carol Reedy thought to herself, This is the worst relationship between two people I've ever seen in my life.

Carol, who was convinced they hated each other, later asked Billy, "What do you get out of this?"

There never was an answer.

Later that year Bill Reedy visited Billy in New York. They stayed at the Regency Hotel, where Billy had lived when he managed the Yankees. Billy asked Reedy to take Jill to the ballpark. Reedy, who from the beginning didn't like her, said he really didn't want to.

Billy said, "Do it for me, will you please? Stop in the dining room if she wants to get something to eat and then bring her to the ballpark." Reedy relented.

"What time should I meet her?"

"Four o'clock."

At four Jill met Reedy in the dining room. Reedy ordered a hamburger and a bottle of beer. After perusing the menu, Jill ordered pressed duck. It was the most expensive item on the menu, Reedy noticed, and after it arrived, she ate very little of it. Reedy hid his disgust.

They hailed a cab to go to Yankee Stadium, and Reedy hid his eyes in embarrassment as Jill complained the whole way there, telling the cabbie which route to take until the driver said, "Lady, I've been driving a cab for thirty-five years. I'll get you to the goddamn ballpark."

Offended, Jill told him, "I'm going to report you. What's your number? I'm Billy Martin's girlfriend."

They got out of the cab. Reedy paid the driver and said, "I'm sorry."

At the ballpark Reedy and Jill sat down in Billy's private box close to the dugout on the third-base side. Jill instructed the usher that no one else be allowed to sit in the box without her permission. Before the start of the game one of Billy's bar-owning friends, Rudy Stephano, arrived with his girlfriend. They sat down next to Reedy and Jill.

Late in the game Reedy told Stephano he had to go to the bathroom. He never came back. Reedy sent a message down to Billy. It said, "I can't take this shit anymore."

Billy sent word back to Reedy where to meet him after the game. Billy stuck his head out of the dugout and told Stephano to take Jill back to the Regency Hotel after the game. Then he went to meet Reedy.

"What's the matter?" Billy wanted to know.

"She's crazy," Reedy told him. "She's flat-assed crazy. She ordered pressed duck for lunch. A hundred dollars. And she picked at it. She didn't want to eat it. It was the prestige. In her mind it was something she should have. And then she was on the cab driver all the way out, and she screamed at the usher. What the Christ is it with this broad, Billy? I can't take this shit. I left her with Rudy."

Billy tried to calm his friend. And he continued to see Jill, taking her with him when the A's were on the road.

A couple of times Carol Reedy was given the task of picking her up at the Pontchartrain Hotel in Detroit. Jill confided in Carol. One time she told her she wasn't going to the ballpark because she and Billy had had a terrible fight. Jill told her that Billy had hit her and that she was really scared. Carol was concerned when Jill told her, "I'm afraid he's going to beat me up bad."

Heather and her family were living in Northern California. Jill was kept secret from Heather. Billy had bought a condominium in the Balboa Beach Club in Del Mar, near where Jill had grown up, and installed Jill there. Periodically Billy would tell Heather he was going to New York, but he would fly south instead.

Vicki Figone, the daughter of Lewis Figone, a childhood friend of Billy's, remembers the time she came to the Oakland airport to pick Billy up. He was scheduled to fly in on Air Cal from Anaheim. She watched Billy walk over to the baggage clerk and hand him a twenty-dollar bill without saying a word. The baggage clerk then pulled off the Air Cal tags and replaced them with United Airline tags. It was all part of the subterfuge to keep his flights south secret from Heather.

Kelly Martin, Billy's daughter, flew down with her baby daughter, Evie, to Newport Beach to spend Christmas 1981 with her dad and Jill. After a couple days Billy got word that there was a problem up north, that he had to fly back to Heather.

Billy said, "Kelly, I have to go. Stay here and entertain her. I'll be back."

Billy left. Jill said to Kelly, "I'd like to take you and Evie to Safari World, but your father didn't leave me any money. And he didn't put any money into my checking account like he said he was going to do. So I just don't have any money until he comes back or until he sends it."

She then asked to borrow a couple hundred dollars from Kelly.

By 1982, Billy's private life was a disaster. He told Bill Reedy, "I got three homes and no place to go."

He had the home at Blackhawk in Northern California, where Heather and her whole family lived. By 1982, Billy was complaining, "What am I going to do with them? I can't even go home and walk around in my underwear. I got them sons a bitches of Heather's living there."

Reedy told him, "You brought them there. Get them out."

Billy had the second home in Del Mar, where Jill lived, but life with Jill was fraught with discord and unrest. He owned a third home in Uniontown, New Jersey, where he lived alone when the A's visited New York to play the Yankees.

According to Bill Reedy, when Billy wanted privacy on the West Coast, "he went home to Berkeley and slept with his mom."

# THE BEGINNING OF THE END

As manager for Oakland, Billy had been Manager of the Year twice in a row in 1980 and 1981, but in 1982 the lack of depth in the A's organization finally caught up with him. His starting pitchers, the strength of the team, broke down one after the other. Critics tried to blame Martin for the bad arms, saying he pitched them too many innings, but the pitchers to a man thought that ridiculous.

Said Steve McCatty, "My God, look back a long time ago. Walter Johnson and those guys were throwing five hundred innings a year. I threw two hundred and forty-something, which isn't any big amount.

"I didn't know what my problem was, what happened in my particular case. The doctors didn't know what it was, and it took eight years to figure it out. I had belaborments inside the shoulder, a muscle on top of the cartilage that was torn, bad tissue in the front and the back. I had some frayed tendons, scar tissue, but then I had a big bone spur under my biceps that nobody ever knew about for eight years.

"Mike Norris got hurt after we had a fight with Seattle that year. He threw at somebody and got knocked down, and later in the game he said he had lost some feeling in his hand, and then he had a nerve problem, and he had surgery on it.

"Rick Langford, one day, threw a pitch and his elbow popped, and Matt Keough hurt his shoulder pitching on a wet day in Baltimore. I remember he

came in, slipped, and said, 'Something happened to my shoulder.' It ended up
he had a slight tear in there.

"All in the same year. So how could they have blamed Billy for that? Personally I would run through a brick wall for the guy. He was fun off the field.
I had a good time with him. He had faults, like everybody else, but again, when
you know what they are, you stay away from them, and you do fine. I enjoyed
him. I had a great time with Billy."

When the pitchers got hurt, the A's couldn't replace them. They stopped
winning, and baseball stopped being fun for Martin, who hated to lose more
than anything in life.

Paul Tabarry, who was Eddie Sapir's assistant, noticed that during the summer
of 1982, Billy was starting to have some serious problems. When he joined the
A's in 1980, he was on the wagon, but that lasted only until April. By 1982 he
was drinking heavily, as he had done when he was with the Yankees. On the
road Billy took Jill, which at times caused him to neglect his baseball duties.

Ordinarily Billy's routine was to meet with his coaches after the game for
several rounds of drinks to talk about the game and what they planned to do
for the next game.

But when Jill was with him, she was jealous of the time he spent with the
coaches, and she would say to Billy, "You aren't going to be with the coaches.
You are going to be with me. That's the way it's going to be."

And that's the way it was.

The players and the front office took notice of Jill because she and Billy
fought loudly and sometimes through the night in their hotel room. Their fighting and screaming, which was constant, could be heard three rooms away.

During the summer Billy called Eddie Sapir. "Eddie," Billy asked, "do we
have a five-year deal or a ten-year deal?" Billy didn't tell him why he was
asking, and Sapir didn't ask, but Sapir had vibes that Billy was no longer happy
in Oakland, that a wedge was beginning to separate him and the A's management.

Sapir told him, "You were right with me when we signed the contract. We
have a five-year deal in writing. You have a verbal commitment for five more.
I don't know if it would hold up in a court of law, and I told you at the time
that you were making a mistake, and you acknowledged making that mistake;
we said we had to live with it, but you felt the ten years were there because the
house deal was for ten years." Sapir told Martin he felt there was probably
enough evidence for a judge to decide the contract was binding for ten years.

Billy asked, "What else is going on?"

Sapir said, "I heard from your accountant that the government is looking for
$200,000."

Billy said, "Why don't you borrow that from Sandy against my sixth year?"

Sandy was Sandy Alderson, whom Walter Haas had hired as general counsel
to the A's. Sandy, a sharp lawyer, had worked for Levi Strauss. Haas had picked
him for his smarts and his love of baseball. It wasn't long before Alderson
became the A's general manager and top decision maker.

Alderson, a man who has always stressed family involvement with the A's, was deeply concerned about the image of the team. He was upset when he was told that Billy, a married man, was squiring his mistress on the road with him. When he learned that their loud fighting was causing the players to talk, he liked it even less.

When Eddie Sapir called A's owner Roy Eisenhardt to ask him for the advance on salary so Billy could pay his IRS debt, Eisenhardt asked Alderson whether he should do it.

Alderson came back with the answer. No.

Eisenhardt informed Billy that the A's would not pay him the money. On August 19 the A's lost a tough game to the Milwaukee Brewers. A key call had gone against them. Before the game was over, Billy and coaches Clete Boyer and Art Fowler walked from the dugout into the clubhouse to Billy's office.

They proceeded to demolish Billy's office. They smashed furniture, threw a large metal chart with all the A's minor league players written on it onto the floor, and punched holes in walls.

Billy was like a tornado, going right across the wall, punching out the photos he had placed up there, including one with Frank Sinatra. The only photo he didn't punch was that of Mickey Mantle. It remained intact, on the wall by itself, while the others were smashed and flung around the room.

The next day Billy showed up at the ballpark with six of his fingers in splints. During the game he was trying to give signals to Clete Boyer at third base when Steve McCatty came over and stood next to him. McCatty had taped tongue depressors to all of his fingers, and as Billy struggled with his splints, McCatty mimicked him, wigwagging the tongue depressors back and forth. The players watched McCatty, laughing behind hands over their mouths.

To Roy Eisenhardt there was nothing funny about it. Eisenhardt tracked down Eddie Sapir at Tahoe. Roy was concerned that Billy's anger had been directed at him and Wally Haas. Sapir said, "No, Roy, none of that was directed personally at you. It was a situation in the game."

About two weeks after Billy trashed his office, George Steinbrenner called the A's and asked permission to talk to Billy about managing in 1983. There is a question whether Steinbrenner's call was made in order to conceal some unethical conduct.

During his previous managing jobs, there were incidents in which Billy had offended the front office and had gotten himself fired—in Minnesota he punched traveling secretary Howard Fox in the face after Fox refused to give him his room key; in Texas he slapped the elderly Bert Hawkins; and in New York he said the famous words about Reggie Jackson and George Steinbrenner, "One's a born liar and the other's convicted." But these actions always had been spontaneous, spur-of-the-moment outbursts.

Martin's pattern of behavior during the final months of the 1982 Oakland A's season might have suggested to an observer that he seemed intent on getting himself fired. There is some evidence that the observer would have been correct, that Billy Martin, in late July, had been offered the job of New York Yankee manager in 1983 by George Steinbrenner—if he could get himself fired.

If this was true it was a clear case of tampering. Owners were not supposed to entice managers of other teams to get themselves fired so they can manage elsewhere.

The evidence Billy had been offered the Yankee job is statements he made to several of his friends.

On the A's final visit to Baltimore in late July, Billy was riding in his limo when he told his chauffeur and friend Tex Gernand that he would be coming back to the Yankees the next year. Billy seemed excited, and so was Tex, because it meant Billy could spend more time riding with Tex. For Tex, who genuinely loved Billy, it also meant an improved payday.

In early August, Billy told Rickey Henderson he would have the Yankee job the next year. Henderson remembers that Billy told him about two weeks *before* Billy trashed his office. The team was on the road, and Rickey and Billy were talking about the falling fortunes of the Yankees.

Billy told Rickey he was going to be the Yankee manager in 1983. "I know I can turn it around," Billy told Rickey.

In early September 1982, the second trip into Detroit for the A's, Billy told Bill Reedy about the Yankee job in 1983. Billy went to see Bill and Carol Reedy at the Hummer. During their conversation Billy told Reedy, "I was talking to George, and he told me the Yankee job was available if I could get myself released by the A's." Billy seemed excited by the prospect. He added, "We've just about made a deal. Now all I have to do is get fired or released."

Reedy thought his friend crazy to want to go back to New York and Steinbrenner. Reedy thought to himself, You have it made where you are in Oakland. They've given you a free hand. You make the deals. Why would you want to go back to New York?

But after this discussion it became clear to Bill Reedy that no matter how any other club treated Billy or how much they paid him, the only place Billy really wanted to manage was in New York with the Yankees. Reedy began to suspect that Billy's tearing up his office and subsequent acts of self-destruction had been premeditated to ensure that he would be fired by season's end so he could go back to working for Steinbrenner.

Martin's behavior the very next evening reaffirmed Reedy's conviction. Pitching coach Art Fowler was talking with Bill Reedy at the Reedys' bar. In the middle of the dining room sat Roy Eisenhardt and Sandy Alderson. The two had been trying to meet with Billy, to talk to him about the team, but Billy had been avoiding them.

On the last road trip Billy had spent all his spare time with Jill, and when Roy Eisenhardt returned to Oakland, he told owner Wally Haas, "We couldn't get to talk to Billy."

"Why?" asked Haas.

"He's with his lady all the time."

Roy Eisenhardt continued his quest to talk to Billy. When Billy saw them, he went over to their table. He was drunk, and when Eisenhardt began saying something to him, in front of his coaches he shouted, "If you fucking Jews don't shut up, I'll send you back to the hotel in a fucking cab."

Reedy ordinarily would have been shocked, but not after what Billy had told him about Steinbrenner giving him the Yankee job if he could get fired. Reedy chuckled as he watched Billy easing his path back to New York. By year's end, Reedy knew, Billy would be a Yankee again. When Billy wanted something badly enough, he got it, no matter how he did it. In that respect, Reedy mused, Billy and George weren't very different.

On September 15, Billy was thrown out of a game in the sixth inning. Still wearing his uniform, he walked across the street to a bar and managed the game from there, watching the game on TV and phoning in instructions.

Roy Eisenhardt, a moralist like Sandy Alderson, was upset that Billy had been involved in the game after he had been thrown out. When he told that to Billy, Billy laughed at him for being naive.

Judge Eddie Sapir, who was intimately involved in Billy's contractual dealings with both the A's and the Yankees, did not believe there was any tampering by George.

He remembered that Billy was "in tears" when he thought he might lose the A's job.

There is no way to reconcile Reedy's and Sapir's recollections. It will remain a mystery. What is clear is that Billy was out of control.

On September 27 the A's were playing the Texas Rangers in Arlington. Billy, Jill, Art Fowler, and Lewis Figone were over at Mickey Mantle's house. Every year the Celebrity Boat Company presented Mickey with a boat, and this year he had arranged for Billy to get one, too.

The doorbell at the Mantle home rang. Mickey answered the door. Billy and Jill entered, and Mickey, who didn't like Jill any more than Billy's other friends did, out of earshot asked Figone, "What the hell did he bring that bitching broad along for?" Figone had no answer. Later that day Jill said something to Mantle, who bent over and pulled down his bathing trunks.

"Kiss that, baby," Mantle told her.

Mickey and Billy posed for pictures in front of Mickey's boat, and then they and Figone stopped at a Mexican restaurant across from the ballpark. Billy sent Art ahead to go with the team from the hotel to the ballpark.

Billy was late for the pregame practice. The players were horsing around, playing the game Flip in the left-field corner, and coach Jackie Moore, who was disgusted with their lack of seriousness, pulled the players off the field.

As luck would have it, the local TV sports announcer was giving an update, and as the camera was panning the field, viewers could see that no A's players were out there when they should have been taking batting practice. Back home in Oakland, the A's brass was watching all this on a satellite feed.

When the coaches were asked why the players weren't out on the field, instead of making an excuse like "It was hot. We wanted to give the guys a break," the A's brass was told the truth, that Billy hadn't been there and the players were horsing around, and that's why they pulled the team off the field.

The next day Roy Eisenhardt gave the New York Yankees and Cleveland Indians permission to talk with Billy.

On October 20, 1982, Eddie Sapir flew to Oakland to talk to Wally Haas and

Roy Eisenhardt to see whether there was anything they could do to solve Billy's tax problem. Sapir knew that Billy had torn up his office, but he was not aware of the other things he had done.

Haas and Eisenhardt told Sapir, "The $200,000 is not an issue, and the length of the contract is not an issue right now, but we are seriously considering making a change, and that's why we're glad you came out to talk to us." They asked Sapir to stay overnight. When Sapir said he had to fly back to New Orleans, they asked that he stay through the evening, offering to fly him back in the Levi Strauss jet afterward.

That evening the A's fired Billy. Roy Eisenhardt told Eddie Sapir, "Eddie, we will not be able to replace Billy as a manager. We're not going to get anybody better than Billy, but sometimes—this is the best way I can explain it to you—you just have to make a change for change's sake and hope that it works good for your club and that the change will take you in the direction you set out to go."

Eisenhardt made it clear to Sapir that keeping Billy any longer would not take them in the direction they wanted to go.

Said Eddie Sapir, "My own personal conclusion was that Roy, Wally, and Sandy got in bed with Billy and truly wanted to be there for ten years. They just found something that got in their craw, and they didn't think they could live with it anymore. I was never privvy to what that was, because Roy and Wally and Sandy never told me anything except how much admiration they had for Billy personally but that they thought they needed a change in order to get to the goal that they wanted to achieve down the line."

Roy Eisenhardt told Sapir, "We're going to be real generous to Billy. The house is his to live in. If it sells for $5 million, we get the 1.5 we have in it, and Billy can have the rest."

When the A's fired him at the end of the 1982 season, Billy had the right to live there for nine more years. All he had to pay was the utility bills. He also had the right to buy it at market value. The way California real estate was going, Billy stood to make a small fortune at the end of the nine years.

At the time Billy was fired, his friend Lewis Figone offered him some good advice. He told Billy, "I called banks and made arrangements for the loan. Buy the house."

Billy told Figone, "Piss on them. I've decided I'm going to make them eat it. I'm going to stay there ten years, and then I'm going to buy it."

Figone warned, "If you do that, you'll have to pay a lot more for it."

Billy told him, "I don't give a goddamn. They'll have to pay all the upkeep and the taxes."

Matty Keough, who pitched for Billy in Oakland and New York and kept close to him afterward, says he believes that the reason Billy didn't buy the house was Jill Guiver.

"If he had bought it," said Keough, "he would have had a foundation on the West Coast, and Jill didn't want him to do that. She wanted him entrenched on the East Coast, where she could surround him with her group of people."

Many of the Oakland players had been very upset when Billy was fired. They didn't know that Billy had apparently arranged with Steinbrenner to return to New York. A number of the players, including Keough, believed that the reason Billy had been fired was because of his open and notorious relationship with his mistress, Jill, a relationship that was an embarrassment to the A's front office.

Lamented Keough, "Billy was happy in Oakland. He was in his hometown. He had it made. And then he met Jill. What sunk Billy in Oakland was Jill. Billy couldn't manage a baseball team and at the same time manage a relationship with her."

Eddie Sapir worked out a very generous settlement with the A's. Sapir felt terrible about the firing. At the same time Sapir thought it odd that Billy seemed elated. Billy never told Sapir about his arrangement with George.

Billy told Sapir, "It's okay. It's okay, Eddie, believe me."

It was okay, because getting fired was just what Billy wanted. Recalled Bill Reedy, "When Billy was fired, there was *never* any remorse of his getting fired at Oakland. Nothing."

Not long after the A's fired Billy, Sandy Alderson's father, John, ran into Billy at the Pink Pussycat sports bar in Scottsdale, Arizona. Sandy's wife, Linda, had undergone surgery several months earlier. John went over to Billy and introduced himself as Sandy's dad, half-expecting Billy to say something nasty to him.

Instead Billy replied, "How is Linda feeling?"

"Fine," John said.

"I'm glad," Billy replied.

Later, when John passed Billy's regards to Linda, she was surprised at his concern. "I never met the man," she said.

Recalled John, "Even though Sandy had fired Billy, Billy had kept up. And he had asked about Linda in just the right way." John Alderson shook his head at Billy's geniality. And why not? Sandy hadn't hurt Billy, but rather had done what Billy had just about begged him to do: fire him.

When Billy was fired at Oakland, Cleveland Indian president Gabe Paul badly wanted him to manage the Indians. Gabe left the World Series to come down to New Orleans to see Eddie Sapir about Billy. According to Sapir, the deal Gabe was offering was unbelievable.

Said Sapir, "Gabe got to see Billy up close with the Yankees, saw that he put tails in the seats, and he needed somebody who could come in and instantaneously make the fans want to come back to the ballpark.

"Gabe was willing to give Billy an attendance clause, big bucks per ticket. Big bucks. And Cleveland hadn't drawn flies. I mean, this was going to be a bonanza. But there were two jobs out there, the Cleveland job, and the Yankee job, and no matter what, if there was a chance to manage the Yankees, that's where Billy's heart was."

Gabe Paul was offering Billy an impressive contract, $1 million for three years to manage. *Plus* the attendance bonus. For the tightfisted Indians such an offer had been unheard of.

Billy considered the offer for three days and turned it down.

The next day he signed with the Yankees and Steinbrenner for Billy III.

During Martin's three-year tenure with the A's, George Steinbrenner had maintained his relationship with Eddie Sapir, Billy, and Jill Guiver. When Martin took the mediocre A's into the playoffs against the Yankees in 1981, the Yankee owner expressed to Sapir his admiration.

Said Steinbrenner, "You know, Eddie, this guy really is incredible. Here we are, playing Oakland, Billy Martin's team. He's just incredible."

Which was exactly what *Time* magazine had said about him on its cover. More incredible, thought his friends, was that after all the polluted water that had gone over the dam between them, after a tearful resignation and an ignominious firing, after all the name-calling and dirty pool, Billy Martin was going back to New York to work once again for George Steinbrenner.

# HEATHER AND
# JILL

After Billy got himself fired by the Oakland A's and rehired by George and the Yankees, the biggest complication in his life was how he was going to handle his dual relationships with Heather Ervolino and Jill Guiver. Heather was living in his home in the Oakland area, and Billy lived with her when the A's were in town.

Jill lived south of Los Angeles in a condo he had bought for her to stay in, and she traveled with Billy when the A's were on the road. The loud, sometimes violent fights between Billy and Jill were the talk of the A's ball club.

Billy juggled his time between the two women. Neither knew about the other. Billy tried hard to keep it that way.

For more than a year Billy successfully kept the knowledge of Jill from Heather and Heather from Jill. Then in early November 1982, Billy flew to New York to film a commercial for American Ankalon carpets. Jill flew from Newport Beach to meet him.

Billy had his private chauffeur, Tex Gernand, pick her up at the airport. In case anyone noticed, Jill's story was that she was a photographer covering Billy's appearance in the commercial.

She told Gernand, "I'm Jill, and I'm doing a story on him." Said Gernand, "I didn't know her as anything else but a professional photographer. But then it kept going, and I could see there was more to it than that."

The evening before the shoot, Billy and Jill went to a party at George Martin's, a New York nightspot popular with athletes. During the festivities, a photographer took a photo of Billy and his escort. The next day the photo appeared on the back page of the *Daily News*. Jill, who was described as "an unidentified woman," could be clearly seen alongside him.

Immediately Heather's relatives living in New York called her to tell her about the photo of Billy and the blonde.

When Billy saw the photo the next day, he was furious. He told Gernand, "I was set up, and George Martin, who I thought was my friend, had something to do with it." Billy was sure George Martin had contacted the photographer in advance of his appearance for the purpose of getting his bar some publicity. Billy decreed to Tex that he would never be seen at George Martin's again.

Billy did the commercial, and around noon met his lawyer, Eddie Sapir, in a little Irish pub. Jill was with him.

Billy excused himself, leaving Jill at the bar. When he got Sapir alone, he said, "Man, can Heather and I get married in New Orleans? Can you find some place, set it all up? Can you arrange everything down there since we're not Louisiana residents? Can we legally get married down there?"

Sapir told him, "If that's what you want to do, sure."

"Would you let Heather know that?" Billy asked.

Sapir said, "You talk about the marriage part, and if you communicate that, I don't mind telling her I can get you a beautiful, complimentary suite at our friend's hotel and arrange for a judge to marry you, plus help you with the licensing procedure and the requirements under Louisiana law."

Sapir was amazed, though he kept his feelings inside. He was Billy's friend, and if this was what Billy wanted, so be it. Later Sapir would say, "Try to figure this out, I didn't want to try. It wasn't any of my business."

Billy got up, called Heather on the phone, and asked her to marry him in New Orleans. During the conversation he told her that the girl in the picture was a girlfriend of Eddie Sapir's. Heather, who was close to Sapir's steady girlfriend (and later wife) Peggy, was furious that Sapir would "cheat" on Peggy. It was a story Heather believed for several months until she finally learned the true identity of the girl in the photo.

Billy walked back to the table and told a flabbergasted Sapir of his marriage proposal. Then Sapir got on the phone with Heather. "Congratulations," Sapir said.

"Eddie, is he serious?" Heather wanted to know.

"He's asking me to get a judge to marry you and find out whatever else you have to do. Sure he's serious."

Martin and Sapir hung up and went back to the bar, where Jill was still waiting.

Billy and Heather Ervolino got married in a small, private ceremony on November 30, 1982, at the Maison Dupuy Hotel in New Orleans. To attend his own wedding, he had to lie to Jill Guiver about where he was going.

Billy had planned a weeklong honeymoon in Las Vegas. But two days into it, he made up a story, telling Heather he had to go to New York. But he didn't fly West to be with Jill. Instead he flew up to Toronto, Canada, to see another of his girlfriends, a woman named Lisa.

Ed Sapir never pretended to understand Billy and his relationships with women. "That was Billy's life, and that didn't interfere with anything I was doing for Billy," said Sapir. "Billy's life was Billy's life, and I always respected what he wanted to do. Nobody was asking me whether I thought it was right, wrong, or indifferent."

Tex Gernand, who was Billy's chauffeur for almost ten years, looked at the marriage to Heather with scorn.

"She was a child who didn't know anything about life," said Gernand. "There was nothing to their relationship. It was like taking a small kid and moving her to a big town and saying, 'I'm being a nice daddy.' I didn't understand the relationship. To me, there was nothing there."

Very, very few people apart from the Sapirs even knew Billy had married. It had taken place in secret, and Billy did what he could to make sure it was kept a secret.

One time when Billy and Bill Reedy were together with a few of Billy's other friends, Bill Reedy almost let slip that Billy had married Heather, but before he could finish the sentence, Billy kicked him hard under the table. Afterward Reedy asked Billy why he had kicked him.

"I don't want anyone to know I'm married," Billy told him. Reedy never brought it up again.

To keep Jill's identity secret, Billy arranged with Eddie Sapir to legitimize her cover story that she was a professional photographer doing a project about him. Sapir, Billy, and Jill determined that the best way to do that was to put together a book of her photographs, something marketable to enhance Billy's image. Jill had taken thousands of photos of Billy. Billy told Sapir, "Put her on the payroll of Billy Martin Public Relations."

Sapir agreed. She arranged a book of her photos. Then, said Sapir with disgust, "She submitted a bill to us that was astronomical. Here we were doing this to try to justify who this lady was, and she was totally uncooperative."

Billy tried using the same story on his mother and sisters. The first time he brought Jill over to his sister Pat's house, he was still married to Heather. Jill arrived toting a camera. Pat took one look at her sexy body and thought, "She's a photographer? This is stupid." But when Jill began taking pictures, Pat reconsidered.

Maybe she is writing an article and taking pictures, she mused.

Just to make sure word of Jill didn't get to Heather, Billy gave his sisters strict orders not to say anything about her.

Younger sister Joan told him, "Who the hell do you think you are telling me what to say?"

Older sister Pat told him, "We've known about it for months."

Said Pat, "Their relationship became public all over Oakland. They were fighting all the time. It was bad. She was bad news right from the beginning.

So many people told him to get rid of her. His good friends were begging him.
"So many people told him, but Billy wouldn't listen."

Heather Martin, quiet and soft-spoken, was a looker who had an affect on men.
Because Billy was very protective and jealous, there was always a chance a
fight might break out when he was with Heather.

Lewis Figone was with Billy on two such occasions.

"It was right after Billy married Heather," said Figone. "We had met them
in Harrah's Club in Las Vegas after they had gotten married in New Orleans.
They were on their honeymoon.

"Billy and I were downstairs in the casino. Heather and my wife and someone
else's wife were talking, and Billy and I were playing a slot machine.

"All of a sudden these three guys walk by us, and they looked at Billy, and
when they walked by Heather, one of them patted her on the butt. And Heather
slapped the guy across the face and hollered.

"Billy went tearing over there, and luckily I grabbed hold of Billy, because
the Yankees had just signed him.

"I said, 'Jesus, Billy, cool it. Not now. That's all you need, to get in a fight.'
And he stopped.

"One of the casino managers was a friend of ours, and he threw the guy out.
But that's how things happen.

"I vividly remember one fight in San Francisco. We were at the St. Francis
Hotel. Billy was with the Yankees as a manager. Howard Wong was with us.
We were sitting in the bar, and a couple guys were drinking, and one of them
walked over to Billy and said, 'Could we buy you a drink?'

"Billy said, 'No, we're fine.' The guy took offense to the fact Billy wouldn't
let him buy him a drink. Then he looked at Heather, and he said, 'What is she
doing with a little pipsqueak like you?' The next thing I know, Billy popped
him. But the guy asked for it. That one never hit the papers. The bartender got
Billy out of there."

Because of the photo in the *Daily News*, the existence of Jill was out in the
open. But Billy successfully deceived Heather, first portraying Jill as Sapir's
girlfriend and later creating the full-fledged cover for her as a photographer
working on a book about him.

When the 1983 season started, Heather remained in Oakland with her mother
and brother. As part of the settlement with the A's, Billy would be allowed to
live in his home at Blackhawk for nine years as long as he—or his family—
were living there. Cynical friends of Billy's say this may have been one reason
Billy married Heather—her presence in the house would allow Billy to continue
to own it. Others said he married her because of his embarrassment after the
*Daily News* photo.

When the Yankees were home, Billy would fly Heather into New York to be
with him. On the road Jill continued to go with him, and sometimes she, too,
would visit him in New York.

There were even occasions when both women came to New York at the same time. Billy, who loved to live on the edge, was in his glory. It was hard on Billy's friends and family because of all the lying and sneaking around and also because they found Jill so difficult and unreasonable when they were with her.

Kelly Martin, Billy's daughter, recalled the great ends Billy went to in order to entertain both Heather and Jill and also to keep them apart. Oprah Winfrey and Geraldo Rivera would have been impressed.

"In '83 Dad and Heather were staying in the Regency," said Kelly, "and Jill was staying at the St. Moritz, that little rinky-dink run-down old hotel. Jill and Merry, her [older] sister, had a room, and their brother, Mark, had another room.

"Dad would come over and be with this one and then go back over and be with that one. I thought, Oh my God.

"Dad said to me, 'Here, you take the credit cards and you and Jill go out, keep her occupied, and you buy Evie [Kelly's daughter] a bunch of pretty things from Grandpa.'

"When it was time to go shopping, Jill got mad because when she called for a limo, she wanted Billy's limo. And Heather had it.

" 'No, no. I want Tex. I want Billy's limo here.'

" 'Sorry.'

"And boy, she just got hot. She said, 'Fuck it. Come on. We're going in a cab. You just tell Tex to pick me up at Macy's.'

" 'We'll send the other limo.'

" 'No, I don't want the other limo. Just tell Tex to pick us up at Macy's. I've got Billy's daughter and we're going shopping. So you just have Tex come and pick us up.'

"So we went shopping, and I bought Evie a couple of little things, a cute little red dress. A pair of Jordache jeans. That was her first pair of Jordache jeans. And that was basically it.

"Jill went into a camera store and bought five or six camera bodies. She bought a fish-eye lens. She bought a lens that was three feet long. She bought a tripod. She bought all kinds of stuff. A few thousand dollars' worth' easy.

"I asked her, 'Why do you need all these bodies? Can't you just snap one off and put it onto the other one? Why do you need so many?'

"She said, 'You need them for different reasons.' Well, fine, wonderful. I wasn't saying anything, 'cause Dad didn't clue me in on what she was supposed to get away with and what she wasn't supposed to get away with. Was I supposed to just say, 'Okay, darling. You've spent enough now. Come on?'

"I didn't know how to act, so I was just kind of taking it all in.

"Jill tried to sign, and they wanted to see her ID. She didn't have ID saying 'Jill Martin.' I had ID saying 'Kelly Martin' So I had to show *my* ID. And that just pissed her off all the more, so then she had to go spend *more* money.

"Afterward we went to the ballpark. Heather was sitting over on the first-base line. We were sitting behind the third-base dugout. And Jill began setting up all the camera equipment. And after that she demanded security protection. She was making a big to-do.

"Billy was married to Heather at the time, but we didn't know that because he wouldn't tell us. And Jill kept asking me to ask him. And I'd say, 'Well, did you get married?' He'd say, 'That's not important right now, Kel.' I'd say, 'Well, come on, Dad, tell me.' He wouldn't even tell me. Finally he told me but told me not to tell her.

"Dad would say, 'God, what am I gonna do? Heather keeps asking about Jill.'

"I said, 'Tell her who Jill is.'

" 'Oh God, I can't do that.'

"He'd say, 'You come up with a lie for me, Kelly.'

"I'd say, 'Nah-ah. Let's just come up with the truth.' I said, 'Why lie? Then you gotta tell another one. Let's just tell the truth, and they'll never believe it anyway. They'll think it's a lie.'

"And Jill kept asking me about Heather. She wanted me to give her Heather's phone number. I said, 'Nah-ah. I don't know what it is.'

"I told Jill, 'They won't even let me in the house at Blackhawk.' I went out there. The grandmother looked out her window and asked, 'What do you want?'

"I said, 'I'm Billy's daughter.'

" 'So, what the fuck do you want?'

"I said, 'It's a hundred and ten degrees out. We just drove out, and I thought maybe I could come in.'

" 'Your dad's not here.'

"I couldn't come in until Heather got out of her shower and came walking halfway down to the stairway to see it was me, and then grandma came down and opened the door. I had to stand there at the entry and talk to Heather right there in the stairwell in her towel."

"One time Dad called me up and he was crying. He said, 'Kelly, what am I going to do?' I said, 'Hey, I say dump 'em both. Get somebody who likes you for Alfred Manuel, that likes you for you.' I said about Heather, 'You don't need this one. My God, I would have to buy this one a beer. She's not even twenty-one.' And as for Jill, I told him, 'You certainly don't need the other one.'

"My dad wanted Jill to be very low-key. That's what he had me with her for. I was supposed to keep her low-keyed, right? Well, how can you keep somebody low-keyed when she had all this camera equipment that stands up over the dugout? And she had all these bullets around us because she had to protect her camera equipment. But also because Heather had security around her. My dad always had security guards around Heather. He had security guards on me when I went to Yankee Stadium.

"But see, Jill wanted it more obvious that they were guarding her. So what better way than to get a tripod that stands up over the dugout and get all these guys standing around to watch it?

"What was I supposed to do? Slap her and say, 'You're not taking that to the ballpark.' Did he want me to knock the camera equipment down? That would have made even more of a spectacle.

"In the middle of the game I could see him looking over at us, just pissed. I mean, he wasn't even looking at the game he was so mad.

"Before the game ended, Jill said, 'You're going to have dinner with us, aren't you?'

"I said, 'Not in your lifetime, darling.'

"After the ball game, Dad was pissed. I mean, he was just fit to be tied because Jill had made such a spectacle of herself by having to have all these security guards around us to protect her camera equipment."

Jill knew about Heather before Heather realized how much of a threat Jill posed to the marriage. Jill began a concerted campaign to split Billy and Heather, and the young girl from the Bronx would be no match for her. Meanwhile, Billy's juggling act would continue off the field, even as he managed on it.

# MOVING ON UP

**W**hen Billy took the once-hapless A's to the top of the division, the man most impressed was George Steinbrenner. When Steinbrenner suggested that Billy break his contract with the A's and come back to the Yankees during the summer of 1982, it was with Billy's understanding that this time George would *really* do right by Billy. Honest Injun. No crossies.

All along what Billy had sought from George was just one thing: an indication that George respected him. When George called Billy and offered him his job back, Billy saw that as George's sign. Another sign from George was that Billy's new contract would give him a lot of money, enough to pay off some steep debts to the IRS and enough to continue his house play with Heather and Jill.

When Billy returned to manage the Yankees in 1983, George gave Billy a multiyear contract that provided that no matter what Billy did, and no matter what George did to Billy, Billy was guaranteed upwards of $400,000 a year. The contract Billy signed in 1983 was for four years, but George's understanding with Judge Sapir was that it would be extended.

To re-sign with the Yankees, Billy got his salary, plus a signing bonus, plus $100,000 in expenses, plus a free apartment in the Regency Hotel, plus a nice car, along with the added carrot that when his managerial days were numbered, Billy would become an important executive in the Yankee organization.

Said Eddie Sapir, "Billy was looking down the pike to the day he would be an executive. Billy knew what was between Billy's ears. Billy knew talent. He was going to be the guy who George was going to rely on, that when George talked about his 'baseball people,' Billy was going to be his 'baseball people.'

"But this wouldn't come until after Billy no longer wanted to manage."

Said Sapir about Billy's contract in 1983, "George never wanted Billy to be an old baseball player who was down on his luck, didn't have any money, and drank too much. George wanted Billy well taken care of. He wanted him to have financial security. George told me, 'Let's not allow our friend to ever be in a position where he's got to worry about where the next dollar is going to come from. I want him to have a very generous check every year from the Yankees.' "

According to Sapir, thanks to George, Billy never again had to worry about income.

Outflow was another story. Billy would need every penny of it. In addition to a whopping bar tab, Billy was supporting Heather and Jill in two different homes, flying first-class all over the country to the two women plus half a dozen others, paying alimony to his former wife Gretchen, and trying to live the life of a rich man.

Pat Irvine, Billy's sister, remembered the change in her brother, how by this time money really mattered to him.

"As a boy, it never bothered him that he didn't have much money," said Pat, "but later on, as he grew up, it started really bothering him. As a kid he was satisfied and happy. He was content with what he had. If Billy needed shoes, his mom bought them. He didn't really know he was underprivileged until he saw others who had more.

"When he was managing Texas, for instance, Bob Short invited him to dinner and insisted on sending his helicopter. In New York, when he started out as a player, he had to learn to wear a tie. No one wore a tie in California. While he lived in New York, he developed a taste for the good life."

One of the attractions George Steinbrenner held for Billy was his veneer of wealth. Billy admired that. George had a home in Tampa and lived in a fancy apartment in the Carlyle Hotel in Manhattan, and when he drove around the city, there was always a town car to transport him. By 1983, when he returned to George permanently, Billy decided he wanted to live the way George lived. He also wanted people to see his wealth.

"Every captain of every room in Las Vegas and every maître d' in every restaurant in New York loved to see Billy Martin, because when Billy was doing good, everybody did good," said Eddie Sapir, who struggled daily with Billy to stem Billy's lavish spending habits.

"If he was out at a fine restaurant, he had to have the finest caviar.

"Billy had an apartment in New York and a $75,000 bill at the Westbury Hotel at the same time because the Westbury was convenient and he liked it there. Billy flew first-class because to fly coach was to take him back to where he once was.

"Billy enjoyed a lot of the finer things in life because at one time, he had those hopes and dreams, but he didn't think he could ever attain that.

"Then one day he found himself with a big contract and security, and he didn't have to worry about money anymore."

In 1983 Billy hired for himself a full-time limousine driven by Tex Gernand. The limo was an expensive adornment, but his friends were pleased with the arrangement because with Tex driving, Billy could drink without endangering others.

George Steinbrenner had wanted Billy to have a chauffeur. He wanted to keep Billy from drinking and driving. He should have been pleased when Billy hired Tex. But incredibly George had gotten into a row with Tex a couple years earlier when Tex was driving for Steinbrenner's closest friend, Bill Fugazy. As a result George hated that Tex was driving for Billy, and Billy's limousine became a sore point with Steinbrenner. Tex riled George further after Tex acquired the vanity plate YANKEE1. When Steinbrenner saw that Tex had it on Billy's limo, George called his political connections to try to take it away from him, to no avail.

Tex, a former New York City policeman who is six foot seven and two hundred fifty pounds, became known to all of Billy's friends as Tex the Driver, and as far as anyone knew, he was also Billy's bodyguard. Had it not been for Gernand, who drove Billy around in New York and often in Boston and Baltimore as well, it's likely Billy would have been in a lot more fights. All it took was one look from the imposing Gernand, who never drank on the job and was usually at Billy's side, and a potential troublemaker thought twice about pursuing a fight with Martin.

"I met Billy in the very beginning of 1981," said Gernand. "I was a cop in New York City for eleven years and left the job. I was with Limousines by Lloyd. Lloyd had heavy connections that got him the Miller Lite account.

"They were doing a commercial at the Teaneck [New Jersey] bowling alley, and I picked up Billy and Bill Specken, who was running the ad campaign.

"Specken said to me, 'Do you realize that's Billy Martin?'

"I wasn't a baseball fan. I said, 'I don't care who it is, as long as the guy tips me.'

"Billy asked Specken if I could be his driver for the rest of the week. Specken arranged it. In 1982, I began my own business, and Billy went with me in '83.

"When I first quit the cops," said Gernand, "I went to Bill Fugazy and got a franchise. I was probably the top booker with Fugazy. I knew how to run a car and do a job.

"During the time I was with him, I was called on to pick up George Steinbrenner at the Plaza Hotel. At that time I had a Town Car, and one of my gimmicks was to put fresh flowers in the back of the car every day. My clients liked it. George didn't. He complained to Fugazy, and I told George and Fugazy to go fuck themselves.

"I said, 'It's my car. I'm paying for it. I'll put fucking nude women in there if that's what I want to do.' End of conversation.

"One thing you have to understand about George, he hates limousines. He doesn't believe they belong in baseball. He rides in a four-door sedan. But Billy didn't want to ride in just a four-door sedan. Billy liked a limo. George wanted for Billy to take transportation. What Billy liked was an out-of-sight car for big bucks. Billy wanted people to look at the car. He grew up poor, and all the time he used to say, 'Look at this dago, look what he's got.' He loved the car. That's why people thought it was his car. 'Come on out and see my car.' He loved it. I didn't mind. I built it for him.

"The first car I designed for him was when he came back to the Yankees in 1983. It was a black Olds. That's the one where I designed the Billy Bar, which became the hottest ticket in the limousine business. I should have had a patent on it. It was the wildest bar at the time, and everybody wanted it, and it was copied by every builder in their limo. The only bad feature was you could only get five people in the back, so they got away from it.

"The first time I met Billy with the first limo, every time we would go to Yankee Stadium, Billy would get ahold of the parking lot attendants and park me right next to George.

"The first day George came out, and he nearly shit because he not only saw the car, but he saw me.

"That was the year they took a picture of Billy leaning on the hood of the limo—'Billy's Back'—that was my limo.

"I took Billy and Judge Sapir to Yankee Stadium for a contract signing, and Steinbrenner and Fugazy were at the table, and naturally Steinbrenner being Steinbrenner, he let Billy know that he would pay for Billy's transportation, but Billy said, 'No, I don't want that. I have my own limo and my own driver to drive it, Tex.'

"Judge Sapir came down after it was over, and he jumped into the back of the limo. He said, 'Tex, you would have been hysterical. Their eyes rolled over three times. Billy put you in the contract, and they were fuming.'

"While the judge was talking, Billy came out, followed by the photographer to take the picture that went with 'Billy's Back,' and behind him were Fugazy and Steinbrenner, and they were so hot they would have burned my windshield. They hated me.

"I remember when Billy gave me the license plate for the limo. It said YAN-KEE1.

"I said, 'What about George?'

"He said, 'Fuck George. That's my car.'

"Billy and George were living at the same hotel, and Billy's car was always out front, because we did the right thing by the doorman. George didn't.

"Billy knew this would happen, and to Billy this was hysterical. Billy said, 'When George sees the plate on this car, he's going to go spastic.'

"I found out through one of George's chauffeurs that when George came out and saw that license plate, he went off the fucking wall. He called Motor Ve-hicles, called state senators, demanding the plate back. He was told, 'You can't get it. It belongs to TMG Limousine.' That's me, Tex M. Gernand.

"With Billy in '83, it was an everyday deal. I was taking Billy to the ballpark. He didn't even have a car. When George gave him a Chrysler New Yorker,

Billy told him, 'Get that piece of shit out of my driveway. I got a limo.' But eventually Billy had to take it. Judge Sapir finally said to him, 'You're spending $6,000 to $7,000 a month.' After that, Billy hired me whenever he could.

"Through the ten years I was with Billy, he didn't have any problems because of me. I was usually there right by his side. I didn't let anyone give him any trouble. Basically the only two were the [Ed] Whitson fight and [the topless bar] Lace, and those were two times when I wasn't with him."

As a client Billy could make life difficult for Eddie Sapir because Billy was the type of person who would agree to anything you asked him to do to your face, but afterward he would rarely keep his word.

One time Eddie, George, and Billy met to discuss Billy's gold limousine. Tex had replaced the black Olds with a gold Caddy. George hated for Billy to be riding in such a fancy car. He wanted Billy to give up his chauffeur and the gold Cadillac, and he offered to pay for a car and driver if Billy would do as he asked.

"It looks like a lounge moving around town," said Steinbrenner. "I'd like to do this for you, Billy."

Billy looked George in the eye and agreed.

But after the meeting Billy said to Sapir, "Look, Eddie, no one else is driving me."

"Billy," said Sapir, "you needed to say that at the meeting with George."

Billy didn't care. Tex was his driver, and that gold Cadillac stretch limo with the license plate YANKEE1 made him feel like a millionaire.

# BILLY AND
# GEORGE

hen he wasn't pursuing sex and luxury, Billy Martin was managing a baseball team. It was his third stint with the Yankees. Before he got fired the first time, Billy generally had his way with George. The second time, after George fired him and broke him, George had his way. But after the Yankees folded in 1982 and failed to respond to anything George tried, he badly needed Billy, and so Billy thought that this time he would have the upper hand in their power struggle.

Whenever George needed Billy, Billy's drinking and his fighting and his sexual escapades became irrelevant. This was one of those times. In addition to Billy's large salary and his apartment in the Regency Hotel, George even allowed Billy to have Art Fowler as his pitching coach.

When they were apart, the two men professed great affection for each other. It was when Billy went back to work for George that George's insecurities caused him to act as he did toward Billy. George had a psychological *need* to show him—and any other manager—who was boss.

George was constitutionally incapable of leaving his manager alone. George constantly had to reassure himself that *no one* knew how to run things better than he, that *no one* was as smart as he, that *no one* was as successful as he, that *no one* was as handsome as he, that *no one* was as powerful as he. He did that by controlling everyone around him, giving instructions before the fact and second-guessing after the fact.

And it wasn't just the manager of the team. The general manager got the same treatment, as did the secretaries, the farm system employees, his AmShip employees, his horse farm employees, his children, the grounds crew, the waiter —anyone who crossed his path. Most of the people he came into contact with had no choice but to accept his behavior if they wanted to remain employed. Including Billy.

George was attracted to Billy because he was famous and was respected for his brilliant baseball mind. ("Teach me the game, Billy.") There was one other thing about Billy that George couldn't replace: Billy knew how to win games better than the other managers he hired.

Billy was attracted to George because George was rich and powerful. There was a part of Billy that was in awe of the way George could treat people so shabbily and get away with it. Billy didn't consider the pain and misery George caused others. He saw only the power. Like a moth to a flame, Billy liked being near power. It was one reason Billy wanted George to like him. He very much wanted George to give him some of that power. What Billy didn't realize was that George was *never* going to give him—or anyone else—*any* of his power.

The fact was that the two men were incompatible. When Billy came back to the Yankees in 1983, he took George at his word that things would be different. But George was the type of person who would say *anything* to get what he wanted, and what he wanted was Billy returning to the Yankees, so he told him things would be different. If you're a control freak, you can't change no matter what promises you make. When Billy saw *nothing* had changed, he held in his resentment of George for only so long, and then he went after George in the papers. Because George's ego was more important than the success of the team, he couldn't abide what he saw as Billy's challenge to his leadership—an act of mutiny—and so he felt he had no choice but to fire Billy for the third time, even though he knew that Billy could help his team win more than any other manager.

Commented Graig Nettles at the time Billy was rehired in 1983, "George and Billy are like Richard Burton and Liz Taylor. They are attracted to each other. They enjoy the glamour of having the other one around. Each respects the other for what he does for a team. Billy likes how George isn't afraid to spend money for players. George respects Billy's ability to walk into a chaotic situation, shake things up, and turn a team into a winner.

"The only question Billy's hiring brings up is the same question that has come up every time Billy manages for George: Will George leave Billy alone so he can do his job? He never has in the past. I really don't see any reason why he should in the future."

In 1983 George and Billy began the season as a twosome sharing a common public enemy: the umpires.

If Billy and George had one character trait in common it was their disdain for authority. Billy felt oppressed by authority. George wanted to be the authority. Billy all his life contended the umpires were against him. George picked up the mantra with a vengeance in 1983.

Billy's behavior toward the umpires was nothing new. Periodically an umpire would miss a call or misinterpret a rule, and Billy would become unglued. Why George got into the act is less clear, though it certainly kept his name in the papers. George's public bitching and moaning about the umpires, the blatant poor sportsmanship exhibited by a team owner, was a yearlong display that embarrassed all of baseball.

Together George and Billy were fined or suspended five times for attacks on the men in blue. This disgraceful campaign began with Steinbrenner's idea to feature Billy's umpire baiting in the 1983 Yankee press guide, the cover of which featured a picture of Billy, his back turned with his uniform number 1 in view, kicking dirt on an umpire.

It's rare when an owner gets fined for on-field behavior. It's rare for an owner to get his name in the paper at all during the course of the season.

In spring training, in a game against the Pittsburgh Pirates, Steinbrenner put on a shocking display of boorishness in front of Mike McAlary of the *New York Post* and Jerry Eskenazi of *The New York Times*.

Eskenazi, who says that covering the Yankees was the most distasteful assignment of a long and distinguished career, remembered the incident.

"I was visiting my mother-in-law in spring training one year when Murray Chass's father died," said Eskenazi. "My editor asked me, 'Jerry, can you hop over to the Yankees?'

"They were playing the Pirates, and during the game I was standing next to George Steinbrenner, who was affable and friendly. This was an interleague exhibition game, and someone was running to first base, and National League umpire Lee Weyer made a call against the Yankees.

"It was the first time I met George Steinbrenner. George was standing with five or six reporters along the first-base line, and he said, 'Those fucking National League homers.' He was the owner of the Yankees. I made a mental note of it.

"After the game, I had a problem. Is a guy allowed to say 'fuck'? And is a guy allowed to say, 'National League homers,' and do I have to write it?

"I said to myself, The man has got the right to some privacy. On the other hand, this is the president of the Yankees. And so I wrote what he said.

"He was also quoted by Mike McAlary of the *Post* blasting the umpires.

"As a follow-up story I called Richie Phillips, the head of the umpires' union, and told him what George had said. I told myself, 'There's no problem telling Rich, because I did write something like that, and it was already public record.'

"And Richie used my comment, not McAlary's, about what George said, quoting me to Lee MacPhail.

"George Steinbrenner called me at home.

"He said, 'Jerry, the thing you told Richie Phillips, it's going to go badly with our friendship.'

"Now remember, I had met him *once*. And he's telling me it's going to go badly with our friendship if I continue to talk to Richie Phillips.

"I thought to myself, You mean I've lost George Steinbrenner as a friend?

"And then George brought up a philosophical question. He said, 'Don't I have a right to be pissed off?'

"I said, 'George, you know better than that. You're the owner of the New York Yankees. You know your national reputation.'

"He said, 'Maybe you're right,' which surprised me. In other words, he was admitting that maybe he should be careful of what he says."

The petulant outburst was childish and unworthy of a team owner. Commissioner Bowie Kuhn fined George $50,000.

During the very first game of the season, Billy lived up to his press guide cover by arguing with the umpires three times. The Yankees lost to Seattle. Afterward Billy said, "Seattle's best player out there today was the second base umpire."

This was mild stuff compared to Steinbrenner's next salvo, which occurred on May 27 in a game at Yankee Stadium against the Oakland A's. George was at the stadium, watching the game on TV. A's pitcher Mike Norris brushed back Dave Winfield, and Winfield charged the mound and began choking Norris. Umpire Darryl Cousins ejected only Winfield.

Steinbrenner called Ken Nigro, the Yankee public relations director, and began dictating a press release attacking Cousins and umpire John Shulock, calling them scabs and "a disgrace."

Bob Fishel, who worked for AL president Lee MacPhail, was watching Nigro take down what Steinbrenner was telling him, and he called MacPhail to report what George had said. In a scene from a Fellini movie, Fishel used the Yankees' Xerox machine to announce to the press that Steinbrenner was going to be punished by MacPhail for his outburst.

Nigro called Steinbrenner to tell him about MacPhail's press release. Steinbrenner then issued another press release to blast MacPhail for not allowing him to exercise his freedom of speech.

Steinbrenner was suspended for a week.

The shooting war between Steinbrenner and MacPhail began on the afternoon of July 24, when George Brett hit what appeared to be a game-winning home run off Goose Gossage, only to have it taken away after Billy got hold of Brett's bat and protested on the grounds that there was too much pine tar on it.

Billy read the umpires rule 1.10b, which decreed that a foreign substance could not be more than eighteen inches up the handle of the bat, and the umpires nullified the home run, and the Yankees went on to win.

Brett went crazy, Kansas City appealed the decision, and four days later MacPhail ruled that the bat had not been doctored, that there was no evil intent in this case, and for the first time in his ten-year rule as American League president he overturned a ruling made by an umpire. Thus, the home run counted, and the Yankees and the Royals were going to have to finish the game from the point of the home run.

Steinbrenner began an indefensible campaign that MacPhail was "anti-Yankee." Said Steinbrenner, "It sure tests our faith in our leadership. If the Yankees lose the American League pennant by one game, I wouldn't want to be Lee MacPhail living in New York. Maybe he should go house hunting in Kansas City.''

The last four outs were to be played on August 18. Billy treated it as a joke. He played Ron Guidry in center field and Don Mattingly at second base. The Yankees surrendered meekly.

On December 23, Bowie Kuhn fined Steinbrenner $300,000 for his remarks about MacPhail. Relieved he hadn't been suspended again, George paid up.

Billy's worst outburst in 1983 occurred several days after Lee MacPhail's ruling. On July 31, in a game against Chicago, Billy went out of his way to make an issue out of the rule book.

The Yankees had been in a slump, and Martin told the players, ''There's no question we were cheated. MacPhail changed the rules against us. But we have to battle back and show we're true Yankees.''

Mad about the umpires to begin with, Martin was ejected by umpire Dale Ford for arguing about the number of warm-up throws catcher Butch Wynegar should get when he replaced Rick Cerone, who had been ejected for accidentally bumping the home-plate umpire after a close play at the plate.

''There's nothing in the rule book that says if a catcher gets thrown out of a game the new guy only can have five throws,'' Billy said correctly.

Umpire Ken Kaiser stepped between them, holding Billy's shirt in one hand and Ford's in the other. When Billy said the magic word that got him ejected, Kaiser went to bring his arm up, got it caught on Ford's shirt, and ripped off all the umpire's buttons up the front.

In the dugout afterward Billy was laughing, but later Billy told reporters he was redeclaring war on the umpires. Billy was in a rage, brought on by alcohol. Martin said that Ford had been out to get him. Wynegar backed his manager.

Ford told reporter Moss Klein his side of the story, that he twice had told Billy to ''Play ball,'' and then tossed him.

Klein returned to Martin and relayed what Ford had said. Martin stood face-to-face with Klein and yelled at him, ''Ford's a stone liar, a flat-out liar, stone liar. He doesn't know the rules. I'm calling the umpire a liar, and I know the commissioner and MacPhail will call me in on it. But I'm telling the truth.''

Lee MacPhail suspended him three days for his comments.

**42**

# FIRED AGAIN

T he détente between George and Billy continued through June 1983. George made suggestions as to what Billy should do with his players. Billy bit his tongue and kept his feelings to himself.

As an example of George's infuriating meddling, he sent Billy a letter dated June 9. In the letter, George offered "a few thoughts about the practices and continuing work during the trip." He told Billy that Andre Robertson needed to work on his bunting, that Roy Smalley needed to practice his fielding at first, that Steve Balboni needed lots of extra hitting, and George underlined the words *extra hitting*. George told Billy he wanted to see Balboni hitting against more left handers so he could "make a decision on him."

George added that all players had to work on bunting, that catcher Rick Cerone should "work on low pitches," that Steve Kemp needed to "work on fly balls," that Lou Piniella and Bobby Murcer should also take fly balls "just to stay in shape."

More: George informed Billy that Don Baylor needed to DH on the road "as much as possible," and that he should use his relievers more if they were going to be effective. All players, moreover, needed instruction on base running, "as we discussed," and the team wasn't stealing enough bases. "Can Robertson be worked with?"

George had "one more thought." Enforce the curfew and maintain strong discipline. If Billy did this, George wrote, "we'll turn it around."

He then asked Billy to either tear up the letter or keep it confidential.

Obviously Billy never tore it up. Billy was a man who always stressed the positive. As indicated by this letter, George concentrated on the negative. This combination of amateurish player critique and "suggestions" for Billy made his life miserable because Billy knew the man had no idea what he was talking about, but at the same time he had the power to fire him if he didn't go along.

The beginning of the end of Billy III came because of Billy's promiscuity, his lack of respect for George's Knute Rockne–like mandates, and his penchant for yessing Steinbrenner and then not doing what he had said yes to, followed by George's anger at what he saw as Billy's challenge to his leadership.

The scenario unfolded in early June. The Yankees had lost their final game of a homestand to the Indians, and Steinbrenner ordered Martin to hold a workout the next day on the team's off day in Milwaukee.

"Will you do that, Billy?"

"Okay," Billy told him, though he had no intention of carrying through on his promise. George always wanted his players practicing on their off days, especially after a loss. Billy felt the players needed the day off. The players sided with Billy.

Don Baylor, a seasoned veteran who had played with Baltimore, Oakland, and California, was incredulous when he saw how vindictively Steinbrenner acted toward the players, ordering punishment drills if a player made an error. Baylor shook his head in disgust that players had to come out at three in the afternoon to practice bunting or fielding or taking ricochets off the outfield wall as punishment.

Said Baylor in his autobiography, "In 1983 that always-'unnamed' authority mandated that we had to work out on every scheduled day off until we were in first place."

Though Billy had told George he would make the players practice when they arrived in Milwaukee, he made the workout voluntary for everyone, including the coaches. Only three players showed up. Billy hadn't even come to Milwaukee. He was back in New York with Jill.

The night before the Yankees were to leave for the trip, Billy told Bill Madden of the *New York Daily News*, "I'm flying out on my own, with my girlfriend Jill. Why don't you join us? I'll meet you at the bar of my hotel at one o'clock."

They met the next day in a bar in New York at one in the afternoon, around the time the players were supposed to be working out in Milwaukee. They had a drink, and Billy and Jill headed for La Guardia Airport to catch the flight to join the team.

Billy told Madden, "I'd appreciate it if you don't write anything about the workout today, because there isn't one. George just doesn't understand that the players need the off days to get their rest. Rather than argue with him, I just said okay and told the players they could work out, talk a little hitting if they wanted."

That night the Yankees were beating Milwaukee 7–1, behind Shane Rawley. In the middle of the game Billy had gotten into a shouting match with a County

Stadium security guard about escorting Jill safely out of the park. While Billy was screaming at the guard, out on the field Rawley was getting hit hard, but Art Fowler could not get Billy's attention.

For the first time in his career, Billy was putting his private life ahead of his job.

The next day Jill couldn't have summoned more attention if she had sat in her seat naked. She sat in the boxes right next to the Yankee dugout wearing a halter top and shorts. She was seated among a sea of spectators, but her blonde hair, sexy curves, and bare midriff made her as noticeable to the reporters in the press box as a diamond in a coal field. They also noticed that during the game Billy sat on the top step of the dugout right below her, and periodically he would reach over to her to take a note that she would pass through the barrier with her toes.

All the reporters saw it. No one wrote about it.

And no one would have, except that the resourceful Henry Hecht, who was writing a column for the *New York Post* at the time, had called Ken Nigro, the Yankee PR guy, to ask about Billy's behavior on the road trip. Nigro, who had his favorites among the reporters, wanted to protect Billy. He told Hecht nothing but then called Bill Madden of the *News* to tell him of Hecht's inquiry.

"Find out if Hecht is onto something," Nigro said.

Reporters as a whole are a suspicious lot. In a world where a big scoop can make a career, you can't afford to be beaten on a story very often. The *News* and the *Post* were very competitive, as each tried to put the other out of business.

Madden suspected that Mike McAlary of the *Post* had tipped off Hecht and that the *Post* was going to run the story about the skipped practice and the notes from Jill's toes.

Madden couldn't afford to be scooped, so Madden called Steinbrenner to get his reaction to the recent events, and that's how Steinbrenner found out about the informal workout and Jill's notes from her toes.

Steinbrenner's immediate reaction was to fire Billy.

"I'm probably going to have to make a change," Steinbrenner told Madden. "What do you think about Yogi managing the team?"

The next day Madden wrote that Martin was facing dismissal and that Yogi was the candidate to replace him. The story ran on page one of the *News*.

Nigro, in trying to learn what Hecht was up to, had caused the story to be printed. As it turned out, Mike McAlary hadn't even talked to Hecht. The industrious, inquiring Hecht had just been fishing for a story. Because of the story, Bill Madden made enemies of both McAlary *and* Billy Martin.

McAlary rushed to tell Billy that Madden had written about the missed practice and the notes from Jill.

"He wrote *what*? How the hell could he write that? Doesn't he know I'm married! I'm married."

The next day Steinbrenner flew to Cleveland, where the Yankees were beginning a series with the Indians, as did Eddie Sapir. They met at Steinbrenner's local hangout, the Pewter Mug. Steinbrenner agreed to give Billy a reprieve—as long as Billy "instilled discipline" in the team.

That afternoon Ed Sapir, working hard to keep the reports of Jill's presence from Heather, told reporters, "Billy has been vindicated. Reports of the girl are unfounded."

After the final game in Cleveland, Steinbrenner got back at Billy. He fired Art Fowler, causing Billy enough personal misery to make him drink hard. The hard drinking made him a little more paranoid and crazy than usual.

The team returned to New York for three games against the Brewers. That Friday, George tried to call Billy at his apartment, but Billy had spent the day in a bar drinking. That afternoon, when Billy arrived at Yankee Stadium, he was booze-whipped. He refused to talk to reporters, and he slammed the door of his office.

Meanwhile, a young woman named Deborah Henschel, an intern for *The New York Times*, was in the clubhouse taking a survey on who the players thought should be on the All-Star team. Henschel was covering the Yankees for the first time. When Billy saw her, she was sitting on a table taking notes. Billy, who would have been first in line trying to hustle Henschel had they been at a bar, had enough girl problems of his own without having to face *this* woman.

Billy, who looked at most women as subservient sexual objects, had always hated the idea of female reporters being allowed in the clubhouse, and he angrily demanded to know what she was doing in the Yankee locker room. She told him about the survey she was conducting. He didn't believe her. In his alcohol-induced state Billy was convinced George had sent her to entrap him in some way so George could fire him.

Billy said later that because she was "wearing a low-cut dress with slits up to here," she didn't look like a working reporter.

Billy barked, "Get your ass out of here."

Henschel, an attractive woman, told other reporters about Billy's behavior and accused Billy of calling her a "hussy." She also accused him of saying, "Suck my cock."

According to Billy, what he had said was, "If you don't like it, you can kiss my dago ass."

Upset with the way she had been treated, she called Steinbrenner in protest. If it turned out that Billy had told a member of *The New York Times* to suck his cock, Steinbrenner vowed, Billy would be gone today.

Steinbrenner questioned coach Don Zimmer, trainer Mark Letendre, and pitcher George Frazier. Zimmer, who knew better than to comment, said he heard nothing. Letendre backed Billy. So did Frazier.

Billy made it through yet another crisis of Steinbrenner's making.

Ultimately it was George's incompetent handling of player personnel combined with his power over the press that got Billy fired this time around. There was no way Billy could ever keep his job as long as his success depended on George's player moves and as long as the reporters kept track of Billy's every move. One fight, one incident, one outburst, and Billy was headlines.

Without the reporters, Billy might have done or said something and the incident might have died. But the competition among the reporters was so great that there was always a reporter or two buzzing around a sotted Billy, waiting for him to slug someone or blast George or do something irrational or intemperate.

In 1983 Billy, unable to handle George, drank more than ever as the disease of alcoholism worsened. In the past Billy had reserved his imbibing for after games. This year he was drinking before games and even *during* games. Players began to notice that Billy's memory wasn't always what it should have been.

Pitcher Shane Rawley could see the effect Billy's drinking had on him.

"Mostly the problem was if we had a day game. I can remember one night [Dave] Righetti and I were out at Oren and Aretski's, a bar in New York we went to every once in a while, and Billy came in with Jill. 'Hi, how are you doing?' He bought us a couple drinks. He was there, and we left.

"In the dugout the next day, we said, 'Hey, Billy, thanks for the drink.' He said, 'What are you talking about?' So I figured maybe he didn't want to talk about it, so we went to the end of the dugout. This was early in the game. We were like, 'Whoa, okay.'

"About the fifth inning, Billy came by and said, 'Oh, now I remember.'

" 'No problem. Okay.' And that was it."

That year Ryne Duren, who had been such a terrible alcoholic that he once drank a case of beer, parked his car on the railroad tracks, and waited to die, several times tried to contact the Yankees to talk to Billy and the players about alcoholism.

"I was trying to get into the Yankee organization to work with the team," said Duren, who is renowned for his work as an alcohol rehabilitation counselor. "Clyde King wanted me to come in, Yogi asked for me to come, others, too, and I would call, but I always got shut off. I never heard anything back. I felt very bad about that, especially in view of my having been given the Yankee Family Award in 1983, which was a way of saying, 'Congratulations on the work you've done since you've gotten out of baseball.' But the Yankees never let me speak in the clubhouse. And my feeling was that it was Steinbrenner who kept me from doing that, because it would be alien to Billy."

Bill Denehy, who pitched for Billy in Detroit and who is also an expert in the field of alcohol-related problems, suggests that George Steinbrenner did not want to rock the boat by forcing Billy into treatment.

Said Denehy, "They are called enablers, and they really want to keep people with an alcohol addiction problem sick. If Billy had stopped drinking and been able to rationalize better and not continue to be a victim, someone who felt he was being used—me against the world—where he could start thinking more clearly, then he could realize what was being done to him, to understand that the pressure and stress was coming upon him as a result of George's actions. In other words, if Billy stopped drinking, he'd quit, leave. He'd see the Yankee job was not the only job. But as long as Billy was drinking, he thought it was.

"Every place Billy went, he was a Yankee. Big deal. Go somewhere else and be successful. But he couldn't. That was the job he *had* to cling to. And so long as he was drinking, he felt he *needed* George Steinbrenner, even though he was being abused by him, even though he was being mistreated. That's all Billy knew, so he felt it was what he needed, and he clung to it.''

The pressure on Billy to keep his job was overwhelming. Adding to this problem was his continued need to keep Jill a secret from Heather and to keep Jill happy.

What made Billy drink so hard was the pressure George was putting on him to win at the same time George was meddling with his team, especially the pitching staff. Firing Art Fowler was bad enough. Without Fowler, Billy's lines of communication with the pitchers were effectively cut off. At the same time Billy began to imagine the other coaches, Jeff Torborg, Don Zimmer, and Sammy Ellis, were plotting against him with George.

But in addition to firing Fowler, George had the habit of destroying the confidence of his pitchers in face-to-face confrontations.

Pitcher Matt Keough, who had just come over to the Yankees, remembered how Steinbrenner treated Jay Howell, one of the Yankees' top young pitching prospects.

"I'll never forget," said Keough, "Jay Howell was pitching for us. He had a wonderful arm. He threw as hard as anybody, had two great breaking balls.

"In this game he got knocked around a little, and Billy took him out of the game.

"We had a lounge at Yankee Stadium, and ten minutes after [Jay] got taken out, I went into the clubhouse to get some coffee, and I could hear a huge commotion in the lounge. Jay was sitting on the couch, and George was standing behind him, calling him names and telling him he couldn't pitch. This was during the game! George was down in the clubhouse airing this poor kid out, calling him names! I thought, Oh, Lord.

"In my mind if an owner will come into the clubhouse during a ball game, there isn't any line he isn't willing to cross in terms of meddling with the ball club.''

Recalled Shane Rawley, "To me Jay had really good stuff, he was learning how to pitch, and he may have felt intimidated by George, as a lot of players do. It's like you're walking on eggshells. You go out there and you think, If I make one bad pitch, I'm going to be jumped on.

"You feel bad enough as it is going out and pitching bad. Nobody wants to go out and get his brains kicked in, and Jay was doing the best he could, but George's presence was a problem for him, and after he left the Yankees, Jay went on to have some great years. I don't think he ever had that opportunity in New York when he was there. But Steinbrenner's actions also hurt Dale Murray, Mike Morgan, and Rick Reuschel as well as others.''

Steinbrenner's impulsive, unthought-out player moves also hurt the Yankees. He didn't have confidence in his young shortstops, Andre Robertson and Bobby Meacham, so after the 1981 season he traded away his superb setup man, Ron Davis, to Minnesota for an over-the-hill Roy Smalley, a player Billy felt the Yankees didn't really need. The loss of Davis hurt the rest of the staff badly.

In 1981, Davis and Goose Gossage were an awesome relief combination. Davis would come in in the sixth or seventh inning, pitch two or three shutout innings, and Goose would finish up. With Davis in the game the Yankees never lost a game in which they were ahead. But Davis took the Yankees to arbitration and won, so Steinbrenner once again let his personal feelings come before what was good for the team, and he traded Davis away.

Despite everything he had going against him—his heavy drinking, George's incompetence, the terrible atmosphere in the clubhouse, the press's hatred for him—in spite of all that, in 1983, Billy once again rejuvenated the team.

The year before, the Yankees had finished four games under .500. In 1983, Billy had them playing pennant-winning ball. The team won ninety-one games, were twenty full games over .500, and would have won the title had George not made his power play to bury Billy in the middle of the season.

At the time Steinbrenner fired pitching coach Art Fowler in late July, the Yankees had a real shot to win the pennant. Once he fired Fowler, everything Billy had worked for went down the drain.

The pitchers, especially, couldn't fathom why Fowler would be fired.

Said Shane Rawley, "Firing Art made no sense to us. It might have been because Billy wasn't listening to what George was trying to tell him to do in playing certain players. Billy would tell him to take a hike. But when George fired Art, it disrupted things. Billy might not say it affected him, but it did affect him. This was one of his best friends, and for no apparent reason, George fired him.

"That was the start of Billy not caring as much about his job as he could have. That being *his* payback to Steinbrenner for what he did to Art.

"We were right on the verge of doing something good, but after George fired Art, in the last month we just couldn't get over the hump, and it was like the last month everyone let down mentally."

The firing of Art Fowler fed Billy's bitterness. Once again, Billy knew, he had done everything asked of him, done a better job than anyone else could have, and George *still* sought to make him look bad and then fire him. Ron Guidry, the Yankee ace, who rarely got in the middle of the George-Billy feuding, was so disgusted when George fired Art that he announced he was dedicating the rest of the season to Fowler.

Billy knew George wanted him to quit. But Billy told Graig Nettles, "He's trying to get me in a pissed-off mood so that I'll quit. But I'm not going to let him force me into quitting. I'm not happy about his firing Art, but there isn't much I can do about it right now."

Art's firing made the irascible Billy even more difficult to play for. The young players were subjected to constant criticism and second-guessing, and with Fowler gone, Billy decided he would be his own pitching coach, ignoring coaches Sammy Ellis and Jeff Torborg, whom he believed to be spies for George.

Once Billy ran the pitchers himself, the staff fell apart emotionally. When Thurman Munson was the catcher, Billy generally let Munson call the pitches.

Without Munson, Billy second-guessed the pitch selection of all but the most veteran pitchers such as Guidry. The pitchers began to resent Billy.

Without Fowler, Billy brought relief star Goose Gossage into the game a batter or two too late. Graig Nettles and some of the other players noticed. But no one had the courage to confront Billy.

When Goose stopped being effective, the team began to lose, and once that happened, some of the pitchers began complaining to George and in the press. Other position players, who felt that either they weren't being used properly or Billy was too tough on them, started talking behind Billy's back. When an owner has complete confidence in the manager, the backbiting becomes irrelevant. Most of John McGraw's players had hated him, but the players knew the owner backed him a hundred percent, so they played, bitched among themselves, and won. But it was as Billy had always said: If the players know they can climb the stairs to the front office, no manager can keep his job.

In September Steinbrenner and GM Murray Cook, whom Billy disliked, called Lou Piniella up to the office to find out if the players were happy with Billy.

Lou, who was loyal to Billy, was furious that George was once again trying to involve him in his games. Lou went and told Billy. Billy cornered Cook, called him a few names, and told him not to try to undermine his ball club again. Billy, powerless before George's coming onslaught, prepared himself for the worst.

In the end the avalanche of stories in the papers planted by George made Billy's firing acceptable to the public. George had learned from the first time he fired Billy. George paved the way with a long string of scathing stories about Billy from "a source close to Steinbrenner."

No manager can keep his job if the owner mounts a campaign to get him fired. If an owner spreads stories in the papers often enough, saying that the manager has lost control of his team, saying that his players no longer want to play for him, saying that the team is in disarray, the fans will eventually believe it.

Jerry Eskenazi, a sportswriter for *The New York Times*, covered the Yankees intermittently during that 1983 season. Eskenazi saw firsthand why it was so difficult to be a reporter covering the Steinbrenner-Martin Yankees. One man was excessively cruel. The other was ornery and on the edge of a nervous breakdown.

For Eskenazi it was his worst, most bizarre experience in a long, distinguished career of journalism.

"It was 1983, the first trip around the circuit," said Eskenazi. "We were in Cleveland, and there was a young kid, an intern twenty-one or twenty-two years old, who was doing a lifestyle piece on Billy Martin.

"The game ended, and the Yankees lost big.

"Someone said, 'Tough loss, Billy,' and he said, 'Yeah,' and the kid said to him, 'Good to be back in pinstripes, Billy, huh?' Billy looked up, and he was holding himself back, so he said, 'Yeah, it's good to be back in pinstripes.'

Then the kid said, 'Great to be a Yankee, right?' Billy said, 'Yeah, great to be a Yankee.' And Billy then went on about how the umpires had jobbed him in this 10–0 loss, the usual harangue, and 'This guy sucks,' but it was low-keyed.

"When Billy stopped, the kid asked another question: 'What did you do during your first night here?'

" 'I had a nice meal at Stouffer's.' And you could see the tension in Billy was rising. His fingernails were getting white. And we were looking at this kid and thinking, Kid, shut up.

"And the kid said, 'So Billy, your team is pretty good this year?'

"Billy jumped up behind his manager's desk. He screamed, 'What the fuck are you talking about? I'm horseshit. We're horseshit. The team is horseshit. The fucking Indians are horseshit. You're all horseshit.' And he ran out of the room.

"The writers wanted to distance ourselves from [the kid]. We were looking down, shuffling our feet. The kid left the room, and five minutes later Billy came back. He was composed.

"He said to us, 'From now on just you four fucking guys. I'm not giving any more fucking interviews. Just you guys. Just my writers.' I thought, *His* writers?

"Billy kept everyone on edge, and there was always a thing of beating out the next guy, because you didn't know what Billy would say. You were always nervous about who had the inside track with Billy, and you were always, on a daily basis—it sounds bizarre—you were calling up the general manager or Steinbrenner to see if [Billy] had his job. After every incident.

"The first thing I would do when I got up in the morning, even when we were on the road, I would read the New York papers. Even in Texas you can get the *Daily News*.

"I'm the kind of writer who likes a complete circle. I like every loose end to be tied up, and I'm never really happy until I've called everyone, and it used to astound me that with all the professionalism I brought to bear, still the first thing in the morning I'd run down to the newsstand. 'What did I miss?' 'Did the guys beat me on something?'

"It was because I didn't feel I had a handle on it. I wasn't the regular beat guy.

"It often surprised me that George would go so heavily with Mike McAlary and Bill Madden. Was it based on circulation? That the ballplayers read them? 'Cause ballplayers, despite their saying they don't read the papers, they read every word.

"When Billy was the Yankee manager, everyone was agitated. There was a constant struggle among the tabloids to get the latest thing he was going to say, what he was thinking, when was George going to or wasn't going to fire him.

"To me it was a defining moment in my covering sports in that I thought I had seen it all, been in situations where nothing would ever get under my skin, and here at the age of forty-five I was getting nervous, afraid of getting beat on stories.

"This trip was coming to a close, and Madden wrote that Billy was going to be fired, and luckily for me, he wasn't. Meanwhile, Billy and I finally had developed a rapport.

"It was the last week of the road trip, and Art Fowler was in the room with him, and Billy said to me, 'They are trying to screw me. I know they're after me. I don't know who it is, but I know they are after me. I know who it is.' And he was talking about the Steinbrenner–Bill Madden relationship, and he talked about how he was going to look into it, because he knew who was out to get him.

"Billy had the sense of the wagons having to be circled, that things were falling apart, that he was out of control.

"In a strange way, and I'm ashamed to admit this, I started to feel some empathy for the guy because he was a man alone. There was a Gary Cooper, *High Noon*, the-town-deserted-him kind of feeling about this guy whom I thought of as a sleazebag, basically a bad person, and now I had empathy with him.''

The players knew best that George's leaks were an effective campaign of propaganda against Billy. One player who was furious about what George was doing was third baseman Graig Nettles.

Said Nettles in his 1983 diary, *Balls*, "Out of the blue, the three New York newspapers quoted 'a reliable source close to the Yankees' as saying that the 'Yankee players are on the verge of rebellion because of Billy Martin.'

"The 'reliable source' was quoted as saying that 'George is feeling pressure to fire Billy because of player dissatisfaction.'

"What was funny about those articles was that all three came out the very same day. Here were Bill Madden in the *News*, Murray Chass in the *Times*, and Henry Hecht in the *Post* all knocking Billy and quoting 'sources close to the Yankees.' If I were a suspicious person, I would almost think that George was up to his old tricks again.

"Articles like this would give George a ready-made excuse to get rid of Billy. I don't know a better way to get rid of a manager than to say most of the players are dissatisfied. For him to plant a story like that wouldn't be exactly ethical, but I wouldn't put it past him.

"The thing that never fails to amaze me is that whenever 'a source close to the Yankees' is quoted, he is never identified, which is the chickenshit way of giving a statement. And worse, the reporters also take the chickenshit way out by allowing 'a source close to the Yankees' to get away with it.

"This way anyone can say anything he wants, no matter how rotten or nasty, because no one will know for certain who said it. If you're going to say something against somebody, at least have the balls to allow yourself to be quoted. And if a reporter is going to write something nasty, he should have the balls to say who said it. Otherwise, who knows what the truth is?

"Also, this way a writer can make up a statement and attribute it to an unnamed source. And I don't put it past a couple of the writers who cover the Yankees to use their own ideas and then write that some 'source' said it.

"It seemed funny, all three papers coming out suddenly blasting Billy, saying there are players who want to leave the Yankees because of him."

Nettles, for one, could not understand why George was even mounting this campaign to fire Billy. Nettles was not yet aware that winning came second to George's personal vendettas. If the team died as a result of his ruining Billy's reputation so he could fire him without criticism, so be it.

"Last year the Yankees finished four games under .500, and this year we're seventeen games above .500, and all the writers are saying how bad we were this year and that Billy should be fired," said Nettles. "I don't understand it. Billy should be given a medal. The team was so screwed up last year that it would have been impossible to turn it around in one year."

Even so, in September 1983, after George had set the wheels in motion for the downfall of the team, he again fired Billy. He hired Yogi Berra to replace him.

Said Graig Nettles, a student of human nature, "I guess George got tired of having to take a backseat to Billy again. I can't think of any other reason why he fired him. Billy made George promise he would keep away from the players, stop making suggestions, in short, butt out. And George did that for a year. And it must have just killed him to be so quiet. Now George can reconnect the phone to the dugout. Now he can come back into the clubhouse to give more of his rah-rah speeches."

When George fired Billy, the press made fun not only of George, who *never* could complete a season without firing his manager, but of Billy as well, for allowing George to humiliate him so badly. Why would Billy allow himself to be humiliated for a third time, despite the excellent job he had done as manager?

The answer, of course, was two-pronged: his pride in being the Yankee manager, and his fat contract. Adding to his woes was a thought process warped by alcoholism. To pay for his women and his jet-setting ways, he needed a lot of money. Billy believed that the only person willing to pay him that money was George Steinbrenner.

Friends warned Billy that the money came with a price. They saw how Steinbrenner would torture him, make him feel small, make him look bad in the press and in the eyes of the public. They warned him about what George was doing to his self-esteem.

Billy didn't care. The Yankees were what he cared about. He loved the Yankees deeply. He had come from nowhere to the New York Yankees, and he never forgot it and the pride it instilled in him. The Yankees had made him something.

Yet the franchise he loved most would hurt him the most.

His friends told him, "Billy, you know you can't get anything out of this guy except money." But it was enough. He needed the money, which would be guaranteed even if he were fired. He hoped the money would give him power.

If Billy had to accept another firing and spend the year 1984 scouting, he could do that for $400,000 a year. And he knew, of course, there was another aspect of George's personality that gave him hope. Billy knew George well enough to understand that before too long George's meddling would drag the team down and that he would need him again as manager.

# 43

# POISONED

**W**hen Billy married Heather Ervolino in late November 1982, he did everything he could to keep the marriage a secret from Jill Guiver. For a number of months he didn't tell anyone, including his daughter, Kelly, his ex-wife Gretchen, or his son, Billy Joe. But during the 1983 season, on one of the road trips when he took Jill with him, she overheard one of the Yankee wives talking about Billy's marriage.

When Jill confronted Billy, he told her he had married Heather because he had felt sorry for her, that she had come from a poor family, that she was young and naive, and that he felt he should take care of her.

Once Jill knew, she became terribly jealous of Heather's position as wife. Looking at Jill's subsequent behavior, one is struck by a sad realization: Billy had entered into a relationship with a woman who, like George Steinbrenner, was a person determined to get her way no matter how she did it.

Jill's first step in her war with Heather was to find out Heather's telephone number. The next step was to begin harassing Heather with phone calls to try to make her stop loving Billy so that Jill could marry him.

Eventually she succeeded in getting Heather's number, and in 1983 Jill began making a series of calls to her. The tenor of the calls was, "He's going to marry me. He's going to divorce you. He doesn't love you. He loves me."

One of Heather's best friends was Peggy Sapir, Eddie's wife, and Heather and Peggy would make girl talk. In one conversation Heather talked about the baby she wanted to have with Billy and wondered why she hadn't been able to conceive, because they didn't use any protection. Heather told Peggy, "I guess it's because Billy's away so often."

One day Heather picked up the phone. It was Jill, who informed her, "You know, Heather, Billy is sterile. He can't have any children."

Heather didn't know what to say. Her response was, "Of course I knew that."

Heather immediately called Peggy Sapir. Heather said, "If it was true, I wanted her to think I knew, and if it wasn't, I just didn't know what to say." She told Peggy, "I was so floored, so caught by surprise, I couldn't believe she was saying this to me."

Said Peggy Sapir, "Can you imagine a wife hearing that from a mistress? What was the purpose of Jill saying that to Heather? I have no idea. But it shows the kind of things she would say and do. I mean, Heather was totally blown away with that."

Billy was able to keep Heather calm by lying to her that Jill didn't mean all that much to him, that Jill was crazy, delusional about their relationship, someone she shouldn't pay any attention to.

For four full years Billy was able to maintain his dual relationships with Heather and Jill.

While Heather lived in the Danville, California, house at Blackhawk that the A's had bought for him, Jill lived in a little house Billy owned on Poppy Street, four houses up from the Pacific Coast Highway in Corona del Mar. It was a small wooden house, perhaps eight hundred square feet, nothing lavish, but it had character, and Jill lived there when she wasn't on the road with Billy.

One of Jill's girlfriends during that period was Kathryn Marrero. According to Marrero, the relationship Billy had with Jill was as stormy as the one Billy had with George Steinbrenner. They fought all the time. They would scream at one another. Billy would become violent, partly because of his suspicious nature and partly because of his drinking. Kathryn well understood what Jill was going through because she, too, was married to a jealous, possessive husband.

"I lived at the Balboa Bay Club in Newport Beach," said Marrero. "After Jill and Billy would have fights, I would go see her, and we would sit and spend time together. When I'd be at Jill's house, the phone would ring, and it would be Billy's daughter, Kelly, or it would be George Steinbrenner, or Billy. We'd sit and drink coffee, and all this stuff would go on around us.

"Jill was crazy about him. It was the roller-coaster excitement. She was in love more than she would be in her whole life, but the down parts were worse than anything that could possibly be. Because that was the way it was with my ex. So I can relate to it, because when you're out of the situation, you look back and say, 'How can anybody in their right mind stay with that person?'

"She was crazy about him. She had this one song by Carly Simon, and it talks about getting drunk at the Plaza, and that was her song to Billy. We'd sit and listen to it.

"But Jill constantly stayed home because she wasn't allowed to leave the house. She had direct lines to everything. She'd call him in the clubhouse. She'd call when he was out in the field. She'd talk to him right then and there.

"She talked to George Steinbrenner whenever she wanted to. Jill and George acted like they were friends. She had a direct line to George, and when Billy and Jill would get in a fight, George was a mediator at times.

"George was always in Billy's life. Even when Billy was in Oakland. I don't think George ever stopped not being in Billy's life.

"When Billy and Jill would have fights, George would intervene sometimes, or he'd call, and sometimes if Jill wouldn't want to speak to Billy, George would call and try to talk to her.

"Billy and Steinbrenner had a love-hate relationship.

"The love part was that Steinbrenner would even get involved in the middle of Billy and Jill's mess and call and try to be the mediator and that kind of garbage. That in itself was amazing. How many men in a powerful position would even get involved in that garbage? They would say, 'Get out of my face. You guys have to take care of this on your own.'

"He used to talk to Jill on the phone, and I knew he talked to Billy and tried to patch things up, and the next thing you know, George and Billy would be fighting tooth and nail and not be speaking to each other. And George would fire him.

"The drinking was the biggest problem because it got Billy out of control. He'd go to the Five Crowns bar a whole lot. That's across the Pacific Coast Highway in Corona del Mar.

"There's a phone booth in front of the Five Crowns, and whenever he'd be mad at her, he wouldn't come to the house, but he'd stay on the phone and sit in that phone booth all drunk, and he'd talk to her on the phone.

"Personally, I did not like Billy. I was rude to him on the phone when he called me in the middle of the night. I did not give in to the whim of Billy Martin. After that, he wasn't keen on me being around Jill. But he wasn't keen on Jill having *any* friends.

"Billy had the upper hand. He was in total control over Jill's life, and Jill is a strong person. At that point all she had was the relationship she had with him. She stayed home all the time. She was home *all* the time.

"I don't know that I consider myself to be one of her best friends. I think I was someone who would come over and bide time with her, someone who was harmless so that Billy couldn't get really angry, because she was lonesome. I mean, she totally loved Billy. I really believe that.

"Billy's friends did not like her because they thought she was a gold digger. But see, Billy did not set Jill up *that* nicely on the Newport Island house that she was living in. When she moved to Corona del Mar, that was when she got her BMW 700 series, and that's when she got her horse. And that was when he finally started making money, but she still did not live *that* lavishly. I know what lavish living is. She was not pampered. To be honest, Billy did not have that much money. He liked people to think he had money. I didn't know Billy's financial status, but I would have guessed that he didn't make more than $400,000 a year. It's not like the guy was rich.

"But I'm sure Billy gave her a sense of power. Even without him not having really that much money, the power of being his girlfriend and going to all these functions was great, I'm sure.

"I am telling the truth, which is they fought like crazy. They loved real hard, and they fought real hard.

"She was nuts about him. For us to sit there on the floor and listen to that song from Carly Simon, and her writing down all the words so she could write it in a little note. . . . Both she and I were crazy about our men. And these guys were not good for us. And it wasn't just totally the power thing. I don't know if she has a history of abuse or why she would want to be with someone who mentally abused her, but she was crazy about him."

On April 15, 1984, the fighting between Billy and Jill escalated until there was an incident that became national news. As a result, Heather found out that Jill meant more to Billy than he had led her to believe.

The evening before, the papers reported, Billy and an unidentified female had returned to Billy's condo in Corona del Mar. According to the paper, the unidentified female (Jill) had locked him out of his home. Someone called the police. Billy had put his fist through a plate-glass window and was arrested on charges of public drunkenness and disorderly conduct. When the police arrived, they found Billy on the lawn of his condo with a bleeding hand and, said the report, "obviously intoxicated, screaming and hollering at a female."

Billy spent four hours in jail and was released on one hundred dollars bond. It wasn't until late October that Billy was acquitted of the charge. Municipal Court Judge Russell A. Bostrom ruled that the incident didn't occur in a public place but on the patio of his home.

Many of Billy's friends blamed Jill for the fight.

Said Peggy Sapir, "I remember when Billy got arrested in Corona del Mar. It was over a stupid horse trailer.

"Jill loved horses. She owned a mare, and she wanted Billy to buy her a horse trailer that had air-conditioning.

"Billy said, 'The goddamn horse doesn't need air-conditioning. I'm not spending any more on that horse. I'm sick of that horse.' And they got in a fight in the car on the way home, and when they arrived home, she locked him out of his own house, and they were screaming and hollering."

Bill Reedy was supposed to meet Billy at the Polo Bar in the Westbury Hotel on Madison Avenue the afternoon of April fifteenth. Billy showed up ten hours late. Reedy was furious. He hadn't heard.

Reedy told him, "You cocksucker, if you're not going to be here on time . . . I've been sitting in this goddamn bar for ten hours. I flew in. If you'd have told me you'd be this late, I could have caught a later flight."

"Fuck you," said Billy. "I'll be down in a minute. I have to take a shower."

Tex Gernand, Billy's driver, came walking in. He said to Reedy, "Didn't you hear?"

"Hear what?"

"It's all over the radio. He just got out of jail."

When Reedy asked Billy about it, he told him, "She wanted a fucking trailer for the horse, and I told her to stick the horse up her ass."

After the incident Billy decided he was ending his relationship with Jill permanently and was returning to Heather.

"Billy tried to break off with Jill so he could save his marriage to Heather," said Peggy Sapir. "Billy refused to communicate with Jill.

"Billy tried to protect Heather from her, unlisted her phone, tried to get [Jill] not to call, even tried to leave her, but when he did that, Jill threatened legal action against him as a way to get back at him.

"She would call our office during the time Billy wouldn't talk to her. She'd say, 'Please, I need to talk to him.' She'd leave 'urgent' messages. I'm convinced that if Jill had left Billy alone, his marriage to Heather would have worked out.

"Jill was like a bulldog. She just kept hanging on. When she threatened him with a palimony suit, he agreed to pay her a lump sum per month for her expenses. He had been doing that anyway. And he started seeing her again. Which was incredible to me.

"One thing Billy Martin detested was change. I mean, it took us forever to finish our business with his business manager, Doug Newton. Billy wanted us to take over for him, but he and Newton dragged on and on before it finally came to an end. Billy wanted it that way.

"Whether it was a wife or a girlfriend, Billy liked stability. He really resented change. That was the reason he wasn't able to really end any relationship. He'd have maintained relationships with Jill and Heather forever except that Jill pushed Billy hard enough to get him to leave Heather.

"Billy loved Heather. He loved Jill. He loved Gretchen. He loved all of these women very much. The only one he never came back to was Lois. Somehow, she was out of the picture."

Billy's daughter, Kelly, was thrilled when Billy told her he was leaving Jill. Kelly had made it clear she didn't like Jill *or* Heather.

Recalled Kelly, "My dad would call me up and say, 'Kelly, what am I gonna do? Heather's good, but this other one just won't leave me alone.'

"I told him, 'Dump them both. They're both too young. Get an old broad, somebody that loves you for Alfred Manuel. Because you're not going to be "Billy Martin" all your life. Who cares about Billy Martin? You're Alfred Manuel, Dad. Find somebody who loves you for you. Not for what the limelight can bring and to be Mrs. Popular. Find somebody who loves you for you. You're a good enough person.' "

On April 26, less than two weeks after Billy's arrest, Billy and Jill signed a palimony agreement.

The document stated, "Guiver must return all credit cards in her possession which are in his name. She would be responsible for her own purchases and legal obligations.

"Martin conveys and transfers to Guiver any and all legal rights to personal property in her possession [a 1982 BMW] deemed to be a gift, and he has to pay all the insurance and bills until the balance is paid off in full."

In addition, Billy had to pay Jill $2,500 a month, commencing April 27, 1984, and proceeding to September 27, 1984.

Upon execution of the agreement, Jill would give up and release all legal rights and claims against Billy.

To the best of her knowledge, said the agreement, Jill was not pregnant at this date.

She signed it on April 24, 1984. Billy signed it on April 30, 1984.

Carol Reedy remembers what happened next.

"That was supposed to be the end of their relationship," said Reedy. "She was supposed to not call Heather, not be calling the house, not try to break up the marriage.

"Then shortly after, she was contacting him again. Leaving 'important' messages, 'Please call,' message after message, and before he made all the payments, he was back with her."

But before that happened, Billy made a concerted effort to patch up his marriage to Heather.

One day Bill Reedy called Carol and asked her to talk to Heather. "I need you to do this for me," said Bill. "Call Heather in California. Billy wants to go home, but he wants to test the waters first."

Carol said to her husband, "Bill, what is this? Tell me right out."

Bill replied, "Tell Heather Billy said he'll be home the day after tomorrow. He just wants her to know."

Carol always liked Heather, and they were always genuinely friendly. One time they had had a good laugh when Heather found out about Jill's horse. Carol wanted to know if Heather was entitled to half the horse.

Heather asked Carol, "Which end of the horse is mine?" Carol told her, "I wouldn't take the end that eats, that's for sure. Take the other half. You can sell the manure."

So when her husband asked her to call Heather and tell her Billy wanted to come home, she did so gladly.

Carol told Heather that Billy would be home in a day or two.

"He'll probably call and tell you himself," Carol said.

Heather said, "No, he won't."

"Why?"

She said, "Well, Carol, Billy and I are not exactly hitting it off. In fact, he's been screwing around on me for a couple of years, and you know her. I know you do." Heather was talking about Jill, of course, and Carol felt pangs of guilt because she *did* know Jill and knew of Billy's relationship with her. Carol thought to herself, Those dirty rats put me up to this, because neither one of them wanted to face Heather.

In the end Carol kept the truth from Heather because she didn't want to hurt her friend, but she felt terrible about doing so.

Billy did return to Heather, but by the summer of 1984 he was also back with Jill, and it wasn't long before Jill irrevocably poisoned Billy against Heather.

"One of the things that was happening," said Peggy Sapir, "Jill was telling Billy that while he was away, Heather was having an affair with a bartender at Blackhawk. Disloyalty was one thing Billy couldn't stand, and when Billy heard that, that helped him make the separation."

Vicki Figone, the daughter of Lewis Figone, Billy's childhood friend, was another of Billy's and Heather's friends, and she could never understand why Billy left Heather. According to Vicki, Billy had bought Jill's story about Heather's infidelity and spread it around himself.

"Heather was true to him, a fantastic girl, so sweet, so kind and nice," said Vicki. "She never messed around on Billy.

"When they broke up, Billy spread the rumor he left Heather because she was fooling around at Blackhawk with the bartender at the golf club. That was a total fabrication and a lie.

"He picked out the guy, and he went around and said he dumped Heather because she was sleeping around with him.

"I remember when Heather and I went to Hawaii, we would go out, and every night we were in bed at nine o'clock because Heather refused to go to a bar or a disco or anywhere where men were around, because she wasn't interested. She didn't care.

"I had been out in Blackhawk with her. The only bar Heather ever went to when Billy was away was down at the country club with the old people. She'd chat with the cocktail waitress. She was friends with her. She'd chat with the bartender. He was married and had kids. She never had an affair with him. That was a lie that Billy fabricated to have a reason to leave Heather. To make her look bad. It was horrible what he did to Heather.

"She was true to him, and she was a fantastic girl. She wasn't with him for the money. He didn't even give her a checking account. She couldn't even sign a check.

"When Heather and I went to Hawaii, I put everything on my credit card, and he'd reimburse me. He never gave Heather money. She never spent anything, either. She barely bought a thing. She was happy with him, taking care of him, being with him."

Bill Reedy was with Billy and Heather the final weekend they were together. It was in December 1984. Reedy had flown to San Francisco to meet with Billy, who had driven from Dallas, Texas, in a Jaguar sports car he had just bought. They were eating at the Washington Square restaurant in San Francisco when a friend of Reedy's came over to their table and asked him what he was doing for lunch the next day.

"I'm having lunch with Billy and his wife." Bam. Billy had kicked Reedy hard under the table. To the end Billy wanted his marriage kept a secret.

The next day Bill Reedy met Billy and Heather at an Italian restaurant on the San Francisco waterfront. They were there to say hello to Joe DiMaggio.

When Billy went to the bathroom, Heather told Reedy, "I wish you'd come more often, Bill. This is the first time he's taken me out in months."

Later Joe DiMaggio came in.

"Hey, Dago, how are you?" Billy asked. They shook hands. Joe's hair was windblown, and immediately the always immaculate DiMaggio went into the bathroom to comb it.

Heather leaned over to Bill Reedy and asked, "What's his name, Joe or John?"

Reedy said to Billy, "Would that take a shot at his ego or what, if you told him that?"

All three laughed.

The next day Billy left their home at Blackhawk and never returned. When the days passed and she didn't hear from Billy, she intuited correctly that their marriage was over.

Said Peggy Sapir, "The fact remains that Billy did not come home, and that was the end of Billy and Heather. And Heather moved on in life. She married a great guy, had four great kids, and she's very happy now. She's as happy as she can be. She had a tremendous amount of love and admiration for Billy, and she was really good for Billy, and she's a wonderful person."

It was an assessment joined by all who knew her.

When I called Heather to talk to her about Billy, she was bitter and seemed badly shaken by the call.

"It was a period in my life I want to forget. There was nothing good about it," she said.

"He insisted my mother, grandmother and brother come live with me. So he could be away more. And he left me with them. That was his motive. Billy mostly kept me in the dark. He knew Jill since 1981. Jill knew what she was doing. He was with her when we got married.

"One day he left, and that was it. It was the best thing that ever happened to me. I could never have had much of anything with him."

Billy would spend the last five years of his life fighting with Jill Guiver and George Steinbrenner and drinking to ease the constant pressure brought upon him by their double-barreled demands. Having a relationship with George *or* Jill over a five-year period was stressful enough. Billy embraced them both. That Billy survived as long as he did was a minor miracle.

# A KICK TO
# THE RIBS

George Steinbrenner rehired Yogi Berra to manage in 1985. Yogi had led the team to a 87–75 record in 1984—good, but still seventeen games behind the Detroit Tigers, who had opened the season winning thirty-five of their first forty games.

When Berra began the 1985 season at the helm, Steinbrenner assured everyone that what the Yankees did during spring training would be meaningless, which is how it should have been all along.

Said Steinbrenner, "I put a lot of pressure on my managers in the past to win at certain times. This will not be the case this spring."

Yogi managed the first sixteen games of the season, was 6–10, and when Berra "defied" George by refusing to schedule a mandatory workout—the same nonsense that had gotten Billy fired in 1983—Steinbrenner fired him after spreading the charge that Yogi had been too "easygoing."

From the start of the season Steinbrenner's mania for attention, control and power seemed to be getting more pronounced, but, like Billy and his alcoholism, George was unwilling to admit he had a problem. Billy's problem hurt himself. George's problem hurt many others and also soured the fortune of the Yankee team.

For the first two weeks of the season George had been threatening Yogi, one of the most revered heroes in Yankees history. Yogi was a Hall of Fame catcher. He had won pennants as manager of the Yankees in 1964 and the Mets in 1973. Yogi Berra was a beloved idol to Yankees fans.

According to pitcher Phil Niekro, Berra's nerves were so shattered by Steinbrenner's constant pressure that in a game against the White Sox he cracked, making inappropriate moves that lost the Yankees the game.

"He's under so much pressure that he can't even think," Niekro said in his book *Knuckle Balls*, a diary of that season, "It almost seemed as if he subconsciously wanted to lose the game just to get all this shit over with."

Steinbrenner had made the fabled New York Yankees into a joke. The Yankee fans who remembered the days of Casey Stengel and Ralph Houk knew that as long as George continued his policy of trading away all the great prospects and firing one or two managers every year, the Yankees would *never* win again. The real Yankee fans knew what Billy knew—that George didn't know enough about baseball to run a team and that he never would because he was too quick to fire the competent people, those who disregarded most of his ridiculous, counterproductive orders.

When Yogi left, it was Steinbrenner's twelfth firing in eleven years, a record for frivolous, destructive management. In running AmShip, Steinbrenner did the same thing, churning executives and secretaries with great gusto, but the public didn't know or care what he did at AmShip. Only the affected employees and their families cared.

George was too powerful to depose. The Yankee fans had no choice but to be subjected to his every devious and destructive whim until George had done to them what he had done to his players: taken away the fun of being a Yankee.

Even bringing Billy back in 1985 generated little enthusiasm among the fans because it had become clear that Billy no longer was the little guy fighting against his powerful boss but rather a man who had sold out his principles to keep his job as Yankee manager.

At the time Billy took over the team, George and he were talking about Billy's future role in the organization. Billy had always argued he should be George's right-hand man, and George began hinting to Billy that such an assignment might become a reality in the future.

At the time Billy was hired in 1985, Billy's lawyer, Ed Sapir, told the press, "Billy is grooming Lou Piniella. That's his role. At the end of the season, don't come asking me, 'What happened to Billy?' I'm telling you right now, George asked Billy to take this club for one year or two to groom Lou Piniella. That is his role right now. He is the manager, and he's grooming Lou Piniella."

According to Sapir, Lou had been one of Billy's key players, and he liked Piniella. And Billy was looking to move up in the Yankee hierarchy. He was envisioning a vice presidency. According to Sapir, Billy didn't want to be full-time manager or full-time general manager. He wanted to be somebody who could troubleshoot for Steinbrenner and make recommendations about all aspects of the team: the minors, players, trades, etc.

No one paid much attention to what Sapir had to say because it sounded so ridiculous. Hire a man to train another man to manage? Move into a front office where the one man making the decisions seemed to use a Ouija board? But Billy had bought into George's mad system, and if he had to jump around, he would do so willingly for all the money he was making.

When Billy took over the team on April 28, the players were just as tepid as the fans about his return. Many players loved Yogi. They respected him for who he once was and how gentlemanly he treated them and everyone around him.

When team leader Don Baylor heard that Yogi had been fired, he kicked a trash can across the clubhouse. Don Mattingly fired a bottle of shampoo across the room. Joe Cowley, that day's losing pitcher, sat in his locker sobbing into a towel, believing the firing to be his fault.

When the Yankees took the bus to O'Hare Airport that afternoon, the bus dropped Yogi off at the terminal so he could fly home to New Jersey. When he stepped off the bus, he was given a resounding ovation by the choked-up players.

"We had become a family under Yogi," said Baylor. "Guys felt greatly for each other, felt we could win it all in '85."

Unfortunately for the players and the fans, George often made moves at inappropriate moments, destroying cohesiveness and dooming the Yankees. Baylor, for one, did not look forward to the switch in managers. He knew that Billy whipped players, and Baylor didn't like to be whipped. He was also aware that when Billy was manager, the players tended to imitate Billy in their private lives.

Baylor said in his book, "What [Steinbrenner] never understood was the players stayed in line because of Yogi. No one ran up and down the halls or tore up hotels. There was no misconduct on airplanes. We respected him too much to do those things. Yogi set a high standard for himself and his players. He was no threat to citizens in a bar because he didn't hang out in bars."

But when Billy first joined the team this time, he fooled everyone. He rarely lost his temper, rarely argued with the umpires. At the same time he injected into the players his winning ways. By the middle of May, Billy's injection of intensity and intimidation had transformed the team. In one game the Yankees were losing 8–0, but they came back to win 9–8 on a three-run home run by Mattingly.

Said Phil Niekro, "We're playing differently under Billy. We're playing like we're pissed off."

When Billy took the job this time, he and George had made one side deal. For years George was in the habit of making forays into the clubhouse, during which he lambasted the players in front of anyone who happened to be there, including the press.

Billy wanted George to stay out of the clubhouse and eschew his rah-rah speeches. George agreed, but there was one provision: Billy had to promise he would fine the players more often. Billy agreed.

Billy had always railed against George's "Mickey Mouse rules," and here was Billy enforcing them. He fined Phil Niekro for giving up a grand-slam homer, fined Rich Bordi a hundred dollars for not trimming his mustache, and fined Bobby Meacham two hundred and fifty dollars for swinging at a first pitch.

The players knew who was responsible, but it still cost Billy respect in their eyes.

Said Niekro in his book, "Instead of coming down to reprimand us personally, George now just calls down to the dugout and has Billy fine us, which is
not normally Billy's style, but it does keep George off his ass."

By June Billy's constant second-guessing of the players, especially of the
pitchers, had everyone on edge. Billy had taken the fun out of the game. And
this time Billy didn't have pitching coach Art Fowler as an intermediary.

After George fired Art during the 1983 season, Art was drinking in a New
Jersey bar, the Bottom of the Barrel, near where Billy lived, when Billy came
in. Art was very drunk.

Art was angry that Billy hadn't fought harder to keep George from firing him.
Art said to Billy, "You didn't fight for me. And I'll tell you this. I don't fucking
need you anymore. You ain't my boss, and you can't tell me what to do."

Billy loved Art Fowler to the day Billy died, but that day Art hurt Billy badly.
When Billy took over for Yogi in 1985, he remembered what Art had told him,
and so he didn't call on Art. He did bring him back in 1988, but by then Art
was drinking too heavily to be much help to Billy, and Billy regretted doing
so.

But without Art to protect them from him, Billy was merciless on his pitchers.

In June Billy publicly berated Don Cooper for throwing Seattle infielder Do-
mingo Ramos a fastball on the first pitch. Ramos had homered into the left-field
stands. (It ended up being the only homer Ramos hit all season.)

Phil Niekro learned from Billy's tirade that no Yankee pitcher was allowed
to throw a fastball on the first pitch to any Latino batter.

According to Niekro, all the Latinos knew it, too.

Said Phil Niekro, "When we were playing California, Juan Beniquez came
walking to the plate, whistling at [Yankee catcher Ron] Hassey, and held up his
index finger, just like Billy does every time a Latin player comes to the plate,
to remind whoever's catching about his first-ball, fastball shit. We all about died
laughing, and Billy just kinda looked at us real strange, like we were the ones
who were screwing up."

The next day Cooper was returned to Columbus. By that time Niekro was
describing Billy as "the maddest of the game's madmen."

By the middle of 1985, Billy didn't need a reason to drink. Between George
and Jill, Billy had demands made upon him every day that reminded him how
powerless he was. Billy drank constantly, both at and away from the ballpark.

At night after games Billy often would get very drunk, and on the road he
and Jill would fight so loudly sometimes they could be heard down the hall of
the hotel. Some days Billy would show up at the park wearing sunglasses. Every
once in a while he would even leave in the *middle* of a game to go to a bar to
drink.

Despite it all, the Yankees were only a couple games behind Toronto as July
became August. Billy Martin, drinking or sober, once again was proving his
greatness as a manager.

Said Phil Niekro in *Knuckle Balls*, "Billy has transformed us. We're smart,
we're aggressive, and we're having fun. Never have I seen this type of spirit

on a ball club before. Right now we're playing like we're all one out there, same uniform, same goal, same hangover.

"When we go out there now, we expect to win, and I can't ever remember having as much fun at any time in my career as I'm having now. I'm proud to be part of this whole thing, and I'm proud to be a Yankee. That's just the kind of pride and respect that Billy breeds. I don't give a shit what's written about him. When you're playing for him, he treats you like a man."

On July 20, the Yankees were only a game and a half back. If George Steinbrenner had sat back and reveled in how well the team was doing, the Yankees would have had a good chance to win the division.

On July 22, George had a major interview opportunity. Howard Cosell invited him to come on the "ABC Game of the Week," seen by millions nationally. National TV brought out George's need to be noticed. Being on national TV meant more to him than winning. Howard Cosell did not have the biggest ego in America. His guest that day did.

George Steinbrenner came on during a game against Toronto on July 22. He had a scoop for the millions of viewers. He told Cosell, "If Dennis Rasmussen doesn't pitch well today, I'm going to send him to the minors."

(Translation: "See what a powerful person I am.")

Rasmussen had pitched excellently going into the fourth inning, when pitcher Joe Cowley, who was listening to the game on a radio hookup, heard Steinbrenner's remark and told Rasmussen, who proceeded to give up five runs in the fifth.

If the Yankees had won, the lead would have been a half a game. Because Toronto won, the lead grew to two and a half games.

Rasmussen hit the showers in time to watch Steinbrenner tell Cosell that he was banishing Rasmussen to Columbus.

After the game Phil Niekro asked pitching coach Mark Connor about the move, but Connor said that neither he nor Billy knew anything about it. Billy, who was supposed to be consulted on player moves, was suitably furious.

The next day Rasmussen's bags sat in a cubbyhole as a mute reminder of Steinbrenner's arbitrary power. Pitchers are a fragile lot. Steinbrenner's treatment of Rasmussen affected the rest of the staff. That day pitcher Ed Whitson lost and Toronto won, and the lead was up to three and a half games. Cowley then lost, Toronto won, and it was up to four and a half.

Said Phil Niekro, "Joe Cowley seems to have lost all his confidence. I think it may all have to do with what happened to Rassy the other night."

Toronto won on the Yankees' off day, then Ron Guidry lost as the Blue Jays were winning again, and suddenly the deficit was up to six.

Making a bad situation of his creation worse, Steinbrenner then fired pitching coach Mark Connor. Billy was surprised, but not upset, because without Art Fowler, he was acting as his own pitching coach anyway.

In baseball the winners are usually the ones with the fewest disruptions during a season. The general rule is that if a team is going good, leave it alone because every time an element on a baseball team is changed, someone is affected, and you never know whether the team will be affected for good or for bad.

In this case the player most affected by Steinbrenner's sudden firing of Mark Connor was pitcher Ed Whitson, who was close to Connor. Whitson had been angry with Billy all season long, but Connor had been an effective buffer between them.

After Connor was fired, Whitson suddenly lost his effectiveness. In his first start after Connor's departure, Whitson pitched four innings and was taken out. He started again, went three innings, and gave up five runs. On August 20 the Yankees gave Whitson a 7–0 lead, but he couldn't hold it.

Whitson finally won on August 25, then on August 31 he again pitched poorly. Billy took him out after four and two-thirds innings. Whitson was angry that Billy didn't let him finish the fifth inning and get the win.

On September 10, Whitson was clobbered by Milwaukee. He gave up twelve hits and eight runs. He still won the game. The Yankees trailed the Blue Jays by only one and a half games.

The Yankees had a four-game series against the Blue Jays on September 12, 13, 14, and 15. The Yankees won the opener, then lost the next two. Whitson started on the 15th. He lasted three innings, and the team lost 8–5. Instead of being two and a half back, the Yankees trailed by four and a half.

George used the loss to pursue a feud with outfielder Dave Winfield. The Yankee star was one of those caring men who felt deeply about giving back to his community. He established a foundation to help underprivileged children, gathering the support of major corporations to help him in his quest to show kids how to reject the lure of drugs. Any team would have been honored to have a Dave Winfield on its team. George Steinbrenner tried to blacken not only Winfield's name but that of his foundation's as well.

As part of his contractual obligation to Winfield, George was obligated to pay the Winfield Foundation $300,000 a year. For reasons Winfield couldn't understand, George twice reneged on his promise, forcing Winfield to sue him for the money. In September 1985, George again had refused to pay, and Winfield again was pressing him for the money.

Without revealing the reason behind his words, the bully in George surfaced. George wanted the public to know that not only didn't the Winfield Foundation deserve his money, but Winfield wasn't even earning his salary.

After the final Milwaukee game, George infuriated key Yankee players like Ken Griffey, Don Baylor, and Winfield, during a diatribe in front of the press in which he said, "Where is Reggie Jackson? We need a Mr. October or Mr. September. My big guys aren't coming through—Winfield, Baylor, Griffey. They're letting us down. That's a fact." Then George referred to Winfield, who that night had driven in his 100th run for the fourth consecutive year, as "Mr. May."

Said Winfield when he was told of George's comments, "There's a feeling among us that we'd like to tell him, 'Shut up. You don't know what you're talking about.'"

Even Don Mattingly, who rarely commented, said: "You've got an owner here who likes to say things. But to belittle us is out of control."

In his book, Don Baylor remembered, "After Steinbrenner ripped the team, we lost focus. We also lost eight straight games, from September 13 to September 20, to fall six and a half games behind."

Nothing hurt the team as much as the time George questioned why Billy had brought Dave Righetti into the game in the fifth inning. George told Tom Boswell of the *Washington Post*, "Ask Billy, but don't tell him who told you to do so."

There were twenty games to play. Billy was extremely unhappy with George's criticism of his players. When he learned that George had publicly second-guessed his managerial decisions, Billy decided to put his personal feelings for George ahead of the welfare of the team. For the first time in their stormy relationship, Billy made moves to show up George.

Right after George had questioned why Billy had brought Righetti into a game too soon, the Yankees were leading 5–3 going into the ninth inning against Cleveland in a makeup game. Starter Brian Fisher began to lose his effectiveness, but Billy sat in the dugout while Fisher was shellacked for six runs as relief ace Righetti waited in vain for the call.

The Yankees flew to Detroit for three games. In the opener Billy allowed the Tigers to hit five home runs and score seven runs against Ron Guidry. And who did Billy bring in? Dennis Rasmussen, far from his best reliever. More eyebrows were raised among the players.

The next night, with Phil Niekro going for career win number 300, Billy let the struggling Niekro pitch the entire game.

Players began questioning among themselves Billy's moves.

Commented Phil Niekro, "Billy's begun to respond in some very strange and detrimental ways.

"George may have pissed Billy off too much this time. 'Cause Billy has gotten really crazy with some of his thoughts and actions."

During the Niekro game Billy made the strangest move he ever ordered as a manager. The game was tied 2–2 in the sixth inning. There were runners on first and third and two out.

The go ahead run was on third when Billy ordered third-base coach Lou Piniella to have Mike Pagliarulo, a left-handed batter, go up to the plate right-handed against lefty pitcher Mickey Mahler. Twice Pags had looked bad against Mahler's sweeping curveballs. Billy felt Pags was overmatched batting lefty and wanted him to stay in defensively. His solution: Bat righty.

At first Pags thought Piniella was kidding. A good soldier, he did as he was told. Batting from the wrong side, he looked lost, taking a called third strike.

The Yankees lost 5–2, and Detroit won the next game, too.

Phil Niekro wrote, "I wonder if Billy really does want out of here or if he's just playing games with George's mind."

By the time the Yankees arrived in Baltimore for the last leg of the road trip, Billy was in a wretched mood. He told reporters that he was passing over pitcher Ed Whitson because Whitson had a sore right shoulder. In twenty-nine games, Whitson's record was 10–8 with a 5.03 earned run average.

Whitson, when told he had a sore arm, began laughing. He said his arm never felt better. In the clubhouse Whitson was furious with Billy, having been shown up by his manager.

"Billy's got one real pissed-off Tennessean on his hands," said Phil Niekro.

That night, in a game the Yankees lost, a foolish blunder by Billy cost the Yankees the game. With the count 3–0 on Lee Lacy, a runner on first, and pitcher Rich Bordi struggling for control, Billy stood on the top step of the dugout and scratched his nose, the sign for a pitchout.

Catcher Butch Wynegar saw the sign but couldn't understand why Billy was calling a pitchout, and he was too cowed to say anything. Bordi pitched out, the runner didn't run, and Lacy walked, bringing up Cal Ripken and Eddie Murray, Baltimore's two best hitters. Both hit run-producing singles to win the game, bringing the Yankees their eighth loss in a row.

After the game Billy said he hadn't been thinking about where he was standing when his nose began to itch, and "I scratched it."

Mentally Billy was cracking up.

After the game Billy headed for the bar of the Cross Keys Inn, where the team was staying. Billy was downing his liquor with pitching coach Bill Monbouquette when two couples approached them. One of the couples had just gotten married. Billy bought them a bottle of champagne.

Around one forty-five in the morning the two couples returned and talked to Billy. When the groom went to the men's room, Billy talked with the man's new wife for a few minutes. After the groom returned, the two walked to a table. Billy was talking to reporters when the groom came back and tapped Billy on the shoulder.

"We've got to talk," he said. "You said something to my wife."

"Get lost, pal."

The groom said, "You told my wife she has a pot belly. I just married her this afternoon."

Billy told him, "I didn't say she had a pot belly. I said this woman here," and he pointed to another woman at the bar, "has a fat ass."

The groom poked Martin again, but this time Martin shoved him back hard. Pitcher Rich Bordi restrained Billy while Rickey Henderson and Dave Righetti stood in front of the groom.

The bar manager ordered the groom to leave. Billy shouted at him, "We'll take this outside."

Billy followed after him, but he had disappeared, leaving Billy feeling empty and unsatisfied.

The next night, the evening of September 22, the Yankees finally broke their losing streak. Under the strain of having to play for Steinbrenner, Billy's paranoia was working overtime. In the lobby of the Cross Keys that night, Billy had something to tell Moss Klein of the *Newark Star-Ledger*.

"I've been set up," Billy confided, his eyes wild and crazy looking.

Billy told Klein that he was certain the groom who had tried to pick a fight with him had been hired by George to get Billy in trouble in order to give George a reason for firing him.

After telling this to Klein, Billy then went out on the town. As was his habit when he was in Baltimore, he had dinner at Bud Paloma's Crab Haven, where he ate steamed crabs. Ordinarily, Billy's driver and bodyguard, Tex Gernand, would have been there to drive him, but that weekend the Mets' Ron Darling had booked the car for a date with a model named Toni, who would eventually become his wife.

Billy told Tex, "Don't worry about it. There's nothing going on. Come on down Sunday, watch the ballgame, and we'll go home Sunday after the game."

Said Gernand, "If I had been down there that Saturday night, the Whitson thing never would have happened, because Billy *never* stayed with the team at the bar when he was with me."

Dale Berra, Yogi's son and a Yankee third baseman, had asked Billy for permission to bring his wife on the road, and Billy gave it to him. After the game Billy had told Dale, "I would love to meet your wife. I'm going to Bud's. I'm going to eat, and afterward I'm coming back to the hotel. If you guys are in the bar having a drink, I'll stick my head in."

When Billy came back from dinner, he walked into the bar of the Cross Keys Inn. Ed Whitson looked up, pointed to Billy, and said, "He's the man who's causing my problems."

Sitting at the next table was Albert Millus, a twenty-nine-year-old Yankee fan from Binghamton, New York, who had traveled to Baltimore with his wife to see the Yankees play. They, too, were staying at the Cross Keys Inn.

Millus stared at Whitson, a large, intimidating man. Whitson, seeing Millus watching him, pointed a finger and asked him, "What business is it of yours?"

Millus was under the mistaken impression that Whitson was one of the Yankees' rookie pitchers. Said Millus, "If I was a rookie making $90,000, I wouldn't be acting like a little kid."

Whitson responded by grabbing Millus by the throat.

When Billy saw Whitson attacking the man, he rushed in and said, "Eddie, you're drunk, you don't need this."

Commented Millus later, "Whitson was going crazy by then." Millus, however, did not think Whitson was drunk.

Billy was the peacemaker. He was trying to stop Whitson from getting in trouble. It was a bad mistake.

Yankee pitcher John Montefusco had known Ed Whitson when they had been together on the San Francisco Giants and the San Diego Padres. The day after Billy took over the team back in April, Montefusco had told Moss Klein, "Watch out for Martin and Whitson. I know Whitson. There's no way—no way in hell—that Whitson will be able to deal with Billy. There's gonna be bloodshed, believe me."

Whitson had complained all season long about Billy calling pitches from the bench and pulling him out of games too soon.

Whitson, moreover, hated the way Billy berated pitchers when they made mistakes. He also felt Billy played favorites. He was *not* one of Billy's favorites. Billy thought Whitson, a free agent whom Steinbrenner paid $4.4 million for five years, was an overpaid journeyman.

Whitson's hatred for Billy was ruling his emotions, and he began swearing at Billy.

Billy kept saying, "That guy's crazy. He's crazy. I just tried to help him. What's the matter with him?"

That further incited Whitson, who was cursing and screaming at Billy. Then Whitson said the wrong word. He called Billy a "motherfucker."

Billy, who could be counted on to begin slugging at the sound of the four magic syllables, without warning punched an unsuspecting Whitson in the face, splitting Whitson's lip.

Catcher Ron Hassey and others separated them. A furious, snarling Whitson was pulled into the lobby.

Billy came looking for Whitson, and when he saw him, he charged after him. Whitson's arms were pinned to his side. As Billy closed in, to defend himself Whitson applied his martial arts training and with his cowboy boots gave Billy a solid karate kick to the body.

Billy doubled over and screamed. Whitson had broken some bones.

Billy said, "Now you did it. I'm going to kill you. I have to do it. I *have* to do it."

Billy was restrained while Whitson was dragged out of the lobby toward the parking lot. Once outside, Whitson got into a fight with Dale Berra. Whitson tore Berra's sweater, and Berra then slugged him in the face.

Inside, Billy broke free of his handlers, and though he had only one operative arm, he headed into the parking lot after Whitson. It was Billy's nature never to stop a fight until he had won. It was war. Whitson became the enemy. Billy was out of control.

When Billy ran outside and Whitson saw him, the big pitcher broke loose and charged Billy, tackling him on the concrete pavement in front of the motel. They were separated by security men. This time Billy suffered a bloody nose.

Billy was screaming, "He's finished. He's gone."

Whitson was screaming, "You tried to bury me. You tried to ruin me."

The cops came, and Billy went back into the bar. A short time later he told reporters he was going back to finish Whitson off. He asked the clerk at the front desk for Whitson's room number. He didn't get it. Billy got on the elevator to go back to his room.

As Billy got off on the third floor, Whitson was getting off the adjacent elevator. Another shouting match ensued as both shouted obscenities at the other before Whitson was hustled into his room.

Billy went to his room, then emerged and told reporters he intended to suspend Whitson without pay.

Standing in the hallway in his underwear, holding his fractured arm, Billy said, "I'm going down there and kick the shit out of that son of a bitch. He's in his room hiding from me. But I'm gonna get him out of there."

Billy told reporters, "Wait around ten minutes. I don't want the security guard to hear this. Go to room 345 [Whitson's room]. You're gonna see a guy get the shit kicked out of him."

Billy called Whitson on the telephone. Coaches Lou Piniella and Willie Horton were with Whitson.

Piniella, Horton, traveling secretary Bill Kane, and a representative of the hotel patrolled the floor until the wee hours in an effort to keep Billy and Whitson apart until the booze wore off.

Finally, Billy went to bed.

Martin had suffered a broken arm and two cracked ribs from Whitson's blows. Worse was the beating his ego had taken.

Billy said he wanted Whitson suspended "for the rest of his life" but soon mellowed. General manager Clyde King sent Whitson home for the remainder of the road trip. When Whitson returned to the team, Billy used him as though nothing had happened.

Bill Kane had been called toward the end of the ruckus as both combatants were herded into their hotel rooms. What Kane remembered most vividly was Billy's tenacity in the face of a far bigger, much younger opponent.

"Billy was a character," said Kane, who always admired Billy. "Whitson was twenty-five years younger and a foot bigger and fifty pounds heavier, and Billy had a broken rib and a broken arm and all Billy kept saying was, 'Let me get back at this guy. If he fights normal, I'll kill him. All he does is kick. This little puss doesn't even know how to fight. All he knows is kicking.'

"That night all the beat writers finally got an idea of why he was so admired, because they saw how really tough he was. When he got into a spot that was not his fault whatsoever, he was going to fight until the very end if he had to die doing it. And they saw this firsthand, and it really did amaze and shock them. They saw firsthand, and I think they looked at Billy in a new light after that. It was unbelievable. Billy even called Whitson on the phone to get him to keep fighting. Billy was so pumped up. We finally got Billy to bed. I calmed Whitson down. I got him out on a six o'clock flight the next day.

"Afterward Billy didn't hold it against him. He figured the guy had too much to drink and was out of his mind. Plus Billy's rib and arm were still broken, and he wasn't ready for him yet.

"The punishment Billy took that night was unbelievable. Maybe it sounds barbaric, but it showed the mettle of the guy."

The team flew to Toronto. Bill Kane called Bill Reedy and asked him to come up and stay with Billy. Reedy drove up from Detroit. Reedy met Billy in the hotel coming down the hallway. When he saw Billy, Reedy thought, Holy shit. Billy looked like he had been in combat.

Said Bill Reedy, "I remember after the Whitson ass-kicking, [Billy] had a cast on his hand all the way up to his elbow, and his ribs were broken. He was spitting blood. And he was really down.

"He was beat up emotionally and physically.

"It was all coming apart. He started to lose the zest for it. He was beat up. He looked like an old man."

A week later Billy was still coughing up blood.

Despite it all, Billy did a remarkable job in 1985, losing to Toronto by but two games. Under Billy the Yankees were 91–54, with a pitching staff that consisted of Ron Guidry, Phil Niekro, Dave Righetti, and a bunch of pitchers scarred by their Yankee experience.

All season long Billy tried to do what George had wanted him to do, but George was the sort of person who was never satisfied, and by the end of the season Billy was looking for a confrontation. Only the entreaties of Eddie Sapir kept Billy from being fired in mid-September.

Remembered Ed Sapir: "In 1985 the Yankees were fourteen games behind Toronto when George told Billy, 'I'll be happy if we can finish a respectable second.' Billy said, 'We're not out of this thing. I ain't trying to finish second. I want to win this son of a bitch.'

"And every day the lead dwindled, and Butch Wynegar hit a big home run to keep them alive until the final two series at the end of the season.

"The Yankees were playing Toronto in the second-to-last series for the division title at Yankee Stadium.

"George had discussed with Billy his doing what amounted to scientific research on the Blue Jays so all the bases would be covered before the start of the series. George wanted the Yankees to be better prepared and have more information. George asked Billy whether he should do it, and Billy told him, 'Do it.' Billy agreed to meet with George in his office the afternoon before the first game of the series.

"The meeting was called for two o'clock. George paid to have the meeting catered so Billy and the coaches could go over the material.

"George didn't attend. He purposely wanted to stay out of the way. At four o'clock George walked into the office where the meeting was supposed to take place, and not a single piece of paper or celery had been touched. It was obvious no one had been there.

"Billy and the coaches had stayed in Billy's office. Billy had taken the position, 'I ain't going up there.'

"George called me and explained it to me. He said, 'Eddie, I'll tell you right now, this is getting crazier by the moment. I think you need to call down to Billy and get him up here.'

"I talked to Billy. Billy said, 'I don't have to go up there and see all that shit. I have my coaches down here. We covered our game plan. We know what we're doing. We don't fucking need all that shit.'

"I said, 'Either explain that to George and tell him you're fully prepared and that you appreciate what he did or get your guys and go up and say, 'We're prepared. We'll look through this. I had wanted to have my meeting downstairs, and now we're happy to come up and see this information.'

"Stick Michael was saying, 'Billy, let's go up.' But Billy wasn't going up.

"George said, 'Eddie, I don't know what to say. I don't know what I'm going to do, but I'm really unhappy and justifiably so.'

"I called Billy, and I said, 'Billy, I'm going to tell you what I honestly believe. I believe you and your coaches should go up to George's office.'

"And Billy and the coaches did, but the entire time they were up there, Billy wouldn't look at George. He listened and went, but when he got there he wasn't there, if you know what I mean. As my associate Paul Tabarry would say, 'The light was on, but nobody was home.'

"That day Joe Cowley got ripped for three quick runs, and Toronto went on to win the division title."

Three weeks after the season ended, George Steinbrenner fired Billy as manager and hired Lou Piniella, as Eddie Sapir had predicted at the beginning of the season.

Steinbrenner fired Billy because of the Whitson fight, but he felt bad about it and so did Billy. Ed Sapir, Billy, and George met right away to plan for Billy's future.

George named Billy a member of the broadcasting staff in 1986. Billy didn't complain. He had two more years running on his personal services contract to George. The money was good, and he needed it.

It was another blow to his self-esteem, but that had been part of the bargain. George had control over his soul. Billy would just have to swallow a little harder. Finally, Billy was saying uncle. George Steinbrenner was his boss. George Steinbrenner was calling the shots. George now owned Billy, as he owned Hopalong Cassady.

According to Ed Sapir, "Billy Martin was a bottom-line guy, and he was looking for security. Billy loved to manage, but he wasn't going to manage Seattle for $125,000 or the White Sox for $125,000 when he was making a lot more with George and filling several important roles in the organization."

As a reward for capitulating, George paid Billy generously. He extended Billy's contract four years for a total of $1.4 million. In the contract Steinbrenner gave Billy an escape clause. He was free to go, no strings attached. But George was paying Billy so much money now, the likelihood of him ever leaving the Yankees was slim. Billy was making more than $300,000 a year to be George Steinbrenner's consultant, TV commentator, manager, scout, or gofer—whichever George preferred at the time.

Said Sapir, "What the public didn't know was after he got fired the third time, Billy and George and I talked about security for Billy, that he was going to stay with the Yankees in one capacity or another for the rest of his life, even if he got fired as manager. There was no question that Billy enjoyed managing the most, but let me tell you, what was best for Billy economically? When Billy was broadcasting or scouting or doing something else for George, he had a lot more time for endorsements and speaking engagements, and he could make a lot more money than when he was the manager.

"So after the third time he was fired, the writers kept referring to it as Billy III and Billy IV and Billy V, but in fact nothing much changed for Billy except the job he had to do for George.

"After he returned to the Yankees for the third time, his role would change, but never his salary. And every time his role changed, Billy got more and more years, which meant more money and more benefits.

"George genuinely liked Billy. George wanted Billy to be well taken care of, and he wanted Billy to have financial security. George told me, 'Look, Eddie, let's don't let our friend ever be in a position where he's got to worry about where the next dollar's gonna come from.'

"I said, 'George, what do you propose?'

"He said, 'I'm proposing that after this contract is up, he'll have a lifetime contract. I want him to have a very generous check every year from the Yankees.'

"George did that."

It was the last contract Ed Sapir negotiated for Billy before Jill Guiver, the other person vying for the control of Billy's soul, replaced the best financial adviser Billy ever had. Jill didn't know it, but Eddie had negotiated millions of dollars in contracts for his client and had never charged Billy a dime. But after Jill worked on Billy to leave Heather, she would create enough animosity to separate Billy from the rest of his friends, including Eddie Sapir. One day the only people left in Billy's life would be Jill, George Steinbrenner, and the one man keeping Billy from collapsing under the strain of being involved with the other two: Bill Reedy.

# BILLY'S DAY

In February George decided what Billy's new role would be in 1986. It was announced that Billy would join Phil Rizzuto and company as a Yankee broadcaster, doing pre- and postgame commentary.

Billy worked hard at his job, making certain not to appear to be second guessing manager Lou Piniella. Billy also stayed out of serious trouble, coming to work hung over more than George might have liked, but free from the pressures of managing, Billy was able to eat and sleep well. He put on weight, looked younger, and usually was in a jocular, happy mood.

Billy's driver, Tex Gernand, saw that behind the smiles was a longing to do the only thing Billy really wanted to do: manage.

"When Billy was announcing, it was great for his health," said Tex, "but he wasn't happy because he wanted to manage more than anything."

From the start of the 1986 season Eddie Sapir began campaigning to get Billy the one tribute Billy had always felt he deserved: a day of recognition. It was an honor long overdue. He had played on seven pennant-winning Yankee teams and had managed the Yankees to a pennant and a world championship. But Billy knew George would never give him a day unless he pushed for it. If he had to beg for his day, he would. Billy had Eddie Sapir talk George into giving him one.

"The idea initiated in Billy Martin's head," said Sapir. "It was something Billy always wanted. Billy asked me if I would pursue it with George when the timing was right, and when the timing *was* right, I got a commitment from George that it would be done, and he did it.

"It was big-time important to Billy. It was wonderful that George did this for Billy.

"If someone had said to Billy Martin, 'Billy, you're going to die and be buried in Yankee Stadium,' he would have smiled. Billy was so Yankees.

"Yankee Stadium was his home. If someone had been ingenious to build a plush residence for the manager in the stadium, Billy would have loved it. All you had to do was look at his driver's license. For address, it said 'Yankee Stadium, Bronx, New York.'

The day designated as Billy Martin Day was August 10, 1986. What the public saw was an outpouring of love and affection for Billy. Behind the scenes there was nothing but acrimony and hurt feelings. The person responsible was Jill Guiver, who had won in her war to wrest Billy away from his wife Heather. Billy appointed Jill to organize his day.

It was a mistake on Billy's part to give her control of the event. Once in control, Jill created hurt feelings among Billy's friends and family, as her actions drove them away.

One of the first to be offended by Jill was Lewis Figone, one of Billy's closest childhood friends. Lewis and Billy were members of a duck hunting club together. They were like brothers. They often hunted and fished, and they loved to play practical jokes on each other.

Figone was asked if their duck club would present something to Billy on his day.

Figone, a wealthy man who owned a garbage disposal firm, said, "No problem at all. It's done."

Figone called Billy and asked him what he wanted.

Billy told him, "I'd like a Ford pickup truck for Jill's horse trailer."

Figone agreed.

Said Figone, "As far as making a presentation at Yankee Stadium, I could care less. We said to him, 'We'll set it up and get it going, and when you come back here, you can pick it up.'

"I didn't talk to her about it. I gave the job to my brother, Clyde. I said, 'You talk to her. I don't want to talk to that bitch.'

"Jill wanted it shipped to Yankee Stadium. She told Clyde something to the effect, 'If we can't do it at Yankee Stadium, there's no point doing it.'

"I said to Clyde, 'Tell her to go to hell. When Billy comes back here, we'll tell him to go get the truck.'

"And that's the way it was left."

Lewis Figone called Eddie Sapir to tell him what the duck club members were proposing. When Sapir reiterated to Jill what they wanted to do, she became angry. Whatever she told Billy, it caused a rift between him and Figone.

Said Sapir, "I can hear the way Jill must have presented this to Billy, because Billy's response was, 'Fuck Figone.' "

It was the beginning of a split in a friendship that had gone back to the days before Billy had become a ballplayer. Jill then treated Figone's daughter Vicki shabbily, perhaps resenting Vicki's closeness to Heather.

As Vicki relates it, Jill was wary of Vicki because she and Heather were good friends. Also, Jill was extremely jealous of other women being in Billy's presence, much the way Billy felt about other men being with her.

"A girlfriend and I flew from San Francisco to New York to be with Billy on his day," said Vicki Figone. "I couldn't get ahold of Billy. When I called, Jill answered. She said, 'What do you want?' I said, 'I'm coming out to the party, and I'm going to bring a girlfriend with me.'

"She said, 'I know you're not bringing a girlfriend, that you're bringing Heather.' She said, 'I know what you're up to. You're going to ruin my party.'

"I had only met Jill once, at Trader Vic's. I said, 'I would never do that, Jill. I'm friends with Heather, but I would never bring Heather out to the party.'

"Then she said, 'I know why you're bringing that girl, to set her up with Billy.'

"I said, 'Come on, Jill. I'm not going to do that.'

"I ended up leaving a message with Jill for Billy to call me. Billy never called me back. So I brought the girl out there anyway

"There was no problem getting into the party, but when I got there Jill came up to me and starting saying things like, 'Vicki, we can be friends,' but I could tell she wasn't being sincere.

"I said, 'You know there's a problem here. I'm friends with Heather, and I don't want to get in the middle. You'll want to question me about Heather. I don't want to get in the middle. I'm not against you. You're Billy's girlfriend, so he obviously likes you, but Heather is my friend, too, and that's where it's at. If you want to give me a call someday and get together, that's fine. I'll meet you for lunch, but you have to understand, I don't want to discuss Billy or anything about Billy. It's just the way it's got to be.'

"I thought everything was fine. That was August 1986. After the party I headed back to school.

"In June 1987, one year later, I was coming back from Europe. I hadn't talked to Billy in a year.

"I called Dad and asked him to get ahold of Billy and tell him I was coming back from Europe. Dad said, 'Billy has a room for you to stay in.'

"Billy met me at the bar of the hotel that night.

"I said, 'Billy, how are you? I haven't seen you in a long time.'

"He said, 'I got some problems with you. You started this shit with Jill. You told her off at my party. How could you do this to me? I'm not very happy with you. You ruined her night because you told her off. As a matter of fact, if you don't apologize to her, I'm never going to speak to you again.'

"I said, 'What are you talking about, Billy?'

"He said, 'All that stuff you told her, that you were on Heather's side, that she was a bitch, all the stuff you said. I'm mad at you, Vicki. And the only reason I got you this room was so I could tell you off tonight.'

"I said, 'Billy, I never said a bad thing to Jill at that party. She is making this up.' I said, 'Billy, I would never do that. And if I was going to tell her off, it sure wouldn't be at a party for you. What she said is a complete lie.'

"He said, 'I've about had it. You're not a friend of mine.'

"I was devastated. I said, 'Billy, this is bullshit.'

"So we sat about three hours, and I tried to explain it, and I think I had him halfway believing that that was a lie. And then we discussed Heather.

" 'How could you still be friends with Heather after she cheated on me?'

"I said, 'Billy, Heather never cheated on you. You cheated on Heather for years. And even if she did cheat on you, big deal.'

"By the end of the night, he said, 'Maybe we can work things out, that you and Jill can be friends.'

"I said, 'Yeah, maybe.'

"That was in July 1987. I went back to Pepperdine College. I didn't talk to him again until November. It was snowing at Tahoe, and I heard Billy was around town. He wasn't managing at that time.

"I thought to myself, I heard Jill likes to ski. I'll try to make everything right and invite her to ski with me. I thought that maybe after the talk at the bar, that Billy had smoothed things out.

"I called up the house, and Jill picked up the phone.

"I said, 'Jill, this is Vicki. Is Billy there?'

"She said, 'You fucking bitch, don't you ever call this house again. You call him at the ballpark like all his other unimportant friends.'

"And she hung up the phone.

"I couldn't believe it. I called my dad. That's when he got mad and didn't call him anymore.

"I didn't talk to Billy again until the birthday before he died. I loved Billy so much I just wanted to get along with whoever he was going out with.

"I called him up to wish him a happy birthday, and he started wimping on the phone. I said, 'I can't have anything to do with you while Jill is in the picture because all she does is tell lies about me.' "

Before Billy's Day would end, Jill would alienate Billy's family members as well.

Pat Irvine, Billy's sister, couldn't understand why Jill treated her, her siblings, and her mother as curtly and rudely as she did.

Recalled Pat, "When we went to New York, Billy said, 'I want you to pick a Broadway show. I'll send a car. They'll take you to dinner and you can go to the show.'

"I said, 'I don't know what is playing there. Why don't you pick one for me?'

"Billy said, 'I'd rather have you pick it, and then the family will go.' I agreed. I spoke to Jill, and I asked her to send me a list or tell me what was playing so I could ask the family which one we wanted to go to.

"She said, 'Absolutely not. You and your family are *not* going to any show.' I said, 'We didn't ask to go. Billy said he wanted to send us to a show and take us to dinner.'

"She said, 'Well, you don't have time for that.'

"I said, 'This is Billy's say, not yours. It's his money and not yours.' But we did *not* go out to dinner, and we did *not* go to the show.

"The night we were there, they had a special party for Billy, and we didn't know that. The family was not invited. Jill made sure none of us went, and a couple of his friends, like Frank Straface from Blackhawk, they didn't go either. A lot of them thought that was a pretty rotten thing to do. We didn't find out about the party until the next day.

"This was our first time in New York, and we sat in the hotel room like a bunch of duds, so finally we hired our own van, and everyone pitched in the money, and the cabdriver was the one who took us all over and showed us New York.

"We went to the ballpark, and that was quite a day, seeing the ballpark. I had never seen Yankee Stadium before that day.

"My mother had fallen and broken her hip, and she was in a wheelchair. She made that effort to go. She should have flown in first class, where she would have had more room. Jill would not allow that. And she wouldn't let Billy Joe go first class either.

"My sister-in-law Betty, [Frank] Tudo's wife, does not fly period, so they were going to go ahead of time on the train, and Billy said that was fine, but Jill stopped it. She would not allow them to go on the train. She said it was too much money for them to go on the train, and if they did not want to go on the airplane, then she could stay home. And that's exactly what Betty did. So Tudo came with us, but she didn't come.

"Constantly Jill would tell us, 'Billy does not have any money.' I said, 'How could you say he doesn't have any money when he's making all kinds of good money from the Yankees? Where does the money go?' She said, 'You don't know, Patsy. He's broke.' I said, 'He has to be spending it on somebody.' I didn't accuse Jill to her face of taking it all. I said, 'He can't be broke, but that's not my business anyhow.'

"Jill said to us, 'We have all kinds of surprises for you when you get here.' We did get a surprise. We got *nothing*—except a ball with his name he signed. We didn't even go see the apartment in the Regency where they lived. We weren't even allowed to see his own home.

"I told her, 'My mother would like to see where he lives.' Jill told me, 'You know, you're not the only ones here. He has a lot of friends, and we do not have the time to be taking you all over the place.'

"Whatever Billy wanted to do for us, she stopped it. And she gave us orders what to wear at the ballpark, what to wear for dinner, like she was talking to little kids.

"I told her, 'You know, Jill, I'm old enough to be your mother. You don't tell me what to do. That is not very polite. My daughters are older than you are.'

"She said, 'I just want to tell everybody what to wear.'

"I said, 'We know how to dress. You're not talking to a bunch of hicks.' But her own sister Merry, she was dressed the complete opposite of everybody else. She looked like a slob. I didn't realize it, but I think she did it deliberately, to show Jill she wasn't going to tell her what to do either."

Bill Reedy and Art Fowler knew Jill better than the others. Reedy never liked her but never made an issue of it with Billy. If that's who Billy wanted to be with, so be it. But Reedy made it a practice to disappear as soon as he saw Jill coming. Art Fowler did likewise.

The night before the ceremony Bill Reedy and Art Fowler stayed up most of the night drinking. The morning of the game a bus had been hired to take everyone to the stadium.

Art Fowler called Bill Reedy. "Are you going out to the fucking ballpark?"

Reedy said, "I don't know. I don't think so. I'll see you downstairs."

Twenty minutes later Reedy met Fowler in the coffee shop. Fowler said, "I'm hungrier than a motherfucker. Let's go across the street and see if we can get a drink." It was eleven-thirty in the morning.

Art said, "I know the guy who owns the place." Art had lived in the Sheraton when he was Billy's pitching coach. They went across the highway for a beer.

Art said, "Do you want to go to the game?" Reedy asked whether the ceremony was going to be on television. Art said yes.

"We're going to sit right here, buddy," Reedy said.

They watched everything on television, had a great time, and waited for Billy to return.

The ceremony on the field went off without a hitch. With his mom sitting next to him in a wheelchair, Billy was presented with a raft of expensive gifts as a packed Yankee Stadium crowd cheered.

When Billy was presented with a pin that had "Number 1" in diamonds, he looked at it, then hesitated.

He walked over to his mother and said, "Here, Ma, this is for you." She took it in her hand and looked at it and saw the "Number 1" in diamonds.

She said, "Thank you, Billy," and she held it tight.

Most important to Billy, his uniform with the hallowed number 1 on the back was being retired along with other famous numbers in Yankee history including 3, 4, 5, 7, 8, 16, and 37. He was joining the Babe, Lou, DiMag, Mick, Yogi, Bill Dickey, Whitey, and Casey in the pantheon of Yankee gods.

The one damper on the afternoon had to do with Jill.

Remembered Eddie Sapir, "She was all dressed up and ready to be introduced as the fiancée, out there with all the hoopla. At the last minute Billy said, 'Tell her no, that only the family is going to go out there.'

"Billy made up a story that George didn't want her there—when it was *he* who didn't want her there.

"That was one reason she came to hate George. [Billy] created this hate between Jill and George. It was based on a lie that Billy told.

"And when Billy didn't let Jill go out on the field on Billy Martin Day and blamed it on George Steinbrenner, that caused problems both for me and for George.

"She had no love for me or Paul Tabarry, because we were doing what Billy wanted us to do, which wasn't always what she wanted us to do, and she certainly had no love for Steinbrenner, because Billy told her George had kept her from going out onto the field.

"So later on, after they became husband and wife, I would tell her, 'Believe me, George is an honest guy. George really likes Billy, and it's all in good faith,' and she had to be in the background saying to herself, 'That fucking Steinbrenner wouldn't let me go out onto that field with my man.' "

Tables were set up for Billy and five hundred of his friends at the Hasbrouck Heights Sheraton after the ceremony and the game. Mickey Mantle and Whitey Ford were on hand, as was Billy's mother, who sang two songs, "O Solo Mio" and "My Man," for Billy.

After the banquet everyone returned to their rooms. Billy's mom and sister Pat were in their hotel room when the phone rang. It was Jill.

She said, "Patsy, I'm sending someone over to pick up the pin."

Pat knew what she was talking about, but she said, "Which pin is that?"

Jill said, "That Number 1 diamond pin. The players gave it to Billy, and he wants it."

Pat said, "Jill, he gave that to Ma on the field."

Jill said, "No, he didn't. He just told her to hold on to it. Billy wants his pin."

Pat said, "I'll tell you what, Jill. You send Billy over and let him ask Ma, and she'll give it to him if he wants it."

Jill said, "You tell her if she gives up the pin, I will give her a stuffed Yankee doll."

Pat said, "Are you kidding? Don't be silly."

Jill then began screaming at Pat, who hung up on her.

Billy's mother asked, "What did she want?"

"One guess, Ma."

Jenny said, "She's not getting it, the bitch."

Said Pat Irvine, "Jill must have called every half hour to get that pin, and I kept telling her, 'If Billy wants the pin, send him over and ask me, and she'll give it to him.'

"But by the end of the evening, I finally said, 'Ma, the pin is not that important. Give it back to him.'

"Ma said, 'He doesn't want that pin. She does.'

"Ma was so disgusted. A guy came over from the ballpark, and Ma gave him the pin to give back to Jill.

"Sometime afterward, when my sister, Joan, saw Jill, she told her, 'Don't you dare ever wear that pin in this house. And if you're wearing it, tuck it away so Mother can't see it.'

"Don't you know she came over wearing the thing! Just out of spite. She is such a spiteful person.

"I am sorry now I ever talked Ma into giving it back, but we didn't want any problems, didn't want any trouble.

"You know, all Billy had to do was get one made for her and send it. It didn't have to be real diamonds. Just fix something up for her. But no, he couldn't put himself out to do that. He had his head so full of [Jill], he didn't have time for anybody else."

\* \* \*

In the fall of 1986 Billy took steps to evict Heather from his home at Blackhawk. Heather sued to try to stop him. In the suit she named Jill Guiver as Billy's paramour.

Heather never wanted much from Billy. Not long after Billy left and never returned, she had found a new man in her life, and though she could have gotten an extra $20,000 in alimony had she waited a few more months to remarry, she chose not to.

She divorced Billy, treating him more generously than he deserved. When she moved out of the Blackhawk home, in order not to lose it back to the A's, Billy had to install another family member. Billy wanted his daughter, Kelly, and his granddaughter, Evie, to move in. Instead, he installed Jill's younger sister, Hope, whom Billy helped send through college.

For Kelly Martin it was the beginning of a bitterness that will color her feelings about her father for the rest of her life.

Said Kelly, "All my life I fought for him just to spend time with me and Evie, and when Billy became the manager of Oakland, I really thought he was going to. But then Jill took him away to New York, and when he said my daughter, Evie, and I were going to move into Blackhawk, I thought, Oh good, it's gonna be great because we'll be able to have you guys out all the time.

"Well, we didn't move into that house. [Jill's] sister Hope moved into that house."

According to Bill Reedy, Billy apparently had an ulterior motive for moving Hope Guiver into his house: sex.

Said Bill Reedy, "Billy made a big deal that if Hope would stay in their Blackhawk home and house-sit, Billy would pay for her college education.

"Shortly after Billy married Jill, I flew to San Francisco to meet Billy. I waited about an hour for Billy to show up, and when he finally arrived, I asked him where he had been.

"In Newport Beach," Billy said.

Billy told Reedy his goal was to have sex with Hope.

"What the hell," Billy told him, "it's all in the family."

Said Kelly Martin, "My dad wanted *us* to stay in the house at Blackhawk. But no, no, Jill wanted Hope out there so Hope could go to college. And my dad wanted Hope. . . .

"I said to him, 'That's your girlfriend's little sister.'

"He said, 'I'm going to get in line.'

"I said, 'I figured you would. Go for it, Dad.'

Kelly thought her father was also after Jill's older sister, Merry.

Even the most disapproving observer might find humor in the scenario of Billy trying to bed the three Guiver sisters even as he was planning to marry Jill.

# A GREAT GIRL

**B**illy enjoyed a second carefree baseball season in 1987. He waited in the wings while George Steinbrenner spent the last few months of 1986 and the entire 1987 season complaining about the inexperience of manager Lou Piniella.

As for his social life, Billy continued his nightly drinking binges, and the arguing and fighting between him and Jill continued unabated.

Bill Reedy visited Billy in Ft. Lauderdale during spring training in 1987. During one violent argument that took place at the Royce Hotel the door to their room was kicked into splinters.

When she got back into the room, she broke the heads off all Billy's golf clubs, after which he threw them at her like spears.

Later that spring training Bill Reedy and his wife's brother, Matt, went to the ballpark for a Yankees night game. Billy wasn't there. Reedy knew he was staying at the Royce Hotel, so they headed there. They went to their rooms, showered and shaved, and then rode the elevator down to the hotel bar to wait for Billy.

The elevator opened. Jill stood there, fire in her eyes. She told him, "Your friend's across the street, and he's ridiculously drunk." As Reedy and Matt got off the elevator Jill got in and and headed back upstairs.

Reedy and Matt went across the street to find Billy. Reedy had never seen his friend falling-down drunk, but after Jill's description he didn't know what he would find.

Reedy found Billy sitting placidly in his usual spot at the end of the bar. He was by himself. To Reedy, Martin seemed his usual cheery self.

"Hey," said Billy, his face lighting up. Reedy mentioned he had run into Jill.

"Fuck her," Billy said. "It's the same old bullshit, ragging my ass. She wants to run this, wants to run that. Wants to know everything. She's even taped our phone calls. And I caught her."

During the 1987 season, when Billy traveled with the Yankees, he stopped taking Jill on the road. Heather was gone, and Jill was now his steady, and his steady didn't go on the road.

In 1987 Billy spent a lot of time with Bill Reedy away from Jill. The two men had started a ham company as a side venture, and when Billy came to Detroit, he would visit the Reedys. Sometimes Bill Reedy would fly off and meet Billy in another town.

While Billy was with Reedy, Jill would call Carol Reedy from New York and try to pump her for information about what the two men were up to. Jill knew more about Billy than some of his other women did. Jill had been Billy's mistress when he was married to Heather; she knew how secretive Billy could be, and Jill was doing all she could do to find out who Billy was seeing behind *her* back.

One time during a trip, when Billy and Bill Reedy were off by themselves somewhere, Jill called Carol.

"Did you know I tried to call Billy and there was no answer?" Jill asked. "I know they had women in the room. You know they did, Carol."

"Okay, so they did," answered Carol, who didn't know any such thing. Carol did know one thing. When she left the message, "Tell Mr. Reedy to call Mrs. Reedy at his leisure," she always got a return call. But Bill and Carol had a relationship. Billy and Jill had a sexual war.

After periods of fierce fighting between Billy and Jill, when Billy was away Jill would call him hundreds of times. She would be frantic. The line would be busy because Billy would take the phone off the hook, or it would ring because Billy would pull the phone plug from the wall. Or Billy would leave word he was accepting no calls, not from anybody, *especially* his wife.

The harder Jill tried to keep tabs on Billy, the harder he fought for his privacy. It was a constant tug-of-war.

On certain occasions Billy took Jill along. A pivotal event in the lives of Billy and Jill occurred in September 1987, when Billy, Mickey Mantle, and Whitey Ford all were hired by the Elkay Truck Leasing Company to be the guest speakers at the company's thirtieth anniversary luncheon.

After the luncheon, which took place in Binghamton, New York, the company president, Michael Klepfer, sat with the three former Yankee stars and listened to them talk about the old times.

At the luncheon Billy introduced his fiancée, Jill Guiver, who sat with Klepfer's wife, Katie, and Mantle's agent, Greer Johnson. At the luncheon Jill, Greer, and Katie talked about their shared love of horses. Katie informed Jill that they had a horse farm at their Binghamton home.

Afterward the burly Michael Klepfer, a former state trooper who was now a wealthy trucking magnate, drove Billy and Jill to the airport. It was the beginning of a friendship that would change the lives of Billy and Jill Martin dramatically.

On October 19, 1987, George Steinbrenner finally got rid of Lou Piniella, citing his lack of experience. Piniella wasn't fired, as expected, but he was promoted to general manager, a job at which he had absolutely zero experience. Billy was named manager of the Yankees for the fifth time.

All through the summer and fall of 1987, Billy talked of marrying Jill. He would ask all his friends, "Should I marry her?" Not a single friend thought he should, but they saw he was addicted to her. They were afraid that if they said, "Don't do it," and he went ahead and did it anyway—as most thought he would—then their relationship with him would be strained.

Bill Reedy, who disliked Jill tremendously, told Billy, "If you want to marry her, marry her." Commented Reedy, "I was afraid to say anything." Besides, Reedy knew, she had her eyes on Billy, and he suspected she was not the type of person to allow her quarry to get away.

Bill Reedy was with Billy in November 1987 when Billy was supposed to join Mickey and Greer for a weekend at the home of Mike Klepfer, but Billy came down with shingles and was in too much pain to make the trip.

During the same period Billy had been invited to a banquet in Rochester for veteran umpire Ken Kaiser. Billy told Reedy he intended to go despite the shingles, which pained him. Jill was worried.

She called and said to Reedy, "Will you talk to him? Tell him not to go because the doctor said he can become blind from it." She added, "And I have too much invested in him."

Her investment finally paid off when, on December 9, 1987, Billy announced to the press he was going to marry Jill Guiver on January 24, 1988.

"I'll be married, and I'll be staying home more. I'll still get mad, but having somewhere to go after the game should help me healthwise."

Billy told reporters, "I met her seven years ago when she took my picture at the ballpark in Anaheim.

"She's a great girl."

# THE WEDDING

The wedding of Billy Martin, age sixty, to Jill Guiver, age thirty-one, took place on January 24, 1988, under a large white tent on the manicured lawn of the Blackhawk Country Club in Danville, California, about a forty-five-minute car ride from San Francisco. To the hundreds of guests in attendance it looked like any other wedding, with bridesmaids and flowers and a wedding cake and a minister.

Behind the facade of joyous expectation lay a submerged feeling of dread experienced by Billy's relatives and closest friends, none of whom wanted him to go through with it.

Jill had been with Billy for seven years now. Billy's friends considered her manipulative, controlling, jealous, vengeful, spiteful, antagonistic to him much of the time, and she spent his money lavishly on herself. The whole time they wondered when he'd give her up. They felt about her the same way they felt about Steinbrenner. Secretly they wished Billy would dump her—a wish on their lips even as the couple walked down the aisle.

A few days before the wedding date, Jill had hosted a weekend for her friends. Most were high school classmates, and equestrians from Southern California. Jill had taken Katie Klepfer, Greer Johnson, and a few other horsewomen out to where her thoroughbred horse, Lucky, was training. She was having problems with it. It had been struck with a disease.

Others in attendance were Bernadette Ross, the wife of radio commentator

Spencer Ross; Greer Johnson, Mickey Mantle's agent and girlfriend at the time; Carol Reedy; and Katie Klepfer. The dinner was sedate and relaxed, far different from Billy's stag party.

Among Billy's male friends who came were Bill Reedy; Mickey Mantle; commentator and former football coach John Madden; Howard Wong; Mickey Morabito; Clete Boyer; a bearded Bill White, the National League president; and trucking magnate Mike Klepfer. Art Fowler wasn't there. He disliked Jill so much he had refused to come to the wedding.

The bachelor party didn't appear to be much different from any other bachelor party. There was a lot of heavy drinking, some pool playing, and much joking and kidding. And of course, on hand was the usual stripper. It was the tone of the party that made it different. Drinking, especially by Billy and Mickey, was unusually heavy, and talk of sex was in the air.

Billy's friends had hired a hoochie-coochie girl who danced around Billy, rubbing herself suggestively against him.

Billy was well in the bag, and before the evening was out, Billy was in his underdrawers leading the woman to a back room. He later returned to the pool table with a big grin.

"Ain't half as good as Jill," Billy told all his friends, some of whom were embarrassed that he could talk so crassly about a woman he was about to marry.

Out of Billy's earshot some of the men were talking about former players with whom Jill had had relationships. Reggie Jackson's name came up. A scout for the Yankees who worked on the West Coast named the A's players she had dated. A former Athletic close to Billy also recalled her involvement with ballplayers before Billy. Mickey Morabito, the A's traveling secretary who was very close to Billy, said, "Jesus Christ, I feel funny. I dated her before Billy, and I'm going to be in the wedding."

There was also a discussion whether, with Billy's famous temper, this marriage, his fourth, would last. They expressed concern that he was marrying this woman, that he "didn't know what he was getting into," that she had set her hooks for Billy and was "landing a big one."

They began talking about organizing a hundred-dollar-a-guess betting pool on how long the marriage would last. Billy even wanted in. He joked, "Give me a hundred."

Mike Klepfer hadn't fully understood why he had been invited, but coincidentally another couple from Binghamton had wanted to visit Las Vegas, so he and Katie decided they would attend the wedding, sightsee in San Francisco, and then continue to Vegas to meet their friends.

Klepfer was new to the jock scene. He was astounded by the predominance of talk about women and sex. What stood out in Klepfer's memory was how often Billy was asked one question: "Why are you getting married?" It was a mystery that no one, including Mickey Mantle, could figure out.

Mickey, who had shared in many of Billy's sexual adventures as a player, drunkenly suggested that perhaps it was a very specific sexual act that Jill did for him that Billy enjoyed.

Thought Klepfer, That's a pretty shallow reason to get married.

Billy's daughter, Kelly, asked Billy over and over why he was marrying Jill.

Said Kelly, "He told me, 'I might as well marry her, 'cause she's not going to go away.' Billy didn't want to be alone. And I kept telling him, 'Dad, why don't you move in with me and Evie? We would love to have you live with us.' And I think he was afraid because he really didn't want us to know how much he drank. But that wouldn't have made any difference to me. I loved him. I didn't care if he drank.''

Billy's sister Pat had a different answer. Said Pat, "Billy's problem was that he was woman-crazy, and usually the wrong kind. One time, years ago, when we could actually sit and talk, I said, 'Why do you pick this type of women? They are nothing but bums. All they are interested in is your money and what you can buy them. Instead of taking them to a show or a fancy dinner, why don't you take them for a hot dog or a hamburger and see how many times they'll date you?'

"He said, 'I pick out this kind of girl because I can't hurt them. If I take out a nice girl, I'll hurt her. How are you going to hurt these women?'

"I said, 'I never really thought of that.'

"Everything he ever pulled on women he got back ten times with this last one. They would argue and fight. Up until the time he married her, all of us were praying, 'Dear Lord, let him find someone else and let's stop the marriage.'

"Up to the last minute when they walked up the aisle, before the ceremony, we were hoping he'd find somebody else and all of a sudden the wedding would be off.

"But Billy had a crazy sense of obligation. If he was going to live with them or be with them, he should marry them, do right by them. Billy really tried to do right by his women, set them up, help their families—and then he'd leave them.''

The highlight of the stag party was a presentation made to Billy of the smashed-in door to his room at the Royce Hotel in Ft. Lauderdale. The manager, a friend of Billy's, had sent it as a wedding present.

Jill, who loved the trappings of wealth, had arranged the wedding. She had a Rolls-Royce bring her and her bridesmaids the quarter-mile from their house to the country club. She hired six parking valets wearing glitzy ersatz Yankee uniforms. A big white tent encased the event. Under the tent was an ice statue of a castle, and on the buffet tables was a feast. Video cameras recorded it all.

The problem was that Billy had wanted a small ceremony. When he had married Heather, the Sapirs had been witnesses in front of a justice of the peace. That was Billy's style. This wedding would cost tens of thousands of Billy's dollars, and he was very unhappy about it. Billy complained bitterly about the lavishness and the cost. He told his sister Pat that if he had had his way, he would have gone to the justice of the peace.

It bothered him that it was more important for Jill to show off with fancy cars and a big display of ostentation than to abide by his wishes. He was upset that she had gotten her way with him. With Jill, Billy rarely got his way. She had a power over him that no one could understand or break. She had wanted a big wedding, and though Billy's relatives grumbled about the cost of having to rent tuxedos and gowns, she didn't care. This was *her* wedding.

Behind a facade of smiles, Billy was in turmoil the entire weekend.

Billy's friends, instead of feeling happy for Billy, felt sorry for him, adding a pervading gallows atmosphere to the occasion that contributed to their heavy drinking.

Mickey Mantle, for one, drank even more than his usual, which was plenty. Just before the ceremony began, Mantle and Mike Klepfer were at the back of the tent talking and drinking wine. Klepfer was holding him up, along with Bill Reedy. Various other friends were there, too.

The subject of the betting pool came up once again. The men first began to discuss making bets based on the number of weeks Billy and Jill stayed married. They then decided they didn't want to be unfair to Billy, so they redesigned the pool on the basis of how many months.

Mickey Mantle drew six months.

Said Mantle, "Bullshit. It ain't gonna last six months." All of Billy's friends started to laugh.

As the merriment filled the tent, the organist began playing "The Wedding March," and the procession began. Mike Klepfer headed for his seat, near Bill White.

"Mike?" asked White. "What the hell's going on back there?"

"You aren't ever going to believe this," said Klepfer, who told him about the marriage pool.

Jill came down the aisle, accompanied by her father. At the altar the bridesmaids and bridegrooms all stood around her. A nattily dressed Billy came down the aisle, followed by best man Mantle, who stumbled and lurched most of the way.

The minister intoned, "Today is a milestone. You will mark a lot of things from today. You're going to find that certain parts of your past will sort of fade away and forever be past. You're going to find parts of your future you will be saying to yourself, It's not what I want, but what do *we* want. It's not what's going to be good for me, but what's going to be good for *us*. Also, a joining of families is taking place today. You bring everybody in your lives to each other. Now many more people are going to enrich your lives, and hopefully, the other way around, many other lives that you're going to strengthen and enrich.

"You've come to a place where you trust what your partner is saying to you, where each can believe it and trust in the other, and that's what's really neat.

"Marriage is hard work, but you try to make it fun."

Billy's friends made wry faces at these empty words. They suspected that this was a marriage to test Billy to his fullest.

One irony would be that in this relationship neither Billy nor Jill ever considered each other's needs or trusted each other for a moment. Another was that after this day, when the "joining of families" was taking place, the two families would never speak to each other again.

The minister then suggested that each praise the other every once in a while, not take each other for granted, and to say "I'm sorry" every once in a while.

He talked about the ups and downs of life. He said, "One of the things you'll be saying when you give your vows is 'Here I am. I give myself to you. I hope I'm going to be good for you. I know we're going to be good for each other.' "

He extended them prayers and good wishes for the future and asked them to exchange wedding vows.

"First, Billy Martin, do you take Jill Guiver, here present, to be your lawful wife?"

Billy: "I do."

"And Jill Guiver, do you take Billy Martin, here present, to be your lawful husband?"

Jill: "I do."

They pledged to make each other happy, to live in harmony and peace so their lives could become one, and to be loyal to each other with all their being.

They exchanged rings.

The minister said, "For anyone who wears a wedding ring, for you the wedding ring has a special meaning. No one knows how good it is, but you do. For a woman, to be loved, devotion. For a man, fidelity. So right now you're not sure what meaning that ring will take on although they do have one meaning right now. You give these rings to each other with a real meaning of pride in your partner and a sense of joy in what you are doing.

"Billy, will you give this ring to Jill?"

Mickey Mantle, whose job it was to try to get the ring on Jill's finger, had been wobbling unsteadily during the entire ceremony. With his duty before him, he grabbed her hand and tried to slip on the ring. But Mickey was so drunk he couldn't do it and had to be helped.

The minister then read a short poem, about friendship in everyday life. The words held hope for happiness for their future. Billy's friends weren't even listening. The words fell on deaf ears. They knew that for Billy and Jill all of it would be meaningless.

Part of the problem was that happiness was something foreign to Billy Martin. Even when he was winning a World Series he didn't feel happiness. And Jill Martin, Billy's friends were sure, would bring him days of nothing but trouble, pain, and sorrow.

The minister read an ancient blessing, "Strong in death and love, relentless as a blazing fire, as the ocean, deep waters cannot quench love, nor floods sweep it away."

After explaining its meaning, he sent them off to "venture into the days of your togetherness."

Just before the end, as the minister was saying the line "to have and to hold from this day forth," Merry Guiver, Jill's older sister, loudly commented, "Yeah, if you can believe that."

There were rumors before Billy's wedding that Billy had been very interested in Merry, a glamorous, statuesque woman with long blonde hair. She was just the type to draw Billy's attention. The whispers were that when Billy made it clear he was going to marry Jill, Merry harbored a hatred for both Billy and Jill.

Billy had told Merry he didn't want her in attendance, but she came anyway, wearing a man-cut tuxedo with pants.

Pat Irvine had already witnessed Merry's anger the day before when she heard Merry tell Billy, "Jill is only marrying you for your money."

The rumors of a prior relationship between Billy and Merry Guiver were rekindled when Merry made her very hostile comment during the ceremony.

Ignoring her, the minister pronounced Billy and Jill husband and wife.

Everyone applauded, but there was no great joy expressed, except by Jill's girlfriends, who were treating her like a queen and acting like schoolgirls.

Immediately after the ceremony Billy and Jill were standing under the tent. There was canvas on the floor, so it wasn't level. A waiter carrying champagne lost his footing, a couple glasses broke, and some champagne spilled on Jill.

She hissed, "You stupid son of a bitch." The guests noticed.

Said Bill Reedy, "While they were walking off the altar, Billy said, 'I suppose the champagne and this shit was your idea, you cocksucker.' They weren't married fifteen minutes.

Mickey Mantle, who overheard, said, "Keep it going. I had an hour in the pool."

Billy and Mickey then began telling war stories. Carol Reedy was standing with her husband, Bill; Billy; and Mickey.

"They were having a good time," said Carol Reedy. "Mickey started talking about these women that Billy and him were with, and what they did with them, describing how they would have sex with more than one girl at one time, climbing in and out of windows, that kind of thing. It was a real sport for those two. Greer and Jill and I were right there listening to this. I ran away. I didn't want to hear any more."

Mickey headed for the buffet, and within five minutes he was lying on the dance floor. He had to be helped back to Billy's house.

Despite the minister's hopes that the two families would become friendly, Jill's seating arrangement made all of Billy's relatives furious. It was like she was slapping them in the face.

Jill had placed her family with the wedding party on one whole side of the buffet room. Billy's small family contingent was relegated to the opposite side of the dance floor in a corner, with Bill White and his wife. Family members noticed that Billy never even came over to say hello to his mother.

Said Pat Irvine's husband, Ken, "Nobody from Billy's family was in the wedding party at all. They didn't put Billy's mother or stepfather into the family pictures. Her mother and sisters were in the pictures. Not Billy and Pat's mother.''

According to Ken, Billy's mom got even by stealing the spotlight. Jenny, who was eighty-five years old, was a good-time gal. At the gathering at Billy's home after the wedding, Billy's mom was the hit of the party.

Jill hadn't wanted friends and family coming back to their house, but Billy insisted. This time Billy got his way. When Jill saw that the guests weren't going to leave quickly, she hissed something at Billy.

''You love your damn horses more than me,'' Billy told her. Jill ran upstairs in a huff.

Pat Irvine was upstairs when she saw Jill come running up to her room. Jill started throwing off her wedding dress. She was furious.

Pat asked, ''What's the matter?''

Jill said, ''We're supposed to leave for Hawaii tomorrow, and I didn't want all these people over here.''

Pat said, ''So what did you ask everyone to come over for?''

She said, ''He had no business inviting anybody over here. I didn't want anybody over here.''

Pat said, ''If you didn't want anybody over here, why did you hire caterers and why are there people fixing drinks?''

Said Pat, ''It turned out that Billy wanted them to come and she didn't.''

While Jill stewed by herself upstairs, Jenny Pisani Martin Downey entertained Billy's guests by singing. Her song was ''My Man,'' and she sang it as the gathering listened attentively.

When Jill finally came back downstairs, an upset Billy said to Jill snidely, ''Well, you got what you want,'' meaning marriage.

Pat, who was standing nearby, looked at Billy quizzically.

Billy looked at Pat and said sheepishly, ''She wanted it, and she got what she wanted.''

When Merry Guiver arrived at the house with her mother, Billy threw her out, shouting, ''I want her out of here.''

''It was obvious Billy and Jill were upset,'' said Ken Irvine, ''but for public consumption they put on a show. Billy made a little speech about his wife and how happy they were going to be, but after most of the guests left, you could see them growing farther and farther apart.''

As Billy's relatives were getting ready to leave, Billy came over to talk to Pat.

''I want to tell you something, Patsy,'' Billy said. ''I'm going to be retiring in a few years. When I retire, I'm going to come home to Blackhawk, and I'm going to stay, because I love it here.

''Give me some time to settle down and get myself together. Then we will be a family. You'll be up here for barbecues. You guys can swim anytime you want.''

He said, ''We will be a family again. I promise we'll all be together again like we used to. Just give me some time.''

Pat, who dearly loved her brother even if she didn't understand him, said, "Billy, take all the time you want."

The night of the wedding Billy and Jill fought so fiercely that they decided to cancel their honeymoon. All night long they fought, keeping Mickey Mantle and Greer Johnson awake with sounds of banging and crashing and shouting and cursing.

In the morning they changed their minds and decided to go. After three days together in Hawaii, they cut the honeymoon short and returned home to New York.

It would not be too long afterward when Billy's sister Pat learned that Billy was going to move from New York City to a farm in Binghamton, New York. When his other sister, Joan, heard that, she told him, "Billy, don't do that. You'll never come back."

He said, "Oh, yes, I will, Patsy."

"No, you won't. Once she gets you there . . ." she warned. "Don't give up your home at Blackhawk, when you love it so."

Billy assured her he would never do that.

# THE LAST
# GO-ROUND

**T**he Yankees didn't win a pennant again in 1987. The fans weren't surprised, nor were the players. As long as George Steinbrenner ran the Yankees, he worked as a powerful hidden opponent against his managers and players. With George's ego the constant, there could be no stability, so at the end of the season, when George removed Lou Piniella as manager and made him general manager and hired Billy again, there was no great feeling of hope. The fans and the players knew that Billy could raise the level of play, but no matter what Billy did, George would find a way to sabotage his efforts and keep the team from winning.

In 1988, after two years of being away, Billy was healthy and optimistic. He had Art Fowler back as his pitching coach, and he felt sure his players could win it all.

But this time not only would Billy have George Steinbrenner to oversee his every move, he also had his new wife, Jill.

The Reedys visited Billy and Jill in Ft. Lauderdale in the third week of February 1988.

They were booked at one of the two Embassy Suites hotels in Fort Lauderdale, where the Yankee team was staying. Billy, Art Fowler, third-base coach Clete Boyer, and Bill Reedy decided to go to the other hotel to drink. The game had ended at around eleven-thirty at night, and the men hit the bar about an hour later.

The phone rang in the bar. It was for Billy. Jill was on the other end of the line checking up on him. Billy ordered the barmaid, "Hang up on this mother." Billy then went over to the telephone, pulled it off the wall, and heaved it across the room.

An hour later, around one-thirty in the morning, the group had to leave because the hotel bar was closing.

Clete Boyer, who had once owned a country-and-western bar in Atlanta, knew of a similar bar that was open in Ft. Lauderdale. Clete and Art went in one car, and Billy and Bill Reedy went in the other.

The bar was a big place, noisy, with couples dancing and a lot of beer being drunk by men wearing cowboy hats.

They ordered a beer at the stand-up bar. A girl came over and asked Billy to dance. Billy put his beer down and went to the dance floor, and as he started back off the floor, one of the patrons, a large man about thirty years old, reached out and jerked Billy and said, "You're dancing with my girlfriend."

Billy, still in a foul mood because of Jill, was ready for action, but Bill Reedy, Art, and Clete moved in quickly to stop any fight. A bouncer, a big good ol' boy, came over.

The patron was angry and asked Billy if he wanted to go outside. Before Billy could answer, Reedy replied, "No, we don't want to go outside."

The bouncer told Billy, "Don't worry about it," and bought the group a drink.

The confrontation ended any fun they were having. Everyone wanted to go home. "The hell with it" was the feeling of the group.

They walked outside. Art and Clete turned left to their car. Billy and Bill Reedy headed to the right to theirs. Waiting outside was the angry cowboy, with a friend. Reedy ordered Billy, "Just keep walking to the car." Art and Clete had seen the men and headed back to protect Billy.

The cowboy kept walking toward them, telling Billy, "I'm going to whip your little ass." Bill Reedy understood Billy Martin couldn't afford to be involved in yet another altercation. He knew what he had to do. When the man was close enough, Bill Reedy slugged him. He went down. The cowboy's buddy fled.

The cowboy rose and started to run. Reedy, Billy, and Art Fowler pursued him into an alley. Art swung, missed, and hit the wall. The guy lashed out, ripping Billy's shirt and sending him into the wall. Billy received a bruise where his face struck the wall. Reedy hit the patron hard, and blood began to flow from the man's face.

Reedy screamed at him, "Are you happy? That's what you wanted. You *wanted* to get your head kicked in."

The cowboy finally left. The bouncer came running over. "I saw it all," he said. "This guy asked for it. Don't worry about it."

Reedy said, "Billy doesn't need any bullshit."

The bouncer understood, but Reedy was worried. When the guy who got beat up learned Billy was involved, Reedy figured he would come back to press charges.

Everyone returned to their hotel rooms for the night. The phone rang in Bill Reedy's room. It was Art Fowler.

"If anyone asks, we're going to say that you did the hitting," Art told Reedy.

In the morning Billy, Bill Reedy, Art, and Clete all caucused just in case there was any media or police fallout. But this time there wasn't any. The guy who had started the fight never returned.

That night Jill, Carol Reedy, and Ruth Fowler were on their way to meet their husbands for dinner. In the car Jill asked Carol, "How do you stay married to somebody all these years?"

Carol said to Jill, "You married a guy—you didn't take a hostage. If you'd think that way, Jill, you'd be better off. You can't take Billy Martin hostage. I've watched a lot of women do that, and they always end up in divorce."

Jill replied, "You don't love your husband the way I love my husband." Then Jill turned to Ruth and asked her the same question.

"Carol's telling the truth," Ruth said.

Jill said, "You guys don't care." Ruth just shook her head. They realized their talking to Jill was fruitless.

In mid-February 1988 Billy and Jill went to New York for the grand opening of Mickey Mantle's restaurant on 59th Street and Central Park South. After the ceremonies, the Martins, the Klepfers, and Mickey Mantle and Greer Johnson got in a limo and were driven to the World Trade Center, where they intended to take the elevator 110 stories up Building Two to Windows on the World for wine and hors d'oeuvres.

When they arrived in the lobby, the maître d' asked if they had reservations. They didn't. He then informed the men that they couldn't go up because they didn't have on jackets and ties.

"Do you know who these men are?" asked Mike Klepfer. "This is Mickey Mantle and Billy Martin."

The maître d' refused to make an exception.

Everyone got back in the limo, and Billy told Tex to drive to Eleventh Avenue where a favorite Italian restaurant of his was located.

Billy ordered scungilli and calimari and shrimp for everyone, and Jill ordered a fish dish.

Mickey, Greer, and the Klepfers sat in expectation for the waiter to bring Jill her food. Greer had described to Mickey and the Klepfers Jill's habit of sending food back, even if it was cooked to perfection.

"She will either complain it's too rare or too well done, and she'll send it back," said Greer. "It *will* go back."

The food came. It was a restaurant owned by a friend of Billy's. Would she send it back? Mickey and Mike Klepfer were tittering under their hands. Billy was telling dirty jokes, but that wasn't why they were laughing. They were waiting for "send it back" Jill to go into her act.

She sent it back. There were winks all around. The food came back. She returned it again. By then she announced she wasn't hungry because of all the bread she'd eaten. She got up and left.

Mike Klepfer got stuck with the bill.

Jill invited Katie Klepfer to Opening Day, April 1988. The Yankees won, and afterward Billy, Jill, and Katie had dinner at a little spaghetti restaurant halfway down the block from the Regency Hotel, where the Martins lived. As they ate, fans came over to the table to congratulate Billy. For Katie Klepfer it was exciting to be part of the hoopla.

That week Katie Klepfer was hosting a big horse show at the Klepfer farm in Binghamton, New York, and she invited both Greer Johnson and Jill to assist in the running of the show. Jill, a talented equestrian, would be a judge.

It was Jill Martin's first look at the Klepfer estate, and she was impressed. Jill's hobby was horses. She dreamed of having a huge spread where she could ride and raise horses. Mickey and Greer had visited Katie Klepfer several times and had told Billy and Jill about her horses and barns. Now Jill was seeing it for herself, and she could see why Mickey and Greer enjoyed coming up to visit the Klepfers. There was a fishing hole and a large barn and the house was beautiful, and it was very peaceful and quiet. Jill couldn't wait to tell Billy about her weekend.

Billy didn't wait long to come. The first Monday the Yankees were off, he and Jill traveled to Binghamton to see the Klepfers. They marveled at their living quarters. On the ground floor of the Klepfer home, the floor below where the Klepfers lived, was a guest quarters with two bedrooms, a large living room, a full kitchen, a fireplace, and a beautiful view of the pond. The Klepfers even provided maid service.

The Klepfers enjoyed having the Martins, though occasionally they noted that Billy and Jill would yell and snip and snarl and snap at each other. But Billy loved to cook, and they loved his salads and veal or lamb and his huge pots of spaghetti. Klepfer noted that when Mickey and Greer visited, even though Mickey liked Katie's chicken and biscuits, at the end of the day he and Greer wanted to get dolled up and be out in public, doing the town, and the Klepfers would take them to local haunts where the owners would keep the gawkers away.

When Billy and Jill came, they preferred to eat at home.

Billy found some quietude at the Klepfers'. He wasn't a man who could sit still for five minutes, but he was able to go to the edge of the Klepfer's pond in the morning with a fishing pole, a box of cigars, and a bottle of vodka, and he could spend the entire day there until the sun went down. He loved to fish, and sitting all by himself he would puff on a stogie and drink and fish for hours by the still water.

Billy particularly liked it when Jill would go off and leave him alone. Billy encouraged Jill to go off with Katie, and the two women would either ride horses or go off to talk horses or drive off to shop in Syracuse.

By getting rid of Jill, he could have some tranquillity. He could also make his phone calls. Billy had girlfriends all over America—in Tampa, Milwaukee, two in Cleveland, Kansas City, Brooklyn, and Toronto. Or he could go off with Mike Klepfer and fish or go to the local bars and drink some more.

The last time Billy was manager he had kept Jill from going with him on the road. This time she was determined to find a way to travel with him. The man she recruited to accomplish her goal was George Steinbrenner.

Jill told Carol Reedy she had discussed with George that Billy was an alcoholic and that he wasn't going to be any good to the Yankees unless he did something about the drinking. Her recommendation was that George send her on the road with Billy so she could keep a close rein on him and prevent him from drinking.

But when Jill traveled with him in 1988, Billy drank worse than ever. When Billy would complain that she was following him around, Jill would tell him, "You can't leave me behind, Billy, because George Steinbrenner wants me there."

According to Bill Reedy, the arrangement didn't last long. Part of the reason was that Jill was formulating big plans for her and Billy—her own horse farm in Binghamton.

By the time the Yankees hit the road in early May, Jill was more interested in visiting Katie Klepfer in Binghamton than in going on the road with Billy. This time, Billy would have been better off if she had been with him.

On May 7, 1988, Billy was thrown out of a 7–6 road loss to Texas in the ninth inning for arguing an umpire's call.

Billy dressed quickly. He and Mickey Mantle took a cab to Lace, a bar where women are known to dance naked, not far from the Arlington ballpark.

Mike Ferraro also went. In the wee hours of the morning Ferraro accompanied an inebriated Mickey into a cab and was supposed to return for Billy. According to Art Fowler, who did not go to Lace that evening, he saw Ferraro go into the hotel and not leave it again.

Billy was by himself in a bar filled with pretty women looking for love and with booze-filled, pugnacious urban cowboys. Before Billy could get out of there, somebody beat him to a pulp.

The story Billy told for public consumption was that three young guys tried to roll him, that they were after his World Series ring. He said that one guy hit him with a pipe and almost took his ear off.

That isn't what happened.

Part of the story had to do with a woman Billy took a shine to. She had a boyfriend in the bar, a big guy who got angry at Billy's friendliness to the girl.

The other part developed from Mickey Mantle's way of infuriating someone and then leaving before the fighting began.

Said Eddie Sapir, "I know exactly what happened at Lace. This was one fight Billy didn't know was going to happen.

"There had been an exchange between Mickey and a couple cowboys who had been dating strippers, motorcycle guys who were just waiting to kick anybody's ass. That was part of having a good time for them.

"The guys said something to Mantle, and he said something back in jest, and then Mike Ferraro took Mickey home, and Billy was left there."

That was typical of the way it was with Mickey Mantle. Said Billy's limo driver, Tex Gernand, "Mickey is a fantastic person in a lot of ways, but he has a way of creating World War II and then leaving before the first bomb is dropped."

Billy would not have stayed if he thought the cowboys were offended by what Mickey had said. Billy thought they had just been joking around. There is also the question of the cowboy who was offended at Billy's conversation with his girl. He may or may not have been part of the group who beat Billy up.

Said Eddie Sapir, "Billy went into the bathroom, and when he got there, he discovered they were waiting for him and that it was going to be bad. These guys got Billy in the bathroom and beat him up, and then they dragged him out the back door, and nobody inside the club knew anything was going on."

Billy said afterward that his attackers knocked him down and "put the boots to me" and then threw him down a flight of stairs and out the back door.

The flight of stairs was adjacent to a stucco wall. The stucco scraped Billy's head like heavy sandpaper on soft wood, almost ripping off an ear and leaving a long trail of blood down the stairs.

"Billy was in horrible shape," said Sapir. "My guess is the motorcycle guys told the doorman, 'Some guy's in the parking lot bleeding to death.' The club wasn't looking for any trouble. They put Billy in the cab, and the cabby took Billy to his hotel."

The cab delivered Billy to the Yankees' hotel at three in the morning. Billy's intention was to return to his room without seeking medical attention. When he arrived back at the hotel, all the guests, including the Yankee players and George Steinbrenner, were waiting in the lobby because of a false alarm.

Trainer Gene Monahan took one look at Billy and raced him to the hospital. Were it not for the false alarm, Billy might have bled to death in his room that night.

Jill was staying at the Klepfers' when the phone calls started to come. Art Fowler called first to advise her that Billy had been hurt. Then Greer Johnson made the first of a series of calls, as Jill tried to get Greer to find out what she could from Mickey.

After the beating Billy needed eighty stitches to close his wounds. His ribs ached. He hurt all over. Billy needed companionship, and he called Gretchen, his second wife, and asked her to come to the hospital.

Billy told Mike Klepfer that they talked meaningfully. He reached out for someone, and Billy was glad Gretchen was there for him.

When Billy got out of the hospital a day later, he flew to New York to retake the helm of the Yankees. He wore dark glasses and tried to cover up the extent of his injuries as best he could.

There was a day off in the season schedule, so Tex drove him from New York to Scranton, Pennsylvania.

"Billy was a mess," said Tex. "I picked him up at La Guardia. I knew he was going to be hurting. I had the bar set up with Chivas scotch and a bottle of club soda, a John Wayne movie in the VCR. He got in the limo. We talked for a few minutes, and I didn't drive five minutes from La Guardia when he was asleep. He never opened his eyes until we got to Scranton. He was hurting real bad."

Mike Klepfer picked Billy up in Scranton and drove him to his home in Binghamton.

When Klepfer saw Billy, he was appalled. Billy looked "gruesome." He was lying down in the backseat of the limousine.

It took all the strength of Tex and Klepfer, who is a powerful, large man, to bring Billy from the limousine into Klepfer's Mercedes. Billy sat in the passenger seat, rolled the seat back, and thanked Klepfer for giving him a place to heal.

"Thanks, pard," Billy said. "Man, I'm really hurting."

Billy was on pain medication and was groggy, and on the way he tried to figure out what story he would tell Jill. He told Klepfer he had seen Gretchen and how much it had meant to him. He said, "That's one helluva woman."

And then he said, "I wish Jill was out of my life. I wish I was back with Gretchen."

Klepfer suggested that Billy take some leave time to heal, but Billy refused despite his pain. His greatest concern was how George Steinbrenner was going to react. Billy was afraid Steinbrenner would fire him again and cut him off.

"I'm in trouble," Billy told Klepfer.

Billy also worried about Yankee GM Lou Piniella. The two were not getting along. Martin worried because Steinbrenner and Piniella had ordered an investigation of his fight. Until the day he was fired, Martin worried about getting canned.

Billy loved managing the Yankees, and he didn't want to lose his job again. More than anything, he wanted to bring the Yankees another championship.

"I'm going to do it," Billy told Klepfer. "I want to make them champions." Then he began to rail about George Steinbrenner. Billy's bitterness began to flow out of him.

"George owns the Yankees for one purpose: the spotlight," Billy said. "He has used the Yankees to get himself into the spotlight. George loves the spotlight. He doesn't care about the sport, doesn't care about anything other than the fulfillment of his ego."

And then Billy told Klepfer how Steinbrenner would have Piniella listening through walls while they talked and Billy would say, "Hey, Lou, you can come in, too," and Lou would come in, and everyone would be embarrassed.

Billy feared George was taping his calls, that he was under intense scrutiny.

"Piss on them," Billy said. "I'm the best. They know it, and if they want to win, they need me."

When they got to Klepfer's home, Billy called Bill Reedy. He wanted Reedy to hire someone to avenge his beating. He told Reedy that the police reports were a lie. He then conjured up a story for Jill that consisted of four men ganging up and jumping him in the men's room.

"I got a couple of good licks in. I decked this one guy," Billy said. It was a story to soothe his ego. Billy got in one shot, and after that the beating was all his. In all his years of bar fighting, Billy had never been beaten so badly. This was even worse than the ass-kicking he had absorbed from Ed Whitson.

As a result of the beating at Lace, George decided it would be a good idea if Jill traveled with Billy when the Yankees went on the road.

The Klepfers quickly became aware that Jill and Steinbrenner were having discussions, because Jill soon learned that the fight was over a woman and that Billy had been visited by Gretchen.

Billy returned to New York for a homestand. The Yankees were off on Monday, so on Sunday night he returned to Binghamton and the comfort of Klepfer's home. And when Billy and the Yankees left New York to go on a road trip beginning in Detroit, Jill went with him, much to Billy's displeasure.

"Billy called me to meet him at Tiger Stadium," said Bill Reedy. "He didn't do that often. Jill was with him, and he didn't want to go back to the hotel, and Art and him got into an argument. Billy wanted Art to come with him, and Art told him he couldn't.

"Billy and Clete [Boyer] and I went down to the Athens bar, which is in Greektown. We went there because it's a quiet spot.

"Well, my beeper was going crazy. Jill and Carol were at the Pontchartrain Hotel. Every time I'd look, Billy would say, 'Who the fuck is that?' 'It's Jill.' Billy said, 'Turn that fucking thing off.' I did.

"We sat there until two in the morning, and he told Clete, 'You know, it's over. He is going to fire us. It's done.'

"Clete said, 'I know. I know, Billy. The motherfucker, I know.'

"And Clete began to defend the job they had done. He said, 'We're second in the league in earned run average. Mattingly has been hurt all year. Willie Randolph, too. We only need . . . '

"Billy said, 'He's going to fire us.' "

Billy's life was a mess. He was kept awake at night by fears that Steinbrenner and Piniella were going to fire him because of what had happened at Lace. He felt constricted because he had his wife on the road with him. Billy complained that Jill, moreover, spent a great deal of his money, and that she was pressing him to look for property in Binghamton in order to build a spread like the Klepfers'. She had walked around the Klepfer property, looked at what Katie Klepfer owned, and told her, "I want a bigger barn. I want a bigger corral."

Katie tried to tell her, "You don't want this. It's a lot of work, a lot of money." But Jill's mind was set.

The pressure on Billy intensified as the Yankee pitching staff went into a tailspin.

On May 30, Billy finally cracked. The play that caused the beginning of the end was a sinking line drive hit by A's shortstop Walt Weiss to Yankee second baseman Bobby Meacham, who was so sure he caught the ball that he threw to shortstop Rafael Santana without even bothering to look to first base, starting the ritual tossing of the ball around the infield. When the umpire at second, Rich Reed, signaled a trap, the runner at first was ruled safe. A big rhubarb ensued.

Watching the replay, announcer Joe Morgan said, "No way this ball was trapped."

Billy asked crew chief Dale Scott to overrule Reed. The four umpires huddled. Scott told Billy he wouldn't overrule the call. Billy screamed at him, "You mean to tell me you didn't see it?"

Scott replied, "I saw it. It was a trapped ball."

Billy threw a tantrum. He went nuts. He swore at Scott, whom he believed was lying.

Umpire Rich Garcia attempted to talk to Billy. He said, "Just calm down. There's no sense getting in trouble on this play."

But Billy would not be calmed. He went over to Scott and told the umpire he was full of shit. Scott tossed him, which gave Billy license to go crazy. Feeling twice wronged, Billy began kicking dirt on Scott's legs. Then he reached down, scooped up some infield dirt with his hands, and flung it at Scott's chest.

On June 2, Billy was fined $1,000 and suspended for three games.

From Oakland, the team went to Baltimore. Billy sat out his suspension in Baltimore. Thursday was an off day, and Billy spent most of it drinking. By the evening, according to sportswriter Bill Madden, Billy was incoherent, slurring his words.

"They think they're the game. They've got too much power."

Madden escorted Billy up to his room.

In response to what they felt was the leniency of the punishment, the umpires vowed a vendetta against Billy. Anytime he stuck his head out of the dugout, they said, he would be ejected. It was implied that he couldn't even go out to talk to his pitchers.

The American League umpires had agreed to this, said Richie Phillips, who represented the umpires' union. Said Phillips, "He's going to have to behave like an altar boy" to stay in games.

On June 6, Billy, not for the first time in his career, threatened to sue the umpires in court.

"You can't gag an American, and I'm not going to be gagged," he trumpeted.

On June 7, baseball commissioner Peter Ueberroth stepped in. Billy apologized for his actions. When Billy went out to talk to Yankee pitcher Charlie Hudson in the first inning, he got a standing ovation from the Yankee Stadium fans.

Behind the scenes, Billy Martin wanted revenge on the umpires.

In front of Mike Klepfer, Billy made a call to one of his friends and ordered him to find a mob triggerman to whack umpire Dale Scott.

According to Klepfer, whoever was on the other end of the phone refused to be involved in any such thing.

Some days later Billy was in Mike Klepfer's office in Binghamton, railing over the phone at his friend for not carrying out the hit on Scott.

"You had every opportunity and you could have done it, and you didn't. You're supposed to be a friend of mine." In disgust Billy hung up on him.

Klepfer was horrified. "Bill," he later told his friend, "you're just going to get yourself in more hot water." Klepfer realized that Martin was far more upset about the umpire situation than he had been about the beating at Lace.

In the end the public pissing match with the umpires was the final straw before Steinbrenner fired Billy.

The real reason Billy got fired was his heavy drinking and the dislike of his behavior by the players. Clyde King, whom Steinbrenner had hired to replace Lou Piniella as general manager when Piniella quit, was sent on the road to watch Billy. Billy for years had made it clear he didn't like King, a Southern gentleman who had never liked Billy.

In baseball if you antagonize enough people, no matter how good you are, you're going to get fired. And if your owner is George Steinbrenner, your chances of staying on become even worse. That's what happened to Billy in 1988.

For weeks Billy had asked the front office to trade or release Tim Stoddard, and he rarely used him. On June 19, in a game against the Cleveland Indians, the Yankees were trailing 4–3 when Billy brought Stoddard into the game. Stoddard had nothing, and to show up George and the Yankee front office, Billy left him in to take a shellacking. Stoddard faced eight batters; there were two hits, five walks, a wild pitch, and an out.

Billy then called in Charlie Hudson before he was warmed up. Hudson came in and gave up a grand slam.

Clyde King was distressed by Billy's behavior. Front-office executives don't like to be shown up by their manager at the expense of their players.

King told Steinbrenner, "My advice to you is we make a change, but only if you make it quickly. It's not too late to save the season, but it's getting close to it. The pitching is a mess, and the team morale is slipping fast."

King suggested replacing Billy with Dallas Green.

But Steinbrenner was afraid of adverse fan reaction, so he decided that Lou Piniella would finish out the season.

Billy was fired a few days later, on June 23, following three losses to Detroit in extra innings. Reliever Cecelio Guante, who had been used too much by Billy, gave up game-losing homers in the first two games, including Alan Trammell's grand slam in game two.

Around noon on June 23, George Steinbrenner fired Billy Martin for the fifth and last time. Lou Piniella, who had resigned as general manager on May 29, returned as manager.

The Yankees had led the American League East most of the year but had suffered through a 2–7 road trip and had lost their lead. The Yankees were an excellent 40–28, a .588 winning percentage, when Billy was canned.

Despite Billy's won-lost record—which was supposed to be the bottom line—Steinbrenner's excuse was that he was worried about Billy's drinking and felt Billy had lost his skills as manager.

"Martin wasn't the same Billy Martin this time," Steinbrenner told reporters.

Said Yankee slugger Jack Clark, "If Billy had stayed as manager, we'd have won the pennant."

By 1988, George Steinbrenner had finally sucked the lifeblood out of Billy Martin. At a time when Billy needed someone to stand up for him and say, "We'll fight your fight, Billy, you just go out and win. And we'll fight this together," George Steinbrenner did what he always did when things got rough—he took the cowardly route, placing the blame on a suitable scapegoat. Once more it was Billy Martin.

And when a disconsolate, dispirited Billy turned to his wife to support him, Jill told him he was a fuck-up, a poor provider, and "a loser." He would spend the rest of his days attempting to have some fun away from her.

About an hour after the announcement that Billy had been fired, calls started to come in to Mike Klepfer's office. Mickey Mantle was the first caller.

"Did you hear? Billy has been let go. We're trying to find a place to get him out. This place is going to be a zoo down here, the reporters and everything."

"Why don't you invite him up here?" asked Mike Klepfer.

It wasn't thirty seconds later when Billy called. He was very emotional, choking back the hurt, sounding as though he was crying.

Klepfer said, "Billy, why don't you get in the car and have Jill drive you up here as fast as you can get here. Get the hell out of New York. I just spoke to Mick. He thinks it would be a good thing for you to come for a little while. Why don't you do it? The press will never find you here. Come on up."

Billy answered, "Okay, maybe I'll do that, pard. I need to be with friends right now."

By five in the afternoon, Billy and Jill arrived in Binghamton with their stack of luggage and three cats.

# THE MOVE TO BINGHAMTON

**T**wo days after Billy was fired, Billy Martin and Bebe Norton, a friend and employee of Mike Klepfer's, sat at the edge of the pond on the Klepfer estate and fished while six hundred equestrians vied for honors. The horsepeople didn't even know who he was, and they wouldn't have cared if they had. The press never got to Billy. Peter Kaye of the *New York Post* tried to interview him, but he was stopped and escorted out.

Billy posed with a string of good-sized largemouth bass he had caught. He tried to smile, but Mike Klepfer couldn't believe the change that had come over Billy since the time he had first met him.

"Standing in front of me was a completely broken Billy Martin," Klepfer said. "Decimated. Destroyed. He was not the same guy. He had no reason to live. He was just broken."

Billy talked very little as he turned his thoughts inward. One conversation that Mike Klepfer remembers vividly concerned Billy's daughter, Kelly, and his granddaughter, Evie. Billy, according to Klepfer, loved Kelly dearly.

"There's a kid," Billy said. "I always gotta take care of her because she ain't never gonna make it, you know." Billy figured that Kelly had gotten a screwing in life and said he had played no small part in that.

"I should have been there more for her," he lamented. Then he talked about Evie and how much he loved her.

"They'll never have anything to worry about," said Billy. "Kelly and Evie are set for life.'' Martin told Klepfer he had left a living trust that would take care of them.

Billy then expressed irritation with his son, Billy Joe, incorrectly labeling him a professional student, a goof-off.

"But that's my son. What are you gonna do? You gotta take care of family."

Billy then began to talk about Jill and why he had married her. He praised her sexual abilities in embarrassing detail.

Appalled, Klepfer said to himself, I've been with guys who've been with prostitutes who have more respect for their women than he does.

Billy would ask Klepfer to "drive me to the store to get a cigar," and the two would go out, enabling Billy to make calls to Bill Reedy or Mickey Mantle or to his girlfriends on Klepfer's car phone.

Billy had a fierce rivalry with Mickey Mantle. His goal, Billy told Klepfer, was to make as much money as Mickey Mantle made. During the years when Mickey was thrown out of baseball for working for the Clarion Casino in Atlantic City, he and Billy had been close buddies. Mickey at the time was making a lousy $100,000. But when Mickey was reinstated and began making his long comeback, earning megabucks from autograph sessions at card shows, Billy began to grow more and more agitated. As long as Billy had the limelight from managing, they could compete financially, but once he was fired, card show operators began negotiating Billy's fees down from $4,000 to $3,200 while Mantle continued to get between $30,000 and $40,000 a show.

It finally hit Billy that Mantle still was what he had always been—the superstar everybody loved—and here Billy was out of work, down and out with so little to look forward to that he began to concoct dreams in his head.

"Donald Trump is gonna buy the Yankees and make me general manager *and* manager," Billy told Klepfer, who sensed this was a fantasy.

Billy had been upset that after he had been beaten up at Lace in Arlington, Mickey had stayed away. One observer said that after a wounded Billy got out of the cab that took him from Lace to the hotel, Mickey got into it, saw the blood all over the backseat, and called the Yankees to say that somebody ought to look in on Billy. If that was so, then why hadn't Mickey noticed the blood, stopped the cab, and come back to attend to Billy himself?

Billy also was bothered that Mickey, no matter what he did, *never* got in trouble. He was like Ronald Reagan—Teflon-coated. Mickey could be standing naked on Broadway with ten naked strippers around him and no one would ever find out. Or if they did find out, no one would think bad of the Mick. All this agitated Billy terribly, and his upset grew when early in his stay with the Klepfers, he called Mickey to ask him to come to Binghamton, only to have Mickey tell him there were some card show appearances he had to make and he wouldn't be able to visit him for a while.

That evening Billy and Klepfer visited Casey's, a Binghamton gin mill. As they sat on their stools, Billy asked Klepfer, "Who do you think my best friend is? Go ahead, tell me."

Klepfer guessed it was Mantle.

"You're wrong. Guess again."

Klepfer, who was close to Mantle, was devastated.

"Mickey is *not* your best friend?"

"No. Guess again."

"Whitey Ford."

"You're wrong. Guess again."

Klepfer said, "Jeez, now you got me. Is it an old friend?"

Billy said, "My best friend is Bill Reedy, and don't you ever forget it." Reedy had called the Klepfers a couple of times, but Mike hadn't realized he was so important to Billy.

Continued Billy, "Bill is a man's man. Mickey—yeah, the old days. We were buddies. But today Bill Reedy is my best friend." And after a few drinks, Billy reiterated what he had said. "Bill Reedy is my best friend."

That night, before they went out, Billy and Mike Klepfer discussed the ground rules for who was to drive.

Said Billy, "If it's my car, I drive. If it's your truck, it's your call. If you're driving and I think you're too drunk, I call a cab. If I'm driving and you think I'm too drunk, you call a cab."

"We were big boys," says Klepfer. "We had it all worked out."

Because Klepfer was the host, he had the prerogative of always insisting they take his truck. Early in their visit Jill had told Mike, "If you're smart, you won't ride with him. You'll always drive. He's nuts."

Klepfer was savvy enough to realize that Billy was a dangerous enough driver sober. One habit Billy had that drove everyone crazy was that if he was driving and having a conversation with a passenger in the backseat, he insisted on looking back at that person when he was speaking.

Behind the wheel Billy had the star's attitude that everyone else should get out of his way, in the same way that Billy would not wait in a line and would expect special treatment. He would buy things without a charge account, and rarely would he carry identification except for his driver's license.

But Billy was sober only perhaps twenty percent of the time he and Mike went out together. The other eighty percent he was legally DWI. Klepfer believed Billy to be a road hazard.

For his part Billy was happy to let Klepfer drive his truck. It was a Ford pickup, and Billy loved it.

After a night of drinking Billy would be three sheets to the wind, and Klepfer would have three beers in him.

"Okay, pard," Billy would say, "you're driving. Your truck."

Billy had expressed such admiration for Mike Klepfer's Ford pickup that Klepfer had arranged for Billy to get one free along with a Bronco for Jill. Klepfer was a business acquaintance of Jack and Gary Cory's, the owners of Cory Ford. Mike and Billy arranged a sweet deal giving Billy the two top-of-the-line vehicles worth $48,000 in exchange for some promotional TV work.

The day they were to make the deal for the vehicles, Billy told Mike, "Let's not take Jill. She'll get in there and muddy the waters. She'll want things for herself. She's a pain in the ass.''

Klepfer watched as Billy and the Corys made their deal. They made up a two-page memo, and they signed it. But according to Mike Klepfer, because they didn't bring Jill along, Jill took it as a personal affront on Klepfer's part. According to Klepfer, the deal marked the end of his relationship with Jill Martin. Where in the past she had been friendly, now there was coldness that he could feel. "She became cold stone, like talking to a brick fireplace," he said.

The Klepfers, who had invited Billy and Jill to come and stay for "a little while," ended up playing host for four stormy months. Befriending the Martins disrupted their lives as Mike baby-sat Billy and Katie did the same for Jill.

In late August 1988 the Martins announced that they had signed a binder to purchase a home in Binghamton.

Earlier that month they had looked at the back of the hill adjacent to the Klepfer estate. Billy demurred. He didn't want a huge place, just a place where he could get away from the limelight of New York when he wanted to. Billy wanted a little retreat to raise some upland birds and ducks, and he wanted a lake on which to fish.

Mike Klepfer's sister, Pat, a real-estate broker, took Billy and Jill around to homesites that were on the market. Despite Billy's desire to buy a small retreat, they settled on a small run-down farmhouse on Potters Field Road on 159 acres of property. It had a five-acre lake. It was a private, off-the-road place to get away.

The farmstead had been owned by a psychiatrist who had committed suicide. The wife was living there alone.

When Bill and Carol Reedy first came to Binghamton, Billy showed Reedy where the psychiatrist had done it. It was to be the Reedys' bedroom during their stay.

"You sleep here," Billy said with a grin. "This is where he sat in his chair and blew his brains out." Added Billy, "It was on that wall where all his brains splattered."

Most of those who had made offers on the place had heard of the suicide and had offered far less than what the widow was seeking, and she kept turning the offers down. Billy and Jill paid her close to what she was asking for the property: $365,000.

On top of that, Jill wanted to completely redesign the house and add a large barn and stables like the Klepfers had. In the tug-of-war between Billy and Jill, Jill's tug was clearly the stronger. What Jill Martin wanted from Billy, Jill Martin got.

**50**

# FIGHTING AND DRINKING

Shortly after Billy signed the contract to buy the house, he and Mike Klepfer went to Sears in the Oakdale Mall in Binghamton to buy tools. Billy didn't even own a hammer.

Billy said, "Jeez, pardner, I don't have any money." He was always hitting Klepfer up for money, two hundred here, four hundred there.

Klepfer told Billy, "Tell you what, we'll buy what you need, and you can owe me and pay me back."

"No problem."

Billy bought hammers, drills, and saws like a kid in a candy store. While Billy was in the store, other customers noticed him and started to come over and chat.

Said one woman, "My husband thinks you're great. He'll never forget 1952. Oh my God, if he knew I was talking to you."

Billy signed a piece of paper and told her, "Give this to your husband, honey. You tell him Billy said hello."

Klepfer marveled at Billy's ability to relate to people, whether they were rich or poor. If it had been Mickey Mantle, Klepfer thought, Mickey would have moved on. He would have put up a wall and gotten away or he would have made sure Klepfer shielded him from the public. But Billy, Klepfer thought, could go from one end of the social strata to the other like a truckdriver shifting gears smoothly.

It was syncromesh, Klepfer thought to himself, marveling. Billy could be talking to Ronald Reagan and then go across the street and have a beer with a truck driver.

The Klepfers couldn't help but notice that Billy's consumption of and need for alcohol was growing. Jill tried to keep track of how much Billy was drinking at home by measuring the amount of liquor left in the bottles at the end of the day, but that didn't stop him.

Whenever Jill would go with Katie to the barn, Billy would run for the Stolichnaya, all the while calling her filthy, disgusting names.

One morning at about half past nine Bebe (Daddio) Norton, a retired truck driver who worked for the Klepfers, was tidying up the property when he saw Billy outside by the pool. It was a record-setting summer, with temperatures in the hundreds, and this day was no different. Billy and Daddio had fished together, and Daddio sometimes washed Billy's car.

"Hey, Daddio, how you doing?" Billy asked him.

"Good, man," Norton replied. "Boy, it's hot out here, ain't it?"

"Here, you want a drink?" Billy asked him. Norton thought Billy had a glass of water.

Daddio said, "Yeah, jeez, give me a swig, will ya?" And he took it, slugged it down, and almost gagged. Billy was drinking straight vodka. It was nine-thirty in the morning.

The Klepfers also observed that his fighting with Jill was escalating. Mike Klepfer's den on the second floor was above the furnace, and the piping of the duct work carried the sound from the Martins' apartment to his den so clearly he was able to hear the battles. If the Martins screamed loudly enough, he was able to hear their words.

Billy's final firing by the Yankees was causing a rift in the marriage. Jill apparently had sold her soul to become the wife of Yankee manager Billy Martin, and now he was the *former* Yankee manager, and she was coming unglued.

She had become irate about the Lace incident, chastising Billy not because he had gotten hurt but because it was jeopardizing his job. And when the umpire situation arose, again Jill was upset, because Billy's job was on the line.

Those around Billy at the time felt that Jill had a series of financial objectives for them. Among those objectives was to get the bills paid, especially money Billy owed the IRS, and to build a horse facility and a nice home. His firing had put all her plans in limbo.

For his part, when they argued, Billy used every piece of dirt on Jill that he could summon up. He threw up to her his knowledge that she had once dated Reggie Jackson. Billy had always hated Jackson, going all the way back to their fateful 1977 and 1978 seasons together.

Another night Mike Klepfer's son Bobby was out by the pool in the backyard when he saw Billy shaking Jill violently. Young Mike wanted to go in and break them up but instead ran upstairs to Katie.

"Ma, they're fighting terrible downstairs," he said. "Let me go down and do something."

Katie said, "Bobby, that's not our business. You stay up here. Do *not* go down there. If they need us, they'll call us. Otherwise, you cannot interfere in a domestic affair."

That fight ended with Billy throwing Jill's expensive camera equipment into the swimming pool.

Afterward Jill came upstairs and apologized. She felt very bad about the disturbance.

The next blowup was an explosion. Billy was drunk, and when Billy was drunk, it wasn't hard to provoke him to fisticuffs.

She started by berating him for having gotten fired from his managerial job. "Look what you've put us into," she began, and she proceeded to tell him what his firing was costing her.

"I don't want to hear it," Billy told her.

She kept at him. "You're going to hear it." And then she said the magic words.

"You're a loser," she told Billy.

Upstairs the Klepfers heard what sounded like a big bang in the guest quarters.

Despite what she had told her son earlier, Katie Klepfer could not maintain her hands-off position. She ran down the stairs to see what had happened. On the way down, Billy passed her going up.

He came upstairs, shook hands with Mike Klepfer in the den, and said, "Pard, I'll see ya."

"Where you going?"

"I'm going to New York. Pard, I'll see ya, buddy."

Mike Klepfer realized Billy was in no shape to drive. He said, "Billy, come on. Wait a minute. I'll call Tex."

Billy said, "No, pard, I'm leaving." Then he said something philosophical that didn't make much sense to Klepfer, something forgotten, and Billy drove off "drunker'n a hoot owl."

When Katie arrived downstairs, she found a bruised woman. Jill had a lump on her head and a welt. She had probably hit a pole that was a structural element of the room she was in. The attack had come so quickly she really couldn't recall what had happened to her. Her neck had been wrenched, probably from a shaking. She had whiplash.

The welt came from Billy's hands. Only a week earlier Mike Klepfer had caught Billy educating Mike's two sons in the fine art of handling women.

"When you're gonna belt a woman," Billy told them, "always keep your hands open. And then you can belt the hell out of them."

It was the one time that Billy made Klepfer so angry he wanted to take Billy on.

Katie went upstairs to see where Billy had gone. Mike told her, "I think he went to New York." Katie went back downstairs and brought Jill upstairs with them.

Jill insisted she was fine, but the next morning she couldn't turn her head.

Katie said, "Jill, we really have to see somebody."

Jill said, "You're right. I want proof that I was hit." Jill began to talk about finding a lawyer to help her get a divorce. She asked the Klepfers about the bases for divorce in New York State.

Katie Klepfer took Jill to her physician. The doctor told her, "The only way we can check you is to send you to the hospital for X rays."

Jill knew she was taking a chance that the media might find out she had checked into the hospital for tests. She went anyway. She left the hospital wearing a neck brace.

When she returned to the Klepfers' home, immediately she removed it. She told Katie, "I really don't need it." But when some friends of the Klepfers came over, Mike and Katie thought it odd that Jill ran downstairs to put it back on while their friends were visiting. As soon as they left, off it came again.

Billy, meanwhile, had vanished, leaving Jill with the Klepfers. It wasn't the first time he had gotten into an argument with Jill, run off to New York, and disappeared for a day or two. Billy could do it, Mike Klepfer realized, because he was able to leave Jill in safe surroundings. Not only was she physically safe, sound, and secure, but the ever-jealous Billy—paranoid and drinking heavily—felt it was a place where she wouldn't be screwing around with anyone else.

This time was not like the other times. In New York the next day Billy called Jill and told her he didn't want to have any more to do with her.

He called Mike Klepfer at his office.

"Billy, where the hell are you? What are you doing?"

"I've had it. I can't stand her. She's driving me nuts, that no-good bitch," Billy said. "I know what she wants. She wants me to build her a goddamn Taj Mahal and, aw, Jesus, she wants a horse barn and she wants . . ." Billy was in a rage. "Man, I've had enough of her."

"Where the hell are you?" Klepfer asked him.

"I'm with a good friend. Someone who cares."

Billy was with old flame Patty Stark, who had married but had remained a phone companion to Billy. Though Patty cared for Billy a great deal, she had remained faithful to her new husband. She would not sleep with Billy, and Billy liked her for it.

Klepfer asked him, "What are you going to do? When are you coming back?"

"I ain't gonna be back."

"What the hell do you want me to do with Jill?"

"You tell her to have a good life." Then Billy said, "I'll see ya, pard. I gotta run." And he hung up.

For about a week Billy wasn't heard from. From New York, Billy flew to Detroit to spend time with the Reedys, then to Marina del Mar to stay a week with Tom Demer, the owner of the marina there. Billy also was seeing a lady friend in the area.

Billy was away a total of three weeks before he returned to Jill in Binghamton. While he was away, he would call Mike Klepfer, who wanted Billy to come back to fulfill the promotional commitments he had made in exchange for the two trucks.

For those three weeks Jill Martin recounted her life to Katie Klepfer. Jill told Katie that she once had been very wealthy, rode around in a Mercedes-Benz convertible, lived in a big house, had horses, and then her father went belly-up and she was thrust into the streets with nothing.

Jill explained that she had met Billy in 1980, that she had left the guy she was engaged to in order to date Billy, that Billy was between Gretchen and Heather, that she was a stewardess for a small airline, and that she had met Billy at an Oakland game doing work as a freelance photographer.

She told Katie that she had known Reggie Jackson and several of the Oakland players and that through Reggie she had gotten an introduction to Billy. She also said that Billy's friend Mickey Morabito, the A's public relations head, had also hit on her.

She explained how after Reggie had gotten her an introduction to Billy, she was trying to get permission from Billy to get on the field to take photographs of Reggie and other players. And when Billy met her, evidently he took a liking to her. Immediately, she said, Billy had asked her out.

"He came on to me like wildfire," Jill told Katie.

Jill then told her she had gone to New York to meet Billy, and at his Western-wear store someone introduced Heather to Jill, introducing Heather as "Billy Martin's fiancée." Jill said she hadn't known.

Soon afterward, Jill told Katie, she had moved in with Billy at Marina del Mar, where Billy had a co-op. At the same time Billy was carrying on a relationship with Heather in Northern California. Then Billy went north and married Heather. Jill didn't find out for more than a year.

"For a year I didn't know he was married," Jill said. Billy, meanwhile, was commuting between the two women.

Katie repeated this part of the conversation to Mike. Mike was astounded.

"If you find this out," Mike said to Katie, "there is only one reason you would marry this man, and that's for material gain. There could be nothing more."

Jill told Katie that to go out with "this son of a bitch Martin" she gave up a handsome, intelligent, college-educated guy who had been working at a local TV station in Los Angeles and was madly in love with her. She was engaged to him, she told Katie, but she I gave him up to go with Billy. The Klepfers remembered that he had become either an actor or "a big executive with one of the major networks."

During the three weeks Billy was away, Jill told Katie every rotten thing she could think of about Billy. She told Katie that Billy had had nine cases of venereal disease. She accused Billy of abandoning her, railing because he wasn't calling her.

"I have bills to pay and no money. I have major decisions to make. Billy was supposed to make the down payment on our new home, but he isn't to be found.

"Please have him come back," Jill told Katie. "He has to tell me what we're going to do. If this is it, we can't go any farther." She was frustrated because she needed his signature for everything.

Billy began calling his friends. He called Mickey Mantle. He talked to Tom Demer in Marina del Mar. He conferred with Bill Reedy, and also with Bill Maybeck, the manager of the Regency Hotel in New York.

During the time Billy was away from Jill, he called one night to talk to his sister Joan.

Billy told his sister, "I ought to leave her."

Joan told Billy, "Cool down and think about it." Later Joan would say that she was afraid if she had told him to leave her and he didn't, he would hold it against her.

His other sister, Pat, told Joan, "You should have told him to leave her." They laughed, but there was little joy in their laughter.

Mike Klepfer called Bill Reedy to find out if there was anything he could do to convince Billy to come back. The Klepfers had Jill living in their home, and they wanted to get rid of her. They wanted to get on with their lives.

After three weeks Billy returned. He signed the contract for the farmstead and made the down payment. The closing would be in October, but Jill announced that they were about to undergo a major reconstruction of the house.

Katie asked her, "Are you going to live in the house during the reconstruction?"

"Oh, no."

"Then it's time we look for a place for you," said Katie. "It's time. It's *really* time."

Katie's patience had run out. Jill had bought a ferret. One time the ferret got loose, ran up the stairs, and while Katie Klepfer sat in a chair, the ferret waddled over and bit her leg.

For four months the Klepfers' housekeeper, Anne, had cleaned up their mess and did the laundry. According to Carol Reedy, Billy Martin gave Jill hundreds of dollars for the housekeeper. According to Mike and Katie Klepfer, the housekeeper was never paid a dime.

Within forty-eight hours Katie Klepfer had found them a place. In a Katie Klepfer–driven whirlwind of activity, against her will Jill packed their belongings, and a couple of the Klepfers' friends moved them to the Hearth on Front Street, where they lived until April 1989.

Jill, furious that she was being thrown out, said to Katie, "Now you're going to find out what it's like to go up against a superstar."

Katie said, "Honey, there's nothing to go up against because I have my husband and I have my family. I don't need anybody else."

Said Mike Klepfer, "I moved them from New York, sent a truck down with two drivers, and moved all their furniture out of the New York apartment to here. I put it all in storage, and then I moved them into their hotel suite while they were waiting for their place to be remodeled. My sister found them a home. I took them to Glenn Small, the senior vice president of the Binghamton Savings

Bank and got them a $65,000 mortgage. I even lent them $13,000 out of my checking account to close the house. I mean, there's nothing we didn't do for them.

"We found them all their contractors, got them a farm tractor, got them a deal for two cars. I mean, I did eighty times for Billy Martin what Billy Martin did for me. And we did it for Jill as well."

# BROKE IN THE
# TAJ MAHAL

**B**illy was intent on revenge. The one baseball concern he had was his fixation on suing the umpires, whom he blamed for running him out of the game.

George Steinbrenner had professed to being sympathetic to Billy with respect to the umpiring dispute. No one pointed out to Billy that it wouldn't have been an issue had Steinbrenner not fired him.

But when Billy told George he intended to pursue a lawsuit, George told Billy, "I will testify in a court of law that the reason I fired you is that you could not operate as manager because of the umpires. They were depriving you of a livelihood. Let's sue them."

Steinbrenner sent a check for $25,000 for Billy to hire a lawyer to proceed. The check was cashed.

According to Bill Reedy, Eddie Sapir was in favor of the suit against the umpires, as were Steinbrenner and Jill. The contrary voice was that of Bill Reedy.

One afternoon Billy and Bill Reedy were drinking at the bar of the Regency Hotel in New York when Cubs broadcaster Harry Caray entered.

Caray sat down with Billy and Bill Reedy. When Billy went off to go to the bathroom, Reedy said to Caray, "I want you to do something for me. When Billy comes back, I want you to bring up the umpire thing."

"What are you talking about?" Caray asked. Reedy told him of the incident, how it had apparently caused Billy to be fired, and told him of Billy's threat of a lawsuit against the umpires.

"Oh geez," Caray said. "He can't do that."

Reedy said, "That's right, because he will never work in baseball again."

Caray said, "And not only that, George Steinbrenner will take him to the altar and dump him. When he's supposed to testify for him, he won't. It's as simple as that with that son of a bitch. How can Billy trust him?"

Billy came back to the table and sat down. Reedy began, "Have you ever mentioned to Harry about the lawsuit?"

Martin said, "What do you mean?"

"Why don't you ask his advice?"

The three men proceeded to discuss the long-term effect on Billy of a lawsuit against the umpires.

Reedy said, "I, for one, am against it. I don't think Billy should do it. No matter how you look at it, Billy is suing baseball. Baseball has been his life."

Caray agreed. He pleaded with Martin to reconsider, and the next day Billy dropped the suit. He called Steinbrenner on the phone to tell him that he was not going to pursue it.

Jill was angry at Bill Reedy for talking Billy out of the lawsuit. She was angry most of all for Bill's having influence over Billy that she didn't have. Jill once told Carol Reedy, "I can't help it. Your husband, it's almost like Billy clears everything with him, never with me, and I'm the one who has to suffer because of the bad decisions that your husband is making."

Bill Reedy, meanwhile, was loaning Billy money while Jill was spending thousands of Billy's dollars on the remodeling of their farm and on her horse.

The Reedys couldn't believe the Martins spent as much as they did on the renovation. Bill Reedy thought, It's a depressed area. You have to go by trailer camps to get there. Billy's friend shook his head at the realization that Billy owed more on the house than it was worth.

Carol Reedy once went to Binghamton for a brief visit and ended up spending ten days there. Carol Reedy, like Jill, Katie Klepfer, and Greer Johnson, had been involved in equestrian competition, as she was growing up in Bloomfield Hills, near Detroit. Carol enjoyed horses and going to horse shows with Jill.

During spring training Jill had told Carol that she had her heart set on buying a particular horse but that the price tag of $15,000 was way too steep.

Now Jill conspiratorially told Carol Reedy, "I got the horse."

"Did you?" Carol said. "I thought you said it was too much money."

"It was," Jill said. "I had some money put aside, and my mother gave me the rest." A few hours later she sheepishly admitted to Carol Reedy, "I'm not going to lie to you. It cost $15,000, but I told Billy it was only $5,000. I told Billy it was money I had put aside for that horse, but Billy doesn't know, so don't say anything."

The horse soon thereafter came down with a bone disease. She donated it to a stable that gives riding lessons to retarded and blind children and took a $15,000 tax deduction.

When she told Billy about it, he thought she was a financial genius. Billy was under the impression that she had paid $5,000 for the horse and then was able to take a $15,000 deduction.

During that same visit Jill was doing her bills, and she asked Carol to help her out by reading the bills to her as she wrote out checks.

One was a barn bill for $5,000. Carol, who knew horses and what they cost, was horrified at the exorbitant cost and said so. After all, Jill owned only one horse.

Jill said, "That's not bad. That includes all the traveling, carting the horse to shows back and forth, his room, board, feed, the vet bill, all my class fees for the horse shows I ride in, plus the horse has been getting therapeutic massages for his nerves."

"Really?"

"Yeah, the horse gets massages at fifty dollars an hour for over a month. That all mounts up."

Carol said, "Christ, Jill, five thousand dollars? For two thousand that horse could live in the lap of luxury."

Billy made about $700,000 a year from the Yankees and other endorsements, but he never had any money because he and Jill spent it like they were millionaires.

Billy was a free spender, tipping waitresses a hundred bucks if he felt generous, taking limousines, flying first-class here and there at his whim to meet mistresses.

Billy had one girlfriend, Lisa, who lived in Toronto. She would call him through Bill Reedy, and Reedy would send her airplane tickets to meet Billy, and then she wouldn't show up. Carol Reedy would go to the airport to get her, and she wouldn't be there. It happened so many times that Carol began calling her the Phantom.

One time Billy had Bill Reedy prepay a ticket so that Lisa could meet him in Minneapolis. Reedy had joined Billy for the weekend, and the two went to the airport to meet her. She wasn't on the plane.

Billy became so incensed that he called Lisa's mother on the phone and asked her, "What kind of daughter did you raise? I'm in Minneapolis waiting for your daughter, and she didn't show up, and son of a bitch, what kind of daughter are you raising?"

When Billy got off the phone, Reedy was laughing. He said, "You told that woman that? You asshole."

Another reason Billy was hurting for money despite the large salary was that Eddie Sapir had been taking a chunk of his paycheck and using the money to pay taxes to the Internal Revenue Service.

Bill Reedy, for one, could never figure out how Billy on his large salary could constantly be broke. Reedy, who disliked and distrusted Jill, blamed her. No longer was Billy master of the checkbook. She oversaw the bank account. She paid the bills, wrote the checks. Billy had little interest in business and was happy to have someone else doing the accounting. Reedy wondered where all that money was going.

In March 1988 Billy came to Detroit to do an election benefit for Bill Reedy's boss, Jack Kelley. Billy paid his own way to Detroit, but when he arrived he sheepishly told Reedy, "I don't have any money."

"What's happened to the goddamn money?" Reedy asked. "You stupid son of a bitch, watch your money."

Billy was hard-pressed to answer.

Reedy ran the fund-raiser, and as his fee for speaking, Billy was paid $10,000. At the end of the day Reedy handed Martin an envelope with the money.

"You prick, if I ever hear that she finds out about this," said Reedy, "I'll never speak to you again. Put it in your goddamn pocket and hide it somewhere so that when you get out of town, you have some spending money."

During the winter of 1988, after Billy and Jill fought and Billy disappeared for a few days, Jill called Bill Reedy. The oil company had refused to deliver oil to the Martins' home in Binghamton because there was an outstanding bill of $1,000. Billy was nowhere to be found. Bill Reedy sent a check so the house would have heat.

Money was flowing in and flowing out. Bill Reedy and his brother-in-law Matt drove with Billy from New York City to a show in Atlantic City. Billy was to get $10,000 to speak at ten the next morning to a gathering sponsored by a swimming pool company.

The next day Reedy, Matt, and Billy sat and ate breakfast at the counter of a restaurant, trying to be inconspicuous. While they were eating, a representative of the swimming pool company came over and gave Billy a check. Billy told him he didn't want a check. Though it was eight o'clock in the morning, the man returned promptly with cash.

After Billy made his speech, he handed Reedy a hundred silver dollars. Billy said, "Let's play one machine. As soon as the two hundred is gone, we're out the door."

They lost the money, and they got in a limousine for the ride back to New York. In the car Billy handed Reedy the envelope with the $10,000 in it.

"Let's count it," he said. They did. The money was there. Billy brought it home to Jill.

A week later Billy called Reedy in Detroit. Billy was at the Bull & Bear bar in Binghamton. He was drunk.

"The money's all gone," Billy said.

Reedy said, "What did she do with the money?"

Billy said, "She paid off the carpenter and paid off the plumber."

Reedy said, "You're putting a lot of money into that house. General Motors pays off in ninety days. Let them do some work, and *then* you pay them."

Bill Reedy chided Billy for paying off the renovation in cash and not refinancing. He told him, "What Jill is doing is paying off the goddamn house as quickly as possible, 'cause when you go south [leave her], she's going to own the son of a bitch, and it'll be paid for."

Billy didn't say a word.

Even after the major renovation of the house was completed, Jill continued to list for Billy other improvements she wanted made. Billy would tell her, "We have lots of time."

But her actions made it seem like she felt time was running out. Certainly she was aware of his previous patterns with his past wives. She saw that Billy had been staying away for longer and longer periods. One of those trips, Billy would not return. He would be gone. It seemed to Bill and Carol Reedy that Jill, understandably, was hedging against that day.

Billy said to Carol, "I just don't understand what is her rush. She wants everything done yesterday. I'm up to my ass in bills from this place. What is the big rush?"

# 52

# THE SPLITTER

**E**d Sapir had been negotiating contracts for Billy since 1980. They were worth millions, but he never took a penny in fees. Whenever Billy got in trouble, Eddie was there for him. He saved Billy after he punched out Ray Hagar in Reno, was there in Baltimore with him after the Ed Whitson mauling, and when needed he flew all over the country to help Billy with his wives, girlfriends, and the rest of his female entourage.

Sapir even had Billy's IRS problems under control, reducing a $200,000 deficit down to nothing by keeping Billy on a budget.

Billy was not an easy client. His philosophy was like that of many stars: It's your fault when you're wrong, and it's your fault when I'm wrong.

One time Billy was out on the West Coast. It was about one in the morning when he called Eddie at home. In New Orleans it was three A.M. Billy needed an airplane ticket.

Billy said, "Could you get the ticket for me and call me back and let me know the details?"

Eddie said, "Sure, let me wake up. Where are you at?"

"I'm in a phone booth. I don't have my glasses. I can't see the phone number."

Eddie said, "Why don't you call me in the morning when you know where you're at so I can do this for you?"

Commented Eddie Sapir, "With Billy, every day was a new day. But it was something we didn't mind doing. Sometimes we didn't enjoy the hour, but the guy was our friend, so we did it.''

Eddie Sapir, like Bill Reedy, was as good a friend a man could ever have.

Because he represented Billy and worked to do what was in the best interests of his client, Eddie often had set-tos with Jill. In an attempt to learn who Billy was seeing on the side, she would call his office in New Orleans to demand Billy's telephone records. Billy, of course, ordered Eddie not to make those records available to Jill, who would call Sapir's law office, talk to the young secretary, call her names and swear at her, and make her cry. But Jill never got those records.

It also bothered Eddie and Paul Tabarry, his associate, that while they were working so hard to pay off his IRS debt, she was dumping thousands of dollars into the house.

Said Paul Tabarry, ''She told me that she was paying the workmen renovating the house by the hour! I told her, 'You don't do that. They'll be out there forever.'

''She said, 'These guys are good. They aren't sitting down.' And maybe they weren't, but to me the first priority was clearing up Billy's IRS debt.''

In early 1989 Jill Martin was able to convince Billy that Eddie Sapir wasn't doing right by him, that *she* could do it better, and it was a testament to Jill's power over Billy that he allowed her to manage his finances.

Once Jill took over for Sapir, the two men no longer had any contact because Billy acted like a coward and felt embarrassed, and rather than face Sapir, he stayed away. Bill Reedy kept in touch with Sapir, telling him that Billy understood and relaying how much Billy loved him. Sapir told Reedy he knew that. By not calling Billy, Ed Sapir knew he was making it easier for Billy to coexist with Jill.

By taking on Billy's financial responsibilities, Jill was taking on a lot. There were times when Carol Reedy actually felt sorry for Jill. She watched as Billy's wife attempted to do the impossible, control Billy's life, keep him from drinking, keep him from his other women, and also try to oversee his business deals. There was no way she could succeed. How could she? She hadn't even graduated from high school.

When on July 14, 1989, the IRS placed a lien on their home, seeking back taxes of $35,564.62, Jill, who had no experience in such matters, was horrified. She thought she was going to lose all she had worked for.

Carol Reedy told her, ''Don't worry about it. All it means is if you sell it, the IRS will get what is owed them. We've had that before.''

''You have?'' Jill asked.

''Hell, yes. It's no big deal. You think Uncle Sam wants to own our apartment?''

When Jill told Carol she wanted to take over Billy's business affairs from Eddie Sapir, Carol told her, ''Let Eddie Sapir run it. Enjoy Billy and have a marriage.''

But Jill felt a need to have as much control as she could muscle.

Jill told Carol Reedy, ''You're stupid for not knowing what's going on in

Bill's life, not knowing what's going on in his bar, not seeing his books. You don't love your husband like I do. You should have your own money. You should be running something.''

When Bill Reedy found out that Billy was no longer going to be represented by Eddie Sapir, he asked him, "How can you? How?"

At that point Billy asked Reedy if *he* wanted to be his agent. Reedy told him, "No fucking way, partner. No. We're doing fine doing what we're doing. That's it. We have a lot of fun, and we're trying to make a buck with our ham company, but you're not going to get me involved with that."

As Bill Reedy saw it, Eddie Sapir's removal was the latest in a string of events that had split Billy's friends from him. She had caused Billy and Lewis Figone to drift apart by insulting Figone *and* his daughter, Vicki. She had gotten between Billy and the Klepfers by her attitude after she was asked to leave.

How Jill treated the Klepfers was one example of her behavior. The Klepfers had put Billy and her up at their home during four months of aggravation and turmoil, asking nothing in return, but when Katie Klepfer moved the Martins out, it was as though nothing that went on before counted for anything.

Jill took the eviction personally. Jill had hated that Billy and Mike Klepfer had become close, and after the Martins moved into their own home, Jill made two assertions.

The most incriminating was one in which Jill told Billy that Klepfer had been "hitting on her." One day Jill had ridden with Mike Klepfer in his truck. She had asked Mike to give her a lift from her house to his, a six-minute trip, and he had obliged.

Jill told Billy that during the trip Mike had said to her words to the effect, "You don't need Billy. I can take care of you. You live with me."

The Klepfers' friends felt it was absurd on the face of it. Mike and Katie Klepfer had a strong marriage. But Jill knew Billy very well. On the strength of Jill's accusation, Billy severed his relationship with Mike Klepfer despite all that Mike Klepfer had done for him.

The second assertion Jill made split Klepfer from his good friend Mickey Mantle. She wrote a note to Mickey at the Preston Trail Country Club saying that Mike Klepfer had been traveling to Atlanta to carry on an affair with Greer Johnson, Mickey Mantle's agent and girlfriend.

"Jill created that rift," said Klepfer. "She was clever because I am in the trucking business, and one of the locations where we dispose of used equipment is Atlanta. And when I was down there, if Greer was around, we'd go out for a bite. It was open. Mickey knew. There was nothing going on.

"And even if I had been so inclined, if I had been a rattlesnake and went after Greer, she was too much of a lady and too much in love with Mickey to participate."

But as a result of Jill's accusation, Mickey had a parting with Klepfer and also held bad feelings for Billy. For several months Billy and Mickey didn't talk. The rift between Mickey and Mike Klepfer never has completely closed.

Mickey, who shunned confrontation, never told Billy what was bothering him but instead withdrew. Billy never knew what Jill had done to hurt their relationship. All Billy knew was that Mickey disliked Jill intensely. Billy and Mickey loved each other, and each was angry that Jill had come between them, but ego kept them apart. Whenever Billy called Mickey, Mickey didn't return his calls.

When Bill Reedy met Billy in New York, Reedy would stay at the Barbizon Hotel, and the two would spend an afternoon sitting in the hotel bar by the window, watching the passing parade of people outside.

The Barbizon was also the hotel where Mickey Mantle would stay, and this one afternoon Reedy noticed that Billy was walking around the street-level bar, looking in all the corners, acting like a detective.

"What are you looking for?" Reedy asked him.

"I'm looking to see if Mike is here with Greer."

Reedy said, "Billy, this is where Mickey lives when he comes here. If the guy was fooling around, do you think he would come here and fool around? Come on. I just don't believe that."

Eventually, Billy and Mickey made up. Mike Klepfer asked Bill Reedy if he would go to Mickey and straighten it out.

Klepfer told Reedy, "This bitch has created a hell of a problem for me, planting that in Mickey's head."

Bill and Carol Reedy were in New York to spend the day with Billy the Sunday after a roast for Billy in Atlantic City. Billy and Bill went to Mickey Mantle's restaurant at around eleven-thirty in the morning and sat in the back room.

When Mickey arrived an hour later, the atmosphere was strained between Billy and Mick.

Mickey showed some tapes of himself hitting during his playing days. Billy had always idolized Mickey as a player. As Billy watched, he said to Reedy, "Watch him fall out when he swings left-handed." It was because of Mickey's bad knee, and he did give ground a little when he swung. "But watch him right-handed. He was the greatest right-handed hitter I ever saw."

Billy and Mickey started telling baseball stories. They began laughing, and Reedy could see it was like old times. Reedy kept quiet, just letting the two old friends talk.

Mickey told Billy, "This new chef makes the greatest fried chicken you ever saw."

Reedy mediated. He told them, "You've been friends for over thirty-five years and you're gonna let some cunt come between you? What the fuck is the matter with you two? I really enjoyed today, and you guys ought to see more of each other."

"Yeah, we ought to go hunting," Mickey said. Billy agreed.

Said Reedy, "You'll be in the blind together, and the important thing is, you'll be together. It's the way it should be."

Both agreed they had been foolish.

"Jesus Christ, I'm sorry," Mickey said to Billy.

After everyone had a great time, around nine at night Jill and Carol Reedy came into the restaurant. Jill had been searching all over for Billy.

Mickey hissed at her. "How the fuck did you find us?"

Jill had also helped alienate Billy from his sisters by repeating to Billy Aunt Ellen's assertion that he had been born an illegitimate child.

"Your mother hadn't really been married at the time of your birth," Jill told Billy. When Billy repeated that to his sisters, Joan and Pat, they became furious with him, and a rift developed.

What Jill did to Billy's daughter, Kelly, was even worse. Because of Jill's actions, Kelly became convinced her father didn't love her anymore.

Said Kelly Martin, "I was really sick, going into the hospital every week, and the doctors couldn't figure out what was wrong with me, and I kept calling Jill and asking her to tell my dad, but he never called me.

"Finally I called Bill Reedy and said, 'Doesn't my father even care about me? I'm going in for surgery in a few days. If it keeps going like this, I only have eight months to live.'

"Bill called my dad and told him, and my dad called me, and he said, 'Jesus Christ, how come I gotta hear it from my friend that there's something wrong with you?'

"I said, 'Because I never can get through to talk to you. Dad, I've called every day for over a month. Sometimes I get a recording. Sometimes I get her.'

"He said, 'I never got any messages. Not one.' "

As for Billy's younger child, his son, Billy Joe, Jill told Billy that the boy was a drug addict, a spendthrift, and a bum. She refused to make the last payment due on his college tuition, an act that could have kept him from graduating, and she did what she could to see that none of Billy's money was spent on him.

One time Billy Joe had gotten into a fight at Texas A&M, and his lawyer called Ed Sapir to say that for $160 he could get the civil and criminal actions dropped.

At that time Jill was insisting on okaying every check Eddie was writing. Her rule was: Any check dispersed for Billy Joe, you call me first.

Eddie Sapir knew in this instance the right thing to do was to pay the money and then call. He wrote a check from his own bank account. Then he called her, and they had a blowup. She wanted to know why he hadn't called to get her permission first.

"I am *never* going to call to get an okay for something like that," Sapir told her.

Sapir later said to Billy, "Look, I know it's your wife, and you have to live with her, but there's no way I'm going to be calling to get an authorization for a hundred and sixty dollars for Billy Joe. I know what you want me to do for Billy Joe."

After Billy left Eddie Sapir in the spring of 1989, he didn't talk to him until October 26, 1989, when Billy came to New Orleans to perform "The Saga of Billy the Kid" with the Binghamton Philharmonic. By coincidence it was also

Eddie Sapir Night in New Orleans. Senators and congressmen attended. New Orleans' legendary singer Fats Domino performed. But what made the night particularly special for Sapir was being able to spend the evening with Billy.

While Peggy Sapir talked with Jill, Eddie and Billy put their heads together and talked all night. Billy expressed how grateful he was that Eddie had stepped down to make it easy on Jill, rather than fight her for control.

Sapir told Billy, "I did it for you. This is what Jill wanted, and I know in a million years you never would have asked me to step down. I just made it easy for you."

Sapir told him, "I will always be there for you."

Billy said he knew that.

Billy spent part of their conversation complaining about how much money Jill was spending on the property, especially on the barn and the horses.

"I have a $300,000 barn!" Billy told Sapir. He added, "The place is nice. There's a lake, but I just can't go out and wet my line every day. It gets old."

Says Eddie Sapir, "I'm convinced Billy wanted to leave Binghamton and leave soon." But, says Eddie Sapir, though he may have wanted to leave, he doesn't think he ever would have.

"He would have yielded to what Jill wanted him to do and lived with the situation and hoped it would change," he said.

When Jill separated Billy and Eddie Sapir, only two of Billy's close friends remained: Bill and Carol Reedy.

By July 1989, Billy would head down to the Bull & Bear bar in Binghamton in the late morning, and by four-thirty Detroit time, after four or five hours of drinking, Billy would call Bill Reedy collect. The phone would ring in Reedy's office in his bar, and it would be Billy. Reedy's phone bills were astronomical.

"What's going on, pard?"

If Reedy wasn't in his office, Billy would call Carol to ask Bill to call him. When Billy learned to call Reedy on Bill's beeper, sometimes Billy would call him from airplanes. Jill was very jealous of Billy's reliance on Bill Reedy for his friendship.

She drove all his friends away, Carol thought to herself. One of these days *we're* going to be the victims.

Said Carol Reedy, "She can't drive me away, because as slick as she is about all those things I'm not, we're solid in our marriage, and no way could she end that. She tried to put doubt in my mind about my husband being faithful to me, but it just didn't work. She finally gave up. She considered me stupid.

"She is a very devious person. I didn't realize it at the time or it would have scared the hell out of me."

Jill would get back at the Reedys in her own time.

**53**

# THE DEATH OF JENNY DOWNEY

**D**uring the 1989 season George Steinbrenner made Billy a roving scout for the Yankees. His job was to go from city to city to scout both the opposing major league players and players in the Yankee farm system. Considering his state of mind, it was a perfect job for Billy.

During 1988, after Billy was fired as manager for the last time, he and Jill fought even more fiercely, and Billy began staying away for longer periods of time.

With Jill tied down to her house in Binghamton, the job gave Billy the perfect opportunity to get away from her, to travel from city to city to visit his many girlfriends and to spend time in bars with Bill Reedy.

As soon as Billy would leave, Jill would begin tracking down his whereabouts in a desperate attempt to keep tabs on him. The more she fought to keep tabs on him, the more he sought to avoid her, and the more afraid she would become that he would leave her. Here was a classically destructive relationship. Jill drove Billy crazy with her calls, and Billy left enough clues of his infidelity to drive to torture this rightfully insecure woman.

On March 16, 1989, Billy was in Tampa, Florida, meeting with George. During the evening, he picked up a hooker, brought her back to his room, had sex and fell asleep. She took his Rolex watch and all his money.

The next day Billy called Bill Reedy, who sent Billy a thousand dollars by Western Union.

Jill found out he had been robbed. She repeatedly asked Carol Reedy, "She was a hooker, wasn't she?" Carol didn't know and said so.

When Billy was on the road, Jill was afraid to leave the house, lest Billy call and she not be home, because she knew he would raise hell and accuse her of being unfaithful. When they were together, Jill diligently avoided eye contact with other men.

Said Carol Reedy, "He couldn't imagine anyone being faithful because he never was."

Billy was insanely jealous, not just of his wife, but of any girl he had gone with. Bill Reedy was sitting with him in a bar one day when Julio Iglesias sang a song on the jukebox.

"Who the fuck played that?" Billy wanted to know.

"Julio Iglesias," said Reedy. "Why?"

"He was fucking Heather." Billy was steaming, ready to explode. The charge was absurd, a product of Billy's paranoia.

"Can I ask you a question, Billy?" said Reedy. "Do you think she was going to sew up her pussy after you left her, you fucking macho prick, you?"

"Fuck you," Martin replied. The anger passed.

When Billy was with his girlfriends, he treated them like gold. There were no problems then. He would see them, make love to them, leave them, and there were no complications or aggravations. He had no responsibilities.

With Jill, he did everything he could to make her feel insecure. The more she tried to keep tabs on him, the harder he would try to escape her detection. It was a cat-and-mouse game played out on the telephone.

One time Billy visited the Reedys in Detroit. Billy and Bill Reedy went to the bar of the Pontchartrain Hotel to drink. Carol Reedy was working at Reedy's Bar on Michigan Avenue at the time.

Jill called Carol to ask where Billy was. Carol didn't realize she wasn't supposed to tell Jill. She informed her that the boys were at the Pontchartrain.

Jill correctly assumed they were at the bar. The phone rang. Jill, knowing Billy wouldn't take the call if he knew she was on the other end, asked for Billy Martin and identified herself as Carol Reedy. Billy took the phone, and when he discovered it was Jill, he pulled the phone from the wall and threw it across the barroom.

Billy began screaming, "Call her up and tell her off and get an attorney and sue her for using a false name, for falsely identifying herself as Carol. Do it."

Bill Reedy knew that when Billy was this hot, he had better obey. Reedy went to another phone. Billy watched him. Reedy dialed Jill. She answered.

Bill Reedy said, "I'm supposed to be bawling you out." They talked a few more minutes, and he hung up. Billy was satisfied.

One time Billy caught Jill taping his phone calls. He couldn't believe she could do such a thing.

Billy called Reedy and asked him to meet him in Columbus, Ohio, where he was scouting. Steinbrenner had sent Martin to scout the Columbus ball club. Reedy arrived first and waited for Billy at the airplane gate.

Billy said, "Hey, wait till I show you something."

They went to the bar and sat down. Billy said, "Fucking Jill."

Reedy said, "What?"

Billy pulled out a cassette tape. Billy said, "I was at home looking for my bag to pack, and I went down to the fucking basement and the phone rings. I figure, Fuck it, I ain't gonna answer the phone. Then, all of a sudden, I hear a click. I thought it was the furnace. I said to myself, 'What the fuck is the furnace doing kicking in in July?' I went over to the furnace, and there was a tape recorder. I played the tape, and you and I were on the fucking tape."

Billy said, "I don't know how long she's been doing this."

Billy and Reedy arranged for Billy to make his personal calls from the Bull & Bear bar if there was call that he didn't want Jill finding out about. Otherwise, the calls from home would be limited to yes/no answers.

Billy went to the winter meetings in Nashville, Tennessee, in November 1989. Representing the Yankees, Billy believed he was authorized to talk to the Toronto executives about a deal, but he was informed by Pat Gillick, the general manager of the Blue Jays, that he didn't have the authority from George to talk to them.

Billy blew up. He flew right out of town.

Billy said to Bill Reedy, "George told me I'm going to have more input. Do you believe that shit?"

Reedy told him, "No, I don't, and neither do you. It's going to be the same old George. That's what you say, 'Same old George.' "

During this period Jill was sending Billy out on the road to do some extra money-making appearances. On December 10, Billy had a speaking engagement in Terre Haute, Indiana, where he was the featured speaker at a fund-raiser for the Indiana State University baseball team.

After his talk, Billy went to drink at Larry Bird's sports bar in Terre Haute. A female patron left her purse on the bar. When another patron accidentally knocked it onto the floor, a two-shot .38-caliber derringer, which was in the purse, went off. The bullet whizzed by Billy's head, missing him by two feet.

Billy flew from Terre Haute to Oakland to visit his mother, who was deathly ill. Billy went to the hospital, where her tiny body lay under white sheets. She had been in and out of consciousness, but she revived long enough to recognize her Billy. Jenny looked up at Billy and patted his hand. She told him how good looking he was. An hour later she was dead.

The phone rang at the Reedy home in Detroit. Carol Reedy picked it up. It was Billy, crying like a baby. His mother had died at age eighty-eight.

Funerals are supposed to bring grieving families together. But Jill had caused such bitter feelings among so many of Billy's relatives and friends that harmony during the three days Billy spent in West Berkeley for his mom's funeral was impossible.

For some time Jill had been giving Billy inaccurate information about his children, Kelly and Billy Joe. She had told Billy that Kelly had a drug problem and was an unfit mother.

Jill had stopped paying Billy Joe's college tuition, telling Billy he was nothing but a professional student, would never get his diploma, was a leech. According to Carol Reedy, Jill accused Billy Joe of trying to live the high lifestyle, saying the boy felt that as the son of Billy Martin he deserved to live that way.

Part of the problem was that Billy was not the kind of father who could talk to his children. He was distant. Often Billy Joe would call Bill Reedy and say, "What can I do? My father thinks" this or that. At the same time Billy would be in Bill Reedy's other ear, saying, "You talk to him. He'll listen to you." Reedy would say, "Leave me out of this. I have enough with my own kids," but Reedy still tried to help. When Billy allowed Jill to cut the boy off, it was Bill Reedy who paid the $600 tuition so Billy Joe could finish at Texas A&M and get his diploma.

Reedy even told Billy he was sending the boy the money. He told Billy, "I'm not doing this behind your back. Jill won't send him any more money. She stopped paying him. I'm going to send him six hundred dollars."

"Okay, go ahead," Billy said.

At the time Reedy wired the money, he asked Billy Joe, "Are you getting into trouble?"

"No."

"Are you doing drugs?"

"No."

"Are you booking horses?"

"No."

Reedy sent the money. Reedy thought Billy Joe to be bright, handsome, everything in a son Billy would have loved. Reedy always told Billy he should have spent more time with Billy Joe than he had, but Billy had trouble with meaningful relationships, and he wasn't much of a father.

"It's a goddamn shame Billy didn't spend more time with him," says Bill Reedy. "Billy Joe is everything Billy Martin would want out of a son."

The evening before his mother's funeral Billy and the family went to an Italian restaurant named Francesco's for dinner in a hotel near the Oakland airport.

Billy Joe sat between Billy and Bill Reedy. Billy Joe turned to Reedy and asked him, "Did my dad ever accuse you of going to bed with Jill?"

Reedy said, "Billy Joe, hell no, to start with, Billy knows I hate her. He knows goddamn well I wouldn't go near her."

Billy Joe said, "Well, he has asked me."

Reedy said, "Well, you little son of a bitch, have you?"

"No, no," said Billy Joe.

Just as the food was being served, Billy accused Billy Joe of not having a diploma.

"She's lying," Billy Joe told his father about Jill's accusation. "And it was Mr. Reedy who sent me the money to finish my last two months." Billy Joe began to cry.

Billy Joe then pulled out a piece of paper.

"Here, Dad. Look. I got it here. She's not telling you the truth."

And then Billy Joe, tears streaming down his face, presented Billy with his diploma from Texas A&M. Billy Joe had been the first member of the Martin family to earn a college degree.

Billy, overcome with emotion, got up and quickly walked out of the dining room toward the hotel lobby. Bill Reedy followed after him. Billy was standing in the hallway, hands in his pockets, staring out the window.

"What do you think?" Billy asked.

"I think she's a fucking liar," Reedy replied. "Let's go eat our dinner with your son."

Billy returned to the table, patted Billy Joe on the back, and dinner resumed.

The next morning Billy and Bill Reedy went out to the home of Billy's daughter, Kelly. Jill had been telling Billy that Kelly Ann was a drug addict, a bum, someone who wanted Billy only for his money.

They arrived at Kelly's home. Reedy saw it was clean, that her granddaughter was well groomed, dressed nicely. It was a three-bedroom apartment, with one of the rooms dedicated to her father.

After the visit Billy and Reedy drove back to the hotel. Billy asked him, "What do you think?"

Reedy said, "I don't see anything here." Reedy, a street guy, had been around the drug scene all his life in inner city Detroit. His senses told him Kelly wasn't involved in any way with drugs.

During Billy's visit to Kelly's home, Billy started crying at the thought of his mom's death. Kelly wasn't sympathetic. All her life she had hated Billy's mother and his sisters, feeling that they had shunned her mother, Lois, and her as well.

Kelly had remained in contact with Billy's father, Alfred Manuel Martin, and his relatives, and over the years they had filled her ears with stories about Billy's mom, whom they had hated just as deeply as she had hated them.

Kelly told Billy, "Dad, come on. Okay, she was your mother. She's gone. It's not the end of your world, because she was never nice to you to begin with."

Kelly recalled her memory of the time when she was about ten when Jenny had asked Billy for money, and when Billy wasn't forthcoming, she had grabbed a belt and started hitting Billy with it as hard as she could, calling him nasty, mean names.

According to Kelly, Billy replied, "I wish I had been around more. I wish I would have gotten to be closer with my dad."

Kelly said, "I wish you would have, too."

Billy said, " 'Cause he was good to you."

"Yes, he was," said Kelly.

When Kelly was a young girl, Al Martin would come over to Lois's house every other weekend and pick her up and take her roller-skating or ice-skating or to a cousin's house. Every Christmas and birthday he sent her a savings bond. Billy's father had died in 1986.

Kelly told her father, "Your mother's dead now. I can tell you the truth. Your father made me promise not to tell you this until she was dead."

She said, "Your mother held a knife to your throat, and she threatened to kill you unless Alfred left. Unless your father left and never came around you again.''

Said Kelly, ''Your mother told Alfred, 'If I ever see you anywhere around, I will kill the boy.' ''

Kelly said, ''That's why your father never came around. It wasn't 'cause he didn't love you. He loved you so much he stayed away. That woman who you thought was so great was going to kill you. Why do you think you lived at your grandmother's? Because she piped up and said she would see that nothing ever happened to you, that she would take care of you. That's why you lived with Nonna.''

Explained Kelly, ''That's why my grandfather made me promise never to tell my dad so long as his mother was alive. Because Billy loved his mother, and Billy's dad didn't want Billy to have nobody. Because Billy didn't have his dad, and Billy's grandfather didn't want Billy to be without his mom, who he cherished.

''As much as she beat my dad and put him down, my grandfather didn't want him to be without somebody he thought loved him.''

Kelly told Billy that several times Al Martin had gone to see his Oakland A's play.

Billy said, ''But he didn't come to me for tickets.''

''No, he wouldn't do that,'' said Kelly. ''He bought his own tickets.''

Kelly says, ''I know that what Al told me was true because his wife, Eva, came up to the Lake Country in the summer and spent time with us, and when I was a little girl I would ask her questions about Billy's mom, and she would get very irate.

''She'd say, 'Why even ask about that woman? That damn bitch caused your grandfather so much pain and grief.'

''Grandpa would say, 'Eva, Eva.'

''Then I'd say to him, 'Why does Grandma get so upset?' And he'd say, 'She's from the Old School. She doesn't like to see people get hurt.'

''I'd say, 'Grandpa, why don't you ever go see my dad? Why didn't you ever go see him when he was little? You came to see me? Didn't you love him?'

''He'd say, 'I loved him very much, honey. One day when you are older, you'll learn why.'

''When I was older, maybe fifteen, I said, 'Grandpa, I'm older now. Can you tell me why now?'

''Grandpa said, 'It's not really important. What's important is that I love your dad, and I love you.'

''Eva said, 'Why can't you tell her the truth, that you loved your son so much that you stayed away so that bitch wouldn't kill him.'

''And that's when they told me. And Grandpa made me promise never to tell my dad until after Jenny had died.''

Kelly told Billy, ''I just don't see any reason why you should fall apart because she's dead. Okay, she was your mother, but at the same time you always fought for her love and attention, the same way I fight for your love and attention, Dad. Why can't you just come back here to California? Leave Jill. Forget her.''

He said, "I'm coming. I promise you."

Kelly said, "I've heard that before. 'We're going to spend time together.' But you know that day never comes. Are you just telling me now because this is what you think I want to hear? Or are you strong enough to do it?''

Billy said, "Yeah, I am. Because you know what, Kelly? She's made us grow apart, when we were close. She made me move back there. I don't want to live back there. I love my Blackhawk house. We could have been together.''

"I know," Kelly said. "That's what you kept telling us, that we'd have barbecues, that you'd come and stay.''

Billy said, "Kelly, I even fixed up the basement of that house in Binghamton for you and Evie to come and live with me.''

Kelly wasn't impressed. She said, "Oh yeah? That would go over real big. Dad, she's afraid of me. She keeps saying to Carol Reedy, 'Stay away from Kelly. She's bad.' ''

Troubled by Kelly's story about his mother, Billy was feeling hostility toward his sisters, Pat and Joan. They were equally furious with him for spreading the untrue story that Jenny had been unwed at the time of Billy's birth.

Joan knew that the story wasn't true because she had in her possession the marriage license for Jenny and Al Martin. Billy had been born more than nine months after the date on the certificate.

Their anger toward Billy increased when, before the funeral service, he informed them that he deserved to inherit his mother's house. He also asked for them to return the World Series rings he had given them.

Says Pat Irvine about Billy's claim that he had paid for the house, "That house was my grandmother's, and before she died, she wanted to give it to my mother, and Mother said, 'No, I'm married with my own house, give it to Joe,' my uncle.

"She said, 'No, I want to give it to you.' Ma said, 'No, give it to Joe.' In that time there was no greed. So my grandmother put the house in my uncle's name. And my uncle, Joe Salvini, lived there. He had been older, never been married, and when he met this lady, my mother said, 'Good, get married.' But he didn't want to live in the house. So my mother and dad bought the house off him. It wasn't for very much money, and my dad remodeled it, and we all moved into that. But Billy never put one penny into it.

"Billy never sent any money to my mom. Never. A couple of times he gave her a thousand dollars. Years ago when it was her birthday. The rest of the times, flowers. There's no central heating in his mom's house. Do you think he cared? You'd think he would have said, 'Gee, let me do something for my family. I'll put in heat for them upstairs. Or maybe add a room to make the home a little bigger.' No no no no. There were a lot of things he could have done, but he didn't. One time he got some carpeting for doing a commercial, and so he carpeted the downstairs. But that was all.''

Lewis Figone says he finds it hard to believe Billy really wanted the house.

Said Figone, "Billy was very upset about losing his mother, and he was very upset about the problems his family had. He told me he was going to go see them after the funeral and really tell them off.

"Billy treated his family good, his mother and father. I know he wasn't *really* going to try to take the house. He was just upset. If his mother had been around, it never would have happened.

"I told him, 'Billy, forget it. You're all upset now.' "

Billy made the demands anyway.

Billy had given his mother the World Series ring from 1953. It had been the fifth World Series win in a row for the Yankees, a priceless treasure. Billy asked for it back.

Even though there was no evidence that Jill was involved, Billy's sisters, who hated Jill, assumed she was behind it.

Said Billy's sister Joan: "Every wife of Billy's wanted my mother's '53 ring. They all thought they could just walk into our house and demand that ring. And my mother was supposed to say, 'Here, sweetheart, you're my daughter.'

Before she died, Jenny told Joan, "Before Jill gets ahold of it, take that fucking ring and throw it in the ocean."

Said Vicki Figone, "It was the day before the funeral, and he wanted the rings back. She had to be behind it, because Billy would never ask for anything back from anybody.

"They had a large family fight."

The sisters were still angry with his comments about their mom being unwed at the time of his birth, so when Billy asked them for his mother's noodle maker, they refused.

At the funeral itself, there was a lot of glaring and bad feelings all around.

If any good came from the weekend, it was the patching-up of the friendship between Billy and childhood friend Lewis Figone.

The night after the funeral, Billy had an opportunity to talk with Figone, whom he hadn't spoken to in a year and a half. Jill had caused the rift between them. During that time Billy often said to Bill Reedy, "I wish Lewis would talk to me." Billy hadn't been aware of *why* Figone was angry with him—that Jill had poisoned the atmosphere by antagonizing both him and his daughter. Billy invited Figone to go to Mickey Mantle's golf outing the following October.

Around the table sat Bill Reedy, Billy, Jill, Billy Joe, Kelly Ann, and Lewis Figone. Jill never opened her mouth.

During that meal Billy leaned over to Bill Reedy and asked him whether he should ask Figone to lend him a hundred thousand dollars. Billy was broke.

Reedy told him, "You just got back talking to the guy. You can't ask him for that."

Said Billy, "I guess you're right."

A couple days after the funeral Billy called the Figone home looking for Lewis, who wasn't in. Vicki answered. According to Vicki, Billy sounded very depressed, like he was going to cry.

Billy said to her, "You know, Vicki, a long time has passed since I have spent any time with your father and all my friends in the Bay Area, and that is going to stop. I'm going to start coming out here more. I'm going to come out right after Christmas. I'm going to spend a lot of time with your dad at the duck club. I miss Matt Keough. I miss my family." Vicki could hear the emotion building within him.

Vicki said, "Billy, you know you really hurt my father. You haven't called. We never hear from you."

Billy said, "This thing with Jill and your family . . ."

Vicki said, "That's beside the point."

"This is all going to change," Billy said. "I'm going to come out to the Bay Area and be with my friends."

Billy was also feeling guilty about the way he had dumped Mike and Katie Klepfer after all they had done for him.

Shortly after the funeral Billy called Mike Klepfer's dad, Ellis, and he told him, "When I get back right after the holidays, you and I and Mike are going out. We're going to bury the hatchet."

The rosary for Billy's mom was held at Ellis Olson Mortuary. It was an old Italian funeral home with a small alcove for the family. Tudo, Joan, and Pat were there. Even Heather came. Mike Norris, the former A's pitcher, came to comfort Billy, who cried off and on. Ruben DeAlba and another Bay Area friend, Choke Mejia, also attended. So did Lewis and Vicki Figone. And Jill.

After the rosary, which was scheduled for eight-thirty, Billy and Bill Reedy and the family went to a seafood restaurant.

Later that evening Billy and Bill Reedy returned to the hotel and sat at the bar from nine-thirty to one in the morning. During their conversation, Billy again asked his friend, "Would you please come for the holidays?" meaning the Christmas holidays, which were only two weeks away.

Billy had broached the subject earlier. As an inducement to the Reedys to leave their family in Detroit and come see him in Binghamton, Billy promised a trip to New York City to go to St. Patrick's Cathedral for midnight mass Christmas Eve.

Bill Reedy earlier had told his wife, Carol, "It's up to you, but I'd like to go." At the funeral of Billy's mother, Reedy saw how shook up Billy was, and he told Carol, "He's taking it hard. We ought to go."

Carol's mother was dying of cancer, but her family thought a trip to New York was a terrific idea because of the planned stop at St. Patrick's for the elaborate Christmas mass. Carol's mom told her, "I'd like to go to that myself." And because her family didn't seem to mind that she was going to Binghamton to be with the Martins, Carol Reedy told her husband, "Let's go."

And so Bill Reedy informed Billy that they would indeed spend the Christmas holidays with them. Billy was grateful.

"Thanks, pard," he said.

After their drinking was done, Reedy said to Billy, "I'm not going to go to the service tomorrow. I said good-bye to your mom tonight. I'm flying out in the morning.''

Billy hugged Reedy and began to cry. "I've lost my pal," Billy said about his mom. "Thanks for coming up. I understand. I'll have Billy Joe drive you.''

Billy, drunk, then left the bar and went up to be with Jill.

# CHRISTMAS DAY

# 1989

**B**illy Martin hated Christmas. He had from the time he was a little boy. He felt poor growing up. Presents were few. The holiday was a reminder that his father had deserted him, that his relationship with his mother could be rocky, their fights at times acrimonious and hurtful. As an adult, whenever Christmas came around, he shunned calling her, angering his siblings.

Said his sister Pat Irvine, "My mother didn't like Christmas either, but yet she would go all out for Christmas, have the big dinners. When Billy was younger, he came, but after he went to New York as a player, all of a sudden, Christmas didn't mean anything. He didn't want to be around people at Christmastime, didn't want to be around all those festivities. He just wanted to be off by himself."

When he was a player, he saw that Yogi Berra would go home to Carmen and his family at Christmas, and Mickey Mantle would go home to Merlyn, as rocky a marriage as they had, and Phil Rizzuto had Cora and his kids, but for many years Billy didn't feel he had anyone to go home to. After he married Gretchen, he would go out and get drunk and come home to kick over the Christmas tree, a reminder of what he didn't have as a youth.

Said Pat, "When he was an adult, everybody wanted Billy to come over. He didn't want to hurt anyone's feelings, so he promised everyone he'd come, say yes to everyone. But he would never show up. After a while, Christmas became too much of a hassle."

Christmas released Billy's inner demons. The holiday haunted him like a recurring nightmare. Once, while he was living with Mike Klepfer, a friend of Mike's, Bill Norton, told Billy of his own aversion for Christmas, and Billy said, "I just don't like to talk about Christmas."

The Reedys had come to Binghamton for the weekend after Billy had promised they would attend Christmas Eve mass at St. Patrick's Cathedral. But Jill had developed a bad cold, and they didn't go. They remained in Binghamton, freezing in the Martin home because of a faulty heating unit.

The day before Christmas, Billy and Jill quarreled over a Christmas card that Heather had sent him. Billy and Bill Reedy spent the day drinking at the Bull & Bear.

Jill began Christmas Day doing what Bill Reedy described as "bitching and nagging." Exactly what she was saying, Reedy cannot remember. He shut the noise out. But Billy heard, and at around eleven-thirty he told Reedy they were "getting the fuck out of here."

Billy and Bill Reedy drove off in Billy's truck to get some kerosene. Billy was raising quail in a brooder out behind the main house, and he needed the kerosene to heat the heater to keep the birds warm.

Once they got into Billy's truck, Billy said to Reedy, "Did you hear her?"

Reedy answered, "Fuck her. Don't pay any attention to her. Carol says a lot of things to me, and I don't fucking listen."

"It's easy for you to say," said Billy. "You're going to be on a fucking airplane and out of here tomorrow."

"You married her," Reedy said. "I didn't. Fuck, don't be mad at me."

Billy said, "This is my last motherfucking winter here, freezing my nuts off."

At about noon they stopped at Workingman's Gas on Front Street. William Simpson, the station manager, told Billy he was out of kerosene and directed him to try the Sunoco Day and Night.

Simpson saw Billy drive off down Front Street toward Binghamton, where they stopped at the Day and Night. Billy bought the fuel, putting it in the bed of the truck. Bill Reedy bought a few supplies, including a toothbrush, some razor blades, a Mounds candy bar, a jar of Vaseline, and he grabbed a pack of matches.

When they left the Sunoco station, they headed to a favorite Billy Martin watering hole, Morey's Tavern. Reedy was surprised that Billy could get a drink Christmas Day. In Michigan the bars closed at nine at night Christmas Eve. When the truck approached Morey's, the sign read, PRIME RIB DINNER, 1 P.M. CHRISTMAS.

Billy said, "If they're serving Christmas dinner, they're serving drinks."

They sat at the bar with four other Christmas drinkers, including a part-time bartender, an older man who used to be a golf pro, and a car salesman at Miller Honda who was there with his Chesapeake Bay Labrador retriever puppy sitting in his lap.

In the bar Billy ordered a Stoliychnaya and Reedy had a screwdriver. After one drink, Reedy switched to Budweiser beer. Reedy, a bar owner, preferred drinking beer out of the can because back home when someone offered to buy him a drink, he had to accept to keep from insulting the offerer and starting a fight. When he drank out of a can, he could take a few sips, then dump it.

Billy talked golf with the pro, whom Billy had met on the local golf course several months earlier. They had played in the same foursome. The pro told Billy he could better his score if he didn't swing quite so hard.

Billy then chatted about raising quail and pheasant with the man with the dog. The man had gone hunting that day, but the snow was too high for his little puppy, so he quit hunting and had come to Morey's for a few beers. He told Billy about his hunting dog, and when Billy asked to see it, he went and got it and showed it around the bar for five minutes.

Billy then talked to Reedy about more personal concerns. He spoke about Billy Joe and about Kelly and said how he realized that what Jill had been saying about them had not been true.

"I can't figure out the reasoning," Billy said. "I don't know why, but she's wrong."

"I'm going to leave her," Martin said. "I'm going to get rid of her. I'm going to fucking get rid of her."

But Reedy knew that Billy saying it and Billy doing it were two different things. After all, he had hit her and sent her to the hospital that summer. She had threatened to sue him for palimony while he was married to Heather. It had all the hallmarks of those sick, needy relationships in which the two partners fight like cats and dogs and keep coming back for more.

It hurt Bill Reedy to think Billy would stay with her.

Billy talked about his future. Billy was still getting paid big money, but his responsibilities with the Yankees were unclear. He talked wistfully about George Steinbrenner making him a vice president, but Reedy didn't believe that was ever going to happen.

Billy also talked about George making him manager again, promising that he would be back, but Reedy saw this, too, as only wishful thinking, a ray of hope to Billy. George had not approached Billy to manage in 1989. Bucky Dent, George's newest protégé, was going to be the manager. But Billy knew it would be just a matter of time before George called Billy to bail him out again.

"I'll be back," Billy said. Reedy nodded. There was nothing to say. Whether he managed again would be entirely at the whim of George Steinbrenner.

Meanwhile, at around noon at the Martin home, Jill was telling Carol that she knew from the phone records that Billy had called Heather's close friend, Semora Landreano, several times.

"Billy says they are only friends, but I don't believe him," Jill said. This time Billy was telling the truth. The woman had spurned his advances, but they had continued as friends.

Jill told Carol, "I want you to look through Bill's little book to see if there are phone numbers of other women."

Carol said she would, figuring she would tell Jill she had looked but had found nothing. Carol well knew that Bill's book contained the phone numbers of *all* of Billy's women friends. In fact, the first time Carol had sneaked a peak into the book, she had confronted her husband, who asked her, "Whose numbers do you *think* they belong to?" He told her the names that went with the numbers.

Later that Christmas Day afternoon, Jill said to Carol, "Come in here. I want you to hear something." While Carol "stood there like a dummy," Jill played a tape of a telephone conversation from the day before, at the end of which Bill Reedy was heard saying to Carol about Jill, "You know the fucking bitch."

Carol was taken aback. She tried to make light of her husband's crass remark.

Reedy had known Jill was taping phone conversations because Billy had told him about it. But Bill Reedy hadn't told his wife. The Watergate burglars have nothing on this one, Carol thought to herself.

Carol was embarrassed, giving Jill an opening to ask Carol questions about things she might know about Billy. In one of their final conversations, Jill wanted to know whether she knew about some woman named Donna from Cleveland.

Donna had written Billy a letter, which Jill showed Carol, and in it the woman said, in effect, "Whenever you get ready to leave her, give me a call, because I know you want to."

Jill was sure that Bill Reedy was keeping the phone numbers for Billy. And Jill was right, but Carol played dumb.

By four o'clock in the afternoon it was snowing heavily, and Carol and Jill began to look out the window toward the driveway to see if Billy and Bill had arrived. They weren't worried, but it was getting late, and there was a Christmas dinner to prepare.

Sitting at Morey's Tavern, Billy decided it was getting late and he might as well go home. It was Christmas, after all, and Jill had a lamb roast in the oven.

Over a final drink Billy switched to a favorite subject: sex. He discussed with Bill Reedy "how much I love to eat pussy." The day before Bill Reedy had bought a box of cigars, and Billy smoked a cigar and talked about his longtime girlfriend Lisa and how much he liked her.

They left the bar and got into Billy's truck. Billy, behind the wheel, wore a baseball cap that said ROCHESTER POLICE DEPARTMENT. He had a workman's glove on his left hand. Reedy sat on the passenger side, his legs sideways because of the lack of legroom. Neither man attached his seat belt. Neither ever wore one.

It was snowing hard. Though it was only five o'clock, it was already dark.

Billy drove easily down to Highway 12A and then turned onto Route 369. Ordinarily Billy turned off at the Ballyhack Road exit, but he and Bill Reedy were talking to each other, and as Billy spoke he looked at Reedy and missed the exit.

"Goddamn it, I missed the turn," Billy said, "but what the hell, there's another turn right up here."

They continued talking. Billy went another quarter mile and took a right on Beartown Road. He had to make a big loop, making a right onto Monkey Run

Road, another right on Vincent Hill, then a right down Hunt Hill Road to Potter's Field Road, where he lived. It was no big deal, an extra five minutes to get home.

It was more hilly going this way, but his was a four-wheel-drive pickup truck. Billy had never had any trouble traversing the country roads in his 4X4. Ford made a powerful truck.

According to Bill Reedy, Billy had taken this route in the past when he anticipated that the police were watching out for him. So many patrons of Morey's Tavern or the Bull & Bear had seen him leave loaded that there had been a stream of phone calls to the police.

A typical call: "My cousin got arrested for DWI last week. Here's Billy Martin getting drunk out here, and you don't do anything about it."

The calls were so numerous that the traffic department decided it had better do something about it. Captain Vasbery of the Fenton police issued a task force order that any officer who saw a blue Ford pickup truck should pull over the driver for any reason.

Billy found out about the order, and twice he went to the Bull & Bear and drank water all day. At the end of the day he pretended to stumble around, got in his truck, and rode home. Both times when he was stopped he was cold sober. Billy always was the ultimate game player.

Had he not missed his usual exit, Billy would have made a left into his driveway. This time, because Billy had missed the exit and had to loop around, he would need to come down Hunt Hill Road, stop at a sign, make a left-hand turn onto Potters Field Road, and then immediately make a right into his driveway.

As Billy was coming to the bottom of Hunt Hill Road, he was talking about his mother. He said to Bill Reedy, "She's with the Lord." While turning left onto Potters Field Road, the truck began to skid sideways.

A dusting of powder covered a road already packed with snow, it was icy, and there was no traction. Billy tried to warn Reedy that the truck was sliding. He wasn't going very fast, so the warning was said with little urgency, either "Look out" or "Hold on." Reedy can't remember which.

As the truck lost control and slid into the ditch, Billy could have stepped on the brake and allowed the truck to settle into it. Had he done so there would have been minimal damage to the truck. But Billy took getting stuck in the ditch as a personal challenge, and rather than stop, he did the opposite. He floored the gas pedal, betting that the faster speed would free the truck from its prison. Moving forward, Billy turned the wheel hard to the left, but the right-side wheels could not escape the ditch. Too late Billy saw the circular shape of a large pipe directly in front of him. He jammed the brake, leaving a footprint on the brake pad. He bit down on the cigar he had in his mouth.

The two right-side tires were still mired in the rut when Billy struck the large culvert, built by his handyman with the permission of the town of Fenton. The force of the impact and the suddenness of the stop left an imprint of the steering wheel lacing on Billy's left glove.

The truck was traveling less than thirty miles an hour when it hit the four-foot-deep culvert, skidded, and landed on its side.

If Billy hadn't erected the huge brick entranceway with the B.M. in brass circles on the wrought-iron fence, he wouldn't have had to build the large culvert, and he wouldn't have been injured badly at all. Billy Martin wanted those huge gates to announce it was Billy Martin's place, and his grandiosity helped do him in.

Upon impact with the culvert, Billy lurched forward, striking the bridge of his nose against the top of the steering wheel. The top of his head then hit the windshield. His abdomen pressed hard against the steering wheel, which mushroomed inward. The impact and the subsequent rebound toward the backrest of the seat caused his neck to snap.

Letting go of the steering wheel, Billy went limp and fell backward. His inert body lay against the back wall of the cab, and since the truck was tilting at a steep angle to the right, he slid down toward the passenger-side door, along with everything else in the truck, including the items he and Reedy had bought: Vaseline, razor blades, a candy bar, a toothbrush as well as the pack of matches obtained from the Sunoco Day and Night food store just before the accident, and Bill Reedy's cigars.

Reedy, sitting on the passenger side, struck his head against the rearview mirror and then the windshield, and after he snapped back from the impact, the right side of his body was compressed under the narrow dashboard. His right leg was pushed straight back, and his right hip was badly injured. Reedy also suffered glass cuts on the second and third fingers of his left hand.

Reedy leaned over and rubbed Billy's face. Reedy thought Billy had been knocked out. Reedy said, "Billy, if you can get up, I can push you out the window."

Billy said nothing and didn't move.

Bill Reedy saw a light from a nearby house in front of him. He didn't realize it, but the light was coming from Billy's house.

Reedy tried to find the switch to flip the headlights from dimmer to brighter, dimmer to brighter, to bring help, but he had never driven the truck before and didn't know where the switch was located.

The first to arrive at the scene was a family who passed by moments after the impact. The father, Peter Piech, found Reedy holding on to the steering wheel of the truck in an attempt to keep the weight of his body from falling against Billy, who sat inert on the passenger side.

When members of the Port Crane Volunteer Fire Department arrived several minutes later, Piech was found holding Reedy by the lapel of his coat to keep him from falling downward in the cab. Billy Martin was still seated in the passenger side of the cab, his neck tilted forward. Bill Reedy, who had been crunched under the passenger side, was in too much pain to exit the truck by himself. He waited for the firemen to get him out.

Among the first questions asked of Reedy was "Who was driving?" It wasn't a stupid question. From the position of the bodies of the two men, it was hard to tell. One set of ambulance personnel wrote in their log, "Driver undetermined." The way the bodies were thrown around, they couldn't figure out who had been behind the wheel at the time of the crash.

But when asked who was driving, Bill Reedy didn't have to think. For ten years he had covered for Billy, even offering to take raps for Billy after fights. Reedy, who loved Billy Martin like a brother, knew Billy would be in real trouble if charged with drunk driving. It didn't occur to Bill Reedy that Billy didn't need his help anymore because he was dead. All Reedy knew was that Billy was out cold and couldn't contradict him.

It had been Bill Reedy's role to protect his friend from unfriendly publicity. He knew that if he said Billy was driving, the national publicity for his friend would be devastating, and it would be a terrible setback for their budding ham company, which had been damaged badly after the beating Billy took at Lace.

Reedy also was certain he hadn't been drinking enough to be classified as drunk, so he answered, "I was driving." Bill Reedy was just doing his usual job of covering up for Billy.

The firemen quickly pulled Billy from the truck. Reedy could not understand why they were rushing. There was no smell of gasoline, no fire, no hint of the need for speed. The chief of the Port Crane Volunteer Fire Department, John Eldred, hoisted Billy over his head to a second volunteer, who passed him back to a third man, whose weak back gave way. Billy's limp body, removed without the aid of a brace or a board, bounced on the ground. These firemen then lifted his abused body onto a board. Billy wasn't moving.

Carol Reedy and Jill Martin could see the commotion at the end of the block-long driveway. They could see men in uniforms and an ambulance. Carol Reedy was wearing sweatpants and a sweatshirt and Billy Martin's hunting jacket. In bedroom slippers she ran down the Martins' driveway to the site of the accident.

When Carol reached the scene, she was shaken when she saw that Billy, who was lying on his back on the ground, appeared to be dead.

When she looked inside the cab of the truck, she could see her husband covered in a blanket. As she ran up to a policeman, she began to feel light-headed. She thought her husband also was dead. The policeman tried to stop her from getting any closer, but when he realized who she was, he began yelling, "No, no. Take the blanket off. Let him talk to her."

Bill Reedy had been covered with a blanket only to protect him from getting hit with glass as rescue workers broke out the left half of the windshield in an attempt to extricate him from the truck.

When the blanket was lifted from Bill Reedy's head, Carol Reedy could see he wasn't dead but was in a lot of pain.

# THE MOTIVE

A frantic Jill Martin's first question to Carol Reedy was "Who was driving?"

Carol Reedy repeated to Jill what Bill Reedy had told investigators. Carol told Jill that Reedy had been driving.

"I hope that no-good son of a bitch goes to jail," Jill screamed.

Carol Reedy was taken aback by Jill's antagonistic ferocity. Wasn't Jill her friend? Carol's only feeling other than numbness and disbelief was sorrow. As she watched Billy lying there inert, she thought she was dreaming. Her friend of many years looked dead, and her husband was seriously injured. Carol wondered what jail had to do with it.

It was freezing cold outside. Carol Reedy went back to the house and drove the Bronco, the Martins' other vehicle, to the end of the driveway.

Jill was bent over Billy, who was lying on the ground motionless. The only evidence of injury was a cut across his nose, which had been struck by the top of the steering wheel. Jill could not understand why Billy wasn't moving.

Jill, now hysterical, said to Carol, "You have to come over here and talk to Billy. He'll come out of it for you." Carol walked over to calm her down. Carol called Billy's name several times. There was no response.

Bill Reedy painfully sat in the crumpled truck as emergency rescue squad members tried to figure out how to extricate him from the vehicle.

The emergency service employees placed Billy's body in the ambulance for the trip to Wilson Memorial Hospital in Johnson City, near Binghamton. Jill went along. She handed the keys to Carol and asked her to bring the Bronco back to the house.

"Give the keys to somebody, but be careful who you give them to," Jill instructed.

Carol got into the Bronco and backed it back up to the house. She ran into the house, grabbed her purse and her boots, and drove back to the end of the driveway.

As the Bronco stopped at the end of the driveway, the emergency service personnel were preparing to extract the injured Bill Reedy from the truck on a board out the driver's side door in order to take him to Wilson Hospital.

At Wilson Hospital, X rays were taken, and Dr. Irwin Rosenberg determined that Reedy was in "pretty good shape" but that Wilson Hospital could not treat him, that he would have to go by ambulance to Upstate Medical Center Hospital in Syracuse.

During the short time Bill Reedy was at Wilson Hospital, a priest went to see him. There was confusion at the time over who was driving the truck, so the priest asked Reedy in confidence who was driving, and Reedy told him that he was, because "if I say Billy was driving, the authorities will crucify him."

The priest told Reedy that Billy had died, that Billy no longer needed protection.

"Nobody can hurt Billy anymore," said the priest.

Reedy stared out silently into space.

Soon thereafter Dr. Rosenberg asked Carol Reedy to sign a release form. In fifteen minutes the ambulance left Wilson Hospital and sped off for Syracuse.

Carol Reedy never left Bill Reedy's side during his ride to the hospital. In the ambulance she suddenly realized that Christmas dinner was still in the oven.

"My God, did anyone turn off the lamb?" she wondered.

While the Reedys were on their way to Syracuse, Jill still had enough sympathy for Carol to call ahead to a friend, Don Ross, whom Carol had met at the Martins' house a couple times.

Carol knew no one in Syracuse, and Ross and his next-door neighbor came and sat and waited for the ambulance to arrive, and after Bill was taken to intensive care, they told Carol there was no reason to stay, that she couldn't see him, and Ross took her to his home for dinner.

While Bill Reedy lay in his hospital bed, Jill called Carol Reedy and told her, "I'm coming up there, and I want some answers from your husband."

Carol was incensed at her tone. Carol told her, "Oh, no you're not, Mrs. Martin. This is one time you're not going to tell me you're going to do anything. You're not coming down to interrogate my husband because to my knowledge you're not with the FBI, and you're not coming here. If you want to come in and look in on him, that would be nice. But you're not going to interrogate anybody in this hospital room while I'm here."

Jill hung up on her.

Jill interpreted Carol's comment to mean that Reedy would not speak with anyone. When Bill's many friends asked Jill whether Bill wanted visitors, she said, "You can go down there, but [Carol] won't let you even talk to him, won't let you in the room."

Recalled Kelly Martin, "Jill told me Bill Reedy was in a coma and didn't want to see me 'cause he felt so bad for killing my dad. Then Jill told the Reedys, 'Don't call Kelly because she hates you for killing her father.' "

Said Tex Gernand, "Three hours after the accident, Jill called and asked me if I could come up. There was a storm that night. I said, 'I have to take a shower. I'll be up as soon as I can.' It took about six hours to get up there.

"I drove back to the Regency Hotel, and that's when I first began to realize there were problems. I couldn't understand why no one was calling Bill Reedy.

"I called Bill Reedy, and he let me know there was trouble. He didn't know why he wasn't getting any calls from [Jill]. He said, 'I'd love to hear from her.' I had been hearing that he wasn't taking any calls. He said, 'No, please have them call.'

"I left Binghamton and drove down the New York State Thruway, and when I came home that night, I called Kelly and Billy Joe and told them to call Bill Reedy, and I gave them the phone number, and then I called Jill to tell her Bill Reedy wanted her to call.

"Jill got livid that I called Bill Reedy and wouldn't tell her what we talked about. She said, 'After all I've done for you and Billy has done for you, how can you do this?'

"I said, 'I'm not doing anything wrong. I'm giving you the same information I've given the kids.'

"Jill said, 'I don't give a shit about the kids. I'm his wife, and I thought we were close.' "

Said Gernand to Jill, "I don't know why this is happening. The only thing I can tell you is what I told them, and this is what I'm telling you: Bill Reedy wants to talk to you and would love to hear from you. I can't say anything more than that."

Gernand finishes, "And with that, she hung up the phone on me. And I never heard from her again—until the week before they put up the headstone for Billy."

The night of the accident Carol Reedy had booked a room in the Holiday Inn in Syracuse. Her husband was in the hospital in intensive care. She had dragged herself to sleep for a few hours, then woke up and started to cry because everything seemed to be closing in on her. Because it was too quiet in the room, she turned on CNN, and there was Mickey Mantle saying, "I have to say something about Bill Reedy. Bill Reedy can drink a truckload of beer and not be drunk. I just want to say that I don't think it happened that way. I think it was an icy road and the conditions were bad, and two friends were out, and it's an unfortunate thing. Ain't no way Bill Reedy was drunk."

Carol Reedy began to sob. This time Mickey had come through even though he knew he would incur the wrath of Jill. Obviously he didn't care.

The next day Mike Klepfer was watching the news on TV when it was reported that Billy had been a passenger in a truck owned by Billy and driven by Bill Reedy.

"I don't believe that," Klepfer said to himself, "not for one minute." Billy had set the rules: "My truck, I drive. Your car, you drive."

"That's bullshit," Klepfer said to himself.

Around eight that night, when investigators asked Bill Reedy about the accident, this time he told them that he had lied to cover for Billy and that the truth was Billy was behind the wheel, that it had been icy, the truck slid into a ditch, and whammo, there was a crash.

Bill Reedy wasn't thinking about legal ramifications. He wasn't a suer, and he had no intention of suing Billy's estate to collect on his hospital bills. As far as Bill Reedy was concerned, it was an accident, a terrible accident, one he wished hadn't happened, but still an accident.

As for lying to prevent a DWI charge, Reedy knew he hadn't had all that much to drink—one screwdriver, a few beers. Billy was the one drinking the hard stuff.

"Who was driving?"

"Billy was."

There wasn't a single friend of Billy's who didn't believe Bill Reedy when he changed his story.

Eddie Sapir remembers that right after Billy died Sapir was sitting at a table at the Regency Hotel in New York City with Mickey Morabito, Mickey Mantle, two others, and Jill.

Said Sapir, "Bill Reedy had just revealed for the first time that Billy was the driver and not him. And all the guys looked at each other, and we all said, 'If Bill Reedy said that, it's true.' We knew the love and affection Bill had for Billy and Billy for Bill, and if Reedy said it, you knew it was true.

"Everybody chimed in. We were in unison. It was a unanimous consensus of the guys there.

"Mickey Mantle said it out loud. He said, 'You know, if Reedy said it, hey, I believe it.' Morabito said it, too."

Billy's friends were dumbfounded when Jill became unglued when she learned Bill Reedy had changed his story. What did she care who was driving?

Her actions had nothing to do with grief for Billy. Ever since they had known her, behind her back they had called her a gold digger. For them, her actions were proof of that assessment.

They saw that she intended to go after Reedy with all the vengeance she could muster, that she had started the wheels in motion to do what she could to make sure Bill Reedy was convicted of being responsible for the death of her husband.

Said Kelly Martin: "She was pressing charges against Bill Reedy. That's absurd. Ridiculous. Everybody knows my father wouldn't have let Bill Reedy drive. He'd have driven himself. Anybody who knows my dad knows he's going to drive."

When Bill Reedy changed his story, Jill was faced with a practical problem.

As long as Bill Reedy was the driver, there was no need for an autopsy on Billy. Without an autopsy, it would not be possible to determine at the time of death whether Billy had been drinking. Having no autopsy would ease the way for her to collect insurance and to seek an award from a negligence lawsuit.

If there had been an autopsy, it surely would have been revealed that Billy's liver was shot. As much as Billy drank, which was most of the time, he couldn't have lasted much longer. Billy was drinking so much at the time of his death that friends were sure that on some level he was killing himself.

Only one test was performed on Billy when he was taken to Wilson Memorial Hospital initially, and that one test indicated that Billy was driving.

Dr. Walid Hammoud had performed a peritoneal lavage, in which a needle was inserted into Billy's body to determine the extent of internal injuries. When the needle was pushed into Billy's abdomen, a significant amount of blood spurted, indicating a strong possibility of a serious, massive abdominal injury, probably caused by Billy's smashing into the steering wheel with great force.

But without an autopsy, there was no corroboration of internal injuries and no proof of liver damage, and any negligence award might be much larger.

Whether or not Jill had considered any of this, she vehemently opposed an autopsy.

The person Jill enlisted to help her in this pursuit was George Steinbrenner.

Dr. Patrick Ruddy, a Broome County coroner, signed the death warrant without ever seeing the body.

It became clear early in the case that Steinbrenner was assisting Jill to make sure no autopsy would take place.

A service was to be held for Billy at the Frank Campbell Funeral Home in New York City when the call came from Broome County requesting an autopsy on Billy. The change in Bill Reedy's story had triggered that request.

Jill contacted George Steinbrenner. The funeral was to be the next day. Couldn't George do something to keep the Broome County DA from performing the autopsy?

Two reasons were cited not to perform an autopsy. The first was that Jill didn't want to postpone the burial service, which had already been scheduled. The second, asserted by George's people, was based on religious grounds. They said Jill was Jewish, that an autopsy was against the Jewish religion.

Paul Tabarry, an associate of Eddie Sapir's, was at the funeral parlor around nine at night when Jill ran up to him, frantic.

Said Paul Tabarry, "Jill popped a cork because Reedy was changing his story. She was very upset mainly because she was trying to bury her husband the next day, and now that might not happen. Number two, I got the impression that Jill was Jewish, and Jewish people don't like autopsies."

Steinbrenner contacted one of his attorneys, who also was in attendance at the funeral parlor. He had been a prosecutor in New York City, and he called a police official at his home and told him what the problem was.

The two agreed that if George's attorney could get an examination out on Long Island, it would be good enough. The problem, though, was transporting Billy. Arrangements were difficult.

George's attorney then came up with the idea of contacting another friend of his, Michael Baden, the former New York City medical examiner. Broome County District Attorney Gerald Mallen agreed that if Baden could examine Billy's body, no autopsy would be necessary.

Around the same time back in Binghamton, Bill Fischer, who had been hired by Jon Blechman, Bill Reedy's lawyer, to investigate the accident, inspected the truck and discovered physical evidence that proved to him that without a doubt that Billy Martin, not Bill Reedy, had been behind the wheel of the truck.

Among the physical evidence he found was a faint but clear impression of a footprint made by a workboot on the brake pedal. When Fischer checked, he found that Bill Reedy had been wearing galoshes with a crisscross pattern on the soles. Billy had been wearing workboots.

When Fischer went to Gerald Mallen to tell him there *was* an issue as to who the driver had been, he suspected that Mallen wasn't calling the shots, that someone higher up in the law enforcement ladder was making the decisions. Fischer had no proof, of course, because back-room politics is done behind closed doors, but the private detective believed that the New York State Police was already participating in the investigation.

Fischer asked Mallen, "Please, Gerry, bring the body back."

"I can't do that. You don't have any evidence."

"Jerry, I can't tell you what the physical evidence is, but there *is* significant physical evidence that indicates there may be an issue as to who the driver is."

"I can't help that."

"You can call back the body."

"No, I can't do that."

"Like hell. You're the chief law enforcement officer in the county. Call it back."

"I'm not going to do it."

"Would you at least have the body X-rayed?"

"I don't know. We'll see."

Howard Rubenstein, a PR man for George Steinbrenner, arranged on behalf of Jill Martin to get Michael Baden to study Billy's body before burial. The Broome County DA's office agreed to let Baden look at Billy.

Jill said to Paul Tabarry, "Promise me you won't let them poke and stick and cut Billy, won't let them invade Billy's body."

Tabarry agreed.

Instead of an autopsy, Michael Baden, a famous pathologist, did a visual inspection of Billy's body. Baden was a figure who loved the spotlight. He had been involved in a number of celebrity murder cases, including the Claus Von Bulow murder case. He was also controversial, and he had stepped down after a political dispute with the mayor of New York.

Baden looked over Billy's body, searching for physical evidence. As Baden examined him, all the time taking pictures, Billy looked as normal as could be. Baden inspected a bruise on his neck. Baden said, "If the man had worn a seat belt, he would have walked away from it."

In interview statements after his exam Baden did not accurately describe the body. He said that Billy's injuries were only on his right side, clear evidence he had been the passenger when the truck crashed and threw him against the passenger-side door. But photos Baden had taken showed injuries on his left side as well.

Around two-thirty in the morning, Baden came to his conclusion, which he wrote into his report:

"His injuries are consistent with Billy being a passenger."

No autopsy was conducted, and the next morning the funeral went on as scheduled.

As long as it could be proved that Bill Reedy was the driver, none of the inconsistencies mattered. Jill Martin was determined to pin Billy's death on Reedy.

Billy's friends knew Jill Martin. As soon as they saw what Jill was doing, they began discussing a possible motive.

The consensus: a big-time money grab. If she could pin it on Reedy, down the road there might be a ton of money to be made suing him, the town of Fenton, and even the Ford Motor Company, whose finance division had paid off the truck Billy had been given by the Cory brothers.

If it could be proved that Billy was driving drunk, that money would be much more difficult, perhaps impossible, to collect.

Said Matt Keough, who knew Jill going back to when Billy had first met her in Oakland: "You gotta figure out what the motive is, and it's pretty simple. If Billy is driving, then she can't claim any money in a civil suit. If Bill Reedy is driving, then she can. That's why she sued him. All she cared about was a guilty verdict, which placed her in a position to go after what she was *really* after— the big lawsuit against Ford."

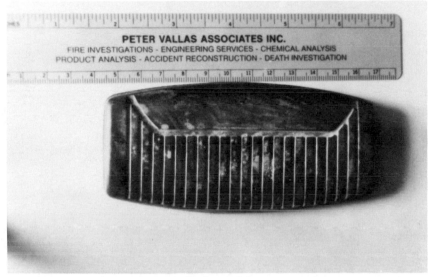

Brake pedal.

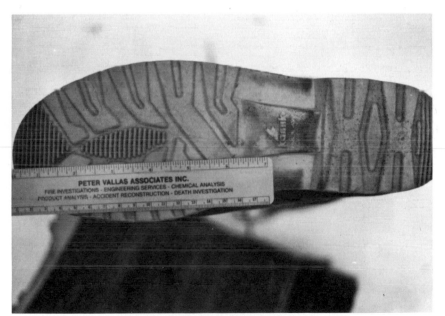

Underside of Billy's boot. (Both photos reprinted by permission of William C. Fischer, Fischer Bureau of Investigation, Endicott, New York)

Location of shift selector shaft. Note the shaft's edge. (Photograph reprinted by permission of William C. Fischer, Fischer Bureau of Investigation, Endicott, New York)

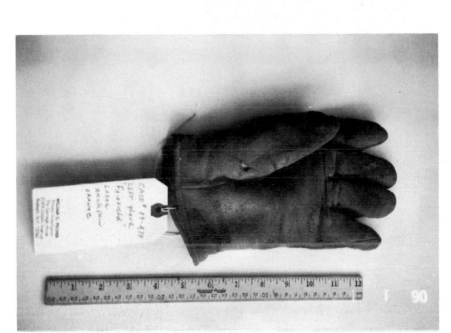

Billy's left-hand glove. Note the black hatch markings near the little finger. Recall that Reedy had an open laceration of his left-hand little finger; this glove had no such laceration.

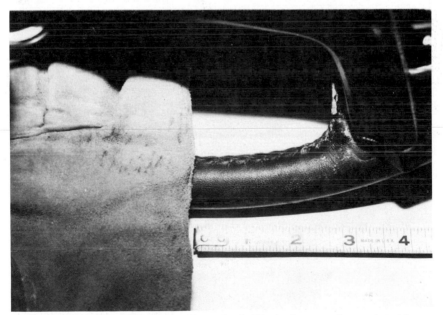

Glove juxtaposed with the steering wheel. (Both photographs reprinted by permission of William C. Fischer, Fischer Bureau of Investigation, Endicott, New York)

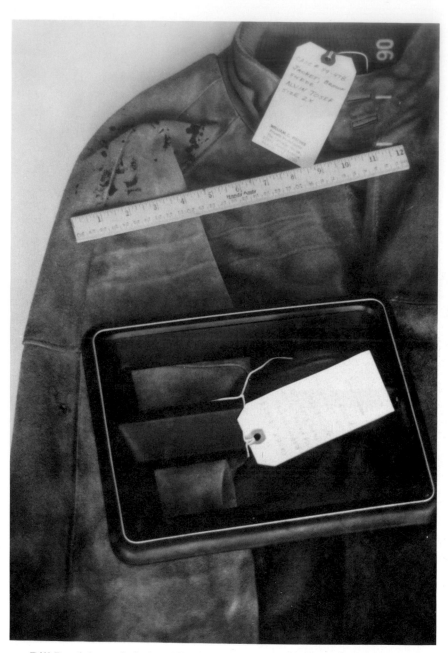

Bill Reedy's suede jacket. Note the horizontal marks on the jacket, and the shape of the radio cover lying on the jacket, just beneath the marks.

Bill Reedy's jacket. There is a nick in the fabric, barely visible here, on the *left* chest (right side of photo, just above the stitching). (Both photographs reprinted by permission of William C. Fischer, Fischer Bureau of Investigation, Endicott, New York)

Interior of the truck, showing dashboard. Note jagged edge of the lower right corner of the dash, just to the left of the radio.

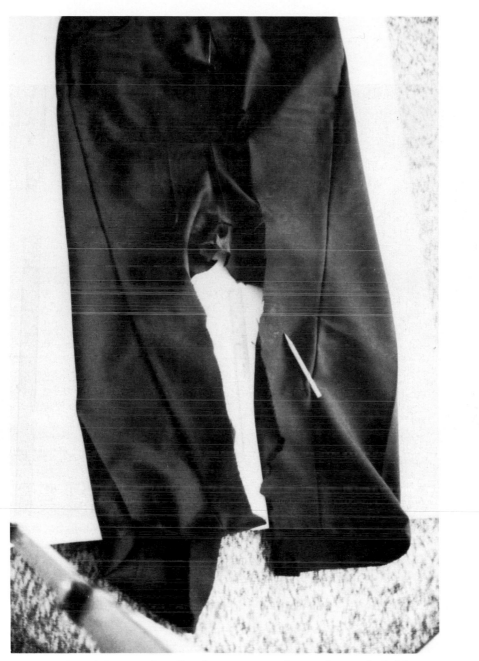

Photo of Reedy's pants. Pencil points to a square impression on the left knee.
(Both photographs reprinted by permission of William C. Fischer, Fischer
Bureau of Investigation, Endicott, New York)

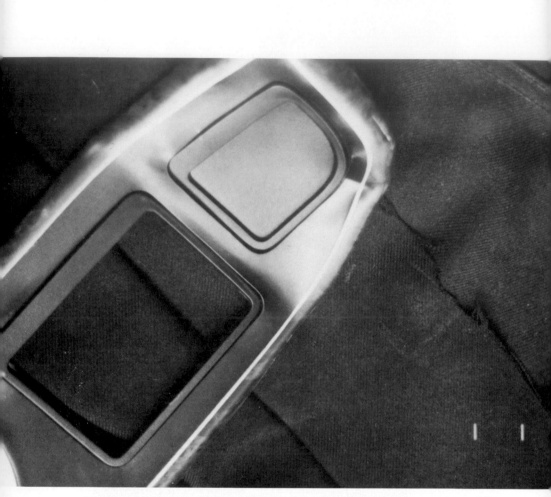

Closeup of fabric bruise, juxtaposed with the dented right lower corner of the driver's side console. (Photograph reprinted by permission of William C. Fischer, Fischer Bureau of Investigation, Endicott, New York)

## 56
·········

# THE FUNERAL

There was an emotional issue surrounding Billy's death that caused a great deal of anger and heartbreak to his friends and family. All of Billy's relatives and friends wanted Billy to be buried in El Cerrito, California, near his west Berkeley home and next to the grave of his mother. They also wanted a closed-casket ceremony, as Billy had specifically requested.

Jill and George Steinbrenner wanted Billy to be buried in Valhalla Cemetery near the burial site of Babe Ruth, and they wanted an open casket.

According to Eddie Sapir, Jill said that after his mother's funeral, Billy was so hurt by the way his sisters had treated him that he told Jill, "If something happens to me, I don't want to go back home."

There's no question that Billy was angry with his sisters when he died. Said Kelly Martin, who had disliked them intensely her entire life, "His sisters, Joannie and Patsy, were just as mean to my dad as possible. They'd tell him how no-good he was, how he didn't do anything for his mother. All he got from them was criticism, and that's why he made me promise to spit in Patsy's face if she came to his funeral.

"I said, 'Dad, I can't do that.'

"He said, 'Kelly, I want you to do that. You have to do that for me. Promise me.'

"I said, 'I can't promise you, Dad.'

"He said, 'It's all I'm asking. That's all I want you to do.'

"I said, 'If she gets in my face, I will.'

"At the funeral I made sure I didn't go anywhere near them, so she didn't get in my face. Because Gretchen raised me that when you go to the ballpark or you're in public, you don't do anything to make your dad look bad. And you don't do anything disrespectful."

Regardless of how Billy might have felt, Billy's sisters say their rift was meaningless, that Billy wanted to be buried with his mom and family. They expressed strong bitterness toward both Jill and George Steinbrenner.

Said Billy's sister Pat, "I was with Billy when he told Jill, 'I want to go where the family's going,' which is next to my mom up at Sunset View Cemetery in El Cerrito, right up on the hill. It's just two miles from the house. We have our plots all in a row. Tudo couldn't get in our row, but he's in our group.

"Billy said to her, 'That's where I want to go.'

"Billy told Joan, who is the plot getter in our family, 'Go find me a plot.'

"She said, 'Okay, I'll do it, but you know, Bill, you have to put that in your will so if something happens, we can do that.' She said, 'You have to pay for the plot, and then you've got it.'

"Billy said, 'No problem. Don't worry about that. I'll do that. Go do it.'

"It never did happen. And he ended up with a funeral he never would have wanted. It was a circus.

"When Billy died, my sister Joan called Jill and told her we wanted Billy to be buried out here in California. We told her Lewis Figone had called to say he would pay to fly Billy's body here. My brother Tudo called her I don't know how many times and said he would give Billy his plot. It wasn't going to cost her a thing.

"If she had really loved Billy, she would have respected his wishes. Billy loved New York, but this is his home. Berkeley is where he belongs, home with his family. Not in New York where nobody will go see him.

"When my dad died, we went every day, taking care of the grave. We would have been there for Billy. No matter how mad he was at us sometimes. Billy'd blow up at us and hate us and wouldn't talk to us, but the next time we'd see him, he'd kiss us and all was forgiven.

"A couple days after Billy died we tried to call George Steinbrenner to see if he would help us get Billy home.

"George Steinbrenner did not even have the courtesy to call us, not even to say he was sorry about Billy's death. He never responded to our calls. We talked to his secretary and got his private number, but he would not return the call.

"For Steinbrenner to stick up for a wife who he didn't like . . . and she *hated* George Steinbrenner. And for him not to talk to the family, not even send a note that he was sorry. That is a bitter thing.

"I don't know which one is more rottener than the other, her or him. And now they kiss each other's butts. She's saying, 'George has been so good to me.' She never liked him. She knew how badly he treated Billy. She ought to be honest and tell the truth.

"The last time he was out here, Billy was talking about Babe Van Huitt and

Howard Noble, who were his childhood friends. Both of them have died, and they are buried near the family, and Billy told us, 'Don't forget, when you go up to the cemetery, make sure you put flowers on Babe, and make sure you put flowers on Howard.'

"Joan said to him, 'For Crissakes, why don't *you* put flowers on Babe and Howard?'

"He said, 'I will. I'll give you the money.'

"But now Billy's buried in New York. You think Jill goes there and brings flowers and takes care of him? No. If she had loved him, she'd have sent him home.

"This way he's dead, and he's by himself. Someone said to me, 'He's with Babe Ruth.' I said, 'The hell with Babe Ruth. Who in the hell cares about Babe Ruth? That's not his home.'

"My uncle Joe died about fifteen years ago. Joe was my mother's brother, a nice little man, never harmed anyone. We went to his rosary, and Billy was sitting next to me, and he said, 'Patsy, do me a favor. When I die, I want a closed casket.'

"I said, 'Billy, we never do that in our family. It's always open.'

"He said, 'No, I want a closed casket. I don't want people coming in and gawking at me while I'm dead. If you guys want to see me, okay, but after that, close it.'

"I said, 'Sure, no problem. As long as we can see you, because we have to kiss you good-bye.'

"I figured if that was what he wanted, he would put it in his will. But he didn't, and then George Steinbrenner went all out and helped Jill make a spectacle of his funeral. I mean, that's okay for a President, but that wasn't what Billy wanted, not the kind of circus atmosphere with Presidents coming, and she's standing there in her fur coat like she's so brokenhearted, and now she's got everything.

"That's how we look at it. We thought, What a joke this whole thing is.

"I was told Steinbrenner was the instigator of all this big hody-do circus, just so he'd get his name in the paper. He's a big show-off. I said, 'You know what he can do with all his money? He can use it as toilet paper if that makes him happy.'

"We debated among the family members whether or not we should go to Billy's funeral, and we decided not to go because of Jill. It would have been too much of a hassle. There would be too many problems with her, and we didn't want this circus atmosphere of the cops saying, 'Who are you? You have to prove who you are.'

"So like I said, I wasn't at the funeral, but we got reports back from the relatives that they had him in a suit, and she had a glass over his coffin and a parade of fans for many hours. And when it came time for the evening service, they changed his clothes.

"My brother would not have appreciated all those people gawking at him. But that's what [Jill] did to him, her and George Steinbrenner.''

Bill Reedy was another who didn't attend the funeral, because he was recuperating from his injuries in the hospital in Syracuse.

Reedy is also bitter toward Jill and George. He is also convinced that Billy should have been buried with his mom in California. He suspects that Steinbrenner was behind the choice of burial site. Said Reedy, "No way she could get that plot next to Babe Ruth by herself. Only someone with George's pull could do that."

According to Reedy, the funeral in New York allowed George "to say he took care of Billy, that he loved Billy. Eat shit. Billy hated that motherfucker. And the picture of Mickey and George and Nixon on the front page of every newspaper in the country made me sick, and a lot of his other friends as well. Mickey told me he would never have gone to that funeral if that was going to happen, using him like a prop."

Ed Sapir found out that Billy had died through the media. He called Jill to express his sympathy and to see what he could do for her. He got her secretary, who Sapir says was very nice. He told the secretary, "Please tell Jill how sorry I am and that I called and that if she feels like talking I'm certainly available."

Eddie wasn't asked to do anything. He says that the Yankees handled not only the service at St. Patrick's but the burial service as well.

According to Sapir, some people were embarrassed for him that he hadn't been asked to be a pallbearer. Sapir's analysis: "Jill's thinking was that I was not really working for Billy anymore."

Eddie's wife, Peggy, wasn't so charitable.

Said Peggy, "[Jill] was jealous over the close relationship that Eddie and Billy had and that was her way of showing who was in charge."

Tex Gernand, Billy's chauffeur, had his own memories of the weekend of the funeral.

Said Tex, "When Billy was working with the judge, I would send a bill at the end of the month, and it got paid. I had to keep it within reason, and if Billy went over, I sucked it up. Because I knew Billy would do something extra for me later. Billy and I knew what our limits were, and I was willing to work within them.

"The last couple years Jill ran things, and I could never get paid on time. If my bill was $2,000, she'd send me a check for $1,100 and carry over the balance. I was a little guy, and it hurt. But I would never say anything to Billy. I didn't want him to have the pressure on him. I figured he had all these problems with his kids.

"Jill would say the kids, Kelly Ann and Billy Joe, were draining Billy dry. What did I know? To hear it from Jill, Billy was helping to support them, and Billy had no money. And for a long time, Billy didn't have much money.

"When Billy Joe flew in for Billy's funeral, I was nervous. Jill had said such bad things about Kelly and Billy Joe, I wondered, What are these two kids going to look like? I figured Billy Joe would have a ring through his nose and was going to do a couple lines of coke in the backseat of the limo. Who knows? I was prepared for a whack job.

"So when I went to pick him up and I started to talk to him, it was, 'How are you doing, Tex?' I couldn't believe it. I was totally in shock. Billy Joe was a sweetheart. If he were my son, I'd love it. So I couldn't understand what was going on.

"And then Kelly came, and she was very nice, and I thought, Who is Jill talking about? And when I talked to Kelly, I learned that Billy and Jill had never sent her a dime. I thought, What kind of bullshit is going on here? I thought, Boy, this is horseshit."

Said Kelly Martin, "Jill didn't want me at the funeral. First she told me there wasn't any space on the plane. She said, 'Sorry, there's no available space on a plane so you won't be able to come to your dad's funeral.'

"And then when I came she didn't want me riding with her and Billy Joe in the limo. If it hadn't been for Billy Joe . . . He said, 'Hey, that's my sister.'

"After the service, we walked out of St. Patrick's Cathedral. We got into the limo, and Tex turned the heat on and some music. As we drove away, the song playing on the radio was 'I'm Leaving Here a Better Man' by Clint Black.

"It was dark, and Jill filled her glass with bourbon and stuck her glass out the window of the limo going down those streets that were completely packed with fans holding banners saying, We Love You, Billy, or We Miss You.

"We were driving out to bury him, and as we went further, another song came on the radio. It was Anne Murray singing 'Brokenhearted Me,' and I started crying.

"There were two people standing in the middle of the freeway, holding up a sign: Yonkers Loves You, Billy. Jill saw them, too.

"She said, 'Well, you know, I loved him, and he loved me.'

"I said, 'No, you didn't love him. My brother loved him. I loved him. My daughter loved him. You didn't love him. You just wanted to get all you could get from him.'

"She said, 'Oh, yes I did. And he loved me.'

"I said, 'No. He was taken in by you because you're strong.' "

The limo drove on toward the Gates of Heaven Cemetery in Valhalla.

Though the sun was out, it was cold as everyone stood around the grave site. Just as the priest prepared his reading, a cloud passed in front of the sun, and it started to snow hard.

Amid the silence, Whitey Ford whispered to Mickey Mantle, "Jesus Christ, right to the very end he had to pull something like this, the little bastard."

After Billy was buried, Jill wanted to wait a little while longer by herself. She asked Tex to shoo away all the fans who had come to see Billy buried and wanted to stay.

Jill yelled, "Get those people away from here. We don't want them here. This is private."

Kelly told her, "Hey, wait a minute, you're wrong. These are his fans. These are the people who loved him. They're out in this snow to pay tribute to him. No, you don't send these people away. You're not doing that."

Tex told them it was okay for them to stay.

After the burial everybody headed over to Bill Fugazy's house, which wasn't far from the cemetery.

Tex couldn't remember how to get there.

Jill threw a fit.

# A PERVERSION OF JUSTICE

**B**efore Bill Reedy changed his story, the Broome County District Attorney's office was interested in only one thing: getting Bill Reedy to plea bargain to a misdemeanor, fine him, suspend his license, get him out of the state, end the press circus, get back to normal.

When Bill Fischer was hired by Reedy's attorney to investigate the accident, one of the first stops he made was to John's Body Shop on Upper Front Street, where he scrutinized Billy's truck. It was clear to Fischer that no one from the district attorney's office had bothered with the truck since on the driver's side sun visor he saw a visible hair sample, which he put in a paper envelope to save as evidence. Until Reedy changed his story there was no reason for the district attorney to look at the truck.

It had not been impounded at the time of the crash. Pieces of it were missing. Some of it had even been lost to souvenir hunters. Fischer was angry at the district attorney for allowing the truck to be left unattended, permitting evidence to be lost or inadvertently tampered with.

The left side of the windshield was missing. Bill Fischer found it. Fischer also discovered an orange left glove that belonged to Billy. On the glove were black markings matching the lacings on the steering wheel. The steering wheel itself was bent in, indicating the driver had crashed into it on impact.

Afraid that the unimpounded truck would be compromised further, he took the glove, the steering wheel, and the brake pedal as evidence.

Fischer called Tom Tynan, the investigator for the district attorney's office, and told him to come down to the garage and get the evidence. Tynan came and secured the truck, using plastic trash bags to protect some of the evidence.

Fischer pointed out what he believed to be a bloodstain on the headliner above the windshield on the driver's side. Tynan said he didn't think it was blood and refused to test it.

And when Fischer told him to take home some of the loose parts, such as the left side of the windshield, the rearview mirror, the brake pedal cover, the knob of the shift selector, a trim piece from the center of the dashboard console, and the steering wheel, he demurred.

"I'm not interested in it," Tynan said. "Take whatever you want." This was some investigation the DA was conducting. But Tynan wasn't anticipating a problem. Reedy had confessed. Who needed evidence?

Fischer, who was a fanatic about these things, told him, "If you're not interested, I'm not going to let it disappear. I'll get it." He took the evidence back to his office.

Once Reedy changed his story, the evidence became crucial, and now the DA's office was in a panic. The state police were putting pressure on Broome County DA Gerald Mallen to convict Reedy, but without an autopsy and without Fischer's evidence, there was no case.

Muddying the waters was Jill Martin, who was so intent on convicting Bill Reedy that she hired her own attorney, Robert Pearl, to do an investigation for the DA. When Bill Fischer returned to continue his examination of the truck, he found a member of the DA's office, Pearl, and an investigator named Stu Bennett, who had been hired by Jill Martin and Pearl to go through the truck.

When Fischer saw Pearl and Bennett, he became aware that Jill Martin was taking full measure to do what she could to convict Bill Reedy.

When the DA discovered he needed Fischer's evidence, they tried the tough-guy approach.

"We want the evidence."

Fischer told Mallen, "Don't ask me. Ask Jon Blechman. He's the attorney. I'm the investigator. I already offered it to your guy. He didn't want it."

"Okay, Fischer, if you don't want to turn it over, we'll execute a search warrant."

Fischer went to see Jon Blechman.

It was at this point that Bill Reedy won—and lost—the case. To get Blechman to turn over the evidence, Mallen threatened Blechman he would add the charge of driving while under the influence, a felony that could have landed Bill Reedy in jail, instead of the charge of driving while impaired, a misdemeanor with a penalty of a small fine, a license suspension for a short period, and no jail time. It was also suggested that they might charge Reedy with criminally negligent vehicular homicide and nail his ass to the cross.

Blechman had a decision to make. One alternative was to keep the evidence, tell Mallen to shove it, and risk the possible incarceration of his client. The other alternative was to hand over the evidence and risk it being altered or destroyed, but get Reedy a guaranteed license to walk. Even if he lost the misdemeanor case, the only thing sullied would be Reedy's reputation.

Blechman and Fischer argued over what to do. On December 27, Fischer told Blechman that they ought to go to the newspapers, tell the reporters that they had evidence Billy Martin was the driver, keep the evidence to themselves, and roll the dice. Fischer felt that with his physical evidence there was no way Blechman could lose the case. The two men had worked together in fifty-six other cases. Their record was 50–6. The odds were in their favor.

Blechman was a Binghamton insider, one of the boys. He had been an assistant district attorney who often played golf and handball and skied with DA Gerald Mallen. He had easy access to the DA's office.

Blechman was aware that Reedy wanted vindication. When Reedy read the stories about the crash in the papers, he had been furious about the way he had been portrayed. When the prosecutor first attempted to make the case go away, he had offered Reedy a deal. If he would plead to driving while impaired, he could pay the small fine and go home.

Because Reedy hadn't been driving, to him a plea bargain was an admission of something he hadn't done.

He told the prosecutor, "Kiss my ass."

When the prosecutor offered Blechman the chance to bargain the case down to a misdemeanor, Blechman knew he had to take the deal.

"If it's a misdemeanor and he loses, so what?" was Blechman's attitude. And from a tactical perspective, it was the right decision.

Fischer knew that by handing over his evidence, whatever advantage they had would be decimated one way or another.

"Anything we gave them they would try to tear apart *not* on its merits but just because they wanted the verdict to go against Bill Reedy," said Fischer.

Bill Fischer took his evidence down to the state police and showed what he had: Billy's glove with the striations that matched the steering wheel, and the imprint of the workboot on the brake pedal.

Then he turned it over to them. At that point the impression was clearly on the brake pedal because Fischer had been very careful to protect it.

When the case came to trial, Fischer says, some of the best evidence had been lost or mislabeled. Moreover, the prosecution had plenty of time to refute Fischer's best evidence in whatever manner it could, plausible or not, fair or not.

"At the trial my evidence came in limping along rather than coming in like thunder," said Fischer.

He added, "Where Jon Blechman won Bill Reedy's freedom from jail was showing them our evidence. Where Jon lost the case was showing them our evidence."

Even with Blechman and Fischer's evidence, the prosecution was aware it might not be able to convict Reedy of driving while impaired. Reedy was a big man, and one screwdriver and three or four beers might impair one man but not impair another. Reedy had been coherent and responsive to questioning when in the hospital.

After Reedy refused to plead to driving while impaired, the district attorney added another charge right before the trial—that the alcohol level in his blood was .10, beyond the legal limit. That was the cutoff: exactly .10. At the hospital he had been tested and was measured at exactly .10. And yet there was supposed to be a .003 margin of error for the test. Reedy was not afforded that margin.

Had Reedy chosen to, he could have skipped the trial entirely without any real penalty—you can't be extradited from another state for a misdemeanor—but he wanted to be cleared. Reedy, moreover, was still working out his emotions over the death of his friend, Billy Martin. He felt obliged to defend himself.

While Jon Blechman was preparing Reedy's case, the prosecutor's case against Bill Reedy was developed by the consultants hired by Jill Martin: attorney Robert Pearl and accident reconstructionist Stu Bennett. Robert Pearl was in daily contact with Gerry Mallen, who allowed him to help, he said, as ''we would any expert witnesses who would be able to help in presenting the case.''

The ''help'' provided by Jill Martin's consultants even included ''educating'' the state's witnesses. One of the key state witnesses at the trial was Dr. Erik Mitchell, who had taken hair samples from both Reedy and Billy Martin. Before the trial Dr. Mitchell took the position that he could determine cause of death but not who was driving.

Pearl learned about Dr. Mitchell's view and was given the opportunity to have Stu Bennett meet with Dr. Mitchell and sway his thinking.

On the stand, Mitchell changed his story. It was Mitchell's testimony that helped swing the jury against Bill Reedy.

Pearl even bragged afterward that this was what won the case.

From the beginning the proceedings smacked of a hanging. The town of Fenton, where Billy Martin had lived, is minuscule. When the array of jurors was rounded up, one of the potential jurors was the judge's son. He was excused, but another potential juror had gone out to the crash site and admitted it, and he was still left on the jury. Of the six jurors, he was the only man.

The trial took place between September 10 and 18, 1990, before the Honorable P. Murray Benjamin in the Fenton Town Hall. P. Murray Benjamin wasn't a lawyer but a justice of the peace. In New York State the concept is the judge should be a man of the people. The problem is that justices of the peace make a lot of reversible procedural mistakes. Benjamin was a Fenton farmer. Though he had been a justice of the peace for a long time, this case was considerably beyond the scope of a trial he ordinarily would preside over.

The courtroom was tiny. There was room for the judge, the jurors, the defense table, the prosecution table, and a handful of spectators.

Bill Reedy was concerned that the remainder of the jury consisted of older women. He had reason to be concerned. They would all feel for the aggrieved widow, who was sitting in the courtroom not ten feet from their line of sight.

P. Murray Benjamin's most unfair decision was in allowing Jill Martin to attend the trial after her first outburst. She had no real connection to the case. She wasn't a participant or a witness. Her only role would be to sit in her seat and cry or carry on or flirt with the jurors to gain sympathy for herself and against Bill Reedy. And that's exactly what she did.

When Jon Blechman suggested that Jill Martin be barred from the trial, P. Murray Benjamin turned him down, saying that as the widow of the decedent she had a right to be there.

To give support to Bill Reedy, Kelly Martin, Billy's daughter, flew in from California. Jill was not pleased to see her.

When Kelly walked into the courtroom, Jill stood there with her mouth open, then ran to get a matron.

"Check her for guns," Jill said. "I know she's gonna try and kill me."

Said Kelly, who like her father was rapier-sharp, "I just flew in from California. Where did I have my gun, in my arsenic bag that I put on the plane? Or did I just send it through the U.S. mail ahead of me? Come on."

The matron checked Kelly's briefcase. There was no gun.

Later Kelly would tell reporters about Jill, "My father was leaving her ass and coming to live with me."

The first day of the trial consisted of a series of witnesses who said that right after the accident, when Bill Reedy was in the truck or the ambulance, he admitted he was the driver of the truck and that he had had "a couple of beers." These words were said over and over again. The other testimony had to do with where Reedy was positioned at the time of impact, which was near the steering wheel with his feet tilting toward the driver's side.

Sheriff's Deputy Steve Glanville testified that Reedy had had slurred speech and running eyes, but Blechman got him to admit that the pain from Reedy's dislocated hip might have been the cause of this.

Glanville was asked how he knew Reedy was driving while impaired. Glanville said he had taken a weeklong class as part of his police training.

The deputy admitted in the years he had worked on the force never to have arrested anyone for driving while impaired. It was the policy of the sheriff's department not to do so.

Glanville said he had Reedy recite the alphabet for him in the hospital room. Jon Blechman got him to say on the stand that he had told Reedy, "You say it better than I can say it."

"So why did you arrest Reedy?" Glanville was asked.

Glanville testified that he had concluded that Reedy had been driving while impaired five and a half months after the crash, after discussing the case with the district attorney.

The next witness was hospital attendant Suzanne Donovan, who testified that she heard Reedy admit to Glanville that he was the driver. She testified that she thought Reedy was impaired because he was acting "impatient."

Tim Kelly testified next. Kelly was a bartender at Morey's. He was off duty and drinking screwdrivers that day with Martin and Reedy. He said Reedy had had four drinks while he was sitting there. On cross-examination Kelly testified that he hadn't really counted the drinks Reedy had taken.

Florence Piech, a witness at the accident scene, testified that when she saw the crash, she went over and talked to Reedy, who was lucid and understandable. Her husband, Peter, was trying to pull Reedy out. Her son, Brent, said Reedy's feet were on the passenger side of the truck when he looked in.

Ronald Stanbro of the New York State Police testified that he had found some hair on the driver's side of the windshield. Because he hadn't done the testing, his purpose was to tell of the existence of the hair.

Prosecuting attorney Kevin Guyette then called Peter Piech, who had come to Reedy's aid until the ambulance arrived. He said Reedy had asked him to hold him up, that he didn't want to press against his friend.

Piech said he had to go into the truck and get the key to unlock the door on the driver's side. Then he helped hold Reedy off Billy's body until the ambulance came.

Piech said that at the time he found him, Reedy was sitting in the middle of the truck with his feet stuck on the hump on the floor on the driver's side. Piech said Reedy was holding himself up by the steering wheel.

Detective Albert Bomysoad, a detective with the Broome County Sheriff's Department, testified that he was at the hospital when a technician took a sample of Bill Reedy's blood.

Bomysoad then identified the passenger side of the windshield of the truck, which he said he transported to the evidence custodian, then to the New York State crime lab. He testified he had a hair sample taken from the Onondaga Medical Examiner's Office, which he matched to the passenger side of the windshield.

H. Chip Walls testified next. He was a forensic toxologist with the Onondaga County Health Department. He testified that Reedy's blood-alcohol level was exactly .10, the cutoff for being legally drunk.

Fire Chief John Eldred was next. Eldred, of the Port Crane Fire Department, was a volunteer fireman who managed the Forest Manor adult community mobile-home park in Port Crane. Eldred testified that he grabbed Billy in a bear hug and passed him over the top of his head out of the truck to another volunteer fireman. That fireman passed Billy to another and then onto a long board. It took him "literally seconds."

Eldred said he thought Billy looked dead. On cross-examination Blechman ate the guy up. Eldred had to admit that he had pulled Billy out of the truck without a cervical collar or board or any other support for his neck.

He was asked whether he knew that Billy's heartbeat and pulse had been obtained in the ambulance. (They had been, meaning that Billy was alive when he'd been yanked from the truck.)

Eldred said he didn't know.

The judge adjourned for the day. Except to repeat its initial admissions, on day one, the prosecution hadn't laid a glove on Bill Reedy.

The next day, at nine sharp, the trial resumed. The first prosecution witness of the day was Charles Lalley, another volunteer fireman, and he, too, testified that Reedy said he was the driver at the time Lalley had come onto the scene. He testified that he helped remove the rest of the windshield, put a cervical collar on Reedy, and with the help of four others extricated him on a board out the driver's door of the truck. He said that two or three times Reedy asked how Billy was.

Thomas Francisco, another volunteer fireman, testified that he smelled the odor of alcohol and that Billy was on the passenger side.

Francisco testified that he was the one who took Billy's body from Chief Eldred, that after he took it he passed it over his head to a volunteer named Pease, and because Pease had a bad back, his knees buckled, and he dropped Billy onto the ground into a ditch.

The paramedics, he said, only then placed Billy on a long board. No neck collar had been placed on him. Three medical technicians then began trying to revive him.

Kelly Martin was sitting in the courtroom next to Carol Reedy. Kelly sat in her seat sobbing.

Volunteer Pease was never called to the stand.

Francisco testified on cross-examination that Reedy asked several times about Billy.

Earl Drury, another fireman, was next. He also testified that Reedy told him he was driving. Drury said he checked Reedy for broken ribs because the steering wheel was pushed in, and he worried that because Reedy said he was the driver, he wanted to see if Reedy's ribs had hit the steering wheel.

The prosecutor asked Drury whether Reedy had broken ribs. Blechman objected that he didn't have the medical training to give a proper answer. The objection was sustained.

Reedy did not have broken ribs.

Drury testified that he smelled alcohol on Reedy's breath. He said Reedy had a gash on his forehead.

On cross-examination he testified that Reedy had bashed his right side but that his anterior chest (the front part) was not injured. This evidence indicated that Reedy had not hit the steering wheel and was not the driver.

Prosecutor Guyette then got Drury to say that if Reedy had hit the steering wheel with his right side, he'd have a bruise there.

Michael Keneckny was next, another volunteer, who had driven the ambulance. He testified that Reedy told him he was driving and that Reedy told him he had had a few drinks.

On Blechman's cross-examination, Keneckny testified that several times Reedy asked how Billy was. He said that the ambulance volunteers told Reedy that Billy was in another ambulance and everyone was doing all they could for him. He said that no one had told Reedy that Billy had died.

The prosecution then entered all sorts of pictures of the crash site and the removal of the truck into evidence.

Everyone broke for lunch.

Tom Tynan was next. He was chief investigator for the Broome County District Attorney's Office. Tynan had not been interested in Bill Fischer's evidence from the truck and had done nothing to secure the truck from souvenir hunters. Reedy had not yet changed his story.

Tynan testified that the windshield came to him for safekeeping after Bill Fischer had discovered that the Chordas brothers, who owned the local garage, had hidden it away along with the sun visors and other pieces of the truck to keep these items safe from souvenir hunters. The windshield was placed into evidence.

The irony here was that had Fischer not learned the whereabouts of this evidence and taken it from the Chordas brothers, the prosecutor would have had no case whatsoever.

Tynan then introduced a hair sample labeled HEAD HAIR—WILLIAM REEDY. He said he took them from the driver's side of the windshield.

The prosecutor never asked him exactly where the hair was found on the windshield. Without knowing where it was found, it had no merit as evidence. Blechman never asked, either, unfortunately, nor did he object that its location had not been determined.

Blechman did beat up on Tynan a little when he got him to admit that there was no proof that this was in fact the windshield from Billy's truck because no one had checked the Vehicle Identification Number to make sure it matched the number on the truck body.

Tynan then revealed that there had been evidence tampering. When Bill Fischer first examined the truck, he found a visible hair on the driver's side sun visor. He took the hair sample, labeled it and put it in an envelope, and it was part of what he and Jon Blechman had to turn over to the prosecutor in exchange for the charge getting dropped from a felony to a misdemeanor. At the time Fischer feared his best evidence would disappear or be tampered with. His fears were realized when Tynan testified that Fischer's hair sample was gone.

On redirect Guyette got Tynan to say that the samples might have been sent to the FBI and that the FBI might have lost it.

Tynan told Blechman he never opened the bag. In court he opened it and looked in. It was empty. The hair samples had been lost or stolen.

Bill Fischer says that evidence-tampering has been a problem for the New York State Police, that a policeman named Robert Lishansky has been indicted on numerous counts of tampering with physical evidence.

Douglas Deedrick of the FBI was next. He testified that he was the hair-and-fiber expert. He testified that the hair on the driver's side of the windshield did *not* match the hair sample taken from Billy Martin.

The problem with this testimony was that the hair samples had been taken in such a haphazard way as to make his testimony worthless.

When a hair sample was taken from Bill Reedy at the hospital, it was labeled as property taken from the deceased, Billy Martin. Was this a sample from Reedy or from Martin? The way it was labeled, the prosecution was able to use it to fit whatever purpose it served. When the FBI analyzed the sample, it didn't know what it was getting, either.

Three hair samples: One sample wasn't precisely located on the windshield, the next was lost or stolen, the third was mismarked.

If Jon Blechman made an error in his cross-examination, it was this: there are seventeen characteristics of human hair. On the stand Deedrick said he had matched Reedy's hair to hair on the driver's side. But no one asked him the following:

"Did you determine medulla size?"

"Did you determine coloration?"

"Did you . . . ?" asking him for a match characteristic by characteristic. Bill Fischer had asked Blechman to do this. For some reason Blechman didn't want to, so Deedrick did not have to give specifics about either the sample of hair taken from Reedy or the sample of hair taken from the driver's side.

Deedrick should have been questioned in order to make him say, "It was gray matched against gray," and so on through seventeen different characteristics. He never was made to do that. All he gave was his opinion, and it went a long way toward convicting Reedy.

Michael Baden was the next witness.

On the stand Baden, testifying for the prosecution, was shown a fourteen-by-twenty-inch color blowup of Billy lying naked and dead, the right side of his face, neck, and side visible down to his chest.

When the photos were shown, Jill began to cry, as did several female members of the jury.

Bill Reedy couldn't look at the photos and asked the prosecutor to turn them around.

Jon Blechman objected to the enlarged photo of Billy as being inflammatory. It was a valid objection. He repeated that this was not a homicide case, not a trial for criminal death. He asked the judge to preview the pictures before showing them to the jury.

The judge called the attorneys into his chambers. At the private hearing Jon Blechman surprised prosecutor Kevin Guyette by telling him that he was going to introduce as evidence another series of photos showing injuries to Billy's left side that Baden had taken but had not produced. Baden had, after hors d'oeuvres at a doctors' convention in New Orleans, given a private showing to his friends of these photos of Billy dead on the slab. A friend of Bill Fischer's had been there and had seen them, and he told Fischer about them. Blechman then put in a discovery demand for the photos.

When prosecutor Kevin Guyette heard that Blechman intended to introduce the previously undisclosed photos by Baden, Guyette called Robert Pearl, Jill Martin's attorney. Pearl went to see the judge.

When Blechman saw what was going on, he left the judge's chambers and went to get Bill Fischer.

"Hurry," said Blechman when he caught up with Fischer in the hall outside the courtroom. "Come with me."

Blechman and Fischer burst into the judge's chambers unannounced to find the Honorable P. Murray Benjamin in a heated discussion with Robert Pearl and Jill Martin.

Pearl was giving the judge explicit instructions that Blechman's photos should not come into evidence because of the protestations of the widow that it would be improper.

Blechman asked the judge, "What's going on?"

The judge explained that Pearl and Jill were arguing against the admissibility of the photographs.

Blechman said, "They're not participants in this trial. I don't know what they are doing in here. If they want to do something, put it on the record."

Blechman and Pearl went into the hallway.

Blechman told him, "What you're doing ex post is improper, and I have half a mind to report you to the Committee on Professional Standards up in the Fourth Department. You have no business tampering with the judicial process. If you want to address the issue [not that he had any standing to do so], you ought to do it on notice with all the parties present and get a stenographer in there."

Said Blechman later, "This back-room secret attempt on his part to influence the judge's decision was totally improper. And I told him so."

Pearl backed down. The photos were allowed to be entered into evidence.

When the trial resumed in front of the jury, everyone could see that Jill Martin was upset and distressed. She was making loud conversation with Robert Pearl in full view of the jury.

When Jon Blechman objected to her disruptiveness, the judge admonished Pearl to keep her quiet, that she'd only be allowed to stay if she kept herself within bounds. She quieted for a while.

The people called Don Loomis, a forensic toxicologist for the New York State Police Department. He was the one who had analyzed the blood sample taken from Bill Reedy. He testified that Bill Reedy's blood-alcohol level was .10.

Court was adjourned for the day.

Dr. Erik Mitchell, the medical examiner in Syracuse, was the last witness for the prosecution.

Dr. Mitchell testified that he had photographed Reedy's body in the hospital, and at the time could not conclude whether Reedy was the passenger or the driver. He testified that he had met with Dr. Baden, and after his discussion with Baden, revised his opinion. In his direct testimony Mitchell didn't mention that Stu Bennett, Pearl's accident reconstructionist, was there. On cross-examination Jon Blechman got him to admit he had been there.

Before he was through, Dr. Mitchell repeated the findings of Stu Bennett as to what caused the injuries to whom and how.

Reedy, said Mitchell, echoing Baden, was the driver, and Billy was the passenger. This matched Baden's conclusion and Bennett's reconstructed hypothesis.

The people rested. Jon Blechman moved to throw out the case based on lack of evidence. Judge Benjamin denied the motion.

The defense called eight witnesses. The first was William Simpson, who testified that he saw Billy driving when he left Workingman's Gas. Alston Morley, a retired golf pro, testified that he was having Christmas dinner with his wife at Morey's when Billy and Reedy were in there drinking. Morley said Reedy had a bottle of beer in front of him, that he wasn't intoxicated.

Andrew Howey was next. Howey, the car salesman who had brought his dog into the bar to show Billy, testified that Reedy was drinking a Budweiser, that he wasn't intoxicated but behaved "like a gentleman."

Court was adjourned.

The next day the first witness was Father Corey Van Kuren, the priest who had informed Bill Reedy that Billy had died. Father Van Kuren testified that there was confusion as to who was driving the truck, so he asked Bill Reedy in confidence who was driving, and Reedy had told him that he said he was the driver, because if he said Billy was driving, the authorities would "crucify him," meaning Billy. Reedy didn't know Billy was dead until Father Van Kuren told him so.

Dr. Melvin Jones was next for the defense. Blechman wanted Dr. Jones to testify about Jill Martin's and George Steinbrenner's efforts to prevent an autopsy.

Dr. Jones was one of four coroners for Broome County. He was the coroner on call the day of the accident. He testified that he had ordered an autopsy but that Jill Martin called to stop it, that George Steinbrenner was offering assistance "in any way possible." He said a lawyer representing Steinbrenner had called him and told him Jill was Jewish, that he was forbidden to perform an autopsy.

On cross-examination the prosecuting attorney said to Dr. Jones, "You did learn, though, that Gerry Mallen requested an autopsy be performed on Billy Martin?"

Jones said, "I understand, but that's hearsay evidence."

Guyette said, "That's hearsay, but talking to the lawyer with regard to a religious objection is not hearsay evidence?"

Blechman objected to this statement as being argumentative.

Guyette began talking to the judge. "I think it's only fair to question him on it," said Guyette.

From the courtroom Jill Martin yelled, "That's right."

The judge said, "I'm going to instruct the witness."

Blechman said, "Excuse me, Your Honor. I'm hearing some comments being made from the part of the courtroom where Mrs. Martin is seated. I think if I can hear what she's saying, I'm afraid the jury can."

Blechman objected to any outbursts in the courtroom and asked the judge to tell her to keep quiet.

The judge asked the spectators not to make comments within earshot of the jury.

Dr. Jones went on to say that upon hearing of Jill's objection on religious grounds, there didn't seem to be any compromise. Guyette got Jones to admit that sometimes a body is examined rather than autopsied.

Dr. Patrick Ruddy, a Broome County coroner, was next. He testified that Jill and a "gentleman from the New York area who didn't identify himself" had called him about not having an autopsy. He said he had signed the death report without viewing the body. He said he had told Jill he would do whatever Dr. Jones wanted him to do.

Bill Reedy finally took the stand next. He testified that he was not wearing gloves on the day of the accident. He identified his right rubber boot. His shirt. His scarf. His socks. His belt. His underwear, Fruit of the Loom. His pants. His jacket.

Reedy said he was the passenger and Billy the driver, and he described what they did that day. He said he wasn't familiar with the route Billy took home. He testified that he was not under the influence of alcohol. He reasserted that Billy drove and he was the passenger.

He described the accident, how he was crushed under the dashboard, how he had reached up to grab the steering wheel to keep from landing on Billy. He spoke about how Billy was in the seat with his back against the wall and his head down. Then Bill Reedy began to cry.

Reedy composed himself quickly, talked about how help arrived, told how he covered for Billy but, when he learned Billy was dead, changed his story. He spoke of how he always had protected Billy, had lied to Jill a lot about what Billy was doing, had covered for Billy when he tried to pick up strange women and got in fights. This was not testimony geared to making a jury of six homebodies from Fenton, five of them women, fall in love with him or Billy.

The more Bill Reedy talked about how much he lied for Billy, the more the jury wondered whether he would lie to save himself.

On cross, to reinforce the notion that Reedy might have been lying, prosecuting attorney Guyette asked Reedy, ''Did you tell the truth and nothing but the whole truth with respect to December 25, 1989?''

''Yes.''

''Nothing that you testified to that you want to change?''

''No.''

The weekend had arrived. The trial had one more day to run.

On September 17, the final day of the trial, the defense put on the stand an expert witness to prove once and for all that Billy Martin was the driver of the truck.

The major obstacle Jon Blechman had to winning the case hinged on convincing the jury that Reedy had lied to protect his friend, that he *really* had been the passenger and Billy the driver.

The primary witness to prove the case was Bill Fischer, the accident reconstructionist hired by Blechman and Reedy.

This is the evidence as Fischer described it to me. The reader should look at the corresponding photos in the insert following page 498 as Fischer describes what happened.

Bill Fischer: ''Let's look at the physical evidence. We'll start with Martin.''

## 1. MARTIN'S RIGHT BOOT

"During the course of the trial, we served a subpoena on Stu Bennett, the accident reconstructionist hired by Robert Pearl. I asked for an examination of Billy Martin's clothing.

"He gave me Martin's right boot, which was a workboot with lug soles, and I put the tip of it in ink and rolled an impression. It matches the impression that's on the brake pedal.

"Here is a picture of the brake pedal. Here is a picture of the underside of Martin's boot." [See photo insert following page 498.]

"You can see there are some striations on the brake pedal. You can see the top part especially of Martin's boot, which is at least a similar, if not identical, configuration of the boot to the brake, and if you take the time to examine the distance between the treads, you'll find they are the same on the boot and on the brake.

"This doesn't necessarily mean that Martin had his foot on the brake at the time the truck hit the wall, but I can say it was the *last* impression on the brake.

"The boot impression on the brake matches the pattern of Martin's boot. You know for a fact it isn't Reedy's boot print."

## 2. SHIFT SELECTOR LACERATION

"Let me take you to something even a little bit more interesting. The stick-shift lever was a high-low, four wheel range shift selector. There was a laceration on the outside of Martin's right leg with striations on it, and although you can't see them in the photo, there are machine-tool marks on the end of that shaft that match. There is no hole in the pants. The laceration was made *through* the pants.

"The fabric was abraded on Martin's pants, but there was no hole through it.

"So you had a shift selector shaft between the two of them, but Martin had a laceration on the outside of the right leg, which is in the exact position of that shift selector shaft, which had the knob bent off it. It's more physical evidence Martin was on the left, or driver's side." [See photo insert following page 498.]

To contradict this evidence, the state claimed that the striations were made by the corduroy fabric on the seat of the truck. It was absurd, but because the state had seen Fischer's evidence in advance, at least they could come up with something, however flimsy.

## 3. MARTIN'S LEFT GLOVE

"Now I am showing you the picture of Martin's left glove, which had on it crosshatched crow's-foot impressions that appear to match the lacing on the steering wheel.

"If you recall, Reedy, who said he wasn't wearing gloves, had a laceration on his left little finger. Billy's work glove had *no* laceration of the left little finger.'' [See photo insert following page 498.]

''I suppose you could argue it was Reedy's work glove, but Reedy came to visit Martin from Detroit for Christmas. How often does a person bring work gloves when he visits a friend for the holidays? He doesn't. This is the only glove I could find in the truck. So here you have a left glove, apparently Martin's, and the impressions on the left glove match the steering wheel lacing on the steering wheel.''

## 4. REEDY'S JACKET

''Now let's look at Reedy. I examined Reedy's jacket, and during the course of the examination I saw some marks impressed into the suede fabric above the right breast and along the sleeve. Interestingly, if you fold the sleeve back across the body, the marks on the sleeve and the right breast form a continuity.'' [See photo insert following page 498.]

''I observed that the linear distance as well as the height between the lines is the same as the radio surround in the truck.

''Now, very important, do you see this little nick of fabric out of Reedy's jacket? There is a little nick on the left side. At first I didn't realize the significance of this when I first took a picture of it or I would have gotten in a little closer. But you can see there is a nick in the material.

''Let me show you a picture of the inside of the truck. You can see the shift selector has been driven through the console, and it has made a crack in the material just ahead of the selector shaft on the right side of the console, and that has bent back, and there is a jagged projection. This jagged projection is the *only* sharp object in the entire interior of the truck. Ford made sure of that. The door handles were recessed, the windshield. There is nothing else sharp.'' [See photo insert following page 498.]

''Now, if you take the sharp object and match it against the left side of Reedy's jacket, you can see that on full impact, here is where the nick would have been on his chest.

''Now I'm going to show you the truck in the ditch. It was lying on its side, so you couldn't open the passenger door. Let's pretend you are the passenger in the truck, and the truck goes in the ditch. What are you going to do with the upper body? You will lean hard to the left to try to maintain your equilibrium. You are trying to stabilize yourself. You are trying to be vertical. Which is how Reedy got his jacket caught on that jagged edge.''

## 5. REEDY'S PANTS

''In a collision, everything goes down. The truck is on springs, the force of the collision has to go somewhere, and it can't go forward anymore because it has hit the headwall, so it goes down.

"I'm the passenger. We are on a bench seat. We're going down in the ditch. The driver is holding the steering wheel. What have I got to hold on to? Whatever is available.

"The only way a passenger can right himself is to lean very hard to the left toward the driver's side.

"Reedy has a square mark on his left knee that is consistent with his trying to right himself." [See photo insert following page 498.]

"As soon as I got on the case, I asked to have Reedy's clothes secured. I looked at his pants, which had been cut off him. In the vicinity of the left knee, you can see a square mark that comes through the front crease. It matches up perfectly with the right bottom corner of the instrument console.

"Note, too, that after the crash he had a nick on his left hand. This would also be consistent with his trying to grab the shift selector lever to keep himself horizontal."

## 6. HOW REEDY HIT THE REARVIEW MIRROR

"Now take a look at a diagram of the impacts on the windshield. This, by the way, is to exact scale.

"You know anything about how glass breaks? There are a couple ways. One is concentric, round circles, and the other is radial, where the lines come out from the center. And you will see there are both radial and concentric fractures around the focus of the impact point. One is here, but there is one right in the middle of the windshield, and a third is here. Why three, you ask?

"If someone were to strike the rearview mirror, the center of the mirror is attached to the windshield. Slam the mirror over in that direction, and that would account for both of these fractures on the right side.

"Let me show you a picture of what appears to be a minute scab on that mirror. There were also smears on it which appeared to be eyelashes.

"Reedy has a laceration on the forehead. What is an object in a truck that is made of glass other than the windshield? The rearview mirror. If the rearview mirror were cracked, it wouldn't tell you anything in and of itself, but it would be consistent with him being the passenger."

## 7. ACCIDENT CONSISTENT WITH MARTIN'S PERSONALITY

"Here is a drawing of the accident site made by the Broome County Sheriff's Department. Notice there is a gap on the left-side pavement where the left-side wheels were not touching the ground.

"In other words, the truck came out of the curve, went into the ditch, the left side shot up in the air, and then it came back down.

"Why did that happen? What would happen if your vehicle was tipped down

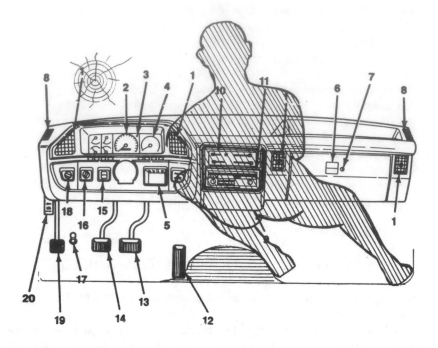

Diagrams of Reedy, pre-impact and full impact. Reedy leans left to stabilize himself as the truck tilts right into the ditch. (Both drawings reprinted by permission of William C. Fischer, Fischer Bureau of Investigation, Endicott, New York)

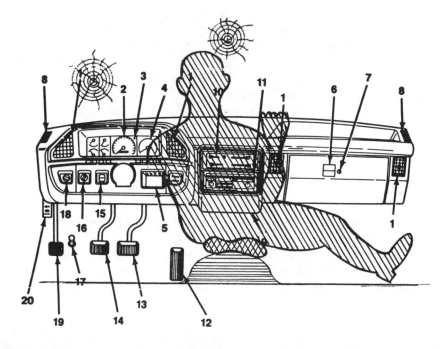

into the ditch and you tried to drive it out? What would happen to the outside tires? They'd come out of the ditch.

"Look at the diagram of the accident. There is a deep ditch on the right side of the road, and at the end of the ditch is a large headwall. In this case the headwall is made of fieldstone.

"The truck came around the curve and slid into the ditch, and then it went a long distance, more than two hundred feet, down the ditch, and ran head-on into the headwall.

"The point is, even if it were very slippery, which it was once the truck was in the ditch, if the driver had attempted to stop the truck, he could have. If he had stepped on the brake instead of stepping on the gas, the truck wouldn't have hit the headwall. It would have come to a stop.

"But the driver of the truck was *not* attempting to brake that truck; he was attempting to drive it out of the ditch at the time it hit the headwall. Why did the driver do that? The guy is dead. I can't ask him. The driver was being obstinate about the truck being in the ditch. It was obvious the truck was buried in a deep ditch and wasn't coming out. But come hell or high water, the driver was saying to himself, I'm going to drive this sucker out of this ditch.

"I know Reedy. I never knew Martin. Reedy is laid-back. I will take a guess that Reedy would have stopped the truck. You knew Martin. Was it like him to say, 'The hell with this sucker. I'm driving her out'? But I'm not trying to match an accident to a man's personality, I'm trying to show the physical evidence."

## 8. THE SEAT WAS PULLED WAY UP

"I am six foot one, over two hundred pounds. Bill Reedy is even bigger than I am. When I got into the truck for the first time, it was obvious to me that I could not steer the truck effectively in the position the front seat was in. It was too close.

"And I checked the railing underneath the seat to make sure it hadn't been stripped on the impact. And it wasn't.

"Let me tell you something about this case. I found a brake impression, which is rare. I found a glove impression, which is *extremely* rare. I found an impression in fabric, which is not uncommon, but if you multiply the probability of finding the boot print on the brake pedal, plus the fabric impression on Martin's glove, plus the nick on Reedy's pants, plus the fabric impression on Reedy's jacket, you are talking 10 million to 1 that anyone could find all this physical evidence in one truck.

"If you ask me, 'How did we lose this case?' I can only laugh."

On the stand Fischer gave the information in a clinical, unemotional manner. Physics ruled. He explained that in order for Bill Reedy to hurt himself in the manner he did, he would have had to slide up under the dashboard until his right hip struck the bottom portion of the dash about where the ashtray was.

He showed that the cuts on Reedy's head came from his having hit the rear-view mirror. He showed how Reedy's jacket had nicks on the left breast from the jagged console projection. He showed how the radio cover made an impression on Reedy's right chest and shoulder. He showed how his left knee hit the instrument console. He showed that the impression on the brake pedal didn't match Reedy's boot.

Then he discussed where Billy was sitting by using some of Dr. Baden's photographs to show that Billy had sustained a bruise across the bridge of his nose from hitting the steering wheel.

He showed the injury on Billy's right hip that was made when he hit the gearshift selector lever. He matched Billy's boot to the impression taken on the brake pedal. He matched the marks on Billy's glove to the cross-hatchings on the steering wheel in color, spacing, and shape. He testified that there was no blood on the glove even though Bill Reedy had sustained an injury on the left hand and had bled. He showed the area where the peritoneal lavage was taken, indicating internal bleeding in Billy's abdomen, which suggested that he had hit the steering wheel with great force.

As a summation to his testimony, Fischer was asked by defense counsel Jon Blechman, "Based on everything that you've shown us here, on the night Billy Martin died, who was driving the vehicle at the time of the accident?"

Fischer, with gusto and flair, said, "Billy Martin."

"And who was the passenger?"

"Bill Reedy was the passenger in that truck."

And as the words came out of his mouth, Jill Martin stood up with tears pouring down her face. She stared at everyone around the tiny Fenton court-room, spun around, and stormed out of the room, slamming the door behind her.

It was grounds for a mistrial. Instead, everyone broke for lunch.

The trial resumed with Kevin Guyette challenging Fischer's conclusions. Guyette sought to refute Fischer by showing that Reedy might have made the impression on his jacket not by hitting the radio console but rather by striking a spot consistent with his being the driver and his going through the steering wheel.

When Fischer said he didn't think Guyette's supposition feasible, Guyette moved on to Fischer's contention that Billy had hit his nose and forehead on the steering wheel. Guyette wanted to know why, if Billy hit the steering wheel, he hadn't broken his nose. He wanted to know how Fischer knew Reedy's swelling chest hadn't been caused by *his* having hit the steering wheel.

He got Fischer to admit that he never marked exactly how far forward or back the seat was at the time of the crash. Guyette made fun of Bill Reedy's size, infuriating Carol Reedy, who glared angrily at Guyette from her seat in the courtroom.

Guyette questioned how Reedy could have hit the rearview mirror had he been the passenger. He asked how Reedy's hair could have been on the pas-senger visor as well as the rearview mirror. Fischer questioned whether it was, in fact, Reedy's hair on the passenger visor. Who knew whose hair it was? said Fischer.

Guyette wanted to know why Fischer hadn't conducted a blood test on a piece of fabric he had found. Fischer became angry. After the DA's office had lost crucial hair samples, *he* was being asked why he didn't conduct a test the DA should have done. Fischer replied, "I could have hid it all from you if I had wanted to."

The big question: If Billy was the driver, how did he end up on the other side of Bill Reedy? Fischer explained it fully.

"How do his legs pass through Mr. Reedy's body to end up on his right when he's sitting spread-eagle on the passenger side of the foot well?"

"They don't. They would have to come down behind his back."

How?

"Gravity."

Guyette asked, "Gravity tucked his legs up and then caused his knees to come up to his chest and then swing his feet around Reedy and then down again?" The prosecutor was trying to rattle Fischer, and he succeeded. Bill Fischer lost his cool.

"Mr. Guyette, I can't explain every conceivable little movement of each person's body for the next few minutes after they're in that vehicle while Reedy's moving around trying to get out of there."

Guyette got Fischer to admit that there was no way of knowing whether Billy applied the brakes in the accident. He asked, "Wouldn't you expect the owner of the vehicle to have his boots match a print on the brake pedal?" He continued, "You do know that both Billy Martin's and William Reedy's footprints appear on the passenger side."

Guyette suggested that Billy was wearing his left glove as he sat in the passenger seat and grabbed the steering wheel at the time of the crash.

Said Fischer, "That's not impossible, unless his left index finger isn't cut."

They discussed the location of the blood on the steering wheel. A recess was called.

They then discussed the gouge made by the gearshift on Billy's body, to no resolution.

Guyette got Fischer to admit that in most criminal cases, he worked for the defense. Fischer admitted that he was actually getting paid. "For my time, not my testimony," he said.

The cross-examination was completed. Fischer had presented all the evidence he had gathered. But Jon Blechman's questions were so unorganized, and Fischer's testimony so fragmented, that the full impact of the testimony didn't reach the overloaded jury.

The last witness was Dr. Irwin Rosenberg, an orthopedic surgeon who had treated Reedy in the hospital.

Dr. Rosenberg testified that a fractured dislocation of a hip, which was what Bill Reedy suffered, is "almost always" incurred by the passenger in an auto crash. He also testified that Reedy had fractured his eighth rib, which was consistent with his being the passenger in a straight-forward accident.

Then Dr. Rosenberg recalled his initial conversation with Reedy at Wilson Memorial Hospital, when Reedy first said he was the driver and then, when he learned Billy was dead, changed his story. It was a convincing recitation by a man with no real interest in the case, a nice way for the defense to finish.

Guyette, on cross, got the doctor to admit that Reedy had changed his story after he had told Reedy that if he didn't and he was convicted he might do jail time.

The summations came on September 18, 1990. Jon Blechman did an excellent job, making all the salient points. Kevin Guyette ridiculed the defense's witnesses one by one.

Kevin Guyette was supposed to have had the burden of proving that Reedy was the driver. In fact, defender Blechman only had to establish reasonable doubt that Reedy had been driving. In front of this jury, he wasn't able to do it. Bill Reedy's initial admission that he was the driver, made over and over, had sunk him.

The jury ruled that Bill Reedy was not guilty of driving while impaired but that he was guilty of driving with an alcohol content of .10 in his blood. He was fined $350. His license was suspended in New York State for six months.

Why did Bill Reedy lose? Anytime you have a jury trial, you never know what the outcome is going to be. That's human nature. And when you have interested parties working against you, it becomes even harder to win.

One significant reason why Bill Reedy was convicted was the work done by Robert Pearl, Jill Martin's attorney, on behalf of the prosecution. Another reason was that the jury had sympathy for Jill Martin, who acted prejudicially throughout the trial.

Said Fischer, "It's apparent that there was a substantial perversion of justice here. We had a strong case from the beginning and blew it. But Jon won Reedy's freedom. It's necessary to be fair to Jon. It's very easy to have twenty-twenty hindsight. Any time you go to court, one side wins, and the other side loses."

Said Carol Reedy, "Billy Martin was a celebrity. People are enamored of these celebrities, regardless of what kind of reputation they have, and I'm not just talking about Billy. Sometimes as people they aren't worth a damn. There is no end to the strange things they do.

"And so the public would rather take the word of the wife of a celebrity, like when Jill Martin went on television and said about Bill, 'This man is lying.'

"There were times when I used to sit and think, My God, what am I going to do with Bill if anything happened to Billy Martin? I really loved Billy. He was like a member of our family. And the way Billy was going, getting his head smashed, getting in fights, I wondered, What would it be like if he left us? And then right around the corner, there it was.

"All this garbage has come down on my husband. I still have yet to say to Jill, 'My husband was very badly hurt in that truck accident, and Billy Martin was driving.'

"Billy Martin doesn't know what happened to Bill because of the accident he caused. He'd be so broken up today knowing what Bill had to go through.''

The close friends of Bill Reedy all know the true story. It hurts them, after all that Bill Reedy had done for Billy Martin over so many years, that Billy's wife would turn around and sue him and cause him such emotional and financial hardship.

"The lovely thing about Bill Reedy," said Mike Klepfer, "is that even though we all know Billy was driving, and even though this has caused Bill a tremendous amount of pain, his attitude is, It was an accident; it was a slippery road. That's Bill's attitude: It wasn't Billy's fault.

"It takes a helluva guy."

Concerning the jury's findings, Judge Eddie Sapir said, "We follow the American system of justice, but having been part of the judicial system for many, many years as a lawyer and as a judge, sometimes things don't work out the way you'd like them to. Sometimes it's hard to prove or disprove something. It happens. Bill Reedy was the guy who was there. He knows the real situation.

"What happened to Bill Reedy is horrible, horrible, because Billy loved Bill Reedy. Reedy loved Billy. Reedy and Carol were going to spend Christmas with their family, but when Billy called and said, 'Hey, big guy, come on up,' Reedy said, 'Come on, Carol, let's go.' And they went."

Said Peggy Sapir, Eddie's wife, "Bill and Carol knew how unhappy Christmas was for Billy, and when he called and wanted him to come, they did what they did because they loved him."

After the trial Bill Reedy returned to Detroit to resume his life without Billy Martin. He lives more quietly now. He hasn't had a drink of any kind since the accident. As a result of his ordeal, he and his son, Billy, Jr., have become closer than they ever were before. In the past Bill Reedy had held it against his son that he had long hair and was a musician. Now none of that matters. He takes his son any way the boy wants to be, and his life is so much richer for it.

As for Carol, her husband stays home now. No more whirlwind drinking trips around the country. He runs his business, and in 1993 he ran for and lost his bid for a seat on the Detroit City Council.

It has been several years since Billy Martin died, and Bill Reedy still misses him, though he is glad to no longer have to answer Billy's phone calls in the middle of the night. He looks forward to Jill Martin's wrongful death lawsuit against him and Ford, secure in his belief that the truth will come out finally. A judge ruled prior to the trial of the suit that nothing that was decided in the first case would have any bearing on the second one. In other words, this time it's the Ford Motor Company against Jill Martin, not just Bill Reedy, and this time the stakes aren't peanuts but millions. This time Jill's relationship with Billy Martin will be open to public scrutiny. This time she'll be a participant, not a spectator. Bill Reedy can't wait for the battle to be joined.

As for Billy, Bill Reedy has no regrets, only fond memories.

"I can rationalize in my own mind when I'm alone thinking about it," said Bill Reedy. "It wasn't his fault. We didn't leave the house with an intent to hurt me, and when we were turning that corner, we were almost home. The damn truck was going only twenty-five miles an hour, and it went erratic, and bam, here we were. It took a tenth of a second.

"I was charged with drunk driving, which was ridiculous, but to me the sadness comes from the final outcome that can never be changed: I lost my friend. The worst thing that could have happened, happened. I can't change that.

"I would rather have Billy back, but I can't have that. I lost what I lost, and that's the end of it. I could never think bad about him. I bust out laughing in the car or at home thinking about the things we did."

Not long after the trial Jill attempted a public humiliation of Bill Reedy on the tabloid television show "A Current Affair." She accused Bill Reedy of not being at Billy's funeral, of not sending flowers, and of not taking her phone calls.

Reedy answered that he was screwed to a bed in a hospital in Syracuse, that his boss sent flowers for his staff, and that he was told by his attorney not to speak to her.

Immediately Jill said, "But they didn't send flowers."

Reedy answered, "Lady, you ain't listening. You ain't never going to listen." And Bill Reedy ripped off the mike and walked off the set.

The Reedys received phone calls of support from bars and sympathizers all over the country. Callers commented that entire bars booed her and cheered him when he got up and stormed off.

After Reedy left, the "Current Affair" reporter walked with Jill Martin to the site of the accident. Said Jill solemnly, "This is the first time I have returned to the scene of the accident."

It was the end of her driveway. What was she talking about? It was the *only* exit from her house. How could she say a thing like that and expect to get away with it?

Vicki Figone watched "A Current Affair" and saw what Jill had tried to do to Bill Reedy on national television. She became so incensed she called Jill at home.

Said Figone, "When she answered, I said, 'Jill, you fucking, lying bitch. I just saw "A Current Affair," and I hope you rot in hell.'

"I didn't identify myself, but she knew it was me, and I couldn't believe she did. She said, 'Vicki, you fucking whore, I hope you rot in hell—right next to Billy.'

"I hung up the phone. First of all, I couldn't believe she knew it was me. Second of all, I couldn't believe she told me to rot in hell right next to Billy. I was floored. I called my dad. I said, 'You're not going to believe this one.'

"It was the last time I ever spoke to her."

# THE VOID

**W**hen Jenny Martin died on December 10 and Billy came West for the funeral, the next day he went to visit the bar owned by Sam Curtain, the husband of his first wife, Lois, and he brought Jill with him.

Curtain, who had raised Billy's daughter, Kelly, since she was a baby, remembered, "Jill seemed like a fairly nice gal. Billy probably spent seventy-five dollars, bought the house a couple of times. Then he said he wanted to talk to me, and we went back into the office. I had a guy sit in for me and tend bar and Billy talked to me about the kids.

"He said, 'Sammy, you don't have to worry. Kelly and Evie, they're well taken care of. They're gonna have plenty of money if I die. I've got this trust fund for both of them.' He said, 'I got plenty. They're both gonna have plenty of money. If I die tomorrow,' he says, 'they're both gonna be rich.'

"And he told me that maybe three times.

"Every once in a while he'd get gassed and he'd call up and he'd talk to Kelly, and he told Kelly the same thing.

"Two weeks before he died, and he told me Kelly would be taken care of at least three times. He had made a point of asking me to go back and sitting down and talking to him about how much money he was going to leave Kelly if anything happened to him.

"I said, 'I'm sure you do, Billy. You wouldn't bullshit me.' And I don't think he would.

"I know he did a lot of crazy things. But never to me or to Lois. He was always real straight with us."

So how to explain that when Billy died, his children got virtually nothing?

Billy's Last Will and Testimony was dated February 11, 1988, initialed on every page, and signed at the end Billy Martin, which certainly indicated that a lawyer close to Billy didn't draw it up but he only signed it, because his important documents drawn up by his lawyers he always signed Alfred M. Martin, not Billy Martin.

The will was prepared by Victoria Huey in Newport Beach, California, and one of the witnesses was Virginia Madden, coach John's wife. The will confirmed Jill's one-half community property interest in their joint property, and gave his entire estate over to the Martin Living Trust, which was signed on the same day.

Under the terms of the living trust that they had set up, Billy's entire estate, with a few minor exceptions, would be held in trust for Jill, who was named as the trustee.

In a letter dated March 27, Jill wrote Kelly and Billy Joe, Billy's children, informing them that after expenses, "the balance in the Trust account at year-end was $8.82."

Billy Martin had told Sam Curtain that he would leave Kelly enough money that she would not have to worry. At the time of Jill's letter, Kelly's share of the trust was $4.41.

Said Kelly Martin, "Dad died, leaving a living trust, and I tried to get ahold of it. My dad supposedly had put away money for Evie to go to college. He said he was putting away so much a month.

"Jill called me in January 1990. She said, 'Quit trying to contact my lawyers, because it's just costing money. I'll send you a copy when I get ready to. If you contest the will, you will not get anything. Your father wanted you to have the diamond Number 1 necklace the Yankee players gave him. There are some other things, too. You'll get all these things upon *my death*.'

"She's thirty-five years old.

"When she finally sent me a copy of the living trust in April, she said that because of taxes, all that was left was $8.82.

"She said to me, 'Your dad died penniless. I'm sorry, but everything had to go to the income tax.' "

Kelly was devastated. Although her father hadn't stood by her much, he was still her emotional support. Without him she was like a ship without a rudder on a very stormy sea. Her disappointment that her father could leave her and not take care of his granddaughter, Evie, as he had promised was heartbreaking.

Said Kelly, "My dad often thanked Sam Curtain for what a good job he did raising me. He said, 'Sam, don't worry. I promise you that Evie and Kelly are well taken care of, that they will have everything. If anything happens to me, I've got it set up where they're well taken care of. They'll be rich, rich, rich.'

"Sam told me, 'That's what makes me so mad about her getting everything.

Your dad promised me that he'd already had everything worked out to where you and Evie would never want for a thing, that you'd be taken care of.'

"The woman [Jill] does whatever she wants to do because she knows that there isn't any way I can fight against her. She wins. No lawyer will take my case without up-front money. I'm still paying for the cost of going to his funeral.

"Somebody's got to stop her, but I just don't know who can, and I've made myself sick worrying about it. This woman came along and took it all and wouldn't give us a thing. She won't even give me his cowboy hat.

"I asked for it, and she said no.

"When I got the letter about the living trust seventeen months after his death, and it said that all that was left was $8.82, I called her. I got her answering machine.

"I said, 'I just got your letter. Apparently, you have won. But if that's what winning is all about, you can have it. Because you know what? You're the one who has to look in that mirror and know what a rotten, fucking snake you are.

" 'But,' I said, 'it probably won't bother you, because you don't have a conscience.' I told her, 'The one thing I know, when I die, I'll never have to see you again. 'Cause you're going straight to hell where you belong. And let you just burn there. Until then, you have a real nice life, because you certainly have wrecked ours.'

"And I hung up. That was the last time I had anything to do with her."

According to Eddie Sapir, Jill had the living trust and the will drawn up without his knowledge. Sapir had put a clause in Billy's contract with the Yankees saying that if Billy died a natural death, his wife would be paid fifty percent of his salary. When Billy divorced Heather and married Jill, Ed Sapir had called Jill to tell her of the substitution.

To Sapir's surprise, Jill told him to call her lawyer in California to check whether the money should be left to Jill or to the living trust that she and Billy had signed.

"I had no knowledge of it," said Sapir, "but I know what my advice would have been. It would have been something I would have pleaded with Billy not to do. It didn't shock me it had gotten done, because knowing Billy, she would have hocked and hocked him until he broke down and signed it."

Ed Sapir later told Lewis Figone, Billy's childhood friend, about the living trust and the will he had signed. Figone said to Billy, "Jesus Christ, Billy, do you know what the hell you're doing?"

Billy said, "Aw, shit, I'm going to sign it and tear it up later."

Of course, Billy never tore it up.

Says Lewis Figone, "And she's in charge of the living trust. Billy didn't have any money on hand, but he had a large pension coming, and she's in complete control over the pension. And his kids are not going to get anything."

As part of her accounting, Jill Martin drew up a schedule of assets and debts left in Billy's estate. The assets totaled $109,512.95. The liabilities totaled $709,741.92, including about $300,000 in state and federal taxes.

On November 30, 1990, Jill Martin did what everyone expected her to do.

She parlayed that trumped-up conviction of Bill Reedy into a whopping lawsuit against the town of Fenton and Ford Motor Credit Company. Bill Reedy was also a defendant, but he doesn't have deep pockets like Fenton and Ford.

As Matt Keough put it, "She is just trying to screw Ford Motor Company."

In her bill of particulars Jill Martin said that because of Reedy's negligence, the negligence of the town, and the negligence of Ford, she was entitled to an award of $11 million based on Billy's past and expected future earnings.

Since Billy's death, Jill is working hard to rewrite history, telling everyone who cares to listen that her marriage to Billy was loving and stable, arguing that if Billy had not died, they would have had twenty more blissful years of marriage.

Jill's behavior enraged Peggy Sapir sufficiently that the normally serene Peggy Sapir called Jill to tell her off.

"If you listen to her now," said Peggy Sapir, "she conveniently forgets that between 1980 and 1987, Billy was seeing and then married to Heather. She'll say, 'For ten years Billy and I this, and Billy and I that. . . .' Well, what about the marriage in between? She likes to say that she didn't know he was married. She is so calculating, so smart. . . . And maybe it was to her advantage not to know, to pretend she didn't know.

"I was so mad at her for distrusting my husband. I felt that Jill had been using him, and I didn't want her to use him anymore. And I just confronted her.

"I told her why she wasn't out there that day at Yankee Stadium when they retired Billy's number.

"I said, 'Because I don't like you, I think you should know some of these things. You talk like everything between you and Billy was perfect, and your marriage was ideal and wonderful. You talk about all this love and this and that, but that's really not the truth. He did things before you and during you. And remember when you were at Yankee Stadium, you know *why* you weren't out there? Because Billy didn't want you out there. Ask Paul Tabarry if you don't believe me. He'll tell you, too.' I felt it was something she deserved from me.

"Oh, she was crying. She said, 'Oh, thank you for telling me now. I don't know why you're telling me this.' "

In the papers Jill filed against Ford, she stated that in 1987, Billy earned a total of $853,797 and in 1988 had made $834,123, and in 1989 he had earned a total of $804,201, and during those three years "the monies or items of value received by Jilluann Martin consisted of all her living expenses, food, clothing, travel, entertainment, jewelry, gifts, home purchases, and furnishings, and for that three-year period totaled $1,926,000."

Those numbers show that the bulk of Billy's income was spent on Jill, leaving little for Billy's own needs or for the future.

According to land records, on January 22, 1991, the $248,000 mortgage on Jill's home in Fenton was paid off in full. But according to Eddie Sapir, Billy did not have mortgage insurance because he simply refused to take the time to make an appointment with a doctor to take the required physical. And according to George Steinbrenner, when Billy died he stopped paying Jill.

When Billy was alive, she was having trouble paying the oil bill. So where did the money come from for her to pay off the $248,000 mortgage?

Bill Reedy could not stand the thought that Evie, Billy's grandchild, would not be able to go to college because Jill was the beneficiary of Billy's money, and on October 18, 1991, Bill Reedy, through his Pals of Billy organization, held a benefit for Evie Martin-Knight at the Westin Hotel in downtown Detroit.

Whitey Ford, Frank Howard, Johnny Blanchard, Ron Guidry, and Hank Aguirre were all there as Bill Reedy raised $35,000 to start a fund for eight-year-old Evie's college education.

Jill Martin, pursuing her vendetta against Bill Reedy, even tried to sabotage the dinner. She wrote to all of Billy's friends to ask them not to attend. In the letter she said she was going to take care of Billy's granddaughter herself.

Referring to Jill's letter, Eddie Sapir told the packed gathering at the dinner honoring Billy, "Don't believe in Santa Claus until the present is under the tree. And because of Bill Reedy, the present is under the tree."

Mickey Mantle to this day has not gotten over the death of his friend. On the golf course, if he makes a particularly good shot, he will comment with his trademark sardonic grin, "Billy's in charge."

As for Kelly Martin, the combination of her father's death and Jill's actions have destroyed her life. In life Jill took Kelly's father across the country, and in death Jill took everything of his that had any meaning to her. During the time Kelly was trying to get a copy of the living trust from Jill, Jill called the California police and told them that Kelly had been harassing her with threatening phone calls.

"Jill sent the cops up to my house," said Kelly. "She told them I was calling her daily with death threats. I've never called her once with death threats.

"I told the cops, 'I'm not a person who's gonna call somebody and say, "I'm going to break your legs." ' One day if I see her, I will probably beat the living shit out of her, but I will do it with my own hands. But I am not planning to go East.

"I've had people say to me, 'Kelly, I'll take care of her. Let me go back and do it.' But no, I can't do that. I have to look in the mirror every day. I can't hurt anybody. I can't deliberately hurt someone even as much as she's hurt me."

"I have a conscience. So I told the cop, 'Why don't you ask her for the tapes? She tapes every conversation. If I'm making these death threats, surely she's got it on tape. So ask her for them. But do me a favor, don't come out here and bother me, 'cause I don't need it.' "

With her father gone, Kelly Martin seems to have lost her zest for living.

"I talk to my dad all the time. I've got a light in my bedroom that goes off and on by itself all the time.

"One night Evie came home from her dad, and she said, 'Mama, can I sleep in your bed?'

"I said, 'Sure.' She said, 'Mama, Grandpa won't turn the light off.'

"I said, 'Well, tell him good night.'

"She said, 'I love you, Grandpa.' And the light went off.

"I haven't been in my right mind since he died. He wasn't supposed to go. I was waiting for him to stop playing baseball, because I hated that damn game.

"I remember after George fired my dad as manager and made him a commentator, he asked if I was going to come down to the ballpark in Oakland and see him.

"I said, 'Sure, Dad.'

"At the end of the seventh inning he was done, and he said, 'Well, I'm going to go. I'll see you later this evening.'

"I said, 'Can't I go, too?'

"He said, 'Don't you want to stay and watch the rest of the game?'

"I said, 'I hate this game. I've always hated this game.' I said, 'I only came to see you.'

"He said, 'You really hate baseball?'

"I said, 'Yeah, I hate it because if it weren't for baseball, I'd have a father.' I said, 'Do you think I like standing in a corridor waiting three hours for a game to end, only to have you lose and have somebody say to me, "Tell Kelly I'll catch her the next time I'm in town?" ' I told him, 'I stood down here with Evie when she was a baby, standing because there were no chairs, only to have you send someone out to tell me that.'

"Baseball was my dad's whole life. He loved it. So I was looking forward to the day when he couldn't manage, that he had to stay home, when we could spend some time with him.

"That's all I ever really wanted."

Billy's death had a devastating affect on his brother, Tudo. The brothers hadn't been speaking for a long time. When Billy was managing Oakland, Tudo asked him for a coaching job. Billy turned him down. When Billy died, Tudo was bedridden for three weeks.

Billy's death left his sisters, Pat and Joan, with a void they have not been able to fill. As adults Billy and his sisters rarely had a meeting of the minds. He seemed so different from them. Pat and Joan continue to struggle to understand their late brother, a man who became a stranger in the family.

"Ma used to tell Billy he ought to go to a psychiatrist and stop drinking," said Joan. "She always harped on it, but he drank.

"If Pat and I knew what was bothering Billy, we could have talked to him, but you couldn't talk to Billy. Not us. We couldn't."

"Nobody in the family could talk to him," said Pat. "Maybe we should have made more demands on him. We never asked him for anything. And that might have bugged him. Other relatives were kiss-butts, pushing themselves on him and acting like big shots. If you did that, Billy felt you were his friend."

Said Joan, "We should have said, 'We're coming to spring training. We're coming to New York. Send us tickets.' "

"And he'd have appreciated us more," said Pat.

"But we didn't want to bother him," said Joan.

"Here we felt we were doing right by not bothering him," said Pat.

"We never called," said Joan.

"Except if he got hurt," said Pat, "and then we sent him a card."

"And if I felt he deserved it," said Joan, "I used to yell at him. One time I said, 'Other people might have to take your shit, but I don't. They have to because of who you are, but I don't.' And I left."

Said Pat, "We never kissed his butt. We treated him like a brother. We *were* proud of him, whether he was right or wrong, and he knew that to the very end."

One of Billy's more curious actions late in his life was his apparent attempt to give his mother's house to the University of California, Berkeley.

Billy had mentioned it to one of the university regents, who mentioned it to a friend of the family. When the friend told Jenny, she said, "They're crazy." When his mom confronted him, Billy denied it. Another relative, however, confirmed that this was Billy's intention, to donate the house to the university as "the birthplace of Billy Martin."

Pat said, "Where does he think Joan's going, out into the street?"

About a month after Billy passed away, Jenny's house, which Jenny had left to Joan, again became the object of attention, this time by Jill.

Jill's lawyer wrote to Pat and Joan to say that Jill was going to sue them for the house Joan was living in and the World Series rings given to them by Billy.

Joanie called Lewis Figone for some advice. She had never been involved with attorneys.

Figone told her, "You have the ring in your possession, don't you? And the house is in your name? She's just bluffing you. Don't even bother calling her back. Forget about it, Joanie. She can't do anything."

Said Joan: "Jill wrote, 'Billy said he wanted me to have the World Series rings, and if you don't return them by a certain date, I'm going to have the authorities look into the circumstances of the house being left to you by your mother.' She wrote that my mother was senile and incompetent when she left the house to me.

"I thought, Oh my God, what am I going to do?

"I got a lawyer. I sent Jill a copy of my mother's will. And that was it. I never heard from her again.

"My lawyer said, 'It's just scare tactics.'

"I said, 'Well, it worked for a while.' And now she has a lawsuit against everybody else she can think of."

Said Pat Irvine, "You don't stop Jill. No one stops her. She has a master plan. And whatever is formed in her head, it's like a map, it's down, and she knows how to do it. I've never met anybody as smart and as calculating as this woman. I know smart people, but not one this devious.

"She was a good actress. This girl should have been in the movies. She would have won an Academy Award. She is *good*. She can turn it on, and then she can switch it off and be mean at the snap of a finger.

"She wanted Billy's money, everything she could get in order to have an easy, glamorous life. She didn't want to live in Blackhawk because it was boring. And Billy loved Blackhawk. He loved that home. He had quiet there, a little knoll where he could sit and think and have quiet.

"But she wanted New York, the high life.

"The only one who could have stopped Jill is the good Lord up above, and I don't think he wants her. As far as I'm concerned, she's the devil's disciple."

As for George Steinbrenner, he finally got nailed after years of trying to ruin his players. What he did this time went over the line of propriety and got him banned from baseball for life, though the ban turned out to be only temporary.

In December 1980 Steinbrenner signed Dave Winfield to a ten-year contract for $23 million. At the time it seemed like Winfield was getting all the money in the world. In the contract was a cost-of-living clause, the impact of which Steinbrenner apparently didn't fully understand when it was signed. When it was fully explained to Steinbrenner, he asked Winfield to rewrite the contract. Winfield refused.

For eight years Steinbrenner whispered nasty comments about Winfield, at times berating him for not playing better. Through it all, Winfield smiled and defended himself by telling the reporters to wait until the end of the year and then look at his numbers.

There were times Steinbrenner forced his managers to bench Winfield, to move him down in the batting order, or to platoon him. Winfield never said a word, but his teammates were furious. The team always suffered for it, and then the manager would have to defy Steinbrenner to get things back where they belonged.

Steinbrenner became more frustrated as he tried to trade Winfield. Beginning in 1986 his star outfielder was a ten-year veteran with five years of service with the Yankees and hence could not be traded without his permission.

Winfield wrote a book that came out in 1988. It revealed what everyone already knew: Steinbrenner was a bad man. In retaliation Steinbrenner ordered Winfield traded. General manager Lou Piniella made a deal to send him to Toronto for Jesse Barfield. He was also talking to Houston about trading him for Kevin Bass. But it was a charade because of Winfield's no-trade status. Winfield kept his cool, making Steinbrenner look foolish.

During the early part of the 1988 season, Steinbrenner kept saying Winfield was a selfish player. Steinbrenner tried to get Willie Randolph and Billy to denounce him. All through the spring, while Winfield did his book promotions, Steinbrenner criticized him for "thinking only of himself." Winfield let all the criticism slide off his back, as usual.

Steinbrenner could not dent Winfield's armor. Like Steinbrenner's buddy, Richard Nixon, who went after the Democrats with dirty tricks, Steinbrenner hired his own dirty trickster to get the goods on his star player.

In January 1989, Winfield sued Steinbrenner for failing to pay the Winfield Foundation the $300,000 that was called for in his contract. Four days later Steinbrenner countersued, charging the foundation with "fraud, wrongdoing, and misappropriations." Steinbrenner accused Winfield of using the money that was supposed to go to needy children and spending it on himself and friends. Steinbrenner also noted that Winfield had not made his $480,000 payment to the foundation and demanded he do so.

Everyone wondered how Steinbrenner could possibly have known about the details of Winfield's foundation. Before long it came out.

A man by the name of Howard Spira, who accused Winfield of loaning him $15,000 at 700 percent interest, had been calling reporters for a year to talk about how Winfield had ruined his life. Winfield denied having loaned him money. Spira proved Winfield was lying by producing a canceled check.

Spira, it turned out, had been the one who had leaked to Steinbrenner the incriminating information about Winfield. For that information Steinbrenner had paid Spira $40,000.

When the news came out, Steinbrenner was investigated by baseball commissioner Fay Vincent. One fact was incontrovertible: George had paid Spira, a known gambler, $40,000. Something else too: Spira had provided George with the damaging information on Dave Winfield.

Vincent was certain the two transactions were connected, putting George in a terrible bind. As in the Watergate situation, George had been caught red-handed doing something truly despicable, but this time it was to one of his players.

Why did George pay Howard Spira $40,000? George asserted a number of different rationales: He said he paid Spira (1) out of the goodness of his heart; (2) because he "felt sorry for the guy"; (3) because he feared that Spira would tell the press that Lou Piniella gambled; (4) because he feared Spira would tell the press that two of his front-office employees had sold stolen Bat Day giveaway items; (5) he feared for his safety.

Fay Vincent dismissed his excuses. He cleared Piniella of any wrongdoing. Commented another baseball executive: "George is really like a cornered rat now if he's dragging Lou Piniella into this."

Said Spira's lawyer, David Greenfield, "This guy changes the story about what happened more often than he changes managers."

Concluded Vincent, "This decision is largely the result of admitted conduct by Mr. Steinbrenner, although there is ample evidence from other sources supporting the conclusion I have reached."

The hearing before the commissioner was supposed to be in closed session. According to Fay Vincent, George was up to his old tricks, leaking the transcript to the papers to gain sympathy from the public.

On July 30, 1990, Fay Vincent and George Steinbrenner signed an agreement: He would be barred from running the Yankees for the rest of his life.

Vincent had ruled that George's conduct was "not in the best interests of baseball." He had told Steinbrenner he intended to suspend him for two years.

But Steinbrenner, in a move he said he made to keep him from losing the vice-presidency of the United States Olympic Committee, asked Vincent to instead ban him for life. Vincent, perplexed, complied. Afterward Steinbrenner said he was "very satisfied with the resolution."

When George bought the Yankees, he had told everyone he was going to be an absentee owner. Now, eighteen years later, he would be.

Announced Vincent, "Mr. Steinbrenner will have no further involvement in the management of the New York Yankees or in the day-to-day operations of that club."

Steinbrenner also agreed not to contest the decision in court.

Said Vincent afterward about Steinbrenner, "I am able to evaluate a pattern of behavior that borders on the bizarre.

"It is apparent to me that Mr. Steinbrenner does not appreciate the gravity of his conduct."

The Yankees were playing the Detroit Tigers when the news of the decision spread throughout the crowd. The fans greeted the announcement with a ninety-second standing ovation.

Kelly Martin called George when the commissioner banned him from the game.

Said Kelly, "I called his office. I told him, 'I just wanted to tell you that I was really sorry that they banned you.'

"He said, 'Oh, thank you. It's very nice of you to say that.'

"I said, 'Well, wait, I didn't finish. I'm just sorry that my dad wasn't here to see it happen. My dad would have loved to have seen you thrown out of baseball.' "

The ink was barely dry on their agreement when George began campaigning to get it lifted. George hired a public relations firm to attack Vincent and his chief investigator, John Dowd. One of George's partners, Leonard Kleinman, then filed a $22 million suit against Vincent, claiming the Vincent hearing was a sham. Kleinman also sought a temporary restraining order, saying the commissioner did not have jurisdiction over him because Steinbrenner's contract did not contain a specific clause agreeing to submit to the power of the commissioner. The judge denied the request.

Fay Vincent said of the lawsuit, "I think it is an imbecilic act which reflects enormous contempt on his part about an agreement he signed." He added, "He is desperate to find ways of attacking it. It's disturbing he's doing what he's doing."

A month after signing his agreement, Steinbrenner was telling reporters he had not been kicked out of baseball, that he had done nothing to justify even a suspension. At this point, it was all bluster. George had signed an agreement banning him for life, and now he was stuck with it.

In an AP article, George sounded like a lost puppy. He told the reporter that he had watched the movie *Hoosiers* forty times. He said he identified with the coach, played by Gene Hackman.

"Here is a guy who has his own way of doing things. The guy stuck to his beliefs despite all the criticism and the team ends up winning. It's my favorite. It makes me feel real good inside."

George admitted to having made "a lot of mistakes. Maybe there were too many managerial changes." He pointed out that five of the nineteen changes in seventeen years involved Billy.

"I loved the guy," said Steinbrenner. "Billy Martin was one of the dearest friends I've ever had." Alas, poor Billy.

As for Spira, in February of 1990 he had made the mistake of writing to George that he would go public if George didn't pay him another $110,000. George's security officer, Philip McNiff, formerly special agent in charge of the Tampa FBI office, turned the letter over to the FBI.

Spira was indicted on eight counts in March 1990. Spira said Steinbrenner promised him not only the $40,000 for his work, but an additional $110,000, a job, and a free room at Steinbrenner's Bay Harbor Inn. Steinbrenner said that the $40,000 was all Spira had been promised and that Spira had been shaking him down for the rest.

Spira's trial took place in April 1991. George took the stand for two hours. He choked back tears. He played his Tiny Tim card, saying about Spira, "I had given him all I was going to give him to start a new life, to help his family, to get away from me."

Unfortunately for Spira, he tended to lose his cool and threaten people. In addition to having five guilty verdicts handed down against him for his dealings with Steinbrenner, he was convicted of extorting money from a Houston lawyer and of threatening a United Airlines employee who had rejected a claim involving lost luggage.

Spira was sentenced to five years in jail.

Spira is still in prison, but George is back running the New York Yankees.

Fay Vincent, who from the start felt that George's self-inflicted lifetime ban was too severe, returned Steinbrenner to baseball's good graces on July 24, 1992, when Vincent announced that George would be reinstated beginning March 1, 1993.

"It's a matter of fairness," said Vincent's assistant, Steve Greenberg.

When questioned by George Vescey of *The New York Times*, Steinbrenner showed no sense of remorse or guilt for what he had done to Winfield.

"Someday the facts will come out," he said. Added Vescey, "Whatever that means."

Two months later, Fay Vincent was out, the victim of a coup. Most of the baseball owners, including Steinbrenner, wanted him out for a myriad of reasons having to do with player relations, scheduling (including his refusal to consider interleague play), distribution of expansion fees, an attempt to limit superstations, and in general, Vincent's insistence on doing what was best for baseball as a whole.

On March 1, 1993, George officially returned, curiously hailed by the sports press as the cure to what was ailing a Yankee team that he had mismanaged for so many years.

At the same time, the American Shipbuilding Company, the company that George built, filed for bankruptcy and laid off almost all of its workers after the Navy canceled contracts for repair work on two oil tankers.

George tried to use his political influence to have the contracts restored, but failed. He threatened to sue. The Navy held firm. It looks like AmShip soon will close up shop.

Though George may have run AmShip into the ground, his control over the Yankees has resumed. The Yankees acted uncharacteristically during his exile. General manager Gene Michael relied on his manager, Buck Showalter, promoted rookies, maintained continuity, and returned the focus where it should have been all along: on the players. Now that George is back, can the usual chaos be far behind?

Reggie is back, too, if only symbolically. George hired Mr. October to be a member of the Yankee front office. Like an abused child, Reggie has come back to Papa.

On August 14, 1993, the Yankees retired Reggie's number 44. Before a large Stadium throng, former Yankee broadcaster Frank Messer read the list of the players in addition to Reggie whose numbers had been retired by the Yankees, including Babe Ruth, Lou Gehrig, Joe DiMaggio, Mickey Mantle, Yogi Berra and Bill Dickey, Roger Maris, Phil Rizzuto, Thurman Munson, Whitey Ford, Elston Howard, and Casey Stengel. Messer read them in order—all except for one former Yankee whose name *was not* mentioned: Billy Martin, number 1.

Thirteen of the fourteen names were read. Only Martin's wasn't. And later, as speeches continued, the camera panned across the numbers, showing them all, from Gehrig's 4 to Ruth's 3 to Mantle's 7 to Stengel's 37 and all the others, and yet faded to black after showing Phil Rizzuto's number 10, cutting off from view the final number: 1.

Had Steinbrenner deliberately ordered Billy, Reggie's nemesis, persona non grata during the ceremony? It certainly appeared so.

Meanwhile, George has let it be known that he wants to move the New York Yankees across the river to the New Jersey Meadowlands. The crime in the South Bronx is bad, he says, and attendance is down. These are his excuses. In 1993, with a competitive team on the field, the Yankees drew 2.4 million fans.

No matter, George wants to move. He wants the same kind of deal Walter O'Malley got from Los Angeles, a gift of hundreds of acres of land and a brand-new ballpark. The $125 million he extracted from New York City in the 1970s to spruce up the Stadium wasn't enough. This time he doesn't want a fixer-upper. After his lease runs out in the Bronx early in the next century, there's a good chance that New York will lose the sports franchise that is such an important part of the city's image and history.

Before too long Yankee Stadium may be but a fond, albeit painful, memory. The House That Ruth Built and Billy Loved could disappear, just as Ebbets Field, the Polo Grounds, Crosley Field, and Forbes Field have vanished. George lives in Tampa, Florida, where there is a spanking new dome awaiting the first team that signs on. The Tampa Bay Yankees? It's no more incongruous than the Utah Jazz.

\* \* \*

Billy Martin's tombstone inscription reads, "I may not have been the greatest Yankee to put on the uniform, but I was the proudest." Against the backdrop of his life—the boyhood dreams of major league stardom, the demons that tormented him, the public fame and private ruin of his life, and the misery of the job he sold his soul to keep—those words ring with tragic innocence.

# AFTERWORD

The saddest aspect of Billy Martin's story is that he didn't have to die so soon. The tragedy was that though everyone knew he was a drunk, no one recognized that he suffered from the disease of alcoholism and took the necessary steps to save him.

As a result, besotted with alcohol, his judgment under a cloud, Billy accidentally killed himself in a one-vehicle accident on December 25, 1989. He was only sixty-one years old.

What happened to Billy Martin happens to millions of Americans each year. Undiagnosed alcoholics, the ten percent of the population that sit in bars and consume fifty percent of the liquor sold in this country, cause a disproportionate number of traffic fatalities each year, either to themselves or to others.

And if alcoholics don't die in car crashes, other causes are from injuries incurred through fighting or gunshot wounds or stabbings. Alcoholism begets violence, and violence begets death. Illness and disease from alcoholism (especially heart and liver disease) end many other lives prematurely.

As explained to me by Irving Kolin, M.D., Clinical Associate Professor, University of Florida, College of Medicine, board-certified in addiction psychiatry, "Typically the alcoholic either gets treatment, or he dies an early death." Statistics say that alcoholics die twelve years earlier than nonalcoholics.

According to Dr. Kolin, the insidious nature of the disease prevents alcoholics (and drug addicts) from getting treatment.

Till the day he died, Billy didn't think he had a problem. He simply denied he was an alcoholic, despite the many hours he spent in bars drinking. Like most alcoholics, Billy was blind to his condition, deluding himself to excuse his erratic behavior under the influence of alcohol.

Billy's friends never sought to get him treatment. Why would they? Most of the friends he chose gathered in bars to drink with him. The rest kept quiet because they knew the fuss Billy would raise if the subject of his drinking even came up.

When Billy and I worked on *Number 1* together back in 1979, Billy was on the wagon. He had just been fired by the Yankees for punching out the marshmallow salesman in Minneapolis, and I suppose he was feeling guilty over booze costing him his job.

For nine months we worked on the book sitting in bars and drinking Perrier with a twist of lime. Billy told me this abstinence was proof he wasn't an alcoholic.

Neither of us knew at the time that the test for alcoholism was not whether he could stop but whether he could keep from starting up again. He couldn't. Shortly after beginning his tenure as manager of the Oakland A's in the spring of 1980, the drinking resumed, and to my knowledge he never went on the wagon again.

According to Dr. Kolin, alcoholics are vulnerable to the disease from birth and especially susceptible if the father was an alcoholic, as Billy's was.

But once alcoholics start drinking, usually it gets worse with the passing of time. There is no known cure, save abstinence, which is usually impossible without the aid of a medically supervised treatment program.

An alcoholic doesn't choose to be one. Billy had no control over the family into which he was born. Billy would have had to understand and accept his genetic predisposition to the disease in order for him to take the steps to enable him to have responsibility for controlling the disease through rehabilitation and recovery.

It wasn't Billy's fault he was an alcoholic. But Billy never took the responsibility to either understand or receive treatment for his alcoholism.

Billy's critics saw Billy as antisocial, weak of character, and lacking moral fiber. Billy's actions certainly suggested such labels, but in fact those are the labels commonly given to alcoholics. Billy was sick, and no one helped him to get better. If he had had heart trouble, his relations, friends, and employers would have sent him to a heart specialist. Billy was terminally ill from a chemical dependence on alcohol. The problem was that none of the people around him recognized his illness, nor did they have a clue how to get him help because they were enmeshed in his disease.

For example, Billy's wives, who apparently had as little understanding of the disease as his bosses, had never forced him to get help. According to Dr. Kolin, wives of alcoholics rarely force their husbands into treatment. They need the paycheck, need him to continue functioning even if impaired by alcohol.

His employers, the team owners, saw his behavior as trouble, and time after time fired him. Even today, alcoholism among baseball players is an extremely serious problem, but far too little is being done to stop it or to get those players with serious drinking problems any help. Baseball and booze: The two have been intertwined since the days of the Babe.

As the years went by, the public witnessed a series of Billy's misadventures beginning when he was a player and continuing through his years as manager. With a couple of exceptions, the common element contributing to each fight was alcohol.

Over the years his functioning became more and more impaired. It got so bad at the end that some of his managerial moves seemed strange and irrational. The criticism mounted, but no help arrived.

For the last ten years of his life, Billy worked under the shabby tyranny of

George Steinbrenner, the owner of the New York Yankees. Because he was an alcoholic, Billy's mechanism for dealing with Steinbrenner's treatment of him was to drink.

The drinking led to antisocial behavior, and this behavior five times ended in his firing, causing Billy to drink harder.

Why did Billy stay with George? In large part because he was an alcoholic. Billy often said that when he wasn't a Yankee, he felt as though he were nothing.

The reality was that Billy Martin was a tremendous baseball talent. If it hadn't been for his disease, he could have gone to any team and flourished. Had he had a broader, healthier perspective, Billy would have seen himself as one of the most talented, brilliant managers in the game. Instead, he measured his self-esteem on George Steinbrenner's terms. At the end his self-esteem was close to zero. Had Billy not died in the accident, it's safe to say that cirrhosis of the liver would have gotten him before long.

Because he was an alcoholic, Billy had no mechanism for handling Steinbrenner's abuse other than drinking. Because he was an alcoholic, he didn't feel he had an option but to suffer the abuse in an unhealthy relationship.

Said Dr. Kolin, ''If Billy had not been an alcoholic, he may not have returned to the Yankees five times. He would have had the option to tell George, 'I quit. You'll be hearing from my lawyer. I'm going to another organization.' ''

Because Billy was an alcoholic, Billy stuck with George, accelerating his misery, his drinking, and his death.

The Billy Martin–George Steinbrenner relationship is one of the most fascinating in the history of sports. The question everyone asks: Why did Billy allow himself to be hired by George five different times? Alcoholism was part of the reason, but not the entire reason.

The great irony, as you have seen in *Wild, High and Tight*, was that Billy Martin, who for most of his career controlled a ballgame like few other managers, lived his life off the field almost totally out of control.

# BIBLIOGRAPHY

*Dynasty*, by Peter Golenbock, Prentice-Hall, 1975; *The Bronx Zoo*, by Sparky Lyle and Peter Golenbock, Crown, 1979; *Number 1*, by Billy Martin and Peter Golenbock, Delacorte, 1980; *Balls*, by Graig Nettles and Peter Golenbock, Putnam, 1984; *Guidry*, by Ron Guidry and Peter Golenbock, Prentice-Hall, 1980; *Billyball*, by Billy Martin and Phil Pepe, Doubleday, 1987; *Whitey and Mickey*, by Whitey Ford, Mickey Mantle, and Joseph Durso, Viking, 1977; *Billy Martin*, by Gene Schoor, Doubleday, 1980; *Damned Yankees*, by Bill Madden and Moss Klein, Warner, 1990; *Pinstripe Pandemonium*, by Geoffrey Stokes, Harper-Collins, 1984; *Reggie*, by Reggie Jackson and Mike Lupica, Villard, 1984; *The Return of Billy the Kid*, by Norman Lewis Smith, Coward, McCann & Geoghegan, Inc., 1977; *Stengel*, by Robert Creamer, Simon and Schuster, 1984; *The Glory of Their Times*, by Larry Ritter, MacMillan, 1966; *The Mick*, by Mickey Mantle and Herb Gluck, Doubleday, 1985; *Damn Yankee*, by Maury Allen, Times Books, 1980; *The Last Yankee*, by David Falkner, Simon and Schuster, 1992; *Steinbrenner's Yankees*, by Ed Linn, Holt, Rinchart, 1982; *Knuckleballs*, by Phil Niekro and Tom Bird, Freundlich, 1986; *Don Baylor*, by Don Baylor and Clair Smith, St. Martin's Press, 1989; *The Billy Martin Story*, by Joe Archibald, Messner, 1962; *Steinbrenner!*, by Dick Schaap, Putnam, 1982; *Sweet Lou*, by Lou Piniella and Maury Allen, Putnam, 1986; *Mr. October*, by Maury Allen, Times Books, 1981; *Casey at the Bat*, by Casey Stengel and Harry Paxton, Random House, 1962; *Thurman Munson*, by Thurman Munson and Marty Appel, Coward, McCann & Geoghegan, 1978.

# NOTES

The research for this book was exhaustive. The information came from researching many thousands of newspaper and magazine articles, the books listed in the bibliography, records from both the Watergate hearings and the Bill Reedy trial, my transcripts of the taped conversations I had with Billy; his mom, Jenny Downey; his agent, Doug Newton; and his lawyer, Eddie Sapir back in 1979 when Billy and I together wrote *Number 1*, plus information from about one hundred interviews, including a taped interview with George Steinbrenner that took place in 1980.

As noted earlier, Jill Martin refused to be interviewed, either at her home or on the telephone. The reason, she said, was the negative treatment of her in *The Last Yankee*, by David Falkner.

**CHAPTER 1. THE DEATH OF BILLY MARTIN**
Interviews with Bill Reedy, Carol Reedy, Bill Fischer, Eddie Sapir, Peggy Sapir, and Kelly Martin.

**CHAPTER 2. THE ZENITH**
Interviews with Billy and Eddie Sapir.
I was given unlimited access to the files of the now-defunct *Oakland Tribune*. My thanks to the *Trib*'s Eric Newton for his assistance.
The Pearl Harbor story was witnessed by Bill Denehy.

**CHAPTER 3. JENNY**
Interviews with Billy, Jenny Downey, Ken Irvine, Pat Irvine, Joan Holland, Ruben DeAlba, Bruno Andrino, Sam Curtain, Lewis Figone, and Trivio Torrez.

**CHAPTER 4. HENRY**
Interviews with Frank Treadway, Robert Sauvey, Bob Stecher, Patsy Stecher, Joe Bennett, Lee Robinson, Ket "Pete" Barber, Paul Hensil, Don Martin, George Steiner, and Jim Beardsley.

**CHAPTER 5. BILLY STENGEL**
Interviews with Billy, Ken Irvine, and Ruben DeAlba.
See also *Stengel*, by Robert Creamer, and *Dynasty*, which I wrote in 1975.

**CHAPTER 6. YANKEE DOODLE DANDY**
Interviews with Billy, Pat Irvine, Phil Rizzuto, Jerry Coleman, the late Eddie Lopat, Whitey Ford, and the late Johnny Lindell.
"I was scared shitless . . . " From *Damn Yankee*, by Maury Allen, page 37.

"I've got two girls who are going to have breakfast with us. . . " *Whitey and Mickey,* with Joe Durso, page 11.

See also *Dynasty* and *Damn Yankee,* by Maury Allen.

### CHAPTER 7. THE MOCK ATHLETE

Interviews with Frank Treadway, Jim Beardsley, Pete Barber, Coke Smith, George Steiner, Paul Hensil, Lee Robinson, Dr. Jack Brody, Steve Blasky, Peter Callahan, Charlie Glass, Bruce Breckinridge, and Don Martin.

### CHAPTER 8. STARDOM

Interviews with Billy, the late Eddie Lopat.

For an account of the trip to Covington, Kentucky, see *The Mick,* by Mickey Mantle and Herb Gluck, page 97.

See also *Dynasty.*

### CHAPTER 9. LOIS

Interviews with Billy, Lois Berndt, Sam Curtain, Pat Irvine, Ken Irvine, and Ruben DeAlba.

Billy loved everyone, "even one of my best friends' wife." See *The Mick*, page 108.

### CHAPTER 10. THE MOCK AIRMAN

Interviews with Major William Jones (a pseudonym), Jeanette Montgomery, Col. Jerry Adams, Lou Lyle, Hal Connors, Sam Romano, and Tom Keyes.

### CHAPTER 11. THE SPARK PLUG

Interview with Billy.

See especially *Dynasty.*

### CHAPTER 12. THE COACH

Interviews with Joe Bennett, Jeanette Montgomery, John LeCorte, Dr. James Hull, Tony DeSabito, Tom Keyes, Ben Froelich, Len Dawson, and Frank Treadway.

### CHAPTER 13. THE BETRAYAL

Interviews with Billy, Bob Turley, Sam Pedone, Whitey Ford, Lewis Figone, Ed Sapir, Bill Reedy, Pat Irvine, and Bill Lane.

For the account of the Weiss-Mantle negotiation after the 1956 season, see *The Mick,* page 145.

### CHAPTER 14. HENRY AND GEORGE

Interviews with Joe Bennett, Frank Treadway, Bill Crippen, Patsy Stecher, and Dr. Jimmy Hull.

The story about the bathroom in the Steinbrenner home was told to me by a good friend who is also a good friend to the contractor. He asked that his name not be used.

### CHAPTER 15. THE ITINERANT

Interviews with Billy and Gabe Paul.

### CHAPTER 16. THE CLEVELAND PIPERS

Interviews with Joe Bennett, Bob Stecher, John McClendon, Jack Adams, Dan Swartz, Ben Flieger, Frank Treadway, Bill Sharman, Dick Brott, Mike Cleary, Louis Mitchell, Ben Warley, Bob Ferry, Jerry Lucas, Mary Stouffer, and Dr. Irving Kolin.

Dick Barnett and Roger Taylor refused to talk to me. When I told them I wanted to ask them about George, their immediate response was to say they were not interested in discussing him, and they hung up on me.

CHAPTER 17. SURVIVAL

Interviews with Billy and Graig Nettles.

For an account of the altercation with the airline steward and then Howard Fox, see *Damn Yankee,* by Maury Allen, page 138. Also *The Last Yankee,* by David Falkner, pages 124 and 125.

Bill Denehy graciously provided me with his interviews he taped in 1981 with Billy, Jim Burris, Art Fowler, Jim Campbell, and Calvin Griffith.

CHAPTER 18. WE WIN—YOU'RE FIRED

Interviews with Billy, Bill Reedy, and Gerald Eskenazi.

CHAPTER 19. HIGH AND TIGHT

Interviews with Billy and Bill Denehy.

CHAPTER 20. A TIGER TITLE

Interviews with Billy and Bill Reedy.

CHAPTER 21. BILL REEDY

Interviews with Bill Reedy and Carol Reedy.

CHAPTER 22. THE LONE RANGER

Interviews with Billy, Lenny Randle, and Roy Howell.

CHAPTER 23. STABBED IN THE BACK

Interviews with Billy, Roy Howell, Ron Pruitt, Lenny Randle, and Matt Keough.

"I was a pawn in Billy Martin's life." From *Damn Yankee,* by Maury Allen, page 165.

CHAPTER 24. THE STEINBRENNER YANKEES

Interviews with Don Martin, Gabe Paul, Bob August, Frank Treadway, the late Mike Burke, Howard Berk, Tom Evans, and Fred Bachman.

CHAPTER 25. AN ADMITTED FELON

Interviews with Jim Polk, Roy Meyers, Chris Jindra, Thomas McBride, Sam Dash, Thomas Evans, Jack Melcher, Robert Sauvey, Herb Kalmbach, Bill Tanner, Judge Leroy Contie, Frank Treadway, Richard Zimmerman, Henry Ruth, and David Dorsen.

See also *Steinbrenner,* by Dick Schaap, and *Steinbrenner's Yankees,* by Ed Linn.

CHAPTER 26. BACK TO THE BRONX

Interviews with Billy, Gabe Paul, and Bill Kane.

CHAPTER 27. A YANKEE FLAG

Interviews with Billy, Graig Nettles, Kelly Martin, Bill Kane, Gabe Paul, Dock Ellis, and Ed Linn.

CHAPTER 28. REGGIE

Interviews with Billy, Peter Callahan, Gabe Paul, Robert Ward, Graig Nettles, and Sparky Lyle.

"That was mistake number one, showing kindness . . ." from *Don Baylor,* by Baylor and Claire Smith, page 175.

See also *Steinbrenner's Yankees,* by Ed Linn, and *Reggie,* by Reggie Jackson and Mike Lupica.

CHAPTER 29. WHAT REGGIE WROTH
Interviews with Billy and Sparky Lyle.
See also *The Bronx Zoo*, by Lyle and me; *Balls*, by Graig Nettles and me; *Thurman*, by Thurman Munson and Marty Appel.

CHAPTER 30. GEORGE VS. GABE
Interviews with Billy, Pearl Davis, and Gabe Paul.
See also *Steinbrenner's Yankees*, by Ed Linn.

CHAPTER 31. A WORLD CHAMPIONSHIP
Interviews with Billy, Gabe Paul, Marty Blackman, and Ed Sapir.
See also *The Bronx Zoo, Balls, Reggie, Thurman, Steinbrenner's Yankees*, and *Sweet Lou*, by Lou Piniella and Maury Allen.

CHAPTER 32. "ONE'S A BORN LIAR, AND THE OTHER'S CONVICTED"
Interviews with Billy, Eddie Sapir, Pat Irvine, Kelly Martin, Bill Reedy, Carol Reedy, Graig Nettles, and Bill Kane.
See also *The Bronx Zoo, Reggie, Thurman, Sweet Lou, Steinbenner's Yankees, Pinstripe Pandemonium*, by Geoffrey Stokes, and *Damn Yankee*, by Maury Allen.

CHAPTER 33. GONE AND BACK
Interviews with Billy, Bill Kane, Graig Nettles, Eddie Sapir, Bill Reedy, Doug Newton, and Kelly Martin.
See also *Reggie* and *Steinbrenner's Yankees*.

CHAPTER 34. JUDGE SAPIR
Interviews with Billy and Eddie Sapir.

CHAPTER 35. "EVERY WHORE HAS HIS PRICE"
Interviews with Billy, the late Cedric Tallis, Billy Joe Martin, Bill Reedy, and Eddie Sapir.
"Every whore has his price, Meat," and following from *Reggie*, pages 258.
See also *Steinbrenner's Yankees*.

CHAPTER 36. BILLYBALL
Interviews with Billy, Doug Newton, Eddie Sapir, and Matt Keough.

CHAPTER 37. BILLY IN LOVE
Interviews with Heather Ervolino Coyles, Pat Irvine, Peggy Sapir, Carol Reedy, Bill Reedy, Vicki Figone, Kelly Martin, Tex Gernand, Eddie Sapir, and Paul Tabarry.

CHAPTER 38. THE BEGINNING OF THE END
Interviews with Bill Reedy, Steve McCatty, Paul Tabarry, Eddie Sapir, Matt Keough, Tex Gernand, Lewis Figone, and John Alderson.
See also *The Last Yankee*, by David Falkner.

CHAPTER 39. HEATHER AND JILL
Interviews with Bill Reedy, Ed Sapir, Heather Ervolino Coyles, Lewis Figone, Paul Tabarry, and Kelly Martin.

CHAPTER 40. MOVING ON UP
Interviews with Eddie Sapir, Pat Irving, and Tex Gernand.

## Chapter 41. Billy and George
Interviews with Billy, Bill Reedy, Eddie Sapir, Graig Nettles, and Gerald Eskenazi.
See also *Pinstripe Pandemonium* and *Damned Yankees,* by Bill Madden and Moss Klein.

## Chapter 42. Fired Again
Interviews with Bill Reedy, Eddie Sapir, Shane Rawley, Ryne Duren, Gerald Eskenazi, Graig Nettles, Bill Denehy, and Matt Keough.
The letter sent to Billy by George was saved by Bill Reedy and given to me.
See also *Damned Yankees, Don Baylor,* and *Knuckleballs,* by Phil Niekro and Tom Bird.

## Chapter 43. Poisoned
Interviews with Heather Ervolino Coyles, Bill Reedy, Carol Reedy, Eddie Sapir, Peggy Sapir, Kathryn Marrero, Tex Gernand, Paul Tabarry, Kelly Martin, and Vicki Figone.

## Chapter 44. A Kick to the Ribs
Interviews with Bill Reedy, Eddie Sapir, Bill Kane, and Tex Gernand.
See also *Knuckleballs, Don Baylor, The Last Yankee,* and *Damned Yankees.*

## Chapter 45. Billy's Day
Interviews with Bill Reedy, Pat Irvine, Ken Irvine, Eddie Sapir, Tex Gernand, Lewis Figone, Vicki Figone, and Kelly Martin.

## Chapter 46. A Great Girl
Interviews with Bill Reedy, Carol Reedy, and Mike Klepfer.

## Chapter 47. The Wedding
Interviews with Bill Reedy, Carol Reedy, Joan Holland, Mike Klepfer, Katie Klepfer, Ken Irvine, Pat Irvine, and Kelly Martin.
In addition, Pat Irvine graciously allowed me to view her copy of the videotape of the wedding.

## Chapter 48. The Last Go-Round
Interviews with Bill Reedy, Carol Reedy, Mike Klepfer, Katie Klepfer, Eddie Sapir, Tex Gernand, and Bill Kane.
See also *The Last Yankee* and *Damned Yankees.*

## Chapter 49. The Move to Binghamton
Interviews with Mike Klepfer, Katie Klepfer, Bill Reedy and Carol Reedy.

## Chapter 50. Fighting and Drinking
Interviews with Mike Klepfer, Katie Klepfer, Joan Holland, and Pat Irvine.

## Chapter 51. Broke in the Taj Mahal
Interviews with Bill Reedy and Carol Reedy.

## Chapter 52. The Splitter
Interviews with Eddie Sapir, Peggy Sapir, Paul Tabarry, Bill Reedy, Carol Reedy, Mike Klepfer, Katie Klepfer, Greer Johnson, Pat Irvine, Kelly Martin, and Billy Joe Martin.

## Chapter 53. The Death of Jenny Downey
Interviews with Bill Reedy, Carol Reedy, Billy Joe Martin, Kelly Martin, Pat Irvine, Lewis Figone, Joan Holland, and Vicki Figone.

CHAPTER 54. CHRISTMAS DAY 1989
Interviews with Pat Irvine, Bill Reedy, Carol Reedy, and Bill Fischer.
See the transcripts of the Reedy trial for added details of the final trip and the crash.

CHAPTER 55. THE MOTIVE
Interviews with Tex Gernand, Carol Reedy, Bill Reedy, Kelly Martin, Mike Klepfer, Eddie Sapir, Vicki Figone, Paul Tabarry, Bill Fischer, and Matt Keough.
Also see the transcripts of the Reedy trial.

CHAPTER 56. THE FUNERAL
Interviews with Eddie Sapir, Kelly Martin, Pat Irvine, Bill Reedy, Peggy Sapir, and Tex Gernand.

CHAPTER 57. A PERVERSION OF JUSTICE
Interviews with Bill Fischer, Bill Reedy, Jon Blechman, Kelly Martin, Peggy Sapir, Mike Klepfer, and Eddie Sapir.
See also the trial transcripts and also *The Last Yankee*.

CHAPTER 58. THE VOID
Interviews with Sam Curtain, Kelly Martin, Eddie Sapir, Lewis Figone, Peggy Sapir, Matt Keough, Bill Reedy, Ken Irvine, Pat Irvine, and Joan Holland.

# INDEX